CW01209865

MACRO-FINANCIAL STABILITY POLICY
IN A GLOBALISED WORLD
LESSONS FROM INTERNATIONAL EXPERIENCE

Selected Papers from
the Asian Monetary Policy Forum 2021
Special Edition and MAS-BIS Conference

Recommended Titles

Digital Currency Economics and Policy
edited by Bernard Yeung
ISBN: 978-981-122-377-8

The Asian Monetary Policy Forum: Insights for Central Banking
edited by Steven J Davis, Edward S Robinson and Bernard Yeung
ISBN: 978-981-123-861-1

MACRO-FINANCIAL STABILITY POLICY IN A GLOBALISED WORLD
LESSONS FROM INTERNATIONAL EXPERIENCE

Selected Papers from
the Asian Monetary Policy Forum 2021
Special Edition and MAS-BIS Conference

Editors

Claudio Borio
Bank for International Settlements, Switzerland

Edward S. Robinson
Monetary Authority of Singapore, Singapore

Hyun Song Shin
Bank for International Settlements, Switzerland

World Scientific

NEW JERSEY · LONDON · SINGAPORE · BEIJING · SHANGHAI · HONG KONG · TAIPEI · CHENNAI · TOKYO

Published by

World Scientific Publishing Co. Pte. Ltd.

5 Toh Tuck Link, Singapore 596224

USA office: 27 Warren Street, Suite 401-402, Hackensack, NJ 07601

UK office: 57 Shelton Street, Covent Garden, London WC2H 9HE

Library of Congress Cataloging-in-Publication Data
Names: Borio, C. E. V., editor.
Title: Macro-financial stability policy in a globalised world : lessons from international experience / editors Claudio Borio, Edward Robinson, Hyun Song Shin.
Description: Special AMPF edition | Hackensack, NJ : World Scientific, [2023] | "Selected papers from the AMPF 2021 edition and MAS-BIS conference"--Title page. | Includes bibliographical references and index.
Identifiers: LCCN 2022037314 | ISBN 9789811259425 (hardcover) |
ISBN 9789811259432 (ebook for institutions) | ISBN 9789811259449 (ebook for individuals)
Subjects: LCSH: Monetary policy. | Globalization.
Classification: LCC HG230.3 .M3364 2023 | DDC 332.4/6--dc23/eng/20221110
LC record available at https://lccn.loc.gov/2022037314

British Library Cataloguing-in-Publication Data
A catalogue record for this book is available from the British Library.

Copyright © 2023 by Bank of International Settlements

All rights reserved.

For any available supplementary material, please visit
https://www.worldscientific.com/worldscibooks/10.1142/12921#t=suppl

Desk Editors: Lai Ann/Nicole Ong

Typeset by Stallion Press
Email: enquiries@stallionpress.com

These published proceedings of the May 2021 Conference, convened by the BIS and MAS, provide a definitive account of the usage of macro-prudential policies. A stellar collection of authors have written five general and ten country/regional Chapters on this subject, with discussant comments on each, all by top names in the field. A great book and a must-read by anyone with an interest in financial regulation.

Charles Goodhart
London School of Economics

The global financial crisis of 2008 prompted a global call for a new financial regulatory framework that regulates the cyclicality of the financial system as a whole rather than its individual parts. Since then, so-called macroprudential regulations have been introduced in many countries to tame financial cycles, with a view to reduce the build-up of systemic financial stability risks and increase financial buffers to absorb shocks when they arrive. This book brings together the wisdom of senior policymakers and academics with hands-on experience in the development of macroprudential policy to draw invaluable lessons for the design and implementation of macroprudential policy. I recommend especially the chapters on country experiences, showing what worked well and what did not.

Luc Laeven
European Central Bank

The COVID pandemic and geopolitical tensions brought significant stability challenges for open economies. The headwinds are prominently characterized by the pick-up in inflation and capital flow volatility. The impact has been significant, but kneejerk policy responses will prove suboptimal. I highly recommend this book as it offers a collection of reasoned insights and systematic analyses on many important policy choices facing EMEs. Adding to its appeal is the accompanying commentaries by independent experts. Differing perspectives can help readers gain a more holistic understanding of the complex policy trade-offs at play.

Jin-Chuan Duan
National University of Singapore

About the Editors

Claudio Borio was appointed Head of the BIS Monetary and Economic Department on 18 November 2013. At the BIS since 1987, Mr Borio has held various positions in the Monetary and Economic Department (MED), including Deputy Head of MED and Director of Research and Statistics as well as Head of Secretariat for the Committee on the Global Financial System and the Gold and Foreign Exchange Committee (now the Markets Committee). From 1985 to 1987, he was an economist at the OECD, working in the country studies branch of the Economics and Statistics Department. Prior to that, he was Lecturer and Research Fellow at Brasenose College, Oxford University. He holds a DPhil and an MPhil in Economics and a BA in Politics, Philosophy and Economics from the same university. Claudio is author of numerous publications in the fields of monetary policy, banking, finance and issues related to financial stability.

Edward Surendran Robinson is Deputy Managing Director of the Economic Policy Group (EPG) and Chief Economist, MAS. He currently heads the EPG which formulates Singapore's monetary policy and conducts macro-financial surveillance. The Group also undertakes research on broader economic and financial issues facing the domestic and external economies. Edward studied Economics/Econometrics at Monash University and the University of Melbourne. He has a particular interest in macroeconometric modelling and continues to be engaged in the developmental work for the suite of MAS models, which are used for both price and financial stability analysis. He has also been involved in other areas of economic policy work including in various inter-governmental work groups, and served as a Board Member of the Competition Commission of Singapore.

Hyun Song Shin took up the position of Economic Adviser and Head of Research at the BIS on 1 May 2014. Before joining the BIS, Mr Shin was the Hughes-Rogers Professor of Economics at Princeton University. In 2010, on leave from Princeton, he served as Senior Adviser to the Korean president, taking a leading role in formulating financial stability policy in Korea and developing the agenda for the G20 during Korea's presidency. From 2000 to 2005, he was Professor of Finance at the London School of Economics. He holds a DPhil and MPhil in Economics from Oxford University (Nuffield College) and a BA in Philosophy, Politics and Economics from the same university.

About the Contributors

Viral V Acharya is the C V Starr Professor of Economics in the Department of Finance at New York University Stern School of Business (NYU-Stern) and an Academic Advisor to the Federal Reserve Banks of New York and Philadelphia. Viral was a Deputy Governor at the Reserve Bank of India (RBI) during 23 January 2017 to 23 July 2019 in charge of Monetary Policy, Financial Markets, Financial Stability, and Research. His speeches while at the RBI were released in July 2020 in the form of a book titled *"Quest for Restoring Financial Stability in India"* (SAGE Publishing India), with a new introductory chapter *"Fiscal Dominance: A Theory of Everything in India"*. At Stern, Viral co-edited the books *Restoring Financial Stability: How to Repair a Failed System*, John Wiley & Sons, March 2009, *Regulating Wall Street: The Dodd-Frank Act and the New Architecture of Global Finance*, John Wiley & Sons, November 2010, and *Dodd-Frank: One Year On*, NYU-Stern and CEPR (released on voxeu.org), July 2011. He is also the co-author of the book *Guaranteed to Fail: Fannie Mae, Freddie Mac and the Debacle of Mortgage Finance*, Princeton University Press, March 2011 and Harper Collins (India), June 2011.

Pierre-Richard Agénor is Hallsworth Professor of International Macroeconomics and Development Economics at the University of Manchester. He has published numerous articles in leading professional journals and made contributions to a wide range of fields and topics in economics, including international macroeconomics, development economics, growth theory, labour economics, financial regulation, gender equality, and poverty analysis. He is the author of several books, including *The Economics of Adjustment and Growth* (Harvard University Press), *Public Capital, Growth and Welfare* (Princeton University Press), *Monetary Policy and Macroprudential Regulation with Financial Frictions* (The MIT Press), and *Development Macroeconomics* (with Peter J. Montiel, Princeton University Press).

Ana Aguilar joined the BIS in January 2019 as a senior economist. Before that, she worked in Banco de México from 1998 to 2018. Most of that time, she was in charge of the monetary policy analysis as the Head of the Directorate of Economic Studies. Ana Aguilar holds a PhD in Economics (2004) by the University of California, Los Angeles (UCLA). She has been lecturer at the Mexico Autonomous Institute of Technology (Instituto Tecnológico Autónomo de México, ITAM), from which she originally got a Bachelor degree in economics.

Muhamad Chatib Basri is a former Minister of Finance of Indonesia. Previously he was the Chairman of the Indonesian Investment Coordinating Board. Dr Basri was also a Vice Chairman of the National Economic Committee of the President of Indonesia. Dr Basri is now the Chairman of the PT Bank Mandiri tbk, and also of the XL Axiata. He teaches at the Department of Economics University of Indonesia and co-founded CReco Research Institute, a Jakarta based economic consulting firm in 2010. He was a Thee Kian Wie Distinguished Visiting Professor at the Australian National University (2016–2017). His expertise is International Trade, Macroeconomics and Political Economy. He was Ash Centre Senior Fellow at the Harvard Kennedy School, Harvard University (2015–2016), Pacific Leadership Fellow at the Centre on Global Transformation, University of California at San Diego (2016), NTUC Professor of International Economic Relation, RSIS, NTU, Singapore (2016). Dr Basri is a member of the World Bank Advisory Council on Gender and Development. He is the author of a number of papers in international journals and actively writes for various leading newspapers and magazines in Indonesia.

Charles Bean is a Professor of Economics at the London School of Economics and a member of the Budget Responsibility Committee at the Office for Budget Responsibility. From 2000 to 2014, he served at the Bank of England as, successively, Executive Director and Chief Economist, and then Deputy Governor for Monetary Policy, serving on both the Monetary Policy and Financial Policy Committees. He also represented the Bank in international fora, such as G7 and G20. Before joining the Bank, he was a member of faculty at LSE and has also worked at HM Treasury. He has served as Managing Editor of the Review of Economic Studies, was President of the Royal Economic Society from 2013 to 2015, and is Chairman of the Centre for Economic Policy Research. He was knighted in 2014 for services to monetary policy and central banking and recently undertook a major review of the quality, delivery and governance of UK economic statistics on behalf of the UK government. He holds a PhD from MIT.

Thorsten Beck is Director of the Florence School of Banking and Finance and Professor of Financial Stability at the European University Institute. He was professor of banking and finance at Bayes Business School (formerly Cass) in London between 2013 and 2021. He is also a research fellow of the Centre for Economic Policy Research (CEPR) and the CESifo. He was professor of economics from 2008 to 2014 at Tilburg University and the founding chair of the European Banking Center from 2008 to 2013. Previously he worked in the research department of the World Bank and has also worked as consultant for — among others — the European Central Bank, the Bank of England, the BIS, the IMF, the European Commission, and the German Development Corporation. His research, academic publications and operational work have focused on two major questions: What is the relationship between finance and economic development? What policies are needed to build a sound and effective financial system? Recently, he has concentrated on access to financial services, including SME finance, as well as on the design of regulatory and bank resolution frameworks. In addition to numerous academic publications in leading economics and finance journals, he has co-authored several policy reports on access to finance, financial systems in Africa and cross-border banking. He holds a PhD from the University of Virginia and an MA from the University of Tübingen in Germany.

Katharina Bergant is an Economist in the Macro-Financial Division of the Research Department at the International Monetary Fund (IMF). In addition to her work on monetary and macroprudential policies, her most recent research focuses on the application of microdata in international financial macroeconomics. Before she joined the IMF, Katharina did a research fellowship at the Harvard Kennedy School. Previously, she worked in the Directorate Economics of the European Central Bank and the Monetary Policy division of the Central Bank of Ireland. Katharina was a Grattan Scholar at Trinity College Dublin where she earned her PhD under the supervision of Philip R. Lane.

Claudio Borio was appointed Head of the BIS Monetary and Economic Department on 18 November 2013. At the BIS since 1987, Mr Borio has held various positions in the Monetary and Economic Department (MED), including Deputy Head of MED and Director of Research and Statistics as well as Head of Secretariat for the Committee on the Global Financial System and the Gold and Foreign Exchange Committee (now the Markets Committee). From 1985 to 1987, he was an economist at the OECD, working in the country studies branch of the Economics and Statistics Department. Prior to that, he was Lecturer and Research Fellow at Brasenose College, Oxford University. He holds a DPhil and an MPhil in Economics and a BA in Politics, Philosophy and Economics from the same university. Claudio is author of numerous publications in the fields of monetary policy, banking, finance and issues related to financial stability.

Valentina Bruno is Professor at the Department of Finance and Real Estate of American University. She holds a Master in Finance and Economics and a PhD in Finance from the London School of Economics. Before joining American University, she worked at the World Bank in the Financial Sector Strategy and Policy Group and in the International Finance Team. Professor Bruno is Faculty Research Fellow at the Center for Economic Policy Research (CEPR) and Faculty Research Member at the European Corporate Governance Institute (ECGI). She has studied topics at the intersection of macroeconomics and finance: global liquidity, capital flows, macroprudential policies and foreign banks. Her recent work has focused on the role of the US dollar in the transmission of global financial conditions. Her research has been published in academic journals including the Review of Economic Studies, Review of Financial Studies, Journal of Monetary Economics, and Management Science.

Agustín Carstens became General Manager of the BIS on 1 December 2017. Mr Carstens was Governor of the Bank of Mexico from 2010 to 2017. A member of the BIS Board from 2011 to 2017, he was chair of the Global Economy Meeting and the Economic Consultative Committee from 2013 to 2017. He also chaired the International Monetary and Financial Committee, the IMF's policy advisory committee from 2015 to 2017. Mr Carstens began his career in 1980 at the Bank of Mexico. From 1999 to 2000, he was Executive Director at the IMF. He later served as Mexico's deputy finance minister (2000–03) and as Deputy Managing Director at the IMF (2003–06). He was Mexico's finance minister from 2006 to 2009. Mr Carstens has been a member of the Financial Stability Board since 2010 and is a member of the Group of Thirty. Mr Carstens holds an MA and a PhD in economics from the University of Chicago.

Yongheng Deng is a Professor and the John P. Morgridge Distinguished Chair in Business in the Wisconsin School of Business, University of Wisconsin–Madison (UW–Madison). Before joining UW–Madison, Professor Deng has served as a Provost's Chair Professor of Real Estate and Finance, Director of the Institute of Real Estate Studies, and Head of the Department of Real Estate at the National University of Singapore (NUS). He was also a Professor in the Department of Finance at NUS Business School and Director of the Lifecycle Financing Research Program at NUS Global Asia Institute. He has served as the 50th President of the American Real Estate and Urban Economics Association (AREUEA), the first and only Asian to be elected President in the Association's over 50 years history. Professor Deng has published his research works in leading economics and finance journals. Some of those journals include *Econometrica, Journal of Financial Economics, Management Science, Review of Finance, Journal of Environmental Economics and Management, Journal of Urban Economics, China Economic Review*. Professor Deng holds a Ph.D. in Economics from the University of California at Berkeley.

Sebastian Edwards is the Henry Ford II Distinguished Professor of International Economics at the University of California, Los Angeles. From 1993 to 1996 he was Chief Economist for Latin America and the Caribbean at the World Bank. He has published 15 books, and over 200 scholarly articles. He was the Co-Director of the National Bureau of Economic Research's "Africa Project." He is a Research Associate at the National Bureau of Economic Research and an Honorary Professor at the Universidad de Chile. His latest book is "American Default: The untold story of FDR, the Supreme Court and the Battle over Gold" (Princeton University Press, 2018). Professor Edwards is currently working on a book titled "*Neoliberalism and Chicago Economics*," to be published by Princeton University Press in 2022. Other books include "*African Successes*," (co-edited with Simon Johnson and David Weil; University of Chicago Press, 2016); "*Toxic Aid: Economic Collapse and Recovery in Tanzania*" (Oxford University Press, 2014); "*Left Behind: Latin America and the False Promise of Populism*" (University of Chicago Press, 2010), and "*Crisis and Reform in Latin America: From Despair to Hope*," (Oxford University Press, 1995). Sebastian Edwards has published two novels and a book of memoirs in Spanish. "*El Misterio de las Tanias*" (Alfaguara 2007) was on the best sellers list in Chile for 29 weeks. "*Un día perfecto*" (Norma 2010) was on the list for 14 weeks. The memoir "*Conversación Interrumpida*" (2016) was also a best seller. Professor Edwards was educated at the Universidad de Chile and Universidad Católica de Chile. He received an MA in economics in 1978, and a Ph.D. in economics in 1981, both from the University of Chicago.

Barry Eichengreen is the George C. Pardee and Helen N. Pardee Professor of Economics and Professor of Political Science at the University of California, Berkeley, where he has taught since 1987. He is a Research Associate of the National Bureau of Economic Research (Cambridge, Massachusetts) and Research Fellow of the Centre for Economic Policy Research (London, England). His most recent books are *The Populist Temptation: Economic Grievance and Political Reaction in the Modern Era* (Oxford University Press, 2018), *How Global Currencies Work: Past, Present, and Future* with Livia Chitu and Arnaud Mehl (November 2017), *The Korean Economy: From a Miraculous Past* *to a Sustainable Future* with Wonhyuk Lim, Yung Chul Park and Dwight H. Perkins (March 2015), *Renminbi Internationalization: Achievements, Prospects, and Challenges*, with Masahiro Kawai (February 2015), *Hall of Mirrors: The Great Depression, The Great Recession, and the Uses — and Misuses — of History* (January 2015), *From Miracle to Maturity: The Growth of the Korean Economy* with Dwight H. Perkins and Kwanho Shin (2012) and *Exorbitant Privilege: The Rise and Fall of the Dollar and the Future of the International Monetary System* (2011) (shortlisted for the Financial Times and Goldman Sachs Business Book of the Year Award in 2011).

Kristin Forbes is the Jerome and Dorothy Lemelson Professor of Management and Global Economics at MIT's Sloan School of Management. She has regularly rotated between academia and senior policy positions. From 2014 to 2017 she was an External Member of the Monetary Policy Committee for the Bank of England. From 2003 to 2005 Forbes served as a Member of the White House's Council of Economic Advisers and from 2001 to 2002 she was a Deputy Assistant Secretary of Quantitative Policy Analysis, Latin American and Caribbean Nations in the U.S. Treasury Department. She also was a Member of the Governor's Council of Economic Advisers for the State of Massachusetts from 2009 to 2014. In 2019, Forbes was named an Honorary Commander of the Order of the British Empire (CBE) by Her Majesty Queen Elizabeth II for services to British economic policy. She was previously honoured as one of the top 25 economists under the age of 45 who are "shaping how we think about the global economy" (by Finance & Development, 2014) and as a "Young Global Leader" as part of the World Economic Forum at Davos. She is currently the Convener of the Bellagio Group, a research associate at the NBER and CEPR, and a member of the Aspen Economic Strategy Group and Council on Foreign Relations. She also serves in a number of advisory positions, such as on the Monetary Policy Advisory Panel of the New York Federal Reserve Bank and on the External Advisory Group of the Managing Director for the International Monetary Fund. Forbes' academic research addresses policy-related questions in international macroeconomics. Recent projects include work on exchange rate pass-through, capital flows, macroprudential regulation, financial crises, contagion, current account imbalances, capital controls, inflation dynamics, foreign investment, and tax holidays. Forbes has chaired research projects on the Global Financial Crisis, Global Linkages and International Financial Contagion. She has won numerous teaching awards and teaches one of the most popular classes at MIT's Sloan School. Before joining MIT, Forbes worked at the World Bank and Morgan Stanley. She received her PhD in Economics from MIT and graduated summa cum laude with highest honours from Williams College.

Linda Goldberg is a Senior Vice President at the Federal Reserve Bank of New York. Linda's main areas of expertise are global banking, international capital flows, and the international roles of currencies. Linda is the co-chair of the International Banking Research Network, Bank for International Settlements Technical Advisor, CEPR Distinguished Fellow, and an NBER Research Associate. Linda is co-editor of the *International Journal of Central Banking* and on editorial boards of the *Journal of Financial Intermediation* and *Journal of Financial Services Research*. She also is on board of the Central Banking Economic Research Association, advisory board of the Academic Female Finance Committee of the American Finance Association, and is the Vice President of the Association of Princeton Graduate Alumni. Linda previously engaged with the World Economic Forum, including as chair and vice chair of the Council on Global Economic Imbalances. Linda has a PhD in Economics from Princeton University, and a B.A. in Mathematics and Economics from Queens College CUNY, where she graduated Phi Beta Kappa and Summa Cum Laude.

Johan Grip was a Senior Economist at Sveriges Riksbank when he wrote the chapter. He previously worked at the Directorate General Economics Department at the European Central Bank and the Economic Affairs Department at the Swedish Ministry of Finance. Johan Grip is a PhD candidate in economics at Uppsala University and he was a visiting scholar at New York University in 2011–2012.

Yiping Huang is Sinar Mas Chair Professor of Finance and Deputy Dean of the National School of Development and Director of the Institute of

Digital Finance (IDF), Peking University. He served as a member of the Monetary Policy Committee at the People's Bank of China during 2015–2018. Currently, he is a member of the External Advisory Group on Surveillance of the International Monetary Fund, and Vice Chairman of Council at the Public Policy Research Center and Research Fellow at the Financial Research Center, both at the Counsellors' Office of the State Council. He also serves as Chairman of the Academic Committee of China Finance 40 Forum, and a member of Chinese Economists 50 Forum. He is Editor of China Economic Journal and an Associate Editor of Asian Economic Policy Review. His research areas include macro economy, financial market and rural development. Previously, he was a policy analyst at the Research Center for Rural Development of the State Council, research fellow and senior lecturer of economics at the Australian National University, General Mills International Visiting Professor of Economics and Finance at the Columbia Business School, Managing Director and Chief Asia Economist for Citigroup, Managing Director and Chief Economist for Emerging Asia for Barclays, and an Independent Director of China Life Insurance Ltd, Minmetal Trust Ltd and Mybank. Prof Huang received his Bachelor of Agricultural Economics from Zhejiang Agricultural University, Master of Economics from Renmin University of China and PhD in Economics from Australian National University.

Yi Huang is Professor of Finance at Fudan University. He was associate professor at the Graduate Institute in Geneva and a research affiliate at the Center for Economic and Policy Research (CEPR). He was professor and Pictet Chair in Finance and Development at the Centre for Finance and Development and an economist in the research department of the International Monetary Fund and a research associate of the Federal Reserve Bank of Dallas and the Institute of Digital Finance of Peking University. He also has been a research fellow at the Bank for International Settlements and Hong Kong Institute for Monetary Research as well as the visiting positions at the Berkeley, London Business School, Imperial College Business School, Cheung Kong Graduate School of Business (CKGSB), Fanhan International School of Finance, and the Massachusetts Institute of Technology. Professor

Huang also serves at the Council on Global Economic Imbalances at the World Economic Forum and Academic Fellow at Luohan Academy, Alibaba Group. Professor Huang's research consists of international macroeconomics and finance, especially the influence of corporation's financing and investment to financial market and labour market. Recent work focuses on credit markets, fintech, and entrepreneurship. His research is published at academic journals such as the Review of Economic Studies and Journal of Finance. Professor Huang gained his Master's degree from the China Center for Economics Research, Peking University, and his PhD in International Macroeconomic and Finance from the London Business School.

Stefan Ingves is Governor of Sveriges Riksbank and Chairman of the Executive Board. Mr Ingves is a Member of the Board of Directors of the BIS and Chairman of the BIS Banking and Risk Management Committee (BRC). Governor Ingves is also a Member of the General Council of the ECB and First Vice-Chair of the European Systemic Risk Board (ESRB). Governor Ingves is Governor for Sweden in the IMF, and Chairman of the Toronto Centre for Global Leadership in Financial Supervision and Board Member of the Nordic-Baltic Macroprudential Forum (NBMF). Mr Ingves has previously been Chairman of the Basel Committee on Banking Supervision, Director of the Monetary and Financial Systems Department at the IMF, Deputy Governor of the Riksbank and General Director of the Swedish Bank Support Authority. Prior to that he was Head of the Financial Markets Department at the Ministry of Finance. Stefan Ingves holds a PhD in economics.

Lana Ivičić is an economist and a financial stability expert at the Financial Stability Department in the Croatian National Bank responsible for development and implementation of macroprudential policy and instruments. Mrs. Ivičić holds a master's degree in economics from Bocconi University, Italy. Her publications include Ivičić, L. and Cerovac, S., 2009, Credit Risk Assessment of Corporate Sector in Croatia, Financial Theory and Practice, Vol. 33 No. 4; Ivičić, L., Kunovac, D. and Ljubaj, I., 2008, Measuring Bank Insolvency Risk in CEE Countries, Croatian National Bank Working Paper.

Mirna Dumičić Jemrić holds a PhD in economics from the Faculty of Economics, University of Split, where she is also a Senior Research Associate. She has started her career in 2004 in the Croatian National Bank and she currently works as the Chief Advisor in the Financial Stability Department. In the meantime, she has also spent three years (2016–2019) working as the Financial Stability Expert at the Macroprudential Policy Division in the European Central Bank. Mrs Dumičić Jemrić has published more than 20 scientific papers and has edited several books.

Anil Kashyap's research focuses on banking, business cycles, corporate finance, price setting and monetary policy. His research has won him numerous awards, including the Order of the Rising Sun 3rd class Gold Rays with Neck Ribbon from the Government of Japan, as well as a Sloan Research Fellowship, the Nikkei Prize for Excellent Books in Economic Sciences, and a Senior Houblon-Norman Fellowship from the Bank of England. Prior to joining the Chicago Booth faculty in 1991, Kashyap spent three years as an economist for the Board of Governors for the Federal Reserve System. He currently works as a consultant for the Federal Reserve Bank of Chicago, and as a Research Associate for the National Bureau of Economic Research and a Research Fellow of the Centre for Economic Policy Research. He is a member of the Squam Lake Group and serves on the International Monetary Fund's Advisory Group on the development of a macroprudential policy framework. Since 2016 he has been an external member of the Bank of England's Financial Policy Committee. Kashyap is a member of both the American Economic Association and American Finance Association, and is on the faculty oversight Board of the Chicago Booth's Initiative on Global Markets and a co-founder of the US Monetary Policy Forum. He regularly speaks on financial crises, Japan, the global economy and the direction of economic policy.

Hwanseok Lee is Deputy Governor of the Bank of Korea. His research interests lie in the monetary policy transmission mechanism and inflation dynamics. After joining the Bank in 1991, he has held various positions, including Director General of the Research Department and

Financial Markets Department, and Director of the Monetary Policy Board Secretariat. He holds a PhD from University of Illinois.

Rosemary Lim is Executive Director of the Macroprudential Surveillance Department at the Monetary Authority of Singapore. The department conducts surveillance of the financial system to identify emerging trends and potential vulnerabilities, and undertakes policy-relevant studies on macro-financial linkages, systemic risk and other financial stability issues. She holds a BSc in Economics from the London School of Economics and an MSc in Finance from Imperial College, London.

Simon Lloyd is a Senior Research Economist in the International Directorate of the Bank of England. He completed his Ph.D. at the University of Cambridge. His research interests span international and monetary economics, and macro-finance. His research has been published in outlets such as the Journal of Banking and Finance and the Review of International Economics.

Tingting Lü is a PhD Candidate at Peking University. She is also Director of Monetary Cooperation Division of Macroprudential Policy Bureau, People's Bank of China. She worked in Legal Affairs Department of People's Bank of China and External Department of Hong Kong Monetary Authority previously. She has mainly engaged in the fields involving RMB internationalisation, opening-up of China's financial market, the liberalization of China's capital account and relevant areas. Ms Lü achieved Bachelor and Master of Laws from Central University of Finance and Economics, and Master of Science in Finance from City University of Hong Kong.

Robert N McCauley does policy-relevant and market-savvy research on international financial markets, the international monetary system and corporate finance. His research spans the international monetary system (exorbitant privilege, Triffin dilemma), reserve management (currency and instrument composition), money, bond and foreign exchange markets (dollar zone, covered interest parity, non-deliverable forwards) and renminbi internationalisation. He combines deep analysis with broad communication: The Financial Times, the Economist, the Wall Street Journal and the New York Times cite his work extensively.

He has enjoyed teaching courses on banking and international finance in business and law schools. He spent most of his career at the Bank for International Settlements and, before that, at the Federal Reserve Bank of New York. He is a non-resident senior fellow at Boston University's Global Development Policy Center and a senior research associate at the Global History of Capitalism project at the Oxford Global History Centre at the University of Oxford. He serves on the scientific committee of the Fondation Banque de France.

Enrique G Mendoza is Presidential Professor of Economics at the University of Pennsylvania and Managing Editor of the Journal of International Economics. He joined Penn in 2013 and served as Director of the Penn Institute for Economic Research from 2014 to 2020. Before that, he was Neil Moskowitz Professor of Economics at the University of Maryland and held positions at Duke University, the Board of Governors of the Federal Reserve and the IMF. He is a 1989 PhD from the University of Western Ontario, an NBER Research Associate, and member of the BIS Advisory Panel and the Latin American Shadow Financial Regulatory Committee. He has served in the NSF Economics panel and in the editorial boards of several journals, including the American Economic Review. In 2017, he was awarded the ECB's Wim Duisenberg fellowship. His research focuses on international capital flows, financial crises, sovereign debt and international business cycles. His main publications include: "Optimal, Time-Consistent Macroprudential Policy," with J. Bianchi, Journal of Political Economy, 2018, "A General Equilibrium Model of Sovereign Default and Business Cycles" with V. Yue, Quarterly Journal of Economics, 2012, "Sudden Stops, Financial Crises & Leverage," American Economic Review, 2010, "Financial Integration, Financial Development and Global Imbalances," with V. Quadrini and J. V. Rios-Rull, Journal of Political Economy, 2009, and "Real Business Cycles in a Small Open Economy," American Economic Review, 1991.

Ravi Menon Mr Ravi Menon was appointed Managing Director of the Monetary Authority of Singapore (MAS) in 2011. He was previously Permanent Secretary at the Ministry of Trade & Industry (MTI) and Deputy Secretary at the Ministry of Finance (MOF). Mr Menon began his career at MAS in 1987. During his 16 years in MAS, he was involved in monetary policy; econometric forecasting; organisational development; banking regulation and liberalisation; and integrated supervision of complex financial institutions. Mr Menon spent a year at the Bank for International Settlements in Basel, as a member of the secretariat to the Financial Stability Forum. A recipient of the Singapore Government's Meritorious Service Medal and Public Administration (Gold) Medal, Mr Menon has served on a variety of boards in the public, private, and people sectors in Singapore. On the international front, Mr Menon is a member of the Financial Stability Board (FSB) Steering Committee. Mr Menon holds a Master's in Public Administration from Harvard University and a Bachelor of Social Science (Honours) in Economics from the National University of Singapore.

Tuomas Peltonen is Deputy Head of the European Systemic Risk Board (ESRB) Secretariat. His main tasks include management of the ESRB Secretariat, systemic risk analysis and its presentation to the ESRB General Board as well as interaction with ESRB members and stakeholders. Prior to the ESRB, Tuomas was with the European Central Bank (ECB) since 2004, where he worked in various positions in the Directorate General Macroprudential Policy and Financial Stability, in the Directorate General Market Operations and in Directorate General International and European Relations. Prior to the ECB Tuomas worked with the Bank of Finland. Tuomas received his PhD (Econ) from European University Institute (EUI), Italy in 2005 and holds BSc and MSc (Econ) degrees from University of Turku. His research interests include macroprudential policy and systemic risk analysis. Tuomas has published several academic articles related to banking, financial stability, financial markets and emerging economies in academic journals like *Journal of Banking & Finance, Journal of Financial Stability,* and *IMF Economic Review.*

Luiz Awazu Pereira da Silva became Deputy General Manager of the BIS on 1 October 2015. Before joining the BIS, Mr Pereira da Silva, a Brazilian national, had been Deputy Governor of the Central Bank of Brazil since 2010. Prior to that, he worked in various positions for the World Bank in Washington DC, Tokyo and southern Africa. He also served as Chief Economist for the Brazilian Ministry of Budget and Planning, and as Brazil's Deputy Finance Minister in charge of international affairs.

Eswar Prasad is the Tolani Senior Professor of Trade Policy and Professor of Economics at Cornell University. He is also a Senior Fellow at the Brookings Institution, where he holds the New Century Chair in International Trade and Economics, and a Research Associate at the National Bureau of Economic Research. He is a former head of the IMF's China Division. Prasad is the author of "*Gaining Currency: The Rise of the Renminbi*" and "*The Dollar Trap: How the Dollar Tightened Its Grip on Global Finance.*" He has testified before numerous U.S. Congressional committees, including the Senate Finance Committee, the House of Representatives Committee on Financial Services, and the U.S.-China Economic and Security Review Commission. He is the creator of the Brookings-Financial Times world index. His op-eds have appeared in the *Financial Times, Harvard Business Review, International Herald Tribune, New York Times, Wall Street Journal,* and *Washington Post.* Prasad is also a Research Fellow at IZA (Institute for the Study of Labour, Bonn). Prasad holds a PhD in Economics from the University of Chicago.

Ramkishen S Rajan is Yong Pung How Professor at the Lee Kuan Yew School of Public Policy, National University of Singapore. Prior to this, he was a Professor of Economics at ESSEC Business School, Asia-Pacific. From 2006 to 2016, he was a Professor of International Economic Policy at George Mason University (GMU) in Virginia, USA. In the past, he has taught at the University of Adelaide in Australia, Claremont McKenna College and Claremont Graduate University in California, Singapore Management University, among other places. He has been a consultant with the APEC Secretariat, Asian Development Bank, Development Bank of Singapore, UN-ESCAP and the World Bank. He holds a B.Soci. Sci. (Hons) from NUS, M.A. from University of Michigan, Ann Arbor and MA and PhD from Claremont Graduate University, California. He specializes in international finance with particular reference to emerging Asia. He has published numerous books, journal articles and book chapters and a number of policy briefs, op-eds and book reviews on various aspects of international economic policy.

Dennis Reinhardt is a Research Advisor in the International Directorate of the Bank of England. He received his PhD in Economics from the Graduate Institute of International and Development Studies, Geneva. His research interests include international finance and banking, the transmission of macroprudential and monetary policies, international capital flows as well as capital controls and financial vulnerabilities. His research has been published in outlets such as the Journal of Financial Economics, the Journal of International Economics and the Journal of Monetary Economics.

Edward Surendran Robinson is Deputy Managing Director of the Economic Policy Group (EPG) and Chief Economist, MAS. He currently heads the EPG which formulates Singapore's monetary policy and conducts macro-financial surveillance. The Group also undertakes research on broader economic and financial issues facing the domestic and external economies. Edward studied Economics/Econometrics at Monash University and the University of Melbourne. He has a particular interest in macroeconometric modelling and continues to be engaged in the developmental work for the suite of MAS models, which are used for both price and financial stability analysis. He has also been involved in other areas of economic policy work including in various inter-governmental work groups, and served as a Board Member of the Competition Commission of Singapore.

Catherine Schenk FRHS, FRSA is the Professor of Economic and Social History at University of Oxford. After undergraduate and Masters degrees at University of Toronto in Economics, International Relations and Chinese Studies, she completed her PhD at the London School of Economics. Since then she has held academic positions at Victoria University of Wellington, New Zealand, Royal Holloway, University of London and University of Glasgow. She has been visiting professor at Nankai University, China, and Hong Kong University and she has spent time as a visiting researcher at the International Monetary Fund and at the Hong Kong Institute for Monetary Research and was 2019 Senior Lamfalussy Fellow at the Bank for International Settlements, delivering the Per Jacobsson Lecture in 2020. She is the author of several books and many articles on international economic relations since 1945 and the development of Hong Kong's international financial centre. She is current President of the Economic History Society and Associate Fellow in international economics at Chatham House and she leads the ERC GloCoBank project on global correspondent banking 1870–2000.

Ilhyock Shim is currently Head of Economics and Financial Markets for Asia and the Pacific at the Representative Office for Asia and the Pacific of the Bank for International Settlements (BIS Asian Office). He joined the BIS in Basel in 2004 as Economist. In 2007–17, he worked at the BIS Asian Office in Hong Kong SAR as Principal Economist. In 2018, he worked at the BIS in Basel as Special Adviser on International Financial Stability Policy in charge of G20 and FSB matters. He began his career as Deputy Director in the Korean government in 1996. In 1997–99, he worked at Korea Ministry of Finance and Economy as Deputy Director in charge of deposit insurance and financial sector restructuring. When Korea chaired the G20 in 2010, he was Advisor to the G20 Affairs Office of the Bank of Korea. He obtained BA and MA in Economics from Seoul National University, and PhD in Economics from Stanford University.

Hyun Song Shin took up the position of Economic Adviser and Head of Research at the BIS on 1 May 2014. Before joining the BIS, Mr Shin was the Hughes-Rogers Professor of Economics at Princeton University. In 2010, on leave from Princeton, he served as Senior Adviser to the Korean president, taking a leading role in formulating financial stability policy in Korea and developing the agenda for the G20 during Korea's presidency. From 2000 to 2005, he was Professor of Finance at the London School of Economics. He holds a DPhil and MPhil in Economics from Oxford University (Nuffield College) and a BA in Philosophy, Politics and Economics from the same university.

Kwanho Shin is Professor of Economics at Korea University. He received his B.A. and M.A. in economics from Seoul National University and Ph.D. in economics from UCLA. He was Assistant Professor at the University of Kansas for four years and occasionally taught at UCLA, Claremont Graduate University and Claremont McKenna College as a visiting professor. He was elected as "One of the Fifty Future Leaders in

Korea" by the Seoul Economic Daily in 2010, a "MaeKyung Economist" by the Maeil Business Newspaper in 2011 and a "Dasan Economist Prize" winner by The Korean Economic Daily in 2020. He also served as a council member for the National Economic Advisory Council from 2010 to 2011. He has published widely on the subjects of business cycles, monetary economics, international finance and labor economics in a number of leading academic journals including *American Economic Review, Journal of Monetary Economics, Journal of Econometrics, Journal of Money, Credit and Banking, Journal of International Economics, Journal of International Money and Finance* and *Journal of Labor Economics*.

Reza Siregar is currently Chief Representative Singapore Office at Institute of International Finance. Previously he was an International Economist Consultant in the IMF Singapore Regional Training Institute. Prior to this, he was an Executive Director and Chief ASEAN Economist for Global Macro Research at Goldman Sachs (Singapore) Pte. He has also held a variety of other positions at the IMF, the Asian Development Bank, the ASEAN+3 Macroeconomic Research Office, the SEACEN Center, and in academia at the Department of Economics, National University of Singapore, and at the School of Economics, University of Adelaide, Australia.

Rhiannon Sowerbutts is a Research Advisor in the Macroprudential Strategy and Support Division of the Bank of England. She received her Ph.D. in Economics from Universitat Pompeu Fabra. Her research interest include macroprudential policy, regulatory arbitrage, international banking flows, banking and banking crises. Her research has been published in outlets such as the Journal of International Economics and Journal of International Money and Finance.

Duvvuri Subbarao was Governor of the Reserve Bank of India for five years (2008–13) finishing his term in September 2013. Prior to that, Dr. Subbarao was Finance Secretary to the Government of India 2007–08 and Secretary to the Prime Minister's Economic Advisory Council 2005–07. He was a Lead Economist in the World Bank 1999–2004. As a career civil servant for over 35 years, he worked in various positions in the state government of Andhra Pradesh and in the central government in New Delhi mostly in the area of public finance management. Dr. Subbarao has written and spoken extensively on issues in macroeconomic management, public finance and financial sector reforms. During his tenure at the Reserve Bank, he was also recognized as a leading exponent of central banking issues from an emerging market perspective. After stepping down from the Reserve Bank of India, Dr. Subbarao was a Distinguished Fellow first at the National University of Singapore and most recently at the University of Pennsylvania.

Alexandre Tombini is currently Chief Representative of the BIS Office for the Americas. Before joining the BIS, he was Executive Director of the Board at the International Monetary Fund for Brazil, Cabo Verde, the Dominican Republic, Ecuador, Guyana, Haiti, Nicaragua, Panama, Suriname, Timor-Leste and Trinidad and Tobago. Previously, he was with the Central Bank of Brazil, where he served as Governor and also in the roles of Deputy Governor for Financial System Regulation and Deputy Governor for Economic Research. He also held positions as a Board member of the BIS and Chairman of the Standing Committee on Budget Resources of the Financial Stability Board. Mr Tombini holds a PhD in economics from the University of Illinois at Urbana-Champaign.

Paul Tucker is a research fellow at the Harvard Kennedy School, author of Unelected Power (Princeton University Press, 2018), and chair of the Systemic Risk Council. For over thirty years he was a central banker, including at the Bank of England; the steering committee of the G20 Financial Stability Board, leading its work on resolving too-big-to-fail firms without taxpayer bailouts; and the board of the Bank for International Settlements, chairing Basel's (then) Committee for Payment and Settlement Systems. He is working on a book on international order and system.

Boris Vujčić is currently Governor of the Croatian National Bank. He holds a PhD in Economics from the University of Zagreb. He has also received diplomas in Economics from the Montpellier University (France) and was a pre-doctoral PhD Fulbright student at the Michigan State University. He joined the Croatian National Bank in 1997, and was Director of the Research Department for three years before becoming

Deputy Governor in 2000, a position to which he was re-appointed in 2006. In July 2012, Mr Vujčić became Governor of the Croatian National Bank for a six-year term of office and was re-appointed for another six-year term of office in July 2018. Mr Vujčić has been a Deputy Chief Negotiator in Republic of Croatia's negotiations with the European Union 2005–2012. He was also a member of the Global Development Network (GDN) Board in the same period, 2005–2012 and a Member of the Steering Committee of the ESRB 2016–2019. He is also a Chairman of the Steering Committee of the Vienna Initiative, since 2016, and a Member of the General Council of the ECB, since 2013. Mr Vujčić's fields of expertise are macro and monetary economics, international finance and labour economics.

Perry Warjiyo is Governor of Bank Indonesia. He was born in Sukoharjo in 1959. After completing his education in the Faculty of Economy, Gajah Mada University (UGM), in Yogyakarta in 1982, Perry continued his education in Iowa State University and successfully gained his Master's degree in 1989 and Ph.D. in 1991. Before serving as the Governor of Bank Indonesia, Perry was the Deputy Governor of Bank Indonesia from 2013 to 2018. Perry also served as the Assistant Governor for monetary, macroprudential, and international policies. He held the position after he served as the Executive Director of Bank Indonesia's Department of Economic Research and Monetary Policy. Before returning to Bank Indonesia in 2009, Perry Warjiyo held an important position for two years as the Executive Director of the International Monetary Fund (IMF), representing 13 member countries in the South-East Asia Voting Group from 2007 to 2009. Perry has a long and brilliant career in Bank Indonesia since 1984, primarily in economic research and monetary policy, international issues, organizational transformation and monetary policy strategies, education and research on central banks, management of foreign reserves and external debts, and the Governor Bureau. Perry's passion for science makes him love to write and he issued several books, journals, and papers on economy, monetary, and international issues.

Arthur Yuen is Deputy Chief Executive of the Hong Kong Monetary Authority (HKMA) in charge of the full range of banking policy, supervision, conduct, and enforcement issues. He joined the HKMA in 1996 as Head of Administration and has since taken up different responsibilities including research and liaison on China economic and market development issues before being appointed Head of Banking Supervision in 2000. He took up the position as Executive Director (Banking Development) in July 2004, Executive Director (Banking Supervision) in June 2005 and Executive Director (External) in July 2008. He was appointed to his present position on 1 January 2010.

Fabrizio Zampolli has been Head of Economics for Latin America & the Caribbean since February 2018 and a member of the team since September 2016. Before that, he was Acting Head of Macroeconomic Analysis (2015–16), principal economist at the Representative Office for Asia & the Pacific in Hong Kong SAR (2014–15) and a senior economist (2009–14). Before working for the BIS, he was an economist in the Monetary Assessment and Strategy Division and a policy adviser in the External Monetary Policy Committee Unit of the Bank of England. He also worked in the External Development Division and the Monetary Policy Strategy Division of the ECB. He holds a PhD from the University of Warwick and a Laurea in Economia e Commercio from the Catholic University of Milan.

Contents

About the Editors ... vii

About the Contributors ... ix

Welcome Remarks: The Quest for an Integrated Macro-Policy Framework ... xxxv
    Ravi Menon

Welcome Remarks: Historical Evolution of Macro-Financial Stability Frameworks and a Search of a New Conceptual Framework ... xliii
    Agustín Carstens

Chapter 1   Macro-Financial Stability Frameworks: Experience and Challenges ... 1
    Claudio Borio, Ilhyock Shim and Hyun Song Shin

    Macro-Financial Stability Frameworks: Experience and Challenges: A Discussion ... 50
    Linda Goldberg

Chapter 2   What Happens in Vegas Does Not Stay in Vegas ... 59
    Anil K. Kashyap

Chapter 3   Macroprudential Policies and the COVID-19 Pandemic: Risks and Challenges for Emerging Markets ... 73
    Sebastian Edwards

	Macroprudential Policies and the COVID-19 Pandemic: Risks and Challenges for Emerging Markets: A Discussion *Eswar Prasad*	121
Chapter 4	Macroprudential Policy during COVID-19: The Role of Policy Space *Katharina Bergant and Kristin Forbes*	129
	Macroprudential Policy during COVID-19: The Role of Policy Space: A Discussion *Valentina Bruno*	175
Chapter 5	Macro-Financial Policy in an International Financial Centre: The UK Experience Since the Global Financial Crisis *Thorsten Beck, Simon Lloyd, Dennis Reinhardt and Rhiannon Sowerbutts*	183
	Macro-Financial Policy in an International Financial Centre: The UK Experience Since the Global Financial Crisis: A Discussion *Paul Tucker*	224
Chapter 6	Sweden's Experience of Deploying Monetary and Macroprudential Policies *Stefan Ingves and Johan Grip*	231
	Sweden's Experience of Deploying Monetary and Macroprudential Policies: A Discussion *Charles Bean*	272
Chapter 7	The "Twin-Pillar" Framework of Monetary and Macroprudential Policies in China *Yiping Huang and Tingting Lv*	277
	The "Twin-Pillar" Framework of Monetary and Macroprudential Policies in China: A Discussion *Yi Huang*	311

Chapter 8	Timely, Sustained and Effective Macroprudential Policy: Exploring the Political Economy of Hong Kong's Prudential Standards in the 1990s *Robert N McCauley and Catherine R. Schenk*	317
	Timely, Sustained and Effective Macroprudential Policy: Exploring the Political Economy of Hong Kong's Prudential Standards in the 1990s: A Discussion *Arthur Yuen*	362
Chapter 9	Macroprudential Policies for the External Sector: India's Approach and Experience *Viral V Acharya*	367
	Macroprudential Policies for the External Sector: India's Approach and Experience: A Discussion *Duvvuri Subbarao*	399
Chapter 10	Legacy of Early Crisis and Incomplete Institutional Reforms on the Financial Sector in Indonesia *M. Chatib Basri and Reza Y. Siregar*	409
	Legacy of Early Crisis and Incomplete Institutional Reforms on the Financial Sector in Indonesia: A Discussion *Perry Warjiyo*	431
Chapter 11	Lessons from Macro-Financial Policy in Korea *Hyun Song Shin and Kwanho Shin*	435
	Lessons from Macro-Financial Policy in Korea: A Discussion *Hwanseok Lee*	470
Chapter 12	Macroprudential Policies and Financial Stability in a Small and Open Economy: The Case of Singapore *Ramkishen S. Rajan, Edward S. Robinson and Rosemary Lim*	479

Macroprudential Policies and Financial
Stability in a Small and Open Economy:
The Case of Singapore: A Discussion 537
Yongheng Deng

Chapter 13 Monetary Policy Frameworks in Latin America:
Evolution, Resilience and Future Challenges 543
*Ana Aguilar, Alexandre Tombini
and Fabrizio Zampolli*

Monetary Policy Frameworks in Latin America:
Evolution, Resilience and Future Challenges:
A Discussion 575
Enrique G. Mendoza

Chapter 14 Leave No Stone Unturned — Macroprudential
Policy in Croatia Between the Global Financial
Crisis and COVID-19 583
*Boris Vujčić, Mirna Dumičić Jemrić
and Lana Ivičić*

Leave no Stone Unturned — Macroprudential
Policy in Croatia Between the Global Financial
Crisis and COVID-19: A Discussion 612
Tuomas Peltonen

Chapter 15 Towards a New Monetary-Macroprudential Policy
Framework: Perspectives on Integrated Inflation
Targeting 617
Pierre-Richard Agénor and Luiz A. Pereira da Silva

Towards a New Monetary-Macroprudential Policy
Framework: Perspectives on Integrated Inflation
Targeting: A Discussion 674
Barry Eichengreen

© 2023 World Scientific Publishing Company
https://doi.org/10.1142/9789811259432_0001

Welcome Remarks: The Quest for an Integrated Macro-Policy Framework

Ravi Menon

Managing Director
Monetary Authority of Singapore

Mr Agustín Carstens, General Manager, Bank for International Settlements, ladies and gentlemen, good afternoon and welcome to this year's special edition of the Asian Monetary Policy Forum featuring the MAS-BIS Conference on Macro-Financial Stability.

Macro-financial stability: Theory trying to catch up with practice

The origins of this conference go back to a conversation that Agustín and I had about 18 months ago on the need to crystallise a coherent policy framework for macro-financial stability.

In the three decades preceding the Global Financial Crisis, the traditional inflation-targeting framework for monetary policy served most economies well, delivering price stability as a basis for sustained economic growth.

That framework is now coming under strain.

- Emerging market economies (EMEs) faced with large and volatile international flows of capital have had to resort to a variety of

policy tools besides traditional monetary policy to achieve both macroeconomic and macro-financial stability.
- The advanced economies faced with rising leverage and growth in financial assets against the backdrop of extremely low interest rates are also looking at macroprudential measures to promote financial stability.

Practice has moved ahead of theory. In the absence of a conceptual framework, central banks of EMEs facing large capital flows have had to experiment with the tools at their disposal — such as foreign exchange intervention, macroprudential policies and capital flow management measures.

- There is now a rich body of policy experiences, especially in emerging Asia, crying for a theoretical framework.
- We need a framework that provides coherence not only across these various policy tools but also with traditional monetary and fiscal policies.

There is an active research agenda at the BIS on such an integrated policy framework. As a practitioner of some of these policies, MAS is delighted and honoured to organise this conference together with the BIS.

What is the big deal with capital flows?

When central bankers from advanced economies meet, they discuss quantitative easing and r* (the natural rate of interest). When EME central bankers meet, they talk about capital flows.

What is the big deal with capital flows?

First, capital flows to EMEs have become quite large.

- Annual gross portfolio inflows have grown to an average 1.3 percent of EMEs' GDP in the eight years following the Global Financial Crisis, compared to an average 0.7 percent during the eight years prior (IMF).

A key driver of the surge in cross-border capital flows has been the prolonged period of near-zero interest rates and highly expansionary monetary policies in the advanced economies. There is empirical evidence that quantitative easing policies in the US have made capital flows to EMEs more procyclical (Fratzscher *et al.*, 2013; Bhattarai *et al.*, 2017; Eichengreen and Gupta, 2014).

Second, capital flows have become more volatile.

- Volatility almost doubled in the three years post-global financial crisis compared to the three years preceding the crisis.[1] Volatility has since remained elevated.

Third, large and volatile capital flows can create some serious trouble for EMEs.

- What flows in can flow out as easily, and such reversals can be disruptive for EME financial markets which are typically not deep enough to smoothly intermediate the flows.

Capital flows can induce exchange rate fluctuations that are disconnected from macroeconomic fundamentals. There is growing empirical evidence that capital flows to EMEs have grown in importance as a driver of exchange rate movements.[2] In particular, capital flows can cause cyclical deviations to exchange rates beyond movements driven by the current account of the balance of payments. In the face of large and volatile capital flows, a freely floating exchange rate can become a shock amplifier rather than a shock absorber.[3]

Capital flows can trigger financial stresses or exacerbate domestic financial vulnerabilities. Strong capital inflows risk fuelling domestic

---

[1] Volatility of capital flows in EMEs rose from an average US$1.2 billion in 2006–2008 to US$2.1 billion in 2009–2011 based on a 12-month rolling standard deviation of GDP-weighted capital flows.

[2] While economies tend to experience additional capital inflows in response to exchange rate appreciation, these inflows could create additional appreciation pressures on the exchange rate. See Ehlers and Takats (2013).

[3] Exchange rates are sensitive to imbalances in financial markets and seldom perform the shock absorption role that is central to traditional macroeconomic analysis. See Gabaix and Maggiori (2015).

credit and asset price bubbles, heightening risks to macro-financial stability in EMEs.

- A recent MAS study found that a 1 percent appreciation of the US dollar is associated with net capital outflows of 0.3 percent of GDP for EMEs in the following quarter (MAS, 2020).

Fourth, large and volatile capital flows are here to stay.

- Ageing populations and slower productivity growth in the advanced economies suggest that the natural rate of interest, r-star, is likely to remain low, making the search for yield and resultant capital flows persistent rather than episodic (Williams, 2016).

Whose problem is it?

In setting monetary policies, should advanced economies take into account the spillover effects on EMEs through capital flows?

It is neither feasible nor desirable for advanced economies' monetary policies to be constrained by considerations of the cross-border spillovers they generate.

- Advanced economy central banks have their own domestic macro-financial stability goals they need to meet and cannot be expected to sub-optimise their policy outcomes.
- Moreover, accommodative monetary policies in the advanced economies have generated positive spillovers to EMEs, through strengthening export demand and enabling conducive financing conditions.

At the same time, it must be recognised that monetary policy latitude in EMEs is to some extent compromised by large capital flows.

- Empirical studies have found that EMEs' monetary policy responds to movements in US interest rates and exchange rates, besides their own domestic macroeconomic conditions.[4]

---

[4] See Finger *et al.* (2019). Other studies find that some central banks' monetary policy space has been eroded by capital flows even under floating rate regimes. See Rey (2016) and Miranda-Agrippino and Rey (2020).

- EMEs should therefore have the flexibility to use the policy tools at their disposal to protect their domestic economies from risks arising from large capital flows.

Some questions for an integrated policy framework

What are some of the questions that an integrated policy framework should seek to address?

The existence of different policy objectives and multiple sources of disequilibria necessitates the use of a range of policy instruments. These can be grouped under three broad buckets: foreign exchange interventions (FXIs), macroprudential measures (MPMs) and capital flow management measures (CFMs).

Determining which tool is appropriate has been a matter of careful judgement, depending on policymakers' objectives, country circumstances, available policy space and the nature of the shock. Policymakers have typically assigned interest rates as an instrument for price stability, MPMs for financial stability, FXIs for exchange rate stability and CFMs for directly curbing capital inflows and outflows.

However, the reality is more complex as policies interact and have overlapping effects.

- For instance, MPMs working through the credit channel can have a dampening effect on aggregate demand and influence the attainment of monetary policy objectives.
- Some countries use CFMs to mitigate capital outflows to stabilise exchange rates, if FXIs prove insufficient.

An integrated policy framework needs to provide greater clarity on these interactions. We need a deeper understanding of how these instruments can complement, substitute or conflict with one another.

- For example, we need to better understand the interactions between monetary policy and macroprudential regulation in achieving both price and financial stability.

One view is that monetary and macroprudential policies are largely complementary and hence should be used together for better results.

- For instance, an IMF study found that tighter MPMs to address financial stability risks are associated with more countercyclical monetary policy responses to macroeconomic shocks (Mano and Sgherri, 2020).

An alternative perspective is that monetary policy can be used to achieve both price and financial stability.

- By setting the price of leverage and influencing risk taking, monetary policy can lean against the build-up of excessive credit and financial imbalances, thus mitigating financial stability risks.
- However, and this is a point I have made elsewhere, monetary policy is too blunt an instrument for addressing specific risks to financial stability, and it can sometimes cause collateral damage to the rest of the economy if it tries to do so (Menon, 2014).

An integrated policy framework could perhaps shed light on the circumstances under which monetary policy could also serve financial stability objectives, and whether there are benefits to jointly calibrating monetary policy and macroprudential policy, as well as how this calibration should be done.

The BIS and IMF have both been undertaking research on these issues. Central bankers have at the same time gained considerable experience in employing an eclectic mix of policy instruments, with varying degrees of success. There is merit in bringing these practical experiences to bear in formulating an integrated policy framework.

Conclusion

Developing effective policy instruments and using them in a coherent fashion will enhance macroeconomic and macro-financial stability. It will help to make financial globalisation safer, especially for EMEs, at a time when there are growing risks of fragmentation in international economic relationships.

Your task is therefore vital. I wish you a fruitful conference ahead.

References

Bhattarai, S, A Chatterjee and W Y Park (2017). "Global Spillover Effects of US Uncertainty", Fed Reserve Bank of Dallas, Working Paper No. 331.

Ehlers, T and E Takats (2013). "Capital Flow Dynamics and FX Intervention", *BIS Papers* No. 73.

Eichengreen, B and P Gupta (2014). "Tapering Talk: The Impact of Expectations of Reduced Federal Reserve Security Purchases on EMEs", *World Bank Working Paper,* No. 6754.

Finger, H and P L Murphy (2019). "Facing the Tides: Managing Capital Flows in Asia", *IMF Asia and Pacific Department Paper Series* No. 19/17.

Fratzscher, M, Lo Duca, M and Straub, R (2013). "On the International Spillovers of US Quantitative Easing", *ECB Working Paper* No. 1557.

Gabaix, X and M Maggiori (2015). "International Liquidity and Exchange Rate Dynamics", *Quarterly Journal of Economics*, 130(3), 1369–1140.

IMF Balance of Payments, IMF International Financial Statistics, MAS calculations.

Mano, R and Sgherri, S (2020), "One Shock, Many Policy Responses", *IMF Working Paper*, WP/20/10.

Menon, R (2014), "Getting in All the Cracks or Targeting the Cracks? Securing Financial Stability in the Post-Crisis Era", Opening Remarks at the Asian Monetary Policy Forum, 24 May.

Miranda-Agrippino, S and H Rey (2020). "US Monetary Policy and the Global Financial Cycle", *Review of Economic Studies*, Volume 87, Issue 6, November, 2754–2776.

Monetary Authority of Singapore (MAS) (2020). "Implications of USD Dominance on Capital Flows and Financial Stability in EMEs", Special Feature 1, *MAS' Financial Stability Review*, December.

Rey, H (2016). "International Channels of Transmission of Monetary Policy and the Mundellian Trilemma", *NBER Working Paper Series*, Working Paper 21852

Williams, J (2016), "Measuring the Natural Rate of Interest: International Trends and Determinants", *Journal of International Economics*, Volume 108, S59–S75

ize
Welcome Remarks: Historical Evolution of Macro-Financial Stability Frameworks and a Search of a New Conceptual Framework

Agustin Carstens

General Manager, Bank for International Settlements

Introduction

It is a real pleasure to join you at this conference. This conference originates from a discussion I had with MD Menon 18 months ago, where we saw eye to eye on the need for better analytical frameworks for the macro-financial themes that are at the centre of this conference. Thanks to the close collaboration between MAS and the BIS, this conference has become a reality.

When MD Menon and I discussed the idea of having this conference, the BIS was in the process of setting out a new mid-term strategy, i.e., BIS 2025. One key aspect of this strategy was to find ways to bring more of the BIS to Asia and to bring more of Asia to the BIS.

As Ravi put it, we embarked on a joint journey to produce more research on macro-financial stability policy. This conference showcases our determination and willingness. With the joint effort from practitioners and academics, we will be able to find the best solutions.

After Ravi's insightful remarks, let me take a different angle. I would like to trace back the historical evolution of macro-financial stability frameworks, which can shed light on the process of how policymakers have managed to adjust policy tools to the evolving reality through past crises.

Let me share some thoughts on the main themes of this conference.

Brief historical overview

We need to learn from the past to improve our policy frameworks in the future. This conference is an opportunity to take stock of how challenges have evolved over the decades.

Ravi rightly pointed out that theory lags behind practice. I would further advance that practice often falls behind actual developments as well. When we carefully examine the history of past crises, we can identify a few major events that were game changers for the set-up of macro-financial stability policy. We need to break the cycle, and to head off the new challenges before they materialise.

In the 1970s, policy was framed in the context of the Mundell–Fleming framework and the Bretton Woods regime. We had closed capital markets and pegged exchange rates. Macro-financial stability relied on prudent fiscal and monetary policy.

One key challenge was the recycling of petrodollars, which led to excessive bank lending and government over-borrowing. The lack of sufficient discipline in fiscal and monetary policy led to capital inflows with currency appreciation and domestic credit build-up. This ultimately cast doubt on the sustainability of currency pegs. With international banks' capital eroded, this model blew up in the 1980s' debt crises. Policymakers were then busy with bank recapitalisation and there the BIS has provided a leadership role.

In the next decade, emerging market economies (EMEs) started to recapitalise their banks. EMEs made tremendous effort to open up their economies, especially their capital accounts. That was under the intellectual impetus of Washington Consensus. The big change back then was the rapid development of capital markets and the securitisation of sovereign bonds. Banks took the back seat, giving way to capital flows in the form of securities. Risks emerged from two sources. On the one hand, capital account liberalisation was coupled with fixed exchange rates, an awkward combination that did not end well. On the other hand, there was insufficient recognition of the importance of banking regulation. Weak domestic banks exposed themselves to currency risk and credit risk. All these risks culminated at the Tequila Crisis, the first in a series of cumulated currency and banking crisis in EMEs.

From late 1990s to 2000s, many countries adopted inflation targeting with flexible exchange rates, amid large effort for policy framework institutionalisation. At that time, banking regulations were enhanced and Basel standards gained greater prominence. The push for development of local currency bond markets facilitated hedging and channelled global investor flows into local currency bonds. Global and regional safety nets were also enhanced. The IMF developed new liquidity tools, such as the Contingent Credit Lines. In Asia, the Chiang Mai Initiative was set up. We had a few good years in the boom before the onset of the 2008 Great Financial Crisis (GFC).

The GFC was a major crisis in advanced economies (AEs) but EMEs managed quite well. This shows that EMEs had learned lessons from the past, done their homework and enhanced their resilience. However, in the aftermath of the GFC, push factors in the form of monetary easing and asset purchase programmes in AEs set in motion the search for yield in securities markets as a major theme affecting EMEs. Local currency government bond markets came of age, and expanded quickly after the GFC. These markets have played a big role in time for the Taper Tantrum in 2013. In this context, foreign exchange intervention both on the spot and forward markets and capital flow management tools have gained traction and have been accepted as mainstream tools to deal with volatile capital flows. Even the IMF has changed its Institutional View. These tools were sanctified by the orthodoxy. At the same time, both AEs and EMEs further developed their macroprudential policy frameworks.

In 2020, the world was hit by the COVID-19 pandemic, which in some ways was a glimpse into the future. We need to take note of it and rethink our policy framework accordingly. The initial shock was mitigated by massive loosening of the US monetary policy. Banks generally entered the crisis with stronger capital and macro-financial stability frameworks played a key role. However, the current highly accommodative policies and favourable global financial conditions should not be taken for granted as something that continue indefinitely. In addition, some new themes have emerged, to which we need to pay particular attention. First, non-bank financial intermediation has been growing rapidly and is largely unregulated. Second, leverage has been rising in capital markets. In addition, dollar funding could become more expensive in the context of faster economic recovery in the US. Finally, search for yield could trigger what we call at the BIS "original sin redux". Countries whose local currency debt is largely held by foreign investors could face heightened capital flow volatilities when market sentiments weaken.

In search of a new conceptual framework

So far, our policy frameworks have worked well. However, are we prepared for the potential game changer in the future? Here we need to think carefully if our frameworks are fit for purpose. We need a conceptual framework that captures how the four new themes that I have just identified above (non-bank financial institutions, leverage, dollar funding, original sin redux) interact with fluctuations in global financial conditions.

Concretely, we will need a new theory that tells us how global financial conditions, which has been argued to be well-proxied by the broad dollar index, affect risk-taking and hence portfolio flows into EMEs even in the absence of currency mismatches on the part of the borrower.

In addition, these new themes or challenges do not concern EMEs only. Dollar funding is a key issue also for AEs — the biggest FX bases are for yen, euro and other AE currencies. Leverage is an important issue that applies more generally. Facing the new challenges, the traditional demarcation between AEs and EMEs is getting blurred.

I hope the discussions we will have here will shed light on these very important questions. We should feel comfortable with what has been built in the last decade, but we still need a healthy periodic debate, and help policymakers to go ahead of the curve.

I am sure the conference will be a success and help us achieve this objective. Thank you.

CHAPTER 1

© 2023 World Scientific Publishing Company
https://doi.org/10.1142/9789811259432_0003

Chapter 1

Macro-Financial Stability Frameworks: Experience and Challenges*

Claudio Borio,[†] Ilhyock Shim[‡] and Hyun Song Shin[§]

Bank for International Settlements
[†]Claudio.Borio@bis.org
[‡]Ilhyock.Shim@bis.org
[§]Hyunsong.Shin@bis.org

Abstract

Since the 2008–2009 Great Financial Crisis, major advanced economies (AEs) have used monetary and macroprudential policies to achieve macroeconomic and financial stability. Emerging market economies (EMEs) have, in addition, combined interest rate tools with FX intervention, macroprudential policy and, sometimes, capital flow management measures (CFMs) to address the challenges from capital flow and exchange rate volatility. This chapter provides an overview of the use of monetary, macroprudential and exchange rate policies, sometimes alongside CFMs, both in AEs and EMEs. It also assesses the extent to which the

---

*The authors thank Anamaria Illes, Taejin Park and Jimmy Shek for their excellent research assistance. The views expressed in this chapter are those of the authors, and not necessarily the views of the Bank for International Settlements.

use of these policies constitutes a holistic macro-financial stability framework (MFSF). We reach three conclusions. First, combining tools has succeeded in improving policy trade-offs. In particular, EMEs have benefited from the joint use of the various policies to mitigate the risks for domestic stability arising from external influences. Second, a holistic MFSF is still a work in progress: a number of challenges remain. Finally, more efforts need to be made to better understand the channels of international spillovers and spillbacks.

1. Introduction

Macrostabilisation policy since at least the Great Financial Crisis (GFC) of 2008–2009 has increasingly emphasised the importance of a macroprudential orientation in policy frameworks. The term "macroprudential" originated from and was then largely developed at the Bank for International Settlements (BIS).[1] In his seminal paper, Crockett (2000) defines macroprudential perspectives and dimensions of financial stability. Major advanced economies (AEs) have expanded their policy toolkit to achieve their goals of macroeconomic and financial stability, in part driven by the need to use macroprudential tools to offset some of the side effects of unusually strong and prolonged monetary easing. Meanwhile, emerging market economies (EMEs) have been exposed to larger swings in capital flows and exchange rates, reflecting in part those monetary policy settings.

A special chapter in the *2019 BIS Annual Economic Report* builds on these themes, but from an EME perspective, by focusing on the monetary policy frameworks in EMEs that incorporate a financial stability orientation on top of the traditional focus on inflation targeting with flexible exchange rates (BIS, 2019). It notes that practice has moved ahead of theory — akin to the way advanced open economies had adopted inflation targeting in the early 1990s. It explains why and how EMEs have combined conventional interest rate tools with FX intervention,

---

[1] For a discussion of the evolution of the "macroprudential" concept, see Clement (2010) and Baker (2020).

macroprudential policy and, in some cases, capital flow management measures (CFMs) to better address the challenges raised by capital flows and associated exchange rate fluctuations.[2] The International Monetary Fund (IMF) has made related efforts to develop so-called integrated policy frameworks (Adrian and Gopinath, 2020; IMF, 2020).

Against this backdrop, the objective of this chapter is two-fold. First, it is to provide an overview of the use of monetary, macroprudential and exchange rate policies, sometimes alongside CFMs, both in EMEs and AEs. Particular attention is paid to policies that aim to moderate the impact of external financial conditions and to the effectiveness of macroprudential tools — the most novel set of instruments. Second, it is to assess the extent to which the use of these various policies constitutes a *holistic* macro-financial stability framework (MFSF),[3] rather than a collection of disparate policy tools. The concept of a MFSF has a long history at the BIS, since the mid-2000s. Chapter VIII of the *BIS Annual Report 2008* stresses that such a comprehensive framework is needed to address the inherent procyclicality of the financial system, domestically and internationally, so as to better reconcile price with financial, and hence macroeconomic, stability.[4]

We reach three main conclusions. First, combining tools has succeeded in improving policy trade-offs. In particular, EMEs have benefited from

---

[2] The G20 Eminent Persons' Group report published in October 2018 prominently mentioned macro-financial stability. In particular, the report recommended that receiving countries assess the impact of global factors affecting capital flows to EMEs and policy options available to EMEs in maintaining macro-financial stability when faced with such challenges. It also recommended that sending countries develop a policy framework that enables them to adopt policies to meet their domestic objectives while avoiding large, adverse spillovers to receiving countries.

[3] An MFSF covers the joint operation of monetary (including FX intervention), micro/macroprudential and fiscal policies to stabilise the economy, based on solid foundations ensured by structural policies (Borio, 2018). While the original concept of a MFSF does not include CFMs, in this chapter we consider them as well given their prominence in certain asset classes, as a complement to other policies designed to address the influence of external financial conditions.

[4] For a comprehensive discussion of the procyclicality of the financial system, see Borio et al. (2001).

the joint use of the various policies to successfully mitigate the risks for domestic stability arising from external influences.

Second, a holistic MFSF is still a work in progress (Borio, 2014). A number of challenges stand out. Fiscal policy has not been properly integrated so far. There is still a lot of controversy over the role of monetary policy in relation to macroprudential policy. Operationally, the different frequencies of business, domestic and global financial cycles set limits to the realistic degree of integration of the various policies. And analytical tools still have some way to catch up with practice so as to better support policy.[5]

Finally, taking a global perspective, more still needs to be done both to better understand the channels of international spillovers and spillbacks and to incorporate them into a holistic macro-financial stability policy framework. Global financial conditions can sometimes transcend balance of payment boundaries and the nomenclature of "sending" countries and "recipient" countries. The currency dimension looms large in this context, as exchange rate movements have real economy impact through changes in external financial conditions that affect domestic outcomes. These channels of transmission mean that the traditional current account-based narratives of adjustment need to be complemented with broader global overlays of risk-taking and financial conditions.

The structure of the chapter is as follows. Section 2 describes the economic backdrop, explaining why the evolution of the global economy has heightened the need for a MFSF and putting the various issues in perspective. Section 3 describes the deployment of macroprudential policies and CFMs. Section 4 discusses the combination of policies in AEs and EMEs, focusing on that of macroprudential and monetary policies in AEs and on how to address capital flows and exchange rate fluctuations in EMEs. Section 5 considers the impact of exchange rate fluctuations on foreign investors' purchase of EME government bonds. Section 6 reviews the evidence on the effectiveness of the measures. Finally, Section 7 discusses the ongoing challenges.

---

[5] An important aspect of a holistic MFSF is macro-financial linkages, that is, the two-way interactions between the real economy and the financial sector. Claessens and Kose (2018) provide a systematic review of the literature on macro-financial linkages.

2. A MFSF: Why its increasing relevance?

The task of macroeconomic policy has always been to stabilise economic fluctuations and ensure low inflation. For much of the post-war period, the main concern was how to address inflation. However, starting around the mid-1980s, financial instability became an increasingly important concern. In this context, financial instability should not just be interpreted narrowly as banking and financial crises, but more broadly as the major financial amplification of business fluctuations. Put differently, if until the mid-1980s it was sufficient to talk about "macroeconomic stability frameworks", since then it has been hard not to add the qualification "financial" to "stability". Since then, both price and financial stability have been necessary conditions for macroeconomic stability.

The reason for this evolution has been a number of far-reaching changes in the nature of business fluctuations (Figure 1). Until the mid-1980s,

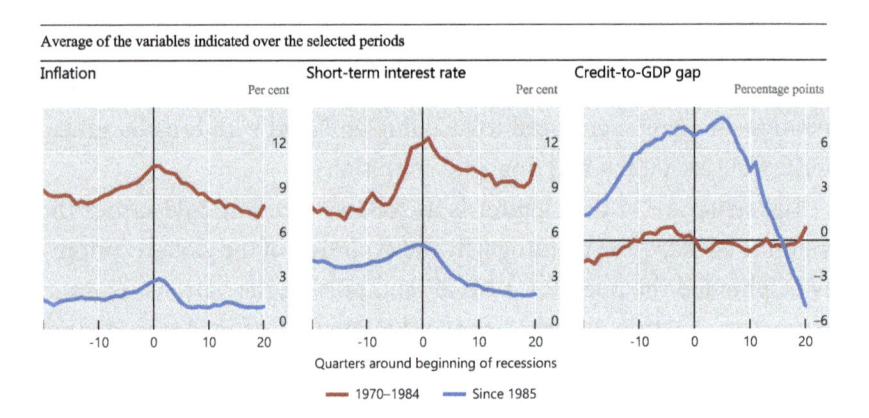

Figure 1. The changing nature of the business cycle.

Note: The horizontal axis denotes quarters around recessions in the business cycles, with the peak date set at zero (vertical lines). Lines show the median evolution across 16 advanced economies and events from 1985 to 2017. The 16 advanced economies are Australia, Belgium*, Canada, Finland*, France, Germany, Ireland*, Italy, Japan, Netherlands*, Norway*, Spain, Sweden, Switzerland, the United Kingdom and the United States. For countries denoted with *, business cycles are dated with a business cycle-dating algorithm. The recession dates are taken from the National Bureau of Economic Research or the Economic Cycle Research Institute.

Source: National data; adapted from Graph 2 in Borio *et al.* (2018); authors' calculations.

the typical recession reflected tighter monetary policy to fight rising inflation. Since then, by and large, inflation has been low and stable, and recessions have been ushered in by the build-up and unwinding of financial imbalances — proxied by the behaviour of the credit gap (the deviation of the credit-to-GDP ratio from a slow-moving trend) in Figure 1. Even in those EMEs that have faced inflationary conditions, the most serious contractions have been greatly amplified by financial forces, both internal and external. Hence, there have been a succession of banking crises, including those in Latin America in the early 1980s and mid-1990s; the Nordic and Japanese crises in the late 1980s and early 1990s; the Asian Financial Crisis in 1997 and the GFC in 2007–2008. Obviously, the most recent pandemic-induced recession is *sui generis*, as it reflects non-economic, exogenous factors.

Two structural factors have arguably played a key role in the evolution of the business cycle. First and foremost, financial liberalisation across borders — domestic and international — <u>and</u> currencies. This has provided much greater scope for financial forces to play a role, typically in the form of self-reinforcing interactions between funding constraints, risk-taking and asset prices, within and across economies. Second, the conquest of inflation, as a result of a mix of more disciplined monetary policy and real-side structural factors, such as globalisation and technology.

Financial factors have been playing a growing role both domestically and internationally. Hence there have been efforts to capture their most important features in a parsimonious way.

Domestically, a popular notion has been that of the *domestic financial cycle*.[6] This denotes the joint expansions and contractions in credit and asset prices that tend to amplify business fluctuations. The measure that has been found to be most useful in this context combines increases in credit and property prices. There is agreement that the financial cycle tends to be longer than the business cycle, traditionally measured as 14–18 years rather than up to 8 years (Figure 2, left-hand panel). Banking crises, and the deepest recessions, tend to occur close to the peak of the cycle.[7] In

---

[6] For a comprehensive discussion of the domestic financial cycle and its properties, see Borio (2014).
[7] There is a large literature showing that financial-cycle proxies are among the most reliable leading indicators of banking crises; e.g., Borio and Drehmann (2009), Gourinchas and Obstfeld (2011) and Schularick and Taylor (2012).

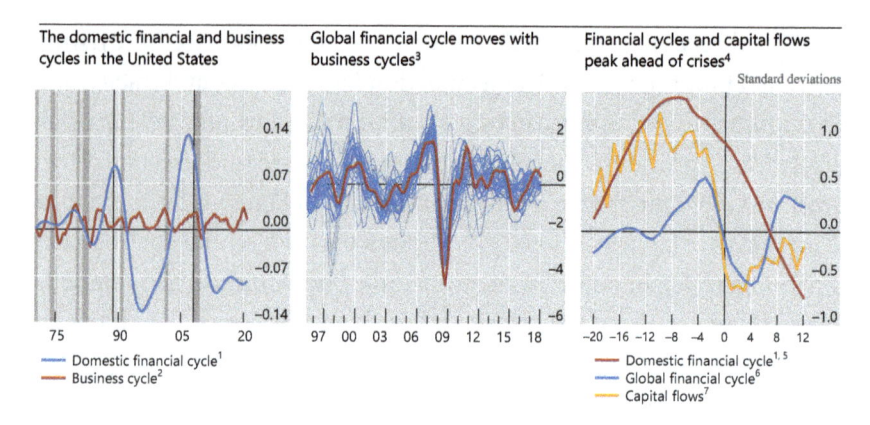

Figure 2. Business cycles, domestic financial cycles and global financial cycles.
[1]The domestic financial cycle as measured by a bandpass filter capturing medium-term cycles in real credit, the credit-to-GDP ratio and real house prices.
[2]The business cycle as measured by a bandpass filter capturing fluctuations in real GDP over a possible window from one to eight years.
[3]The red line is a composite global financial factor from Aldasoro et al. (2020) based on a large cross section of asset prices and gross capital flows. The blue lines are individual business cycles of 29 countries. Both sets of lines are constructed based on a bandpass filter capturing fluctuations over a possible window from 5 to 32 quarters. The global financial factor is lagged by two quarters.
[4]The horizontal axis denotes quarters around crises, with the start date set at zero (vertical lines). The average of the relevant variable is taken at the specific quarter across all crisis episodes available for the respective indicators.
[5]Normalised by country-specific mean and standard deviation.
[6]The composite global factor combines the price-based global financial factor of Miranda-Agrippino and Rey (2015) with a quantity-based factor based on total external flows to 31 countries.
[7]Gross capital inflows, scaled by GDP, normalised by country-specific mean and standard deviation.
Note: The shaded areas in the left-hand panel indicate recessions; the solid black lines indicate the start of a banking crisis as defined by Laeven and Valencia (2018).
Source: IMF, Balance of Payments; Aldasoro et al. (2020); Miranda-Agrippino and Rey (2015); national data; authors' calculations.

addition, recent empirical evidence indicates that financial cycle proxies tend to be among the best predictors of recessions across both AEs and EMEs (e.g., Borio et al., 2021).

Internationally, ebbs and flows in capital flows and the associated fluctuations in exchange rates have been the focus of much academic and policy work. Terms such as sudden stops (Calvo, 1996) or capital flow bonanzas (Reinhart and Reinhart, 2008) have become very popular in the literature. More recently, the concept of a *global financial cycle* has gained prominence as a summary measure of global financial conditions (see, e.g., Scheubel *et al.* [2019]).[8] In all of these characterisations, the main force behind capital flows has been "push" factors, of a global nature and largely driven by US policy, given the unchallenged supremacy of the US dollar as an international currency.

While quite distinct, the domestic and global financial cycles are related (Aldasoro *et al.*, 2020). They are distinct in so far as they involve only a partly overlapping set of asset prices and quantities, but also because they evolve at different frequencies: high-frequency risk-on/risk-off phases aside, the global financial cycle tends to evolve at business cycle frequencies and co-moves with them (Figure 2, centre panel). That said, the two cycles tend to come together around crises and big recessions (Figure 2, right-hand panel). This has implications for the degree and shape of the integration of the various policies that make up a MFSF (see below).

Regardless of whether the global financial cycle is considered a useful summary measure,[9] the channels through which external influences have made themselves felt on domestic financial conditions have changed over time. Three developments merit particular attention, notably as regards EMEs. First, at least ever since the Asian Financial Crisis, a shift from foreign currency to local currency borrowing in EMEs (see, e.g., Hofmann *et al.* [2020a]). The shift has affected mainly governments and the corporate sector to a far lesser extent. Second, especially since the GFC, a move away from bank credit to market-based financing — what has been termed the "second phase of global liquidity" (Shin, 2013). Third, and closely related, a growing participation of foreign investors

---

[8] Rey (2013) has used the term and measured it based on asset prices only; see Aldasoro *et al.* (2020) for a detailed comparison of the notions of the two cycles, domestic and global.
[9] For a sceptical view, see Cerutti *et al.* (2019).

in domestic currency bond markets, with their investments largely on an unhedged basis in order to enhance yield — a form of carry trade (Avdjiev et al., 2018).

These shifts have affected, in particular, the role of the exchange rate as an amplifying mechanism through currency mismatches. Simply put, mismatches have tended to migrate from *borrowers'* to *investors'* balance sheets — what has been referred to as a shift from "original sin" to "original sin redux".[10] As a result, while the development of local currency bond markets has helped shield EMEs from the ebbs and flows of global financial conditions, it has not insulated them altogether. Increases in local currency bond yields and domestic currency exchange rate depreciations tend to go hand-in-hand when financial conditions tighten. This means that investors incur a double whammy, which can in turn amplify their retrenchment. All these have highlighted further the role of the US dollar as a global risk factor for EMEs, operating not just through borrowers', but also through investors' balance sheets.[11]

The growing relevance of domestic and external financial factors explains the evolution of policy frameworks. Domestically, central banks have increasingly complemented monetary policy with macroprudential tools as a means of better reconciling the pursuit of price and financial stability over longer horizons, and better handling the intertemporal trade-offs involved. Externally, central banks have increasingly resorted to FX intervention and, occasionally, to CFMs to achieve the same goals. Here, FX intervention can play a dual, quasi-macroprudential role (BIS, 2018). FX accumulation during capital flow surges builds up buffers for use when the tide turns. And, by relieving some of the pressure to reduce

---

[10] The term "original sin redux" was coined by Carstens and Shin (2019).

[11] The discussion highlights another insight that sheds light on MFSF — the need to shift the focus from net financial flows (e.g., the current account) to gross financial flows and balance sheets (Borio and Disyatat [2011]; Adrian and Shin [2010]; Obstfeld [2010]; Lane and Milesi-Ferretti [2001], following in the early footsteps of Kindleberger [1956]). This is the natural result of shifting attention from inflation and traditional macrostabilisation to financial stability. Moreover, the focus transcends the "triple coincidence of the unit of analysis, decision-making unit and currency area", as firms and currencies straddle borders in a globalised world (Avdjiev et al., 2016a). It is only in the context of interlocking and multiple-currency balance sheets that such behaviour and risks can be properly assessed.

interest rates in order to contain the currency appreciation, it can dampen the corresponding easing of domestic financial conditions (Borio, 2014).

Beyond common elements, there are substantial differences in the deployment of tools across countries. All have been increasingly relying on macroprudential measures. However, the role of FX intervention, let alone CFMs, differs markedly. In AEs, FX intervention has been employed more sparingly and only largely to offset the impact on inflation and output of exchange rate pass-through to prices and exports. In EMEs, the impact of capital flows and exchange rate fluctuations on domestic financial conditions — the financial channel — has played an important role. This partly reflects structural differences in financial systems, as those in EMEs are not as developed and hedging opportunities there are more limited. Moreover, even EMEs themselves differ individually in terms of the extent to which they rely on FX intervention and CFMs. Beyond country-specific structural and institutional features, this reflects different views concerning the merits of floating exchange rates (BIS, 2020, 2021).

3. MFSFs: Deployment of macroprudential and capital flow management measures

By far, the most distinctive new tool in the policy toolkit used to reconcile price and financial stability has been macroprudential measures.[12] Their use has grown rapidly in AEs and EMEs alike (Figure 3).[13] Many EMEs have also used CFMs to deal with challenges from excessive capital flow volatility. In this section, we provide an overview of macroprudential measures deployed by AEs and EMEs during 1995–2020 and also a summary of CFMs taken in 2000–2019 by nine EMEs.

---

[12] To be sure, many of these measures had been used in the past *before* being termed "macroprudential". In fact, some harked back to the credit controls popular in the 1960s and 1970s, during the era of financial repression and when central banks paid more attention to credit aggregates. That said, their deployment as part of a more systematic effort to address *financial* stability is of more recent vintage.

[13] The sample includes 56 countries, of which 33 are EMEs and 23 AEs, since 1995. It covers a total of 1,502 macroprudential measures as well as 913 additional monetary or regulatory measures seemingly used from a macroprudential perspective (e.g., reserve requirements intended to restrain credit expansion). In this second case, of course, the line is blurred.

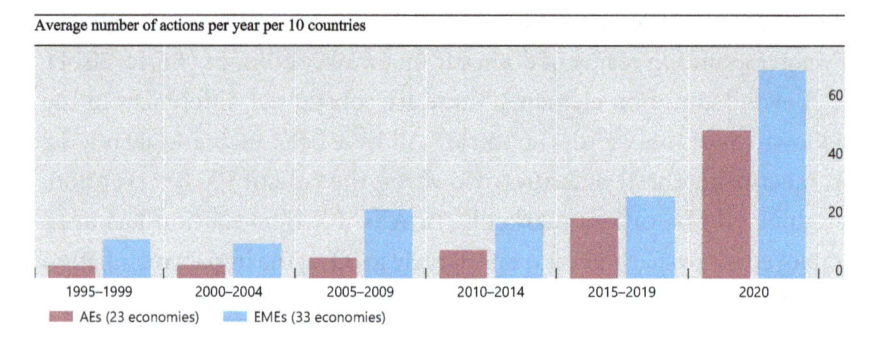

Figure 3. Increased use of macroprudential measures.
Source: Budnik and Kleibl (2018); Reinhardt and Sowerbutts (2016); Shim *et al.* (2013); FSB Covid-19 policy action database; IMF, Integrated Macroprudential Policy (iMaPP) Database, originally constructed by Alam *et al.* (2019); national data; authors' calculations.

3.1. *Experience of using macroprudential measures between 1995 and 2020*

Figure 4 provides an overview of how 56 AEs and EMEs used macroprudential measures targeting different types of credit between 1995 and 2020. Among different types of monetary, prudential and fiscal instruments, "loan-to-value (LTV) limits and loan prohibitions" and "debt service-to-income (DSTI) limits, debt-to-income (DTI) limits and other lending criteria" targeting housing, consumer or household credit were used most frequently by the 56 economies over the sample period (Figure 4, upper panel). The sample economies also frequently used "non-cyclical (structural) systemic risk capital surcharges (such as domestic systemically important bank surcharges, other systemically important institution surcharges and systemic risk buffers)", "risk weights on housing or consumer loans" and "housing-related taxes".

Overall, EMEs were more active in using macroprudential measures than AEs. Among the EMEs, 14 central and eastern European countries took the largest number of policy measures during 1995–2020, followed by nine emerging Asian economies. However, when we calculate the average number of macroprudential actions per country per 10 years, nine emerging Asian economies were the most active users of macroprudential tools among the seven AE and EME regions, followed by central and

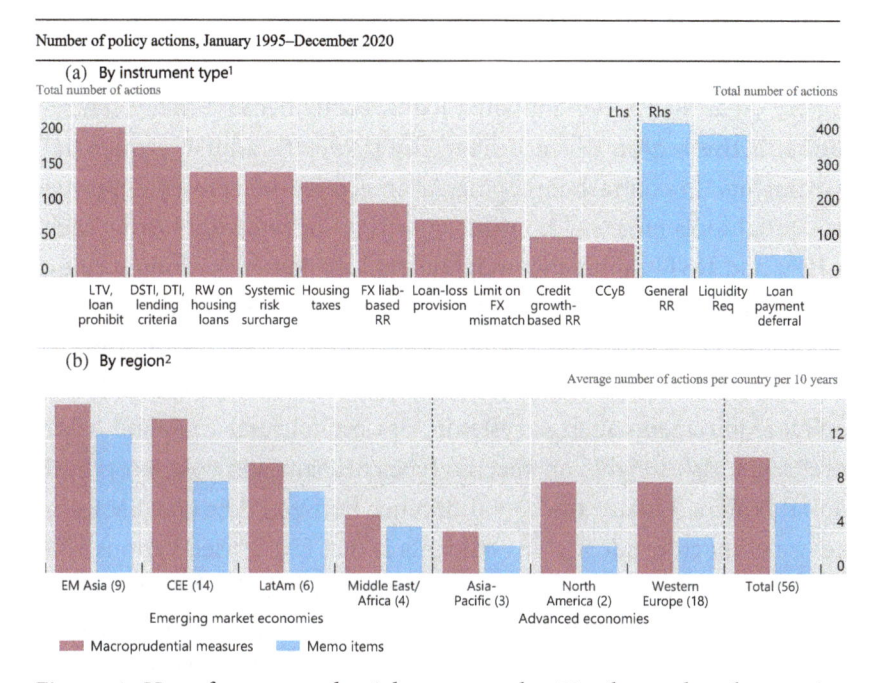

Figure 4. Use of macroprudential measures by 56 advanced and emerging market economies.

[1]LTV means the maximum loan-to-value ratio. DSTI means the maximum debt service-to-income ratio. DTI means the maximum debt-to-income ratio. Systemic risk surcharges are non-cyclical (structural) systemic risk capital surcharges such as domestic systemically important bank surcharge, other systemically important institution surcharge and systemic risk buffers. RR means reserve requirements. CCyB means countercyclical capital buffer. Liquidity requirements include the minimum liquidity coverage ratio, the minimum net stable funding ratio, the minimum liquid asset ratio and the maximum loan-to-deposit ratio.

[2]The figures in brackets on the horizontal axis indicate the number of economies in each region.

Source: Budnik and Kleibl (2018); Reinhardt and Sowerbutts (2016); Shim *et al.* (2013); FSB Covid-19 policy action database; IMF, Integrated Macroprudential Policy (iMaPP) Database, originally constructed by Alam *et al.* (2019); national data; authors' calculations.

eastern European countries and Latin American countries (Figure 4, lower panel). Among AEs, Western European countries were the most active users in terms of both the total number of actions and the average number of actions per country per 10 years.

There are also regional differences in preferred instruments. Latin American economies relied mostly on reserve requirements targeting general credit or FX-denominated loans, partly because many central banks in the region did not have the power to adjust prudential instruments. In contrast, emerging Asian economies actively deployed prudential tools targeting housing, consumer or household loans such as LTV and DSTI limits, risk weights and loan-loss provisioning rules. Central and Eastern European economies were more balanced in their use of macroprudential instruments. Among AEs, Western European countries relied predominantly on prudential tools, especially on capital requirements such as systemic risk capital surcharges and other surcharges, risk weights on specific types of loans and countercyclical capital buffers. Finally, one key difference between AEs and EMEs in the use of macroprudential instruments is that EMEs used various FX-related instruments (such as FX-denominated liability-based reserve requirements, limits on currency mismatch, FX positions and FX-denominated loans, and FX liquidity requirements), while AEs rarely used such instruments.

Now we consider how frequently the macroprudential measures were used over the 26 years. Figure 3 shows that both AEs and EMEs steadily increased their use of macroprudential measures between 1995 and 2019. During the period, EMEs took more actions per year than AEs, but the gap became smaller over time and reached a comparable level in 2015–2019. Facing unprecedented shocks in 2020 due to the Covid-19 pandemic, both AEs and EMEs deployed a wide range of policy instruments to prop up credit provision to and reduce the burden of households, firms and the financial sector. As a result, both AEs and EMEs took more than twice the number of macroprudential actions per year in 2020, compared to that during the period of 2015–2019.[14]

Figure 5 shows how the 56 AEs and EMEs undertook tightening and loosening actions over the cycles between 1995 and 2020. During normal

---

[14] Notably, almost all economies covered in the sample introduced temporary loan payment deferral/suspension or moratorium in March–May 2020, to support the household and corporate sectors during the COVID-19 crisis. Box 1 provides a more detailed analysis on various types of policy measures introduced after the outbreak of the COVID-19 pandemic.

Tightening and loosening actions over time

Tightening (+) / loosening (-)

■ Total tightening ■ Total loosening ■ Net tightening

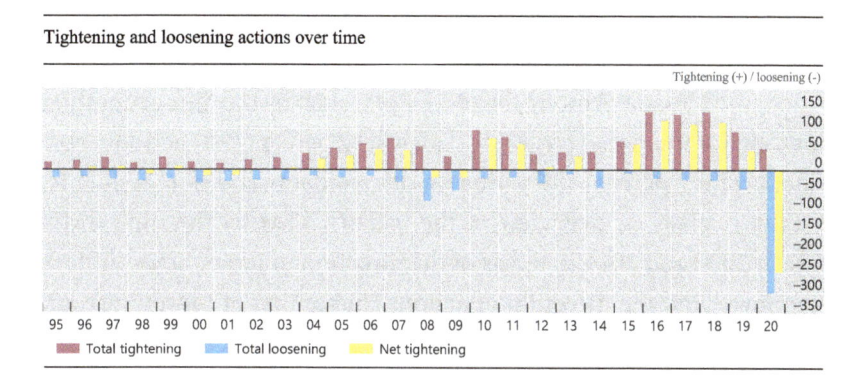

Figure 5. Number of macroprudential policy actions by 56 advanced and emerging market economies.
Source: Budnik and Kleibl (2018); Reinhardt and Sowerbutts (2016); Shim *et al.* (2013); FSB Covid-19 policy action database; IMF, Integrated Macroprudential Policy (iMaPP) Database, originally constructed by Alam *et al.* (2019); national data; authors' calculations.

times, and especially in the run-up to the GFC as well as between the GFC and the Covid-19 crisis, the sample economies took far more tightening actions than loosening ones. In contrast, during crisis years such as the Asian Financial Crisis in 1998, the GFC in 2008–2009 and the Covid-19 crisis in 2020, both AEs and EMEs took more loosening actions than tightening actions to support economic recovery. It should be noted that, as shown in Figure 3, the surge in tightening actions between 2015 and 2019 is mainly explained by the implementation of capital requirements by both AEs and EMEs, in line with Basel III rules such as capital surcharges on domestic systemically important banks (D-SIBs) and countercyclical capital buffers. Most economies loosened such capital requirements in 2020, when faced with the Covid-19 shock.

3.2. *Experience of selected EMEs using CFMs between 2000 and 2019*

In addition to macroprudential measures, many EMEs used CFMs targeting banking, bond, equity, real estate, direct investment and other flows. Some AEs such as Australia and Canada also used CFMs targeting real estate flows. In this section, we focus on CFMs used by the following nine EMEs represented in the subsequent chapters of this book: China, Hong Kong SAR, India, Indonesia, South Korea, Singapore, Brazil, Mexico, and Croatia. Among the 653 CFMs taken by the nine economies, 61 percent (399 actions) targeted residents, 32 percent (207 actions) non-residents and 7 percent (47 actions) both residents and non-residents.

Table 1 gives an overview of the use of CFMs by the nine EMEs between 2000 and 2019 in terms of the direction of target flows (inflows vs outflows) and the direction of actions (tightening or loosening), and thus their overall impact on domestic credit (decrease or increase credit). The number of CFMs loosening inflows and that of CFMs tightening inflows are more or less balanced in most economies. One exception is India, which continuously liberalised its banking and portfolio inflows over the past two decades. As a result, over the sample period, India deployed five times more actions of loosening capital inflows than those of tightening capital inflows (i.e., 24 CFMs tightening inflows vs 124 CFMs loosening inflows). A few other economies also exhibited some imbalances between tightening and loosening actions. In particular, Croatia used more CFMs loosening inflows than those tightening inflows, partly because of its accession to the euro area and the resulting liberalisation of various restrictions on capital accounts. In contrast, Hong Kong SAR and Singapore took more CFMs tightening inflows (mostly real estate inflows

Table 1. Capital flow management measures taken by nine selected EMEs, 2000–2019.

	CN	HK	IN	ID	KR	SG	BR	MX	HR	Total[a]
Total number of CFMs	129	10	212	31	84	8	72	18	69	633
Decrease domestic credit	78	7	80	21	61	8	41	7	30	333
Tightening inflows	36	7	24	17	28	7	31	5	17	172
Loosening outflows	42	0	56	4	33	1	10	2	13	161
Increase domestic credit	51	3	132	10	23	0	31	11	39	300
Loosening inflows	46	3	124	7	23	0	22	8	32	265
Tightening outflows	5	0	8	3	0	0	9	3	7	35

[a]Among the 653 actions in the dataset, 20 actions affect both capital inflows and outflows at the same time. Since it is difficult to classify these actions in terms of tightening or loosening flows, we do not include them in this table.

Source: CFM database in Chantapacdepong and Shim (2015); IMF, Annual Report on Exchange Arrangements and Exchange Restrictions (AREAER) 2001–19; national sources; authors' calculations.

by using housing-related taxes) than loosening inflows, mainly out of their concerns over too much foreign capital flowing into their property markets. Finally, we observe far more actions of loosening capital outflows than of tightening them, mainly because many of these EMEs were in the process of liberalising capital account restrictions on residents' outflows over the sample period.

Now, we focus on how the EMEs used financial stability-motivated (i.e., countercyclical) CFMs between 2000 and 2019. In particular, we consider 298 CFMs aiming to tighten or loosen banking, bond, equity and real estate inflows from foreign banks and investors, to EMEs. Here, we consider eight EMEs excluding India since most of the CFMs taken by India were motivated by structural reasons such as capital account liberalisation. The black line in Figure 6 shows that the eight EMEs on net took policy actions to tighten banking and real estate inflows in the years leading up to the GFC (from 2004 to 2008), and then loosened them in 2009 after the GFC. Between 2010 and 2012, facing strong capital flows from AEs, EMEs on net tightened CFMs, before they loosened the measures in 2013 and 2014 during and after the taper tantrum. Such patterns of tightening and loosening actions match well with capital flow and exchange rate dynamics and the incidence of crises: EMEs on net tightened CFMs during strong capital inflow periods and loosened them during strong capital outflow periods, generally in a countercyclical manner.

Finally, in terms of the types of instruments, we can broadly classify instruments used for CFMs into the following four categories: (1) quantitative limits, (2) qualitative restrictions, (3) taxes and (4) minimum holding periods. Around half of CFMs in our database involve quantitative limits on capital inflows or outflows, while around two-fifths of CFMs involve qualitative changes such as allowing certain types of investors to enter certain segments of markets. In addition, jurisdictions such as Brazil, Hong Kong SAR, India, Indonesia, Korea and Singapore imposed or adjusted taxes on financial transactions involving borrowing from non-residents or foreign investment in domestic financial assets and real estate. Finally, countries such as China, India and Indonesia tightened or loosened minimum holding period requirements for foreign investment in domestic bonds, equities and real estate as well as minimum maturity requirements for external borrowing by residents.

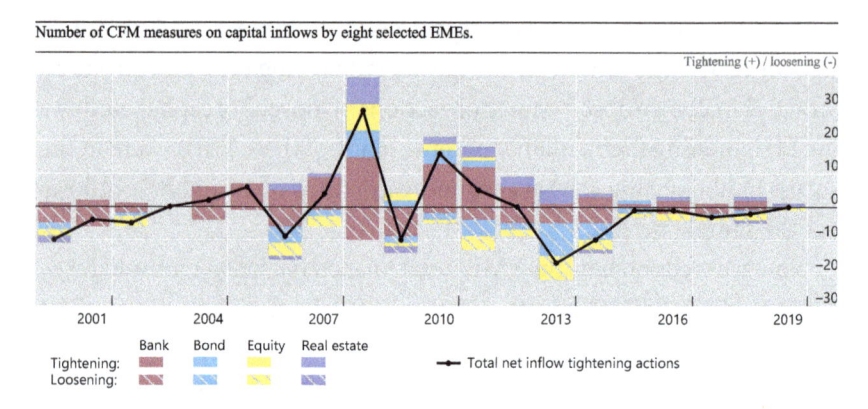

Number of CFM measures on capital inflows by eight selected EMEs.

Figure 6. Financial stability-motivated CFMs: tightenings and loosenings.
Source: CFM database in Chantapacdepong and Shim (2015); IMF, Annual Report on Exchange Arrangements and Exchange Restrictions (AREAER) 2001–2019; national sources; authors' calculations.

4. MFSFs in practice

4.1. *Combining monetary policy and macroprudential measures in AEs*

In this section, we investigate how AEs have jointly used monetary and macroprudential policies. In particular, we focus on how several major AEs kept monetary policy loose and tightened macroprudential policy between the GFC and the COVID-19 crisis in early 2020,[15] and show how macroprudential buffers built up since 2015 paid off in 2020.

Figure 7 shows the policy rates, long-term government bond yields as a proxy for quantitative easing policy, and the use of macroprudential measures for the US, four selected Eurozone countries, Japan, the United Kingdom and Canada. We find that most major AEs kept monetary policy loose or continued to loosen their monetary policy after 2010, while generally tightening macroprudential policy. Such a policy mix by AEs is in line with the situation highlighted in Borio and Shim (2007) who stress that when the scope for monetary policy to lean against the build-up of financial imbalances is constrained by the backdrop of low and stable

---

[15] Facing strong foreign investor inflows to their domestic real estate markets, AEs such as Canada also used tax measures targeting foreign investors. In this section, we focus on AEs' use of domestically oriented macroprudential measures.

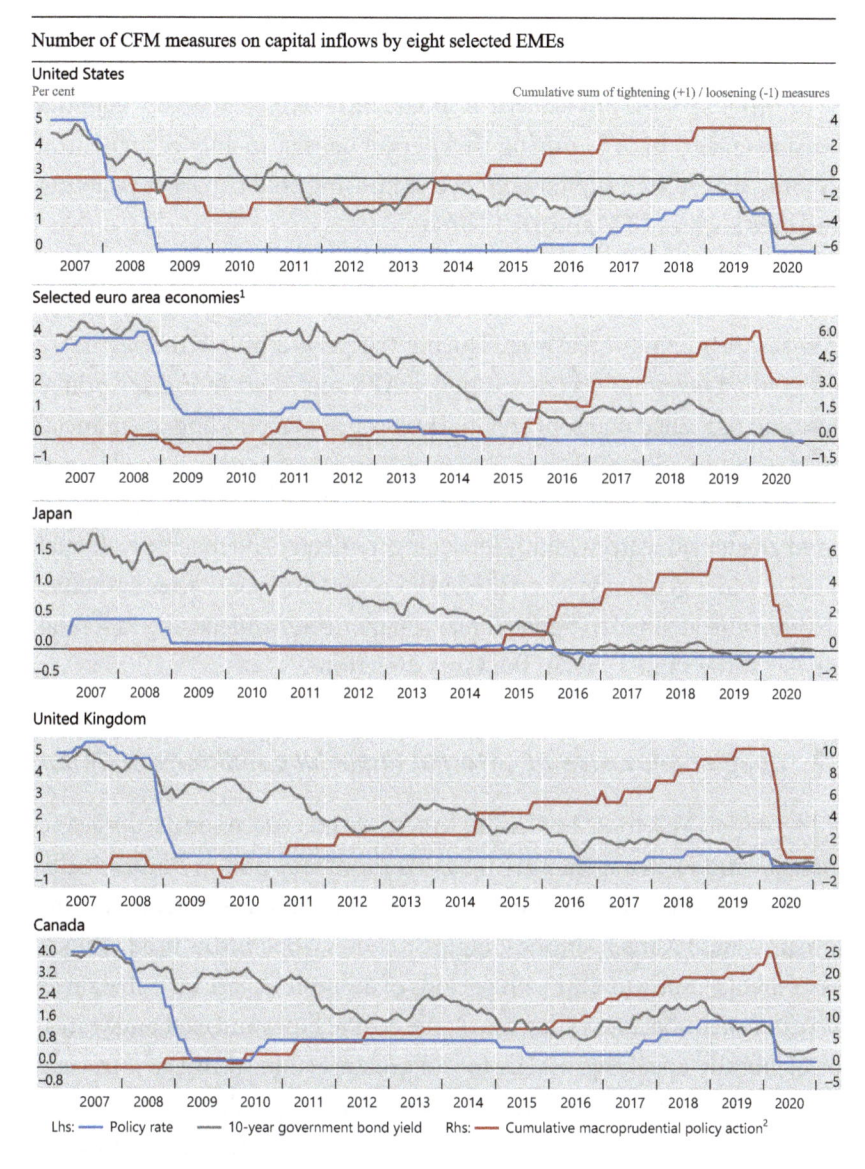

Number of CFM measures on capital inflows by eight selected EMEs

Figure 7. Policy rates, long-term yields and macroprudential measures in advanced economies.
[1]Simple average of DE, ES, FR and IT.
[2]Cumulative sum of tightening (+1) and loosening (−1) actions. For the four euro area countries, the average value of the cumulative sum for each country.
Source: Budnik and Kleibl (2018); Reinhardt and Sowerbutts (2016); Shim et al. (2013); FSB Covid-19 policy action database; IMF, Integrated Macroprudential Policy (iMaPP) Database, originally constructed by Alam et al. (2019); Bloomberg; national data; authors' calculations.

inflation, macroprudential measures designed to restrain the build-up of such imbalances can make the financial system better able to withstand the unwinding of the imbalances. It should be noted that macroprudential measures taken by AEs during this period consist mainly of structural systemic risk-related capital buffers and housing credit/market targeting measures such as LTV and DSTI limits.

A relevant issue for AEs is how far they should use the monetary policy to deal with domestic financial imbalances, rather than relying exclusively on macroprudential measures. During the period of low interest rates and gradual economic recovery, major AEs kept their monetary policy loose and tightened macroprudential policy to avoid building up financial imbalances. In contrast, when they faced a severe financial or real shock such as the GFC in 2008–2009 or the COVID-19 crisis in 2020, major AEs found greater value from jointly loosening monetary and macroprudential policies. More generally, when the business and financial cycles coincide, AEs are more inclined to tighten or loosen monetary and macroprudential policies at the same time, in the same direction.

4.2. *Special relevance of external financial conditions in EMEs*

Unlike major AEs, most EMEs aim to achieve macroeconomic, domestic financial and external stability by using monetary policy, domestically oriented macroprudential measures, financial stability-motivated CFM measures and FX interventions. Figure 8 shows when EMEs used various instruments jointly to deal with periods of domestic financial imbalances and external imbalances such as volatile capital flows and exchange rates.

Generally speaking, EMEs found greater value from the joint use of monetary policy, domestically oriented macroprudential measures, financial-stability–motivated CFM measures and FX interventions in the same direction, when they faced strong capital outflows and excessive volatility in exchange rates. In this section, we consider 17 EMEs in Africa, Asia, Latin America and the Middle East. Figure 8 shows how the 17 EMEs changed policy rates, took macroprudential measures and conducted FX intervention between 2003 and 2020.

Macro-Financial Stability Frameworks   21

Average intensity of policy measures[1]   Tightening (+) / loosening (–)

Policy rate change ■ Macroprudential action ■ FX intervention ■

Net number of EMEs[2] **that tightened or loosened policy instruments**[3]   Tightening (+1) / loosening (–1)

Policy rate change ■ Macroprudential action ■ FX intervention ■

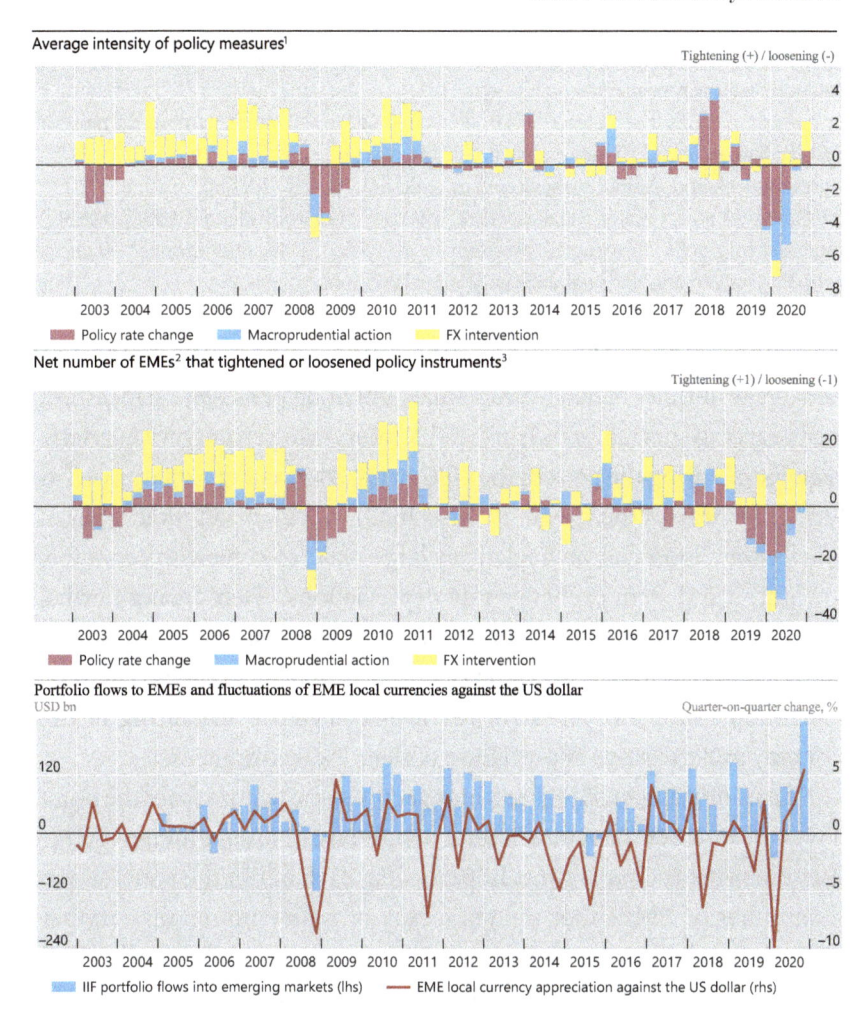

Portfolio flows to EMEs and fluctuations of EME local currencies against the US dollar
USD bn   Quarter-on-quarter change, %

IIF portfolio flows into emerging markets (lhs) ■   EME local currency appreciation against the US dollar (rhs) —

Figure 8.   Policy rate change, macroprudential measures and FX intervention by EMEs.

[1] Policy rate change = average quarterly change in the policy rate in percentage points across 17 EMEs divided by 50 basis points; macroprudential action = sum of tightening (+1) or loosening (–1) actions by an EME, averaged across 17 EMEs; FX intervention = average value of the percentage change in total FX reserve assets in US dollars excluding gold across 17 EMEs normalised by its standard deviation, where a positive value means purchasing foreign currency and selling local currency, and a negative value selling foreign currency and purchasing local currency.

[2] 17 EMEs: AR, BR, CL, CN, CO, HK, ID, IN, KR, MX, MY, PE, PH, SG, TH, TR and ZA.

[3] Policy rate change = the number of EMEs that increased the policy rate (+1) over a quarter, minus the number of EMEs that decreased the policy rate (–1) over the same quarter; macroprudential action = the number of EMEs that tightened macroprudential

Figure 8. (*Continued*) policy on net (+1) over a quarter, minus the number of EMEs that loosened macroprudential policy on net (–1) over the same quarter; FX intervention = the number of EMEs that increased FX reserve assets (+1) over a quarter, minus the number of EMEs that decreased FX reserve assets (–1) over the same quarter.
Source: Budnik and Kleibl (2018); Reinhardt and Sowerbutts (2016); Shim *et al.* (2013); FSB Covid-19 policy action database; IMF, Integrated Macroprudential Policy (iMaPP) Database, originally constructed by Alam *et al.* (2019); IMF, *International Financial Statistics*; Datastream; national data; authors' calculations.

The upper panel of Figure 8 shows the average change in the policy rate, the average number of macroprudential tightening or loosening measures and the average normalised change in FX reserves in percent on a quarterly frequency. During the peak of the GFC in Q4 2008 and Q1 2009 as well as during the peak of the Covid-19 crisis in Q1–Q2 2020, all three types of policies were loosened on a relatively large scale, to cope with economic downturns and stem exchange rate depreciations. Even during normal times, especially a few years before and after the GFC, the opposite was true: EMEs on average increased policy rates, tightened macroprudential instruments and increased FX reserves to avoid overheating of the economy and excessive appreciation of their local currencies.

The middle panel of Figure 8 looks at the same feature from the point of view of whether many EMEs tend to tighten or loosen different policy instruments at the same time. In particular, each bar in the panel shows the number of EMEs that tighten a type of policy minus the number of EMEs that loosen the policy type, every quarter. Each bar therefore can take a value of between –17 and 17. When a bar for a policy points upward (i.e., takes a positive value), more EMEs tightened rather than loosened the specific policy type. A longer bar means that more EMEs on net tightened or loosened the specific policy at the same time. Similar to the upper panel, a relatively large number of EMEs took coordinated loosening actions during crisis periods, while EMEs more often than not tightened all three policies during normal periods. Finally, during normal times with steady capital inflows, the number of EMEs increasing FX reserves was larger than that of EMEs increasing policy rates or tightening macroprudential instruments. Especially in several quarters in 2004–2008 and 2010–2011, all or almost all the 17 EMEs increased FX reserves at the same time.

In addition, it should be noted that we need to differentiate between macroprudential measures that specifically target external sources of vulnerabilities (e.g., the global financial cycle and capital flow surges/stops) and those that target domestic financial imbalances and the domestic financial cycle. An issue here is the different frequencies of the two cycles (domestic vs global), and hence the assignment of the various tools.

5. Original sin, original sin redux and policy implications for EMEs

In EMEs, capital flows and exchange rate changes affect domestic conditions via various financial channels. In 1990s, currency mismatches were prevalent in EMEs, because foreign borrowing by EMEs was mostly international banks' US dollar loans. Several financial crises of EMEs in the 1990s involved the sudden halt of international banks' US dollar loans to EMEs. Since then, many EMEs have shifted their external financing from banks to bond markets. Importantly, external bond financing is increasingly denominated in domestic currency, although currency mismatches still exist in the balance sheets of governments and corporates in EMEs (for details, see Hofmann *et al.* [2020a, 2020b] and Hördahl and Shim [2020]).

Original sin refers to an economy not being able to borrow in its domestic currency, as pointed out by Eichengreen and Hausmann (1999), driven by currency mismatches on the borrowers' balance sheet (often combined with maturity mismatches). It manifests itself through the interaction of exchange rate fluctuations, capital flows and government/corporate borrowing via loans and bonds denominated in foreign currencies (mainly in the US dollar). For example, Avdjiev *et al.* (2016b) show the strong relationship between the strength of the US dollar and cross-border bank lending in US dollars.

In contrast, original sin redux, driven by currency mismatches on foreign investors' (or lenders') balance sheet, focuses on the impact of exchange rate fluctuations on EME local currency bond markets via bond inflows. Original sin redux was especially relevant when EMEs witnessed strong portfolio capital outflows from their bond markets in March and April 2020, during the peak of the COVID-19 crisis. In response, many EME central banks introduced bond purchase programmes partly to stabilise their bond markets and fill the gap created by foreign investors' sale of local currency bonds, and partly to support fiscal policy needed to revive the economy hit by the COVID-19 pandemic.

In this section, we first consider original sin in terms of the impact of exchange rate fluctuations on foreign investors' purchase of EME foreign currency-denominated government bonds. We then provide evidence of original sin redux by estimating the impact of exchange rate fluctuations on foreign investors' purchase of EME local currency government bonds. Finally, we discuss the policy implications.

Recent BIS research provides evidence that the US dollar works as a gauge of global investors' risk appetite and especially as an EME risk factor (see, e.g., Avdjiev *et al.* [2018] and Hofmann and Park [2020]). We show evidence that the broad US dollar index explains foreign investors' purchase of local and foreign currency bonds generally better than the bilateral US dollar exchange rate against an EME's currency. The broad US dollar index can be viewed as a proxy for global investors' risk appetite, while the bilateral exchange rate captures both the strength of the US dollar as a global factor and the strength of an EME's local currency as a local factor.

5.1. *Original sin redux in EME local currency bond markets*

Recent studies such as Hofmann *et al.* (2020b) show that EME local currency bond spreads and the exchange rate of EME currency against the US dollar move in lockstep. To explain a channel through which exchange rate fluctuations affect local currency bond yields or spreads, we consider the impact of fluctuations in the bilateral US dollar exchange rate or the broad US dollar index on EME bond purchases by an individual EME bond fund. In addition, we compare the relative strength of the two exchange rates in explaining EME bond purchases and changes in EME local currency bond spread.

The left-hand panel of Figure 9 shows that, when we consider 20 EMEs for which data on local currency bond yields are available, a 1 percent appreciation (or deprecation) of the broad dollar index has about three times stronger effects on a mutual fund's sale (or purchase) of an EME's local currency government bonds divided by total net assets (TNA) of the

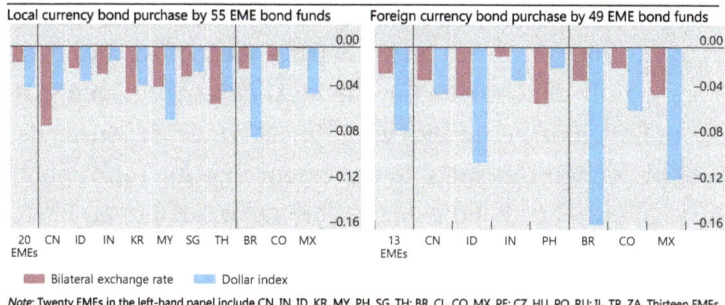

Figure 9. Impact of a 1 percent appreciation of the US dollar on EME bond purchases.
Note: Twenty EMEs in the left-hand panel include CN, IN, ID, KR, MY, PH, SG, TH; BR, CL, CO, MX, PE; CZ, HU, PO, RU; IL, TR, ZA. Thirteen EMEs in the right-hand panel include CN, IN, ID, PH; BR, CL, CO, MX, PE; HU, RU; TR, ZA.
Source: Bloomberg; EPFR; BIS; authors' calculations based on Hofmann *et al.* (2021).

fund than a 1 percent appreciation (or deprecation) of the bilateral exchange rate of the EME currency against the US dollar has. In terms of economic magnitude, the results imply that when the broad dollar index appreciates by 5 percent this month (i.e., other currencies depreciate against the US dollar), a global EME local currency bond fund sells an EME's local currency bonds by 20bps of the fund's TNA over the next month. If the fund is holding the EME's bonds worth 2 percent of TNA, then it decreases its holdings of the EME's bonds from 2 percent to 1.8 percent.

When we consider seven individual economies in emerging Asia (Figure 9, left-hand panel), we find that a stronger dollar captured by both exchange rates (i.e., depreciation of an EME's currency) is associated with a sale of the EME's local currency government bonds by global EME bond funds. For the three Latin American economies in the panel, a 1 percent broad dollar index appreciation has a much stronger impact on the purchase of local currency bonds than a 1 percent bilateral exchange rate appreciation has.

5.2. *Original sin in EME foreign currency bond markets*

In many EMEs, foreign currency-denominated bonds are an important source of financing for governments and corporates. Compared to bank loans, long-term bonds are less subject to maturity mismatch, but still subject to currency mismatch on the balance sheet of borrowers whose assets are mainly denominated in the local currency. Given that the majority of EME foreign currency government bonds are issued offshore and held by foreign investors, to the extent that the funds obtained from foreign currency bond issuances are repatriated to an EME, the funds become a source of capital inflows to the EME. Therefore, it is important to understand how sensitive foreign investors' purchases and sales of foreign-currency-denominated bonds issued by EMEs are as a manifestation of original sin.

The right-hand panel of Figure 9 shows that, when we consider 13 EMEs for which data on foreign currency bond yields are available, a 1 percent appreciation (or depreciation) of the broad dollar index has around three times stronger effects on a fund's sale (or purchase) of an EME's foreign currency government bonds over TNA than a 1 percent appreciation (or depreciation) of the bilateral exchange rate of the EME currency against the US dollar has. Considering four individual economies in emerging Asia, we find that a stronger dollar captured by both exchange rates (i.e., a depreciation of an EME's currency) is associated with a sale of the EME's foreign currency government bonds by global bond funds, and that the broad dollar index has a stronger impact on the purchase of all EMEs' government bonds than the bilateral exchange rate has, except for the Philippines.

5.3. *Policy options to deal with original sin and original sin redux*

As we show in Section 4, since the 1990s EMEs have deployed various types of policies to deal with exchange rate and capital flow volatility related to borrowing from foreign banks and investors. In particular, they used FX intervention to stabilise exchange rate fluctuations by addressing the source of the problem when their currencies appreciated or depreciated. Some regional central banks also used CFMs including prudential measures targeting FX exposure, together with FX intervention, to slow down strong capital inflows, albeit less frequently over time. Some other jurisdictions implemented macroprudential policy to build up buffers in the domestic financial system during good times and mitigate the build-up of financial imbalances such as excessive credit growth and asset price booms due to capital inflows. Finally, a smaller number of central banks in EMEs also adjusted their policy rate to help maintain external stability.

Specifically to deal with original sin involving foreign currency bond financing, central banks and other financial authorities in EMEs have taken policy measures to reduce currency mismatches or FX positions on the balance sheet of the borrowers (either governments or corporates), for example, by slowing down the issuance of foreign currency bonds by corporates during boom periods. By contrast, during periods of dollar funding stress, financial authorities have relaxed prudential regulation on FX borrowing. For example, China and South Korea introduced such measures at the peak of the COVID-19 crisis in 2020.

In order to deal with original sin redux in the local currency bond market, central banks and other financial authorities need to monitor the extent of currency mismatch on the balance sheet of foreign investors (i.e., unhedged exposure of foreign investors to local currency assets) and conduct stress tests against severe outflow scenarios. Also, to make hedging more easily available and less expensive to foreign investors, policymakers can make efforts to develop onshore FX derivatives markets. During severe stress periods, central banks may consider intervening in bond markets or both the FX and bond markets at the same time to alleviate concerns of foreign portfolio investors. Finally, over the long run, EMEs will need to develop a domestic institutional investor base which is not subject to currency mismatch problems.

As empirical evidence provided in this section shows, collective investment vehicles domiciled and/or headquartered in Europe or the US are important investors in EME local and foreign currency bond markets. Therefore, it will be important for national authorities to continue international discussions on the possibility of introducing prudential rules or risk management guidelines on non-bank financial institutions, which are active in cross-border portfolio investment. In particular, national authorities may consider enhancing the microprudential liquidity risk management practice of collective investment vehicles, especially those investing in less liquid EME assets, for example, by promoting them to hold sufficient cash buffers in good times (see Schrimpf *et al.* [2021]). An equally important point, in view of the tendency of EME mutual funds and ETFs simultaneously entering or exiting EME asset markets, is that it will be beneficial for financial authorities to consider the possibility of introducing macroprudential calibration of liquidity management rules for collective investment vehicles headquartered or domiciled in their jurisdictions.

6. MFSFs: The effectiveness of macro-financial measures

Since the GFC, many academic and policy papers have examined the impact of macroprudential measures on various types of domestic credit, asset prices, GDP and inflation. More recently, a growing literature looks at the cross-border impact of macroprudential policy.

Empirical evidence on the impact of macroprudential measures on overall bank risk suggests that macroprudential measures have been generally successful in strengthening the banking system's resilience. For example, Gambacorta and Murcia (2017) show that capital or reserve requirements on particular types of loans can change the relative price of different forms of credit, affect the composition of credit and thus reduce the overall riskiness of banks' loan portfolio. Recent econometric studies gauging the impact of macroprudential measures on bank risk (e.g., Aguirre and Repetto [2017], Altunbas *et al.* [2018] and Gómez *et al.* [2017]) suggest that such macroprudential measures contribute to a more resilient financial system.

There is a large literature showing that certain types of macroprudential measures have moderated financial booms. For example, Claessens *et al.* (2013) use a sample of around 2,800 banks in 48 economies over the period of 2000–2010 and find that maximum LTV and DSTI ratios as well as limits on credit growth and foreign currency lending tended to reduce bank leverage and asset growth during booms but that few policies stopped declines in bank leverage and assets during downturns. Kuttner and Shim (2016) use a sample of 57 economies over the period of 1980–2012 and investigate the effectiveness of nine non-interest-rate policies on house prices and housing credit. They find that introductions of or reductions in the maximum DSTI ratio and increases in housing-related taxes have significant negative effects on housing credit and house price growth. They also find that loosening the policy instruments is ineffective in increasing housing credit or house price growth.

Using the sample of macroprudential measures described in Figure 4, we run panel regressions across a broad set of AEs and EMEs and measure the impact of the most frequently used types of macroprudential measures on general credit to the non-financial sector and on housing credit extended by banks. In line with most other cross-country studies, we define three dummy variables: one for both tightening (+1) and loosening (−1) actions; another only for tightening (+1) actions; and the other only for loosening (+1) actions. Figure 10 shows the coefficients on five different macroprudential dummy variables in the general credit regressions, while Figure 11 shows those on five different macroprudential dummy variables in the housing credit regressions. Asterisks on the bars indicate statistical significance of the coefficients.

Figure 10 shows the impact of all macroprudential measures targeting total credit (including reserve requirements on general liabilities, liquidity requirements and loan payment deferrals/moratorium on general credit in the memo items) on real general credit growth as well as the impact of the macroprudential measures using the following four types of instruments: (1) reserve requirements on capital inflows or FX liabilities; (2) loan-loss provisioning rules on general credit; (3) limits on FX mismatches or FX positions and (4) general credit growth limits.

Limits on FX mismatches or FX positions and limits on general credit growth have economically significant impacts on general credit growth. The coefficients showing the four-quarter effects of tightening or loosening both types of limits are statistically significant. In addition, a relaxation of loan-loss provisioning rules has positive effects on general credit growth in the next quarter. In contrast, policy actions which tighten or loosen capital flow- or FX liability-based reserve requirements are economically and statistically insignificant. Finally, when we consider all macroprudential measures targeting general credit, tightening actions significantly reduce

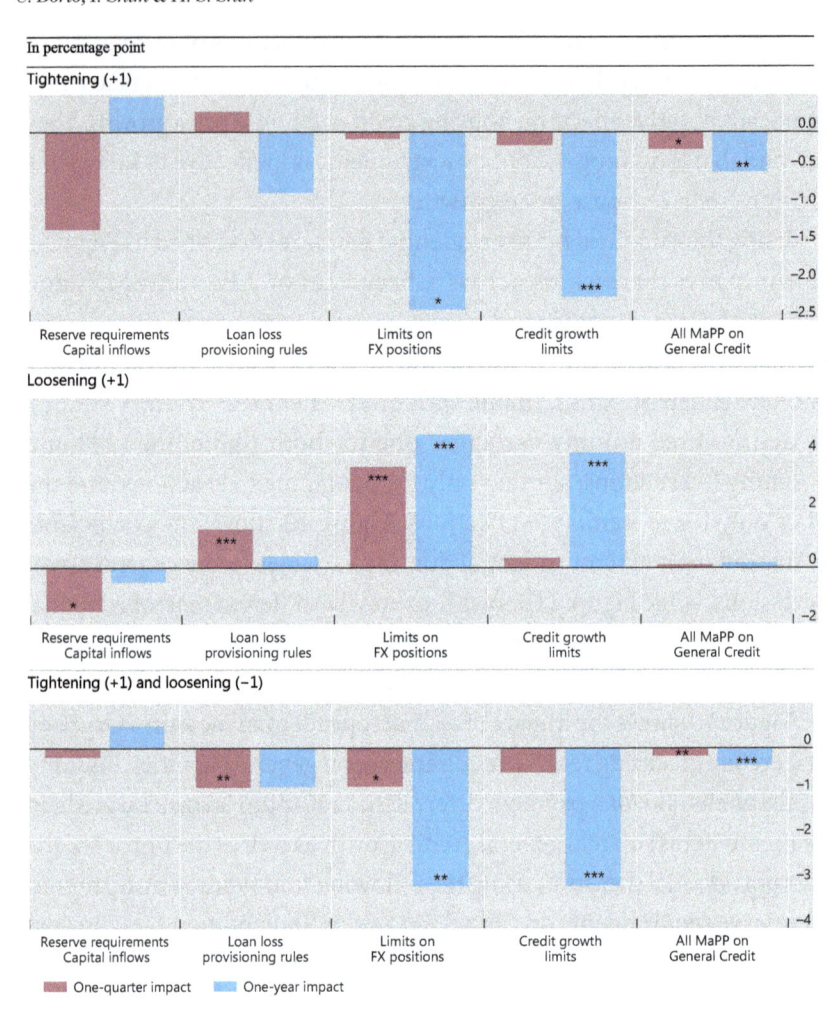

Figure 10. Impact of selected types of macroprudential measures on general credit growth.

Note: General credit data are for 43 economies, from BIS' data on total credit to the non-financial sector. The bars show the coefficients on the macroprudential policy dummy variables in panel regressions with country fixed-effects and the policy rate (2 lags) and real GDP growth (4 lags) used as control variables. The blue bar for loosening credit growth limits shows a 2-quarter cumulative impact. ***, ** and * mean statistical significance at the 1 percent, 5 percent and 10 percent level, respectively.

Source: Budnik and Kleibl (2018); Reinhardt and Sowerbutts (2016); Shim *et al.* (2013); FSB Covid-19 policy action database; IMF, Integrated Macroprudential Policy (iMaPP) Database, originally constructed by Alam *et al.* (2019); CEIC; Datastream; BIS credit statistics; national data; authors' calculations.

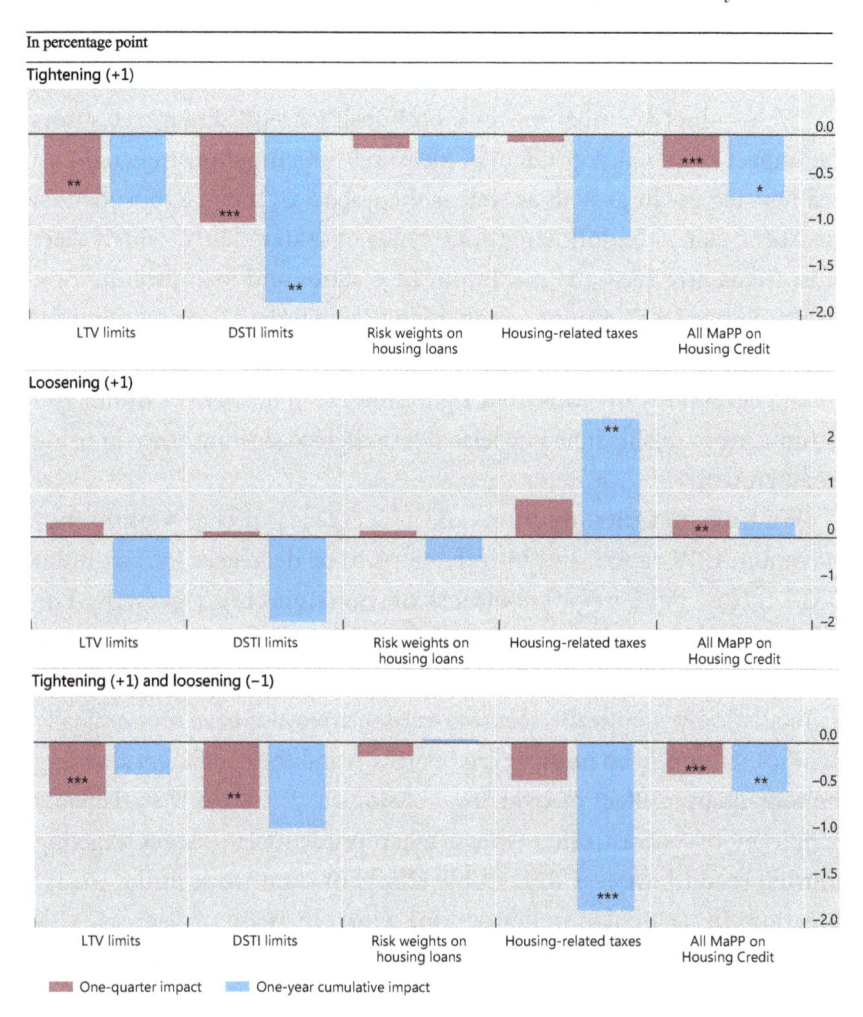

Figure 11. Impact of selected types of macroprudential measures on housing credit growth.

Note: Housing credit data are from national sources for 54 economies. The bars show the coefficients on the macroprudential policy dummy variables in panel regressions with country fixed-effects and the policy rate (2 lags) and real GDP growth (4 lags) used as control variables. ***, ** and * mean statistical significance at the 1 percent, 5 percent and 10 percent level, respectively.

Source: Budnik and Kleibl (2018); Reinhardt and Sowerbutts (2016); Shim *et al.* (2013); FSB Covid-19 policy action database; IMF, Integrated Macroprudential Policy (iMaPP) Database, originally constructed by Alam *et al.* (2019); CEIC; Datastream; national data; authors' calculations.

general credit growth, but loosening actions do not significantly increase general credit growth.

We conduct a similar exercise on housing credit. Figure 11 shows the impact of all macroprudential measures targeting housing credit on real housing credit growth as well as the impact of the macroprudential measures using the following four types of instruments, which were most frequently used: (1) maximum LTV ratios and loan prohibitions; (2) maximum DSTI ratios and other lending criteria; (3) risk weights on housing loans and (4) housing-related taxes. The results from housing credit regressions indicate that tightening LTV and DSTI limits and introducing or raising housing-related taxes helped slowing down housing credit growth.

We find that introductions of or decreases in (i.e., tightening) maximum LTV ratios, and introductions of or decreases in maximum DSTI ratios, have negative effects on housing credit growth. The coefficients showing the one-quarter effects of tightening LTV limits, and the one-quarter and four-quarter effects of tightening DSTI limits, are also statistically significant. Housing-related taxes also have economically significant impacts on housing credit growth and the coefficient showing the four-quarter effect of reducing housing-related taxes is statistically significant. In contrast, other types of macroprudential measures targeting housing credit have less discernible effects or even work in the wrong direction. In particular, policy actions which increase or decrease risk weights on housing loans are economically and statistically insignificant, so are policy actions which loosen LTV and DSTI limits. These results are broadly in line with the findings of similar cross-country empirical studies.

Similar to monetary policy measures, macroprudential measures affect economic activity by changing the cost of borrowing or modifying households' or firms' access to finance. A relatively small number of studies such as Richter *et al.* (2019) find that tightening macroprudential measures tends to reduce output growth, but evidence of their effect on inflation is mixed.

In a financially integrated world, developments in one country may give rise to systemic risk in another. As low interest rates and unconventional monetary policy actions in the large AEs post-crisis result in large capital flows to EMEs and small open AEs, international spillovers may also result from macroprudential measures. For instance, Buch and Goldberg (2017), Reinhardt and Sowerbutts (2015) and Tripathy (2017) find that bank regulation of multinational banks in their home countries affects the banks' lending standards elsewhere. Also, Claessens *et al.* (2021) show that a net tightening of domestic macroprudential measures increases non-bank financial institutions' (NBFI) activities and decreases bank assets, raising the NBFI share in total financial assets. They also find that a net tightening of macroprudential measures in foreign jurisdictions leads to a reduction of the NBFI share, which indicates a decrease in NBFI assets and an increase in banking activity domestically. Such findings of the presence of externalities and international spillovers of domestic macroprudential policies call for international coordination.

As shown in the previous section, CFMs used for prudential purposes can complement FX intervention in dealing with capital flows and thus financial imbalances. Recent empirical studies generally show that CFM tools are sometimes effective in slowing down targeted flows but that the effects tend to be temporary and leakages abound (see Bruno *et al.* [2017]). Such CFM tools are often used when other types of tools do not successfully moderate capital flows.

There is no consensus on which types of CFM tools are macroprudential in nature and which are not, but recently a few papers have started to investigate the effectiveness of FX-related prudential measures. Frost *et al.* (2020), in considering 83 countries over 2000–2017, find that capital inflow volumes are lower where FX-based macroprudential measures have been activated, but that the imposition of capital controls does not have a significant effect on the volume or composition of capital inflows. Aguirre and Repetto (2017) assess the impact of capital- and currency-based macroprudential measures on credit growth at the bank-firm level, using credit registry data from Argentina for the period 2009–2014. They find that a tightening of the capital buffer and the limits on foreign currency positions generally moderates the credit cycle, and that the currency-based measure appears to have a quantitatively more important impact.

Box 1: Experience of EMEs using macro-financial policy measures during the COVID-19 crisis

The COVID-19 crisis served as a stress test on macro-financial stability frameworks across EMEs. Facing an unprecedented shock, EMEs responded by combining a broad range of measures, including new ones, and weathered the shock successfully. In particular, most EME central banks used the full range of pre-crisis policy tools (so called, conventional monetary policy), often on a greater scale and with a wider scope than in the past. A small number of them adjusted CFMs to moderate capital outflows and support US dollar borrowing by domestic financial institutions. Some central banks also expanded liquidity provision including in US dollars to non-banks, conducted asset purchases and established lending programmes targeted at sustaining credit to the private non-financial sector (so called unconventional monetary policy).

The top and middle panels of Figure 12 show how 24 EMEs used various monetary policy tools, macroprudential measures and FX intervention from January to December 2020, in terms of the average intensity of policy measures across the EMEs and the net number of EMEs that tightened or loosened each type of policy. For monetary policy, we focus on the following four types of instruments: policy rate, reserve requirement, lending operations and bond purchases. In particular, and in contrast to experience in AEs, bond purchases were not used to change the stance of policy but, overwhelmingly, to stabilise markets. For macroprudential policy, we consider all categories of instruments except reserve requirements. Finally, we measure FX intervention by monthly percentage change in FX reserves in US dollars. For data on lending operations and asset purchases by central banks, we use the Covid-19 monetary policy database in Cantú et al. (2021). The stacked bars show monthly changes in policy rates, reserve requirements, lending operations and asset purchases as well as macroprudential measures and FX intervention. If policy actions aim to decrease (increase) the amount of credit, they are viewed as tightening (loosening) actions. The bottom panel shows portfolio capital flows to EMEs and the EME-only US dollar index.

We find that some EMEs started to lower policy rates at the early stage of the COVID-19 crisis in February 2020, that almost all EMEs cut policy rates in March by an average size of 66 basis points, and that EMEs continued

> **Box 1: (*Continued*)**
>
> to cut rates until August or September. From September 2020, some EMEs started to raise policy rates gradually. The patterns were similar for reserve requirements. Central banks' purchases of government and corporate bonds started in March or April, and such purchases continued to increase on average until October. Finally, lending operations were introduced or expanded from February. Almost all EMEs in the sample announced either an introduction or expansion of lending operations, on average, 2.2 times in March and 1.5 times in April. Notably, EME central banks continued to expand lending operations until the end of 2020. These four types of monetary policy tools were used mainly to support economic recovery from the Covid-19 shock in 2020.
>
> Macroprudential measures were relaxed alongside monetary policy from February to October 2020, indicating that the tools were used mainly to increase the capacity of domestic financial institutions to provide credit to the economy (i.e., to ease credit supply constraints and avoid deleveraging). In doing so, there was a need to strike a delicate balance between supporting economic activity and preserving banks' soundness (Borio and Restoy, 2020).

7. Outstanding challenges

While the multifaceted policy frameworks have served EMEs well, there is still room for further reflection and improvement. Consider sequentially the range of policies, their integration, the analytical support and the international dimension.

One policy that has not yet been fully included in the framework is *fiscal policy*. To be sure, its relationship with inflation and external stability has been analysed extensively over the years. Likewise, there is a consensus that keeping fiscal policy on a sustainable path is essential for macroeconomic stability. That said, its relationship with financial stability, and the domestic financial cycle in particular, merits further attention. Moreover, the importance of this issue varies across countries, depending on how disciplined fiscal finances are. For instance, fiscal constraints have been very prominent in Latin America and less so in emerging Asia.

Net average intensity of EME policy actions.[1]

Tightening (+) / loosening (−)

- Policy rate change
- Lending operation
- Macroprudential action
- Asset purchase
- Reserve requirement
- FX intervention

Net number of EMEs that implemented policy actions.[2]

Tightening (+1) / loosening (−1)

- Policy rate change
- Lending operation
- Macroprudential action
- Asset purchase
- Reserve requirement
- FX intervention

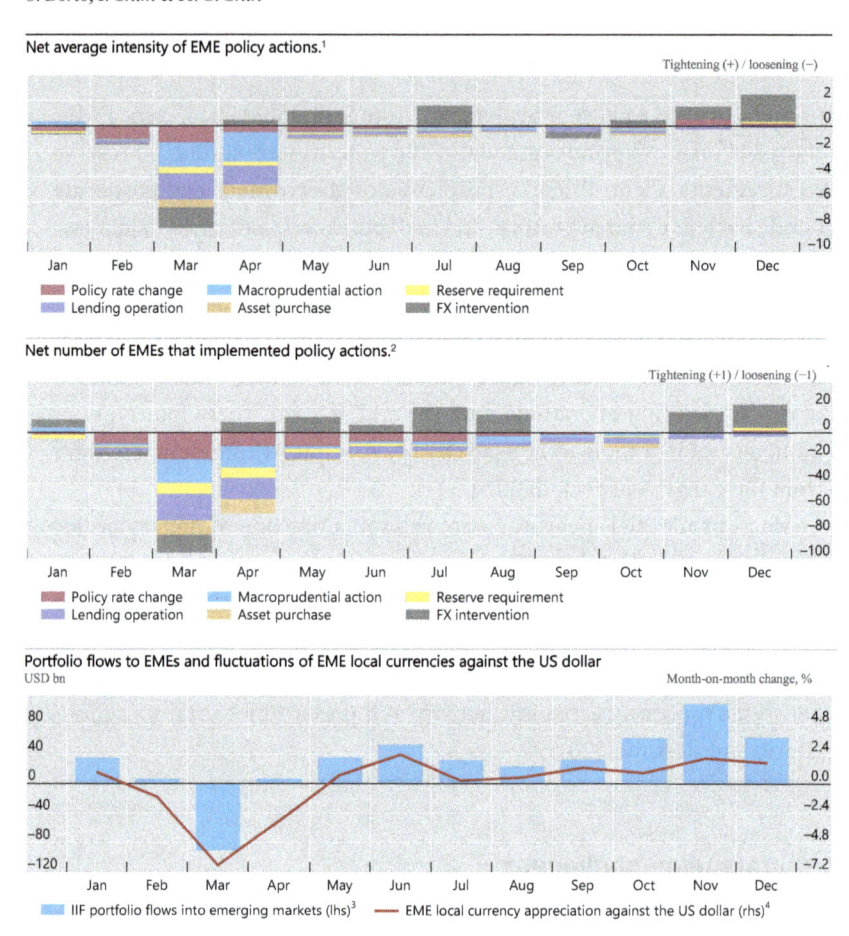

Portfolio flows to EMEs and fluctuations of EME local currencies against the US dollar
USD bn — Month-on-month change, %

- IIF portfolio flows into emerging markets (lhs)[3]
- EME local currency appreciation against the US dollar (rhs)[4]

Figure 12. Use of monetary and macroprudential policies and FX intervention by EMEs in 2020.

[1]Policy rate change = percentage point changes divided by 50 basis points; macroprudential action, reserve requirement, lending operation and asset purchase = the number of tightening (+1) or loosening (−1) actions; FX intervention = percentage change of total foreign currency reserve assets excluding gold across 24 EMEs normalised by its standard deviation, where a positive value means purchasing foreign currency and selling local currency, and a negative value selling foreign currency and purchasing local currency.

[2]Policy rate change = the number of EMEs that increased the policy rate (+1) minus the number of EMEs that decreased the policy rate (−1); macroprudential action, reserve requirement, lending operation and asset purchase = the number of EMEs that tightened the policy on net (+1) minus the number of EMEs that loosened the policy on net (−1); FX intervention = the number of EMEs that increased FX reserve assets (+1) minus the number of EMEs that decreased FX reserve assets (−1).

Figure 12. (*Continued*) ³From IIF Total Portfolio Flows Tracker. Sum of net non-resident purchases of stocks ("portfolio equity flows") and those of bonds ("portfolio debt flows") in EMEs.
⁴Trade-weighted US dollar Index only including emerging market economies.
Note: 24 EMEs = AE, AR, BR, CL, CN, CO, CZ, HK, HU, ID, IL, IN, KR, MX, MY, PE, PH, PL, RO, SA, SG, TH, TR and ZA.
Source: Budnik and Kleibl (2018); Cantú *et al.* (2021); Reinhardt and Sowerbutts (2016); Shim *et al.* (2013); Board of Governors of the Federal Reserve System; BIS Covid-19 monetary policy database; FSB Covid-19 policy action database; IMF, Integrated Macroprudential Policy (iMaPP) Database, originally constructed by Alam *et al.* (2019); Institute of International Finance; IMF, *International Financial Statistics*; Datastream; national data; authors' calculations.

A couple of aspects stand out (Borio *et al.*, 2021). First, domestic financial booms can hugely flatter the fiscal accounts. Financial booms lead to an overestimation of potential output and growth, are revenue-rich and hide the build-up of contingent liabilities, broadly defined, especially if the subsequent bust goes hand-in-hand with a banking crisis and a major recession. The ensuing increases in public debt have historically been over 20 percentage points of GDP and, in extreme cases, 100 percentage points or more (Laeven and Valencia, 2018). At a minimum, this weakens the creditworthiness of the sovereign and constrains its policy room for manoeuvre.[16] Second, the sovereign itself can be a source of banking stress. The sovereign-bank doom loop has attracted particular attention following the euro area crisis (CGFS, 2011), but such events were quite common in EMEs in the past, not least because of a large, albeit declining, portion of foreign-currency denominated debt (Velasco, 1987; Calvo and Mendoza, 1996; Corsetti *et al.*, 1999). Some diagnostic tools have been developed to measure cyclically adjusted fiscal balances and to capture contingent liabilities in real time (e.g., Borio *et al.*, 2017; 2021). However, there is ample scope for improvement. Similarly, addressing the sovereign-bank nexus through regulation and supervision has proved very contentious (Basel Committee on Banking Supervision, 2017).

---

[16] The cases of Ireland and Spain stand out. Both countries were held up as examples of fiscal probity during the financial expansion: they ran apparent "fiscal surpluses" and their debt-to-GDP ratios were falling. Once the banking crisis broke out, both also faced a sovereign crisis.

Growing experience with the deployment of *macroprudential tools* has clarified their strengths and weaknesses. Through construction, the tools can boost resilience by increasing the size of buffers in the financial system. To varying degrees, they can also constrain the build-up of domestic financial imbalances. Even so, there is a risk of overestimating their effectiveness. It may be quite difficult to deploy them with sufficient stringency and timeliness: political economy considerations loom large, inducing a certain "inaction bias".[17] In addition, the tools operate largely through banks: the tools have not as yet been designed for the growing non-bank financial intermediation sector. In fact, even in countries where they have been deployed aggressively, the tools have not always prevented the emergence of traditional signs of financial imbalances (Figure 13).

Given the limitations of macroprudential tools, it stands to reason that *monetary policy* could play a complementary role. After all, monetary policy sets the universal price of leverage in a given currency area and operates fundamentally by influencing financial conditions — the very factors that shape financial expansions. There is a consensus that keeping interest rates low for long contributes to risk-taking and the build-up of financial vulnerabilities as well as having broader side effects. And it is becoming increasingly clear that the issue is not so much "leaning against the wind" once signs of financial imbalances become apparent — by then it is too late — but adopting a policy that takes financial factors systematically into account.[18] That said, it is not yet clear how best to operationalise such a strategy — a serious problem especially for those central banks with monetary policy mandates that explicitly include financial stability. As of now, there is agreement only on the need to lengthen the horizon over which to control inflation, thereby gaining some flexibility.

---

[17] One way of addressing the bias is to rely more on the structural, not necessarily time-varying, aspects of the tools, e.g., setting low but state-invariant LTV or DSTI limits, relying on non-market values to measure them, etc. Lower levels reduce the extent to which higher asset prices or incomes can elicit additional credit; see Borio *et al.* (2001) for a more extensive discussion.

[18] As Stein (2013) has aptly put it, it is not a question of "leaning against the wind" as monetary policy "is the wind". For a concrete example of such a systematic strategy, in the form of an augmented Taylor rule, see Borio *et al.* (2019).

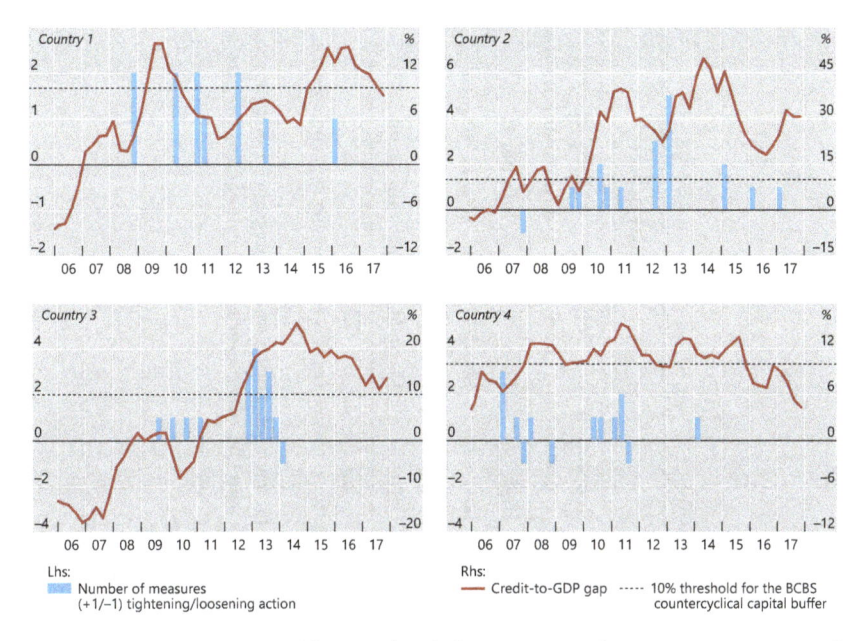

Figure 13. Some signs of financial imbalances even where measures are used actively.
Source: Borio (2018).

This points to another issue — the effective *degree of integration* of the various tools in policy implementation (Borio and Disyatat, 2021). It is sometimes assumed, at least in the formal models designed to shed light on policy, that all instruments are deployed simultaneously. However, in implementing policy, this is neither feasible nor desirable. As the business cycle, financial cycles (domestic and global) and day-to-day external market conditions evolve at different speeds, so does the arrival of useful information (Table 2). For instance, since financial vulnerabilities build-up only very slowly, a quarterly frequency may be reasonable for monetary policy decisions, but not for macroprudential ones, which are in fact taken at longer intervals. Similarly, the flexibility of the tools varies: at one end, adjustments to macroprudential policies or CFMs generally involve a long process; at the other end, FX intervention and, possibly, changes in interest rates can be done with little or no decision lag.

This means that there is a natural hierarchy of policies and an unfortunate tendency to consider them in isolation. Macroprudential and

Table 2. Temporal dimensions of policy tools.

Tools	Frequency of economic process	Transmission lags	Implementation lags	Reputation costs	Policy horizon	Frequency of adjustment of tools
Macroprudential measures	Low	Long	Large	High	Long	Infrequent
FX intervention	High/Medium[1]	Negligible	Negligible	Low	Short/Medium	(Very) Frequent
Monetary policy	Medium	Medium[2]	Negligible	Moderate	Medium/Long	Frequent
Capital flow management measures	Medium/Low[3]	Short/Medium	Medium/Large	High	Short/Medium	Infrequent

[1]High in the case of concerns about excessive market volatility; medium in the case of potential exchange rate misalignments.

[2]Defined with respect to output and inflation objectives. In the case of financial market objectives, such as the exchange rate, the transmission lags would be much shorter, while for financial stability concerns, the transmission lags would be much longer.

[3]Concerns about impact of capital flows on financial conditions tend to revolve around their consequence for output, and hence medium frequency. Concerns about impact on financial vulnerabilities are primarily low frequency. That said, policy concerns at times could be quite immediate, such as in the case of forestalling abrupt capital outflows.

Source: Borio and Disyatat (2021).

CFM measures are a kind of fix point for the rest. FX intervention is carried out on an as-needed (or formula-based) basis, possibly several times a day. And adjustments in interest rates fall in between.[19] It seems possible to articulate a more integrated framework. For instance, distinguishing clearly between strategic and tactical FX intervention — the former at frequencies closer to the global financial cycle and the business cycle; the latter at a higher frequency more in line with day-to-day changes in market conditions. However, in the end, the main adjustment margin is in monetary policy, which can take a broader view and incorporate the other influences. Here, the policy horizon is indeed critical. In fact, at medium-term frequencies, the business and domestic financial cycles tend to co-move closely (Figure 14), and it is the medium-term component of the business cycle that accounts for a larger fraction of output fluctuations. This suggests that a longer horizon for monetary policy would be necessary and justified for this policy to play a more active role.

This takes us to the role of *analytical tools*. Analytical tools are necessary to support policy. They provide a frame of reference and help to quantify trade-offs. All policies, including run-of-the-mill monetary policy, rely on a suite of models. And, indeed, models are being rapidly developed to serve as references for macro-financial stability frameworks.[20] But what is specific in this domain is that no single satisfactory model as yet exists to forecast and carry out counterfactual policy exercises.

One reason is that no practical model can meaningfully capture endogenous cycles, let alone cycles of structurally different frequencies. This reflects in part differences in intellectual perspectives: while central bank economists working in the financial stability area tend to take the financial cycle as the basis for their analysis, those advising on monetary policy largely ignore it. Moreover, both groups tend to rely on the shock-propagation-return to steady state macroeconomic paradigm: this rules out meaningful endogenous cycles, in which expansions sow the seeds

---

[19] This characterisation does not apply to Singapore, where FX intervention is used to enforce an (undisclosed) exchange rate band. In fact, one can think of changes in the gradient of the band as the key tool, akin to the interest rate in a Taylor rule.

[20] For examples of BIS' recent modelling efforts, see Agénor and Pereira da Silva (2021), Cavallino and Sandri (2019), Cavallino *et al.* (2021) and Hofmann *et al.* (2021).

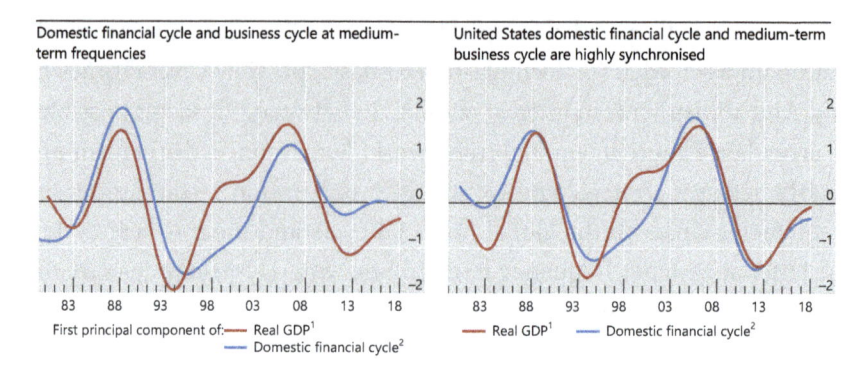

Figure 14. The domestic financial cycle and the medium-term business cycle are synchronised.
[1] Frequency-based (bandpass) filters capturing medium-term cycles (window: 32 to 120 quarters), plotted with a four-period lag.
[2] Domestic financial cycles are measured by frequency-based (bandpass) filters capturing medium-term cycles in real credit, the credit-to-GDP ratio and real house prices.
Source: Aldasoro *et al.* (2020).

of subsequent contractions. Cross-fertilisation has improved, but it has generally not yet narrowed the gap sufficiently. No doubt this area will see substantial progress in the years ahead; in the meantime, any analysis will have to be more partial and/or qualitative.

What about the *international policy dimension*? Historically, this has always been the hardest nut to crack. Spillovers and spillbacks take centre stage, alongside the different perspectives of individual countries. Further progress would need to proceed along two complementary lines (BIS, 2015). First is improving domestic MFSFs. If individual countries put in place effective domestic frameworks, the scope for disruptive spillovers diminishes. Second is addressing residual spillovers and spillbacks more systematically. This involves a range of possible approaches of increasing ambition: enlightened self-interest, in which individual countries seek to take spillovers and spillbacks into account — a particular responsibility for the largest jurisdictions with international currencies; occasional joint decisions, on both interest rates and foreign exchange intervention, beyond well-honed crisis responses; and possibly new global rules of the game to help instil greater discipline in national policies (e.g., Rajan, 2016).

Progress has been uneven so far. Microprudential regulation and supervision has a long tradition of close coordination; Basel III is just the latest example. Because of the macroprudential overlays in the agreement, co-ordination has now been extended to macroprudential tools, notably the countercyclical capital buffer. Its design seeks to align the incentives of home and host jurisdictions, with a view to limiting negative spillovers and regulatory arbitrage. It can set an example for other tools, whenever cross-border spillovers are a cause for concern. In the monetary policy domain, there is less of a tradition of co-ordination and obstacles to tighter co-operation are higher. That said, over the last decade or so, there has been a keener recognition of spillovers and spillbacks. And central banks have strengthened their co-operation at times of stress, as illustrated by the more extensive use of central bank FX swap arrangements. All of these steps are most welcome, but also highlight the scope for further progress.

References

Adrian, Tobias and Gita Gopinath (2020): "Toward an Integrated Policy Framework for open economies", IMF Blog, July.

Adrian, Tobias and Hyun Song Shin (2010): "Financial intermediaries and monetary economics", Chapter 12, in Benjamin M. Friedman and Michael Woodford (eds.) *Handbook of Monetary Economics*, Vol. 3, pp. 601–650, Elsevier B. V., Amsterdam, Netherlands.

Agénor, Pierre-Richard and Luiz Pereira da Silva (2021): "Towards a New Monetary-Macroprudential Policy Framework: Perspectives on Integrated Inflation Targeting", Chapter 14 in this book.

Aguirre, Horacio and Gastón Repetto (2017): "Capital and currency-based macroprudential policies: An evaluation using credit-registry data", *BIS Working Papers*, no. 672, November.

Alam, Zohair, Adrian Alter, Jesse Eiseman, Gaston Gelos, Heedon Kang, Machiko Narita, Erlend Nier and Naixi Wang (2019): "Digging deeper — evidence on the effects of macroprudential policies from a new database", *IMF Working Paper*, no. 19/66.

Aldasoro, Iñaki, Stefan Avdjiev, Claudio Borio and Piti Disyatat (2020): "Global and domestic financial cycles: Variations on a theme", *BIS Working Papers*, no. 864, May.

Altunbas, Yener, Mahir Binici and Leonardo Gambacorta (2018): "Macroprudential policy and bank risk", *Journal of International Money and Finance*, Vol. 81, pp. 203–220.

Avdjiev, Stefan, Valentina Bruno, Catherine Koch and Hyun Song Shin (2018): "The dollar exchange rate as a global risk factor: Evidence from investment", *BIS Working Papers*, no. 695, January.

Avdjiev, Stefan, Robert N McCauley and Hyun Song Shin (2016a): "Breaking free of the triple coincidence in international finance", *Economic Policy*, Vol. 31(87), pp. 409–451.

Avdjiev, Stefan, Wenxin Du, Catherine Koch and Hyun Song Shin (2016b): "The dollar, bank leverage and the deviation from covered interest parity", *BIS Working Papers*, no. 592, November.

Baker, Andrew (2020): "Tower of contrarian thinking: how the BIS helped reframe understandings of financial stability", Chapter 4, in C Borio, S Claessens, P Clement, R McCauley and H S Shin (eds.) *Promoting Global Monetary and Financial Stability; The Bank for International Settlements After Bretton Woods, 1973-2020*, pp. 134–167, Cambridge University Press, Cambridge, United Kingdom.

Bank for International Settlements (2015): "The international monetary and financial system", Chapter V, Annual Report 2014/15, June.

——— (2018): "Moving forward with macroprudential frameworks", Chapter IV, Annual Economic Report 2018, June.

——— (2019): "Monetary policy frameworks in EMEs: inflation targeting, the exchange rate and financial stability", Chapter II, Annual Economic Report 2019, June.

——— (2020): "Capital flows, exchange rates and policy frameworks in emerging Asia", a report by a Working Group established by the Asian Consultative Council of the Bank for International Settlements, 27 November.

——— (2021): "Capital flows, exchange rates and monetary policy frameworks in Latin American and other economies", a report by a group of central banks including members of the Consultative Council for the Americas and the central banks of South Africa and Turkey, 15 April.

Basel Committee on Banking Supervision (2017): "The regulatory treatment of sovereign exposures", discussion paper issued for comment, 7 December.

Borio, Claudio (2014): "The international monetary and financial system: Its Achilles heel and what to do about it", *BIS Working Papers*, no. 456, September.

——— (2014a): "The financial cycle and macroeconomics: What have we learnt?" *Journal of Banking and Finance*, Vol. 45, pp. 182–198, August.

——— (2014b): "Monetary policy and financial stability: What role in prevention and recovery?" *Capitalism and Society*, Vol. 9, no. 2, article 1.

——— (2018): "Macroprudential frameworks: experience, prospects and a way forward", speech on the occasion of the BIS Annual General Meeting in Basel, 24 June.

Borio, Claudio, Juan Contreras and Fabrizio Zampolli (2020): "Assessing the fiscal implications of banking crises", *BIS Working Papers*, no. 893, October.

Borio, Claudio and Piti Disyatat (2011): "Global imbalances and the financial crisis: Link or no link?" *BIS Working Papers*, no. 346, May. Revised and extended version of "Global imbalances and the financial crisis: Reassessing the role of international finance", *Asian Economic Policy Review*, Vol. 5, 2010, pp. 198–216.

——— (2021): "Integrated policy frameworks: The constraints of policy horizons and adjustment frequencies", *SUERF Policy Notes*, No. 246, June.

Borio, Claudio, Piti Disyatat and Phurichai Rungcharoenkitkul (2019): "What anchors for the natural rate of interest?" *BIS Working Papers*, no. 777, March.

Borio, Claudio and Mathias Drehmann (2009): "Assessing the risk of banking crises — revisited", *BIS Quarterly Review*, March, pp. 29–46.

——— (2019): "Predicting recessions: Financial cycle versus term spread", *BIS Working Papers*, no. 818, October.

Borio, Claudio, Mark Farag and Fabrizio Zampolli (2021): "Tackling the fiscal-financial stability nexus", *BIS Working Papers*, forthcoming.

Borio, Claudio, Craig Furfine and Philip Lowe (2001): "Procyclicality of the financial system and financial stability: Issues and policy options", *BIS Papers*, no. 1, pp. 1–57.

Borio, Claudio, Marco Lombardi and Fabrizio Zampolli (2017): "Fiscal sustainability and the financial cycle", in L Ódor (ed), *Rethinking Fiscal Policy after the Crisis*, pp. 384–413, Cambridge University Press, Cambridge, United Kingdom.

Borio, Claudio and Fernando Restoy (2020): "Reflections on regulatory responses to the Covid-19 pandemic", *FSI Briefs*, no. 1, April.

Borio, Claudio and Ilhyock Shim (2007): "What can (macro-)prudential policy do to support monetary policy?" *BIS Working Papers*, no. 242, December.

Bruno, Valentina, Ilhyock Shim and Hyun Song Shin (2017): "Comparative assessment of macroprudential policies", *Journal of Financial Stability*, Vol. 28, February, pp. 183–202.

Buch, Claudia and Linda Goldberg (2017): "Cross-border prudential policy spillovers: How much? How important? Evidence from the international banking research network", *International Journal of Central Banking*, Vol. 13, no. 2, pp. 505–558.

Budnik, Katarzyna and Johannes Kleibl (2018): "Macroprudential regulation in the European Union in 1995-2014: Introducing a new data set on policy actions of a macroprudential nature", *ECB Working Papers*, no. 2123, January.

Calvo, Guillermo (1996): "Capital flows to developing countries in the 1990s: causes and effects", *Journal of Economic Perspectives*, Vol. 10, Spring, pp. 123–139.

Calvo, Guillermo and Enrique Mendoza (1996): "Mexico's balance-of-payments crisis: A chronicle of a death foretold", *Journal of International Economics*, Vol. 41, pp. 235–264.

Cantú, Carlos, Paolo Cavallino, Fiorella De Fiore and James Yetman (2021): "A global database on central banks' monetary responses to Covid-19", *BIS Working Papers*, no. 934, March.

Carstens, Agustín and Hyun Song Shin (2019): "Emerging market economies and global financial conditions: 'Original Sin' redux", *Foreign Affairs*, 15 March.

Cavallino, Paolo, Boris Hofmann and Nikhil Patel (2021): "Capital flows and monetary policy trade-offs in emerging market economies", mimeo.

Cavallino, Paolo and Damiano Sandri (2019): "The expansionary lower bound: Contractionary monetary easing and the trilemma", *BIS Working Papers*, no. 770.

Claessens, Stijn, Swati Ghosh, and Roxana Mihet (2013): "Macroprudential policies to mitigate financial system vulnerabilities", *Journal of International Money and Finance*, Vol. 39, pp. 153–185.

Cerutti, Eugenio, Stijn Claessens and Luc Laeven (2017): "The use and effectiveness of macroprudential policies: New evidence", *Journal of Financial Stability*, Vol. 28, pp. 203–224.

Cerutti, Eugenio, Stijn Claessens and Andrew Rose (2019): "How important is the global financial cycle? Evidence from capital flows", *IMF Economic Review*, Vol. 67, pp. 24–60.

Chantapacdepong, Pornpinun and Ilhyock Shim (2015): "Correlations across Asia-Pacific bond markets and the impact of capital flow measures", *Pacific-Basin Finance Journal*, Vol. 34, September, pp. 71–101.

Claessens, Stijn, Giulio Cornelli, Leonardo Gambacorta, Francesco Manaresi and Yasushi Shiina (2021): "Do macroprudential policies affect non-bank financial intermediation?" *BIS Working Papers*, no. 927, February.

Claessens, Stijn and M Ayhan Kose (2018): "Frontiers of macrofinancial linkages", *BIS Papers*, no. 95, January.

Clement, Piet (2010): "The term 'macroprudential': Origins and evolution", *BIS Quarterly Review*, March, pp. 59–65.

Committee on the Global Financial System (2011): "The impact of sovereign credit risk on bank funding conditions", *CGFS Papers*, no. 43, July.

Corsetti, Giancarlo, Paolo Pesenti and Nouriel Roubini (1999): "What caused the Asian currency and financial crisis?" *Japan and the World Economy*, Vol. 11, pp. 305–373.

Crockett, Andrew (2000): "Marrying the micro- and macro-prudential dimensions of financial stability", remarks at the Eleventh International Conference of Banking Supervisors held in Basel on 20–21 September, *BIS Review* 76/2000.

Eichengreen, Barry and Ricardo Hausmann (1999): "Exchange rates and financial fragility", in: *New Challenges for Monetary Policy*, Proceedings of the Economic Policy Symposium sponsored by the Federal Reserve Bank of Kansas City, Jackson Hole, pp. 319–367.

Frost, Jon, Hiro Ito and René van Stralen (2020): "The effectiveness of macroprudential policies and capital controls against volatile capital inflows", *BIS Working Papers*, no. 867, June.

Gambacorta, Leonardo and Andrés Murcia Pabón (2017): "The impact of macroprudential policies and their interaction with monetary policy: An empirical analysis using credit registry data", *BIS Working Papers*, no. 636, May.

Gómez, Esteban, Angélica Lizarazo, Juan Carlos Mendoza and Andrés Murcia Pabón (2017): "Evaluating the impact of macroprudential policies on credit growth in Colombia", *BIS Working Papers*, no. 634, May.

Gourinchas, Pierre-Olivier and Maurice Obstfeld (2011): "Stories of the twentieth century for the twenty-first", *NBER Working Paper*, no. 17252, July.

Hofmann, Boris, Nikhil Patel and Steve Wu (2021): "The original sin redux: A model-based evaluation", paper presented at the *BIS-BOE-ECB-IMF Conference*, April.

Hofmann, Boris and Taejin Park (2020): "The broad dollar exchange rate as an EME risk factor", *BIS Quarterly Review*, December, pp. 13–26.

Hofmann, Boris, Ilhyock Shim and Hyun Song Shin (2020a): "Emerging market economy exchange rates and local currency bond markets amid the Covid-19 pandemic", *BIS Bulletin*, no. 5, April.

——— (2020b): "Bond risk premia and the exchange rate", *BIS Working Papers*, no. 775, April.

——— (2021): "Bond fund flows to EMEs and the dollar", mimeo.

Hördahl, Peter and Ilhyock Shim (2020): "EME bond portfolio flows and long-term interest rates during the Covid-19 pandemic", *BIS Bulletin*, no. 18, May.

International Monetary Fund (2020): "Toward an integrated policy framework", *IMF Policy Paper*, no. 2020/46, October.

Kindleberger, Charles P (1965): "Balance-of-payments deficits and the international market for liquidity", *Princeton Essays in International Finance*, no. 46, May.

Kuttner, Kenneth N and Ilhyock Shim (2016): "Can non-interest rate policies stabilize housing markets? Evidence from a panel of 57 economies", *Journal of Financial Stability*, Vol. 26, pp. 31–44.

Lane, Philip and Gian Maria Milesi-Ferretti (2001): "The external wealth of nations: measures of foreign assets and liabilities for industrial and developing countries", *Journal of International Economics*, Vol. 55, pp. 263–294.

Laeven, Luc and Fabian Valencia (2018): "Systemic banking crises revisited", *IMF Working Paper*, no. 18/206.

Miranda-Agrippino, Silvia and Hélène Rey, "US Monetary Policy and the Global Financial Cycle", *NBER Working Papers*, no. 21722, November 2015.

Obstfeld, Maurice (2010): "Expanding gross asset positions and the international monetary system," Remarks at the Federal Reserve Bank of Kansas City symposium on "Macroeconomic Challenges: The Decade Ahead," Jackson Hole, Wyoming, 26–28 August.

Rajan, Raghuram (2016): "New rules for the monetary game", *Project Syndicate*, 21 March.

Reinhardt, Dennis and Rhiannon Sowerbutts (2015): "Regulatory arbitrage in action: evidence from banking flows and macroprudential policy", *Bank of England Staff Working Papers*, no. 546, September.

Reinhart, Carmen M and Vincent R Reinhart (2008): "Capital flow bonanzas: An encompassing view of the past and present", *NBER Working Paper*, no. 14321, September.

Rey, Hélène (2013): "Dilemma not trilemma: The global financial cycle and monetary policy independence", paper presented at the Federal Reserve of Kansas City Economic Policy Symposium "Global Dimensions of Unconventional Monetary Policy", Jackson Hole, 22–24 August.

Richter, Björn, Moritz Schularick and Ilhyock Shim (2019): "The costs of macroprudential policy", *Journal of International Economics*, Vol. 118, May, pp. 263–282.

Scheubel, Beatrice, Livio Stracca and Cédric Tille (2019): "The global financial cycle and capital flow episodes: A wobbly link?" *ECB Working Paper*, no. 2337, December.

Schrimpf, Andreas, Ilhyock Shim and Hyun Song Shin (2021): "Liquidity management and asset sales by bond funds in the face of investor redemptions in March 2020", *BIS Bulletin*, no. 39, March.

Schularick, Moritz and Alan Taylor (2012): "Credit booms gone bust: Monetary policy, leverage cycles, and financial crises, 1870–2008", *American Economic Review*, Vol. 102, no. 2, pp. 1029–1061.

Shim, Ilhyock, Bilyana Bogdanova, Jimmy Shek and Agne Subelyte (2013): "Database for policy actions on housing markets", *BIS Quarterly Review*, September, pp. 83–91.

Shin, Hyun Song (2012): "Global banking glut and loan risk premium", Mundell-Fleming Lecture, *IMF Economic Review*, Vol. 60(2), pp. 155–192.

——— (2013): "The second phase of global liquidity and its impact on emerging economies", Keynote address at the Federal Reserve Bank of San Francisco Asia Economic Policy Conference, San Francisco, 3–5 November.

Stein, Jeremy C (2013): "Overheating in credit markets: Origins, measurement and policy responses", speech at the research symposium sponsored by the Federal Reserve Bank of St. Louis on "Restoring Household Financial Stability after the Great Recession: Why Household Balance Sheets Matter", St. Louis, Missouri, 7 February 2013.

Tripathy, Jagdish (2017): "Cross-border effects of regulatory spillovers: evidence from Mexico", *Bank of England Staff Working Papers*, no. 684.

Velasco, Andres (1987): "Financial crises and balance of payments crises: A simple model of the Southern Cone experience", *Journal of Development Economics*, Vol. 27, pp. 263–283.

© 2023 World Scientific Publishing Company
https://doi.org/10.1142/9789811259432_0004

Macro-Financial Stability Frameworks: Experience and Challenges: A Discussion

Linda Goldberg*

Federal Reserve Bank of New York

Macro-financial stability frameworks have come a long way in a short time. Claudio Borio, Ilhyock Shim and Hyun Song Shin have provided a thoughtful contribution on the topic with a focus on the rich expanded toolkit that has been developed towards achieving credit and financial stability. The chapter has a particular emphasis on the external developments and ways that the toolkit engages with related financial stability challenges. The survey contained therein is comprehensive, covering types of tools, details on business and financial cycles and some of the challenges that remain towards setting the overall policy framework. The authors provide an excellent background for the broader themes and contributions covered in the MAS-BIS Conference on Macro-financial Stability Policy in a Globalised World, with other contributions targeting thematic issues, advanced economy and emerging market country experiences and emerging policy frameworks.

As the authors have provided three main arguments, my comments on their chapter mirror this organisation. The initial key point raised by

---

* The comments are those of the author, and do not necessarily reflect the views of the Federal Reserve Bank of New York or the Federal Reserve System.

the authors is that emerging market economies (EMEs) have benefited from the joint use of policies to successfully mitigate the risks for domestic stability arising from external influences. I agree that the initial evidence is positive. However, my remarks below also emphasise that it is very difficult to identify the effects of specific policies and, so far, also challenging to judge which of the many policies applied both by the sender and recipient countries of international financial flows have been most important for financial stability improvements. The second key point developed by the authors is how a holistic macro-financial stability framework is still a work in progress. This is indisputable. In addition to the themes emphasised by the authors, more work is needed on a full policy evaluation cycle. This broader cycle, I will argue, could include, ex-ante, the conditions to be satisfied for rolling back changes. Such ex-ante frameworks could provide policy consistency, perhaps limit induced distortions and actions that might reduce the benefits that come with a country's international financial integration. The third key point argued by the authors is that, from a global perspective, more is needed on understanding international spillovers and spillbacks. This is certainly true. Yet, many credit-related macroprudential tools are for country-specific and sectoral credit issues. The evidence of first-order effects of these tools for international capital flows is both weaker and mixed in terms of signs of influence. The policy framework, if specifically meant to address external spillover and spillback effects, may need to have more of a clear delineation between capital flow management and macro-prudential tools. The framework might also acknowledge how much might be gained from attention within source countries to the shock absorption capabilities and risk management frameworks of financial firms involved in international capital flows.

Joint use of policies to mitigate risks from external influences

As the authors discuss, EMEs have benefited from the joint use of policies to mitigate domestic stability risks from external influences. Nonetheless, it is an open question to what extent this argument in practice applies to macroprudential instruments. Macroprudential instrument applications, to date, are perhaps not as quantitatively important for influencing cross-border international capital flows.

Research studies of the cross-border lending effects of prudential instruments through banks show substantial heterogeneity in the effects. Borrower-based tools are more effective for credit, so likewise for associated risks. In addition, if prudential instruments are used for domestic microprudential purposes, it is not even clear that having a credit growth response in aggregate is even desirable.

Buch and Goldberg (2017) take as a starting point the absence of systematic evidence that establishes whether spillovers are common, important and support or hinder the attainment of policy goals. In an initiative of the International Banking Research Network (IBRN), 15 country teams examined domestic effects and international spillovers of prudential instruments using detailed confidential microbanking data. In addition, researchers from the Bank for International Settlements (BIS) and from the European Central Bank (ECB) provided cross-country perspectives. The analyses focus on evidence for international policy spillovers through multiple channels: *inward* transmission addresses how *foreign* regulations affect the *domestic* activities of domestic banks or foreign affiliates (bank branches or subsidiaries) located in the host country; *outward* transmission to foreign economies addresses the effects of foreign policies on the *foreign* activities of a reporting country's global banks. All country teams implemented the same baseline regression models for analysing inward or outward transmission. In addition, country teams addressed issues specific to their banking markets or banks' business models. In some cases, teams differentiated adjustment of lending by their global banks' branches (which are subject to the capital requirements of their parents) versus subsidiaries (which are, in addition, subject to regulations in the host country). The analytics utilised a new database developed by the IBRN and the International Monetary Fund (IMF), described in Cerutti *et al.* (2017) with prudential instruments covered including: capital requirements, concentration limits, interbank exposure limits, loan-to-value ratio limits and changes in reserve requirements.

Three key observations about prudential spillovers that are immediately of interest from analytical and policy perspectives are emphasised by Buch and Goldberg (2017) from examining these 17 studies. First, some countries observe that prudential instruments spill over internationally and through banks via lending growth. Empirical specifications that focus on international spillovers along the intensive margin and over a time horizon of several quarters detect significant international spillovers in about a third of the specifications. The baseline specifications provide a lower bound of regulatory spillover effects. As the analyses omit large and bank-specific outliers, they do not capture potentially large adjustments along the extensive margin, representing entry and withdrawal of banks from foreign markets. Moreover, as the meta-analysis summarises results from a common empirical approach imposed across countries, the identified spillovers also exclude other potentially important country- and sector-specific dynamics that individual country analyses document. Second, heterogeneity in spillovers through lending is common. This heterogeneity is at the bank level, where prudential instrument effects on lending can each differ with the balance sheet characteristics and business models of the banks participating in international lending. These same characteristics do not appear to be as important for the inward transmission of foreign policies into the domestic lending of global banks. Across these studies using quarterly data on lending activity of individual banks in their jurisdictions, cyclical considerations do not appear as important for the spillovers of regulations to international lending activity. Third, the economic magnitudes of international spillovers of policy thus far have not been large on average. However, the pattern of results highlights the potential for larger and more consequential spillovers as the use of macroprudential instruments increases.

Overall, the evidence drawn from across the 17 IBRN studies, considering a range of country experiences with international spillovers of prudential instruments through bank lending growth, does not point to a one-size-fits-all channel or even direction of transmission that dominates spillovers. This set of findings provide reason for pause when arguing that domestic prudential instruments, when considered for use in altering pressures for international capital flows, will be a consistent and well-understood part of a policy toolkit.

Instead, another key area of policy emphasis could be on the contributions of regulatory changes. In the post–Global Financial Crisis period, many important regulatory developments have led banks to hold more capital, manage their liability structure to focus less on short-term and interbank funding, maintain better liquidity and stronger risk management practices and test robustness through being subjected to more stringent and regular stress testing. Banks involved in global capital flows have also shifted towards direct lending to customers across borders or through their local branches or subsidiaries within the EMEs, with this type of lending tending to be less sensitive to the global factor and changes in risk sentiment (Buch and Goldberg, 2020). Moreover, international banking activity has transitioned towards stronger banks.

A consequence of these changes in the strength of global and international banks is that advanced economy global banks have credit responses to risk conditions that have declined in amplitude, as shown in the work by Avdjiev et al. (2020) on the shifting drivers of global liquidity flows through banks and nonbanks. In addition, another policy emphasis in mitigating domestic stability risk from external influences is the institutional reforms and market deepening that has occurred in many emerging markets, helping to support a shift toward local currency funding, and reducing the incidence of "original sin" in debt financing.

Holistic macro-financial stability still a work in progress

The authors correctly and thoughtfully argue that tremendous progress has been made on macro-financial stability framework. Indeed, these advances owe much to a collaborative effort across the international policy community, for example, with broad workplans across the BIS, IMF, Financial Stability Board (FSB), G-20 and other organisations to develop, understand and refine toolkits. Collaboration with the academic community also has been essential. The FSB explicitly surveys progress in "building and implementing macroprudential frameworks and tools", highlighting developments around establishing regulatory frameworks for macroprudential oversight and enhancing system-wide monitoring and use of instruments. Examples such as countercyclical capital buffers, housing tools and stress tests are deemed to be advancing well.

Nonetheless, challenges remain around this overall framework. As I already noted in the context of the cross-country studies, the first challenge is assessing the effectiveness of specific tools and calibrating them for their purpose.

There is an additional large gap. While tremendous efforts certainly have been made to advance the state of frameworks, some of these frameworks are unfinished with respect to giving ex-ante guidance on when to implement, how to adjust levels of instruments over time and how to be specific ex ante about when ex post tools will be deactivated over the cycle. Other challenges remain around improving communications, a theme that was discussed relatively early in this development in CGFS (2016). Finally, there is a risk that tools are unnecessarily distorting and applied over time more like industrial policy. As it is possible for tools to be misapplied over time in second or third best ways, for goals beyond the original intent, the net benefits of the toolkit can be greatly diminished.

More studies needed on understanding international spillovers and spillbacks

The final main theme addresses which macroprudential tools address credit largely due to the "global financial cycle". For this question, it is important to step back and observe some of the key empirical findings from the still growing literature on the global financial cycle. These include the observation that the main cyclical responses to common external factors such as advanced economy monetary policy and shifts in risk sentiment are visible in credit prices, and much less so in credit quantities (Miranda-Agrippino and Rey, 2020a, 2020b; Cerutti *et al.*, 2019; Goldberg and Krogstrup, 2019). In this case, a policy challenge is around the relative distortions and welfare consequences of price versus quantity movements that are induced by external factors.

As financial flows have evolved, some of the most sensitive forms of international capital flows are diminished relative to prior to the Global Financial Crisis. Interbank and short-term credit had been highly responsive but have become less dominant. Moreover, the direct lending through banks to non-financial borrowers, whether appearing in cross-border flows or extended through the local affiliates of foreign banks, has played a larger role. The effects of the global financial cycles have likewise shifted over time for reasons still being explored in the literature, with this linked to types of common shocks (Buch *et al.*, 2021) and also to quantitative easing being found to have weaker international spillovers (Curcuru *et al.*, *forthcoming*).

Final remarks

Claudio Borio, Ilhyock Shim and Hyun Song Shin have written a comprehensive and thought-provoking chapter. As countries work more with the macroprudential toolkit, the importance of the main themes carefully articulated within this chapter will continue to be underscored. With these experiences, the effectiveness, as well as weaknesses, of the tools will be better known, and policymakers will continue to refine the frameworks for their use.

References

Avdjiev, Stefan, Leonardo Gambacorta, Linda Goldberg and Stefano Schiaffi (2020): "The shifting drivers of global liquidity", *Journal of International Economics*, Vol. 125, 103324, July.

Buch, Claudia, Matthieu Bussiere and Linda Goldberg (2021): "Macroprudential policy in the wake of the coivd-19 crisis: international spillovers and coordination issues", Banque de France *Financial Stability Review*, pp. 71–81, March.

Buch, Claudia and Linda Goldberg (2017): "Cross-border prudential policy spillovers: How much? How important? Evidence from the International Banking Research Network", *International Journal of Central Banking*, Vol. 13, supplement 1, pp. 505–558, March.

Buch, Claudia and Linda Goldberg (2020): "Global banking: Towards an assessment of benefits and costs", *Annual Review of Financial Economics*, Vol. 12, pp. 141–175, November.

Committee on the Global Financial System (CGFS) (2016): "Objective-setting and communication of macroprudential policies", *CGFS Papers*, no. 57, Bank for International Settlements, November.

Cerutti, Eugenio, Stijn Claessens and Andrew K. Rose (2019): "How Important is the Global Financial Cycle? Evidence from Capital Flows", *IMF Economic Review*, Vol. 67(1), pp. 24–60, March.

Cerutti, Eugenio, Ricardo Correa, Elisabetta Fiorentino and Esther Segalla (2017): "Changes in Prudential Policy Instruments: A New Cross-Country Database", *International Journal of Central Banking*, Vol. 13, supplement 1, pp. 477–503, March.

Curcuru, Stephanie E., Steven B. Kamin, Canlin Li and Marius Rodriguez (forthcoming): "International Spillovers of Monetary Policy: Conventional

Policy vs. Quantitative Easing", *International Journal of Central Banking* (earlier version as Board of Governors of the Federal Reserve System *International Finance Discussion Papers*, No. 1234, August 2018).

Goldberg, Linda and Signe Krogstrup (2019): "International Capital Flow Pressures", *NBER Working Paper*, no. 24286, October.

Miranda-Agrippino, Silvia and Hélène Rey (2020a): "US Monetary Policy and the Global Financial Cycle", *Review of Economic Studies*, Vol. 87(6), pp. 2754–2776, November.

Miranda-Agrippino, Silvia and Hélène Rey (2020b): "The Global Financial Cycle After Lehman", *AEA Papers and Proceedings*, Vol. 110, pp. 523–528, May.

CHAPTER 2

© 2023 World Scientific Publishing Company
https://doi.org/10.1142/9789811259432_0005

Chapter 2

What Happens in Vegas Does Not Stay in Vegas

Anil K Kashyap*

Booth School of Business, University of Chicago
Financial Policy Committee, Bank of England

Abstract

I identify several structural weaknesses in the global financial regulatory architecture and offer several suggestions about how they could be addressed. One important theme is that the interconnections in the system mean that problems in one jurisdiction spillover over to other jurisdictions, so cross-border cooperation is essential in dealing with these issues.

1. Introduction

I have been a fan of this conference since its founding, but it always falls during the quarter when I am teaching, so I have never been able to attend in person. So it is an honour to be able to give the virtual keynote address. Much of my thinking on these issues has been influenced by my participation in the Task Force on Financial Stability (Hubbard *et al.*,

---

*The opinions expressed here are that of the author alone and do not represent the views of the Bank of England or any of its policy committees. The author wishes to thank, without implying they share his views, Darrell Duffie, Lee Foulger, Jane Gladstone, Grainne McGread, Kathryn Judge, Ralph Koijen, Donald Kohn, Victoria Saporta, Jeremy Stein and Carolyn Wilkins for conversations on these issues.

2021). I do not want to imply that I am speaking for the other members of the Task Force. After you hear what I have to say, you will realise why I want to be clear that all these opinions are solely my own!

There are many references regarding the risks to financial stability as emanating from reckless gambles that some people and institutions are willing to take without worrying about the consequences for others. Las Vegas is often referred to as the gambling capital of the world and it had a great marketing slogan to encourage people to come gamble and have a good time, "What happens in Vegas, stays in Vegas."

The theme of my remarks is that the financial stability analogy with gambling breaks down when it comes to financial regulation. Instead, due of the interconnected nature of the global financial system in the regulatory domain, I want to argue that what happens in Vegas *doesn't* stay there. In particular, regulatory loop holes whether in one jurisdiction, or risks that are unattended to in one place, tend to spread beyond their point of origin.

I will split the talk into two parts. I will start by going through four examples that span a variety of financial stability risks. They are all drawn from recent experience so they exist despite the many helpful reforms that followed the 2008 Global Financial Crisis (GFC). I am hoping that the examples will serve two purposes. The first is just to shine some light on some problems that are in plain sight and are yet to be addressed. The second is to demonstrate that these problems are so pervasive as to be indicative of a process problem within the current global regulatory architecture.

Unfortunately, as is often the case, it is easier to identify problems than it is to solve them. Thus, while I will close with some recommendations, I am under no illusion that my suggestions will completely address these problems. At best, maybe they will help kick off a conversation that will generate momentum for a larger rethink of what the next required steps in regulation can be.

2. Example 1: Treasury market dysfunction in the US

My first example is the widely studied market turmoil in March 2020. I am sure that this episode is now familiar to all of you so I will not dwell on the details of what happened, though there are two recent analyses (Hall, 2021; Vissing-Jorgensen, 2021) that helped me better appreciate some aspects of that episode. So if you have not seen those, I suggest you do. For the purposes of today, I will just stipulate that there were a variety of factors that contributed to a surge in selling of US treasury securities in the middle of March 2020 and that resulted in a sharp rise in Treasury yields even as equity prices were plunging and measures of volatility were spiking. Critically, the dislocations in Treasury prices spread to other government bond markets around the world and the spillovers were material.

The Treasury market stabilised when the Federal Reserve began buying Treasury securities in unprecedented amounts, starting on 19 March, when it purchased US$70 billion that day and then continued at that pace until the end of the month. I include Figure 1 because I doubt most members of the public or Congress realise that the Federal Reserve bought more Treasury securities as part of its market stabilisation efforts in the first and second quarters of 2020 than it did in its three rounds of quantitative easing in the aftermath of the GFC!

It is commendable that the Federal Reserve was so quick and aggressive in stepping in to stem the problems in this market, but the episode underlined structural weaknesses that had been lurking for some time, and that are likely to re-emerge in circumstances much less catastrophic than a once-a-century global pandemic. Figure 2 reproduces some calculations from Duffie (2020). Darrell has been warning about the

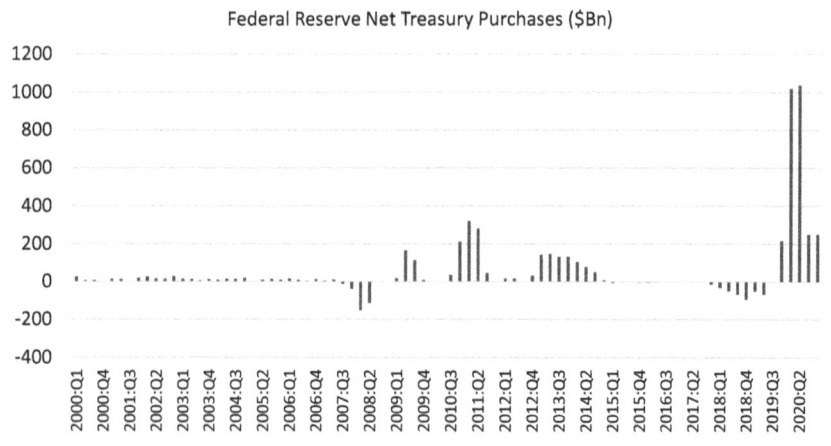

Figure 1. Federal reserve monthly net purchases of treasury securities ($Billions).
Source: Federal Reserve.

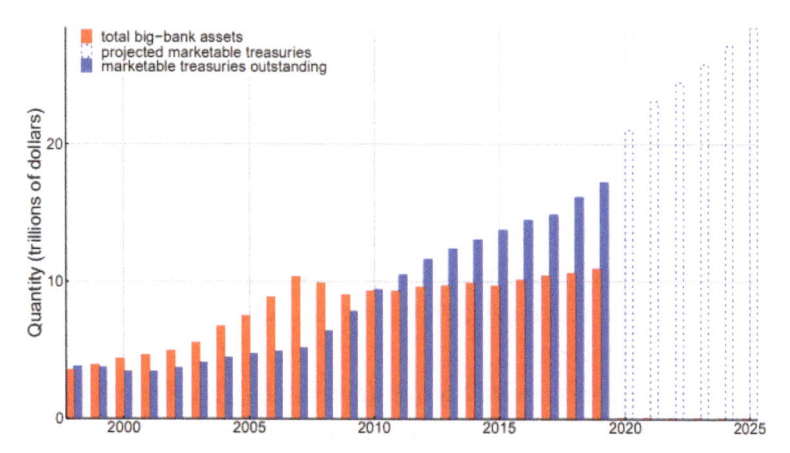

Figure 2. Treasury market size compared to dealer balance sheet capacity.
Note: In blue shows year-end total outstanding amounts of marketable Treasuries, 1998–2019 (data: FRED), with projections for 2020–2025 based on federal deficit projections made 13 April 2020 by the Committee for a Responsible Federal Budget. In red are shown the total assets of the holding companies of Goldman Sachs Group, Morgan Stanley, Merrill Lynch, Lehman Brothers, Bear Steams, Bank of America, JP Morgan Chase, Citigroup, and Wells Fargo, from 10K disclosures.
Source: Duffie (2020).

dangers of relying on the dealers to intermediate for this market for some time so this risk did not simply appear out of nowhere. (See for instance Duffie (2018) for similar concerns.)

It now seems that there is an emerging consensus that central banks may need to set up some type of standing facility to help deal with government securities market turmoil of the sort we saw in March 2020. The design of these facilities will be up to the individual central banks, shaped to fit particular market characteristics and legal guideposts. Clearly there is a public good aspect for the global financial system to make sure that these markets are fit for the purpose. The US authorities also have strong incentives to improve the functioning of the Treasury market.

It is less clear that in whatever reforms emerge, the US will fully internalise the concerns that other countries might have about reach of those measures. For instance, over the last several years, there has been talk of creating a standing Federal Reserve facility for repurchase agreements (e.g., Andolfatto and Ihrig (2019)). However, even if one is set up, access to the facility would presumably be determined by the Federal Reserve and it is hard to know how access decisions will be made. We do know that some countries that would have liked to access to swap lines have not been able to secure them. I am not suggesting that the Federal Reserve has an obligation to offer access to its facilities (or swap lines) to anyone that wants one. I am just not sure how much transparency there will be on these kinds of decisions and the extent to which domestic political concerns may play a role. In particular, whether Congress would judge that this is a purely technical exercise that can be left to the Fed and other central banks is unclear.

Perhaps my concerns will prove unwarranted, but I think this case does illustrate how unilateral decisions in one country can have important stability implications for other countries. In the regulatory domain, what happens in Vegas doesn't stay in Vegas.

3. Example 2: The challenges in tracking cross-border activity of non-banks

The failure of Archegos Capital Management is another high-profile event that has received attention. This family office reportedly had assets of roughly $10 billion, yet according to the *Financial Times* generated losses of the same order of magnitude for its prime brokers (Table 1).

There are three things about this saga that I find striking. First, Bill Hwang, the owner of Archegos, had been banned from trading in Hong Kong SAR for four years and had paid a fine to the SEC for insider trading. Yet, he was able to establish prime brokerage relationships with multiple

Table 1. Estimated losses from Archegos.

Bank	Size of Loss
Credit Suisse	$5.4 billion
Nomura	$2.9 billion
Morgan Stanley	$911 million
UBS	$861 million
MUFG	$270 million
Mizuho*	$90 million

*Estimates in advance of company disclosures
Source: Company disclosures.

global systemically important banks. According to the *Financial Times*, Credit Suisse made only $17.5 million in fees in the year prior to the firm's collapse, but the collapse cost Credit Suisse $5.4 billion.[1] So my first question is what should we conclude from seeing someone with this kind of record, who is not a particularly profitable client, continue to gain access to so much funding from so many large institutions?

The second startling thing about this case is that once the trouble at Archegos arrived, many of the exposed banks caucused about what to do and they reached very different decisions. Goldman Sachs (and possibly others) managed to untangle themselves while taking little or no losses, while we can see from Table 1 that others did not. It would be interesting to know about the margining practices at the various firms that were doing business with Archegos and, more generally, to find out why the responses were so different. For instance, were there policies in place that were simply followed at the firms that escaped the losses or was this due to discretionary actions of particular managers?

The third remarkable thing is that it seems most of the brokers that were left with large losses were headquartered outside of the US, where Archegos was based. One wonders what the supervisors in the various countries knew about their banks' exposure to Archegos? Maybe it is just a coincidence that the foreign banks were the ones that were most exposed. Perhaps, the same forces that make these large complex organisations so difficult to manage also create special challenges for home supervisors to fully monitor their overseas activities?

4. Example 3: The inability to monitor shadow banking activity

My third example is the large build-up of corporate debt that is ongoing and, in particular, the surge in leveraged lending that has been underway for some time. The Federal Reserve, the Office of the Comptroller of the Currency and the Federal Deposit Insurance Corporation were sufficiently concerned about this, that in 2013 they issued guidance to the banks cautioning against originating loans that would be larger than four times the borrower's earnings before interest, taxes and

---

[1] See Morris and Walker (2021).

depreciation.[2] At the time, they noted that growth in the sector was worrisome. In October 2017, the Government Accountability Office concluded that this guidance amounted to regulatory rule and should have been subject to Congressional review. That decision meant that the agencies needed to start that process in order for the guidance to be legal, which essentially halted it.

After the 2017 period, the loans continued to grow briskly and continued to be flagged as a financial stability concern.[3] The Bank of England's Financial Policy Committee (FPC) routinely cited leveraged loans as a source of concern. For instance, the FPC's November 2018 Financial Stability Report noted that

> "The pickup in issuance of leveraged loans at the global level reflects strong creditor risk appetite and loosening underwriting standards. The share of so-called 'covenant-lite' loans — where investors do not require borrowers to maintain certain financial ratios — has reached record highs. Other traditional investor protections in loan documentation (such as restrictions on borrowers' ability to transfer collateral beyond the reach of the lender) have also been relaxed, potentially increasing losses to lenders in the event of default."

The Federal Reserve, in its inaugural Financial Stability Report issued in November 2018, also warned of deteriorating underwriting standards.

Despite all the attention that leveraged lending was attracting, the remarkable thing that I would like to point out is that all parties agree that there is no commonly accepted definition of what constitutes a leveraged loan, much like there was no single definition of a subprime loan before the GFC. Hence, in the two financial stability reports that were issued in the same month, the Fed and FPC differed in their estimated size of the market by nearly a factor of two: the Fed cited the outstanding stock as $992 billion

---

[2] See Board of Governors of the Federal Reserve System (U.S.) (2013) for details.
[3] The *Wall Street Journal* reports that issuance through 20 May 2021 was proceeding at the fastest pace since 2005. See https://www.wsj.com/articles/issuance-of-bundles-of-risky-loans-jumps-to-16-year-high-11621849782?mod=hp_lista_pos4 (accessed 24 May 2021).

and the FPC estimated it to be about $1.8 trillion.[4] Subsequently, it seems that most estimates have converged to the higher figure.

It worries me that, at a time when many observers were focussing on this market, we were unsure about whether it was closer to a one- or two-trillion-dollar risk. As the old joke goes, pretty soon we will be talking about real money!

Furthermore, we still have poor information about exactly who holds this debt. If the economy does slow sometime soon, and downgrades ensue, we would not be well-sighted as to whether any holders might be forced to sell.[5] Kundu (2021) shows that forced selling by some collateralized loan obligation (CLO) managers has happened in the past and if a large fire-sale were to occur, it would likely impair the ability of firms to roll over financing or obtain new funding of this sort.

This example highlights a problem that featured prominently during the GFC. Once activity shifts away from the banking system, our ability to track it deteriorates. It will be sad if some part of the shadow banking system were to be at the centre of the next crisis and the authorities had to explain to the public and Congress that part of the reason is that we did not have a proper measurement system in place.

5. Example 4: Ambiguities in existing bank regulation

While the progress in shoring up bank regulation after the GFC has been substantial, there are still some issues with the current regime.

A casual observer might think that capital regulation for banks is pretty thoroughly worked out and that there are no glaring loopholes by which banks can avoid having instruments that are not loss absorbing counted as capital. As such, I found it surprising that software assets can

---

[4] See Table 2 in the Board of Governors of the Federal Reserve System (2018) and page 42 of the Bank of England (2018).
[5] I was surprised to see that the GAO in December 2020 issued another report suggesting that as of September 2020 the regulators "had not found that leveraged lending presented significant threats to financial stability" (see U.S. Government Accountability Office (2020)). I think the risks still remain and continue to deserve close scrutiny. The report did note that the FSOC does not have good tools for dealing with a problem, were one to develop in this space.

potentially count towards capital. Apparently, this is possible because intangible assets are supposed to be deducted from capital, but the definition of intangible capital depends on accounting rules that differ between the US and elsewhere. In the US, some software assets can be deemed tangible assets and hence do not need to be removed from capital. In Europe, this is not the case. Nonetheless, after the US opted not to subtract some software assets, the EU authorities followed suit. The EU decision is not compliant with the Basel rules, which permit such discretion only to the extent that it accords with local accounting rules.

So if you think I misspoke, let me say this again: European banks are now allowed to count some investment in software as capital (contrary to the Basel rules). As you would expect, when other regulators have tried to verify that somehow the recovery value of software for a firm that was in trouble could be a source of loss absorbency, they find no evidence of that being the case (Bank of England, 2020).

This ruling was just made in December 2020, and as far as I can tell, the rules have not been in place long enough for any weak banks to seriously exploit them. However, it would be tragic if by doing so a bank were able to maintain or launch a risky cross-border business that later unravelled in a way that spilled into another country.

Perhaps equally surprising is that the EU also has a concept of "maximum harmonisation" which holds that member states are forbidden from modifying new regulations, even if the proposed modification were to make the rule more stringent, for example by requiring higher capital levels. This is apparently intended to prevent dangerous races to the top! When I first joined the FPC, I had to have this explained several times because I could not possibly see how this was a good idea, but it continues to this day.

6. Potential solutions

I hope this range of examples has convinced you that despite the regulatory progress made since the GFC, there is still plenty of unfinished work to do. Having pointed out all these issues, let me close by offering a few ideas about how to proceed. Here are four recommendations that I think would be stability enhancing.

First, and probably most importantly, it would be desirable for all advanced economies to create (and/or empower existing) financial stability committees. As Edge and Liang (2019) have emphasised, while most advanced economies now have some sort of financial stability oversight group, in most cases they are relatively toothless. The more diplomatic way of putting this is to quote Edge and Liang who say "the evidence suggests that countries are placing a relatively low weight on the ability of policy institutions to take action and a high weight on political economy considerations in developing their financial stability governance structures". This may require opening up dialogues with legislatures.

This kind of change would help in two ways. First, it would create entities that at least stand a chance at keeping up with the inevitable evolution of the financial system. Second, it might mean some of the specific risks that I have identified could be remedied. For example, I cannot believe a properly empowered financial stability committee would permit software to count as loss-absorbing capital.

If a complete overhaul is infeasible in some cases, it might be helpful for an international organisation to produce an assessment of what types of existing authority is going unused in different economies. It would be powerful to compile this information in a single report that compared jurisdictions and created a common scorecard. Having the specialised technical knowledge of the relevant legislation in many different countries is something that academics are unlikely to possess. Consequently, if this is going to happen, it will probably require the work of a large team.[6] My conjecture from the case I know best — the US — is that even without any major legislation, there are some steps that could be taken that would be useful and having a comparative document pointing that out could prod some action.

A second suggestion is to accelerate reforms to enhance data collection authority, at least in jurisdictions with globally systemic financial institutions. The Office of Financial Research (OFR) in the US in principle

---

[6] Perhaps the International Monetary Fund could draw on it existing Financial Sector Assessment Program reports to do this.

could be more active in eliminating data gaps. For instance, the Director has the authority to subpoena any data from financial institutions that might be needed to achieve its mission. That authority has never been used and there are some doubt whether it would withstand a challenge. Nonetheless, the recommendation of the Task Force on Financial Stability (2021) to reorient the OFR to focus more on data gaps would, in my view, be a good change.

The problem with identifying data on holdings of leveraged loans is just one way in which ownership information is frustratingly incomplete. For example, we also know relatively little about corporate bond ownership. These holdings are scattered across the globe and, absent a high degree of cooperation, we are not going to get this information. Thus, we need better data collection in many countries. A first step would be to create a good template that covers the data that need to be measured and begin to get the different jurisdictions to collect that information on a consistent basis.

Another information request that I would make is for a forensic investigation of what went wrong at the various brokers that were serving Archegos. Again, there is no obvious institution that has both access to the relevant information and a mandate to do this kind of thing.[7] Perhaps this could be undertaken via a collaboration of the various stability committees? Or maybe this could done as a special project by the International Monetary Fund with cooperation of the regulators? Precisely because we have such a poor picture of the collective exposure of the various brokers to Archegos, getting a comprehensive picture of what happened is essential for understanding this episode.

Finally, in terms of the Treasury market, one proposal that intrigues me included in recommendations of both the Task Force on Financial Stability (2021) and the Group of Thirty Working Group on Treasury Market Liquidity (2021) is to explore the possibility of having the Federal Reserve become a member of the Fixed Income Clearing Corporation (FICC, the clearing entity operated by the Depository Trust and Clearing Corporation). By doing this, the Fed would face only the triple A-rated

---

[7] The Financial Stability Board includes the relevant domestic regulators to do it, but is not designed to undertake this kind of project.

FICC as a counterparty, and yet could potentially engage in repurchase agreements or cash-market trades of Treasury securities with a much wider range of counterparties than it can currently interact with. The Fed could control the pricing and terms of repos in which it participates, so that it could set different rules for institutions based on how tightly they are already supervised. The full feasibility of this would need to be studied; however, this could prove to be a way to relatively quickly set up a facility.[8]

Thanks again for the opportunity to share these thoughts. I look forward to your questions.

References

Andolfatto, David and Jane Ihrig (2019). "Why the Fed Should Create a Standing Repo Facility." Last modified 6 March 2019. https://www.stlouisfed.org/on-the-economy/2019/march/why-fed-create-standing-repo-facility. Accessed 4 July 2022.

Bank of England (2018). *Financial Stability Report*, Issue 44, November.

Bank of England (2020). "PRA statement on the EU requirement on prudential treatment of software assets." https://www.bankofengland.co.uk/prudential-regulation/publication/2020/statement-prudential-treatment-software-assets. Accessed 16 May 2021.

Board of Governors of the Federal Reserve System (U.S.) (2013). *Interagency Guidance on Leveraged Lending*. Washington, D.C.: Board of Governors.

Board of Governors of the Federal Reserve System (2018). *Financial Stability Report*, November.

Duffie, Darrell (2018). "Post-Crisis Bank Regulations and Financial Market Liquidity." Thirteenth Baffi Lecture, Banca d'Italia, Rome, Italy, 31 March. https://www.darrellduffie.com/uploads/policy/DuffieBaffiLecture2018.pdf. Accessed 4 July 2022.

Duffie, Darrell (2020). "Still the World's Safe Haven? Redesigning the U.S. Treasury Market After the COVID-19 Crisis." https://www.brookings.edu/research/still-the-worlds-safe-haven/. Accessed 4 July 2022.

Edge, Rochelle M. and J. Nellie Liang (2019). "New Financial Stability Governance Structures and Central Banks." Hutchins Center Working Paper

---

[8] See Hauser (2021) for some of the other issues involved in setting up such facilities. I do not mean to downplay the complexity in designing such facilities.

at Brookings 50, Washington, D.C. https://www.brookings.edu/wp-content/uploads/2019/02/WP50-updated.1.pdf. Accessed 4 July 2022.

Group of Thirty Working Group on Treasury Market Liquidity (2021). *U.S. Treasury Markets: Steps Toward Increased Resilience.* https://group30.org/publications/detail/4950. Accessed 4 July 2022.

Hall, Jon (2021). "Building Financial Market Resilience." Speech, Cardiff Business School, Cardiff, May 19, Bank of England. https://www.bankofengland.co.uk/speech/2021/may/jon-hall-building-financial-market-resilience. Accessed 4 July 2022.

Hauser, Andrew (2021). "Why central banks need new tools for dealing with market dysfunction." Speech, *Thomson Reuters Newsmaker*, 7 January, Bank of England. https://www.bankofengland.co.uk/speech/2021/january/andrew-hauser-speech-at-thomson-reuters-newsmaker.

Hubbard, Glenn, Donald Kohn, Laurie Goodman, Kathryn Judge, Anil Kashyap, Ralph Koijen, Blythe Masters, Sandie O'Connor, and Kara Stein (2021). *Task Force on Financial Stability*, supported by Hutchins Center on Fiscal and Monetary Policy at the Brookings Institution, the Initiative on Global Markets at the University of Chicago Booth School of Business. https://www.brookings.edu/wp-content/uploads/2021/06/financial-stability_report.pdf. Accessed 4 July 2022.

Kundu, Shohini (2021). An Economic Analysis of Collateralized Loan Obligations. PhD Dissertation, University of Chicago.

Morris, Stephen and Owen Walker (2021). "Credit Suisse Made Just $17.5m in Archegos Fees in Year Before $5.4bn Losses." *Financial Times*, 2 May, https://www.ft.com/content/429f2cd2-db55-42b8-a65c-a228cdb3089d. Accessed 4 July 2022.

U.S. Government Accountability Office (2020). *Financial Stability Agencies Have Not Found Leveraged Lending to Significantly Threaten Stability but Remain Cautious Amid Pandemic*, GAO-21-167. Washington, DC, 2020. Accessed 16 May 2021 https://www.gao.gov/assets/gao-21-167.pdf.

Vissing-Jorgensen, Annette (2021). "The Treasury Market in Spring 2020 and the Response of the Federal Reserve." *Journal of Monetary Economics*, Vol. 124, pp. 19–47.

CHAPTER 3

© 2023 World Scientific Publishing Company
https://doi.org/10.1142/9789811259432_0006

Chapter 3

Macroprudential Policies and the COVID-19 Pandemic: Risks and Challenges for Emerging Markets*

Sebastian Edwards

Henry Ford II Professor, UCLA
Research Associate, NBER

Abstract

This chapter deals with COVID-19 and macroprudential regulations in emerging markets. It documents the build-up of a sturdy macroprudential structure during 2009–2019, and the relaxation of regulations in 2020–2021, as part of the effort to deal with the sanitary emergency. The chapter explains that, in every country, regulatory forbearance played a key role in the response to COVID-19; discusses capital controls as macroprudential instruments; argues that rebuilding the macroprudential fabric is important to reduce the costs of future systemic shocks; and

---

*This is a revised version of a paper presented at the MAS-BIS Conference "Macrofinancial Stability Policy in a Globalised World: Lessons from International Experience," 26–28 May 2021. The author has benefitted from long conversations with past and current central bankers and regulators. The author would like to thank José De Gregorio, Joaquín Cortez, Roberto Steiner, Alberto Naudon, Fernando Losada, and Miguel Savastano. Luis Cabezas provided very able research assistance. He thanks, in particular, Eswar Prasad, his discussant at the conference, as well as other (Zoom) participants for their very useful comments.

maintain that post-COVID-19 regulations should incorporate the risks associated with digital currencies.

But now, ah now, to learn from crises...
Walt Whitman (1891–1892)

Deposit banks, which maintain [...] 100 percent reserves, simply could not fail, so far as depositors were concerned, and could not create or destroy effective money.
Henry Simons (1934)

1. Introduction

"Macroprudential regulation" is a relatively new concept in economic policy discussions. It appeared for the first time in the *New York Times* during the early days of the Great Financial Crisis, on 22 August 2008. The *Times* reported that at the annual Jackson Hole conference of central bankers, academics and policy pundits, the Fed Chairman, Ben Bernanke, had stated that there was a need for stepping up "macroprudential regulation". This, explained the Chairman, "would involve an attempt by regulators to develop a more fully integrated overview of the entire financial system". The key operational terms in Bernanke's statement were "fully integrated" and "entire financial system". The idea was to go beyond the strength and weaknesses of individual banks and financial institutions, and to focus on the entire sector, taking into account explicitly those linkages that could, under certain circumstances, result in contagion and severe damage to (or collapse of) the payments system and financial edifice. Of particular concern was the fact that, historically, credit had been pro-cyclical, dramatically increasing during economic expansion and declining abruptly during hard times. Credit booms were often accompanied by a relaxation of loan standards and safeguards, and many times ended up in severe crises.[1] In the years that followed, several articles on the subject appeared in the popular press, with the largest number of stories published, in the *New York Times,* during 2010 and 2014.

---

[1] Examples include the savings and loans debacle in the 1980s and the Great Financial Crisis (GFC) of 2008–2009.

The origins of the concept, however, go back several decades. Some central banks said, very sporadically in internal documents, as early as 1979. In the academic world, and according to Journal STORage (JSTOR), Rainer Stefano Masera was the first one to use it, in a 1981 article on the Euromarkets published in the *Giornale degli Economisti* (Masera, 1981). It would take almost 20 years for the concept to appear again in an academic publication. The IMF's economist Don Mathieson referred to it in a 1998 book review published in the *Journal of Economic Literature* (Mathieson, 1988). As I argue below, Chile was an early adopter of what we call macroprudential policies today, but the regulations put in place after the 1982 banking/currency crisis were not labelled as such.

Increased policy attention on macroprudential policies was at the centre of the Basel III Regulatory Accord of November 2010. A global Bank for International Settlements (BIS) survey found that, between 2000 and 2007, less than five central bankers' speeches per year mentioned "macroprudential" regulations or policies. During 2008, the year of the Great Financial Crisis, the number of speeches increased to almost 40. By 2011, the number had catapulted to more than 200 per year.[2] By now there is a voluminous literature on macroprudential policies (MaPs). Much of the work has been done at the BIS, the International Monetary Fund (IMF) and at individual central banks (see the references section of this chapter for details on some of the most salient contributions). Theoretical models that provide justification for the use of MaPs include, among others, Allen et al. (2018) and Farhi and Werning (2016). These two influential papers show that there are many circumstances under which traditional policies are unable to safeguard the financial system from bad states of the world. In those cases, pointed interventions, including setting limits to banks' exposure, building countercyclical buffers and slowing down international capital movements, provide, in principle, efficient second best solutions.[3]

---

[2] An interesting question is whether the 1933 Chicago Plan on Banking Reform, which included the idea of 100 percent reserve requirements on deposit-taking banks, could be considered an early precursor of MaPs. In his 1934 pamphlet on laissez faire, Simons (1934, p. 64) wrote that "deposit banks, which maintain [...] 100 percent reserves, simply could not fail, so far as depositors were concerned, and could not create or destroy effective money".

[3] Forbes (2019). For overall discussions on MaPs, see also Hanson et al. (2011) and Berner et al. (2011).

The concerns behind MaPs are somewhat different in advanced economies (AEs) from those in emerging markets (EMs). In the former, the goal is to protect the financial system (including the shadow banking sector) from domestic exuberance during booms, from loose lending practices during expansions and from internal asset bubbles.[4] Of course, every one of these issues is important in EMs. In fact, because in poorer nations banks tend to be less capitalised, the dangers of exuberance can be larger than in AEs. However, in EMs, there are additional concerns related to cross-border capital flows, foreign currency loans and deposits, currency mismatches in the banking sector and balance sheet effects stemming from large devaluations. That is, in EMs, the global dimension of MaPs is more central than in AEs.

When looking at the problem through an EM's lens, it is possible to organise the objectives of MaPs under three *interrelated* categories (of course, a similar list can be produced for the AEs):

- To build a sturdy and resilient financial system that is able to withstand aggregate shocks, including abrupt surges of capital inflows, sudden stops, current account reversals, housing and other asset bubbles, terms of trade shocks, changes in risk appetite by global financial investors, large exchange rate changes and other real or financial shocks stemming from abroad;
- To assure that domestic credit booms do not lead to banking overexposure and, eventually, to financial and currency crises. This means building *countercyclical reserves and buffers* that will slow down credit expansion during expansions and will help maintain credit flows during downturns;
- To reduce structural vulnerabilities in the banking/financial system, in order to avoid possible "contagion" spreading across institutions. This means that in designing the MaPs, regulators should take into account interconnected relations both in the traditional and in the shadow banking and financial sectors. An issue of particular concern is avoiding currency mismatches between bank assets and liabilities.

---

[4] A tremendous amount of work on the subject has been done at the ECB and other central banks, including the Bank of Canada and the Bank of England.

As a number of authors have documented, major macroeconomic disruptions, including currency and banking crises, can be extremely costly in terms of output collapses, bankruptcies and heightened unemployment. A very important historical example — and one that triggered an early implementation of what we call MaPs today — is the 1982 crisis in Chile, an episode that forced the government to bail out the entire banking system at enormous costs. The roots of this catastrophe were related to excessive risk-taking by newly privatised banks in an environment of a recently liberalised financial market. Banks borrowed internationally in massive amounts — the current account deficit climbed to 12 percent of gross domestic product (GDP) in 1981 — in order to finance a spectacular real estate boom and other investments in non-tradable sectors. Once the peso was devalued in June 1982, borrowers were unable to pay and (most) banks became insolvent. What made the episode particularly interesting was that the government had put in place (very) strict controls on capital inflows and had regulated individual financial institutions tightly. One of the consequences of this early crisis was the adoption, in Chile, of fully integrated regulations covering the complete financial sector. The purpose of these policies, which included controls on capital inflows, loan-to-value (LTV) limits and other measures aimed at avoiding currency mismatches between deposits and loans, was to make sure that another systemic crisis would not happen. Like Moliere's *Bourgeois Gentilhomme*, who spoke prose without knowing it, Chile's regulators had invented MaPs without realising it or giving them a name, and without knowing that the policies would become generalised a few years later.[5]

The purpose of this chapter is to analyse MaPs from the perspective of emerging markets. My main interest is to analyse the role played by MaPs in the policy response to the COVID-19 sanitary emergency that started in 2020, and the challenges that regulators are likely to face in the immediate post–COVID-19 period. Throughout the chapter, I focus on the experiences of 12 countries: China, South Korea, Malaysia, the Philippines, Singapore and Thailand in East Asia, and Argentina, Brazil,

---

[5] On the Chilean crisis of 1982 and the policy changes it elicited see, for example, Edwards and Edwards (1991). On the costs of crises see, for example, Kaminsky and Reinhart (1999).

Chile, Colombia, Mexico and Peru in Latin America.[6] Although the emphasis is mostly on pandemic-related effects, in Section 6 is mentioned, briefly, a development that was unfolding, rapidly, even before the sanitary crisis: the adoption of digital currencies by central banks. The question is: how are CBDCs likely to affect financial stability?

The rest of this chapter is organised as follows: Section 2 deals with the MaPs landscape before the pandemic. Section 3 concentrates on the response to the pandemic between March 2020 and May 2021 (the time of the conference). The core part of Section 3 is an analysis of the regulatory relief implemented to deal with the emergency. It is shown that, in every country, regulations were relaxed in order to facilitate the provision of assistance to firms and families. Section 4 focuses on the MaPs in the post-pandemic period, in particular on three specific challenges, including the increase in non-performing loans (NPLs) and the need to recapitalise banks. It is argued that lessons learned during the pandemic will be useful in further advancing towards a more complete MaPs architecture. Section 5 discusses controls on cross-border capital flows, a topic that refuses to die in discussions and debates regarding MaPs. Finally, Section 6 presents some concluding remarks. The Appendix provides a minimalist model of MaPs.[7]

---

[6] There has been consensus among analysts for some time now that South Korea has joined the ranks of the advanced countries. However, in order to maintain uniformity of coverage with respect to other studies, it is included in this analysis.

[7] Before proceeding, a word about this paper and "real-time" developments. During the period I have been working on this document, the world's sanitary, political, financial and economic conditions have been changing rapidly; there have also been changes in MaPs, both in the AEs and in some of the EMs. Analysts, policymakers and officials working at multilateral organisations have constantly updated (and changed) their views about the future. Consider the following important developments that unfolded during a few days in late March–early April, 2021. First, Standard & Poor's downgraded Chile's sovereign credit rating from A+ to A. It would not be surprising that between the conference and the publication of the proceedings, further downgrade actions are taken by the major rating agencies in a number of EMs. Historically, in most regions there has been a close connection between the ratings of the sovereign and those of domestic banks. Second, on March 30, 2021, the IMF adjusted its discourse regarding the EMs, stating that the world should be prepared for an "emerging markets debt crisis" (*Financial Times*, 31 March 2021, p. 3). Third, in early 2021, the People's Bank of China decided to step up its MaPs, and released a resolution directing banks "to curb lending as fears rise over property boom" (*Financial Times*, 5 April 2021, p. 1).

2. The macroprudential landscape before the pandemic

As Forbes (2019) has pointed out, it is not straightforward to translate the overall goal of "systemic financial stability" into specific policies. Different authors — and different central banks and regulatory agencies, for that matter — tend to emphasise different mechanisms, transmission channels and angles. Many times these differences are the result of particular experiences and the country's own history. However, an important common element, present in almost every country and region, has been the creation of a dedicated institutional apparatus to deal with the evaluation of systemic risks, and with the implementation of MaPs. In the majority of countries, these functions are shared by two or more institutions, typically the central bank and a financial/banking regulator that sometimes also cover insurance companies. This institutional and governance arrangement, which on the surface appears to be routine, becomes very important during a crisis, when urgent and coordinated decisions have to be made.

A useful way of organising the discussion is to consider a production function for "systemic financial stability". This process consists of combining several regulatory tools or instruments to achieve a certain level of financial protection or sturdiness. At a very general level, regulatory instruments may be substitutes or complements. A well-known production function that satisfies this requirement is the CES:

$$s = A \left(\sum_{j=1}^{k} \lambda_j R_j^\rho \right)^{k/\rho}$$

Where s is "financial stability", which can be measured by some type of index, and the R_j are the different regulatory instruments, which play the role of "inputs". This particular function is homogeneous of degree k, and the elasticity of substitution between any two regulatory instruments is constant and equal to $\sigma = \left[1/(1-\rho) \right]$.

In this setting, a higher s — i.e., higher financial stability — will reduce the probability and the cost of a major financial/currency/banking crisis. However, a higher "financial stability" index may also have a negative effect on economic growth during good states of nature by reducing credit availability and introducing other distortions in the capital market. The policymaker faces two problems: to select the level of *s* that maximises the level of expected real income across all states of nature and to determine which instruments (and in what proportion) to activate/use in order to achieve the optimal level of *s*. The optimal mix of instruments will depend, as usual, on two factors: (1) The expected "marginal contribution" of each of the instruments to systemic financial stability *s*; and (2) The expected marginal cost of deploying each instrument, in terms of (possible) negative impact in economic growth during good states of nature. Of course, there is no need for these marginal costs and benefits to be the same across countries, or to be constant through time. Different countries will, generally, choose different combinations of the R_i's to achieve their desired level of "stability protection." See the Appendix for a model along these lines.

In a recent report, the BIS provides a comprehensive list of instruments and tools deployed in 55 countries in the last 23 years (BIS, 2018). The analysis identified 845 specific MaP actions, which may be grouped into four broad categories:

- Measures aimed at ensuring *capital adequacy*;
- MaPs geared at *protecting the level of liquidity* of the financial system;
- Policies that establish quantitative *limits to banks' exposure to risk*;
- Restrictions setting *limits to foreign currency exposure* of the financial system (*capital controls*).

2.1. A map to MaPs

Tables 1 and 2 present a summary of MaPs in place in the 12 countries covered by this study, as of December 2019, just before the eruption of the pandemic.[8] A total of 19 specific instruments have been considered, which have been grouped into the four categories listed above: capital

---

[8] In its 2018 *Annual Report* the BIS provided a comprehensive list of tools and macroprudential policies implemented in 55 countries during the last 23 years (BIS, 2018).

Table 1. Macroprudential policies in selected East Asian countries, 2019.

	China	Korea	Malaysia	Philippines	Singapore	Thailand
A. Capital Adequacy MaPs						
Risk-weighted capital requirements (CR)	✓✓	✓✓	✓✓	✓✓	✓✓	✓✓
Capital requirements FX positions						
Capital requirements by sector	✓✓		✓✓	✓✓		✓✓
Countercyclical capital buffers (CCyB)		✓✓		✓	✓✓	
Capital Conservation Buffer	✓	✓✓	✓	✓✓	✓✓	
Limits on dividend if capital is low	✓✓	✓✓		✓✓	✓✓	
Profits capitalization	✓✓	✓✓		✓✓	✓✓	
B. Liquidity protection MaPs						
Cyclical reserve requirement ratios	✓		✓	✓		
Higher RRRs for FX positions or non-resident capital inflows	✓✓					
Marginal RRRs on cars and motorcycle loans & mortgages		✓✓				
Higher liquidity ratios on domestic or foreign currency loans (LCR)	✓✓	✓✓	✓✓	✓✓	✓✓	✓
Dynamic provisioning (Cyclical provisioning for NPLs)	✓✓		✓✓			✓✓
C. Quantitative Limits on Banks' Exposure						
Buffer for systemically important financial institution	✓✓	✓✓		✓✓	✓✓	✓✓
Caps on Loan-to-value (LTV) ratios	✓✓	✓✓	✓✓	✓✓	✓✓	✓✓
Caps on Debt-to-income (DTI) ratios	✓✓	✓✓	✓✓	✓✓	✓✓	✓✓
Caps on FX exposure & currency matching of loans to deposits	✓✓	✓✓	✓✓	✓✓		✓✓
Limits on the exposure to derivatives		✓✓				
D. MaPs to Limit Foreign Exchange Exposure						
Foreign exchange reserves	✓✓	✓	✓✓	✓	✓✓	✓✓
Limits on cross border capital flows	✓✓	✓	✓✓	✓✓	✓	✓✓

Source: Alam et al. (2019), BIS (2011–2019, 2017), Cerutti et al. (2017), Corbacho and Shanaka (2018), and individual central bank publications.

Table 2. Macroprudential policies in Selected Latin America, 2019.

	Argentina	Brazil	Chile	Colombia	Mexico	Peru
A. Capital Adequacy MaPs						
Risk-weighted capital requirements (CR)	✓✓	✓✓	✓✓	✓	✓✓	✓✓
Capital requirements FX positions		✓✓				✓✓
Capital requirements by sector	✓✓	✓✓		✓✓		✓✓
Countercyclical capital buffers (CCyB)	✓	✓			✓✓	✓✓
Capital Conservation Buffer	✓	✓✓			✓✓	✓✓
Limits on dividend if capital is low	✓	✓			✓✓	✓✓
Profits capitalization	✓	✓				
B. Liquidity protection MaPs						
Cyclical reserve requirement ratios		✓✓		✓		✓✓
Higher RRRs for FX positions or non-resident capital inflows	✓✓					✓✓
Marginal RRRs on cars and motorcycle loans & mortgages						✓✓
Higher liquidity ratios on domestic or foreign currency loans (LCR)	✓✓	✓✓	✓	✓✓	✓✓	
Dynamic provisioning (Cyclical provisioning for NPLs)	✓✓	✓✓	✓✓	✓✓		
C. Quantitative Limits on Banks' Exposure						
Buffer for systemically important financial institution	✓✓	✓✓	✓	✓	✓✓	✓✓
Caps on Loan-to-value (LTV) ratios	✓✓	✓✓	✓✓	✓✓	✓✓	✓✓
Caps on Debt-to-income (DTI) ratios	✓✓	✓✓	✓✓	✓✓		
Caps on FX exposure & currency matching of loans to deposits	✓✓	✓✓	✓✓	✓✓	✓✓	✓✓
Limits on the exposure to derivatives			✓✓			
D. MaPs to Limit Foreign Exchange Exposure						
Foreign exchange reserves	✓	✓✓	✓✓	✓✓	✓✓	✓
Limits on cross border capital flows						

Source: Alam et al. (2019), BIS (2011–2019, 2017), Cerutti et al. (2017), Corbacho, and Shanaka (2018), and individual central bank publications.

adequacy, liquidity protection, limits to risk exposure and foreign currency exposure.[9] Instead of attempting to develop a numeric indicator to measure the depth and coverage of each instrument, a "softer" and "fuzzier" approach has been taken: for each instrument in every country assigned zero, one or two "ticks" are added. No tick means that particular instrument had not been deployed or activated; one tick means that instrument had been partially activated or was in the process of being activated; two ticks means that instrument was in place and in use in December 2019.[10]

These tables show that there is a great diversity of experiences across nations. No two countries in the sample that are exactly alike; each has its own idiosyncratic set of MaPs. The tables also show that, in spite of this diversity, there are some common elements across countries. In particular, every country has deployed instruments in each of the four broad categories depicted above. This suggests that, based on their own financial, economic and political reality, each of these countries has decided to follow a particular path to achieve financial protection and stability.

Some of the macroprudential instruments in Tables 1 and 2 are aimed at providing "structural" protection, while others provide cyclical safeguards. An important distinction established by the Basel Committee refers to "capital conservation buffers" and "countercyclical capital buffers" or CCyB. The former is additional capital over and above the CET1 capital ratios, while the latter is related to the aggregate credit cycle. Once the conservation buffers are deployed fully (2.5 percent of CET1 capital), banks with resultant low CET1 capital ratios face restrictions on earnings distributions (including dividend payments and large bonuses

---

[9] Filling this table is a major task, as in a number of cases the regulations are rather vague and the details on implementation are incomplete. It is interesting to note that 6 out of the 12 countries considered in this study are members of the Basel Committee, the institution that, arguably, has pushed harder for the implementation of macroprudential regulations: Argentina, Brazil, China, South Korea, Mexico, Singapore. In addition, Chile and Malaysia are observers of the Committee.

[10] At some point, I attempted to use a measure with greater granularity, but the information available makes the exercise difficult. Some instruments, however, are susceptible to being measured quite precisely. These include reserve requirement ratios and LTV ratios. See Alam *et al.* (2019) and Rojas *et al.* (2020) for studies that use these "hard" metrics.

to executives). According to the Basel Committee, capital conservation buffers "must be capable of being drawn... [but] banks should not choose to operate in the buffer range simply to compete with other banks and win market share" (BIS, 2019, p. 7/20). For internationally active banks, the CCyB is calculated "as a weighted average of the buffers deployed across all jurisdictions to which it has credit exposure" (BIS, 2019).

As noted, the role of CCyB is to reduce the amplitude of the credit cycle by keeping credit growth in check during booms and maintaining the credit flow during downturns. In the Basel Committee member countries, the regulator is supposed to judge periods of excessive credit growth that could result in system-wide risk, and deploy the countercyclical capital buffer requirements. "This will vary between zero and 2.5 percent of risk weighted assets" (BIS, 2019, p. 8/20). The activation and release of CCyB is asymmetric: when a regulator decides to raise the buffers, it should pre-announce the decision 12 months in advance. Reductions in the CCyB, however, may take place immediately. By December 2019, the six member countries of the Committee in our sample, had adopted CCyB, but had not activated them fully.[11]

Tables 1 and 2 also show that most countries enacted some MaP instruments aimed at maintaining liquidity. A particularly important tool is the LTV ratio. The main role of this instrument is to safeguard the banking system from housing price cycles, of the type that has affected a number of countries in East Asia and Latin America during the last few decades.

Concerns about real estate prices (and potential bubbles) are particularly serious in countries where an important proportion of credit is funded in foreign currency. Many of the regulations in Tables 1 and 2 are aimed at avoiding exposing banks to situations where foreign-currency-denominated loans finance non-tradable industries and sectors. A number of the Latin American countries in this study — Chile (1982), Mexico (1994), Brazil (1998), Argentina (2002) — were affected by large devaluations that wrecked the local banking sector. The recent directive (April 5, 2021) by the People's Bank of China on restricting credit was

---

[11] After the eruption of the pandemic, Chile, an observer, postponed the implementation of the Basel III directives until December 2022.

triggered by deep concerns on a property boom. That was also the case in New Zealand's recent (2021) reinstatement of LTV ratios.

As may be seen from Tables 1 and 2, 5 out of the 19 instruments are aimed, explicitly, at reducing risks related to foreign currency exposures. Throughout history, a common concern has been that allowing for unlimited foreign funding of domestic banks will fuel speculations and destabilise domestic asset markets. For instance, this was a recurrent theme in South Korea and Chile during the early 1990s (Edwards and Edwards, 1991; Park and Park, 1993).

2.2. Assessing MaPs' effectiveness: Selective review

Do MaPs work? Have they accomplished their goals? From a methodological point of view, answering these questions is a challenging endeavour. Some of the difficulties include the following: (1) There are no generally accepted *broad* quantitative measures or indexes on the extent, coverage and intensity of the policies. (2) There is no clear control group, as almost every country has taken some MaP-related action in the last 10 years or so. (3) There are no obvious counterfactuals. And (4), with the exception of the pandemic, an event that is still unfolding, there are no clear episodes of incipient crises that have been avoided because of the MaPs. In spite of these limitations and difficulties, a number of scholars have made valiant efforts to analyse the effectiveness of the MaPs. Most of these efforts involved analysing the effect of the deployment of MaPs on credit growth, consumption and indebtedness. Although a thorough review of the rapidly growing literature is beyond the scope of this chapter, in the rest of this section, a selective and important set of pertinent contributions is discussed.

A number of studies have analysed whether the implementation of MaPs has reduced the amplitude and period of the credit cycle. Most of these analyses combine historical data — the scope of the cycle in past years — with cross-country information. Indeed, this type of analysis is the basis for the BIS influential "credit gaps" indicator. Gambacorta and Murcia (2020) and Barroso *et al.* (2020) found some evidence that MaPs helped stabilise the credit cycle in Argentina, Brazil, Colombia, Mexico and Peru, and contributed to reducing the risk associated with mortgage lending in Brazil. Bruno *et al.* (2017) used data for 12 East Asia economies and found that MaPs were effective in slowing down banking inflows and, thus, reduced the overall vulnerabilities of the financial sector. According to Dell'Ariccia *et al.* (2012), MaPs helped reduce the amplitude of credit cycles. During the boom, credit grows more slowly in countries with active MaPs, and the costs associated with credit busts are smaller in those countries.

As it was previously indicated, in BIS (2018) report, and as documented in Tables 1 and 2, an important class of MaPs is geared at setting limits to banks' exposure by restricting LTV ratios, and other metrics that capture liquidity and vulnerability across the industry. Choi *et al.* (2011) concluded that more restrictive LTV ratios resulted in a lower housing (mortgage) debt to GDP ratio in Hong Kong. Using a VAR analysis, Tillmann (2015) found that reducing the maximum LTV and "debt-service-to-income" ratios reduced consumption credit, relative to GDP, in Korea. Richter *et al.* (2019) used data for 56 countries over 20 years to analyse the effects (both costs and benefits) of making LTV ratios more restrictive. Their "narrative approach" indicates that tightening the ratio has modest effects on output and inflation. More specifically, a reduction of the maximum LTV ratio by 10 percentage points lowers output in the emerging markets (in their sample) by approximately 1.1 percent after four years. The effects on inflation are negligible. The authors estimate that this effect is similar to what would be generated by a rise in the monetary policy rate of 26 basis points.

Alam *et al.* (2019) introduced a new and very comprehensive data set on MaPs for 134 countries for the period 1990–2016.[12] The authors analysed how some of the more general MaPs affected credit, indebtedness and consumption. They found that instruments that targeted loans reduced household debt (relative to the counterfactual) and had a dampening effect on consumption. Their most interesting results referred to the nonlinear impact of LTV limits on household debt. In addition, and in line with nonlinear models, they found that the initial value of the LTV ratio mattered: this meant that countries that already had tight LTVs were likely to benefit from emphasising other instruments.

---

[12] Interestingly, the data coverage begins when, as noted in Section 1 of this chapter, very few Central Banks were discussing MaPs as such.

In a recent paper, Rojas et al. (2020) found that, when properly identified, one of the most popular MaPs, namely changes in banks' reserve requirements, were costly. According to their analysis, increases in banks' reserve requirements led to a decline in the level of economic activity. Bush et al. (2021) used data for Chile, Mexico and Russia to analyse the extent to which changes in the monetary policy rate in the US affected the domestic financial markets in these countries. Their results were mixed and inconclusive. Interestingly, the authors found that in some countries MaPs targeting the asset side of banks' balance sheets tended to magnify the effects of foreign-policy shocks. Cantú et al. (2020) reported the results of a BIS study that used data for Australia, Indonesia, New Zealand, the Philippines and Thailand, and focused on supervisory bank-level data. They found that, on average, stricter MaPs reduced "excessive" consumer credit growth. They also found that the effects were asymmetrical, with tightening having a larger effect than easing. Interestingly, only a few of the multi-country and multi-policy studies included capital controls in the group of MaPs evaluated. And yet, many politicians and policymakers across EMs tended to think of them as effective policy tools to protect the domestic financial market from extraneous shocks.

3. The pandemic and the MaPs

Regulatory forbearance has been a key component of the global economic response to the COVID-19 pandemic. It has allowed banks and other financial institutions to continue operating in a "quasi normal" mode, without calling back loans from firms severely affected by COVID-19. It has also permitted banks to provide new loans to families and firms in need. A key question is whether the vast regulatory relaxation of 2020–2021 will leave (some) emerging markets in a vulnerable position, without the required tools to face future and imminent shocks. The fact that in the middle of 2021, the IMF and other official institutions had not detected major weaknesses in most financial sectors, but this is not necessarily a sign that everything will be well in the near future. Indeed, it is highly likely that once the emergency is over, and moratoria and regulatory forbearance are over, there will be a need to deal with a large increase in non-performing loans (NPLs) and the recapitalisation of banks. It will also be necessary to reconstruct those MaPs that have been released in order to fight the pandemic. Actual outcomes will depend on a number of factors, including the nature of the shocks stemming from the global economy; see Section 4 for a discussion.

This section documents the policy response for the 12 countries covered by this study, beginning with regulatory relief and then moving to the monetary and fiscal responses. The section ends with an assessment of the health of the financial sector a year after the World Health Organization declared a worldwide pandemic.

3.1. Regulatory relief and forbearance

Table 3 provides a summary of some of the most important regulatory relief measures undertaken by the 12 countries under study, after the eruption of the pandemic (February 2020–March 2021). As may be seen, these actions are related to every one of the four categories of MaPs defined in Section 2 and summarised in Tables 1 and 2. There have been relaxations to capital adequacy requirements, to regulations aimed at protecting liquidity, to quantitative limits to banks' exposure and, to a lesser extent, to limits to foreign exchange exposure. These changes in the regulatory framework were implemented by both central banks and regulatory agencies. While in most countries, the different official bodies involved in the regulatory process coordinated their actions, in some, there were tensions and misunderstandings. In Table 3, the measures highlighted in grey refer to loan moratoria and/or to relaxations of the requirements for classifying loans, including the relaxation of the requirement of labelling those with pass due payments as NPLs.

Instead of repeating the information in Table 3, it is useful to focus on one country from each region, by way of example. In what follows, Malaysia and Colombia are discussed.

As may be seen, in Malaysia there was a reduction in reserve requirements for banks, relaxation of LTV ratios, moratoria on loan payments by distressed companies and forbearance on supervisory compliance by banks. The combination of these policies with the ample government guarantees programme, that will be discussed later on and

Table 3. Regulatory forbearance and regulatory relief measures in selective East Asian and Latin American countries through March 2021.

China	• Local banks allowed to provide limited uncollateralized small and medium-sized enterprise (SME) loans. • Delay of loan payments permitted. • Loan size restrictions for online loans eased. • Tolerance for higher NPLs and reduced NPL provision coverage requirements. • Relaxation of regulations on insurers for bond investments.
South Korea	• Temporary easing of rules on share buybacks. • Temporary easing of loan-to-deposit ratios for banks and other financial institutions. • Temporary easing of the domestic currency liquidity coverage ratio for banks. • Easing collateral requirements for net settlements in the BOK payments system.
Malaysia	• Lowered the Reserve Requirement Ratio (RRR) to 2 percent. • Temporary eased regulatory and supervisory compliance on banks to help support loan deferment and restructuring. • Regulatory relief measures for public-listed companies. • Enhanced protection of distressed companies against liquidation. • Loan-to-Value requirement for third mortgages eased. • Targeted loan payment moratorium for borrowers affected by pandemic. • Banks to provide repayment flexibility to SME affected by COVID-19.
Philippines	• Temporary relaxation of requirements on compliance reporting • Temporary relaxation on penalties on required reserves. • Temporary relaxation of provisioning requirements. • Relaxation of prudential regulations regarding marking-to-market of debt securities. • Loans to SMEs to be counted as part of banks' reserve requirements. • Temporarily reduced SMEs loans credit risk weights to 50 percent. • Assigned zero risk weight to loan exposures guaranteed by the Philippine Guarantee Corporation. • Loans to certain large enterprises recognised as forms of alternative compliance with banks' reserve requirements. • Increased the limit on banks' real estate share of loan portfolio from 20 percent to 25 percent.

Table 3. (*Continued*)

Singapore	• Selected regulatory and supervisory programs revised to enable financial institutions to better deal with issues related to the pandemic. • Wider range of collateral accepted. • Domestic banks allowed to pledge eligible residential property loans as collateral. • MAS expanded the range of collateral that banks in Singapore can use to access US$ liquidity.
Thailand	• The BOT relaxed regulations regarding classification of borrowers • Relaxed levels of loan loss provision to accelerate debt restructuring. • Borrowers not yet classified as NPL or classified as NPL due to COVID-19 can classified as normal if they make repayments in accordance with a debt restructuring agreement, which would not considered be a Troubled Debt Restructuring (TDR). • Reduced lower minimum credit card and revolving repayments from 10 percent to 5 percent in 2020 and 2021 and 8 percent in 2022. • Three-month moratorium on personal loans (installment payments), car loans and motorcycles. • Three-month moratorium on principal repayments for housing, SME and micro-finance loans with consideration on a case-by-case basis for lower interest payments.
Argentina	• Lower reserve requirements on bank lending to households and SMEs. • Temporary easing of bank provisioning needs. • Temporary easing (extra time) of bank loan classification rules. • Stay on bank account closures due to bounced checks.
Brazil	• Lower reserve requirements and capital conservation buffers. • Temporary relaxation of provisioning rules for banks. • Lower capital requirements for small financial institutions. • Banks allowed to reduce provisions for contingent liabilities stemming from loans to SMEs.
Chile	• Central Bank regulations for bank liquidity made more "flexible". • Relaxation of the liquidity coverage ratio on a case-by-case basis. • Special treatment of provisions for deferred loans (CMF measure). • Mortgage guarantees accepted as collateral for SME loans. • Timetable for the implementation of Basel III standards revised.

(*Continued*)

Table 3. (*Continued*)

Colombia	• Reserve requirement applicable to savings and checking accounts lowered from 11 to 8 percent; RRRs on savings accounts cut to 3.5 percent. • Loans less than 30 days over-due re-profiled (maturity was extended). • Viable borrowers can postpone payments to 30 June 2021 to 31 August 2021. • Countercyclical provisions have been released. • SFC authorised certain related-party transactions for fund managers.
Mexico	• Reduced the mandatory regulatory deposit. • Temporary relaxation in accounting standards allowing credit providers to defer loans for up to four or six months. • Committee on Liquidity Banking Regulation outlined temporary flexibilities on liquidity requirements for banks, permitting the use of up to 50 percent of the capital buffer and announcing temporary flexibilities.
Peru	• Reduced reserve requirements for banking sector. • Financial institutions allowed to modify the terms of their loans to households and enterprises affected by the COVID-19 without changing the classification of the loans.

Note: Highlighted measures refer to loan moratoria and/or relaxation on loan classification (including NPLs).
Source: IMF "Policy Responses to COVID-19," https://www.imf.org/en/Topics/imf-and-covid19/Policy-Responses-to-COVID-19#C, and individual central banks.

is summarised in Table 6, allowed Malaysia to put in place an active and aggressive programme for dealing with the pandemic.

As the information in Table 3 shows, Colombia also implemented significant adjustments to its regulatory framework once the sanitary emergency was declared. As in Malaysia, there were reductions in reserve requirements to banks, extended maturity to loans, postponement of dates for loan repayments and relaxation of countercyclical provisions. As will be seen in the Section 3.2, Colombia's ability to enact an aggressive fiscal program has been affected by the rating of its sovereign debt (BBB–).

As noted, CCyB is one of the most important MaPs. The majority of the countries in this study had implemented the regulation but had not built the CCyB up before the sanitary emergency. That is, the regulation was in the books, but its rate was still at zero. This means that for the countries in Table 3, it was not possible to release the CCyB buffer stocks, as was done in many (but not all) AEs. In the countries in this study, most of the relief, in terms of capital requirements, came through structural relaxations. Interestingly, this was not a unique situation in the EMs; it also happened in many AEs. As De Guindos (2021) has pointed out, in March 2020 in the Eurozone, CCyBs amounted to only 0.2 percent of risk weighted assets, a long way from the proposed 2.5 percent.

The strengthening of regulations in the decade that followed the GFC (2009–2019) allowed the banking sectors across regions to respond to the pandemic, without succumbing. The extent and massiveness of the response — see Tables 4 and 5 for details — were possible because

Table 4. General government fiscal balance or general government net lending/ borrowing (as percentage of GDP).*

	(1) 2010	(2) 2012	(3) 2015	(4) 2019	(5) 2020	(6) 2021	(7) 2025
East Asia							
China	−0.36	−0.30	−2.79	−6.31	−11.89	−11.78	−8.14
Korea	1.47	1.49	0.52	0.37	−3.24	−2.33	−2.54
Malaysia	−4.32	−3.10	−2.55	−3.69	−6.53	−4.67	−3.14
Philippines	−2.25	−0.29	0.59	−1.78	−8.06	−7.31	−6.06
Singapore	5.69	7.34	2.86	3.84	−10.77	1.17	2.61
Thailand	−1.07	−0.86	0.13	−0.82	−5.21	−4.92	−1.89
Mean	−0.14	0.71	−0.21	−1.40	−7.62	−4.97	−3.19
Median	−0.72	−0.30	0.33	−1.30	−7.30	−4.80	−2.84
Latin America							
Argentina	−1.39	−3.02	−6.00	−4.47	−11.42		
Brazil	−3.82	−2.52	−10.25	−6.01	−16.78	−6.52	−5.90
Chile	−0.36	0.68	−2.08	−2.65	−8.71	−4.01	−1.55
Colombia	−3.30	0.16	−3.52	−2.51	−9.48	−6.20	−0.90
Mexico	−3.98	−3.73	−4.00	−2.35	−5.80	−3.40	−2.50
Peru	0.12	2.05	−2.13	−1.37	−9.41	−4.31	−1.70
Mean	−2.12	−1.06	−4.66	−3.23	−10.26	−4.89	−2.51
Median	−2.35	−1.18	−3.76	−2.58	−9.44	−4.31	−1.70

*General government fiscal balance or general government net lending/ borrowing is calculated as revenue minus total expenditure.
Source: World Economic Outlook database, IMF.

Table 5. General government gross debt (as percentage of GDP).*

	(1) 2010	(2) 2012	(3) 2015	(4) 2019	(5) 2020	(6) 2021	(7) 2025
East Asia							
China	33.92	34.39	41.49	52.63	61.70	66.53	78.07
Korea	29.49	35.04	40.78	41.92	48.41	52.24	64.96
Malaysia	51.21	53.79	56.97	57.24	67.58	66.03	62.00
Philippines	47.59	45.69	39.64	36.97	48.86	52.51	59.33
Singapore	98.70	106.74	102.30	130.02	131.19	132.35	137.11
Thailand	39.83	41.93	42.56	41.10	50.45	56.37	56.87
Mean	50.12	52.93	53.96	59.98	68.03	71.01	76.39
Median	43.71	43.81	42.02	47.28	56.08	61.20	63.48
Latin America							
Argentina	43.45	40.44	52.56	90.38	96.69		
Brazil	63.05	62.20	72.57	89.47	101.40	102.76	104.41
Chile	8.56	11.95	17.28	27.91	32.81	37.51	47.98
Colombia	36.50	33.97	50.42	52.29	68.23	68.07	59.52
Mexico	41.96	42.65	52.78	53.75	65.54	65.60	64.91
Peru	25.34	21.17	24.07	27.12	39.48	39.13	37.80
Mean	36.48	35.39	44.95	56.82	67.36	62.61	62.92
Median	39.23	37.20	51.49	53.02	66.89	65.60	59.52

*Gross debt consists of all liabilities that require payment or payments of interest and/or principal by the debtor to the creditor at a date or dates in the future. This includes debt liabilities in the form of SDRs, currency and deposits, debt securities, loans, insurance, pensions and standardised guarantee schemes and other accounts payable.
Source: World Economic Outlook database, IMF.

of generalised regulatory relief. This raises a number of important questions related to how to rebuild the strength of the respective banking sectors. This includes how to deal with debt moratoria and NPLs, how to recapitalise banks and how to rebuild the MaPs architecture.

3.2. *Fiscal and monetary policy response*

In order to provide a more complete picture of the role of MaPs in the response to the pandemic, this section provides a brief analysis of the evolution of monetary and fiscal policies.

Tables 4 and 5 present data on fiscal policy for the 12 countries under study. Table 4 shows the evolution of the general government balance from 2010 through 2020, and includes projections by the IMF for 2021 and 2025. Table 5 contains data on gross public sector debt relative to GDP for the same period.[13] These two tables capture vividly the magnitude of the fiscal effort.

As may be seen from Table 4 on the central government balance, the response was particularly large in East Asia, where the median government balance went from a surplus of 0.33 percent of GDP in 2015, to a deficit of 7.3 percent of GDP in 2020. The two countries with the lowest fiscal response in the combined sample were South Korea and Mexico. Table 4 also shows that according to IMF projections, in 2025 all East Asian countries, except Malaysia, will have a larger deficit than in 2019. In Latin America, on the other hand, the IMF projects that in 2025, the public sector deficit will be lower in Chile and Colombia and slightly higher in Mexico and Peru. (A limitation of these projections, however, is that they may reflect the *wishes and hopes* of the IMF, rather than the most probable scenario.)

As may be seen in Table 5, in every country, debt increased significantly after the sanitary emergency.[14] Some of the highlights of Table 5 are:

(1) Contrary to what many people think, the mean and median level of debt were significantly higher in East Asia than in Latin America. This was the case in 2010, was still so in 2021, and according to the IMF, is projected to continue into 2025.

(2) The IMF forecasts that only 3 out of the 12 countries will have a lower debt to GDP ratio in 2025 than in 2021: Malaysia, Colombia and Peru. A key question, which will be addressed in Section 4 is whether these very large debt will affect the vulnerability of these

---

[13] The IMF also presents data and forecasts for net debt for some (but not all) countries in our sample.

[14] One of the consequences of this very large increase in public sector debt is that the rating agencies have raised concerns about the quality of sovereign securities, and have placed many countries in a "negative outlook" and/or are considering downgrades; see Section 4 for details.

countries' macro and financial situation, including the stability of the financial sector.
(3) In 2010, Chile was a clear outlier with a debt ratio below 10 percent, a situation that has changed importantly since 2019.[15]

Table 6 presents a summary of government debt guarantees to corporations, small and medium-sized enterprises (SMEs) and other firms. The provision of these guarantee schemes provides an important bridge between fiscal policy, monetary policy and regulatory forbearance. Because the government guarantees the obligations, banks are able to renew or restructure existing debts, and/or provide new loans to firms in need. For governments, an attractive aspect of these programs is that loan guarantees are usually "below the line" in public sector balance sheets.

Table 7 presents the evolution of central banks' policy rates between the fourth quarter of 2019 and the first quarter of 2021. As may be seen, in every country there were rapid interest rates cuts; the depth of these cuts was reflected in the fact that in the first quarter of 2021, the policy rate was below 1 percent in three Asian countries (South Korea, Singapore and Thailand) and in two of the Latin American nations (Chile and Peru).[16] The highest policy rate was in Mexico, a country that, paradoxically, had the largest cuts at 300 basis points (the initial rate was a very high 7.25 percent). As part of their monetary response, most of the countries in this study have expanded the type of securities that central banks are allowed to purchase, as well as the collateral that can be accepted from commercial banks. Also, as is discussed in Section 3.1, and reported in Table 3, the majority of the central banks in this study have reduced reserve requirements and relaxed other quantitative restrictions — many of them of the MaPs type — as a way of expeditiously increasing liquidity.

Table 8 contains data on total bank credit to the private non-financial sector, relative to GDP, in the years 2012, 2015, 2019, and in the third quarter

---

[15] During that year Chile's debt over GDP was outside the +/− 1.65 standard deviations interval, corresponding to 90 percent probability, for Latin America. However, for 2025, the IMF projections place Chile squarely inside that interval.

[16] In contrast with many of the AEs, the central banks in this study are not severely affected by the problem of the "zero lower bound" in policy rates. The discussion that follows excludes Argentina, a country with a mid-double-digit rate of inflation.

Table 6. Provision of debt guarantees to corporations, SMEs and other firms in sectors affected by the pandemic.

China	• Government support "below the line" in the budget includes guarantees for SMEs of RMB 400 billion (0.4 percent of GDP).
Korea	• Supplementary budget contemplated up to KRW 10.9 trillion loans and guarantees for business households and support local governments.
	• Expanded lending, partial and full guarantees and collateralisation of loan obligations to SMEs, small merchants, mid-sized firms and selected large companies.
	• KDB to support seven industries (airlines, shipping, shipbuilding, autos, general machinery, electric power and communications) with funds raised by government-guaranteed bonds.
Malaysia	• RM 50 bn government fund for loan guarantees for working capital to benefit COVID-19–affected firms.
Philippines	• Funds for credit guarantees and stand-by financing totalling 0.8 percent of 2020 GDP.
	• Credit guarantee program for small businesses and agriculture sector amounting 0.7 percent of 2020 GDP.
Singapore	• Several state-guarantee schemes, up to a total of EUR 4 billion or 4.4 percent of 2020 GDP, covering both SMEs and large firms.
Thailand	• The government guarantees loans to tourism-related sectors for two years; guaranteed may be extended for up to eight years for a 1.75 percent per year fee.
Argentina	• Government guarantees for bank lending to micro, small and medium enterprises for the production of foods and basic supplies.
Brazil	• Working Capital Program to preserve business continuity (CGPE) of micro, small and medium-sized companies and a 40 billion Brazilian real emergency line that aims at supporting the payroll costs of SMEs by Central Bank. Emergency Access to Credit Program — the FGI-PEAC by the Government of Brazil — that gives guarantees to participating financial institutions on loans provided to SMEs.
Chile	• Credit-guarantee scheme that would potentially support loans for up to US$24 billion.
Colombia	• National Guarantee Fund, supported new credit lines for corporates and SMEs in the sectors most seriously affected by the pandemic.
Mexico	• Development banks provided liquidity support and guarantees for up to 250 billion pesos.
Peru	• Government guarantees partially backed loans for up to 1 percent of GDP to support restructurings for households and SMEs.
	• Two government-guaranteed lending programs for SMEs and the tourist sector.

Source: IMF "Policy Responses to COVID-19," https://www.imf.org/en/Topics/imf-and-covid19/Policy-Responses-to-COVID-19#C, and individual central banks and regulatory agencies.

Table 7. Central bank policy rates (percent).

	(1) Q4 2019	(2) Q1 2020	(3) Q2 2020	(4) Q3 2020	(5) Q4 2020	(6) M1 2021
East Asia						
China	4.15	4.05	3.85	3.85	3.85	n.a.
South Korea	1.25	0.75	0.50	0.50	0.50	0.50
Malaysia	3.00	2.50	2.00	1.75	1.75	1.75
Philippines	4.00	3.25	2.25	2.25	2.00	2.00
Singapore	2.13	1.68	0.78	0.70	1.08	0.86
Thailand	1.25	0.75	0.50	0.50	0.50	0.50
Latin America						
Argentina	55.00	38.00	38.00	38.00	38.00	38.00
Brazil	4.50	3.75	2.25	2.00	2.00	2.00
Chile	1.75	1.00	0.50	0.50	0.50	0.50
Colombia	4.25	3.75	2.75	1.75	1.75	1.75
Mexico	7.25	6.50	5.00	4.25	4.25	4.25
Peru	2.25	1.25	0.25	0.25	0.25	0.25

Source: BIS, except for Singapore, where IMF data are used.

of 2020. The pattern that emerges is clear: credit increased significantly in every country in the sample. As with fiscal policy, the East Asian countries have been significantly more aggressive in terms of monetary policy than the Latin American nations. The median increase in credit in 2020, relative to 2019, was 10 percent in East Asia and only 6.5 percent in Latin America. In fact, the Latin American country with the most expansive monetary policy — Chile — had a lower expansion in credit to the private sector (5.2 percent of GDP) than almost any of the Asian countries in the sample. At the macro level, and in spite of the very significant expansions of central banks' balance sheets and government debt, the IMF does not predict inflation to pick up, in the near future, in the countries covered in this study.

3.3. Health of the financial sector after the pandemic: The IMF and the rating agencies

Since 2009, multilateral institutions have been tracking the health of the financial sector in a large number of countries. The IMF, for

Table 8. Credit to private non-financial sector from banks as percent of GDP.*

	(1) 2012	(2) 2015	(3) 2019	(4) 2020-Q3
East Asia				
China	129.2	152.8	165.7	183.6
South Korea	120.1	121.1	138.6	149.9
Malaysia	124.1	132.5	130.9	142
Philippines	26.5	33.7	42.6	44.5
Singapore	107.7	116.4	114.1	122.5
Thailand	108.2	117.1	112.5	123.2
Mean	102.6	112.3	117.4	127.6
Median	114.2	119.1	122.5	132.6
Latin America				
Argentina	15	14.2	12	12.1
Brazil	62.5	66.8	62.7	67.2
Chile	74.6	81.8	87.8	93
Colombia	38.2	46.6	45.9	50.4
Mexico	15.6	17.8	19.9	21.4
Peru	28.0	35.4	36.0	44.7
Mean	39.0	43.8	44.1	48.1
Median	33.1	41.0	41.0	47.6

*In the case of Peru, the data corresponds to credit to private sector from banks. For Philippines it corresponds to credit to private non-financial sector from universal and commercial banks.

Source: BIS except for Peru and Philippines that corresponds to individual central banks.

example, follows 12 core financial soundness indicators for deposit-taking institutions. These include regulatory capital to risk-weighted assets, NPL (net of provisions) to capital, NPL to total gross loans, liquid assets to total assets, liquid assets to short-term liabilities and net open position in foreign exchange to capital. In mid-2021, the IMF had not detected significant deterioration in the financial health of the countries under study.

Table 9. Non-performing loans to total gross loans, in percentage terms.*

	(1) 2010	(2) 2015	(3) 2019	(4) 2020
East Asia				
China	1.13	1.67	1.86	1.94
South Korea	0.59	0.46	0.25	0.24
Malaysia	3.35	1.61	1.53	1.39
Philippines	3.38	1.89	1.97	3.43
Singapore	1.41	0.92	1.31	n.a.
Thailand	3.89	2.68	3.13	3.27
Latin America				
Argentina	2.12	1.74	5.75	4.52
Brazil	3.11	3.31	3.11	2.38
Chile	2.69	1.87	2.06	1.72
Colombia	2.86	2.85	4.17	4.51
Mexico	2.04	2.52	2.09	2.02
Peru	3.03	3.93	3.37	3.47

*The data in column (4) corresponds to data for 2020Q3, except for China, South Korea, Mexico and Peru that have available data until 2020Q2.
Source: Financial Soundness Indicators, IMF.

Table 9 presents data on NPLs to total gross loans, as reported by the IMF[17] and focuses on four points in time: (1) 2010, approximately 18 months after the eruption of the GFC; (2) 2015, a year when things were returning to normal; (3) 2019, the year before the pandemic; and (4) 2020Q3, the latest data point available. These data show that in most Asian nations NPLs declined significantly between 2010 and 2015 and

---

[17] Non-performing loans (NPLs) are defined in different way in different countries. The IMF recommends that loans are classified as NPL when (1) payments of principal and interest are past due by 90 days or more, or (2) interest payments equal to 90 days interest or more have been capitalised (reinvested into the principal amount), refinanced or rolled over (payment delayed by agreement), or (3) evidence exists to reclassify them as non-performing even in the absence of a 90-day past due payment, such as when the debtor files for bankruptcy. The BIS and the European Banking Authority use slightly different criteria. See Ari *et al.* (2020).

stayed approximately at the same level until 2019. The data also show that after the pandemic was declared and regulations on banks were relaxed, only one country — the Philippines — experienced a significant increase in NPLs as a proportion of gross loans. The Latin American experience was somewhat different, as only two countries — Argentina and Chile — experienced a decline in NPLs after 2010, and only one country — Colombia — experienced a significant increase in NPLs in the first year after the pandemic. These low ratios were, in part, the result of moratoria and regulatory forbearance measures like the ones described in Table 3, and highlighted in grey.

In a recent study, Ari *et al.* (2020) analysed the dynamics of NPLs in 88 banking crises since 1990. The authors defined *large* NPL ratios as those in excess of 7 percent. According to this criterion then, as of late 2020, none of the countries in this study had NPLs which approached this "high level". This research also shows that the growth of NPLs lags the eruption of a crisis, and that after a crisis, NPLs increase by three times relative to their pre-crisis levels; more than 80 percent of crises eventually result in NPLs in excess of 7 percent of loans. In Section 4, it is argued that the pace and fashion in which these NPLs are recognised and addressed will be key for future stability.

During 2020, the rating agencies took significant actions lowering the ratings of a number of financial institutions, both banks and nonbanks, from around the world. The following quote from Standard & Poor's regarding Latin American banks is telling:

> "Banks are facing Negative Rating Momentum… This is because of pernicious effects of the pandemic, oil price shock, and market volatility."

Table 10 presents data on the evolution of Standard & Poor's outlooks for East Asian and Latin American banks between 2019 and 2021. It is useful to compare the situation in February 2021 and December 2019. As may be seen, in East Asia, the number of banks with a "negative outlook" more than doubled during this period; and the number of banks with a "credit watch negative" outlook increased from 0 to 2. The situation in Latin America was not very different, except that the number of banks with a "credit watch negative" outlook went from 9 to 0. However, the

Table 10. Standard & Poor's Outlook for East Asian and Latin American Banks: 2019–2021.

	East Asia					Latin America				
	Credit Watch Negative	Negative Outlook	Stable	Positive Outlook	Credit watch Positive	Credit Watch Negative	Negative Outlook	Stable	Positive Outlook	Credit watch Positive
Dec-2019	—	9	84	7	—	9	17	55	19	—
May-2020	—	17	83	1	—	2	41	57	—	—
Oct-2020	3	19	78	—	—	—	43	57	—	—
Feb-2021	2	20	76	—	1	—	37	63	—	—

Source: Standard & Poor's.

number of banks in the more meaningful category of "negative outlook" more than doubled from 17 to 37. Equally concerning is the fact that in both regions, the number of banks with a "positive outlook" has gone to zero in recent months.

Historically, there has been a close correlation between individual banks' ratings and sovereign ratings. Table 11 presents data on sovereign ratings in April 2021 by Standard & Poor's for the 12 countries covered in this study. In addition to the ratings themselves, the table includes indicators on S&P's views of the strengths of each country according to six metrics. In each of these categories, the score goes from 1 for very strong, to 6 for (very) weak. The data show that according to the rating agencies (Moody's and Fitch present a similar picture), East Asia presents lower risks than Latin America. In the former, the lowest rating is BBB+ (the Philippines and Thailand) and only one country has a negative outlook. In contrast, in Latin America, only one nation (Chile) has a rating in the "As," and in this case there has been a recent (late March 2021) downgrade. Moreover, at the time of this writing, two of the six Latin American countries have negative outlooks.

The overall message in this section is that, although in the middle of 2021 (i.e., as of the time of this writing) there were no indications of *significant stress* in banking sectors, there are developments that point to

Table 11. Standard & Poor's sovereign ratings, East Asia and Latin America, April 2021.*

Issuer	Sovereign foreign currency ratings	Institutional	Economic	External	Fiscal/budget performance	Fiscal/debt	Monetary
China	A+/Stable/A-1	3	3	1	4	2	3
Korea	AA/Stable/A-1+	3	1	1	1	4	2
Malaysia	A-/Negative/A-2	3	4	2	3	5	2
Philippines	BBB+/Stable/A-2	4	4	1	3	3	3
Singapore	AAA/Stable/A-1+	1	1	1	1	1	1
Thailand	BBB+/Stable/A-2	4	4	1	3	3	2
Argentina	CCC+/Stable/C	6	5	6	6	5	6
Brazil	BB-/Stable/B	4	5	2	6	5	3
Chile	A/Stable/A-1	2	4	4	2	1	2
Colombia	BBB-/Negative/A-3	3	4	6	3	4	3
Mexico	BBB/Negative/A-2	3	5	2	3	4	3
Peru	BBB+/Stable/A-2	3	4	3	2	2	3

*The different characteristics of sovereign debt are rated, in the different columns from 1 for strongest to 6 for weakest.

Source: Standard & Poor's.

an increase in NPLs in the (near) future. The question is not only whether banks have enough capital to withstand the prolongation of the crisis but also whether the regulatory relaxation has to be undone, and if so, how fast. It is interesting to note that some advanced countries have already begun to unwind the regulatory forbearance triggered by the pandemic. For example, on 1 March 2021, the Reserve Bank of New Zealand announced that "LVR restrictions will be reinstated at the same level as prior to the onset of COVID-19, with a further tightening of investors' restrictions taking effect on 1 May 2021".[18] This policy measure is partially the result of concerns of New Zealand regulators about housing prices, which had increased by 22.8 percent between February 2020 and February 2021. In a similar vein, on 19 March 2021, the Federal Reserve announced that it would let the relaxation introduced in June 2020 to the Supplementary Leverage Ratio (SLR) expire in May 2021. (Consistent with what was discussed above regarding the multiplicity of institutions dealing with regulations, the press release indicating the end of the relaxation of the SLR was a joint release by the Federal Reserve, the Federal Deposit Insurance Corporation, and the Office of the Comptroller of the Currency.)

4. Risks and challenges after the pandemic

Pandemics do not end suddenly; they recede slowly as a result of successful vaccination programs and/or herd immunity. Once the COVID-19 pandemic is "officially" over, the world economy will look very different from how it looked like in March 2020. Debt ratios will be significantly higher than what many analysts think is reasonable or sustainable; central banks' balance sheets will be much larger than at any point in the past and the regulatory landscape will be less protective and less binding than just before the pandemic. A return to "normality" — and even the adoption of a "new normal" — will require dialling back almost every policy undertaken to combat the pandemic. Indeed, doing it will leave the world better prepared to face new threats, including possible future pandemics. An important question is whether this

---

[18] See https://www.rbnz.govt.nz/regulation-and-supervision/banks/macro-prudential-policy/loan-to-valuation-ratio-restrictions.

process of "dialling back" should be gradual or fast, and what the newly acceptable normal policy stances will be.

Regarding MaPs, there will be a need to turn back the regulatory forbearance adopted during the emergency and to continue to strengthen the regulatory architecture. This process is likely to be complex and face some political economy difficulties. In addition, and in light of the analysis in Section 3.3, the authorities will face the task of dealing with NPLs and banks' recapitalisation. Also, in many countries there will be substantial changes in social conditions, with higher poverty levels and higher income inequality; many of the distributive changes will be associated with the uneven effect of the pandemic across industries and regions.

Trying to predict the future evolution of the global and regional economies is, of course, well beyond the scope of this chapter. However, and for the sake of completeness, it is useful to discuss briefly the possible sources of disturbances and shocks to the countries analysed, in the immediate post-pandemic period and the role of MaPs under different scenarios. In analysing these challenges and risks it is useful to distinguish between shocks and developments coming from abroad and those of domestic origin. The bottom line is rather obvious: independently of future developments and of where risks will materialise, it is important to rebuild the pre-existing MaPs architecture, to deal with NPLs and to recapitalise banks.

4.1. Potential short-term systemic shocks

At the time of the conference, the greatest potential (and interrelated) risks to the EMs coming from the global economy were: (1) a possible resurgence of global inflation; (2) a major correction in asset prices around the globe; (3) a decline in the appetite for risk by global investors; (4) generalised downgrading action by the rating agencies; and (5) large terms of trade changes. Three months later, the inflationary risk appears to be materialising, as is the "change in appetite" risk.

These potential shocks, either jointly or on their own, are likely to result in higher interest rates in the EMs and currency devaluations in many countries. The consequences of these developments will depend on the size of the pass-through coefficient, and on whether domestic central banks follow the Federal Reserve when it raises interest rates.[19] In a recent column, Martin Wolf, an influential *Financial Times* commentator, wrote on 17 March 2021:

> "The combination of a huge U.S. fiscal loosening with sharper than expected monetary tightening might destabilise emerging economies. This happened before, notably in the 1980s debt crisis."

In thinking about the future, it is important not to downplay possible political developments. In particular, in a number of countries, there has been unhappiness with the way in which the pandemic was handled, and with the extensive and long lockdown. In most countries, inequality and poverty have increased, and political pressures for increasing expenditures and providing social support may increase in the future. In a recent statement released prior to the Spring Meetings, the IMF has warned of possible social unrest as a result of deteriorating social conditions and rising inequality.

4.2. NPLs and banks' recapitalisation

One of the most salient pieces of information in Table 3 refers to NPLs and provisioning; see the highlighted bullets. As noted earlier, in most countries, there has been a relaxation of the requirement to record NPLs and make provisions; across countries and regions, many loans are under moratorium. Once the emergency is over, banks across the world — and not only in the EMs — will have to face this situation, making sure that the appropriate provisions are made, and, when needed, banks' capital is replenished. What makes the current situation quite unique, from a historical point of view, is that NPLs are distributed very unevenly across sector; not surprisingly, they are very large in hospitality and personal services.

---

[19] In a recent empirical investigation, Edwards (2012) found that most central banks in Latin America tend to follow the Fed. They incorporate, implicitly, the Fed's policy rate in their own Taylor Rules. The same study concluded that East Asian central banks had historically been more independent, and did not react in a clear and unpredictable way to Fed actions.

In a recent paper, Ari *et al.* (2020) analysed the relation between NPLs and economic growth in a large group of countries over several decades. Their results indicate that NPL resolution is essential for countries to recover promptly from a crisis. Lingering and high NPLs are associated with deeper recessions and slower recoveries. Six years after a crisis, real GDP in countries with high/unresolved NPLs (where, as noted above, "high" is defined as higher than 7 percent of loans) is six percentage points lower than in countries that have not experienced "high NPLs".

Although there is no detailed analysis on the 12 countries considered in this study, it is possible to learn from history and from recent experiences in other regions. The 1997–1998 East Asian financial crisis and the succession of Latin American crises have shown that banks have a tendency to delay acknowledging NPLs, in order not to impact their profit and loss (P&L) statements. As a number of authors have pointed out, this may result in the survival of so-called "zombie firms", or companies that operate in spite of the fact that, according to fundamentals, they are not viable (Edwards, 2010; Harwood *et al.*, 1999; Kasinger *et al.*, 2021). The costs of maintaining these moribund firms on life support can be very high and contribute to new and severe crises.

Historically, this type of situation with massive and non-provisioned NPLs has been tackled in a variety of ways, including through the creation/encouragement of a secondary market for loans, the creation of "bad banks" that concentrate on NPL, the conversion of debt to equity and the issuance of new equity that results in the dilution of banks' control. This latter solution is often resisted in EMs, where particular groups/families tend to own controlling blocks of shares, and where banks are part of much larger industrial/financial/technological/commercial concerns. Although discussing the details of each of these possible solutions is beyond the scope of this chapter, there is little doubt that EMs (and AEs for that matter) should prepare for moving in this direction.

However, historical experience also shows that none of these approaches is, on its own, a panacea. In a recent paper, Kasinger *et al.* (2021) made the following point regarding the pandemic, and the use of a secondary market for loans as a way of dealing with NPLs in the Eurozone:

> "Assuming an extremely severe pandemic scenario, all or many banks lose capital simultaneously. This potentially leads to fire-sales as all

banks find themselves on the sell side of the secondary loan market. The resulting market imbalance may invalidate the supportive role of the secondary loan market for banks with NPLs. In fact, a one-sided secondary loan market will pull banks down further as the resulting loan pricing will feed into a downward spiral, infecting loan valuation on banks' balance sheets even for otherwise healthy banks. Thus, a self-enforcing process of falling secondary prices, lower loan asset values and loss of capital may develop that destabilises the financial system at large."

These concerns appear to be relevant to most of the EMs in this study.

5. Capital controls: Musings on an instrument that refuses to die

For a long time, policymakers have been concerned about the disruptive effects of large surges in capital inflows. These concerns have been centred on three issues:

(1) Large inflows tend to generate (temporary) real exchange rate overvaluation, with Dutch Disease type of effects on the local industry.
(2) Historically, in the vast majority of countries these inflows have been intermediated by the banking system and have financed massive credit booms, including major expansions in real estate investment. This may result — and in many historical episodes has resulted — in currency mismatches in banks' balance sheets. Liabilities are denominated in foreign currency and loans are either denominated in domestic currency or granted to non-tradable sectors, generating a situation of severe vulnerability in the financial sector.
(3) Sudden stops in the capital inflows, and the concomitant reversals in current account balances, result in large devaluations that create havoc in the economy. The effects of these currency crises are particularly severe when there are large "balance sheet" effects in the banking sector.

These concerns explain why many scholars and policymakers have argued that capital account liberalisation in the EMs should be undertaken gradually and in ways that avoid the problems discussed above. See, for example, Prasad and Rajan (2008).

Controls on capital inflows may be considered an early form of macroprudential regulations. In fact, in many countries, capital controls on inflows are at the top of the list of regulations favoured by politicians. It is (very) possible that once the pandemic is over, and an effort is made to rebuild the MaPs, many countries will consider (re)instating capital controls.[20]

5.1. *Chile's "first generation" capital controls*

The idea of controlling capital inflows was first put into effect in Chile. The notion was that by slowing down inflows it was possible to reduce banks' exposure to foreign currency risks, and protect them from the potential costs of "sudden stops" and currency devaluations.

Chile's controls on inflows during the 1990s are well known and have been studied quite profusely (Forbes, 2007; Edwards and Rigobon, 2009; Caputo and Saravia, 2018). What is less known is that Chile had an earlier experience — in the mid- to late 1970s — with these types of policies. These "first generation" controls on inflows did not work well, and the country ended up facing a massive and extremely costly currency and banking crisis in 1982.

Starting in 1974, a year after general Augusto Pinochet deposed President Salvador Allende, capital movements were controlled through an array of mechanisms. All capital moving into the country had to be registered with the central bank. Foreign lenders who wanted future access to foreign exchange faced additional restrictions in the form of minimum maturities and maximum interest rates. Foreign loans with maturities below 24 months were forbidden (the exception was trade credit), and those with maturities between 24 to 66 months were subjected to non–interest-yielding reserve requirements ranging from 10 percent to 25 percent of the value of the loan (Edwards and Edwards, 1991,

---

[20] On controls and macroprudential regulations, see Frost *et al.* (2020). On the Chinese approach to managing capital flows, see Prasad and Wei (2005).

p. 55). However, controls on inflows were not the only tool used by the Chilean authorities in an effort to protect the banking sector from foreign-exchange–related excesses. Quantitative restrictions on banks' exposure, very similar to modern MaPs, were also in place.

In spite of these controls, and because of the very large interest rate differentials, massive flows of foreign capital came into the country. Between 1978 and 1982, net capital inflows amounted to almost 8 percent of GDP. Many of those funds were used by large industrial/financial conglomerates — the so-called *grupos* — to finance the acquisition of newly privatised companies and banks and to finance a real estate boom.

In June 1982, and after having run a gigantic current account deficit (12 percent of GDP), Chile could not defend its fixed peg any longer and devalued the peso. In spite of the controls and the other policies, the devaluation resulted in a generalised collapse of the banking sector. After demurring for some months, the government ended up bailing out the whole banking system at a cost of close to 40 percent of GDP. The main lesson from this episode was that it was not only important to manage the amount of the flows but also critical to make sure that there were no currency mismatches on banks' balance sheets and to be concerned about the sectors where those funds were being deployed (the key was whether they generated earnings in foreign currency).

5.2. "Second generation" Chilean controls on capital inflows

In the early 1990s, and after having recovered from the 1982 crisis, Chile was once again subjected to very large capital inflows. The lesson, however, had been learned, and a sturdier system of unremunerated reserve requirements (URR) was put in place, and supplemented by stricter restrictions on currency mismatches of banks.

"Second generation" Chilean-type controls on inflows were later implemented in a number of countries, including Thailand (in 2006) and Colombia (in 2007). An important feature of this type of capital controls on inflows is that they act as a tax and, thus, introduce a wedge between domestic and international interest rates. If the domestic interest rate for a k-months investment is denoted by i_k, and the implicit tax by μ_k, then it follows that (where i is the international interest rate; in order to simplify the exposition, risk premia issues are assumed away):

$$i_k = i + \mu_k$$

Given the reserve requirement ratio on the inflows, it is possible to calculate the (approximate) tax equivalence of these controls. Assume that the investor will keep his funds in the country for k months. Assume, further, that if k is lower than some maturity h, the investor needs to deposit a fraction u of the funds in the central bank. Then, the tax equivalent to the URR is given by:[21]

$$\mu_k \approx i\left(\frac{u}{1-u}\right)\left(\frac{h}{k}\right)$$

In a paper that evaluated the effectiveness of Chile's controls on inflows, De Gregorio *et al.* (2000) computed the tax equivalence of URRs in Chile. For a maturity of one month, the tax equivalence was 31 percent. It did decline rapidly for longer maturities, however. For instance, for six months' maturity the tax equivalence was slightly above 5 percent. For a maturity of 12 months, it was only 2.6 percent (see also, Edwards and Rigobon [2009] and Edwards [1999, 2003]).

In their empirical analysis, De Gregorio *et al.* (2000) reached a number of conclusions that were relevant for any country relying on controls on inflows as a form of MaP. Their most important findings may be summarised as follows:

- Because of the controls, Chile was able to maintain a significant policy interest rate differential with the rest of the world: "We only find a significant effect on the central bank interest rates, which suggests that the URR was indeed used more intensely to accompany monetary tightening".
- The impact on longer-term rates was not clear. It appeared that after 18 months' maturity the effect was very small, not significantly different from zero.
- The effects of the URR on the real exchange rate (RER) were not conclusive, in the sense that different estimation techniques yielded

---

[21] This ignores the presence of other taxes. In Chile, in fact there were other costs to foreign investors.

somewhat different results. This let the authors believe that using controls on inflows was not the best policy for dealing with short-term real exchange rate appreciation. The authors pointed out that one of the possible reasons for not finding much of a connection between the URR and the RER was the existence, at the time, of an exchange rate band in Chile. On URR in a band-based exchange rate regime, see Edwards and Rigobon (2009).
- One thing that the URR did for sure was to change the composition of flows, reducing short-term flows and increasing longer-term ones. This, on its own, provided some stability protection to the financial system, which would not be subjected to sudden reversals of hot capital. The total magnitude of inflows aggregated across maturities, however, did not appear to change.
- With time, market participants found a large number of loopholes, reducing the effectiveness of the capital controls.
- One of the main reasons why capital controls were somewhat successful in Chile was that they were supported by the right type of fiscal policy, which provided the required overall credibility to macroeconomic policy in the country.

Of course, the positive effects, or benefits, of the URR should be compared to the distortionary costs that they introduced in the form of a tax. One of the obvious consequences of these taxes was that they might impact the ability of certain firms to tap the capital market. The controls resulted in higher domestic cost of capital. In a detailed analysis using data from the stock exchange in Chile, Forbes (2007) found that the controls imposed a severe cost to smaller firms. She concluded that as a consequence of the URR policy, smaller traded firms faced a significant financing constraint and had a higher shadow cost of capital than larger firms that could circumvent the controls (see also Caputo and Saravia [2018] and Edwards and Rigobon [2009]).

6. Concluding remarks

The COVID-19 pandemic tested the efficiency and resilience of the macroprudential regulation edifice that had been built in virtually every country since the year 2008. It is not an exaggeration to say that the system has passed the test with good marks. Banks were better prepared than in the previous crises. Relaxing many of these regulations has been a key component of the response to the pandemic by governments around the world (see Table 3).

The fact that the MaPs have proven to be sturdy, so far, does not mean that policymakers can lower their guard. In fact, there is much to do going forward, both in evaluating at a very detailed level the functioning of the current system, and in preparing countries/jurisdictions for future shocks. Some of the key or core questions going forward are:

- When to rebuild the MaPs and return to the pre-COVID-19 situation?
- How fast to rebuild this regulatory framework?
- In light of the experience of the last 18 months, is the pre-COVID-19 situation adequate, or is there a need for a sturdier edifice?
- How to handle NPLs once the current regulatory forbearance is over? If banks need to be recapitalised, how fast is that to be done?
- Is there a need to make changes to the current capital controls landscape?

When thinking about these issues, it is important for policymakers to realise that after the "great regulatory forbearance of 2020–2021", most countries' financial sectors are more vulnerable. For the emerging markets, a particularly important question is whether they would be able to survive possible short-term global shocks during the next year or so. Four of the possible shocks identified in this chapter are: (1) a surge in global inflation that results in early and significant action by the Fed and the ECB; (2) an important correction in asset prices around the globe; (3) a substantive decline in risk appetite by global investors and (4) generalised downgrade action by the rating agencies.

Other (interrelated) questions and issues related to the future strengthening of the MaPs include:

- Should "headroom" or "space" be built into the MaPs in the future?
- Coordination across countries in the same region to release the MaPs, in case of global shocks.

- How to avoid the "stigma" associated with releasing MaPs?
- Coordination between regulators and central banks regarding monetary policy during a systemic crisis.
  - How to deal with "dash to cash"
  - Central bank intervention in the currency market to avoid abrupt devaluations.
  - Rebuilding international reserves.
- Use data from the pandemic to rethink different MaPs. For instance, in the US, there is a significant positive correlation between the request for payment suspensions and the loan-to-income (LTI) ratio. Borrowers with an LTI of 4 were twice as likely to opt for suspensions and those with LTIs of approximately 2.5.
- Develop the right MaPs to face the effects of the increasing adoption of Central Bank Digital Currencies (CBDCs).[22]

Appendix

The simple analytics of MaPs

The basic analytical principles governing the design of optimal MaPs are outlined here. The analysis is kept at a minimalist level, and no attempt is made to obtain closed-form solutions or to calibrate a full-fledged model. More complete analysis may be found in the technical and theoretical literature, including, for example, in Allen *et al.* (2018) and Farhi and Werning (2016).

Consider the case where there are two states of the world: "Bad" (B) and "Good" (G). A "bad" state is characterised by a macroeconomic crisis (banking and currency) and is costly. The probability of being in the "bad" state is p_B, and depends on a number of exogenous and policy variables, including the degree of "sturdiness" or "stability" of the financial sector. The strength of the financial system captured by a "stability" index denoted by s.

$$p_B = f(s, x_1, x_2, \ldots)$$

---

[22] See the references section for some recent contributions on CBDCs: Auer and Böhme (2020); Auer *et al.* (2021); BIS (2020, 2021); and Bordo and Levin (2019).

s is the result of regulatory measures, including MaPs; see below. A higher s reduces the probability of falling in the bad state of the world. However, through a restriction of credit to the private sector, a higher s has a negative effect on growth. Consider the following equations for aggregate (real) income in the good state of the world y_G:

$$y_G = y_0 + \alpha dK$$

where, dK is capital accumulation or net investment; α is the marginal productivity of investment for the economy as a whole. As noted, a higher s results in lower investment.

$$dK = g(s,\ldots); g' \leq 0.$$

There are a number of possible channels through which this may happen. For instance, in the case of controls on capital inflows the channel would be higher domestic interest rates.

Real income in the bad state of the world is a fraction β of y_G.

$$y_B = \beta y_G; 0 \leq \beta \leq 1.$$

The policy problem is to select the value of s that maximises the level of expected real income across both states of the world.

$$y = y_G - p_B(y_G - y_B)$$

where $(y_G - y_B) = G$ is the income gap between good and bad states of the world, or the cost of a crisis measured in real income. We assume that stricter regulations — i.e., higher s — reduce the cost of a macro/banking/currency crisis: $\frac{dG}{ds} \leq 0$.

The first-order condition states that s should be set at the point where the expected marginal benefit of regulations, measured by the reduced probability and lower cost of a crisis, is equal to the expected marginal cost of s, captured by the (negative) effect on economic activity:

$$\frac{dy_g}{ds} = p'_B G + p_B G',$$

where G' and p'_B are the derivatives of the income gap and probability of a bad states with respect to the regulations measure s. Both derivatives are negative.

In order to close the model, we need to define more explicitly three relationships: (1) the precise mechanisms through which changes in the extent of regulations (including MaPs) affect credit availability and investment (and thus real income); (2) the way (and extent) in which a higher *s* reduces the cost of a bad state of the world and (3) the determinants of the probability of a crisis, including the marginal effect on this probability of tighter regulations. A multinomial logit model is, possibly, the most expeditious way of dealing with this last issue. Under that assumption, if there are *j* determinants of the probability of a crisis or bad state of the world, then:

$$p_B = \frac{1}{1+e^{(b_0+b_1x_1+\ldots+b_jx_j)}}$$

where one of the x_i is the "stability" index *s*. Other determinants of the probability of falling into a bad state include the fiscal stance of the sovereign, whether the country in question is suffering from real exchange rate overvaluation and the external balance, among other.

Once the level (or intensity of regulations) of *s* is determined, the authorities have to decide which specific regulatory tools they will use to achieve that optimal *s*. A simple way of thinking about this is to consider a production function for *s*. The (possible) inputs are the different type of regulatory tools discussed in the literature on MaPs and listed in Tables 1 and 2 of this chapter. A general formulation is given by a multifactor CES:

$$s = A\left(\sum_{j=1}^{k} \lambda_j R_j^\rho\right)^{k/\rho}.$$

The R_i are the different regulatory tools, which are assumed to be substitutes. This particular function is homogeneous of degree *k*, and the elasticity of substitution between any two regulatory instruments is constant and equal to $\sigma = \left[1/(1-\rho)\right]$. A special, simpler and possibly more intuitive case is that of a Cobb–Douglass function for *s*:

$$s = R_1^{a_1} R_2^{a_2} \ldots R_k^{a_k}.$$

In this case, the first-order condition for the optimal use of each instrument R_i is given by:

$$\frac{\left(a_1 s / R_1\right)}{MC_1} = \frac{\left(a_2 s / R_2\right)}{MC_2} = \cdots = \frac{\left(a_k s / R_k\right)}{MC_k},$$

where MC_j is the marginal cost (in terms of effect on the functioning of the financial system) of deploying instrument j to achieve a certain level of financial stability, s.

References

Alam, Z., Alter, A., Eiseman, J., Gelos, G., Kang, H., Narita, M., Nier, E., & Wang N., (2019). Digging deeper — Evidence on the effects of macroprudential policies from a new database. IMF Working Paper 19/66.

Allen, F., Barlevy, G., & Gale, D. (2018). A theory of leaning against the wind. Federal Reserve Bank of Chicago Working Paper 2017–16.

Ari, A., Chen, S., & Ratnovski, L. (2020). The dynamics of non-performing loans during banking crises: a new database. European Central Bank Working Paper Series 2395.

Auer, R., & Böhme, R. (2020). The technology of retail central bank digital currency. *BIS Quarterly Review*, March, 85–100.

Auer, R., Monnet, C., & Shin, H. S. (2021). Permissioned distributed ledgers and the governance of money. BIS Working Paper 924.

Barroso, J., De Araujo, D., & Gonzalez, R. (2020). Loan-to-value policy and housing finance: Effects on constrained borrowers. *Journal of Financial Intermediation*, **42**, 100830.

Berner, R., Kashyap, A., & Goodhart C. A. E. (2011). The macroprudential toolkit. *IMF Economic Review*, **59**(2), 145–161.

BIS (Bank of International Settlements) (2010). Guidance for National Authorities Operating the Countercyclical Capital Buffer. Basel Committee on Banking Supervision.

BIS (Bank of International Settlements) (2011–2019). Progress report on Basel III implementation. Basel Committee on Banking Supervision.

BIS (Bank of International Settlements) (2017). Macroprudential frameworks, implementation, and relationship with other policies. BIS Papers 94.

BIS (Bank of International Settlements) (2018). Annual Economic Report.

BIS (Bank of International Settlements) (2019). RBC — Risk-based capital requirements. RBC30 — Buffers above the regulatory minimum. Basel Committee on Banking Supervision.

BIS (Bank of International Settlements) (2020). *Project Helvetia: Settling tokenized assets in central bank money*. BIS, Innovation Hub.

BIS (Bank of International Settlements) (2021). *Central banks of China and United Arab Emirates join digital currency project for cross-border payments*. Press Release 23 February.

Bordo, M. D., & Levin, A. T. (2019). Improving the monetary regime: The case for US digital cash. *Cato Journal*, **39**, 383.

Bruno, V., Shim, I., & Shin, H. (2017). Comparative assessment of macroprudential policies. *Journal of Financial Stability*, **28**, 183–202.

Bush, G., Gómez, T., Jara, A., Moreno, D., Styrin, K., & Ushakova, Y. (2021). Macroprudential policy and the inward transmission of monetary policy: The case of Chile, Mexico, and Russia. *Review of International Economics*, **29**(1), 37–60.

Cantú, C., Gambacorta, L., & Shim, I. (2020). How effective are macroprudential policies in Asia Pacific? Evidence from a meta-analysis. BIS Papers chapters, in Bank for International Settlements, *Measuring the effectiveness of macroprudential policies using supervisory bank-level data*, Volume 110, 3–15. Bank for International Settlements.

Caputo, R., & Saravia, D. (2018). The monetary and fiscal history of Chile: 1960–2016. University of Chicago, Becker Friedman Institute for Economics Working Paper 2018–62.

Cerutti, E., Claessens, S., & Laeven, L. (2017). The use and effectiveness of macroprudential policies: New evidence. *Journal of Financial Stability*, **28**, 203–224.

Choi, H., Fong, T., Li, K., & Wong, E. (2011). Loan-to-value ratio as a macroprudential tool — Hong Kong's experience and cross-country evidence. Hong Kong Monetary Authority Working Papers 1101.

Corbacho, A., & Shanaka J. P. (Eds.) (2018). *The ASEAN Way: Sustaining Growth and Stability*. Washington, DC: International Monetary Fund.

De Gregorio, J., Edwards, S., & Valdés, R. (2000). Controls on capital inflows: Do they work? *Journal of Development Economics*, **63**, 59–83.

De Guindos, L. (2021). "Macroprudential policy after the COVID-19 pandemic." Panel contribution at the Banque de France/Sciences Po Financial Stability Review Conference 2021 "Is Macroprudential Policy Resilient to the Pandemic?"

Dell'Ariccia, G., Igan, D., Laeven, L., Tong, H., Bakker, B., & Vandenbussche, J. (2012). Policies for macrofinancial stability: How to deal with credit booms. IMF Staff Discussion Note 12/06.

Edwards, S., & Edwards, A. C. (1991). *Monetarism and Liberalization: The Chilean Experiment*. Chicago: University of Chicago Press.

Edwards, S. (1999). How effective are capital controls? *Journal of Economic Perspectives*, **13**(4), 65–84.

Edwards, S. (2003). Exchange rate regimes, capital flows and crisis prevention. in Feldstein, M. (Ed.). *Economic and Financial Crises in Emerging Market Economies*, 31–77. Chicago: University of Chicago Press.

Edwards, S. (2010). *Left Behind: Latin America and the False Promise of Populism*. Chicago: University of Chicago Press.

Edwards, S. (2012). The Federal Reserve, the emerging markets, and capital controls: A high-frequency empirical investigation. *Journal of Money, Credit and Banking*, **44**, 151–184.

Edwards, S., & Rigobon, R. (2009). Capital controls on inflows, exchange rate volatility and external vulnerability. *Journal of International Economics*, **78**(2), 256–267.

Farhi, E., & Werning, I. (2016). A theory of macroprudential policies in the presence of nominal rigidities. *Econometrica*, **84**(5), 1645–1170.

Forbes, K. (2007). One cost of the Chilean capital controls: Increased financial constraints for smaller traded firms. *Journal of International Economics*, **71**, 294–323.

Forbes, K. (2019). Macroprudential policy: What we've learned, don't know, and need to do. *American Economic Review Papers and Proceedings*, **109** (May), 470–475.

Frost, J., Ito, H., & Van Stralen, R. (2020). The effectiveness of macroprudential policies and capital controls against volatile capital inflows. BIS Working Papers 867.

Gambacorta, L., & Murcia, A. (2020). The impact of macroprudential policies in Latin America: An empirical analysis using credit registry data. *Journal of Financial Intermediation*, **42**, 100828.

Hanson, S. G., Kashyap, A. K., & Stein, J. C. (2011). A macroprudential approach to financial regulation. *Journal of Economic Perspectives*, **25**(1), 3–28.

Harwood, A., Litan, R. E., & Pomerleano, M. (Eds.) (1999). *Financial Markets and Development: The Crisis in Emerging Markets*. Washington, D.C.: Brookings Institution Press.

Kaminsky, G. L., & Reinhart, C. M. (1999). The twin crises: The causes of banking and balance-of-payments problems. *American Economic Review*, **89**(3), 473–500.

Kasinger, J., Krahnen, J. P., Ongena, S., Pelizzon, L., Schmeling, M., & Wahrenburg, M. (2021). Non-performing loans-new risks and policies? NPL resolution after COVID-19: Main differences to previous crises, SAFE White Paper No. 84.

Masera, R. S. (1981). Comments on Helmut W. Mayer's paper. In Colloquium on The European Capital Market: Problems and Outlook. *Giornale degli Economisti e Annali di Economia*, 9/12.

Mathieson, D. (1988). Review on Ralph C. Bryant's Book, *International Financial Intermediation*. *Journal of Economic Literature*, **26**(3), 1210–1211.

Park, Y. C., & Park, W. A. (1993). Capital movement, real asset speculation, and macroeconomic adjustment in Korea. In Reisen H. and Fischer, B. (Eds.). *Financial Opening*, 93–115. Paris: Organization for Economic Co-operation and Development.

Prasad, E., & Wei, S. J. (2005). The Chinese approach to capital inflows: Patterns and possible explanations. NBER Working Paper 11306.

Prasad, E. S., & Rajan, R. G. (2008). A pragmatic approach to capital account liberalization. *Journal of Economic Perspectives*, **22**(3), 149–172.

Richter B., Schularick, M., & Shim, I. (2019). The costs of macroprudential policy. *Journal of International Economics*, **118**, 263–282.

Rojas, D., Vegh, C., & Vuletin, G. (2020). The macroeconomic effects of macroprudential policy: Evidence from a narrative approach. NBER Working Paper 27687.

Simons, H. C. (1934). *A Positive Program for Laissez Faire: Some Proposals for a Liberal Economic Policy*. Chicago, IL: University of Chicago Press.

Standard & Poor's (2020). "Latam financial institutions monitor 3Q2020: Climbing out of a deep plunge." https://www.spglobal.com/ratings/en/research/articles/201021-latam-financial-institutions-monitor-3q2020-climbing-out-of-a-deep-plunge-11695035.

Tillmann, P. (2015). Estimating the effects of macroprudential policy shocks: A Qual VAR approach. *Economics Letters*, **135**, 1–4.

Whitman, W. (1891–1892) *Leaves of Grass*. David McKay, Philadelphia.

Macroprudential Policies and the COVID-19 Pandemic: Risks and Challenges for Emerging Markets: A Discussion*

Eswar Prasad

Cornell University
Brookings Institution
NBER

This chapter by Professor Sebastian Edwards provides a convincing and compelling narrative about how emerging market economies (EMEs) have used regulatory forbearance on macroprudential policies, as well as modifications of some aspects of these policies, to help their economies buffer the impact of the pandemic and assist in their subsequent recoveries. The chapter contains a detailed listing of the various types of actions taken by central banks and other regulatory agencies in the group of 12 diverse countries included in the sample. It shows how in every one of these countries regulatory authorities actively used macroprudential policies as a policy tool operating in tandem with monetary and fiscal policies to limit financial and economic damage from the pandemic. The study also has an interesting forward-looking element. Edwards notes that new financial technologies, especially central bank digital

---

*This note draws on parts of the discussion in Prasad (2021).

currencies (CBDCs) issued by major central banks, could complicate the conduct of regulatory policies in EMEs.

It is worth pointing out at the outset that the sample of countries analysed in the chapter includes not just EMEs but, as noted by the author, a couple of countries that are now considered advanced economies (Korea, Singapore). This is in fact in keeping with the spirit of the analysis in the study, which is equally relevant to small open economies. Some key characteristics are common to these two groups of economies — exposure to external shocks as well as limited monetary policy autonomy in the face of global financial cycles.

One issue that the analysis raises is about the stringency of the policy measures. This issue is related to the literature on capital account liberalisation, to which Professor Edwards himself has made important contributions. Many countries have de jure capital controls but the intensity of enforcement of these controls often varies across countries and, even within the same country, over time. De facto capital account openness measures often paint a very different picture than that portrayed by de jure controls. In a similar vein, the enforcement of macroprudential regulations might itself vary over time, which could give regulators an additional degree of freedom in propping up their financial systems at times of stress. Of course, this in turn hinges on how binding the constraints imposed by macroprudential regulations are in normal times. These are not easy issues to tackle empirically but could be important in interpreting changes (or lack thereof) in macroprudential measures at different stages of the business cycle.

Most EMEs still tend to have bank-dominated financial systems, and macroprudential regulations tend to focus on this part of the financial system. Thus, another question raised by Professor Edwards' study is whether the changes in macroprudential measures are relevant to other parts of the financial system, including bond and equity markets. In his chapter, there are indications of some measures that seem to transcend the boundaries of the banking system. This distinction might be relevant for further work that builds on the analysis in this chapter.

In fact, in many EMEs, it is not just capital markets but also the informal financial system, including shadow banks, that play a major role in financial intermediation. The reach of traditional macroprudential tools is more limited when it comes to addressing this part of the financial system, but could become particularly important in periods of economic stress because it is these institutions that often support small and medium-sized enterprises that are most vulnerable to adverse economic shocks.

Professor Edwards rightly points out that, despite the severity of the COVID-19 shock and the ensuing global recession, financial systems around the world, including in the economies covered in his sample, held up fairly well. While this outcome might be the result of measures put in place in the aftermath of the global financial crisis, supplemented with forbearance during the recent difficult period, an equally important question is whether the financial system provided adequate support to the economy. In other words, did the forbearance prop up credit growth to businesses and households?

Of course, it is difficult to construct a counterfactual about what would have happened to credit growth in these economies in the absence of such forbearance, but this question is ultimately one that will have to be addressed in broader retrospective analyses of this episode. It is possible, and indeed likely, that the structure of a country's financial system makes a big difference in the outcomes of forbearance measures on economic activity (rather than on just the financial system itself). For instance, in economies with a largely state-owned banking system, forbearance might have been more effectively coupled with government persuasion for banks to increase the provision of credit and support real economic activity. In an economy with mostly privately owned banks, in contrast, one would expect regulatory forbearance that was expected to be temporary to have limited effect on the behaviour of those banks, particularly if the regulatory constraints were not tightly binding before the pandemic shock hit.

Professor Edwards rightly emphasises the interplay between macroprudential measures and capital controls in EMEs and small open economies. In fact, the two are often difficult to tell apart in the context of regulators endeavouring to limit the risks of foreign currency financing of their corporations and financial institutions. This part of the chapter, which draws on the author's extensive academic and policy expertise, is particularly interesting and nicely combines analytical insights and the practical experiences of countries such as Chile in dealing with financial system vulnerabilities that are related to cross-border financial flows.

In the latter sections of the chapter, Professor Edwards provides a forward-looking discussion of how some novel financial technologies, especially digital currencies, might complicate regulatory policies in EMEs and small open economies. This is an area that will undoubtedly consume more of the attention of financial and other regulators in the years to come and it is commendable that the chapter draws attention to them.

Recent technological developments have implications for the structure of financial markets as well as for banks and other financial institutions. The biggest impact of the new financial technologies is likely to be on payment systems, including at the retail, wholesale (interbank) and cross-border levels. Each of these categories is subject to disruptive change or, at a minimum, substantial change that could affect the business models of institutions intermediating such payments.

The development of new cross-border payments systems and other channels that facilitate capital flows could benefit EMEs in many ways. Remittances and inward investment flows could increase, with the costs of such transactions falling, and the settlement and verification of transactions becoming quicker and more efficient. More broadly, foreign capital could help boost investment and growth in these economies if domestic markets effectively funnel this capital into productive investment opportunities.

These developments could also increase the efficiency and stability of financial markets but could equally well create new risks and amplify them in certain circumstances. The structures of financial markets and institutions will also be affected, with even the viability of some traditional institutions coming into question. In particular, commercial banks could face challenges to their business models as Fintech shifts the balance of power between traditional commercial banks and newer forms of intermediation by non-bank/non-financial institutions. The key challenge such developments pose for policymakers and regulators is how to balance the benefits of financial innovation with management of risks.

New and relatively friction-free channels for cross-border financial flows could exacerbate policy spillover effects across economies. These new channels could not only amplify financial market volatility but also transmit it more rapidly across countries. This is a particular concern for EMEs and small open economies that are already subject to whiplash effects on account of conventional and unconventional monetary policy actions of the major advanced economy central banks, particularly the Federal Reserve. In other words, the availability of more efficient conduits for cross-border capital flows could intensify global financial cycles and all the domestic policy complications that result from them.

Digital currencies could lead to more such conduits and the simultaneous erosion of capital controls. While governments around the world try to limit the use of cryptocurrencies for avoiding capital controls, it is unclear if and how long such measures will remain effective in the face of strong economic incentives for capital flows. And it is not just private cryptocurrencies that provide conduits for evasion of capital controls.

It is clear that both official and private channels for cross-border capital flows are expanding. Official channels — such as the cross-border payments system that the central banks of Canada, Singapore and the United Kingdom have been collaborating on — will make such flows easier while allowing governments to modulate these flows and reduce the risk of illegitimate financial activity. Private channels, on the other hand, could become increasingly difficult to monitor and manage, especially if they are created and used by informal financial institutions that will be harder to regulate.

A passive approach to cryptocurrencies and CBDCs is not a viable option for most EMEs. Some of the issues brought to the fore by these developments, especially the implications of new cross-border payments systems for quicker and easier international flows of capital, are particularly relevant for EMEs. These countries already have to deal with substantial capital flow and exchange rate volatility, partly related to spillovers of monetary and other policies from the US and other advanced economies. These challenges could become greater if new payments systems and digital currencies increase both the volumes and fluctuations in cross-border capital flows and make capital controls less potent, adding to such volatility.

Similarly, while none of the G-3 central banks (US Federal Reserve, European Central Bank, Bank of Japan) has so far indicated any concrete plans to issue CBDCs, that prospect is one that countries in this region need to prepare for. Such a development, which could make it easier to hold and transact in major global currencies, could exacerbate the problem of dollarisation that many of these countries are already grappling with. All three central banks have already indicated openness to the idea of issuing CBDCs, implying that these changes may not be that far off into the future. And it is not just the G-3 central banks that matter in this context. Indeed, shifts to electronic currencies would make it easier to use even currencies of smaller reserve currency economies other than the G-3 as mediums of exchange and stores of value if there remains little trust in domestic currencies.

Moreover, while cryptocurrencies issued by large and financially powerful multinational corporations such as Amazon and Facebook might not gain traction in advanced economies with trusted fiat currencies, such financial innovations have the potential to displace domestic fiat currencies in some EMEs. In light of these considerations, and given the BIS' explicit support for CBDC, the advent of both official and unofficial digital currencies that have the potential to disrupt the viability of fiat currencies of certain EMEs might happen relatively soon, leaving policymakers only limited time to prepare for these developments.

Regulatory policy in EMEs, and indeed in virtually all economies, will need to evolve rapidly in order to evaluate and regulate both institution-specific and systemic risk generated by financial sector activities of non-bank financial institutions and non-financial corporations. With Fintech firms and even regular commercial enterprises playing a larger role in various aspects of financial intermediation, the regulatory architecture could soon develop lacunae that affect financial stability in times of macroeconomic stress. Another aspect of financial stability is related to crisis management, particularly in the context of changes to financial market structures. For instance, liquidity injections to smooth over periods of financial market stress would be harder if non-bank financial institutions not directly connected to the central bank became more important players than commercial banks.

To sum up, Professor Edwards has provided both (1) a useful overview of how EME regulators reacted and the flexibility they demonstrated during a very difficult period during and in the aftermath of the COVID-19 pandemic and also (2) a set of lessons that EME regulators and other policymakers should take from the episode, especially in the context of the transformations being wrought by new financial technologies, including digital currencies. This study will undoubtedly serve as a benchmark for further research in an area that is topical and is of both academic and policy relevance.

Reference

Prasad, Eswar S., 2021, *The Future of Money: How the Digital Revolution is Transforming Currencies and Finance*, Cambridge, MA: Harvard University Press.

CHAPTER 4

Chapter 4

Macroprudential Policy during COVID-19: The Role of Policy Space*

Katharina Bergant[†,**] and Kristin Forbes[‡,§,¶,††]

[†]*International Monetary Fund*
[‡]*MIT-Sloan School of Management*
[§]*NBER*
[¶]*CEPR*
[**]*kbergant@imf.org*
[††]*kjforbes@mit.edu*

Abstract

This chapter uses the initial phase of the COVID-19 pandemic to examine how macroprudential frameworks developed over the past decade performed during a period of heightened financial and economic stress. It discusses a new measure of the macroprudential stance that better captures the intensity of different policies across countries and time. Then it shows that macroprudential policy has been used countercyclically — with

---

* This paper was prepared for MAS-BIS Conference on "Macro-financial Stability Policy in a Globalised World: Lessons from International Experience", held on 26–28 May 2021. The authors wish to thank the conference participants, and especially Valentina Bruno, for helpful comments and suggestions. We thank JPMorgan for sharing data on EMBI spreads and Dalya Elmalt for excellent research assistance. The views expressed here are those of the author(s) and do not necessarily represent the views of the IMF, its Executive Board, its management or any other organisations that the authors are affiliated with.

stances tightened during the 2010s and eased in response to COVID-19 by more than previous risk-off periods. Countries that tightened macroprudential policy more aggressively before COVID-19, as well as those that eased more during the pandemic, experienced less financial and economic stress. The ability of countries to use macroprudential policy, however, was significantly constrained by the extent of existing "policy space", i.e., by how aggressively policy was tightened before COVID-19. The use of macroprudential tools was not significantly affected by the space available to use other policy tools (such as fiscal policy, monetary policy, FX intervention and capital flow management measures), and the use of other tools was not significantly affected by the space available to use macroprudential policy. This suggests that although macroprudential tools are being used countercyclically and should therefore help stabilise economies and financial markets, there appears to be an opportunity to better integrate the use of macroprudential tools with other policies in the future.

1. Introduction

The 2008–2009 Global Financial Crisis (GFC) prompted interest in the use of macroprudential tools to improve the resilience of financial systems and stabilise economies. A growing body of literature is beginning to evaluate how these tools work, if they can accomplish their goals and if they have been adjusted appropriately. One challenge in evaluating the use of macroprudential policy to date has been the limited incidence of recessions and financial crises in the decade over which these tools have been more widely adopted. The early stages of COVID-19, however, provide an occasion to evaluate how recent adjustments in macroprudential policy performed during a period of heightened financial market stress and a collapse in economic activity. This chapter uses this event to explore how countries adjusted macroprudential policy in response to an extreme "risk-off shock", what factors affected the use of macroprudential tools and whether adjusting macroprudential policy affected the use of other policies. The results highlight the importance of creating "policy space", i.e., of tightening macroprudential policy before a negative shock in order to be able to use the tool when needed.

After the GFC, it was hoped that a more proactive use of macroprudential tools could reduce the build-up of systemic risk over time, mitigate the amplification of shocks across the financial system and support credit and liquidity during downturns. Certain macroprudential tools would be in place during all phases of the financial cycle in order to ensure sufficient buffers, while other tools could be used countercyclically (tightened during booms and loosened during slowdowns) to stabilise fluctuations in financial flows and real activity. A number of academic papers documented the potential benefits from a more proactive use of macroprudential policy, a literature well summarised in Bianchi and Mendoza (2018), Borio *et al.* (2020), Brunnermeier *et al.* (2013), Claessens (2015), Engel (2016) and Galati and Moessner (2018).

As countries around the world have increased their use of macroprudential tools, a rapidly growing body of research has evaluated if these tools have been effective (well summarised in Araujo *et al.* [2020], Cerutti *et al.* [2017] and Forbes [2021]). Although this literature is still in its infancy, and there are imposing challenges to empirical analysis, the evidence suggests that these tools have had some success in attaining certain direct goals that tend to decrease vulnerabilities (such as reducing domestic credit growth and bank exposure to foreign currency borrowing), but have been less effective in other areas (such as limiting international capital flows). The evidence on whether macroprudential tools can accomplish their ultimate goals of strengthening the resilience of financial systems to shocks and mitigating amplification effects is supportive on net, but more tenuous, partly due to the limited business cycle downturns and financial crises since these tools were widely used. Several papers have also argued that although adjustments in macroprudential policy have been positive, implementation has been slow and more limited than would be required to provide meaningful protection (see Edge and Liang [2017], Forbes [2019, 2021] and Hanson *et al.* [2011]). Moreover, although the direct effects, spillovers and leakages from macroprudential policies suggest they should be coordinated with other policy tools (Agénor and Pereira da Silva, 2018;

Bruno *et al.*, 2017; Forbes *et al.*, 2017; and Richter *et al.*, 2019), there is little evidence to date on whether this is occurring.

The sudden and widespread impact of COVID-19 is the first occasion to test whether a decade of general tightening in macroprudential policy provided meaningful protection against an extreme negative shock. Had countries tightened macroprudential policy enough that these tools could be loosened meaningfully? Did the greater use of macroprudential tools mitigate the financial and economic stress from COVID-19 — either by reducing the imbalances that could aggravate the shock or by providing a countercyclical tool that could mitigate the impact? Could the use of macroprudential policy substitute for the use of other policy tools that may not have been available (such as lowering interest rates if the policy rate was already at the effective lower bound)? And did the space to use macroprudential policy to adjust to COVID-19 reduce the need for countries to use other policy tools? This chapter provides a first look at these questions during the COVID-19 shock in the first half of 2020.

The chapter begins by discussing challenges in measuring macroprudential policy using metrics that are comparable across time and especially across countries. Despite impressive new data sets compiled by several researchers and institutions, capturing different intensities of macroprudential policy continues to be an imposing challenge. To address this challenge, this chapter uses several measures of macroprudential policy. First, to capture a country's macroprudential stance before COVID-19, it uses a new index recently developed in Bergant and Forbes (2021) and Chari *et al.* (2021) that combines three popular macroprudential tools: the Countercyclical Capital Buffer (CCyB), the Loan-to-Value ratio (LTV) and a measure of the FX macroprudential stance. Second, to track recent adjustments to macroprudential policy in response to COVID-19, it uses new data from the IMF Policy Tracker, which records changes in policy (but does not provide details on the types of changes). Finally, it supplements these broader measures of macroprudential policy with more detailed information on one tool, the CCyB, which is consistently measured across countries and available through 2020. The chapter then documents the gradual tightening in different macroprudential measures before COVID-19, followed by a widespread and rapid loosening of these tools as an early part of the response to COVID-19 — a much more aggressive use of macroprudential policy than during other "risk-off" periods over the last decade.

The next section of the chapter explores the relationship between different measures of "stress" and macroprudential policy. It begins by showing that countries which tightened macroprudential policy more aggressively before COVID-19 tended to have lower levels of financial stress (measured as the increase in CDS spreads or bond yields) and lower levels of economic stress (measured as the reduction in expected GDP growth in 2020) during the COVID-19 shock. Then it shows that countries which experienced heightened levels of market and financial stress also eased macroprudential policy more aggressively in the initial stages of the pandemic. These results are correlations and not formal empirical tests, but they are consistent with the goals and structure of macroprudential policy; strengthening macroprudential policy can reduce the build-up and amplification of risk to make an economy more resilient to shocks, and easing macroprudential policy in response to a shock can alleviate financial and economic stress. All in all, these patterns suggest that macroprudential tools are being used countercyclically and in the direction expected.

The chapter then goes a step further to more formally estimate what factors affected the use of macroprudential policy during COVID-19, as well as if the use of macroprudential policy affected the use of other major policy tools. It finds that the most important factor determining whether a country eased macroprudential policy (or just the CCyB) during COVID-19 was if the country had tightened policy (or just the CCyB) more aggressively before the pandemic. Other variables — such as the extent of financial or economic stress, the spread of COVID-19 or a wide range of other country characteristics — were generally not significant in predicting the use of macroprudential policy. Also noteworthy, more space to use other policies — including monetary policy, fiscal policy, FX intervention and capital flow management policies — did not affect a country's decision to adjust macroprudential policy during COVID-19. Likewise, using macroprudential policy more aggressively (either by tightening more before COVID-19, or easing more in the early stages of the pandemic), did not significantly affect a country's use of other policies (including fiscal policy, various forms of monetary policy and

FX intervention). In other words, there appeared to be little relationship between a country's use of macroprudential policy and its use of other policies, so the space to use any of these other policies did not meaningfully affect the use of macroprudential policy (and vice versa).

These results have a number of important implications. Macroprudential tools appear to have been used as intended — tightened during the risk-on period before COVID-19 and loosened during the risk-off shock of the pandemic. The patterns in the data are consistent with macroprudential policy providing a countercyclical benefit and mitigating economic and financial stress — although this is simply a correlation and could be caused by other factors and differences in country characteristics. Most important, countries were only able to use macroprudential policy aggressively if they had actively tightened policy before the pandemic; this highlights the importance of building policy space to use a range of policy tools (Bergant and Forbes, 2021). The results also suggest, however, that despite increased attention to the interactions between different policies, and especially between monetary and macroprudential policy, there is not yet active coordination of these tools. This may reflect different institutions responsible for the use of different policy tools, or simply that different policies are set with regards to specific goals and do not take into account the spillovers to and interactions with other policy tools.

The remainder of this chapter is as follows. Section 2 discusses our measures of the macroprudential stance and changes in macroprudential policy during COVID-19. Section 3 documents various correlations between macroprudential policy and economic and financial stress. Section 4 is the primary contribution of the chapter, documenting the role of pre-existing policy space in determining the use of macroprudential policy during COVID-19, as well as the minimal interactions between macroprudential policy adjustments (and space) and the use of other policies in response to the pandemic. Section 5 concludes.

2. Measuring the macroprudential stance across countries and over time

One of the biggest challenges for cross-country empirical research on macroprudential policy has been obtaining data that is comparable across countries and time. As countries began to pay more attention to their macroprudential frameworks and adjust macroprudential tools more actively, however, several researchers and institutions have begun to compile cross-country databases tracking macroprudential policy adjustments. The most comprehensive early efforts include data on seven tools from an IMF survey described in Lim *et al.* (2011); data on macroprudential tools and capital flow management measures (CFMs) in Asia-Pacific economies in Bruno *et al.* (2017); detailed data on 12 tools from another IMF survey described in Cerutti *et al.* (2017); data on housing-sector tools in Shim *et al.* (2013) and Kuttner and Shim (2016); data focused on foreign-exchange exposures discussed in Ahnert *et al.* (2021) and information on governance structures for adjusting macroprudential tools in Edge and Liang (2017). More recently, the BIS and ESRB have compiled information on one widely used macroprudential policy tool — the CCyB. To date, the International Monetary Fund has compiled the most comprehensive time-series database that includes adjustments to a range of macroprudential tools: the Integrated Macroprudential Policy (iMaPP) database, described in Alam *et al.* (2019). This combines information from a number of pre-existing surveys with a new IMF annual survey and country-specific data to provide detailed information on a range of macroprudential tools for 134 countries from 1990–2018. Most recently, as many countries adjusted policy aggressively in response to the COVID-19 pandemic, several institutions started to track changes in macroprudential regulation in real time, such as the IMF's Policy Tracker (discussed in more detail below).[1]

Despite these impressive efforts towards better measuring and tracking macroprudential policy across countries, the existing data suffers from one imposing challenge: capturing different intensities of macroprudential policy. Most of the data discussed above only tracks if a country changes its policy — not the intensity of any change or the starting point. Further complicating any comparisons, not only have different countries relied

---

[1] For more information, see https://www.imf.org/en/Topics/imf-and-COVID-1919/Policy-Responses-to-COVID-19.

on different macroprudential tools, even adjustments in the same tool in two countries could imply very different changes in their overall macroprudential policy stances. More specifically, a given tool could have different binding thresholds in different countries, could be focused on different segments of the financial sector and could have different effects based on the structure of the financial system and level of enforcement. Something as specific as adding a "limit on FX lending" could be a modest or severe tightening based on the level at which it is set, and it could have very different effects if it is a limit on FX lending relative to a bank's overall loan portfolio, its FX assets or just with respect to FX mortgage lending. Even more complicated is comparing the magnitudes of changes in different types of tools. For example, how can a change in the CCyB be compared to a change in rules on lending for high LTV mortgages or tighter liquidity regulations on systemically important financial institutions (SIFIs)?

Given these challenges, most empirical studies do not incorporate the intensity of changes in macroprudential policy and instead simply analyse the effects of any tightening in any tool (measured as a +1) and the effects of any easing (measured as a –1). This amalgamation of very different macroprudential actions into dummy variables biases studies against finding any effect of macroprudential regulation. Other studies (such as Bergant *et al.* [2020] and Forbes [2021]) address this challenge by creating measures of the overall macroprudential stance by aggregating changes in macroprudential policies over time. This is an improvement but is also problematic, as some countries adjust macroprudential policy often but in small increments (such as China), while others adjust policies infrequently but in larger and more meaningful steps. This can also make it difficult to compare the overall intensity of different countries' macroprudential stances across time (as well as across countries).

Therefore, in order to measure differences in macroprudential stances across countries as well as across time, this chapter focuses on a new index that attempts to balance the trade-offs in capturing intensity, comparability across countries and time and the diversity of macroprudential tools. This new index, which was recently developed in Bergant and Forbes (2021) and Chari *et al.* (2021), combines three popular macroprudential tools: the

CCyB,[2] the LTV from the iMaPP database[3] and the FX macroprudential stance.[4] All three components of the index are scaled based on their standard deviations and then given equal weight. We focus on these three measures as they incorporate adjustments in three of the most widely used tools and they also target three risk areas that are a focus of macroprudential policy: countercyclical risk in banks, the housing sector and international exposures (with the latter a particularly important focus of macroprudential policy in many emerging markets). This index also includes the only two measures of intensity that are comparable across countries (the CCyB and LTV ratio). The disadvantages of the index are that it does not incorporate other tools that may be used in certain countries, and it only has limited information on adjustments made in response to COVID-19 (as only the CCyB data extends through 2020).

To better understand how macroprudential policy has changed over time, the upper panel in Figure 1 provides a graphical representation of these three components of our index of macroprudential policy (the CCyB, LTV ratio and FX macroprudential stance) since 2000. It shows that most countries did not start adjusting their CCyBs until after 2013, and accelerated tightening around 2017 until the COVID-19 pandemic. Adjustments in LTV ratios and FX regulations were spread more evenly over time, with the latter being tightened significantly before the GFC. Again, both reached their peak stringency at the end of the sample and there is no cross-country data available yet on how they were adjusted in response to COVID-19. The lower panel of Figure 1 provides the resulting index of the macroprudential stance from combining these three tools,

---

[2] Data for changes in the CCyB is from the BIS (available at: www.bis.org/bcbs/ccyb/, accessed November 2020) and ESRB (available at www.esrb.europa.eu/national_policy/ccb/html/index.en.html, accessed November 2020). The data is cross-checked with data from Chen and Friedrich (2020).

[3] From the iMaPP database described in Alam *et al.* (2019). We express the LTV ratio as 100-LTV so that a higher value denotes a tighter stance (to correspond with the other indicators).

[4] The FX macroprudential stance is calculated by aggregating the net number of changes in FX-related tools in the iMaPP database since 1990; this includes any changes in macroprudential policy regarding capital requirements on FX-loans; limits on FX lending or rules or recommendations on FX loans; and limits on net or gross open FX positions, limits on FX exposures and FX funding, and currency mismatch regulations.

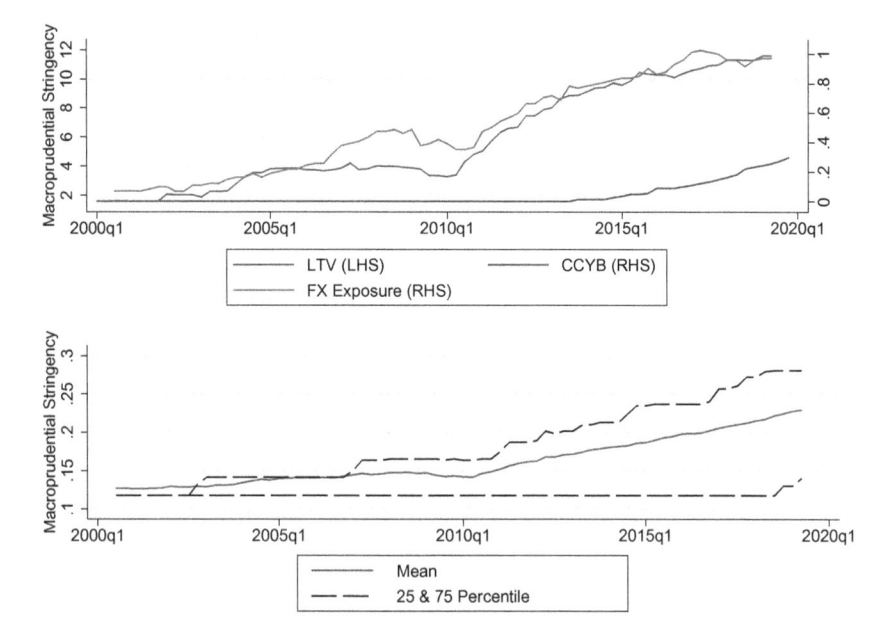

Figure 1. Measures of the macroprudential stance over time.

Note: The upper panel shows three measures of the macroprudential stance: average levels of the CCYB, the LTV ratio (expressed as 100-ratio), and the stringency of FX regulations, which includes the cumulative use of limits on foreign currency lending, limits on gross open FX positions (including currency mismatch regulations) and reserve requirements on foreign currency assets. The lower panel is the mean, 25th and 75th percentile of the overall index of macroprudential stringency (constructed using the three data series in the top graph, as described in Section 2).

Source: Data in the upper panel based on Alam *et al.* (2019), except the levels of the CCyB, which are from the BIS and the ESRB. Data in the lower panel are calculated as discussed in Section 2.

as well as the range of values in our sample of 74 countries. It shows the slow rate of tightening in macroprudential policy before 2010, and then a gradual tightening in average macroprudential stances up to the pandemic.[5] The panel also captures the range in stances across countries, a variation which grows over time and could be important for empirical analysis of the impact of macroprudential policy during COVID-19 (and which is explored later in this chapter).

---

[5] Data is not available on all components of the index to extend this measure through 2020.

One shortcoming of this macroprudential policy index, however, is the limited information on changes in macroprudential policy in response to COVID-19. Therefore, we supplement the analysis below with a timelier data source: the IMF Policy Tracker. This database catalogues changes in a range of monetary, fiscal and financial policies in response to COVID-19, but has the disadvantage of only recording any macroprudential action in the form of dummy variables, such that it is unable to capture the intensity of any changes or a country's initial policy stance. With that caveat, we measure changes in macroprudential policy after the start of the pandemic with three different variables: (1) a dummy if the country reports any loosening in macroprudential policy in the IMF Policy Tracker; (2) a dummy if the country reports adjusting its CCyB in the IMF Policy Tracker; and (3) changes in the CCyB ratio (discussed above).[6]

The resulting changes in macroprudential policy in response to COVID-19 according to these three indicators are shown in Figure 2 and suggest that countries responded to the pandemic with widespread loosening of macroprudential policy. A large proportion of countries report loosening macroprudential policy: 72 percent of advanced economies and 61 percent of emerging markets. Focusing on just the CCyB, this was loosened in 44 percent of advanced economies, but only 16 percent of emerging markets. Many countries (particularly in emerging markets) had not activated the CCyB or had it set at a low level before 2020, such that the average change in the CCyB ratio shown at the right of the Figure 2 was fairly small (0.46 pp for advanced economies). If you only consider the countries that reported adjustments to their CCyB, however, the loosening in the ratio was fairly aggressive; the average size

---

[6] For the CCyB data, the BIS and ESRB do have data updated until 2020 (which we use for adjustments in the pandemic period). There are several countries that report a loosening in CCyB in the IMF Policy Tracker, but do not show a loosening in the BIS and ESRB data. We check these examples with country-specific sources, and in most cases, this reflects countries that reduced some type of buffer on selected institutions, but not a macroprudential CCyB on the entire banking system. For example, the Netherlands reduced a CCyB for selected SIFIs, and by different amounts for each institution. In these cases, we do not adjust the raw data. The only exceptions are for two countries not included in the BIS and ESRB dataset: Morocco (which lowered its CCyB from 2.5 percent to 2.0 percent) and Kazakhstan (which lowered its CCyB by 1 pp for all institutions, starting from 2 percent for all institutions, or higher for SIFIs).

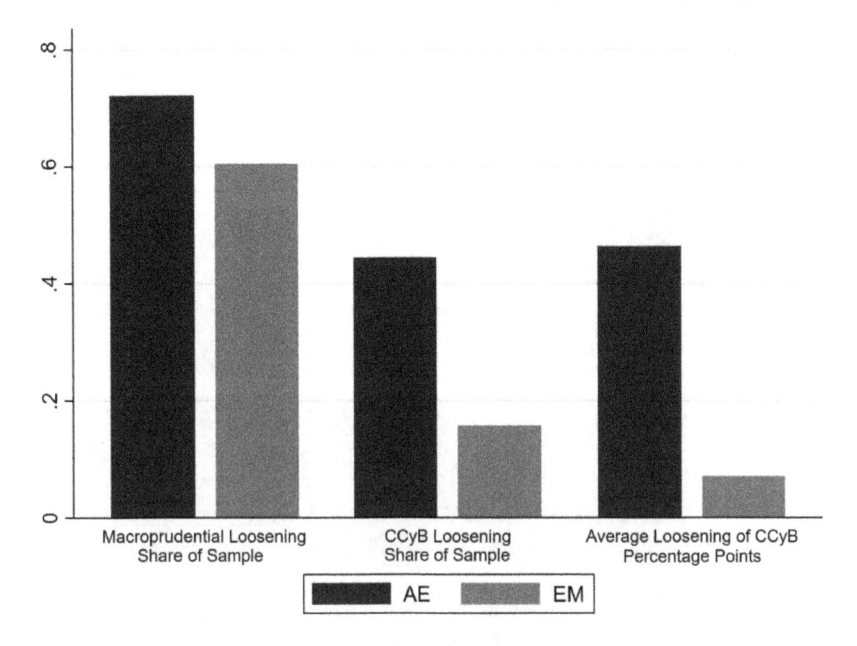

Figure 2. Macroprudential response to COVID-19.
Note: *Macroprudential Loosening* and *CCyB Loosening* report the share of advanced economies and emerging markets that eased each policy during 2020Q1–2020Q2. *Average Loosening of CCyB* reports the average decrease of the CCyB in percentage points across all countries (including those that did not adjust the CCyB).
Source: All data based on scrapped data from the IMF's Policy Tracker, except the average loosening in the CCyB is based on BIS and ESRB data.

of loosening was 1.17 pp, ranging from 0.25 pp (for Germany) to 2.50 pp (for Sweden).

Table 1 provides more country-specific information and puts these adjustments in a historical context; it reports each individual country's adjustments in macroprudential policy (in overall macroprudential policy or just the CCyB) during the COVID-19 window (the first six months of 2020), during the Taper Tantrum in 2013, and during the risk-off period around the commodity shock in 2015.[7] Each cell is coloured green if the

---

[7] Changes in macroprudential policy are measured using the macroprudential index discussed above, except for the COVID-19 window, which uses the dummy indicator from the IMF policy tracker (as data to construct the macroprudential index is not available). For each episode, data for changes in the CCyB is from the BIS and ESRB.

142 K. Bergant & K. Forbes

Table 1. Individual macroprudential actions during three risk-off periods.

Region	Economy	COVID-19 Macroprudential Loosening	COVID-19 CCyB Easing	Taper Tantrum Macroprudential Loosening	Taper Tantrum CCyB Easing	2015 Commodity Shock Macroprudential Loosening	2015 Commodity Shock CCyB Easing
Advanced Economies	Australia						
	Austria						
	Belgium						
	Canada						
	Cyprus						
	Czech Republic						
	Denmark						
	Estonia						
	Finland						
	France						
	Germany						
	Greece						
	Hong Kong SAR						
	Iceland						
	Ireland						
	Israel						
	Italy						
	Japan						
	South Korea						

Macroprudential Policy during COVID-19 143

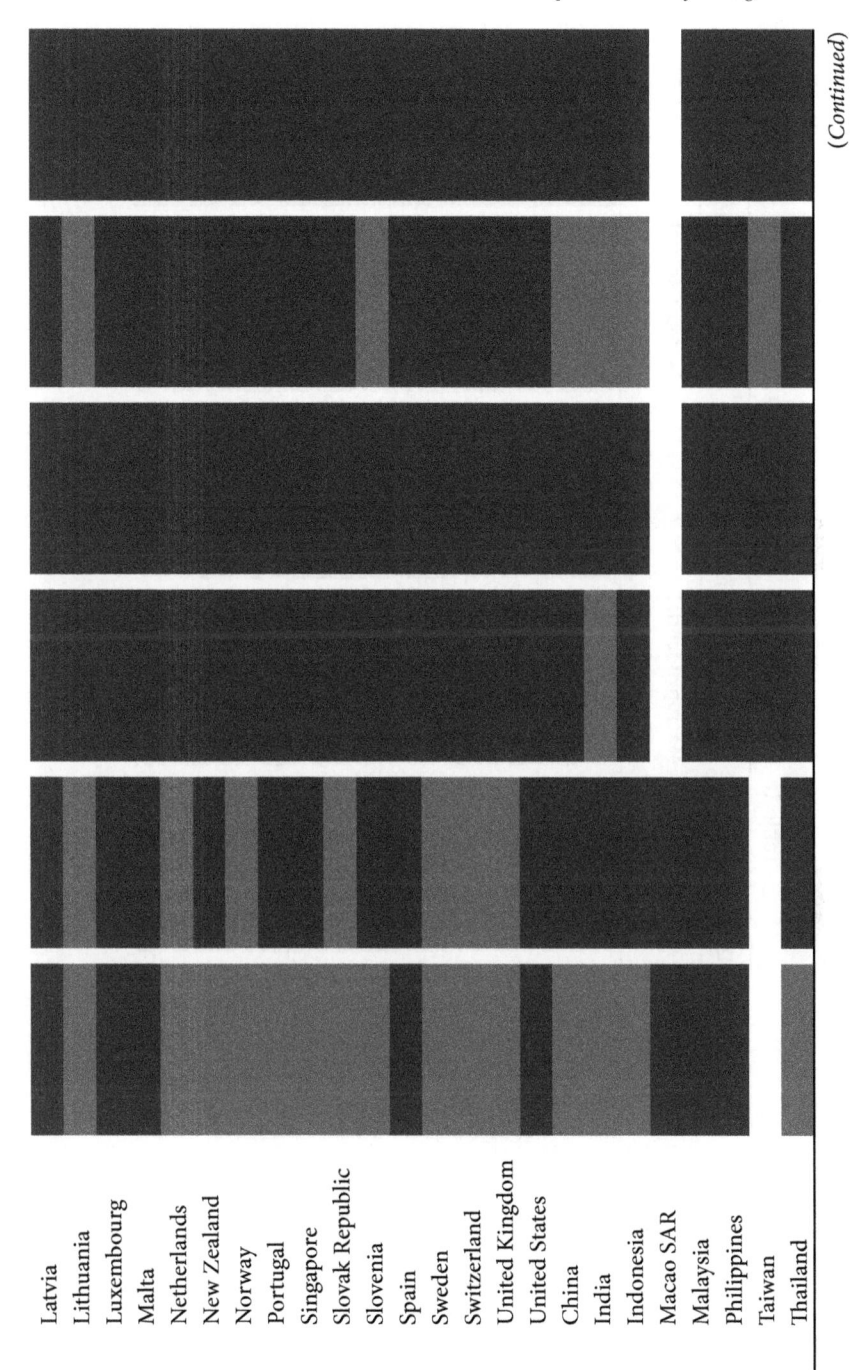

Latvia
Lithuania
Luxembourg
Malta
Netherlands
New Zealand
Norway
Portugal
Singapore
Slovak Republic
Slovenia
Spain
Sweden
Switzerland
United Kingdom
United States
China
India
Indonesia
Macao SAR
Malaysia
Philippines
Taiwan
Thailand

Emerging Asia

(Continued)

Table 1. (Continued)

Region	Economy	COVID-19 Macroprudential Loosening	COVID-19 CCyB Easing	Taper Tantrum Macroprudential Loosening	Taper Tantrum CCyB Easing	2015 Commodity Shock Macroprudential Loosening	2015 Commodity Shock CCyB Easing
Emerging Europe	Albania						
	Belarus						
	Bosnia and Herzegovina						
	Bulgaria						
	Croatia						
	Hungary						
	Northern Macedonia						
	Poland						
	Romania						
	Russia						
	Serbia						
	Turkey						
	Ukraine						

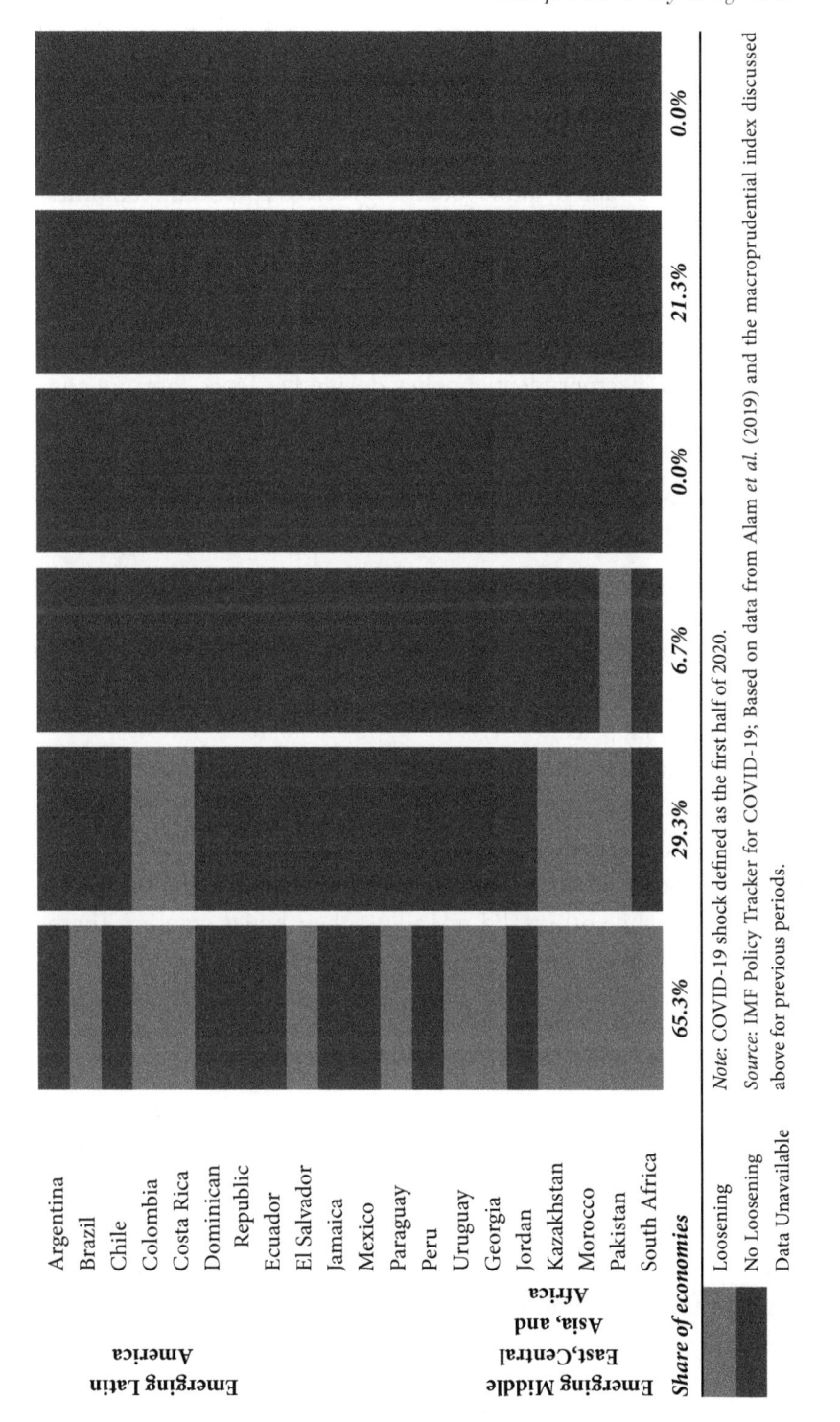

Macroprudential Policy during COVID-19   145

Emerging Latin America	Argentina
	Brazil
	Chile
	Colombia
	Costa Rica
	Dominican Republic
	Ecuador
	El Salvador
	Jamaica
	Mexico
	Paraguay
	Peru
	Uruguay
Emerging Middle East, Central Asia, and Africa	Georgia
	Jordan
	Kazakhstan
	Morocco
	Pakistan
	South Africa
Share of economies	65.3% 29.3% 6.7% 0.0% 21.3% 0.0%

- Loosening
- No Loosening
- Data Unavailable

Note: COVID-19 shock defined as the first half of 2020.
Source: IMF Policy Tracker for COVID-19; Based on data from Alam et al. (2019) and the macroprudential index discussed above for previous periods.

country loosened macroprudential policy, and red if there was no change or a tightening. As shown in the aggregate statistics in Figure 2, a large share of the countries loosened their CCyB and overall macroprudential policies during COVID-19. This was not specific to any region or country group, as Table 1 shows loosenings across advanced economies and emerging markets, as well as all geographical areas in our sample. In fact, 65 percent percent of the countries loosened macroprudential policy according to the index, and 29 percent for just the CCyB. In contrast, the right-hand side columns of the table suggest that far fewer countries eased macroprudential policy during the Taper Tantrum and 2015 Commodity Shock; only 7 percent and 21 percent of countries eased any macroprudential tool during the two earlier periods, respectively, and none loosened the CCyB. Overall, this comparison underscores the unprecedented wave of macroprudential loosening during COVID-19 across the globe. This widespread easing in macroprudential policy may have reflected the outsized nature of the COVID-19 shock in 2020, but it also may have reflected the increased stringency of macroprudential stances since 2015 that made this type of aggressive easing of policy possible in the first place.

These findings raise a number of questions. Did these adjustments in macroprudential policy provide meaningful support during this period of unprecedented financial and economic stress? What caused some countries to loosen macroprudential policy aggressively in response to COVID-19 — while others did not adjust their policy stances? These questions are explored in the remainder of this chapter.

3. Macroprudential policy and country-specific stress during COVID-19

The sharp and sudden impact of COVID-19 in the spring of 2020 provides a unique window to examine the relationship between macroprudential policy and different measures of economic and financial stress. In fact, for many countries it was the first test of how changes in their macroprudential framework would perform during a severe, negative shock. This section explores if countries that had stronger macroprudential buffers before the pandemic fared better during the early stages of COVID-19, as well as if countries that experienced a larger financial or economic shock were more likely to ease their macroprudential buffers.

Macroprudential policies are closely linked to periods of financial and economic stress through several channels. One key goal of tightening macroprudential policy is to prevent the build-up of vulnerabilities in the financial sector that could generate crises, or that could amplify the impact of an initial shock and generate more widespread stress. Working in the other direction, when a financial system is under stress, loosening macroprudential policy could help alleviate pressure in the financial system and mitigate any corresponding contraction in credit and liquidity. Academic research has found some evidence supporting these various links between macroprudential policy, the build-up of risks and financial stress. For example, several papers show that macroprudential policy tools can affect credit growth, household leverage, house prices and FX exposures — all of which correspond to the build-up of systemic risk (i.e., Ahnert et al., 2021; Alam et al., 2019; Cerutti et al., 2017; Claessens et al., 2013; Acharya et al., 2021).[8] Belkhir et al. (2020) show that tightening macroprudential policy reduces the probability of a banking crisis, and Bergant et al. (2020) show that a tighter macroprudential stance can significantly dampen the impact of global financial shocks. There is more limited evidence, however, on whether a loosening in macroprudential policy can alleviate financial stress and amplification effects — undoubtedly reflecting the lack of such episodes since macroprudential tools became more widely adopted.

The sharp impact of the COVID-19 pandemic on financial markets in March 2020, followed by the realisation that the pandemic and associated mobility restrictions would lead to a sharp contraction in economic activity, provides a unique occasion to evaluate the effects of macroprudential policy. More specifically, we focus on two different measures of country-specific "stress" during COVID-19: in terms of financial markets ("financial stress") and real GDP growth ("economic stress"). We measure "financial stress" using sovereign CDS spreads

---

[8] The literature also acknowledges leakages and spillovers from macroprudential policies (e.g. Ahnert et al. [2021] and Aiyar et al. [2014]).

(5-year, US$) from Bloomberg and comparing levels at end-2019 to the country-specific "peak stress" in the first half of 2020.[9] If CDS data is not available, we perform the same calculation using the EMBI+ bond index from JPMorgan. We measure "economic stress" as the change in each country's forecast of 2020 real GDP growth between January and June 2020, according to the IMF's World Economic Outlook updates.[10] In each case, we calculate the measures so that a higher value indicates more "stress" (i.e., greater *increase* in financial market spreads and greater *reduction* in growth, respectively). Appendix Figure A.1. shows the distribution of the "financial stress" and "economic stress" variables, as well as a "health stress" variable used later on in the chapter.

Figure 3 shows the simple correlation of each measure of stress with the pre-COVID-19 macroprudential stance (calculated using the index of the CCyB, LTV ratio and FX stance discussed above and shown in the lower panel of Figure 1). The left-hand panel appears to show a negative slope — suggesting that countries with looser macroprudential stances also experienced the highest levels of *financial* stress (as measured by the increase in spreads). Similarly, the right-hand panel also suggests that countries with a looser macroprudential stance experienced higher levels of *economic* stress (as measured by downward revisions in their forecast for 2020 real GDP growth). The pairwise correlations with the pre-COVID-19 macroprudential stance are both negative and significant, at −0.25 and −0.34 for financial and economic stress, respectively. The panels also show, however, that there are some outliers with high levels of stress (especially financial stress), which could be driving these negative and significant correlations. To test for the impact of these outliers, we drop the three highest "stress" values for each graph, and the raw correlations are still significantly negative (at −0.43 and −0.29, respectively).

---

[9] We use an average of the absolute change and percent change for each country to capture the magnitude of the effect as well as the magnitude relative to the starting level; this avoids overstating the "stress" in advanced economies that have very low CDS spreads such that a small change would imply a huge increase in stress if only focusing on percent changes.

[10] The January 2020 forecast was done at the end of 2019 when the pandemic was believed to be contained to China and not expected to have a meaningful global effect.

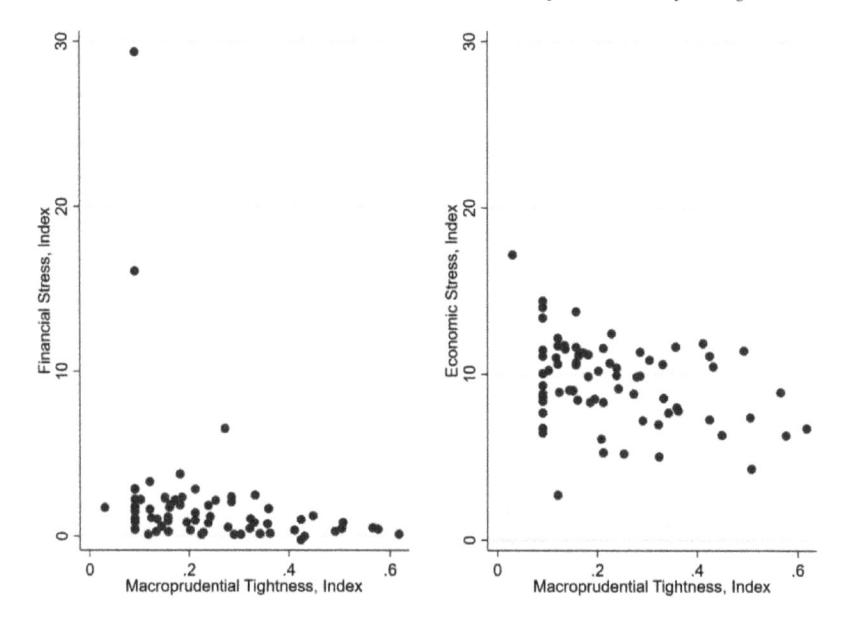

Figure 3. Pre-pandemic macroprudential stance and stress during the early stages of COVID-19.

Note: The *Financial Stress* index is an equally weighted combination of changes and percent changes from end-2019 to the "peak stress" in the first half of 2020 for sovereign CDS spreads (5-year, US$) from Bloomberg, and if this is not available, from the EMBI+ bond index. The *Economic Stress* index is the change in each country's forecast 2020 real GDP growth between January and June, according to the IMF's World Economic Outlook updates. *Macroprudential Tightness* is the value of the macroprudential index from end-2019 and described in Section 2, with a higher value indicating a tighter macroprudential stance.

Source: *Financial Stress* measure based on data from Bloomberg and JPMorgan; *Economic Stress* measure based on data from the WEO database; *Macroprudential Tightness* is calculated using data from Alam *et al.* (2019), the BIS and ESRB.

Stronger macroprudential policies may not only prevent the build-up of systemic risk but they can also support the functioning of financial markets and broader economic activity by being loosened when a negative shock affects the economy. Ghosh *et al.* (2017) show that countries have loosened macroprudential policies in the past in response to global financial shocks. Figure 4 explores if this also occurred during the initial phases of COVID-19 (i.e., the first six months of 2020). In the left-hand panel, the bar graph shows the average financial stress (in blue) and

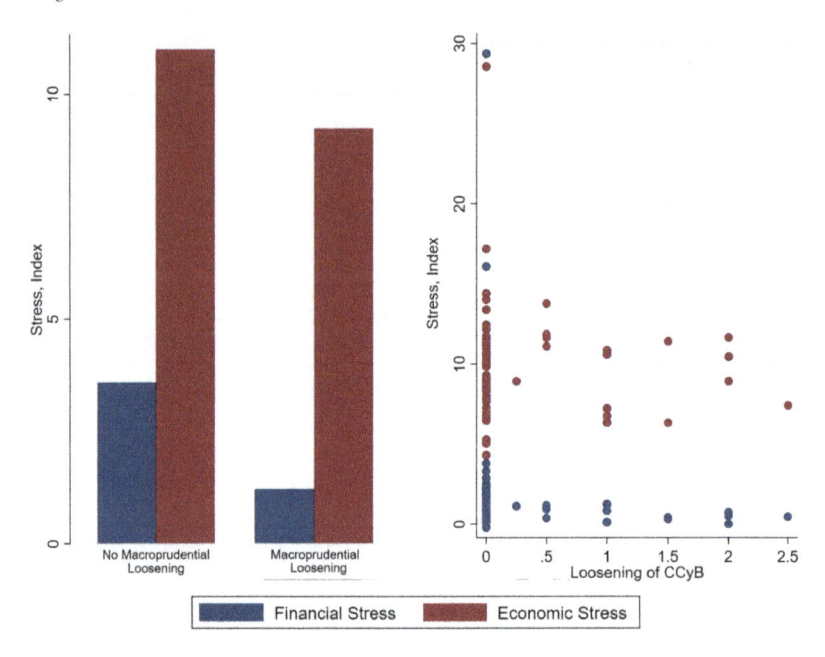

Figure 4. Macroprudential loosening and stress during the early stages of COVID-19.

Note: The *Financial Stress* index is an equally weighted combination of changes and percent changes from end-2019 to the "peak stress" in the first half of 2020 for sovereign CDS spreads (5-year, US$) from Bloomberg, and if this is not available, from the EMBI+ bond index. The *Economic Stress* index is the change in each country's forecast 2020 real GDP growth between January and June, according to the IMF's World Economic Outlook updates. *Macroprudential Loosening* is a dummy if a country reported a macroprudential loosening in the period 1 January 2020–31 June 2020 in the IMF Policy Tracker. *Loosening of CCyB* is the change in the CCyB in percentage points.

Source: *Financial Stress* measure based on data from Bloomberg and JPMorgan; *Economic Stress* measure based on data from the WEO database; *Macroprudential Loosening* based on data from the IMF Policy Tracker and *CCyB* data from the BIS and ESRB.

economic stress (in red) depending on whether the country loosened macroprudential policy in the first months of the pandemic or not. The averages of both measures of stress are lower for countries that loosened macroprudential policies. This pattern is also found when we focus on just changes in one macroprudential tool — the CCyB. The right-hand panel of Figure 4 shows a scatter plot of countries' financial stress (in blue) and economic stress (in red) relative to how much they lowered the CCyB in the first half of 2020. There appears to be a slight negative slope for each stress measure, and countries that did not loosen their CCyB had the highest levels of financial and economic stress. The correlations between the stress measures and reductions in the CCyB are clearly negative (at −0.17 and −0.08 for financial and economic stress, respectively), but insignificant.

Although these figures and the corresponding correlations are clearly not formal empirical tests, the patterns are consistent with the evidence from before COVID-19 and theory on how macroprudential tools should work. The negative correlation between the tightness of the macroprudential stance before COVID-19 and the extent of financial and economic stress experienced during the pandemic are consistent with the hypothesis that strengthening macroprudential policy can reduce the build-up of risk and make an economy more resilient during a crisis. Similarly, the negative correlation between the extent to which countries loosened macroprudential policy (measured broadly or just for the CCyB) during the pandemic and the extent of financial and economic stress are consistent with the hypothesis that loosening macroprudential policies can alleviate stress once a shock hits. It is important to emphasise, however, that this section only shows correlation and not causation; an omitted variable, such as institutional quality, could drive both sets of correlations. In order to better understand these relationships and test these hypotheses more formally, it is necessary to move to the more formal regression analysis in the next section of the chapter.

4. Macroprudential policy, policy space and other policy choices

This section more formally analyses the determinants of changes in macroprudential regulation during the early stages of the pandemic, including any interactions between macroprudential regulation and other policies. It draws on the literature examining the determinants of fiscal and monetary policy, which focuses on the role of existing "policy space" to enable a country to use certain tools to respond to negative shocks. Then the section explores how previous macroprudential actions (and the resulting policy space) and other variables affected the use of macroprudential policy during COVID-19. Next, it tests if pre-existing space for other policies affected a country's use of macroprudential tools, and finally whether initial macroprudential space affected the use of other policy tools. To the best of our knowledge, this is the first study to test for the role of policy space in the use of macroprudential regulation, as well as to understand the use of macroprudential policy during COVID-19.

4.1. Related literature

This section builds on a literature that examines the extent to which different policies are used in response to shocks and highlights the importance of policy space. Most of this literature focuses on how fiscal space can constrain the use of fiscal policy. For example, Ghosh et al. (2013) and Kose et al. (2017) discuss different approaches for defining fiscal space, and Auerbach and Gorodnichenko (2017) provide an excellent review of the literature and an analysis of the interaction between fiscal stimulus and fiscal space at different stages of the business cycle. Romer and Romer (2018, 2019) show that having more fiscal and monetary policy space (measured by debt to GDP and if interest rates are above zero, respectively) leads to significantly better economic performance after periods of stress, partly because monetary and fiscal policy can be used more aggressively to support the economy. Romer and Romer (2019) argue that this constraint from fiscal space occurs partly because of the impact on market access, and partly through policymaker decisions (such as the need to abide by EU or IMF conditionality rules). These conclusions agree with Jordà et al. (2016), who analyse a longer period to show that countries with lower debt ratios respond to crises with more aggressive fiscal stimulus (through financial rescues as well as conventional tax cuts and spending increases), leading to smaller output losses. The conclusion from this literature is that maintaining fiscal space during normal times can be a valuable insurance in the sense that it allows stronger responses to financial crises and recessions.

More recently, several papers have focused on the role of policy space in areas other than fiscal policy and the interaction between policy space and the use of different policy tools. For example, as interest rates have fallen near zero in many countries, there has been increased attention to the limited space available for conventional monetary policy and the potential for unconventional tools to provide additional stimulus (Bernanke, 2020). There has also been increased attention to how limited policy space for one tool could affect the use of other policy tools. For example, when monetary policy is constrained by the lower bound, and especially if the efficacy of unconventional monetary policy tools is uncertain, this could provide a greater justification to use countercyclical fiscal policy (Eggertsson, 2011; Woodford, 2011; Drautzburg and Uhlig, 2015; Furman and Summers, 2020). Related research also shows how monetary policy that affects borrowing costs will affect fiscal space and a country's ability to use fiscal stimulus (Aizenman *et al.*, 2019; Auerbach and Gorodnichenko, 2017). Bartsch *et al.* (2020) provide an overview of these issues around the optimal mix of countercyclical fiscal and monetary policy, highlighting how the debate has changed with policy rates near their effective lower bounds in many countries.

Finally, related research also explores the interactions between the use of macroprudential and monetary policy — including through international spillovers. More specifically, as macroprudential policy has become more widely used, countries that are concerned about overheating in certain sectors (such as the housing market), could tighten macroprudential policy to address these concerns directly and thereby provide monetary policy with greater flexibility to focus on its inflation (and if relevant employment) mandate.[11] Central banks that do not have the institutional framework to use macroprudential tools may need to raise interest rates sooner during recoveries to address growing financial risks. Overall, the literature agrees that monetary and macroprudential policies should not be separated (Adrian and Liang, 2018), but also emphasises that we do not yet have a clear sense of the trade-offs (Martin *et al.*, 2021). One of the few papers to attempt to better understand these trade-offs is Richter *et al.* (2019), which evaluates how changes in LTV ratios affect

---

[11] For a discussion of the interaction between monetary and macroprudential policies in the UK, see Kohn (2017), and for a model of how macroprudential and monetary policy can complement each other, see Caballero and Simsek (2019). The IMF's integrated policy framework (as in Basu *et al.*, 2020) provides policy recommendations based on a theoretical model of the interaction of monetary policy and macroprudential taxes on housing.

output and inflation — and thereby optimal monetary policy. From an international viewpoint, there is also evidence that macroprudential policy can provide a buffer against the impact of changes in monetary policy abroad, thereby providing greater monetary policy independence and avoiding having monetary policy exacerbate the adverse effects of changes in global financial conditions on the domestic economy (as shown in Bergant *et al.* [2020] and Aizenman *et al.* [2017]).[12]

4.2. *Macroprudential policy and macroprudential policy space*

In order to more formally test the factors determining a country's use of macroprudential policy ($\Delta MP_{i,t}$) during COVID-19, we build on our discussion in Section 3 and estimate the following empirical specification:

$$\Delta MP_{i,t} = \beta \cdot PS_{i,t-1} + \gamma \cdot ST_{i,t} + \delta \cdot CC_{i,t-1} + \varepsilon_{i,t} \qquad (1)$$

for each country i over the pandemic window t (the first six months of 2020). The first explanatory variable ($PS_{i,t-1}$) measures available policy space at end-2019 before COVID-19 (initially just for macroprudential policy, and in later tests for other policy tools). The second set of variables ($ST_{i,t}$) measures the "stress" to the economy during the initial stage of the pandemic, and the third set of variables ($CC_{i,t-1}$) is additional controls at end-2019 (or the latest date before that if end-2019 data is not available). Equation (1) is estimated as a probit when $\Delta MP_{i,t}$ is a dummy variable indicating any change in macroprudential policy, and is estimated using OLS when $\Delta MP_{i,t}$ is a quantitative value. All regressions include robust standard errors.

---

[12] This literature builds on evidence that many emerging markets — even if they have flexible exchange rates — tend to increase their policy rates in response to monetary tightening in the US even after controlling for inflation dynamics (Obstfeld *et al.*, 2005; Aizenman *et al.*, 2016; 2017; Han and Wei, 2018; Cavallino and Sandri, 2020; and Bhattarai *et al.*, 2020). There is also an extensive literature on how changes in macroprudential policy generate spillovers to other countries (Agénor *et al.*, 2017; Agénor and Pereira da Silva, 2019; Avdjiev *et al.*, 2016; Buch and Goldberg, 2017; and Forbes, 2021) and how regulations can interact with monetary policy to aggravate these spillovers (Forbes *et al.*, 2017).

More specifically, we focus on changes in macroprudential policy during COVID-19 using three measures: a dummy indicating whether the country changed macroprudential policy; a dummy indicating whether the country loosened the CCyB and the magnitude of the change in the CCyB (in percentage points). The dummy variables are from the IMF Policy Tracker and information on the CCyB from the BIS and ESRB, as discussed in Section 2. In our initial regressions, *Policy Space* ($PS_{i,t-1}$) is measured using the latest data available for our index of the macroprudential stance (described in Section 2) before 2020, which is composed of three popular macroprudential tools (the level of the CCyB, the level of the LTV and an index of FX regulations). For the regressions predicting changes in the value of the CCyB, however, the stance is measured by the initial level of the CCyB (at end-2019). To measure country-specific stress (*ST*) we use three measures: "financial stress" and "economic stress" (both described in Section 2), as well as "health stress". The latter is measured as the number of reported cases of COVID-19 per 1000 people from Oxford's Coronavirus Government Response Tracker (OxCGRT). In each case, a higher value indicates more "stress" (i.e., greater increase in financial market spreads, greater reduction in growth, or greater incidence of COVID-19 cases).

The final set of variables (CC_i) controls for other country characteristics from before the spread of COVID-19. Given the limited degrees of freedom in this cross-section analysis, we only include six controls for our baseline: a dummy variable equal to one for countries with a fixed exchange rate (based on the classification in Ilzetzki *et al.* [2019][13]); another dummy for emerging markets (based on IMF definitions); the ICRG index of institutional quality (from the Worldwide Governance Indicators); a measure of trade openness (exports plus imports as a share of GDP, from the IMF); exposure to commodity prices[14]; country credit rating (calculated as a numerical index based on Fitch country ratings)

---

[13] The data ends in 2016, and we assume the exchange rate regime has not changed through 2019. We define a fixed exchange rate regime using the "coarse classifications" and define countries as fixed if they have a moving band that is narrower than or equal to +/−2 percent (classification #11) or anything more restrictive.

[14] Exposure to commodity prices is measured as the volatility in the commodity terms-of-trade index from 2008 to 2018, based on the data in Gruss and Kebhaj (2019).

and the log of income per capita (from the IMF's World Economic Outlook database). Our final dataset includes 75 countries, of which 37 are advanced economies and 38 emerging markets.

Table 2 shows results predicting changes in our three measures of macroprudential policy during COVID-19 as function of macroprudential policy space, the three stress measures and other country characteristics. The one consistently significant coefficient is for pre-existing policy space. Countries with a tighter macroprudential stance before the pandemic, whether measured by the broad index of the macroprudential stance or the level of the CCyB, were significantly more likely to ease macroprudential policy during the initial stages of the COVID-19 pandemic. Moreover, columns (9)–(12) suggest that not only were countries with more space more likely to ease, but they lowered their CCyB by significantly more than countries which started with a lower CCyB. In some sense, these results are not surprising. Countries that had not tightened macroprudential policy more aggressively (or previously raised the CCyB above zero), would have had less ability to ease regulations (including lowering the CCyB). The magnitude of the coefficients, however, suggests that the effects of creating policy space, even through a modest tightening of policy before a shock, can be important. The coefficients suggest that a one percentage point tightening in the macroprudential policy index before COVID-19, would increase the probability of easing macroprudential policy at the start of the pandemic by 2.2 percent. Therefore, an increase of one standard deviation in the macroprudential space before COVID-19 would correspond to an increase in the probability of loosening macroprudential measures during the pandemic by 30.3 percent. Columns (9)–(12) suggest that for every 1.00 pp higher CCyB buffer as of end-2019, countries lowered the buffer by 0.68–0.69 pp.

Moreover, the significant role of pre-existing macroprudential policy space stands in sharp contrast to the general insignificance of most of the other coefficients in Table 2. The extent of stress — whether in financial markets, the decline in GDP growth, or spread of COVID-19 — has no significant effect on a country's decision to adjust macroprudential policy after controlling for the extent of macroprudential space. Most other country characteristics are also not consistently significant at the 5 percent level. The only exception is that countries which are

Table 2. Macroprudential policy and macroprudential policy space.

	Loosen Macroprudential Policy (dummy)				Loosen CCyB (dummy)				Loosen CCyB (pp change)			
	(1)	(2)	(3)	(4)	(5)	(6)	(7)	(8)	(9)	(10)	(11)	(12)
Macroprudential Policy Space												
MP Index or CCyB Level	6.899*** (1.989)	5.677*** (1.921)	5.810*** (1.960)	6.678*** (2.246)	4.559*** (1.221)	3.728** (1.568)	4.562*** (1.585)	4.727*** (1.537)	0.677*** (0.0959)	0.674*** (0.0939)	0.685*** (0.0854)	0.685*** (0.0858)
Stress Variables												
Financial		−0.0953 (0.0605)	−0.160 (0.115)	−0.133 (0.114)		−0.340* (0.201)	−0.148 (0.297)	−0.116 (0.277)		−0.00213 (0.00170)	−0.00107 (0.00367)	−0.00106 (0.00370)
Economic		−0.0184 (0.0676)	−0.0198 (0.0705)	−0.0731 (0.0718)		0.0426 (0.0922)	0.0226 (0.0935)	0.00663 (0.0999)		−0.00327 (0.0136)	−0.0194 (0.0154)	−0.0204 (0.0151)
Health		−0.0292 (0.0615)	−0.0250 (0.0596)	0.0109 (0.0620)		0.0241 (0.0586)	0.0127 (0.0644)	0.0260 (0.0708)		0.0262* (0.0156)	0.0225* (0.0120)	0.0231* (0.0123)
Other Country Characteristics												
Fixed ER dummy			0.232 (0.441)	0.0925 (0.426)			0.791* (0.449)	0.754* (0.451)			0.112 (0.0724)	0.111 (0.0735)
Institutional quality			−0.0491 (0.0636)	−0.0166 (0.0673)			−0.0638 (0.0671)	−0.0515 (0.0642)			0.00461 (0.00917)	0.00476 (0.00902)
Trade openness			0.0128 (0.399)	0.0429 (0.438)			−0.247 (0.341)	−0.265 (0.343)			−0.111* (0.0617)	−0.111* (0.0617)
Commodity dependence			−0.0768 (0.135)	−0.126 (0.121)			−0.00391 (0.134)	−0.0167 (0.140)			−0.0532** (0.0239)	−0.0535** (0.0244)
Credit rating			−0.00765 (0.0848)	−0.0512 (0.0878)			0.0731 (0.0942)	0.0543 (0.0957)			−0.0190 (0.0136)	−0.0194 (0.0133)
Income per capita (log)			0.218 (0.402)	−0.538 (0.653)			0.386 (0.368)	0.168 (0.504)			0.135* (0.0774)	0.127 (0.0959)
EM dummy				−1.686* (0.876)				−0.545 (0.812)				−0.0189 (0.103)
Observations	73	69	67	67	73	69	67	67	70	65	63	63
Adj. R-squared	0.213	0.230	0.258	0.307	0.170	0.212	0.253	0.259	0.798	0.804	0.832	0.829

Note: Policy space measured by the macroprudential index described in Section 2, except for the regressions in columns (9)–(12) where it is measured by the level of the CCyB. Columns (1)–(8) estimated using a probit and columns (9)–(12) using OLS. All regressions include robust standard errors. See text for variable definitions. *, ** and *** denote significance at the 10%, 5% and 1% level, respectively.

more sensitive to commodity price movements made fewer changes in their CCyBs — although this undoubtedly reflects the fact that most commodity-reliant countries had not previously raised their CCyB. There is also some evidence (albeit only significant the 10 percent level in some specifications), that countries with fixed exchange rates were more likely to loosen macroprudential policy during COVID-19, and emerging markets and countries that were more open to trade were less likely to adjust macroprudential policies.

4.3. *Macroprudential policy and other policy space*

If pre-existing macroprudential policy space was the most important determinant of whether countries adjusted macroprudential policy in response to the pandemic, did the policy space for other variables also matter? More specifically, if countries were constrained in their ability to use other policy responses to COVID-19, would they be more likely to adjust macroprudential policy? As discussed above, could adjustments in macroprudential policy partially substitute for adjustments in monetary policy when monetary policy is constrained by policy rates being near the lower bound? To test for the role of "other policy space" in the use of macroprudential policy, we estimate a variant of Equation (1), now by adding controls for "other policy space" ($OPS_{i,t-1}$), i.e., for other policy tools in addition to the amount of space for macroprudential policy.

$$\Delta MP_{i,t} = \beta \cdot PS_{i,t-1} + \alpha \cdot OPS_{i,t-1} + \gamma \cdot ST_{i,t} + \delta \cdot CC_{i,t-1} + \varepsilon_{i,t} \qquad (2)$$

We focus on the space for four other policies: fiscal, monetary, FX intervention and capital controls. To control for the amount of fiscal policy space, we use general government gross debt to GDP from the World Bank[15] and to control for the amount of monetary policy space, we use

---

[15] Romer and Romer (2019) argue that debt-to-GDP ratios are a useful measure of fiscal policy space as they are slow-moving and less cyclically sensitive (as compared to measures such as budget balances or financing costs) and they capture past policy decisions and "more long-run features of a country's policymaking process". The World Bank data is available at: https://www.worldbank.org/en/research/brief/fiscal-space.

the central bank policy rate.[16] To control for the amount of space for FX intervention and capital controls, we use the ratio of FX reserves to GDP (from the IMF) and an index of controls on capital inflows or outflows from Fernandez *et al.* (2016).[17]

Table 3 reports results when we estimate Equation (2) and continue to control for macroprudential policy space (using the same measures as above), but also control for fiscal and monetary policy space, for FX and capital control space, and then for the space of all four additional policies simultaneously. The first row shows that the results on the importance of macroprudential policy space still hold; countries that had tightened macroprudential policy more aggressively before COVID-19 were significantly more likely to ease macroprudential policy (by each measure) when the pandemic began. In most cases, however, the space available to use other policies had no significant relationship with a country's decision to ease macroprudential policy. The only exception (significant at least at the 5 percent level) is the policy space for FX intervention. Countries that had larger FX reserves (relative to GDP) reduced their CCyBs by less. This could reflect that countries that are more vulnerable to exchange rates movements and thereby accumulate larger reserve buffers are also less likely to ease macroprudential buffers during a shock, or it could reflect that more of the EMs that accumulate FX reserve buffers are also less likely to have raised (or even instituted) a CCyB before the pandemic. Perhaps most noteworthy, there is no evidence that countries relied more heavily on adjustments to macroprudential policy when they had less space to use other policy tools.

4.4. *Macroprudential policy space and other policy choices*

Even if the space available to use other policy tools did not affect a country's decision to adjust macroprudential policy during the early stages of COVID-19, did the ability to adjust macroprudential policy

---

[16] Data from Haver Analytics for most countries, and from the official central bank website for Costa Rica and from the BIS for China. We have also repeated the analysis using the shadow interest rate based on Krippner (2015) instead of the policy interest rate, with no meaningful impact on the results.

[17] Updated as of June 2019, with data through 2017. We use the 2017 value as the pre-COVID-19 level.

Table 3. Macroprudential policy and other policy space.

	Loosen Macroprudential Policy (dummy)			Loosen CCyB (dummy)			Loosen CCyB (pp change)		
	(1)	(2)	(3)	(4)	(5)	(6)	(7)	(8)	(9)
Policy Space									
MP Index or	5.514**	5.153**	4.950**	4.258**	4.261**	4.084**	0.675***	0.727***	0.714***
CCyB Level	(2.202)	(2.137)	(2.410)	(1.673)	(1.660)	(1.744)	(0.0938)	(0.0885)	(0.0984)
Fiscal	0.00136		0.00198	0.00575		0.00456	0.000952		0.00114
Space	(0.00506)		(0.00533)	(0.00659)		(0.00655)	(0.00103)		(0.00121)
Monetary	0.0453		0.112*	−0.0150		−0.0134	−0.00148		0.000131
Space	(0.0545)		(0.0646)	(0.0936)		(0.108)	(0.00251)		(0.00267)
FX Reserves		0.0104	0.00978		0.00880	0.00973		−0.00233**	−0.00256*
Space		(0.00842)	(0.00897)		(0.0100)	(0.0102)		(0.00111)	(0.00132)
Capital Control		0.805	1.656*		−0.890	−1.082		0.157	0.202*
Space		(0.896)	(1.003)		(0.681)	(0.765)		(0.117)	(0.105)
Stress Variables									
Financial	−0.302	−0.288	−0.563**	−0.144	−0.186	−0.168	−0.00190	0.00281	0.00268
	(0.224)	(0.323)	(0.253)	(0.307)	(0.323)	(0.334)	(0.00375)	(0.00277)	(0.00289)
Economic	−0.0152	0.0265	0.0466	0.0204	0.00950	0.00170	−0.0189	−0.0176	−0.0145
	(0.0731)	(0.0780)	(0.0833)	(0.0875)	(0.0956)	(0.0876)	(0.0141)	(0.0169)	(0.0150)
Health	−0.0199	−0.0531	−0.0410	0.0154	0.0220	0.0154	0.0203	0.0232*	0.0216
	(0.0626)	(0.0607)	(0.0629)	(0.0573)	(0.0665)	(0.0594)	(0.0123)	(0.0132)	(0.0139)

Other Country Characteristics

Fixed ER dummy	0.220 (0.449)	0.405 (0.478)	0.612 (0.523)	0.854* (0.476)	0.840* (0.466)	0.927* (0.493)	0.108 (0.0789)	0.0795 (0.0624)	0.0692 (0.0694)
Institutional quality	-0.0466 (0.0715)	-0.0565 (0.0725)	-0.0306 (0.0862)	-0.0744 (0.0663)	-0.0795 (0.0665)	-0.0937 (0.0773)	0.00363 (0.0111)	0.00923 (0.00767)	0.00927 (0.00964)
Trade openness	-0.0250 (0.431)	-0.313 (0.520)	-0.508 (0.582)	-0.301 (0.336)	-0.408 (0.454)	-0.474 (0.458)	-0.129* (0.0696)	-0.0334 (0.0462)	-0.0405 (0.0587)
Commodity dependence	-0.0560 (0.144)	0.0894 (0.182)	0.105 (0.181)	0.00952 (0.132)	-0.00366 (0.141)	-0.00108 (0.146)	-0.0526** (0.0256)	-0.0770*** (0.0255)	-0.0772*** (0.0267)
Credit rating	0.00514 (0.0910)	-0.0335 (0.0940)	-0.0486 (0.101)	0.0469 (0.101)	0.0802 (0.0982)	0.0570 (0.0998)	-0.0251 (0.0183)	-0.0197 (0.0146)	-0.0231 (0.0196)
Income per capita (log)	0.251 (0.455)	0.518 (0.469)	0.832 (0.536)	0.550 (0.413)	0.274 (0.389)	0.427 (0.442)	0.175* (0.103)	0.128 (0.0814)	0.170 (0.107)
Observations	**65**	**60**	**58**	**65**	**60**	**58**	**61**	**56**	**54**
Adj. R-squared	**0.281**	**0.273**	**0.325**	**0.259**	**0.255**	**0.269**	**0.828**	**0.871**	**0.870**

Note: Macroprudential policy space measured by the macroprudential index described in Section 2, except for the regressions in columns (7)–(9), where it is measured by the level of the CCyB. Columns (1)–(6) estimated using a probit and columns (7)–(9) using OLS. All regressions include robust standard errors. See text for variable definitions. *, ** and *** denote significance at the 10%, 5% and 1% level, respectively.

affect countries' decisions to use other policies? As an initial look, Figure 5 graphically represents the relationship between countries' use of other policies in the early stages of COVID-19 and the stringency of their macroprudential policy stance before the pandemic. We focus on two forms of unconventional monetary policy (asset purchases and the activation of swap lines): fiscal policy, conventional monetary policy (changes in the policy rate) and unconventional monetary policy through asset purchases and the activation of swap lines (defined in more detail below). The raw correlations in the figure show a mixed picture. There is a slightly negative correlation between the macroprudential

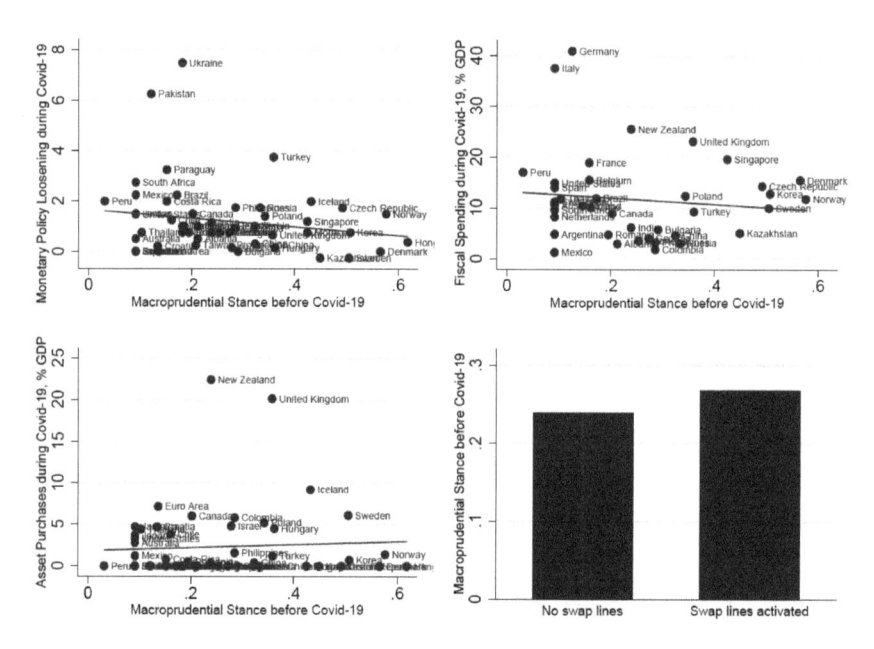

Figure 5. Macroprudential stance and other policies.

Note: Monetary Policy Loosening is changes in policy interest rates based on data from Haver. *Asset Purchases* are calculated as a percent of GDP based on purchase data from central banks' websites for AEs and Fratto et al. (2021) for EMs. *Fiscal Spending* is the change in the 2020 fiscal balance in response to COVID-19 (as a percent of GDP) from the IMF Policy Tracker. *Swap Lines* are a dummy variable if the country activated a swap line with another country from the IMF Policy Tracker. All policy responses are calculated over the first six months of 2020 unless noted otherwise. The macroprudential stance is the broad macroprudential index described in Section 2 using data from Alam et al. (2019), the BIS and ESRB, with a higher value indicating a tighter macroprudential stance.

stance before COVID-19 and the use of fiscal policy and conventional monetary policy. In other words, countries with tighter macroprudential policy before the pandemic conducted less expansionary fiscal policy and decreased their policy rate less, consistent with the hypothesis that countries with more space to adjust macroprudential policy did not need to adjust other policies as aggressively in response to COVID-19. On the other hand, the lower two panels of Figure 5 show that this relationship reverses for unconventional monetary policy; countries with a tighter macroprudential stance before the pandemic conducted more asset purchases and might have been slightly more likely to activate swap lines with a foreign central bank. All of these graphs are just raw correlations, however, and do not control for country characteristics and other omitted variables that could explain these different patterns. For example, countries that tightened macroprudential policy more before COVID-19 also tended to be advanced economies and had lower interest rates before the pandemic, and thereby had less space to adjust policy interest rates in response to COVID-19.

In order to better understand these relationships, it is necessary to control for other country characteristics, including the space available to use other policies that could act as a substitute or complement to macroprudential policy. To test this, we estimate an equation similar to Equation (2), now focusing on the determinants of "Other Policies" ($\Delta OP_{i,t}$) instead of macroprudential policy ($\Delta MP_{i,t}$), and still including a control for existing space for macroprudential policy ($PS_{i,t-1}$), existing space for other policies ($OPS_{i,t-1}$), and the full set of controls for different measures of "stress" and other country characteristics:

$$\Delta OP_{i,t} = \beta \cdot PS_{i,t-1} + \alpha \cdot OPS_{i,t-1} + \gamma \cdot ST_{i,t} + \delta \cdot CC_{i,t-1} + \varepsilon_{i,t} \qquad (3)$$

More specifically, ($\Delta OP_{i,t}$) is the adjustment to fiscal policy, monetary policy (changes in conventional or unconventional policy), or FX intervention during the first six months of 2020. (We do not report results for adjustments in capital controls as so few countries adjusted these controls that there are not sufficient observations for estimation.) Fiscal policy is the change in the 2020 fiscal balance in response to COVID-19 (as a share of GDP), as measured in June 2020 relative to end-2019, and thereby measures additional fiscal support relative to what was planned at end-2019.[18] This includes both "above-the-line" and "below-the-line" spending. Monetary policy is measured using three measures: the change in the central bank's policy rate (from Haver Analytics); the size of the country's asset purchase program relative to GDP over this period (from central bank websites and Fratto et al. [2021]); or whether the country activated a swap line with another country (from the IMF Policy Tracker). Finally, FX intervention is measured as a dummy equal to 1 if the country reports using FX reserves in the IMF's Policy Tracker (which could imply purchases or sales of FX reserves). For each policy response, we also control for the policy space ($OPS_{i,t-1}$) for the relevant action using the measures discussed above: fiscal policy space is measured using general government gross debt to GDP; monetary policy space is the central bank policy rate and FX intervention policy space is the ratio of FX reserves to GDP. Macroprudential policy space ($PS_{i,t-1}$) continues to be measured by the level of the macroprudential policy index at end-2019.

The results from estimating Equation (3) are reported in Table 4.[19] The top row suggests that macroprudential policy space had no significant effect on the use of fiscal policy, monetary policy (through adjustments to policy rates, QE or swap lines) or FX intervention during the early stages of the pandemic. This suggests that even if countries had previously tightened macroprudential policy (and therefore had space to use this tool), this did not meaningfully affect their use of other policies.

Also noteworthy is the second row in the table, which reports the role of *Other Policy Space* ($OPS_{i,t-1}$). As found for macroprudential policy, the use of policies can be significantly affected by the space available for that policy. For adjustments to the policy interest rate and FX intervention, the positive coefficients agree with those for macroprudential policy; countries with more policy space were more likely to use the given policy. More specifically, countries with a higher level of the policy interest rate and larger FX reserves (relative to GDP) were more likely to lower

---

[18] From the Fiscal Monitor Database of Country Fiscal Measures in Response to the COVID-19 Pandemic, with data through June 12.
[19] For the regressions predicting the use of fiscal policy, we exclude Japan. Japan is such a larger outlier that it can influence the significance of estimates and generate results that are not robust to minor changes; see Bergant and Forbes (2021) for more details on the impact of this outlier.

Table 4. Macroprudential policy space and other policy tools.

	Fiscal Stimulus	Monetary Stimulus Policy Rate	QE	Swaps	FX Intervention (dummy)
	(1)	(2)	(3)	(4)	(5)
Policy Space					
MP Index	−0.463	−1.311	3.279	−0.485	2.600
	(10.66)	(0.999)	(5.290)	(0.459)	(2.450)
Other Policy	−0.0789	0.387***	−0.288	0.0360	0.0544***
Space	(0.0500)	(0.0983)	(0.218)	(0.0311)	(0.0134)
Stress Variables					
Financial	−0.598	−0.0140	−0.135	0.0341***	−0.184**
	(0.575)	(0.0199)	(0.0873)	(0.0121)	(0.0925)
Economic	0.790	0.0880	0.429	−0.0481	0.0821
	(0.471)	(0.0848)	(0.301)	(0.0385)	(0.0894)
Health	−0.119	3.78e−05	−0.212	2.19e−05	0.0831
	(0.331)	(0.0505)	(0.243)	(0.0371)	(0.0713)
Other Country Characteristics					
Fixed ER	0.475	0.465	−2.471	0.105	0.104
dummy	(3.121)	(0.435)	(1.716)	(0.199)	(0.602)
Institutional	0.553	0.00153	−0.0719	0.0105	−0.184**
quality	(0.392)	(0.0547)	(0.257)	(0.0272)	(0.0923)
Trade	−1.626	0.0479	−1.468**	0.0615	−2.312***
openness	(2.369)	(0.233)	(0.721)	(0.112)	(0.730)
Commodity	−0.0813	−0.126	−0.109	−0.0764**	−0.0700
dependence	(0.450)	(0.140)	(0.259)	(0.0316)	(0.175)
Credit	−0.781	0.0229	−0.0889	−0.00608	−0.249*
rating	(0.837)	(0.0734)	(0.247)	(0.0431)	(0.131)
Income per	3.466	0.114	1.706	0.276	0.926*
capita (log)	(2.280)	(0.261)	(1.124)	(0.189)	(0.503)
Observations	37	47	47	44	50
Adj. R-squared	**0.214**	**0.556**	**0.121**	**0.140**	**0.417**

Note: MP Index measures macroprudential policy space using the macroprudential index described in Section 2. Other Policy Space measured by the debt/GDP ratio in column (1), by the policy rate in columns (2)–(4), and by the ratio of FX reserves to GDP in column (5), all for end-2019. All columns estimated using OLS, except columns (4) and (5) estimated using a probit. All regressions include robust standard errors. See text for variable definitions. *, ** and *** denote significance at the 10%, 5% and 1% level, respectively.

interest rates or use some type of FX intervention in the early stages of the pandemic, respectively. Also not surprising is the negative coefficient on QE; countries with more policy space (as measured by a higher policy rate) were less likely to use QE (although the coefficient is not significant). More surprising is the negative coefficient on the role of fiscal space for the use of fiscal stimulus; this suggests that countries with higher debt ratios did not use significantly less fiscal stimulus in response to COVID-19. This agrees with results in Bergant and Forbes (2021) that fiscal space did not seem to constrain a country's ability to respond to the negative shock of COVID-19 with a large fiscal stimulus. This is a change from research examining earlier time periods, which has traditionally found that fiscal space is an important constraint on a country's ability to respond to negative shocks (as shown in Romer and Romer [2018, 2019]).

This series of results suggests that although policy space for a given policy tool is often important for the use of that tool — especially for macroprudential policy, adjusting policy interest rates and FX intervention — the policy space for other tools is generally not a significant determinant. Countries were more likely to ease macroprudential policy in response to COVID-19 if they had previously tightened macroprudential policy more aggressively, but their decision was not significantly affected by their ability to use other tools. Similarly, although the use of other tools (such as monetary and FX policy) was significantly affected by whether a country had previously created space to use that tool, the use of these other tools (as well as fiscal policy) in response to COVID-19 was not affected by whether macroprudential policy had previously been tightened to create space to use this regulatory tool. Although economic models suggest that the ability to use one type of tool could affect the optimal use of other policy tools, these spillovers and interactions do not appear to have been powerful during the initial phases of COVID-19.

5. Conclusions and implications for global spillovers

Although many countries have been using macroprudential policy more actively since the GFC, the economic and financial dislocation created by COVID-19 provided the first global shock to test how these new macroprudential tools and broader frameworks would perform under a period of severe stress. Although the pandemic is far from over, the initial evidence suggests that the macroprudential frameworks developed over the last decade are largely working as expected. Banks, which have been the primary focus of most macroprudential regulations, not only withstood this severe shock, but did not amplify the shock to other segments of the economy as occurred during the GFC.[20] Moreover, this study shows that countries have been using macroprudential policy countercyclically, tightening policy during the recovery period starting in the mid-2010s, and then easing macroprudential policy aggressively in response to COVID-19. The empirical analysis suggests that countries which had created more macroprudential policy space (by tightening more aggressively before COVID-19), were also able to ease more aggressively in response to the pandemic. Creating macroprudential policy space in advance was important in order to be able to use this tool actively during a severe negative shock.

The evidence also suggests, however, that having the space to use macroprudential policy more actively is not yet affecting the use of other policy tools, and that having the space to use other policy tools is not yet meaningfully affecting the use of macroprudential policy. More specifically, countries that had more space to support their economies through fiscal policy, interest rates, FX intervention or capital controls did use macroprudential policy in a significantly different way during COVID-19 (even controlling for different degrees of macroprudential space). Similarly, countries which had greater space to adjust macroprudential policy did not meaningfully change their use of policy interest rates, quantitative easing, FX intervention, fiscal policy or FX swaps. This suggests that macroprudential policy is not yet being actively used as a substitute or complement to these other tools, and there may be opportunities to better coordinate the use of these tools in

---

[20] Of course, this is with the important caveat that banks also received substantial support through liquidity programs, subsidised lending programs, and reductions in interest rates in most economies — all of which would further stabilise banks and reduce any amplification effects. See English *et al.* (2021).

the future.[21] For example, as shown in Bergant and Forbes (2021), policy space is an important determinant of the use of a number of these policy tools. If countries were limited in their ability to build policy space in the use of certain tools (such as by raising policy interest rates), could they partially compensate for this by putting more emphasis on creating macroprudential policy space, and then adjusting macroprudential policy instead of other policies that are more constrained?

Finally, although this study provides evidence on the use of macroprudential tools during COVID-19 and the potential spillovers to the use of other policy tools, it does not address the spillovers from macroprudential policy to the non-bank financial system and to other economies.[22] There is increasing evidence that macroprudential policies can help strengthen domestic banking systems, but create externalities to other financial entities and spillovers to other countries (as discussed in other papers in this volume).[23] The shifting of financial risks, liquidity and exposure from the banking sector to the non-bank financial sector likely contributed to the market instability that occurred in March 2020, which in turn prompted widespread easing in macroprudential policy. On the other hand, if tighter macroprudential regulations improved the resilience of domestic financial systems to the COVID-19 shock, this should also have had positive spillovers to the broader domestic economy as well as to other countries. These multifaceted interactions and spillovers should all be considered when adjusting macroprudential policy — as well as the importance of policy space as highlighted throughout this chapter.

---

[21] Bruno et al. (2017) go one step further to discuss challenges when monetary and macroprudential policies are working in opposite directions — such as when one of these tools provides an incentive for economic agents to borrow more, while the other tool simultaneously provides an incentive to borrow less.

[22] For evidence on the international spillovers of macroprudential policies, see Agénor et al. (2017), Agénor and Pereira da Silva (2019), Ahnert et al. (2021), Aiyar et al. (2014), Avdjiev et al. (2016), Buch and Goldberg (2017), Forbes (2021) and Reinhardt and Sowerbutts (2015).

[23] For evidence on the spillovers to non-bank financial entities, see Chari et al. (2021) and Forbes (2021). Also see Bertaut et al. (2021) for evidence from the mutual fund sector on how vulnerabilities in the non-bank financial sector can amplify the impact of global shocks.

Appendix

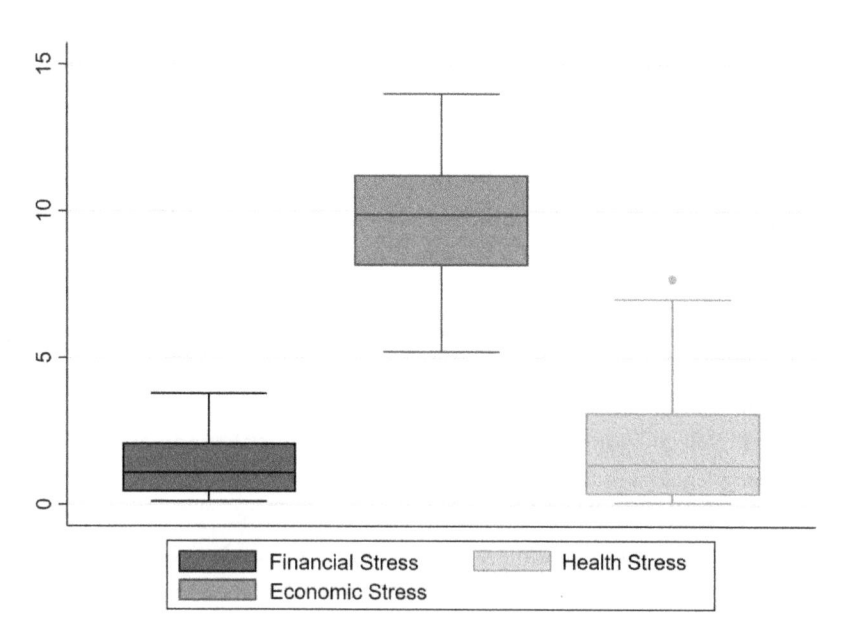

Figure A.1. Country-specific stress variables.

Note: Country-specific stress variables for the first half of 2020. *Financial Stress* is an equally-weighted combination of the (i) percentage change and (ii) absolute change of the CDS spread (or the EMBI spread if the CDS is not available) from end-2019 to the peak level in the first six months of 2020; *Economic Stress* is the change in the real GDP forecast for 2020 from January to June 2020; *Health Stress* is the number of confirmed COVID-19 cases per 1000 people. Data is winsorised at the 5 percent and 95 percent level.

Source: CDS from Bloomberg; EMBI from JPMorgan; Real GDP forecasts from WEO database; Confirmed COVID-19 cases per 1000 people from Oxford's Coronavirus Government Response Tracker (OxCGRT).

References

Acharya, Viral, Katharina Bergant, Matteo Crosignani, Tim Eisert, and Fergal McCann. 2022. "The Anatomy of the Transmission of Macroprudential Policy." *Journal of Finance*, 77(5): 2533–2575.

Adrian, Tobias and Nellie Liang. 2018. "Monetary Policy, Financial Conditions, and Financial Stability." *International Journal of Central Banking* 14(1): 73–131.

Agénor, Pierre-Richard and Luiz Pereira da Silva. 2019. "Global Banking, Financial Spillovers, and Macroprudential Policy Coordination." *BIS Working Papers* No. 764.

Agénor, Pierre-Richard and Luiz Pereira da Silva. 2018. "Financial Spillovers, Spillbacks, and the Scope for International Macroprudential Policy Coordination." *BIS Papers* No. 97.

Agénor, Pierre-Richard, Enisse Kharroubi, Leonardo Gambacorta, Giovanni Lombardo and Luiz Pereira da Silva. 2017. "The International Dimensions of Macroprudential Policies." *BIS Working Papers* No. 643.

Ahnert, Toni, Kristin Forbes, Christian Friedrich, and Dennis Reinhardt. 2021. "Macroprudential FX Regulations: Shifting the Snowbanks of FX Vulnerability?" *Journal of Financial Economics* 140(1): 145–174.

Aiyar, Shekhar, Charles Calomiris, and Tomasz Wieladek. 2014. "Does Macroprudential Regulation Leak? Evidence from a UK Policy Experiment." *Journal of Money, Credit and Banking* 46(1): 181–214.

Aizenman, Joshua, Menzie Chinn, and Hiro Ito. 2016. "Monetary Policy Spillovers and the Trilemma in the New Normal: Periphery Country Sensitivity to Core Country Conditions." *Journal of International Money and Finance* 68, 298–330.

———. 2017. "Financial Spillovers and Macroprudential Policies." *NBER Working Paper* 24105.

———. 2020. "Financial Spillovers and Macroprudential Policies." *Open Economies Review* 31: 529–63.

Aizenman, Joshua, Yothin Jinjarak, Hien Thi Kim Nguyen, Donghyun Park. 2019. "Fiscal Space and Government Spending and Tax-Rate Cyclicality Patterns: A Cross-Country Comparison, 1960–2016." *Journal of Macroeconomics* 60: 229–252.

Alam, Zohair, Adrian Alter, Jesse Eiseman, Gaston Gelos, Heedon Kang, Machiko Narita, Erlend Nier, and Naixi Wang. 2019. "Digging Deeper — Evidence on the Effects of Macroprudential Policies from a New Database." *IMF Working Paper* No. 19/66.

Araujo, Juliana, Manasa Patnam, Adina Popescu, Fabián Valencia, and Weija Yao. 2020. "Effects of Macroprudential Policy: Evidence from over 6,000 Estimates." *IMF Working Paper* WP/20/67.

Auerbach, Alan and Yuriy Gorodnichenko. 2017. "Fiscal Stimulus and Fiscal Sustainability," in *Fostering a Dynamic Global Economy.* Proceedings of the Kansas City Federal Reserve Banks Annual Symposium at Jackson Hole, Wyoming, 24–26 August 2017.

Avdjiev, Stefan, Cathérine Koch, Patrick McGuire and Goetz von Peter. 2016. "International Prudential Policy Spillovers: A Global Perspective." *BIS Working Paper* No. 589 (October).

Bartsch, Elga, Agnès Bénassy-Quéré, Giancarlo Corsetti, and Xavier Debrun. 2020. "How Can Monetary and Fiscal Policies Work or Fail Together?" *Geneva Reports on the World Economy* 23.

Basu, Suman, Emine Boz, Gita Gopinath, Francisco Roch, and Filiz Unsal. 2020. "A Conceptual Model for the Integrated Policy Framework." *IMF Working Paper* No. 20/121.

Belkhir, Mohamed, Sami Ben Naceur, Bertrand Candelon, and Jean-Charles Wijnandts. 2020. "Macroprudential Policies, Economic Growth, and Banking Crises." *IMF Working Paper* No. 20/65.

Bergant, Katharina, Francesco Grigoli, Niels-Jakob Hansen, and Damiano Sandri. 2020. "Dampening Global Financial Shocks: Can Macroprudential Regulation Help (More than Capital Controls)?" *CEPR Discussion Paper* DP14948.

Bergant, Katharina and Kristin Forbes. 2022. "Policy Packages and Policy Space: Lessons from COVID-19." Mimeo.

Bernanke, Ben. 2020. "The New Tools of Monetary Policy." *American Economic Review* 110(4): 943–983.

Bertaut, Carol, Valentina Bruno and Hyun Song Shin. 2021. "Original Sin Redux." Working Paper available at: https://papers.ssrn.com/sol3/papers.cfm?abstract_id=3820755.

Bhattarai, Saroj, Arpita Chatterjee, and Woong Yong Park. 2020. "Global Spillover Effect of US Uncertainty." *Journal of Monetary Economics* 114(October): 71–89.

Bianchi, Javier, and Enrique Mendoza. 2018. Optimal Time-Consistent Macroprudential Policy. *Journal of Political Economy* 126: 588–634.

Borio, Claudio, Marc Farag and Nikola Tarashev. 2020. "Post-crisis International Regulatory Reforms: A Primer." *BIS Working Papers* No. 859, April.

Brunnermeier Markus, Thomas Eisenbach, and Yuliy Sannikov. 2013. "Macroeconomics with Financial Frictions: A Survey." In *Advances in Economics and Econometrics: Tenth World Congress of the Econometric Society*, Vol. III, ed. D Acemoglu, M Arellano, E Dekel, pp. 3–94. Cambridge, UK: Cambridge University Press.

Bruno, Valentina, Ilhyock Shim, and Hyun Song Shin. 2017. "Comparative Assessment of Macroprudential Policies." *Journal of Financial Stability* 28(Feb): 183–202.

Buch, Claudia and Linda Goldberg. 2017. "Cross-Border Prudential Policy Spillovers: How Much? How Important? Evidence from the International Banking Research Network." *International Journal of Central Banking* 48(March): 505–558.

Caballero, Ricardo and Alp Simsek. 2019. "Prudential Monetary Policy." *NBER Working Paper* 25977.

Cavallino, Paolo and Damiano Sandri. 2020. "The Open-Economy ELB: Contractionary Monetary Easing and the Trilemma." *CEPR Discussion Paper* DP14683.

Cerutti, Eugenio, Stijn Claessens, and Luc Laeven. 2017. "The Use and Effectiveness of Macroprudential Policies: New Evidence," *Journal of Financial Stability* 28: 203–224.

Chari, Anusha, Karlye Dilts-Stedman, and Kristin Forbes. 2021. "Spillovers at the Extremes: The Macroprudential Stance and Vulnerability to the Global Financial Cycle." NBER Chapters, in: *NBER International Seminar on Macroeconomics 2021*, National Bureau of Economic Research.

Claessens, Stijn. 2015. "An Overview of Macroprudential Tools." *Annual Review of Financial Economics* 7: 397–422.

Claessens, Stijn, Swati Ghosh, and Roxana Mihet. 2013. "Macro-prudential Policies to Mitigate Financial System Vulnerabilities." *Journal of International Money and Finance* 39: 153–185.

Drautzburg, Thorsten and Harald Uhlig. 2015. "Fiscal Stimulus and Distortionary Taxation." *Review of Economic Dynamics* 18(4): 894–920.

Edge, Rochelle and J. Nellie Liang. 2017. "New Financial Governance Structures and Central Banks." *Hutchins Center Working Paper* #32.

Eggertsson, Gauti. 2011. "What Fiscal Policy is Effective at Zero Interest Rates?" *NBER Macroeconomics Annual* 25(1): 59–112.

Engel, Charles. 2016. "Macroprudential Policy in a World of High Capital Mobility: Policy Implications from an Academic Perspective." *Journal of the Japanese and International Economies* 42(Dec): 162–172.

English, William, Kristin Forbes and Angel Ubide. 2021. *Monetary Policy and Central Banking in the Covid Era*. CEPR ebook, introductory chapter. Available at: https://voxeu.org/content/monetary-policy-and-central-banking-covid-era.

Fernandez, Andrés, Michael Klein, Alessandro Rebucci, Martin Schindler, and Martín Uribe. 2016. "Capital Control Measures: A New Dataset." *IMF Economic Review* 64: 548–574.

Forbes, Kristin. 2021. "The International Aspects of Macroprudential Policy." *Annual Review of Economics* 13(August): 203–228.

Forbes, Kristin. 2019. "Macroprudential Policy: What We've Learned, Don't Know, and Need to Do." *American Economic Review Papers and Proceedings* 109(May): 470–475.

Forbes, Kristin, Dennis Reinhardt, Tomas Wieladek. 2017. "The Spillovers, Interactions, and (Un)intended Consequences of Monetary and Regulatory Policies." *Journal of Monetary Economics* 85: 1–22.

Fratto, Chiara, Brendon Harnoys Vannier, Borislava Mircheva, David de Padua, Hélène Poirson. 2021. "Unconventional Monetary Policies in Emerging Markets and Frontier Countries." *IMF Working Paper* No. 2021/014.

Furman, Jason and Larry Summers. (2020). "A Reconsideration of Fiscal Policy in the Era of Low Interest Rates." Working Paper, available at: https://www.piie.com/system/files/documents/furman-summers2020-12-01paper.pdf

Galati, Gabriele, and Ricchild Moessner. 2018. "What Do We Know About the Effects of Macroprudential Policy?" *Economica* 85 (340): 735–770.

Ghosh, Atish, Jun Kim, Enrique Mendoza, Jonathan Ostry, and Mahvash Qureshi. 2013. "Fiscal Fatigue, Fiscal Space and Debt Sustainability in Advanced Economics." *The Economic Journal* 123(Feb): F4–F30.

Ghosh, Atish, Jonathan D. Ostry, and Mahvash S. Qureshi. 2017. "Managing the Tide: How Do Emerging Markets Respond to Capital Flows?" *IMF Working Paper* No. 17/69.

Gruss, Bertrand and Suhaib Kebhaj. 2019. "Commodity Terms of Trade: A New Database." *IMF Working Paper* No. 19/21.

Han, Xuehui and Shang-Jin Wei. 2018. "International Transmissions of Monetary Shocks: Between a Trilemma and a Dilemma." *Journal of International Economics* 110: 205–219.

Hanson, Samuel, Anil Kashyap, Jeremy Stein. 2011. "A Macroprudential Approach to Financial Regulation." *Journal of Economic Perspectives* 25(1): 3–28.

Ilzetzki, Ethan, Carmen Reinhart, and Kenneth Rogoff. 2019. "Exchange Arrangements Entering the Twenty-first Century: Which Anchor will Hold?" *The Quarterly Journal of Economics* 134(2): 599–646.

Jordà, Òscar, Moritz Schularick, and Alan M. Taylor. 2016. "Sovereigns versus Banks: Credit, Crises, and Consequences." *Journal of the European Economic Association* 14(1): 45–79.

Kohn, Donald. 2017. "Cooperation and Coordination across Policy Domains." *Bank of England Speech,* 19 September.

Kose, M. Ayhan, Sergio Kurlat, Franziska Ohnsorge, and Naotaka Sugawara. 2017. "A Cross-Country Database of Fiscal Space." *World Bank Policy Research Working Paper* 8157.

Krippner, Leo. 2015. *Zero Lower Bound Term Structure Modeling: A Practitioner's Guide*. New York, New York: Palgrave-Macmillan.

Kuttner, Kenneth and Ilhyock Shim. 2016. "Can Non-Interest Rate Policies Stabilize Housing Markets? Evidence from a Panel of 57 Economies." *Journal of Financial Stability* 26(October): 31–44.

Lim, Cheng Hoon, Francesco Columba, Alejo Costa, Piyabha Kongsamut, Akira Otani, Mustafa Saiyid, Torsten Wezel, and X. Wu. 2011. "Macroprudential Policy: What Instruments and How to Use Them? Lessons from Country Experiences." *IMF Working Paper* No. 11/238.

Martin, Alberto, Caterina Mendicino, and Alejandro Van der Ghote. 2021. "On the Interaction Between Monetary and Macroprudential Policies." *ECB Working Paper* No. 2527.

Obstfeld, Maurice, Jay Shambaugh, and Alan Taylor. 2005. "The Trilemma in History: Tradeoffs among Exchange Rates, Monetary Policies, and Capital Mobility." *Review of Economics and Statistics* 87(3): 423–438.

Reinhardt, Dennis and Rhiannon Sowerbutts. 2015. "Regulatory Arbitrage in Action: Evidence from Banking Flows and Macroprudential Policy." *Bank of England Working Paper* No. 546.

Richter, Bjorn, Moritz Schularick, and Ilhyock Shim. 2019. "The Costs of Macroprudential Policy." *Journal of International Economics* 118(2): 263–282.

Romer, Christina and David Romer. 2018. "Why Some Times Are Different: Macroeconomic Policy and the Aftermath of Financial Crises." *Economica* 85(337): 1–40.

Romer, Christina and David Romer. 2019. "Fiscal Space and the Aftermath of Financial Crises: How it Matters and Why." *Brookings Papers on Economic Activity*. Spring: 239–331.

Shim, Ilhyock, Bilyana Bogdanova, Jimmy Shek, and Agne Subelyte. 2013. "A Database for Policy Actions on Housing Markets." *BIS Quarterly Review*, September: 83–95.

Woodford, Michael. 2011. "Simple Analytics of the Government Expenditure Multiplier." *American Economic Journal: Macroeconomics* 3(1): 1–35.

© 2023 World Scientific Publishing Company
https://doi.org/10.1142/9789811259432_0009

Macroprudential Policy during COVID-19: The Role of Policy Space: A Discussion

Valentina Bruno

Kogod School of Business
American University

Macroprudential polices (or "macro-pru") have become a popular tool to address systemic risk especially after the Global Financial Crisis (GFC). South Korea is one example of macro-pru being successfully in action. In June 2010, South Korea introduced a series of macroprudential measures aimed at moderating the procyclicality of the banking sector, especially cross-border banking sector liabilities (Bruno and Shin, 2014). In the chapter, Bergant and Forbes use the COVID-19 event as a natural experiment to examine how more than a decade of macro-pru policies have performed in the presence of an exogenous shock. Bergant and Forbes use a comprehensive dataset that combines three macro-pru tools (countercyclical capital buffer, loan-to-value-ratio and FX intervention), augmented with the most recent macro-pru adjustments. The study is a timely and very important work that highlights differences in macro-pru preparedness across countries.

Before delving into the findings, it is important to provide some background. The COVID-19 shock was significantly different from the 2007–2008 shock because it did not originate from the banking sector, and the banking sector itself had proven resilient during the COVID-19 shock.

Macro-pru gets a lot of credit in strengthening the capital and liquidity positions of banks. For instance, the leverage of broker dealers, one of the culprits of the GFC, has dropped by more than half since the onset of the 2007 crisis. However, risk has progressively evolved and moved from banks to non-banks in several ways. Easy financial conditions have fuelled the build-up of leverage and currency mismatches of firms. Non-financial firms have behaved like financial firms by providing credit domestically (Bruno and Shin, 2020a). Another example is related to the March 2020 stress in the US Treasury market. Since 2018, some investors had taken increasing leveraged positions in some government bond markets, to seek arbitrage differences in the basis trade. The basis trade came undone in March during the dash for cash (Schrimpf *et al.*, 2020), when hedge funds engaged in basis trades significantly unwound their positions (Barth and Kahn, 2021). The Federal Reserve intervention in the Treasury and repo markets helped restore financial stability.

The COVID-19 shock was also significantly different from the previous episodes of financial distress in emerging markets characterised by the cliché of capital outflows and US dollar appreciation. The Federal Reserve and other central banks intervened massively to alleviate the stress in the financial sector. The Federal Reserve dollar swap facilities were particularly important in restoring liquidity in the dollar funding market. All in all, the central bank responses helped ease financial conditions and curbed US dollar appreciation. Figure 1 shows how financial conditions during the COVID-19 event were significantly different from the past episodes. As a result, emerging market economies were able to loosen monetary policy aggressively.

In the context of the above background, Bergant and Forbes find that macro-pru has been used effectively. Countries that tightened macro-pru policy more aggressively before COVID-19 had lower levels of financial stress (measured by the increase in CDS spreads) and lower levels of economic stress. However, there seems to be little relationship between a country's use of macro-pru and other policies, and the space to use other policies did not affect the use of macro-pru (and vice versa). This observation resembles the evidence in Bruno *et al.* (2017) who find that non-interest rate monetary policy tools were used in a complementary way with monetary policy during the first phase of

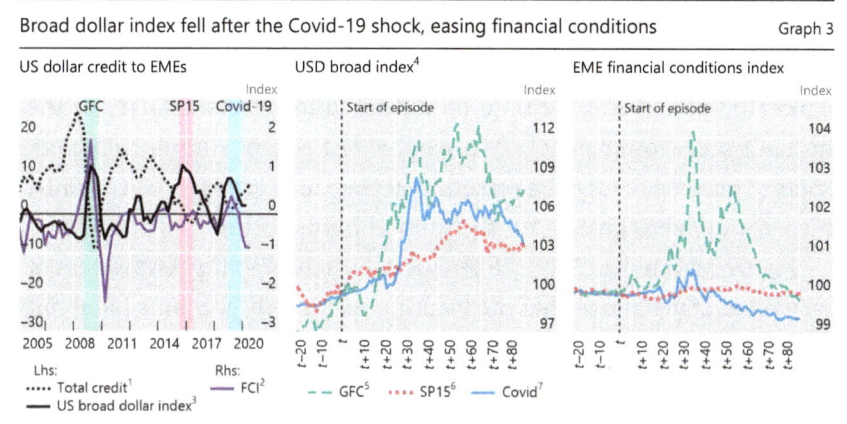

Broad dollar index fell after the Covid-19 shock, easing financial conditions   Graph 3

[Graph: US dollar credit to EMEs; USD broad index⁴; EME financial conditions index]

Lhs:
····· Total credit¹
—— US broad dollar index³

Rhs:
—— FCI²

– – GFC⁵   ····· SP15⁶   —— Covid⁷

¹ Annual growth of USD-denominated credit to non-banks in EMEs. ² Annual growth of trade-weighted broad USD index. Higher values correspond to an appreciation of the dollar. ³ Annual growth of the Goldman Sachs Financial Conditions Index defined as a weighted average of riskless interest rates, the exchange rate, equity valuations and credit spreads, with weights that correspond to the direct impact of each variable on GDP. Higher values represent a tightening in financial conditions. Average of financial conditions index of BR, CL, CZ, HU, ID, IN, MX, MY, PH, PL, RU, TH, TR and ZA. ⁴ Time measured in days. Index = 100 in t. Shaded area corresponds to duration of the stress episode. Each episode lasts three months. ⁵ 7 Sep 2008. ⁶ 1 Nov 2015. ⁷ 2 Feb 2020.

Sources: Federal Reserve Bank of St Louis, FRED; Bloomberg; Consensus Economics; Datastream; Dealogic; Euroclear; Thomson Reuters; Xtrakter Ltd; national data; BIS locational banking statistics; BIS effective exchange rate statistics; BIS calculations.

Figure 1.   Broad dollar index fell after the COVID-19 shock, easing financial conditions.
Source: Aguilar and Cantú (2020)

global liquidity (pre-2007), but less so after 2009. Bruno et al. (2017) argue that when monetary policy and macro-pru measures are pulling in the same direction (opposite directions), banking inflow measures are successful (not successful) in slowing down foreign flows. This happens because, when monetary policy and macroprudential policies pull in the opposite directions, economic agents are being told to borrow more and to borrow less simultaneously.

Bergant and Forbes's core result is that the most important factor determining whether a country eased macro-pru during COVID-19 was if the country had tightened policy before the pandemic. Other factors, such as the extent of financial stress or country characteristics, did not significantly predict the use of macro-pru tools during COVID-19. In perspective, fewer countries eased macro-pru during the Taper Tantrum than during COVID-19. I think it is important to analyse this result in the context of the abovementioned background related to the composition of the financial system and central banks' interventions.

The role of non-banks in the financial sector

Figure 2 shows the ratio of total assets to GDP for all the US commercial banks (top panel) and the ratio of mutual funds assets to GDP for the mutual funds (lower panel). We see that the size of commercial bank assets compared to GDP has essentially plateaued after the GFC, whilst this has not been the case for the mutual funds sector.

Figure 3 from the 2020 IMF Financial System Stability Assessment of the United States shows that the banking sector only accounts for about 20 percent of overall financial system assets in the US, with pension and mutual funds jointly accounting for about 40 percent. Yet, macro-pru policies mostly target the banking sector.

US mutual funds play an important role in emerging markets, too. Figure 4 shows the outstanding market value (in USD billion) of government bonds denominated in local currency by three investor types

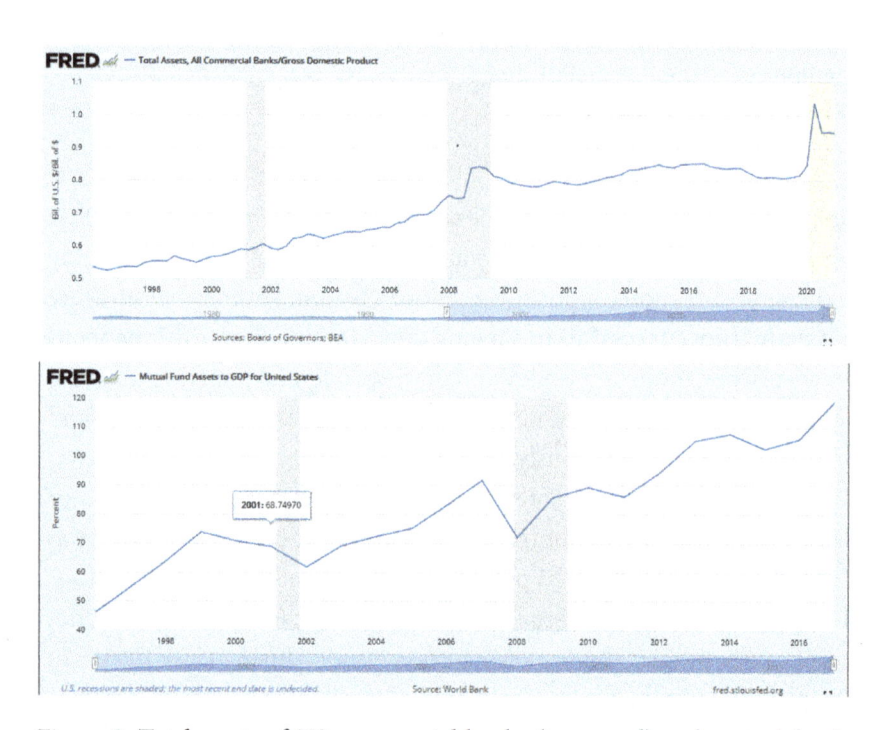

Figure 2. Total assets of US commercial banks (top panel) and mutual funds (bottom panel).
Source: FED FRED.

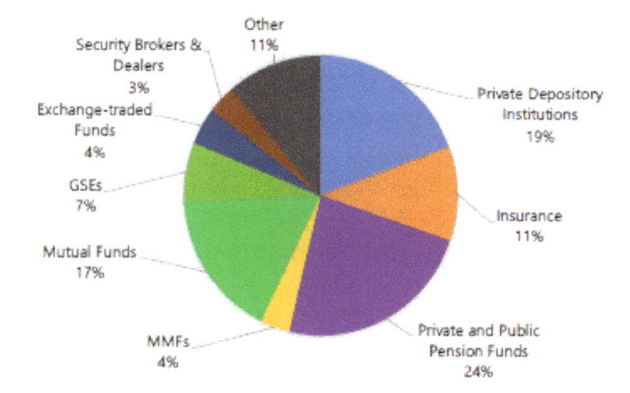

Figure 3. Financial sector composition (in percent of total).
Note: Data as of 2019 Q4. MMF stands for money market funds.
Source: IMF.

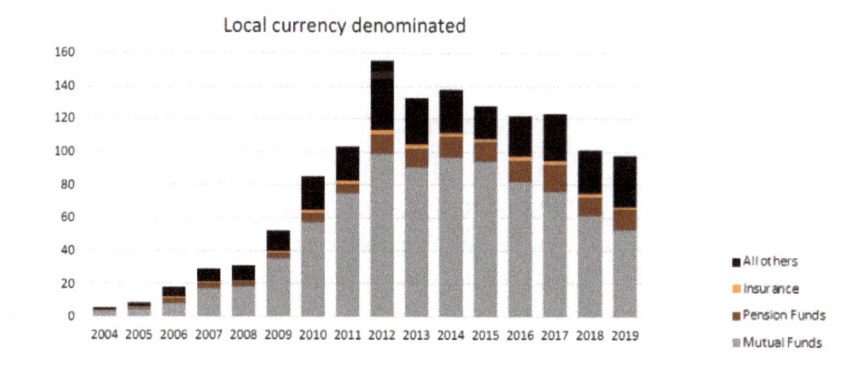

(USD billion)

Figure 4. Mutual funds stand out as the largest holder of EME bonds.
Source: Bertaut *et al.* (2021).

(mutual funds, insurance pension funds). The category "All Others" groups the other investor types (depository institutions, other financials, other funds and non-financial entities). Year 2012 is the high-water mark of US investors' holdings before the period of dollar strength and EME stress between 2013 and 2016. It is striking to observe that more than half of the holdings are by US mutual fund investors. US mutual fund flows go hand in hand with local spread movements.

All in all, the message here is that depository institutions are not the only players both in the US and non-US financial sector. As macro-pru tools mostly target banks, the question on how to reduce systemic risk and financial sector vulnerabilities remains.

The role of the exchange rate for macro-pru

Figure 5 shows the four-quarter growth rates of bank lending in dollars to emerging market borrowers, as well as the four-quarter growth rate of total credit activity. The negative correlation between dollar credit growth and the dollar exchange rate is notable, especially after the GFC. When the dollar is strong, lending in dollars slows. The financial channel of exchange rates (Bruno and Shin, 2015) explains the mechanism behind it. Global banks have a diversified loan portfolio to borrowers around the world. A broad-based depreciation of the dollar results in a lower tail risk in the bank's credit portfolio and a relaxation of the bank's Value-at-Risk (VaR) constraint. The result is an expansion in the supply of dollar credit through increased leverage. In this way, a broad depreciation of the dollar is associated with greater risk-taking by banks — and vice-versa, when the dollar appreciates, credit supply slows.

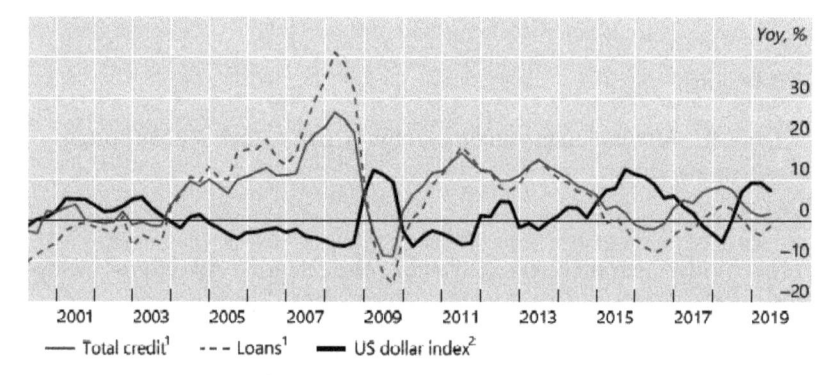

[1] Annual growth of US dollar-denominated credit or loans to non-banks in EMEs.   [2] Annual growth of the Federal Reserve Board trade-weighted nominal dollar index, major EMEs.
Sources: Datastream; Dealogic; Euroclear; FRED; Thomson Reuters; Xtrakter Ltd; national data; BIS locational banking statistics; BIS effective exchange rate statistics; BIS calculations.

Figure 5.   US dollar credit to EMEs.
Source: Bruno and Shin (2020b).

Typically, episodes of financial stress go hand in hand with dollar appreciation, increased risk aversion and tightened financial conditions. The COVID-19 episode was different. The actions of the central banks of advanced economies curbed US dollar appreciation, restored global liquidity and eased financial conditions (see Figure 1). Thanks to these actions, emerging markets were able to ease macro-pru tools to support banks' capacity to lend.

All in all, the message here is that the coordinated policy actions curbed US broad dollar appreciation, calmed the turmoil in financial markets, limited financial stress and created ideal conditions to ease macro-pru policies. Creating macroprudential policy space in advance is important; however, only in the presence of ideal financial conditions will countries be able to use macro-pru actively during a severe negative shock.

Concluding remarks

Whilst it is important to drill down in the macro-pru tools and policy space, it is equally important to understand the context in which these macro-pru actions are originated. The roles of non-banks and of the exchange rate as a global factor show the complexity embedded in the financial system. The events during the turmoil in the US Treasury market are illustrative of how the risk has moved from banks to non-banks. Drilling-up, the expansionary policy action of the Federal Reserve in response to the pandemic (and the subsequent downward trajectory of the dollar) is a very important background feature behind the pandemic experience. The Federal Reserve intervened as the *deus ex-machina* and helped a speedy recovery in global financial conditions.

As Bergant and Forbes demonstrate, macro-pru has been used countercyclically and strengthened the resilience of the financial system. Macro-pru works, but at the same time, we should also reflect on the context in which macro-pru works, on the bigger picture related to the role of non-US banks and, more generally, to the role of the US dollar. Accommodative financial conditions coupled with a weaker dollar — fuelling a greater risk-taking capacity of market participants through the financial channel of exchange rates — help connect the dots during

COVID-19 and put the Federal Reserve at the centre of the mechanism as the international liquidity provider.

References

Aguilar, Ana and Carlos Cantú, 2020, "Monetary Policy Response in Emerging Market Economies: Why Was It Different This Time?" BIS Bulletin #32.

Barth, Daniel and R. Jay Kahn, 2021, "Hedge Funds and the Treasury Cash-Futures Disconnect", OFR Working Paper.

Bertaut, Carol, Valentina Bruno, and Hyun Song Shin, 2021, "Original Sin Redux", Working Paper (available on SSRN).

Bruno, Valentina and Hyun Song Shin, 2014, "Assessing Macroprudential Policies: Case of Korea", *The Scandinavian Journal of Economics* **116**(1), 128–157.

Bruno, Valentina and Hyun Song Shin, 2015, "Cross-Border Banking and Global Liquidity", *Review of Economic Studies* **82**(2): 535–564.

Bruno, Valentina, Ilhyock Shim, and Hyun Song Shin, 2017, "Comparative Assessment of Macroprudential Policies", *Journal of Financial Stability* **28**: 183–202.

Bruno, Valentina and Hyun Song Shin, 2020a, "Currency Depreciation and Emerging Markets Corporate Distress", *Management Science*, **66**(5): 1935–1961.

Bruno, Valentina and Hyun Song Shin, 2020b, "Dollar and Exports", BIS Working Paper 819.

International Monetary Fund, 2020, "United States: Financial System Stability Assessment", Country Report No. 20/242.

Schrimpf, Andreas, Hyun Song Shin, and Vladyslav Sushko, 2020, "Leverage and Margin Spirals in Fixed Income Markets During the Covid-19 Crisis", BIS Bulletin #2.

CHAPTER 5

Chapter 5

Macro-Financial Policy in an International Financial Centre: The UK Experience Since the Global Financial Crisis*

Thorsten Beck,[†,‡] Simon Lloyd,[§] Dennis Reinhardt[§] and Rhiannon Sowerbutts[§]

[†]*Florence School of Banking and Finance, European University Institute*
[‡]*Centre for Economic and Policy Research*
[§]*Bank of England*

Abstract

We describe the macroprudential and monetary policy environment in the UK. We highlight the UK's position as an international financial centre, and the implications for inward and outward spillover effects of monetary and prudential policy actions. These spillovers pose particular opportunities

---

*Any views expressed are solely those of the authors and so cannot be taken to represent those of the Bank of England or to state Bank of England policy. This paper should therefore not be reported as representing the views of the Bank of England or members of the Monetary Policy Committee, Financial Policy Committee or Prudential Regulation Committee. The authors thank Paul Tucker for suggestions in an insightful discussion, as well as attendees of the MAS-BIS Conference 2021 on "Macro-financial Stability Policy in a Globalised Word: Lessons from International Experience". The authors are also grateful to Stuart Berry, Amy Cheung, Richard Harrison, Ed Manuel and Tom Rhodes for useful comments.

and challenges for policymakers, and we explain how they have motivated specific developments to the Bank of England's modelling framework. We also present novel empirical evidence that monetary policy actions in the UK have outward spillover effects through cross-border lending that can, in part, be mitigated by macroprudential actions in receiving countries.

1. Introduction

In the years following the Global Financial Crisis (GFC), policy authorities in the UK have drawn on a range of tools to help maintain financial and monetary stability — the combination of which we henceforth refer to as "macro-financial stability". As in many other countries, these tools were not used prior to the GFC in the UK, and great effort has gone into understanding their transmission mechanisms in the last decade.

The framework for financial stability, in particular, has been overhauled since the GFC, with a host of reforms — including the creation of a resolution regime for banks, structural reforms to the banking sector and the development of the prudential policy toolkit — being undertaken. For this chapter, the most relevant reform has been the creation of a Financial Policy Committee (FPC) of the Bank of England to oversee the stability of the financial system as a whole, thus taking a systemic view. Alongside this, powers of individual bank supervision, which were previously based in a separate institution, were moved to the Bank of England's Prudential Regulation Authority (PRA).

Focusing on the Bank's financial stability objective, the FPC sets macroprudential policy in the UK. To date, their primary policy tool has been the countercyclical capital buffer (CCyB). The FPC sets the UK CCyB rate so that banks and certain investment firms hold an amount of capital in proportion to their UK real-sector exposures. The FPC has also used tools in the housing market to limit the build-up of aggregate debt. Recent years have seen innovations to the CCyB — in particular, the issuance of forward guidance on the CCyB from March 2020 in the context of the COVID-19 pandemic emergency measures.

While the institutional setup for monetary policy has not undergone such a marked overhaul since the GFC, the Bank's Monetary Policy

Committee (MPC) has gone beyond traditional short-term policy rates — which first reached historically low levels in March 2009 and, in more recent years, have been lowered further. The "unconventional" monetary policy tools used by the MPC encompass purchases of government bonds on the secondary market, corporate bond purchases and forward guidance about the future path of the monetary policy rate.

These macroprudential and monetary policy tools are set against the backdrop of the UK as an International Financial Centre (IFC), hosting major financial activities, with a significant share performed by foreign international banking groups. The UK's position as an IFC, with links to the rest of the world, creates opportunities and challenges for the macro-financial policy framework. On the one hand, changes to the global economic environment could affect the economy and financial stability of the UK through UK-based banks' exposures to vulnerable economies, as well as broader macroeconomic spillovers, such as trade and asset prices. On the other hand, the economic events in the UK can generate spillovers to the rest of the world and, in turn, spillbacks that impact the UK.

With such a global reach, the safety and openness of the world economy, and international financial stability more broadly, are of primary importance for UK macro-financial stability. In the years after the GFC, the preservation of this "public good" has required a commitment to institution building both internationally and domestically (Bailey, 2021). The global Financial Stability Board (FSB), with a mandate to promote international financial stability underpinned by strong regulation, has been supported by other standard-setting bodies — including the Basel Committee for banks, IOSCO for markets, the IAIS for insurance, and the CPMI for payment and markets infrastructure. In addition to contributions to these global bodies, the Bank of England has sought to develop its own modelling tools to account for the influence of global conditions on the UK's macro-financial outlook when setting its policy tools.

The backdrop of global interconnectedness leaves open the possibility that UK policy tools, such as its monetary and macroprudential measures, could interact with similar tools used elsewhere. For example, a policy action in the UK, with the aim of improving financial-sector resilience domestically, may have additional effects abroad that could, in turn, spill back to the UK — amplified or dampened by policy actions abroad. These global policy interactions are the subject of a nascent academic literature, to which our work contributes.

In this chapter, we survey the UK's macro-financial policy framework, discussing how the UK's position as an IFC has influenced its policymaking framework and analysing the relevance of global policy interactions. We do so, first, by outlining the UK's recent experience in deploying macroprudential and monetary policies to maintain domestic financial and price stability — in particular in the years following the GFC up to the COVID-19 pandemic. We then discuss the modelling tools that have been developed to help analyse risks arising from international spillovers and spillbacks. We then provide novel evidence to assess the spillover effects of UK policies through UK banks' cross-border lending and study how UK policies interact with other policies enacted abroad.

Formally, we study how changes in UK monetary policy can generate spillovers through UK-based banks' external lending. Tighter UK monetary policy is associated with a sizeable reduction in cross-border lending from the UK. However, we find that this spillover is materially offset by prudential policy actions in destination countries, helping to insulate them partially from these spillovers.

The remainder of this chapter is structured as follows. In Section 2, we discuss the institutional and political economy background for monetary and macroprudential policies in the UK. Specifically, we discuss the role of MPC, FPC and PRA in policymaking and their interaction (including through overlapping committee membership). In Section 3, we focus on the UK's role as an IFC, with a large number of cross-border bank subsidiaries and branches and a high share of cross-border lending. Section 4 offers a literature survey on the global spillover effects of monetary and prudential policy actions. Section 5 presents empirical evidence on the outward spillover effects of UK monetary policy actions and the role of prudential policy in mitigating their impact. Section 6 concludes.

2. Monetary and macroprudential policy in the UK

This section describes the institutional framework within which the Bank of England sets macroprudential and monetary policy, highlighting some of the institutional changes within the supervisory architecture and major policy actions taken by the Bank's Committees since the GFC.

While the capital of the Bank is held by the Treasury Solicitor on behalf of HM Treasury, it is usually considered to be an operationally independent Central Bank, free from everyday government interference. This has been reinforced in the Bank of England Act 1998, which defines the Bank's objectives. The Act covers, amongst other things, the Bank's monetary and financial stability objectives.

In relation to monetary policy, the Bank has a mandate to maintain price stability — currently defined as targeting consumer price index inflation at 2 percent. With relation to financial policy, the FPC is charged with contributing to UK financial stability primarily by identifying, monitoring and taking action to remove or reduce systemic risks with a view to protecting and enhancing the resilience of the UK financial system. In addition, for both monetary and financial policy, the Bank has a secondary objective to support the economic policy of the UK government, including its objectives for growth and employment.

The functions that underpin these objectives are principally, but not entirely, discharged by the MPC and the FPC — which we focus on in this chapter — as well as the PRA. While the PRA took over microprudential supervision from the Financial Services Authority (FSA) in 2012, the FPC focuses on macroprudential oversight. Although each Committee is independent of one another, there is significant overlap in membership and all three are chaired by the Governor of the Bank of England. This institutional structure, and array of available policy tools for financial stability, was formed after the GFC in the context of the Basel III process. The Bank forms part of the Basel Committee of Bank Supervision and the FSB.

The institutional structure provides for independent decision structures and processes across monetary, macroprudential and microprudential policies, in line with arguments that:

(1) consolidating responsibilities in one institution can help to avoid coordination failure and account for the interdependence of the policies;
(2) monetary policy authorities can benefit from supervisory information when forming monetary policy decisions; and

(3) supervisors can benefit from the independence and reputation of the central bank in a consolidated structure.

Other countries (e.g., some of the Nordic countries) have independent monetary and prudential authorities, based on arguments that:

(1) the reputation of the central bank and, in turn, its credibility and effectiveness could be negatively impacted by damages to the reputation of the supervisor following bank failures; and
(2) there could be distortions in decision-making, such as deviation from the optimal conduct of monetary policy in an attempt to preserve the stability of financial institutions.

Having separate Committees with individual policymaking responsibilities, like the Bank, can help to address this second concern.[1]

2.1. *Monetary policy*

The MPC was founded in 1997 and granted operational responsibility to set policy instruments to achieve its inflation target by the Chancellor of the Exchequer. The Committee comprises nine members — the Governor, the three Deputy Governors for Monetary Policy, Financial Stability, and Money and Banking, the Chief Economist and four external members appointed directly by the Chancellor. A non-voting representative from HM Treasury attends the MPC's policy meetings as an observer.

There are eight scheduled MPC meetings each year, though additional meetings can be held at any time if warranted. The MPC sets the Bank's monetary policy tools, by majority vote, at these meetings. Bank staff brief the Committee on the latest data and analysis on the economy — including an assessment of the global economy and the channels through which global events might spill over to the UK — ahead of their policy decision.[2] In its early years, the Committee voted solely on the level of the Bank of England base rate (Bank Rate). Figure 1 plots the path of Bank Rate since

---

[1] For a comprehensive discussion and literature survey, see Ampudia *et al.* (2019).
[2] The MPC has met eight times a year since 2015, but prior to this it met more frequently.

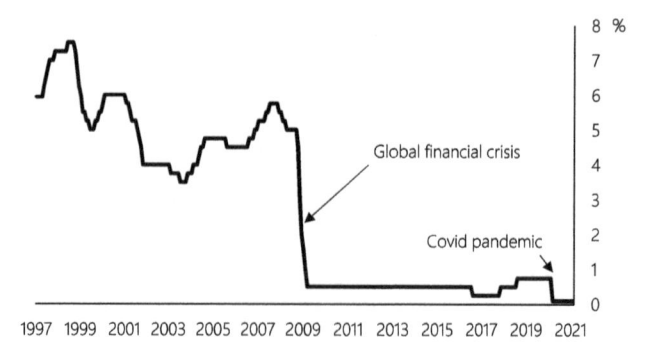

Figure 1. UK official Bank Rate history.
Source: Bank of England.

the MPC's creation in mid-1997. While there have been changes to the monetary framework over the years, in the current system Bank Rate determines the interest rate paid to commercial banks with accounts at the Bank of England. In turn, a change in Bank Rate can transmit to the macroeconomy by influencing other interest rates in the economy and thus altering incentives for households and businesses to consume and invest.[3]

As was the case in other major advanced economies, the GFC motivated innovations to the UK's monetary policy framework in order to achieve the MPC's remit. As Figure 1 shows, the MPC cut Bank Rate significantly. In March 2009, it reached the then-historical low level of 0.5 percent, spurring the development of "unconventional" monetary policies aimed at providing additional monetary stimulus by lowering long-term interest rates when the short-term policy rate was at, or close to, its effective lower bound.

Quantitative easing (QE) — large-scale purchases of financial assets financed by the creation of central bank reserves — was a major component of the Bank's unconventional policy toolkit, first introduced in March 2009. The MPC made £200bn of asset purchases during 2009–2010, with UK government bonds (gilts) making up the vast majority of assets purchased. These gilts were purchased on secondary bond markets, predominantly from dealers acting on behalf of non-bank

---

[3] The "monetary transmission mechanism", which summarises how changes in Bank rate can influence the macroeconomy, is described in Bank of England (1999).

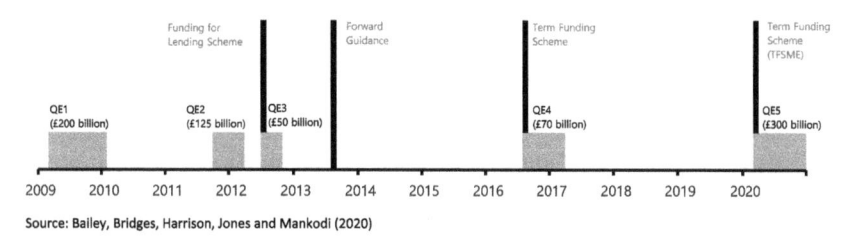

Figure 2. A timeline of Bank of England unconventional monetary policies. *Source*: Bailey et al. (2020)

private sector institutions such as insurance companies and pension funds. Figure 2 summarises subsequent rounds of QE enacted by the Bank, including additional purchases in August 2016 following the EU withdrawal referendum.

In response to the economic disruption from the COVID-19 pandemic, the MPC extended its QE programme further from March 2020. This accompanied a Bank Rate cut to 0.1 percent, a new historical low, as well as coordinated policy action by the FPC — discussed in Box 1. At the start of 2021, the total stock of assets purchased as part of the Bank's QE programme stood at £745bn, including both government and corporate bonds.

2.2. Macroprudential policy

With primary responsibility for protecting and enhancing the resilience of the UK financial system to systemic risks, the Bank's FPC has powers to set a range of macroprudential tools, including powers of recommendation to reduce risks to financial stability.[4] The Committee was formed in the aftermath of the GFC, modelled on the MPC, as part of a new system of regulation to improve financial stability after the crisis. The FPC normally has 13 members. Six of them are Bank of England staff: the Governor, four Deputy Governors and the Executive Director for Financial Stability Strategy and Risk, five external members,

---

[4] Formally, the FPC has powers of direction in respect of sectoral capital requirements for UK firms, a leverage ratio requirement for UK firms, loan-to-value and debt-to-income limits for UK mortgages on owner-occupied properties and loan-to-value and cover ratio limits for UK mortgages on buy-to-let properties.

the Chief Executive of the Financial Conduct Authority (FCA) and one non-voting member from HM Treasury.

An interim FPC first met on a quarterly basis in June 2011, although the Committee was granted its powers in 2013 following amendments made to the Bank of England Act 1998 by the Financial Services Act 2012. Like the MPC, the FPC is briefed by Bank staff — on, amongst other things, the key systemic risks to the UK, including an assessment of global risks and the channels through which these might spillover to the UK — ahead of their policy decision.

Since 2016, the FPC has set a CCyB rate for the UK, with the primary objective of ensuring that the banking system is able to withstand stress without restricting essential services, such as the supply of credit, to the real economy. The FPC's task is not to achieve resilience at any cost.[5] The buffer is therefore intended to be varied — both up and down — in line with systemic risk in the banking system. By increasing the CCyB when risks are judged to be increasing, banks have an additional cushion of capital with which to absorb potential losses, enhancing their resilience and helping to ensure the stable provision of financial intermediation services. When credit conditions weaken, the CCyB can be reduced to free-up capital for banks, mitigating a potential contraction in the supply of lending to households and businesses. The FPC aims to act early and change the CCyB gradually, thus reducing its economic costs in terms of lending. Banks will, in general, have 12 months after the FPC decides to increase the buffer before the higher rate must be used for calculating institution-specific capital buffers. A decision to decrease the CCyB, on the other hand, takes effect immediately.

The CCyB applies to all banks, building societies and investment firms (other than those exempted by the FCA) incorporated in the UK on their relevant UK exposures and is applied at both individual entity and consolidated group levels. Reciprocity provisions apply also to internationally active banks in jurisdictions that have implemented the Basel III regulatory standards. At the same time, the Bank of England reciprocates other countries' CCyB rates on UK banks' foreign exposures.

---

[5] Its actions should not, in the provisions of the Financial Services Act 2012, have "a significant adverse effect on the capacity of the financial sector to contribute to the growth of the UK in the medium or long term".

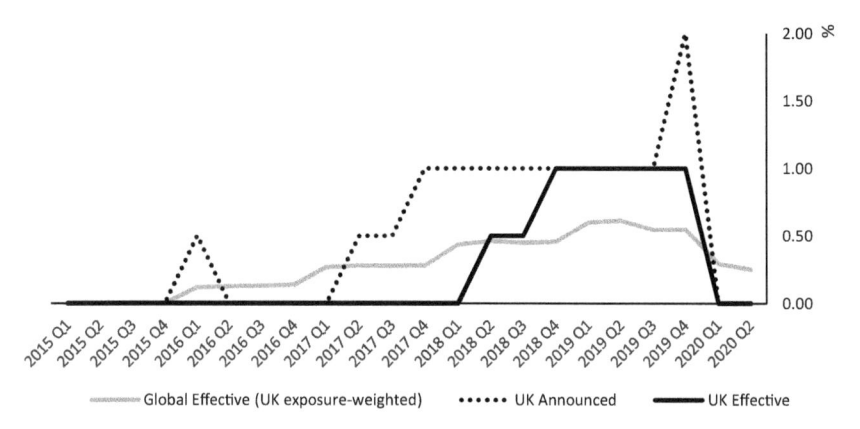

Figure 3. The UK CCyB rate in global context.
Note: Effective CCyB rates. Information up to 2020 Q2. The global (excluding the UK) effective rate are foreign CCyB's weighted by UK-owned banks consolidated exposures to the non-bank non-financial sector in foreign countries.
Source: ESRB, HKMA, BIS, national authorities' websites.

Figure 3 presents a history of the announced and effective UK CCyB rate in a global context.[6] The countercyclical nature of the buffer has been demonstrated on two occasions in the UK. First, following the UK referendum, the planned 0.5 percentage point increase in the rate was reversed in July 2016, with the announced rate returning to 0 percent. In June 2017, the FPC raised the UK CCyB rate from 0 percent to 0.5 percent and in November 2017 to 1 percent. In December 2019, a further increase to 2 percent (effective December 2020) was announced. In March 2020, however, the FPC decided to reduce the rate to zero, as part of a coordinated package of pandemic crisis measures adopted by the Bank of England (see Box 1).

The UK CCyB rate only applies to relevant UK credit exposures. This means that an increase in the UK CCyB does not fully pass through to an increase in capital requirements. The particularly international nature of the UK banking system means that a 1 percent increase in the UK CCyB rate leads to an increase of around 0.4 percent in capital requirements on average. There is obviously considerable heterogeneity for individual

---

[6] Owing to a one-year implementation lag, not all of the announced UK CCyB rate announcements have applied in practice.

banks in the UK with some — particularly the small building societies — being highly UK-focused while other UK banks are much more globally focused.

In addition to the CCyB, the FPC has also recommended measures on mortgages. Notably an affordability test for mortgages based on an interest rate stress and a portfolio limit of 15 percent on the number of mortgages that can be extended at a loan-to-income (LTI) ratio of 4.5 or greater.

In addition to formal powers such as the CCyB and its LTI limits, the FPC has also been active in a number of areas through its regular communications and coordination with other Committees and regulators. For example, in July 2016, the FPC and MPC held a joint meeting on the leverage ratio in July 2016 (discussed in Box 2), and coordinated their responses to the Covid pandemic in 2020 (see Box 1). More recently, the FPC has been working closely with the FCA, HM Treasury and counterparts in the FSB to develop common approaches to enhance the resilience of the non-bank financial system.

Box 1: Coordinated policy actions to respond to COVID-19 shock in 2020

While the three committees take decisions independently, the overlap in membership allows close coordination in crisis times, such as in March 2020, when the three committees took a number of complementary policy actions to address the economic fallout from the COVID-19 pandemic. Specifically, the MPC reduced the Bank Rate by 50 basis points to 0.25 percent and introduced a new Term Funding scheme with additional incentives for small and medium-sized enterprises, financed by the issuance of central bank reserves. The FPC reduced the UK countercyclical capital buffer rate to 0 percent of banks' exposures to UK borrowers with immediate effect (from previously 1 percent and reversing a further increase to 2 percent scheduled for December 2020). At the time, the FPC also provided "forward-guidance" that it expected to maintain the 0 percent rate for at least 12 months, so that any subsequent increase would not take effect until March 2022 at the earliest. Finally, the PRA set out expectations that all elements of banks' capital and liquidity buffers can be drawn down as necessary to support the economy, while at the same time banks should not increase dividends or other distributions, such as bonuses, in response to these policy actions.

> **Box 1: (*Continued*)**
>
> The joint announcement of these decisions by the three committees signalled to markets that the different authorities are cognisant of the impending risks of the pandemic for the economy and a certain element of "whatever it takes" in their response. It also reassured observers of a common and coordinated policy response that clearly takes into account the interactions of prudential and monetary policy actions.
>
> The joint response by the different policy committees of the Bank of England mirrors that of other authorities. For example, the Governing Council of the ECB announced additional longer-term refinancing operations and more favourable terms for the targeted longer-term refinancing operations, starting in June 2020, additional asset purchases and a continued commitment to extraordinarily low interest rates the same day as the Supervisory Board of the ECB announced that banks under its direct supervision can fully use capital and liquidity buffers, including Pillar 2 Guidance.

2.3. Bank supervision

The Bank supervises individual banks through the PRA. The PRA's general objective is to promote the safety and soundness of PRA-regulated firms, and in advancing that objective the PRA must seek to ensure that firms carry out their business in a way which avoids any adverse effect on the stability of the UK financial system, and seek to minimise such an impact from a firm's failure. The PRA has a secondary objective to facilitate, insofar as reasonably possible, effective competition in the markets for services provided by PRA-authorised persons in carrying on regulated activities.

The Prudential Regulation Committee of the PRA consists of the Governor of the Bank of England, Deputy Governors for Financial Stability, Markets and Banking, and Prudential Regulation, the Chief Executive of the FCA, a member appointed by the Governor with the approval of the Chancellor and five other external members appointed by the Chancellor.

Box 2: Changes to the leverage ratio: An example of macroprudential and monetary policy interaction

Since 2015 the FPC has had powers of direction over the leverage ratio. This included a minimum leverage ratio, a leverage ratio buffer for systemically important banks and a countercyclical leverage ratio buffer.

At its meeting on 1 July 2016, following the referendum on leaving the European Union, the FPC agreed in principle that central bank reserves should be excluded from the measure of exposures used to calculate banks' leverage ratios.

The FPC had been reviewing the leverage ratio and considered that there was a potential macroeconomic cost to including central bank reserves in the leverage ratio because it could affect the ability of the banking system to cushion shocks and draw on central bank liquidity facilities. In addition, in circumstances where central bank balance sheets expanded, for example via QE, regulatory leverage requirements could effectively tighten.

In the market turmoil after the referendum, this issue became more relevant. Central bank reserves could have increased as a result of the Bank's additional indexed long-term repo operations — which gave banks the ability to exchange certain less liquid assets for liquidity from central bank reserves, or if banks had chosen to use their pre-positioned collateral to take advantage of the Bank's additional liquidity facilities. In addition, future decisions by the MPC (who had not yet been able to meet) over the expansion of QE could also lead to an increase in reserves. All of these could have led to a tightening in the leverage ratio constraint for banks via an increase in reserves.

However, announcing this exclusion of central bank reserves from the leverage ratio could have been interpreted as a signal of the future path of monetary policy. While there is considerable overlap between members of the FPC and MPC, monetary policy is not in the FPC's remit. Ahead of their policy announcement on 12 July 2016, the FPC scheduled an additional joint meeting with the MPC on 6 July 2016 to discuss the issue. The decision was taken to exclude the discussion on central bank reserves from the original FPC Record — published on 12 July 2016 — and in its Financial Stability Report — published on the same date. Instead, the decision was published after the MPC's decisions were announced on 4 August 2016.

3. The UK's position as an international financial centre

While the decisions of the MPC and FPC are made within their respective remits, the UK's position as a major IFC is an important feature of the environment in which the Committees set their policy tools. The UK financial services industry — spanning financial institutions and associated professional services — is a particularly sizeable component of the UK economy, both in terms of GDP contribution (6.9 percent in 2019) as in terms of total assets (five times GDP).

The UK's role as an IFC means that it is highly connected with the rest of the world. These connections also go beyond service trade linkages. The UK is host to over 200 international banks, and UK-based banks — spanning foreign branches and subsidiaries — have over US$5 trillion in cross-border claims. The UK stands out amongst other international banking hubs with the highest cross-border claims (Figure 4), and the cross-border lending of UK-based banks spans a wide range of countries (Figure 5). In addition, almost 50 percent of assets are held by foreign-owned banks, compared to less than 20 percent in the US or 4 percent in Japan. These foreign affiliates undertake a multitude of different activities, in particular investment banking and trading, but also cross-border lending.

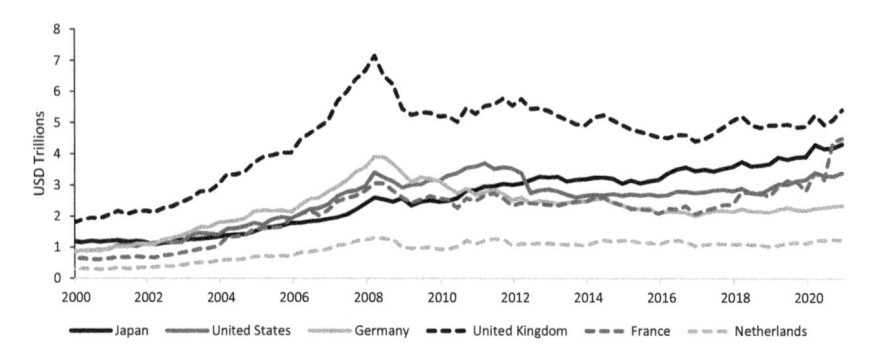

Figure 4. Total cross-border claims of major international financial centres.
Source: Bank for International Settlements International Banking Statistics.

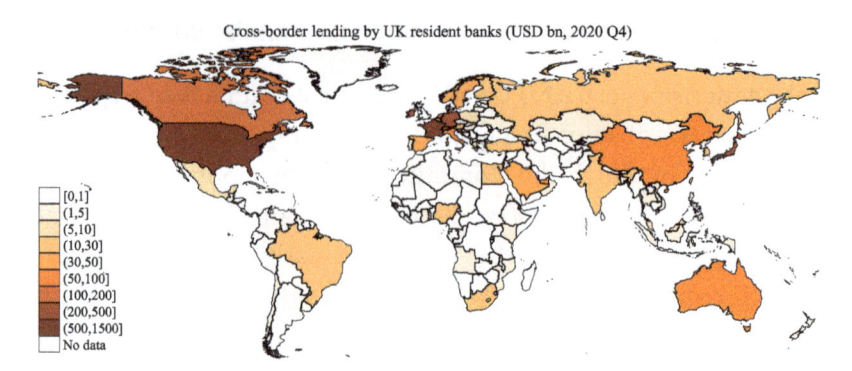

Figure 5. Heat map of UK-based banks' cross-border claims.
Source: Bank for International Settlements International Banking Statistics.

3.1. *Quantifying spillovers*

In light of these sizeable, and in many cases growing, interconnections for the UK economy, it is unsurprising that a large body of work has been developed seeking to quantify the influence of spillovers to the UK. Regardless of the transmission channel studied, a key takeaway is that foreign events can have significant spillover effects to the UK economy and financial system.

Focusing on the contribution of global developments, Cesa-Bianchi *et al.* (2021) find that around half of the variation in UK economic activity, and almost all variation in a summary measure of UK financial market conditions, can be explained by global shocks over the period 1997–2019. This is consistent with the notion of a "global financial cycle" (Miranda-Agrippino and Rey, 2020), characterised by cross-country co-movement in asset prices and international financial flows. Consistent with this, Cesa-Bianchi and Sokol (2017) demonstrate that an adverse US financial shock, which triggers a sharp and persistent contraction in the US economy, can quickly transmit internationally, leading to an increase in credit spreads and a slowdown in economic activity in the UK.

Turning to shocks emanating from specific countries, Gilhooly *et al.* (2018) quantify the spillover effects that could emanate from a slowdown in the Chinese economy. Their modelling encompasses trade and financial linkages, and considers how amplification mechanisms — which could plausibly operate in the event of a particularly large shock — could further increase the impact on the UK from an economic crisis within China.

Given its global nature, the UK banking sector offers an additional, and distinct, channel for cross-border spillovers, with particular consequences for macro-financial stability. Hills *et al.* (2019) examine the effects of US and euro area monetary policy on banks' lending in the UK, establishing evidence for both a bank funding and bank portfolio channel in the UK. Similarly, Forbes *et al.* (2017) show that increases in microprudential capital requirements in the UK can reduce international bank lending, and this effect can be amplified by some unconventional monetary policies.

In addition, the international nature of UK-based banks creates the opportunity for domestic, or foreign, events to have onward spillovers via the UK, creating potential spillbacks for the UK economy and financial system. Bussière *et al.* (2020b) study the influence of euro-area monetary policy on UK-based banks' cross-border lending, capturing both inward spillovers from Europe to the UK and onward spillovers from the UK. They demonstrate that tighter euro-area monetary policy can significantly reduce cross-border lending by French-owned affiliates in the UK.

3.2. *Accounting for spillovers in the macro-financial modelling toolkit*

In light of the wealth of evidence documenting the influence of cross-border interlinkages on the UK economy, a range of tools have been developed to account for them within the macro-financial toolkit. Indeed, the UK's role as an IFC is an important feature of the Bank's financial stability strategy. The global importance of the UK financial system means the actions of the UK authorities contribute to domestic, as well as international, financial stability — with the latter potentially spilling back to the UK economy. Therefore, the UK's institutions and markets must be a source of strength for the global system and able to be relied on by others, with standards of resilience needing to reflect this.

As part of its broader framework for financial stability, the FPC distinguishes between risks which are "crystallising" — or likely to crystallise — in the short term versus "vulnerabilities" which build up in the longer term and could amplify the effects of any shock to the financial system (Brazier, 2019). In order to assess resilience to a risk crystallising, the Bank has developed a stress-testing framework (Bank of England, 2015).

The Bank's Annual Cyclical Scenario (ACS) examines the potential impact of a hypothetical adverse scenario on the health of the banking system and individual institutions within it. In doing so, the ACS allows the FPC and PRA to assess the banking sector's resilience to a range of adverse shocks and ensure they are adequately capitalised, not just to withstand those shocks, but also support the real economy if a stress does materialise.[7]

In part, motivated by evidence that global variables predict domestic financial crises and economic downturns (see Cesa-Bianchi et al. [2019] and Bluwstein et al. [2020] for recent examples), the ACS has been tailored to account for the influence of global factors on the UK. The overall stress test is constructed from country and region-specific profiles, which contribute to an overall world profile. These profiles can then influence the UK stress through a range of macro-financial spillover channels.

The first stage of the stress test involves "risk assessment", gauging vulnerabilities in each region (Fisher and Rachel, 2016). The severity of the stress-test scenario for each region is then adapted to reflect its risk assessment. For a country where economic or financial vulnerabilities are judged to be more elevated, the stress scenario is thus more severe, reflecting the higher probability of a larger downturn.

In the second stage of the stress-test build, country-specific and regional profiles are combined to form an overall global scenario. At this stage, profiles can be decomposed to distinguish between domestic shocks and shocks emanating from abroad. This decomposition accounts for a range of spillover channels, including trade and financial linkages, and reflects differential linkages between countries (see, e.g., Dieppe et al. [2017]).

By modelling these spillover channels in the stress-test scenario, the FPC can examine the effect of bank losses emanating from domestic shocks and those emanating from foreign risks. As an example, Figure 6 summarises the decomposition of the UK GDP hit in the 2019 ACS. The larger externally-generated fraction reflects two things: first, the UK's exposure to foreign shocks, in part due to its position as an international financial centre; second, the severity of domestically generated GDP hits in other countries, in particular those with a higher risk assessment.

---

[7] Owing to the challenges from COVID-19, the Bank's ACS was paused in 2020 and "Desktop" and "Reverse" stress tests were used instead — although the underlying frameworks are similar.

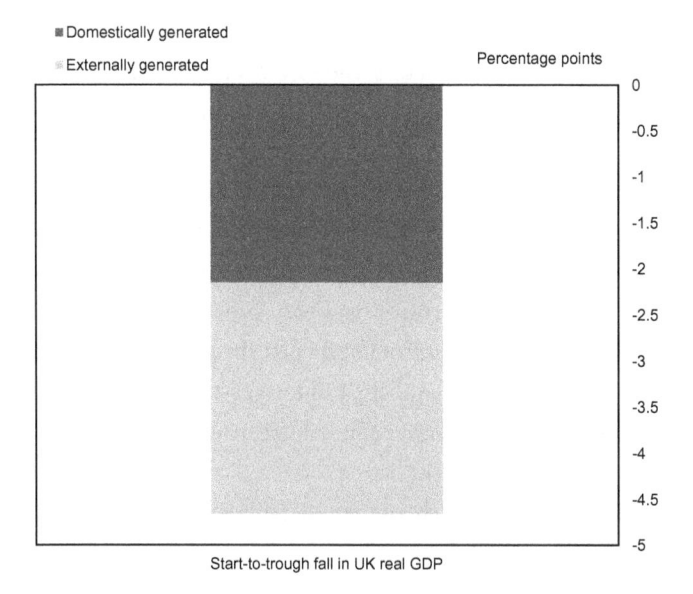

Figure 6. Decomposition of UK GDP stress in 2019 Annual Cyclical Scenario. *Source*: Bank of England (2019).

The FPC can then respond to these UK and global risks by using the results from the stress tests as an input into its setting of the UK CCyB rate, while the PRA can use these results to set bank-specific capital buffers.

Additional modelling tools have been developed to monitor vulnerabilities at a quarterly frequency. In a speech entitled "The Grand Unifying Theory (and practice) of Macroprudential Policy", Carney (2020) characterises the "policy problem" for the FPC's setting of macroprudential policy as minimising the following loss function L:

$$\min_{\rho_t} L \equiv E_t \left[\sum_{i=0}^{T} \beta^i \left(f(G@R_{t+i}) - \phi y_{t+i} \right) \right]$$

where ρ_t denotes the set of macroprudential policy tools set at time t, E_t is the expectations operator that probability weights all future states of the world conditional on information available at time t, β is the discount factor and T is the FPC's time horizon.

The FPC's primary objective is captured by the first term, a function of $G@R_t$, "GDP-at-Risk". GDP-at-Risk measures tail risks in the economy, summarising GDP growth outturns associated with a particular point in the distribution of GDP growth — typically the 5th percentile following Adrian *et al.* (2019). Reflecting this, the FPC seeks to set policy by, in part, minimising some function $f(\cdot)$, where $f'(\cdot) > 0$, of GDP-at-Risk.

The secondary objective of the Committee is summarised in the second term, where $\varphi > 0$ and y_t is the central GDP forecast. Alongside minimising GDP-at-Risk, the Committee must trade-off the potential economic costs of its policy actions in its overall policy setting. These trade-offs are typically intertemporal too. For example, a decision to increase the CCyB might be associated with short-term economic costs, in the form of reduced bank lending, but longer-term benefits for macro-financial stability, in the form of reduced macro-financial vulnerabilities and thus "lower" GDP-at-Risk.[8]

GDP-at-Risk is not directly observed, so it is important that the FPC can accurately estimate it over time in order effectively minimise the specified loss function. Aikman *et al.* (2019) outline the Bank's approach to estimating GDP-at-Risk and find that credit booms and property price booms can pose material downside risks to GDP growth at horizons of three to five years. They further show that such downside risks can be partially mitigated by increase the capitalisation of the banking system.

Given the myriad global spillover channels relevant to the UK discussed above, this macroprudential policy problem has an inherently international dimension. A downturn abroad can spill over to the UK through both UK banks' foreign exposures and broader macroeconomic channels, such as trade and financial markets.

Recent work has sought to account for these cross-border transmission channels in the Bank's GDP-at-Risk framework (Lloyd *et al.*, 2021). The globally-augmented GDP-at-Risk model of Lloyd *et al.* (2021) exploits data on bilateral trade and financial linkages to reflect heterogeneous cross-country transmission of macro-financial risks. The model includes three key "international" variables — foreign-weighted credit-to-GDP growth, a measure of foreign-weighted financial conditions and foreign-weighted lagged GDP growth — that capture a combination of near- and medium-term vulnerabilities and control for the global macroeconomic environment. They find that tighter foreign financial conditions are

---

[8] Where "lower" GDP-at-Risk pertains to reduced left-tail risks to GDP.

associated with more severe domestic GDP downside tail-risks in the near term (less than one year), while faster credit growth abroad significantly increases domestic tail-risks at medium-term horizons (from one to five years). In addition, Lloyd *et al.* (2021) demonstrate that including foreign variables in the model — over and above domestic ones — leads to a significant improvement in GDP-at-Risk estimates. This has important implications for policy: by accurately estimating GDP-at-Risk, the FPC can more effectively set policy to minimise the loss function specified above.

The globally-augmented model can also highlight the causal implications of foreign developments for domestic GDP-at-Risk. Decomposing UK GDP-at-Risk estimates into contributions from foreign and domestic "shocks", Lloyd *et al.* (2021) find that foreign shocks drive around 70 percent of variation in UK GDP-at-Risk as the three-year horizon. Figure 7 demonstrates this, plotting the time series decomposition of UK GDP-at-Risk into domestic and foreign drivers.

In summary, the UK's position as an IFC has repercussions for sources of fragility. This, in turn, means that regulators, both micro- and macroprudential, need to account for spillovers in the macro-financial framework. This is done by including global shocks and their potential spillover effects in the ACS, with the results being used as input into the FPC's decisions on the CCyB.

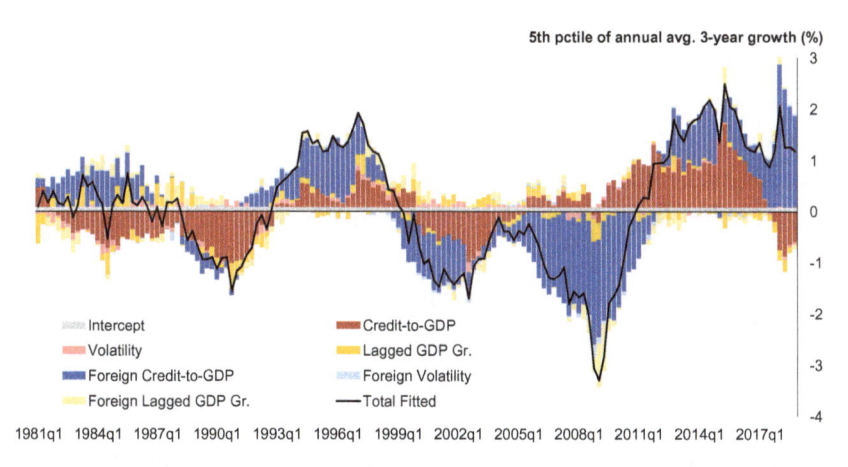

Figure 7. Decomposition of three-year-ahead UK GDP-at-Risk into foreign and domestic shocks.
Source: Lloyd *et al.* (2021).

4. International effects of policies and their interactions

An expansive literature has documented an increasing synchronisation of financial cycles across countries over the past decades. Among others, Rey (2015), Passari and Rey (2015) and Miranda-Agrippino and Rey (2020) have shown that global factors are behind a significant share of movements in a large cross-section of cross-border capital flows, asset prices and credit growth. These studies have also shown that as flexible exchange rates cannot insulate the domestic economy from the global financial cycle, the "trilemma" of monetary policy might be reduced to a "dilemma" between open capital accounts and monetary policy autonomy. Alternatively, macroprudential policy can serve as tool to mitigate the impact of global financial cycles on domestic banking systems and macroeconomy, while flexible exchange rates can absorb external shocks.

Given the status of the UK as global financial centre, it is not surprising that it is among the European economies most exposed to the global financial cycle (Figure 8). The exposure of the UK's capital flows to the global financial cycle is only matched by the exposure of Ireland, Belgium and the Netherlands.

One of the primary channels through which the global financial cycle affects cross-border capital flows, asset prices and credit growth are global financial institutions. Specifically, Cetorelli and Goldberg (2012a,b) provide evidence that internationally active banks manage their liquidity on a global scale, thereby contributing to international shock transmission and contagion and how the existence of an internal capital market for global banks increases the international propagation of domestic liquidity shocks due to a substitution effect between internal and external lending. It is important to stress, however, that while contributing to the international transmission of shocks, global liquidity management by international banks can also constitute a stabilising factor for banks' operations in times of financial stress, as intragroup funding may act as a substitute for volatile interbank funding (see, e.g., Reinhardt and Riddiough [2015]).

A second important systemic risk dimension associated with the cross-border activities of banks stems from the way in which global liquidity conditions affect banks' leverage and risk-taking through

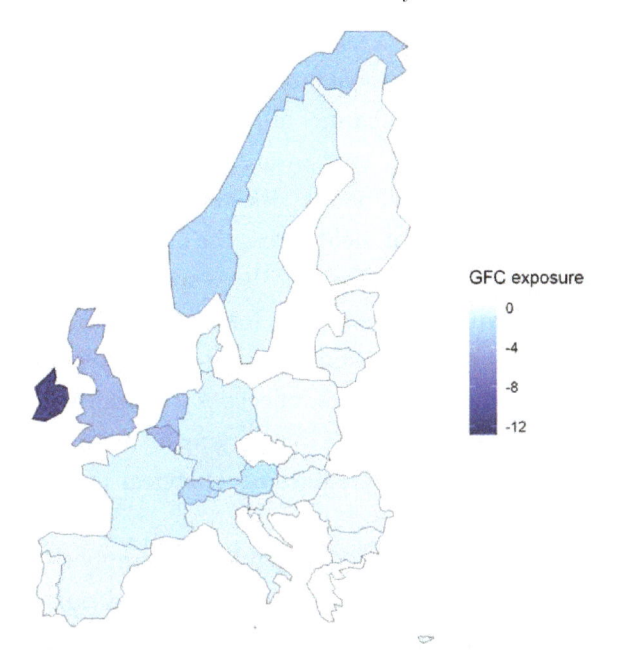

Figure 8. Exposure of European economies' capital flows to the global financial cycle.
Note: The Figure relies on ESRB calculations based on data from the IMF International Financial Statistics and Habib and Venditti (2019). The data period is 1990 Q2–2018 Q3. Capital flows are normalised by GDP. The map shows the country-specific response intensity of total gross capital flows (as percentage of GDP) to a one standard deviation shock in global risk using the global financial cycle indicator devised by Habib and Venditti (2019). The exposure intensity is derived from a country-specific regression of total gross capital inflows (as percentage of GDP) on the lagged global financial cycle indicator. The regression specification also includes one lag of the dependent variable to account for serial correlation and a constant.
Sources: Portes *et al.* (2020).

currency depreciation and appreciation. Bruno and Shin (2015) show theoretically and empirically the existence of a "risk-taking channel" of currency appreciation: global banks lend to corporate borrowers in US dollars, thus introducing a link between exchange rates and financial stability: an appreciation of the local currency leads to local borrowers having stronger balance sheets, which decreases borrowers' credit risk and increases banks' lending capacity and thus risk-taking by banks. A dollar appreciation, however, is associated with deleveraging by global banks and an overall tightening of global financial conditions.

Further, the risk-taking channel of monetary policy has shown to have important cross-border spill-over effects. Time variation in US policy rates influences global banks' risk perceptions, and lower rates encourage them to search for yield across the global spectrum of risky assets (Kalemli-Ozcan, 2019). There is also a spillover of US monetary policy to domestic banking systems (e.g., Ioannidou et al., 2015; Lee et al., 2020). Coman and Lloyd (2019) show that prudential policies can help to reduce the macro-financial spillover effects of US monetary policy and the associated global financial cycle in emerging markets. Loan-to-value (LTV) ratio limits and reserve requirements appear to be particularly effective prudential tools.

Finally, the global operations of banks also imply that domestic macroprudential policies may create inward and outward cross-border spillovers, resulting in a potential need for international policy coordination by macroprudential authorities. For the pre-crisis period (1999–2006), Aiyar et al. (2014) find that UK banks reduced cross-border lending in response to increases in domestic capital requirements, while Berrospide et al. (2017) show that changes in US prudential policies affects lending by large US global banks to foreign residents, while changes in foreign prudential policies affects lending growth in the US through foreign branches and subsidiaries, while also affecting cross-border lending by US banks. Hills et al. (2017) find that prudential actions taken abroad do not have significant aggregate spillover effects on bank lending in the UK, but disaggregated sectoral effects: for instance, when a foreign authority tightens LTV standards, UK affiliates of banks owned from that country expand their lending to U.K. households. Using aggregate cross-country data, Avdjiev et al. (2017) also report evidence for outward spillovers in relation to borrower-based measures (LTV ratio changes) and, consistent with Aiyar et al. (2014), domestic banks increased cross-border lending after a tightening of LTV ratios at home.[9]

---

[9] Several of the papers mentioned in this paragraph were part of an International Banking Research Network project, summarised by Buch and Goldberg (2017).

The literature discussed in this section suggests that because of the status of the UK as global financial centre, it is both exposed to foreign shocks (inward spillovers) and can generate outward spillovers. In response to inward spillovers, the UK can use macroprudential tools, while recipient countries can use also such tools in response to outward spillovers. However, simultaneous changes in macroprudential tools, such as those during the COVID-19 crisis and discussed in Box 3, can generate positive spillover effects. In Section 5, we will explore more specifically the outward spillover effects of UK monetary policy, in interaction with macroprudential policies in foreign countries.

Box 3: Countercyclical capital buffers during the COVID-19 crisis

As discussed in Box 1, the Bank of England, the ECB and many other prudential authorities lowered capital and liquidity requirements for the banks under their supervisions. Most strikingly, CCyB rates were lowered across the board.[10] While these decisions were taken independently and primarily with domestic objectives, cross-border banking links (and reciprocity arrangements) provided important spillover effects. As reported by Reinhardt and van Hombeeck (2020), banks around the world held around $73bn of capital due to CCyBs effective in 2019Q4, almost half ($32bn) due to banks' foreign exposures.

The reduction of CCyBs around the globe also lowered effective CCyB rates for UK banks with foreign exposure as shown in Figure 9. The Bank of England FPC's decision to lower the UK CCyB rate to zero has also contributed to the reduction in required capital holdings for foreign banks. Reinhardt and van Hombeeck estimate a total capital release of $64bn by 2020 Q2, with $24bn of this reduction due to foreign exposures, which may support up to $530bn in new lending to businesses globally.

This experience has shown that not only has the CCyB framework introduced after the Global Financial crisis served as an effective tool in response to the COVID-19 shock, but the almost simultaneous release of capital buffers by many countries created positive international spillover effects.

---

[10] It is important to note that in the euro area, CCyB rates are under national rather than ECB authority.

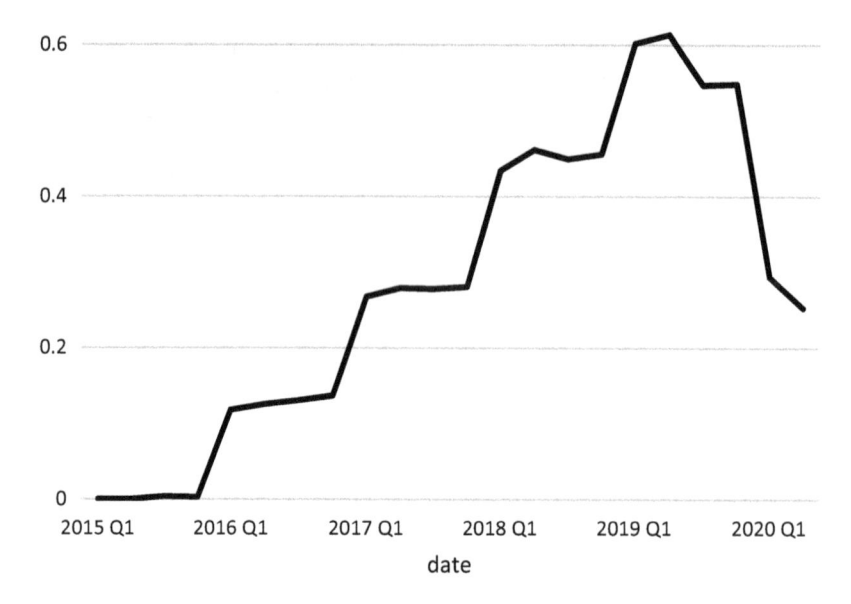

Figure 9. UK exposure-weighted foreign effective CCyB rate (percent).
Note: Foreign CCyBs weighted by UK-owned banks consolidated exposures to the non-bank non-financial sector in foreign countries.
Source: Reinhardt and van Hombeeck (2020) based on BIS Consolidated Banking statistics (https://www.bis.org/statistics/consstats.htm), ESRB (based on national authorities) and HKMA (https://www.hkma.gov.hk/eng/key-functions/banking/banking-legislation-policies-and-standards-implementation/countercyclical-capital-buffer-ccyb/).

5. Empirical analysis on UK monetary policy interactions with macroprudential policy in receiving countries

In this section, we focus on the transmission of UK monetary policies through UK-based banks' cross-border lending behaviour and, in turn, how macroprudential policies taken in receiving countries may offset or amplify any possible effects. The section follows the setup used in International Banking Research Network studies on prudential policy interactions, summarised in Bussière *et al.* (2020a).

5.1. *Data*

We combine panel data on UK-based banks' cross-border lending (as used e.g., in Forbes *et al.*, 2017) with UK monetary policy shocks (Cesa-Bianchi *et al.*, 2020) and macroprudential policy actions based on data from the

IMF's Integrated Macroprudential Policy (iMaPP) Database, described in Alam *et al.* (2019).

To identify the UK monetary policy shocks we use, Cesa-Bianchi *et al.* (2020) estimate a structural vector auto-regression using high-frequency "surprises" as an instrument in line with the existing literature (Gertler and Karadi, 2015). The monetary policy surprises are measured using intraday moves in Sterling futures in a 30-minute window around Bank of England monetary policy events (e.g., policy announcements). The short-time horizon over which these surprises are computed helps to isolate news about monetary policy from other types of news that could affect interest rates. In addition, the futures rate reflects expectations of the average short-term interest rate three to six months after the announcement. Importantly, because variation in the second quarter-ahead futures rates captures variation about the expected future path of policy rates, it can capture changes in monetary policy expectations while the short-term policy rate is at its effective lower bound. In the context of our sample, this is important, because the UK policy rate was at its effective lower bound from 2009Q1 to the end of our sample. To construct quarterly time series for the shocks, we sum them in a given quarter.[11]

The iMaPP database collects data for changes in a range of macroprudential policies taken in 134 countries from 1990 to 2018. The data assigns the value of +1 to a given prudential policy if it was tightened in a specific period, the value of –1 if it was loosened, and 0 if no change occurred. For LTV ratio limits, there is also information on the intensity of the change, as the data records the average size of LTVs across countries. We first focus on the aggregate quarterly sum across all measures. In our baseline specification for prudential policy, we exclude reserve requirements as, in some countries, these are used for monetary policy, not prudential, purposes.[12] We then disaggregate into the most frequent actions taken in advanced and emerging market economies, i.e., capital requirements, conservation buffers, measures to mitigate risks in

---

[11] Importantly, the statistical properties (i.e., mean, standard deviation, persistence) of our quarterly-frequency surprises are not significantly different to the meeting-frequency surprises

[12] In particular, they have been used extensively in emerging economies as alternative to monetary policy in response to capital inflows (Claessens *et al.*, 2013; IMF, 2012; Montoro and Moreno, 2011; IMF, 2011).

SIFIs, limits to LTVs, limits to the debt-service-to-income ratio (DSTI), loan restrictions, the CCyB and reserve requirements.[13]

Bank balance sheet data including external lending data come from the Bank of England's statistical reporting forms. The raw lending data is volatile in its raw form. We therefore employ several cleaning techniques in order to only focus on quantitatively significant links, which may vary at the intensive margin between UK banks and receiving countries. Specifically, we keep only links for which cross-border lending is either at least £100mn in size or 1 percent of a bank's total lending portfolio (if at least £10mn in size).[14] To alleviate the effect of outliers, we winsorise the dependent variable at the 10 percent level so that the growth rates lie within a −100 percent/+100 percent range. Control variables are winsorised at the 1 percent level.

Table 1 contains the summary statistics for the data entering the regression analysis. The sample period is 1998 Q2 to 2018 Q1.

Table 1. Summary statistics.

Variable	Mean	SD	Min	Max	Obs
Dependent variables					
Cross-border lending growth	0.08	0.42	−0.49	1.00	167628
Monetary Policy and Global Factors					
UK monetary policy shocks	−0.01	0.09	−0.27	0.26	167628
UK monetary policy shocks	−0.01	0.37	−0.88	0.74	167628
VIX	20.56	7.74	10.30	58.32	167628
Prudential Policy					
Aggregate Index(Pru_j, t−4)	0.85	1.91	−6.00	13.00	167628
Bank balance sheet characteristics					
Log total assets	16.10	1.95	6.08	20.96	167628
Capital ratio	0.08	0.11	−0.09	0.53	167628
Liquid assets ratio	0.45	0.26	0.01	1.10	167628
Core deposits ratio	0.16	0.20	0.00	0.85	167628
Commitments ratio	0.47	0.28	0.00	1.29	167628
Domestic Macro Controls					
GDP Growth (Annual)	0.027	0.030	−0.056	0.107	167628
Credit Growth (yoy)	0.022	0.067	−0.182	0.250	167628

---

[13] See also Figure 3 in Alam et al. (2019).

[14] Furthermore, we only consider observations of bank lending pairs if the stock of lending exceeds a share of 0.2 percent in the current or the preceding quarter's total stock of external lending (rather than large percent changes relative to small stocks).

5.2. Methodology

Our first specification aims to assess UK monetary policy spillovers through UK-based banks' external lending:

$$\Delta Y_{b,j,t} = \alpha_0 + \sum_{k=0}^{K} \alpha_{1,k} MP^{UK}_{t-k} + \alpha_2 X_{b,t-1} + \alpha_3 Z_{j,t-1} + \alpha_4 G_{t-1} + f_b + f_j + \epsilon_{b,j,t} \quad (1)$$

where $\Delta Y_{b,j,t}$ is the growth of cross-border lending by bank b to country j at quarter t; MP^{UK}_{t-k}. denotes the UK monetary policy shock; $X_{b,t-1}$ is a vector of time-varying *bank* control variables; $Z_{j,t-1}$ includes other time-varying *receiving country* control variables, which might co-move with domestic prudential policies — including controls for domestic demand, in our baseline specification we use lagged annual nominal GDP growth and credit growth; f_b are bank fixed effects; and f_j are receiving country fixed effects. Because the main coefficient of interest in Equation (1) $\alpha_{1,k}$ loads on UK monetary policy, which is the same for all banks b and receiving countries j, we cannot include time fixed effects in the regression. Nevertheless, to capture global time-varying factors that may contaminate our estimates of monetary policy spillovers, we include global macroeconomic controls G_t such as the VIX and US monetary policy surprises. Standard errors $\epsilon_{b,j,t}$ are clustered at the bank-time level.

Second, when assessing the interactions of UK monetary policy with receiving-country prudential policy $Pru^{dest}_{j,t}$, we alter our specification to include bank-time fixed effects $f_{b,t}$. These time fixed effects absorb the direct effect of UK monetary policy spillovers and the global controls G_t, but control for *all possible* globally time-varying factors that could otherwise contaminate estimate of the interaction coefficient of interest. The baseline specification for assessing the interaction is therefore:

$$\Delta Y_{b,j,t} = \alpha_0 + \alpha_1 Pru^{dest.}_{j,t-4} + \sum_{k=0}^{3} \alpha_{2,k}(MP^{UK}_{t-k} \cdot Pru^{dest.}_{j,t-4}) \\ + \alpha_3 Z_{j,t-1} + f_{b,t} + f_j + \epsilon_{b,j,t} \quad (2)$$

In addition to the definitions above, $Pru^{dest}_{j,t-4}$ is a measure of the stance of destination-country prudential policy. We include both the level of the prudential policy stance, as well as its interaction with UK monetary policy. We include the former to account for the direct effects of prudential policy on inflows to the receiving country. For instance, Reinhardt and

Sowerbutts (2015) show that countries experience capital inflows for up to four quarters following a tightening in capital requirements.

Our baseline measure cumulates all prudential policy actions, excluding reserve requirements, in a country over a two-year period. Importantly, we only account for prudential policy actions enacted prior to the UK monetary policy action of interest — reflected by the $t-4$ lag on the prudential policy measure. This mitigates the possibility that our estimates capture a (potentially endogenous) response of receiving-country prudential policy in response to a UK monetary policy surprise. In our baseline specification, we investigate the four-period effect of UK monetary policy. So, our prudential policy measure, $Pru^{dest}_{j,t-4}$ captures cumulated prudential policy actions in a country j over two years from $t-11$ to $t-4$. The regression also includes bank-time fixed effects to absorb all unobserved variation impacting a bank's lending over time to all countries.

In relation to our main hypotheses, we expect that a surprise UK monetary policy tightening will (on average) reduce UK-based banks' external lending, reflected by $\hat{\alpha}_{1,k} < 0$ in Equation (1). In response to a surprise UK monetary policy, we also expect that a country with a tighter prudential policy stance prior to the surprise — higher $Pru^{dest}_{j,t-4}$ — should (on average) face a smaller negative spillover than a country with looser prudential policy, reflected by $\hat{\alpha}_{2,k} > 0$ in Equation (2). The coefficient $\alpha_{2,k}$ can be interpreted as the influence of an additional prudential policy tightening on the cross-border spillover of UK monetary policy relative to its mean.

5.3. Results

The first column of Table 2 summarises our main results for the spillover effects of UK monetary policy through UK-based banks' cross-border lending. Column 1 indicates that a surprise UK monetary policy tightening significantly reduces UK-based banks' external lending growth. In particular a one (0.25) percentage point UK monetary policy surprise reduces UK banks' external lending, on average, by 18.4pp (4.6pp) over one year.[15] This finding is in line with the previous literature, including Kalemli-Ozcan (2019).

---

[15] Over our sample period, the minimum UK monetary policy surprise in a given quarter is minus 27bp, and the maximum surprise is plus 26bp.

Table 2. Monetary policy spillovers through UK banks' external lending, and interactions with receiving-country prudential policy.

	(1) No Interaction	(2) Interaction	(3) Interaction with Time FE	(4) Interaction with Bank-Time FE
$\sum_{k=0}^{0} MP_{t-k}^{UK}$	−0.000179	−0.00232		
p-value	0.991	0.883		
$\sum_{k=0}^{1} MP_{t-k}^{UK}$	−0.0919***	−0.106***		
p-value	0.0006	0.0001		
$\sum_{k=0}^{2} MP_{t-k}^{UK}$	−0.185***	−0.202***		
p-value	0.0000	0.0000		
$\sum_{k=0}^{3} MP_{t-k}^{UK}$	−0.184***	−0.196***		
p-value	0.0000	0.0000		
$\sum_{k=0}^{0} (MP_{t-k}^{UK} \cdot Pru_{j,t-4}^{dest})$		0.0195	0.0273*	0.0264*
p-value		0.125	0.0528	0.0694
$\sum_{k=0}^{1} (MP_{t-k}^{UK} \cdot Pru_{j,t-4}^{dest})$		0.0607***	0.0830***	0.0803***
p-value		0.0042	0.00032	0.0008
$\sum_{k=0}^{2} (MP_{t-k}^{UK} \cdot Pru_{j,t-4}^{dest})$		0.0691**	0.117***	0.109***
p-value		0.0160	0.0002	0.0009
$\sum_{k=0}^{3} (MP_{t-k}^{UK} \cdot Pru_{j,t-4}^{dest})$		0.0527	0.108***	0.105***
p-value		0.116	0.0035	0.0063
$Pru_{j,t-4}^{dest}$		−0.0058***	−0.0005	−0.0008
		(0.0007)	(0.0008)	(0.0008)
VIX_{t-1}	−0.0007***	−0.0011***		
	(0.0002)	(0.0002)		
$\log(Total\ Assets)_{t-1}$	−0.0262***	−0.0232***	−0.0119***	
	(0.0026)	(0.0026)	(0.0027)	
$Capital\ Ratio_{t-1}$	−0.1049***	−0.1016***	−0.0817***	
	(0.0280)	(0.0278)	(0.0270)	
$Liquid\ Asset\ Ratio_{t-1}$	−0.0012	0.0007	−0.0029	
	(0.0111)	(0.0110)	(0.0108)	
$Core\ Deposits\ Ratio_{t-1}$	−0.0093	0.0014	0.0130	
	(0.0177)	(0.0177)	(0.0173)	
$Commitment\ Share_{t-1}$	−0.0035	0.0017	0.0131	
	(0.0092)	(0.0092)	(0.0090)	

(Continued)

Table 2. (*Continued*)

	(1) No Interaction	(2) Interaction	(3) Interaction with Time FE	(4) Interaction with Bank-Time FE
Annual GDP Growth$^{dest}_{j,t-4}$	0.4369***	0.4224***	0.3932***	0.3787***
	(0.0461)	(0.0459)	(0.0521)	(0.0553)
Credit to GDP Growth$^{dest}_{j,t-1}$	0.1684***	0.1696***	0.1129***	0.0962***
	(0.0159)	(0.0159)	(0.0167)	(0.0174)
US Monetary Policy shocks	Yes	Yes	N/A	N/A
Fixed Effects	Bank, Receiver	Bank, Receiver	Bank, Receiver, Time	Bank-Time, Receiver
Observations	167,628	167,628	167,628	166,431
R-squared	0.0124	0.0130	0.0178	0.1393
Adjusted R-squared	0.00928	0.00987	0.0142	0.0485

Note: Dependent variable is quarterly growth in cross-border lending. The prudential policy measure is the sum of prudential policy actions (excluding reserve requirements) over a two-year period. Standard errors, in brackets, are clustered by bank and time.

Columns 2–4 show the mitigating effect that macroprudential policies in the receiving country can have on the spillover effects of UK monetary policy actions. Here, we present our headline estimate of the interaction between recipient-country prudential policies with UK monetary policy for UK banks' cross-border lending.[16] The prudential policy measure here sums all actions (excluding reserve requirements) over a two-year period in advance of the UK monetary policy event. An additional prudential policy tightening action in the recipient country, in advance of a surprise UK monetary policy tightening, can offset spillovers to lending growth by about 10pp over a one-year period in our preferred specification

---

[16] Column 2 presents an intermediate specification between Columns 1 and 3, including monetary policy spillovers and interactions with receiving country prudential policy at the same time. This is achieved by excluding time fixed effects, which would otherwise absorb the monetary policy terms. In this regression, which is not preferred because of the exclusion of time fixed effects, the interaction term is significant up to a three-quarter horizon.

including bank-time fixed effects. Although these numbers appear large, in comparison to the monetary policy spillover, it is important to note that our monetary policy surprise measure does not capture changes in overall levels in interest rates and, unlike the spillover coefficient, our interaction coefficient is identified conditional on time fixed effects.

In Table 3, we explore whether the UK monetary policy spillovers, and interactions with recipient-country prudential policy, differ depending on the ownership type of the bank. To do this, we estimate regressions (1) and (2) for three types of bank: (1) UK-owned, (2) foreign subsidiaries and (3) foreign branches. Building on Bussière *et al.* (2021), we hypothesise that the spillover and interaction effects are likely to be stronger for foreign-owned banks (i.e., subsidiaries and branches) than UK-owned banks on the grounds that long-term bank-lender relationships are most likely to be located at a bank's headquarters. In contrast, affiliates in major IFCs may concentrate on short-term lending or lending with synergies to financial transactions — in turn, associated with larger spillovers and interactions.

The results presented in Table 3 support this hypothesis. Focusing on UK-owned banks, Columns (1) and (2) show that both the spillovers of UK monetary policy and the interactions with recipient-country prudential policies are insignificantly different from zero at all horizons. In contrast, the results for foreign subsidiaries and foreign branches — in Columns (3)–(4) and (5)–(6), respectively — are strongly significant. They indicate both that tighter UK monetary policy is associated with a subsequent reduction in foreign-owned banks' external lending and that tighter recipient-country prudential policies can partially offset these spillovers. Together this supports our hypotheses for the differences between UK- and foreign-owned lenders.

The results so far lend support to the view that countries with a more developed prudential policy toolkit are better placed to shield themselves against the global financial cycle. But which prudential tools are most effective? Next, we explore the differential interaction effects of specific prudential policy tools, using the decomposition in the Alam *et al.* (2019) dataset.

Following Borio (2010) and Claessens *et al.* (2013), we divide macroprudential policies into more long-standing "structural" measures and those taken over the cycle. Reserve requirements are investigated

Table 3. Interactions by type of lending.

	(1)	(2)	(3)	(4)	(5)	(6)
	\multicolumn{2}{c	}{UK-Owned}	\multicolumn{2}{c	}{Foreign Subsidiaries}	\multicolumn{2}{c}{Foreign Branches}
	No interaction	Interaction	No interaction	Interaction	No interaction	Interaction
$\sum_{k=0}^{0} MP_{t-k}^{UK}$	−0.0120		0.0207		−0.00299	
p-value	0.740		0.547		0.879	
$\sum_{k=0}^{1} MP_{t-k}^{UK}$	−0.0952		−0.0963		−0.0893***	
p-value	0.130		0.108		0.00827	
$\sum_{k=0}^{2} MP_{t-k}^{UK}$	−0.133		−0.290***		−0.164***	
p-value	0.125		0.000268		0.000398	
$\sum_{k=0}^{3} MP_{t-k}^{UK}$	−0.127		−0.300***		−0.160***	
p-value	0.196		0.00114		0.00250	
$\sum_{k=0}^{0} (MP_{t-k}^{UK} \cdot Pru_{j,t-4}^{dest})$		0.00871		0.0291		0.0308*
p-value		0.784		0.396		0.0974
$\sum_{k=0}^{1} (MP_{t-k}^{UK} \cdot Pru_{j,t-4}^{dest})$		0.0802		0.112**		0.0699**
p-value		0.122		0.0467		0.0226
$\sum_{k=0}^{2} (MP_{t-k}^{UK} \cdot Pru_{j,t-4}^{dest})$		0.0905		0.151**		0.0991**
p-value		0.217		0.0445		0.0174
$\sum_{k=0}^{3} (MP_{t-k}^{UK} \cdot Pru_{j,t-4}^{dest})$		0.0933		0.147*		0.0934*
p-value		0.290		0.0850		0.0593
Fixed Effects	Bank, Receiver	Bank-Time, Receiver	Bank, Receiver	Bank-Time, Receiver	Bank, Receiver	Bank-Time, Receiver
Observations	26,812	26,672	39,852	39,494	100,921	100,222
R-squared	0.0167	0.1358	0.0151	0.1379	0.0129	0.1413
Adjusted R-squared	0.0116	0.0657	0.0100	0.0460	0.00928	0.0438

Note: Dependent variable is quarterly growth in cross-border lending. The prudential policy measure is the sum of the respective prudential policy actions over a two-year period. Standard errors, in brackets, are clustered by bank and time.

separately as discussed. Again, we cumulate actions over a two-year period in advance of the UK monetary policy impulse.

The results in Columns 1–4 of Table 4 show only weak evidence for structural prudential measures significantly offsetting some of the spillover effects from a surprise UK monetary policy tightening through UK-based banks' external lending. Most strongly, the coefficient estimates on the interactions between monetary policy and capital requirements are statistically significant at the 10 percent level out to the three-quarter horizon. For SIFI measures, there is a significant short-term offset at the contemporaneous level which fades after two quarters. The limited effects of structural measures are maybe not surprising as increases in capital requirements affect usually the supply of credit rather than the demand, and the measure we have is of direct lending from UK banks (which are not directly affected by structural measures in recipient countries). There is also some evidence (e.g., Reinhardt and Sowerbutts, 2015) suggesting that an increase in capital requirements leads to an increase in borrowing from foreign sources for about a year, and this may be affecting our results, although we do attempt to control for this by using a one-year lag on prudential policy.

Columns 5–9 of Table 4 shows clear evidence that previously implemented cyclical prudential policies affecting particular loans and in particular housing loans can act to significantly offset the effect of UK monetary policy shocks. For LTV and DTI limits as well as loan restrictions the interaction with monetary policy is significant at the one-year horizon. The measured effect is strongest when considering the measure for LTV limits which takes into account the intensity of the regulation in Column 6.[17] The results suggest that a country with a 10pp lower LTV limit experiences an around 2.7pp smaller reduction in lending growth from UK banks following a monetary tightening in the UK by 0.25pp.

For the CCyB, we record positive though insignificant point estimates for the interaction effects. This might be because of several reasons including the fact that up to 2017 Q1 (the latest date prudential policies enter our sample at t–4) the CCyB has been implemented at positive

---

[17] The measure in Column 6 is the average LTV at the end of the quarter as of t–4.

Table 4. Types of prudential policies.

	(1)	(2)	(3)	(4)	(5)	(6)	(7)	(8)	(9)	(10)
		Structural Measures				Cyclical Measures				Reserve Requirements
Prudential Policies	Capital Requirements	Conservation Buffer	SIFI	Liquidity Req	LTV	LTV Limits (up is loosening)	DSTI	Loan Restrictions	CCyB	RR
$\sum_{k=0}^{0}(MP_{t-k}^{UK}\cdot Pru_{j,t-k}^{dest})$	0.0494	0.133	0.341*	−0.0250	0.0285	−0.0036**	0.0875*	0.0681	0.353	0.0171
p-value	0.135	0.418	0.0852	0.616	0.433	0.0275	0.0555	0.339	0.301	0.136
$\sum_{k=0}^{1}(MP_{t-k}^{UK}\cdot Pru_{j,t-k}^{dest})$	0.101*	0.0640	0.381	0.0688	0.135**	−0.0075***	0.183**	0.266**	0.736	0.0263
p-value	0.0754	0.820	0.278	0.397	0.0252	0.00418	0.0199	0.0204	0.270	0.191
$\sum_{k=0}^{2}(MP_{t-k}^{UK}\cdot Pru_{j,t-k}^{dest})$	0.142*	−0.174	0.243	0.0912	0.153*	−0.0114***	0.251**	0.408***	0.960	0.0408
p-value	0.0672	0.630	0.601	0.430	0.0676	0.00123	0.0223	0.00723	0.353	0.152
$\sum_{k=0}^{3}(MP_{t-k}^{UK}\cdot Pru_{j,t-k}^{dest})$	0.128	−0.202	0.592	0.0271	0.168*	−0.0109***	0.260*	0.382**	0.812	0.0433
p-value	0.157	0.615	0.269	0.849	0.0923	0.00959	0.0570	0.0307	0.510	0.211
$Pru_{j,t-4}^{dest}$	−0.0021	−0.0077*	−0.0157***	0.0004	−0.0006	−0.0001	0.0027	−0.0021	−0.0040	0.0005
	(0.0020)	(0.0044)	(0.0060)	(0.0034)	(0.0021)	(0.0002)	(0.0036)	(0.0029)	(0.0098)	(0.0012)
GDP and Credit Growth (dest)	Included	Included	Included	Included	Included	Included	Included	Included	Included	Included
Fixed Effects	Bank-Time, Receiver	Bank-Time, Receiver	Bank-Time, Receiver	Bank-Time, Receiver	Bank-Time, Receiver	Bank-Time, Receiver	Bank-Time, Receiver	Bank-Time, Receiver	Bank-Time, Receiver	Bank-Time, Receiver
Observations	166,431	166,431	166,431	166,431	166,431	159,283	166,431	166,431	166,431	166,431
R-squared	0.1392	0.1392	0.1393	0.1392	0.1393	0.1436	0.1392	0.1393	0.1392	0.1392
Adjusted R-squared	0.0484	0.0484	0.0485	0.0484	0.0484	0.0497	0.0484	0.0485	0.0484	0.0484

Note: Dependent variable is quarterly growth in cross-border lending. The prudential policy measure is the sum of the respective prudential policy actions over a two-year period. Standard errors, in brackets, are clustered by bank and time.

rates only in five countries. Compared to the other cyclical measures the CCyB also targets a much broader category of lending and there is a large implementation lag (one year usually) after the announcement.

Finally, in Column 10, we examine reserve requirements. The point estimates are positive but not significant suggesting a limited role for past tightening in reserve requirements to offset foreign monetary policy shocks. As discussed, conceptually, results might be harder to interpret given reserve requirements are often also used for monetary purposes. In fact, they might change as a response or in parallel to UK monetary policy depending on the degree of economic linkages, making it hard to draw firm conclusions on reserve requirements with the setup at hand.

6. Conclusion

This chapter has discussed the institutional structure of monetary and prudential policy decision-making in the UK, as well as policy decisions in these areas over the past decade. Given the UK's status as an IFC, global shocks and their spillover effects are explicitly taken into account in the monitoring and policy process. We have discussed the rapidly expanding literature on the importance of the global financial cycle and the role of macroprudential policy tools in mitigating spillover effects from monetary and regulatory policy decisions in core countries, such as the US, euro area and the UK.

Using data on UK-based banks' external lending, we have presented findings that UK monetary policy surprises have a significant spillover effect on other countries, as a tightening surprise causes a significant fall in external lending. Taking macroprudential policies, especially borrower-targeted policies, can offset a considerable part of that spillover. In this sense, we find support for the thesis that (macro)prudential policies can help insulate countries from the global capital flows cycles. The wide variety of policy instruments which have been developed by policymakers suggests that there is merit in exploring not just, whether macroprudential policy can insulate a country from the credit cycle but which ones are more effective. We find that LTV limits, which affect credit demand, appear to be particularly effective in offsetting the spillovers from UK monetary policy.

References

Adrian, Tobias, Nina Boyarchenko and Domenico Giannone, 2019. Vulnerable Growth. *American Economic Review*, 109(4), pp. 1263–1289.

Aikman, David, Jonathan Bridges, Sinem Hociolgu Hoke, Cian O'Neill and Akash Raja, 2019. Credit, capital and crises: A GDP-at-Risk approach. Bank of England Staff Working Paper, No. 824.

Aiyar, Shekhar, Charles W. Calomaris and Tomasz Wieladek, 2014. Does Macro-Prudential Regulation Leak? Evidence from a UK Policy Experiment. *Journal of Money, Credit and Banking*, 46(S1), pp. 181–214.

Alam, Zohair, Adrian Alter, Jesse Eiseman, Gaston Gelos, Heedon Kang, Machiko Narita, Erlend Nier, and Naixi Wang, 2019. Digging Deeper — Evidence on the Effects of Macroprudential Policies from a New Database. IMF Working Paper, No. 19/66.

Ampudia, Miguel, Thorsten Beck, Andreas Beyer, Jean-Edouard Colliard, Agnese Leonello, Angela Maddaloni and David Marques-Ibanez, 2019. The architecture of supervision. ECB Working Paper Series, No. 2287, May.

Avdjiev, Stefan, Catherine Koch, Patrick McGuire and Goetz von Peter, 2017. International Prudential Policy Spillovers: A Global Perspective. *International Journal of Central Banking*, 13(2), pp. 5–33.

Bailey, Andrew, 2021. The case for an open financial system. Speech at the Financial and Professional Services Address, Mansion House, 10 February.

Bailey, Andrew, Jonathan Bridges, Richard Harrison, Josh Jones and Aakash Mankodi, 2020. The central bank balance sheet as a policy tool: Past, present and future. Bank of England Staff Working Paper, No. 899, December.

Bank of England, 1999. The transmission mechanism of monetary policy. *Bank of England Quarterly Bulletin*, May.

Bank of England, 2015. The Bank of England's approach to stress testing. October.

Bank of England, 2019. Key elements of the 2019 stress test, https://www.bankofengland.co.uk/news/2019/march/key-elements-of-the-2019-stress-test. March.

Berrospide, Jose M., Ricardo Correa, Linda S. Goldberg and Friederike Niepmann, 2017. International Banking and Cross-Border Effects of Regulation: Lessons from the United States. *International Journal of Central Banking*, 13(S1), pp. 435–476.

Bluwstein, Kristina, Marcus Buckman, Andreas Joseph, Miao Kang, Sujit Kapadia and Özgür Şimşek, 2020. Credit growth, the yield curve and financial crisis prediction: Evidence from a machine learning approach. Bank of England Staff Working Paper, No. 848.

Borio, Claudio, 2010. Implementing a macroprudential framework: Blending boldness and realism. BIS Research Papers.

Brazier, Alex, 2019. Financial resilience and economic earthquakes. Speech at the University of Warwick, 13 June.

Bruno, Valentina and Hyun Song Shin, 2015. Cross-Border Banking and Global Liquidity. *Review of Economic Studies*, 82(2), pp. 535–564.

Buch, Claudia M. and Linda S. Goldberg, 2017. Cross-Border Prudential Policy Spillovers: How Much? How Important? Evidence from the International Banking Research Network. *International Banking Research Network*, 13(S1), pp. 505–558.

Bussière, Matthieu., Cao, Jin, de Haan, Jakob, Hills, Robert, Lloyd, Simon, Meunier, Baptiste, Pedrono, Justine, Reinhardt, Dennis, Sinha, Sonalika, Sowerbutts, Rhiannon, and Konstantin Styrin, 2020a. The Interaction Between Macroprudential Policy and Monetary Policy: Overview. *Review of International Economics*, 29(1), pp. 1–19.

Bussière, Matthieu, Robert Hills, Simon Lloyd, Baptiste Meunier, Justine Pedrono, Dennis Reinhardt and Rhiannon Sowerbutts, 2020b. *Le Pont de Londres*: Interactions Between Monetary and Prudential Policies in Cross-border Lending. *Review of International Economics*, 29(1), pp. 61–86.

Carney, Mark, 2020. The grand unifying theory (and practice) of macroprudential policy. Speech at University College London, 5 March.

Cesa-Bianchi, Ambrogio and Andrej Sokol, 2017. Financial shocks, credit spreads and the international credit channel. Bank of England Staff Working Paper, No. 693.

Cesa-Bianchi, Ambrogio, Fernando Eguren-Martin and Gregory Thwaites, 2019. Foreign Booms, Domestic Busts: The International Dimension of Banking Crises. *Journal of Financial Intermediation*, 37, pp. 58–74.

Cesa-Bianchi, Ambrogio, Gregory Thwaites and Alejandro Vicondoa, 2020. Monetary policy transmission in the United Kingdom: A High Frequency Identification Approach. *European Economic Review*, 123, pp. 103–375.

Cesa-Bianchi, Ambrogio, Rosie Dickinson, Sevim Kösem, Simon Lloyd and Ed Manuel, 2021. No economy is an island: How foreign shocks affect UK macro-financial stability. *Bank of England Quarterly Bulletin*, Q3.

Cetorelli, Nicola and Linda Goldberg, 2012a. Liquidity Management of U.S. Global Banks: Internal Capital Markets in the Great Recession. *Journal of International Economics*, 88(2), pp. 299–311.

Cetorelli, Nicola and Linda Goldberg, 2012b. Banking Globalization and Monetary Transmission. *Journal of Finance*, 67(5), pp. 1811–1843.

Claessens, Stijn, Swati R. Ghosh, and Roxana Mihet, 2013. Macro-prudential policies to mitigate financial system vulnerabilities. *Journal of International Money and Finance*, 39, pp. 153–185.

Coman, Andra and Simon Lloyd, 2019. In the Face of Spillovers: Prudential Policies in Emerging Economies. ECB Working Paper Series, No. 2339, December.

Dieppe, Alistair, Georgios Georgiadis, Martino Ricci, Ine Van Robays and Björn van Roye, 2017. ECB-Global: Introducing ECB's global macroeconomic model for spillover analysis. ECB Working Paper Series, No. 2045, April.

Fisher, Jack and Lukasz Rachel, 2016. Assessing vulnerabilities to financial shocks in some key global economies. Bank of England Staff Working Paper, No. 636.

Forbes, Kristin, Dennis Reinhardt and Tomasz Wieladek, 2017. The Spillovers, Interactions, and (Un)intended Consequences of Monetary and Regulatory Policies. *Journal of Monetary Economics*, 85(C), pp. 1–22.

Gertler, Mark and Peter Karadi, 2015. Monetary Policy Surprises, Credit Costs, and Economic Activity. *American Economic Journal: Macroeconomics*, 7(1), pp. 44–76.

Gilhooly, Robert, Jen Han, Simon Lloyd, Niamh Reynolds and David Young, 2018. From the Middle Kingdom to the United Kingdom: Spillovers from China. *Bank of England Quarterly Bulletin*, May.

Habib, Maurizio M and Fabrizio Venditti, 2019. The global capital flows cycle: Structural drivers and transmission channels. ECB Working Paper Series, No. 2280, May.

Hills, Robert, Dennis Reinhardt, Rhiannon Sowerbutts and Tomasz Wieladek, 2017. International Banking and Cross-Border Effects of Regulation: Lessons from the United Kingdom. *International Journal of Central Banking*, 13(2), pp. 404–433.

Hills, Robert, Kelvin Ho, Dennis Reinhardt, Rhiannon Sowerbutts, Eric Wong and Gabriel Wu, 2019. The International Transmission of Monetary Policy Through Financial Centres: Evidence from the United Kingdom and Hong Kong. *Journal of International Money and Finance*, 90(C), pp. 76–98.

Ioannidou, Vasso O., Steven Ongena and Jose-Luis Peydro, 2015. Monetary Policy, Risk-Taking and Pricing: Evidence from a Quasi-Natural Experiment. *Review of Finance*, 19(1), pp. 95–144.

Kalemli-Özcan, Sebnem, 2019. U.S. Monetary Policy and International Risk Spillovers. NBER Working Papers No. 26297.

Lee, Seung J., Lucy Q. Liu, and Viktors Stebunovs, 2019. Risk-Taking Spillovers of US Monetary Policy in the Global Market for US Dollar Corporate Loans. International Finance Discussion Papers, No. 1251.

Lloyd, Simon, Ed Manuel and Konstantin Panchev, 2021. Foreign Vulnerabilities, Domestic Risks: The Global Drivers of GDP-at-Risk. Bank of England Staff Working Paper, No. 940.

Miranda-Agrippino, Silvia and Hélène Rey, 2020. U.S. Monetary Policy and the Global Financial Cycle. *Review of Economic Studies*, 87(6), pp. 2754–2776.

Passari, Evgenia and Hélène Rey, 2015. Financial Flows and the International Monetary System. *The Economic Journal*, 125(584), pp. 675–698.

Portes, Richard, Thorsten Beck, Willem Buiter, Kathryn Dominguez, Daniel Gros, Christian Gross, Sebnem Kalemli-Ozcan, Tuomas Peltonen and Antonio Sánchez Serrano, 2020. The Global Dimensions of Macroprudential Policy. Reports of the Advisory Scientific Committee 10.

Reinhardt, Dennis and Steven J. Riddiough, 2015. The Two Faces of Cross-Border Banking Flows. *IMF Economic Review*, 63(4), pp. 751–791.

Reinhardt, Dennis and Rhiannon Sowerbutts, 2015. Regulatory arbitrage in action: Evidence from banking flows and macroprudential policy. Bank of England Staff Working Paper No. 546.

Reinhardt, Dennis and Carlos van Hombeeck, 2020. With a little help from my friends: counter-cyclical capital buffers during the Covid-19 crisis. Bank Underground, 25 August. https://bankunderground.co.uk/2020/08/25/with-a-little-help-from-my-friends-counter-cyclical-capital-buffers-during-the-covid-19-crisis/.

Rey, Hélène, 2015. Dilemma not Trilemma: The Global Financial Cycle and Monetary Policy Independence. NBER Working Paper, No. 21162.

Macro-Financial Policy in an International Financial Centre: The UK Experience Since the Global Financial Crisis: A Discussion

Paul Tucker

Research Fellow, Harvard Kennedy School

The chapter by Thorsten Beck and coauthors invites comments at many levels. I shall engage at just three.

First, the study effectively assumes that there has been a macroprudential policy in the UK and elsewhere, by which I mean a systematic policy informed by articulated principles and capable of being picked up by a statistical study. That is not the same thing as occasionally using statutory powers to tweak something termed the countercyclical capital buffer. A useful starting point would be whether there is a systematic reaction function, feeding back from variables plausibly bearing a robust relationship, via resilience in intermediaries or borrowers, to systemic stability.

A problem in this area — across jurisdictions — is little or no transparency. We do not know the changes over any 12-month period in the tangible common equity required by regulation and, importantly, discretionary prudential supervision for specific banks. For all we know, in particular cases de facto net requirements could move in the opposite direction from headline regulatory requirements (e.g., by changing components of Pillar 2 requirements, or approving changes in model risk weights). Until we know that, some healthy skepticism is warranted about both policy and, unavoidably, studies of this kind.

I did not anticipate this hazard when, with Matt Hancock, who had left the Bank of England to go into politics (and at the time of the conference was the UK's cabinet-level Health Secretary), I led efforts to reconfigure the institutional architecture of Britain's stability regime. Transparency in prudential supervision seemed an obvious necessary step, but we should have asked Parliament to stipulate some demanding requirements in legislation.

Nevertheless, moving to my second set of points, with the data to hand, the Beck *et al.* study has two results. First, it says that if there is a surprise tightening in UK's monetary policy, there is a reduction in lending overseas. And second, to the extent that there is such a reduction, there is less of a reduction or even perhaps no reduction in lending to borrowers in countries that have tightened their own prudential policies over the preceding 12 months or so.

So an interesting and important question is: what are the stories behind this? One possibility is that the results capture a manifestation of the risk channel of monetary policy; or, in the vaguer terms of market participants, this is the carry trade. The story would simply be that the sterling yield curve has moved up relative to other yield curves, and so fewer resources chase after extra (risk-unadjusted) return elsewhere. Other things being equal, capital-constrained banks will choose to do a bit more lending where the yield curve has moved up (which in the study means at home), taking as given all the kinds and degrees of myopia or other elements of stupidity that involves.

Now, the point of that remark is not to say I believe that this story should be true. But rather that if that were the story, then the result is not about monetary policy surprises as such because any rise in the yield curve over the course of a month relative to the yield curve elsewhere would be enough, on that kind of story, to generate the kind of effect the study picks up. Of course, such shocks could be about the expected path of monetary policy but that is not a given.

Also, to the extent that relative monetary policy expectations are a (or the) key driver, the shocks would not all be delivered in surprise moves in immediate monetary policy settings. It might, therefore, be worth saying that, as a general matter, I do not greatly like the study's method of identification, preferring the Romers' narrative approach, because it cannot distinguish between shocks to the objective, shocks to the reaction function (for a given objective, say because of altered views on the monetary transmission mechanism) and shocks or news about the monetary policymaker's (in this case the Bank of England MPC's) views on the outlook for the economy without any changes in either the objective or the reaction function.

But to the extent that this is what you look at, one might expect the action to be driven by the third of those things: news about the outlook or the Bank of England's view of the outlook. But that underlines the question of why, if what is going on is a carry-trade-like phenomenon, it is only the Bank of England's view of the outlook that matters. What about the data that come out during the month and the market's take on that, meaning the market's shifting expectation and risk assessment of what the monetary policymaker will end up doing down the road (despite its own current view)? For such points to be kicked into touch, the results have to explained with a different kind of story, which is why I want to underline that it is hard to know what to make of the study's first finding, and its robustness, without a story.

Turning to the other element in the chapter's findings, the equivalent question is why, faced with a domestic monetary tightening, UK banks should tighten credit conditions less for borrowers in foreign countries that have tightened prudential policy over the previous 12 months than to countries where prudential policy has not been tightened. One possible story around that, although I think it would be an incomplete story at best or perhaps even flawed, would be that it is because the countries that have tightened prudential policy are more attendant to risk and therefore less risky. Then, as mentioned in the chapter, banks with constrained capital would steer more of their lending abroad towards the less risky destinations (so banks *are* alert to risk, which might make us pause given history!)

But my last sentence contains an elision, because I have shifted from *changes* in prudential policy to *levels* in prudential policy. To the extent that the best story behind the study's second result is a story about the actual or perceived risk of the country in which a borrower is domiciled and operating, that would typically be a story about levels at risk, not about changes in policy. Of course, changes matter because they affect relative levels, but that cannot be enough. One can imagine circumstances — I saw them, including sadly in Britain, during my former central-banking life — where a country has horribly inadequate prudential policies, and there is a tiny prudential tweak in the right direction but it leaves the system horribly fragile. Where so, it is not obvious that a recipient state tightening its prudential policy would always affect lenders' supply schedules unless they are incompetent or myopic (which of course is not uncommon), or the destination's resilience now is (and perhaps already was) adequate in levels terms, or it is at least better than other even more risky destinations and all that matters to lending choices is relative risk among borrowers rather than risk relative to safe assets.

So, on the study's results, the kinds of story that immediately come to my mind raise as many questions as they answer. But I want to suggest something else because my immediate thoughts when I saw what the authors were doing were quite different and I think this is possibly a problem with such regressions. A broad form of the background question is: How will lending abroad be affected by what's happening locally (in this case in the UK)?

Imagine circumstances where there is a nasty adverse local (demand) shock to the UK that does not affect the resilience of the banking system, but does weaken aggregate demand, and is met with an easing of monetary policy. Then I would expect, other things being equal, something like the study's finding to hold: that, other things equal, relative to more neutral conditions, internationally active local banking units would lend more abroad rather than at home because of relative yield curve shifts, plus reduced domestic credit demand.

However, now let us consider another shock — local or global — that again prompts an interest rate cut from the monetary authority, and again shifts down the local currency yield curve, but this time it does significantly impair locally operating banks' capital, to the point where they might need assistance of various kinds from the authorities. In those circumstances, I would expect some home bias in lending to kick in, banks cutting back more on lending abroad than on lending at home (for all sorts of reasons, not excluding the wishes of the government providing any support to the afflicted banking system).

However, here we bump into whether domestic and foreign banks would behave differently, and among the latter whether there is a difference between branches (assuming no locked in local resources) and subsidiaries. In other words, in such studies — and possibly in this one — the definition of local banks might matter. Big picture, I am not sure if a home-bias story would capture the incentives and economic choices of the local (in this study, UK) branches of overseas banks. It is a story that would definitely apply — to the extent that it applies at all — to UK-domiciled units of UK-domiciled banking groups. And, in terms of my priors, whether it applies to UK subsidiaries of overseas groups might actually vary according to all sorts of things which I do not have time even to sketch.

My third set of remarks concerns why policy organisations are interested in any of this at all. Of course, partly because the world is a mysterious place and economists want to research things. But I mean, how is the underlying policy regime and its purpose conceived here? In that respect, I was struck by the first sentence in Chapter 11, which I suspect is far from atypical in describing the purpose of macroprudential policy as being to "moderate the procyclicality of the financial system and thereby secure the resilience and stability of the financial system as a whole" (Shin and Shin, 2021).

Well, I do not doubt that, positively, that is one description of what people would like to do. Normatively, I think it is the wrong way around, at least in current and (regrettably) foreseeable conditions. Casting the purpose of macroprudential policy that way implicitly assumes that the background regime of base (or static) requirements for resilience in the system is adequate, leaving policymakers to make dynamic adjustments with some kind of mean reversion (and maybe occasional permanent recalibrations). That would be like operating monetary policy with anchored medium-to-long run inflation expectations (which is why, by the way, I suspect macro-oriented researchers are inclined to think of *macro*prudential in this way: the basic job is done, and all that remains is dynamic stabilisation policy). But I believe that the necessary background condition — an adequate base regime for ensuring systemic resilience — does not hold, for reasons set out elsewhere (including before I left office quite some years ago). On this view, it would be much better to think of dynamic macroprudential policy as helping, given a flawed base regime, to ensure that the financial system is resilient and so reduce the procyclicality of the financial system (which has things the other way round from the default assumption in the burgeoning macroprudential literature). If that is broadly correct, there is a social cost in proceeding otherwise, including in research programmes.

Why so? For all sorts of reasons, but I will highlight just one. The paper by Thorsten Beck and coauthors starts off with a GDP-at-Risk framework. What we are really focused on in this set up is GDP (aggregate incomes), and of tail risks to GDP somewhere down the road. It is an alluring thought, as researchers with a macro toolkit can project the severity of the tails, stemming from financial imbalances, of the probability distribution for economic activity, as an input to taking policy action to head off such tail events (Aikman *et al.*, 2021).

The idea is useful. The data on which most such work is based are not. First, when, as is not unknown, the state steps in on time to head off an economic collapse, the averted disaster is not in the GDP-data time series, but the rescue might still destabilise a country's social and political harmony, perhaps partly through measures to recoup the fiscal outlay, and partly because of a sense of gross injustice.

Second, and more profoundly, the time series do not capture another, even less visible type of financial instability: near misses. Here it is worth recalling, especially if it has been overlooked, that when the telco debt bubble burst in late 2002, two of the largest firms in the world were said to be precariously positioned. Following up such near misses is as vital as it gets in this field: GDP-at-Risk will not pick them up because there was neither rescue nor severe downturn. During COVID-19, there might have been less dramatic near misses.

My point is not to object to GDP-at-Risk but to observe that it does not take seriously the problem in designing and operating a regime for stability; a challenge not yet overcome, at risk of slipping out of view, and one which presents an important test, and therefore opportunity, for researchers.

References

Shin, Hyun Song and Kwanho Shin (2021): "Lessons for Macro-Financial Policy in Korea." Paper presented at the AMPF 2021 and MAS-BISs conference in May 2021.

Aikman, David, Jonathan Bridges, Sinem Hacioglu Hoke, Cian O'Neill and Akash Raja (2021): "Credit, Capital and Crises: A GDP-at-Risk Approach", *CEPR Discussion Paper*, no 15864, March.

CHAPTER 6

© 2023 World Scientific Publishing Company
https://doi.org/10.1142/9789811259432_0012

Chapter 6

Sweden's Experience of Deploying Monetary and Macroprudential Policies*

Stefan Ingves[†] and Johan Grip[‡]

[†]*Governor, Sveriges Riksbank*
[‡]*Senior Economist, Sveriges Riksbank*

1. Introduction

This chapter focuses on macroprudential policies in Sweden, a country that for a couple of decades was marked by macroeconomic volatility, with recurrent exchange rate instability and a deep, home-grown, financial crisis in the early 1990s. The crisis, however, paved the way for far-reaching political decisions. Following a string of economic reforms, of which some had clear links to macroprudential policymaking, the country has shown relative resilience in the face of ensuing global economic challenges. However, even in the direct aftermath of a crisis, momentum can falter and necessary reforms fall by the wayside, as illustrated by the lack of proper crisis management capabilities when Sweden experienced the Global Financial Crisis (GFC). Furthermore,

---

*The authors thank Mattias Hector, David Farelius, Björn Lagerwall, Olof Sandstedt, Annika Svensson, Jakob Winstrand, Jonas Niemeyer and Gary Watson for valuable comments and suggestions. The opinions expressed in this chapter are the authors' own and cannot be regarded as an expression of the Riksbank's view.

while the reforms in Sweden successfully stabilised government debt, private debt was left unchecked for a long time.

A delayed implementation of the macroprudential policy mandate, with a designated authority under the auspices of the government, contributed to an unencumbered increase of household indebtedness in Sweden.

However, even with a more rapid implementation, it was unlikely that the growing indebtedness would have been brought fully under control. This reflects that macroprudential policy is not a panacea. In the absence of reforms to address the root causes of a problem, in the Swedish case a dysfunctional housing market, macroprudential measures will always be second-best.

The chapter also takes a wider geographical perspective and looks at how macroprudential cooperation in the Nordic–Baltic region has evolved in the face of increasing financial integration. While most countries in the region are members of the European Union (EU) and some have adopted the euro as their currency, a few countries are not members of the EU but are part of the EEA (European Economic Area). Irrespective of the relationship with the EU, the countries in the region need to take into account EU policy when implementing macroprudential policy. While the overall developments in EU law and cooperation are beyond the scope of this chapter, EU policy is referred to in the chapter when particularly relevant to regional developments.

The close Nordic–Baltic regulatory cooperation proved to be extremely useful in containing the fallout of the GFC and the subsequent Baltic crisis, as well as managing different idiosyncratic problems with a cross-border element. Regular contacts to create a mutual understanding of the challenges each part faces are necessary not only to achieve efficiency in policymaking in a cross-border environment but is also key to building the personal trust needed to manage crises.

The chapter is structured as follows. In Section 2, we discuss how financial crises have highlighted vulnerabilities in Sweden and the Nordic–Baltic region, the evolution of macroprudential policy and the relevant remaining vulnerabilities. Section 3 describes the institutional setup in Sweden. In Section 4, we show how institutionally diverse the Nordic–Baltic region is and how regional cooperation nonetheless is effective in the region.

We then move on to Sections 4 and 5 to outline a few instructive policy actions with respect to monetary and macroprudential policy and examine their efficacy. The chapter then concludes by identifying the main lessons learnt from these recent experiences in Sweden and the Nordic–Baltic region in Section 6.

2. Past crises and the evolution of macroprudential policy

To properly understand Sweden's current institutional framework, and how it has evolved, one cannot overlook the role of crises in instigating structural reform.

In particular, the Swedish banking crisis in the 1990s prepared the political ground for the implementation of several important institutional and structural changes to bring increased stability and a longer-term perspective to economic policymaking. As will be shown, some important measures turned out to be temporary and short-lived, but, all in all, the reforms meant that Sweden could cope relatively well with the GFC.

2.1. *The Swedish banking crisis in 1990s paved the way for important reforms*[1]

During the post-war era, Sweden had several different kinds of fixed exchange-rate regimes.[2] During the Bretton Woods era from 1951–1973, the Swedish economy developed strongly at the same time as inflation was also relatively low. However, after the collapse of the Bretton Woods regime, a period of more unstable economic development followed. As illustrated by numerous exchange rate devaluations, economic policies in the 1970s and 1980s were not in line with the requirements of the chosen regime. Fiscal policy in particular did not reflect the need for countercyclical restraint in order to avoid overheating and excessive

---

[1] The description of the Swedish banking crisis is based on Englund (1999). For a more detailed account, the interested reader is directed to read the full paper.

[2] 1951–1973: Bretton Woods; 1973: Membership of the European Currency snake; 1977: Leaves the snake and links currency to trade-weighted basket of currencies; 1991: Unilateral link to ECU.

wage inflation. Financial markets were still considered mainly domestic in nature, despite the growing globalisation of trade and finance. Swedish banks, and credit markets in general, were heavily regulated, with capital controls being kept in place much longer than in many other countries. Banks, insurance companies and other institutions were also subject to lending ceilings and placement requirements (liquidity ratios). However, despite strict regulation, banks found ways of circumventing it. In the early 1980s, in a context of a global trend towards greater openness and transforming financial markets that made regulation increasingly inefficient, the credit rules were questioned. As Englund (1999) writes, "The stage was set for deregulation" and the deregulation of credit markets began in the first half of the 1980s, with an important stage being the phasing out of the lending ceilings in 1985. However, the resulting credit expansion was not met with tighter fiscal policy. Since monetary policy at the time was aimed at maintaining the fixed exchange rate, overall economic policy became too expansionary.

Consequently, in the 1990s, Sweden experienced a "home-grown" crisis fuelled by a commercial real estate bubble that burst,[3] partly due to a tax reform that made it more expensive to borrow.[4] The price fall in real estate was clearly aggravated by distressed sales exacerbated by low equity in the real estate sector, made possible by the lending spree following the deregulation. The commercial real estate crisis led to financial distress for major lending institutions (a solvency crisis) and required government interventions.[5] At the time, Sweden had no formal deposit insurance (or a resolution framework), but the government announced that it guaranteed[6]

---

[3] By the end of 1990 the real-estate index had fallen by 52 percent, and in 1991 prices in downtown Stockholm fell by 35 percent and by another 15 percent the following year. However, the market dried up as valuations fell, making the estimates of the "true" drop in prices uncertain.

[4] Interest rates after taxes increased after interest-rate deductions were lowered from 50 percent to 30 percent.

[5] By the end of 1991, losses were running at 3.5 percent of lending and at the peak of the crisis in the final quarter of 1992 at 7.5 percent of lending, about twice the operating profits of the banking sector. Over the period 1990–1993, total accumulated losses came to nearly 17 percent of lending (Englund, 1999).

[6] By and large, the government followed the principle of reducing moral hazard by saving the banks with a minimum of wealth transfer to the original shareholders.

all forms of bank debt and the Riksbank provided liquidity support. A Bank Support Agency was created[7] to manage distressed banks and two banks had to be taken over by the government, while others received subsidies or guarantees.[8]

At the end of 1992, following the crisis of the European exchange-rate mechanism (ERM), the Swedish krona was left to float after several attempts to defend the fixed exchange rate. In somewhat simplified terms, the 1990s crisis could be described as "Things abroad were more or less OK, but Sweden was not".[9] The crisis provided an important wake-up call for the general public — as a small open economy you need to have your house in order — and paved the way for far-reaching economic reforms. These included a reformed budget process where key elements were a surplus target for the entire government sector, an expenditure ceiling for central government and a pension[10] reform. The reforms achieved stable government finances through fiscal discipline. The monetary policy

---

[7] In Sweden, all the main political parties agreed on the framework for crisis resolution. The framework included a structure to expedite and coordinate responses between the relevant authorities while preserving the integrity of each authority. A new authority was created — the Bank Support Authority (BSA). Before making a decision, the BSA had to obtain the approval of the Riksbank (central bank), the Swedish Financial Services Authority, and the National Debt Office. If agreement was not achieved — this happened only rarely — the issue was referred to the Ministry of Finance. Experience shows the importance of adequate legislation and institutions to tackle weak banks. Lacking these tools, Sweden had to improvise.

[8] The banking crisis led to credit losses of nearly SEK 125 billion in 1990–1993. When the banking system was threatened and the Government intervened, the Bank Support Authority paid out SEK 65 million in bank support of which 98 percent went to two banks: Nordbanken and Gotabanken.

[9] Between 1990 and 1993, the registered unemployment rate increased from about 1.4 percent to 8.2 percent and GDP fell by approximately 5 percent. The government budget deficit exceeded 15 percent of GDP in 1994 and the debt-to-GDP ratio rose to around 75 percent (starting from around 40 percent of GDP at the beginning of the crisis).

[10] The reform was very far-reaching and brought about by the fact that the system at the time was economically and demographically untenable, which could ultimately have jeopardised the Swedish economy. The new contribution-defined system with fictitious pension rights in a distribution system was innovative, and this type of system was even given its own name — Notional Defined Contribution (NDC).

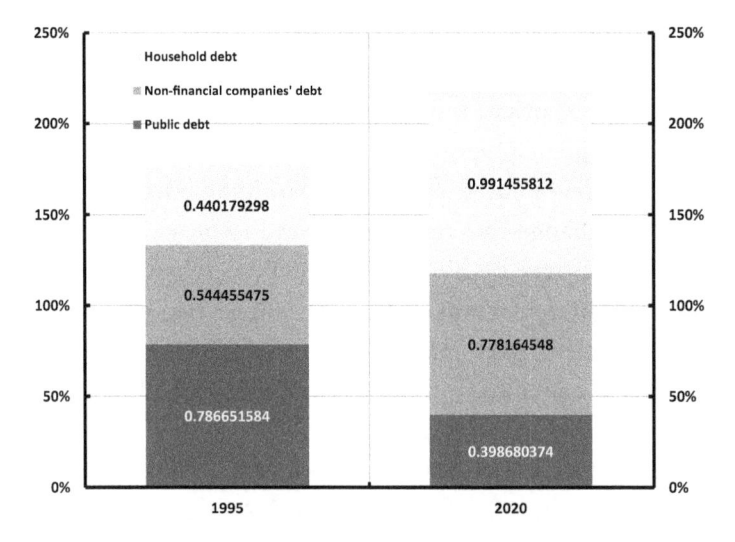

Figure 1. Debt-to-GDP ratio in Sweden; divided into public, household and non-financial corporate debt.
Source: Statistics Sweden.

framework shifted[11] from maintaining a fixed exchange rate to a floating exchange rate with an inflation target, and in 1995 Sweden joined the EU. However, although clearly ambitious, the reforms stopped short of addressing some issues that eventually proved crucial — while government debt was stabilised and put on a clear downward trend, private debt was left unchecked (illustrated in Figure 1).

2.2. Sweden was better prepared, but the GFC shed light on important shortcomings

In the run up to the GFC, the major Swedish banks increased their risk exposure by expanding in the Baltic region as the Baltic States opened up within the context of EU integration. The risks rose substantially due to the increasing imbalances resulting from the uncontrolled growth of the region's economies. Among other things, the credit expansion was

---

[11] The new Sveriges Riksbank Act of 1999 meant that the Riksbank gained greater independence. A new Executive Board was appointed to make decisions on monetary policy and the price stability objective was confirmed by law. The inflation target was introduced in 1993 and began to apply in 1995.

extreme, with lending volumes increasing by 40 percent to 70 percent per year during 2005–2007 (Swedish National Audit Office, 2011). In Riga, apartment prices increased by a factor of four in just three years. Another sign of a high-risk level was that private borrowing was often done in foreign currency, predominantly in euro. This exposed borrowers to exchange-rate risks and proved to be an especially toxic cocktail as salaries rose by 20 percent to 30 percent per year, while the countries had different kinds of fixed exchange-rate policies.[12] Even though banks were in principle shielded from the exchange rate risks, the arrangement contained a considerable credit risk, should the fixed exchange rate prove unsustainable.

In the early days of Swedish banks' expansion into the Baltic region, Swedish authorities considered the risks limited. After some time, concerns increased as the imbalances in the Baltic economies grew, and in 2005 the Riksbank began warning about the build-up of risks in the Baltics.[13]

When the GFC hit, the Swedish economy was in much better shape than in the beginning of the 1990s, due to the earlier reforms. However, our crisis management toolbox was unfortunately back to what it was when we entered the 1990s crisis, since both the temporary legislation created to handle the 1990s crisis and the Bank Support Agency had ceased to exist. As luck would have it, many of the individuals in central positions during the 1990s crisis were still working (in other central positions) during the GFC and could act based on previous experience with basically the same legal framework for crisis management as before.

Being a small open economy, Sweden was still affected by the GFC, as falling European demand had a large negative effect on our export sector and consequently on the Swedish economy. The Swedish banking sector also felt the effects of the GFC but, unlike the domestic crisis in the 1990s, this time it did not suffer major credit losses at home. Instead, it was lending in the Baltic region that led to losses.[14] The low level of confidence in financial markets and considerable uncertainty over developments in the Baltic

---

[12] This raised the risk of currency devaluations leaving households with a higher debt burden, as their debt was denominated in foreign currency.
[13] See The Riksbank's Financial Stability Report 2005:2 as documented in, e.g., Study Group of the Committee on the Global Financial System (2016).
[14] See, e.g., Ingves (2010).

countries, in particular related to concerns over the viability of the fixed exchange rate regimes in the three countries, made it difficult or impossible for Swedish banks to obtain funding from the financial markets. Due to the global nature of the crisis, international collaboration and coordination were an important part of handling the crisis. On a domestic level, measures adopted by the Riksbank (Riksbank, 2020), the Ministry of Finance, FI (the Swedish financial supervisory authority) and the Swedish National Debt Office were decisive in restoring confidence. Moreover, by providing liquidity to other central banks in the region, the Riksbank played its part to ensure that urgently needed liquidity was made available prior to more long-term solutions coming into effect. For example, the swap agreement with the Latvian central bank acted as a bridge to funding from the IMF. Therefore, the crisis never turned into a full-blown domestic solvency crisis, but rather a liquidity crisis that fortunately could be managed. The GFC experience for Sweden can be summarised as "Things abroad were not OK, but Sweden was", and we came out of the crisis without experiencing a long recession.

2.3. *The evolution of macroprudential policy*

The GFC had illustrated some important shortcomings of the global financial regulatory system. One of these was the apparent lack of a systemic perspective when looking at risks and appropriate tools to handle these risks — and the huge costs such omissions could cause. This issue ended up high on the global regulatory reform agenda, with the G20 and Financial Stability Board (FSB) taking on a leading role.

On a European level, a new structure for financial supervision comprising two pillars was created in 2010, one focussing on macroprudential policy and the other on microprudential supervision. The first pillar included the creation of the European Systemic Risk Board (ESRB), not only engaging in the analysis of macroprudential risks but also promoting the development of macroprudential frameworks at the national level. The second pillar included three new European Supervisory Authorities (ESAs), comprising European Banking Authority (EBA), European Securities and Markets Authority (ESMA) and European Insurance and Occupational Pensions Authority (EIOPA). The new ESAs work in parallel with a network of national financial supervisors. Sweden, as a member of the EU, is bound by the regulation developed and agreed at the European level when implementing macroprudential policy.

2.3.1. The macroprudential mandate

An early accomplishment of the ESRB was to issue a recommendation for all EU countries to give an authority, or a council, the mandate to implement policies addressing the build-up of systemic risk, i.e., macroprudential policies. Among other things, the macroprudential authority should be equipped with appropriate instruments to achieve its objectives and be independent from the political bodies and the financial industry.[15]

The need for independence is linked to the fact that macroprudential measures are generally speaking not popular with the groups that are most affected, not least households. If the measures are effective, they limit the amount households can borrow and thus what they can afford to buy. By doing so, they reduce the overall price level of housing and the associated indebtedness of households.[16] As macroprudential policies are unpopular and affect large groups of voters, a conflict of interest for politicians often arises when governments need to decide whether a new requirement should be implemented or not. It can lead to a preference "not to rock the boat" and avoid upsetting the electorate, delaying, or avoiding altogether, the implementation of measures aimed at reducing the build-up of systemic risk — i.e., an inaction bias.

Against this background, central banks, as independent authorities, appear well placed to perform the role of macroprudential authority. They can never disregard the build-up of systemic risk, because a financial crisis affects the economy, the payment system and the transmission channel for monetary policy. Furthermore, monetary policy influences housing prices, credit growth and the general level of risk taking in the economy —

---

[15] Independence from political considerations to avoid inaction bias and independence from the financial industry to avoid regulatory capture.

[16] Everyone would prefer it if only *they* could borrow unconstrained, while the rules constrained others' borrowing capacity. Then they could win the bidding by taking on more debt, but at a lower overall price point. This is an example of a coordination problem that macroprudential policy can influence, by imposing restrictions that limit the amount of debt households can borrow when they bid on an object.

i.e., financial stability. As central banks are used to overseeing the level of risk in the system as a whole, they are well positioned to spot potential leakages and can act pre-emptively, avoiding political considerations that could lead to inaction.

The ESRB recommendation stopped short of saying that central banks should be the designated authority responsible for macroprudential policy. However, the recommendation says that central banks should play a leading role.

2.3.1.1. The macroprudential mandate in Sweden

Despite rising levels of household debt in Sweden (see Figure 2) and repeated warnings[17] from the Riksbank, the government did not appoint a macroprudential authority until 2014. Contrary to most other EU countries, the central bank, i.e., the Riksbank, did not receive

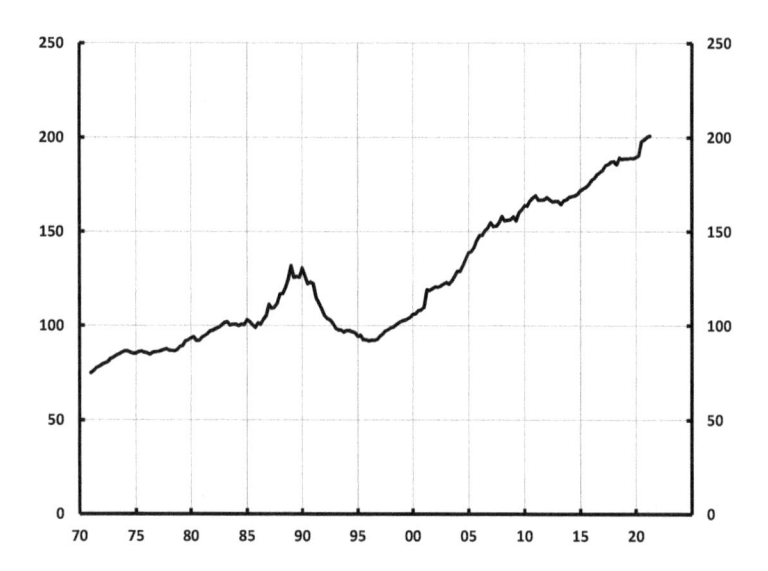

Figure 2. Household debt-to-income ratio.
Note: Total household debt as a share of disposable household income added together over the last four quarters. The final observation refers to Q1, 2021.
Source: Statistics Sweden and the Riksbank.

---

[17] The Riksbank had emphasised the risks associated with increased household debt since 2004. See e.g. "The mortgage market from a Riksbank perspective" 2004, "House price developments and monetary policy" 2005 or "Introduction on monetary policy" 2006.

a mandate for macroprudential policy. Instead, and deviating from the recommendation of the ESRB, the mandate was given to FI, with the government having the final say in some cases (borrower-based measures) on whether or not a proposed measure can be implemented. Around the same time, the Financial Stability Council was formed to discuss issues related to systemic risk; see Section 3 on the institutional setup in Sweden. However, being a discussion forum only, the council did not receive any formal mandate regarding macroprudential measures.

It turned out, however, that even though FI was given the macroprudential mandate, this did not allow the authority to implement borrower-based measures. When FI first tried to implement an amortisation requirement in 2015, the mandate was challenged by a local court and the legal framework for macroprudential policy had to be updated by the parliament. This resulted in a considerable delay and the amortisation requirement was not implemented until the summer of 2016; two and a half years after the mandate was first put in place and over 10 years after the Riksbank first started to warn about the build-up of systemic risk associated with household debt. With the macroprudential mandate in place and the legal framework sorted out, the mandate was once again amended in 2018 to enhance the toolbox for macroprudential polices aimed at households (borrower-based measures). A second amortisation requirement came into effect during the spring of 2018. However, the policy mix of low interest rates (real and nominal) and borrower-based measures that only affect new mortgages has not been enough to stop the dramatic rise in household debt and the associated rise in housing prices. This illustrates that macroprudential policies can only slow the tide of rising household debt; as long as the underlying structural problems on the housing market remain unaddressed, we should not expect the risks to decrease by themselves (see the next section).

2.4. Structural weaknesses — (too) challenging for macroprudential policy

2.4.1. A dysfunctional housing market

For a long time, increased indebtedness among households in Sweden has gone hand-in-hand with the strong development of prices on the housing market (see Figure 3). This is due, in part, to a poorly functioning housing market and a tax system that, from a financial stability perspective, leaves much to be desired. A Swedish economist, Assar Lindbeck, pointed out the dysfunctionality of the Swedish housing market for decades (Lindbeck, 1963, 1967; also see, e.g., Bentzel *et al.* [1963]).

His insider–outsider theory of labour economics also provides a fitting model to illustrate the fundamental problem of the Swedish housing market, which is characterised by those on the inside who have capital, higher incomes, connections, time and knowledge of how the system works. Conversely, those on the outside have little or no capital, lower incomes, no connections, insufficient time and limited knowledge of how the system works.

The rent control system contributes to inefficient utilisation of the housing stock and there are also limitations to the supply of housing. Weak competition in the construction sector, an insufficient supply of land for new construction and comprehensive and complicated planning processes have long impeded housing construction. The limited supply

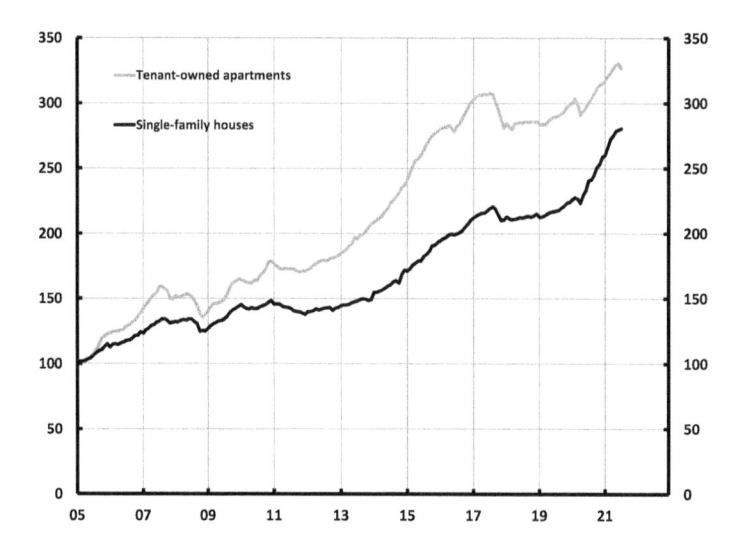

Figure 3. Price developments on the Swedish housing market.
Note: Housing prices refer to an index where January 2005 = 100. Seasonally adjusted prices.
Source: Statistics Sweden and Valueguard.

of housing over a longer period has contributed to higher housing prices and thereby to higher indebtedness among households. In addition, a tax system that focusses more on transactions than ownership, in the form of stamp duties and the taxation of capital gains on housing sales, makes it more expensive to move and therefore does not promote mobility on the housing market. The ensuing lock-in effect results in a further reduction of market supply.

Reducing the risks linked to household indebtedness requires solving the long-standing fundamental problems in the Swedish housing market. Examples of feasible measures include reviewing the regulations regarding the production of new housing, the rent-setting system, the taxation of capital gains and property and interest deductions. So far, the political will to address these issues has been limited. A general lesson to be drawn from this unfortunate inaction bias is the same as after the Swedish banking crisis. As Englund (1999) writes, "Policy choices become very difficult at a stage when the need for major structural reforms has built up for too long".

If such measures are not implemented to the extent necessary, new macroprudential policy measures may need to be introduced, or the measures already implemented may need to be tightened. However, resolving the fundamental problems in the housing market is a better way forward than further macroprudential policy measures.

2.4.2. A large cross-border banking system

Sweden has a large banking system that is concentrated around a few interconnected major banks with large exposures to housing and commercial real estate.[18] Consequently, in the event of a crisis, problems in one bank, or in the property sector, risk rapidly spreading to the entire banking system, potentially threatening the stability of the financial system. Another potential vulnerability is the fact that the major banks in Sweden obtain much of their funding via international capital markets,

---

[18] The major Swedish banks have large exposures to one another, primarily through interbank loans and holdings of covered bonds. Risks arising in a single bank's operations can therefore easily spread to the other major banks. During the GFC, uncertainty over future loan losses in individual banks spilled over to the others.

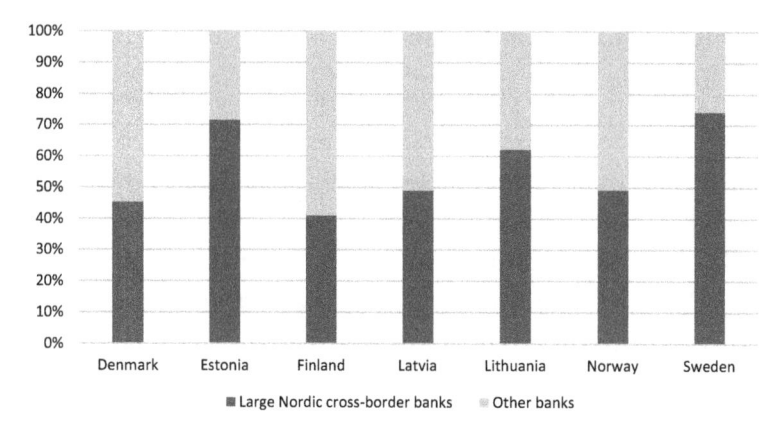

Figure 4. Share of lending to the public.
Note: Large Nordic cross-border banks include Danske Bank, DNB, Nordea, Handelsbanken, SEB and Swedbank. Other banks include Luminor (Estonia).
Source: Bank reports and Sveriges Riksbank (2018).

which means the banking system is sensitive to developments in these markets.

The Swedish banking system is also very much cross-border. Banks with subsidiaries and branches in several countries play an important role in the financial markets of the Nordic and Baltic countries and require the reciprocation[19] of macroprudential policy to ensure the effectiveness of the measures taken. In the Nordic–Baltic region, large cross-border banking groups have very considerable market shares in seven of the eight countries (Iceland being the exception). At present there are three Swedish banking groups, and one each from Denmark, Estonia, Finland and Norway. The relative importance of the large Nordic banking groups in the region is illustrated in Figure 4.

Cross-border banking groups provide benefits and improve efficiency in the financial system. At the same time, they increase the risk that a problem arising in one bank, or banking group, can affect financial stability in more than one country. Agreements on information-sharing and cooperation between central banks and other authorities are therefore important to prevent financial crises.

---

[19] The section on regional cooperation discusses the issue of reciprocation in more detail.

3. Institutional setup in Sweden

The aim of Section 2 was to provide a basis for the rest of the chapter by discussing some more general features of the Swedish economy and the evolution of the macroprudential mandate. In this section we will discuss, in a little more detail, the specific institutional setup regarding financial stability and macroprudential policy in Sweden. It should be noted that, when pursuing macroprudential policy, the Swedish authorities are bound by developments in EU policy. As such, the financial stability authorities in Sweden participate in various groups at the EU level to discuss issues related to macroprudential policy.[20]

3.1. *Authorities responsible for financial stability*

As can be seen in Figure 5, although being a small open economy, the Swedish institutional setup for financial stability and macroprudential policy is highly decentralised, with dispersed responsibilities — the Ministry of Finance, FI, the Riksbank and the Swedish National Debt Office all have a shared responsibility for keeping the financial system

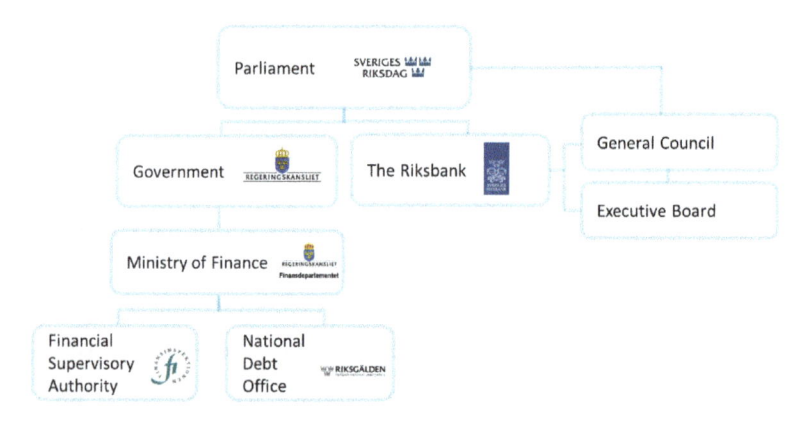

Figure 5. Institutional setup for Swedish authorities responsible for financial stability.
Source: The Riksbank.

---

[20] For example, working groups within the ESRB.

stable. How they are governed is illustrated in Figure 5. The authorities have different roles and responsibilities, but the interaction between them is central, for both preventing and managing financial crises.

3.1.1. The Ministry of Finance

The Ministry of Finance is responsible for primary legislation for matters relating to the stability of the financial system, consumer protection in the financial markets, national debt policy, pension savings and the regulation of companies, trade and services in the financial markets.

3.1.2. The Riksbank

The Riksbank is an authority under the Riksdag, the Swedish parliament. The Riksbank's objectives are to maintain price stability and financial stability. In practice, the two objectives are closely interlinked. Without a stable financial system, it becomes difficult to conduct effective monetary policy to maintain price stability, as the transmission mechanism will be hampered. Likewise, the economic consequences of a financial crisis would directly affect price stability, economic growth and employment.

3.1.2.1. Monetary policy

According to the Sveriges Riksbank Act, the objective of monetary policy is "to maintain price stability". The Riksbank has interpreted this objective to mean a low and stable rate of inflation. More precisely, the Riksbank's target is to hold inflation in terms of the CPIF[21] around 2 percent a year.

The Riksbank's main monetary policy tool is the repo rate. In some situations, the repo rate may need to be supplemented with other measures from the monetary policy toolbox, to ensure that monetary policy has an effective impact. The toolbox also includes, e.g., balance sheet operations that can be deployed to help meet the monetary policy remit. The

---

[21] CPIF is the consumer price index with a fixed interest rate. The target for monetary policy is that the annual change in the CPIF shall be 2 percent, that is, the same level previously applied to the CPI.

Riksbank's balance sheet mostly consists of securities in Swedish kronor. This item has grown substantially since 2015 due to the purchases of, above all, government bonds. In conjunction with the coronavirus pandemic of 2020–2021, the Riksbank's balance sheet has increased further as, in addition to Swedish government bonds, the Riksbank has also purchased Swedish covered bonds, municipal bonds and commercial papers.[22]

In line with EU treaties, the Riksdag has given the Riksbank an independent status.[23] This means that the Executive Board of the Riksbank makes the monetary policy decisions without instruction from other parties. By delegating the task of maintaining inflation at a low and stable level to the Riksbank, the Riksdag has ensured that monetary policy is based on a long-term perspective and that there is a sound basis for the credibility of the inflation target.

3.1.2.2. Financial stability

The Riksbank also has a mandate from the Riksdag to promote a safe and efficient payment system. The Riksbank's interpretation of this is that it shall act to promote stability in the Swedish financial system as a whole. The mandate also includes issuing banknotes and coins. In addition, the Riksbank provides an electronic payment system, RIX, which handles large-value payments between banks and other actors in a safe and efficient way. In the event of a crisis, the Riksbank can provide liquidity support to the financial system through its role as a lender of last resort.

The Riksbank analyses the stability of the financial system on a continuous basis in order to detect, at an early stage, changes and

---

[22] At the same time, monetary policy lending has been increased to alleviate the effects of the coronavirus pandemic on the Swedish economy.

[23] Central bank independence is also safeguarded within the European Union where the Treaty on the Functioning of the European Union stipulates that the European Central Bank (ECB) "shall be independent in the exercise of its powers". Significantly, this independence extends to the national central banks of the EU, meaning no individual EU Member State can unilaterally amend or repeal independence.

vulnerabilities that could lead to disruptions. The analysis focuses primarily on the major Swedish banking groups, the functioning of the financial markets and the financial infrastructure required for the payments and the financial markets in Sweden to function smoothly.

The Riksbank, like most other central banks, holds gold and foreign currency reserves, not least to be able to provide temporary liquidity assistance in foreign currency at short notice. As a consequence, foreign exchange reserves are mostly maintained in the currencies in which emergency liquidity assistance may be needed and in assets that can rapidly be converted into liquid funds, such as government bonds.

It is worth noting that the Riksbank does not dispose of any formal preventive financial stability tools of a macroprudential nature. Apart from the interest rate, which is blunt and not considered a macroprudential instrument, its financial stability arsenal is more adapted to managing existing crises than preventing them from materialising.

3.1.3. FI (Finansinspektionen), micro- and macroprudential policy

As Sweden's financial supervisory authority, FI's operations are governed by the Government's Letter of Appropriation. In this document, the Government outlines the general objective of FI's operations and its assignments.[24]

3.1.3.1. Microprudential policy

FI's role is to promote stability and efficiency in the financial system as well as to ensure effective consumer protection. It authorises,[25]

---

[24] FI's operations are also governed by an ordinance which details the authority's specific objectives, assignments and responsibilities and by an operational ordinance that describes the joint assignments and responsibilities applicable to all authorities.

[25] Operations that involve offering financial services require a permit granted by FI. FI issues regulations and general guidelines and assesses whether existing legislation needs to be amended.

supervises[26] and monitors[27] all companies operating in Swedish financial markets such as:

- Banks and other credit institutions;
- Securities companies and fund management companies;
- Stock exchanges, authorised marketplaces and clearing houses;
- Insurance companies, insurance brokers and mutual benefit societies.

FI monitors and analyses trends in the financial market. It assesses the financial health of individual companies, the various sectors and the financial market as a whole. It also examines the risks and control systems in financial companies and supervises compliance with statutes, ordinances and other regulations.

As microprudential supervisor, FI is responsible for capital and liquidity requirements, such as, e.g., the countercyclical capital buffer (CCyB) or risk-weight floors.

FI is also tasked with supervising financial companies that are subject to the Anti-Money Laundering Act.

3.1.3.2. Macroprudential policy

The mandate for macroprudential policy means that FI can, and should, suggest measures to counteract financial imbalances. When FI proposes a new borrower-based measure, the government makes the final decision on whether the measure should be implemented or not.

To handle vulnerabilities related to excessive household debt, FI could deploy two different categories of measures. First, FI can introduce lender-based measures, such as stricter capital or liquidity requirements. These measures serve to increase the resilience of the banking system, but they typically only have a modest impact on lending

---

[26] FI also supervises compliance with the Swedish Insider Act, investigates cases of suspected offences and share price manipulations. It also conducts onsite investigations at branches of Swedish companies located in other EU countries.

[27] FI monitors that companies disclose complete and clear information to the consumers and ensure that routines for such information function satisfactorily. In addition to monitoring, it also drafts rules for financial reporting by financial companies.

and the underlying risks involved. Second, to curb the systemic risks associated with excessive household debt, FI can use borrower-based measures, which have more of a direct impact on the vulnerabilities linked to household borrowing.

3.1.4. The Swedish National Debt Office, framework for resolution and deposit insurance

In 2016, the Debt Office was appointed resolution authority under the EU Bank Recovery and Resolution Directive[28] and is therefore responsible both for preparing for crises in banks and for managing them. The Debt Office sets a minimum requirement for own funds and eligible liabilities for each bank to ensure that there are sufficient resources to write down or convert into equity if a bank is in crisis.

The Debt Office is also responsible for maintaining and managing the following funds that can be used in relation to bank failures:

- The resolution reserve;
- The deposit insurance fund;
- The stability fund.

3.1.4.1. The resolution reserve

The resolution reserve may be used for a bank in resolution, for example, to provide temporary financing or contribute to the recapitalisation of the institution under certain circumstances. However, this assumes that shareholders and creditors have first covered a substantial part of the costs. Each year, the banks and institutions pay a fee to the resolution reserve.[29] The fee shall be paid as long as the balance of the resolution reserve is less than 3 percent of the total guaranteed deposits of the banks

---

[28] The resolution regulations apply in all EU countries and were developed based on the lessons learned from the GFC of 2008–2009, which resulted in considerable costs to society. The aim of the resolution regulations is to safeguard financial stability and mitigate the costs of any future crisis.

[29] The resolution fee was collected for the first time in 2016.

and institutions. A standardised model is used to set the fees for smaller institutions, while larger institutions pay a fee in proportion to the risk that their potential failure poses to the financial system. Fees are determined in accordance with an EU regulation on resolution fees. However, it is worth noting that, like the stability fund, the resolution reserve does not consist of an actual fund, but is a claim on the government in the form of a special account at the National Debt Office. Fees paid to the different funds become part of the financing of the budget. This means that if there is a need to use the resolution reserve, or the stability fund, this will require government borrowing. This may not be a problem in the case where the underlying stress is of an idiosyncratic nature. However, if there is a general financial crisis, this may turn out to be difficult.

3.1.4.2. The deposit insurance fund

Under the deposit insurance scheme, the state will compensate depositors up to a maximum of SEK 1,050,000 per person if their bank or institution fails. As with the resolution reserve, all banks and institutions that are members of the deposit insurance scheme pay an annual fee to the Debt Office. The fees are then transferred to the deposit insurance fund, which is managed by the Legal, Financial and Administrative Services Agency (Kammarkollegiet). If assets in the fund are insufficient to pay compensation, there is a possibility to borrow from the Swedish state. Such loans shall be repaid by the subsequent collection of additional fees from institutions.

3.1.4.3. The stability fund

The stability fund was set up in the context of the GFC to finance support measures for the financial system. The banks and institutions paid annual fees to the fund until 2016, when the stability fee was replaced by the resolution fee. Part of the stability fund's assets were then also transferred to the resolution reserve. The stability fund remains in place to finance precautionary government support measures by the Debt Office.

3.1.5. The financial stability council

Not least due to the shared responsibility for promoting financial stability in Sweden, interaction between the authorities is important both in preventive work and in the event of a crisis materialising. The Financial Stability Council was established partly as a reflection of this.

The Financial Stability Council is an information-sharing forum with representatives from the government (Ministry of Finance), the Riksbank, FI and the Swedish National Debt Office. The Council meets regularly to discuss financial stability issues, the need for measures to prevent financial imbalances from building up and, in the event of a financial crisis, the need for crisis measures. The Council is *not* a decision-making body. The government and the represented authorities of the Council decide independently, within their own particular remits, which measures are to be taken.

The minister responsible for financial markets chairs the Council meetings with the heads of each authority concerned present. These meetings normally occur twice a year. Minutes of the Council's meetings are made public within two weeks of them taking place. Were a financial crisis to occur, the Council would meet more frequently to discuss the need for crisis measures.

The Financial Stability Council's work is administered by a preparatory group that meets monthly to prepare and plan the work for the Council, and more often should financial instability occur.

4. Regional differences and cooperation

The Nordic–Baltic countries are very diverse in terms of their institutional setup. Neighbouring countries have different types of links to the EU, and cooperation across different jurisdictions can be a complex matter. Nevertheless, Nordic countries have a long history of economic collaboration and the Nordic–Baltic countries are now continuing this successful tradition.

4.1. *Nordic–Baltic differences*

Even though the Nordic–Baltic countries are similar in many ways, the Nordic–Baltic region is institutionally quite heterogeneous. As shown in Figure 6, all countries are members of the EU except Iceland and Norway. Finland and the three Baltic countries have adopted the euro and are thus also members of the banking union. Denmark is pursuing a fixed exchange rate while Sweden, Norway and Iceland all have floating exchange rates.

There are also differences between the countries when it comes to who has been given the role as designated macroprudential authority (see Figure 7). While both Norway and Denmark have put their finance ministries in charge of macroprudential policy, in Finland, Latvia and Sweden the same role is performed by the supervisory authority. In Estonia, Iceland and Lithuania, the central bank is the designated authority. A further complication is that a clear, agreed nomenclature of what constitutes micro- and macroprudential supervision is lacking,

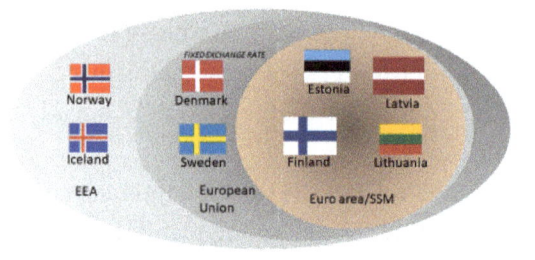

Figure 6. Different characteristics of the Nordic–Baltic countries.
Source: Ingves *et al.* (2020).

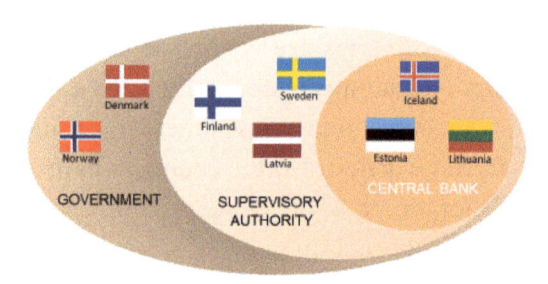

Figure 7. Designated macroprudential authority in the Nordic–Baltic countries.
Source: Ingves *et al.* (2020).

resulting in sometimes differing responsibilities for comparable measures among the group of countries.

4.2. Regional cooperation

The fact that the region has been dominated by a handful of large cross-border banks has created incentives for cooperation between financial stability authorities in the region. While Nordic central banks have a very long history of cooperation in various forms, the collaboration with the Baltic central banks evolved during the GFC. Regional cooperation was key to promoting effective crisis management during the GFC. For example, in May 2008, the central banks of Denmark, Norway and Sweden entered into swap agreements with the central bank of Iceland. Later in 2008, the Riksbank and the Danish central bank agreed on swap arrangements with the Latvian central bank as a bridge to funding from the IMF. Furthermore, a swap agreement was also concluded between the Riksbank and the Estonian central bank in 2009. These agreements led to a deepened cooperation, a continuation of a longer history of cooperation, in the Nordic–Baltic region as the GFC subsided. Several regional groups have since been set up, not only between central banks but also between supervisors, resolution authorities and finance ministries.

4.2.1. Regional groups of cooperation[30]

An important forum of cooperation in the macroprudential area is the Nordic–Baltic Macroprudential Forum (NBMF). This forum was created in 2011 at the initiative of the Riksbank and brings together central banks and supervisory authorities at the senior level in biannual meetings. The task of the NBMF is to discuss risks to financial stability in the region and the implementation of macroprudential policies to counter such risks. The forum also discusses topical issues — with relevance from a macroprudential perspective — that are discussed in other international forums.

---

[30] The following section is based on Ingves *et al.* (2020).

The NBMF has proven to be an important informal forum for discussion of financial stability risks and macroprudential measures. It has enabled central banks and supervisors to meet regularly and discuss issues of mutual interest. It has promoted an increased understanding of cross-border issues and more in-depth analysis of the detailed implementation of the various macroprudential measures. As it provides a regional perspective, it supplements European groups such as the ESRB. In order for macroprudential policy to be effective in an environment with a high degree of cross-border banking and banks operating in the form of branches, the issue of so-called reciprocation of macroprudential policy becomes important.[31] A host supervisor can only ask the home supervisor of a branch to reciprocate a measure, i.e., to also increase capital requirement in its own jurisdiction for exposures of the branch. In the absence of such reciprocation, the measures become less effective.[32] The close cooperation between the Nordic–Baltic authorities, not least in the context of the NBMF, has led to reciprocation working well.[33]

The Nordic–Baltic countries have also established close cooperation in the area of crisis management. In 2010, the Nordic–Baltic Stability Group (NBSG) was established between finance ministries, central banks and supervisory and resolution authorities (see Table 1). The NBSG was the first stability group in Europe. The main focus of the NBSG has been to discuss and exchange information on a regular basis on important issues related to financial stability concerns in the region. Another main task has been to prepare and hold regular financial

---

[31] For example, if a country is hosting a number of foreign branches and sees the need to increase capital requirements for a particular exposure, the national designated macroprudential authority does not have jurisdiction over the exposures in the foreign branches.

[32] For some measures, such as CCyB up to 2.5 percent of CET 1 capital, reciprocity is mandatory. Reciprocity becomes especially important for risk-weight floors and systemic risk buffers as these measures lack mandatory reciprocity.

[33] The most common request for reciprocation in the Nordic–Baltic region is for a measure that has been used as a risk-weight floor for mortgages (article 458). This should be seen in light of the importance of residential real estate markets for Nordic and Baltic banks and financial stability risks in general.

Table 1. Groups and forums concerning financial stability in the Nordic–Baltic region.

Forum/Group	Mandate	Membership
Nordic–Baltic Macroprudential Forum (2011)	Discusses financial stability risks and macroprudential measures.	The central bank and supervisory authorities in the Nordic–Baltic countries.
Nordic–Baltic Stability Group (2010)	Focuses on crisis resolution issues and crisis simulation exercises.	Finance ministries, central banks, supervisory and resolution authorities in the Nordic–Baltic countries.

Source: The Riksbank.

crisis simulation exercises. In January 2019, a major financial crisis management exercise was carried out in the Nordic–Baltic region.[34] The cross-border exercise in 2019 was the first time the European Bank Recovery and Resolution Directive was tested in a truly cross-border setting, involving both authorities within the banking union and authorities outside of it. The exercise involved around 300 individuals from 31 different authorities of Denmark, Estonia, Finland, Iceland, Latvia, Lithuania, Norway and Sweden as well as relevant European Union authorities. In addition to the active participants, a staff member of the International Monetary Fund observed the simulation.

5. Policy actions

In this section, we will look at macroprudential measures that have actually been taken. The focus of the discussion will be on Sweden and

---

[34] A working group, under the chairmanship of a representative of the Riksbank, had prepared the simulation. The two-day exercise simulated the need for liquidity provision as well as resolution of two fictitious regional banks. The exercise provided a wealth of experiences that the authorities continue to discuss, including a number of challenges. One such challenge was the communication between home and host authorities and information sharing within the supervisory and resolution colleges of the fictitious banks involved in the simulation. In the scenario setup, the home authorities of both banks were outside of the euro area and hence the banking union, while both banks had subsidiaries in countries within the banking union.

actions taken to address the risks associated with mortgage lending, although a summary of measures taken in the Nordic–Baltic region will also be provided. We begin by providing a brief background to the build-up of systemic risk connected to housing and the policy measures taken to reduce this vulnerability. As a background to the discussion, it should be noted that measures taken by European countries, although formally taken by national authorities, are heavily influenced by the existence of the European superstructure briefly described in Section 2.

5.1. *Background to macroeconomic measures in Sweden*

As noted earlier, the Riksbank has an objective to maintain price stability and promote a safe and efficient payment system. This means avoiding periods of financial distress, as well as keeping inflation close to the target. In the short run, there can be a trade-off between striving for financial stability and keeping inflation around the target, e.g., where rising inflation is not a concern but a tighter monetary policy stance is motivated on stability grounds, also referred to as "leaning against the wind". Leaning against the wind is a special case where a central bank *can* pursue a tighter stance without having to defend the credibility of the inflation target. The Riksbank applied a mild version of this kind of strategy, in the aftermath of the GFC until around mid-2014. At that time, when inflation expectations were showing signs of becoming unanchored, monetary policy had to be altered to focus solely on inflation.[35] The repo rate was lowered, and in 2015 went negative for the first time ever, and a QE programme was launched to safeguard the credibility of the inflation target and to anchor inflation expectations to the target once again. In the immediate aftermath of the change to a more expansionary monetary policy stance, FI did not have a working legal mandate for macroprudential policy applied to households despite having been given the formal responsibility for macroprudential policy in general.

---

[35] See Monetary Policy Report (2013).

This unfortunately left the field wide open for household debt to increase even more when interest rates were lowered.[36]

5.2. *Macroprudential policies in Sweden*

To reduce the risks associated with high and increasing household debt in Sweden, a number of macroprudential measures have been introduced.[37] As mentioned in Section 3, these measures can be grouped into lender-based measures, such as stricter capital or liquidity requirements to increase the resilience of the banking system, or borrower-based measures, to curb the systemic risks associated with excessive household debt. Lender-based measures typically only have a modest impact on lending and the underlying risks linked to household indebtedness. Borrower-based measures have a more direct impact on the build-up of vulnerabilities and work by limiting households' scope for borrowing in the bank's credit assessments.[38]

---

[36] The legal mandate for macroprudential policy was formally in place from 1 January 2014 but when FI first attempted to introduce an amortisation requirement for mortgage lending, the legality of the measure was questioned by a local court. The attempt to introduce an amortisation requirement was questioned by the same court on two consecutive occasions during 2015. Not until the legal mandate was updated could the amortisation requirement be implemented on 1 June 2016, two and a half years after the mandate was first implemented.

[37] FI generally only motivates borrower-based measures as macroprudential.

[38] A large part of Swedish banks' lending consists of mortgage loans to Swedish households and banks are obliged to conduct credit assessments to ensure that borrowers can meet their commitments, both at the time of borrowing and in adverse scenarios. As part of this, banks draw up so-called discretionary income calculations. When calculating discretionary income, the bank estimates how much (disposable) income the household will have left after taxes, interest expenses, amortisation, operating costs and maintenance costs for the property (or fees for an apartment building) and other living expenses are deducted. To "pass" the discretionary income calculation, a household has to achieve a sufficient margin after expenses. In addition to a discretionary income calculation, the credit assessment consists of a credit report, i.e., a statistical risk assessment based on the borrower's credit record and other data, a qualitative assessment of the borrower's debt servicing ability and the collateral item's location and standard.

5.2.1. *Borrower-based measures*

A special feature of macroprudential measures focused on mortgages is that, at least in Sweden, they only affect *new* mortgages, i.e., mortgages taken out after the requirement comes into effect. Therefore, the measures initially only affect the flow of new mortgages. This kind of macroprudential measure, discussed in more detail below, should therefore be implemented sooner rather than later when risks start to appear, since it takes a long time for the requirements to apply to the entire stock of mortgages. In contrast, an interest-rate change has an effect on the entire stock of debt,[39] including unsecured loans. Similarly, if the government decides to change interest deductions or property taxes, that would affect all households (who own a property) and the entire stock of debt.

5.2.1.1. Loan-to-value limit

After the GFC, FI issued a recommendation for a loan-to-value (LTV) limit. This was motivated by consumer protection concerns, as the macroprudential mandate had not been introduced yet. The LTV limit was set at 85 percent for mortgages and has remained unchanged since its introduction in 2010. The recommendation means that any loan taken by a household above the LTV limit, to purchase a home, cannot be secured against a property. A loan above the LTV limit has to be an unsecured loan, with a shorter duration and a higher interest rate.

5.2.1.2. Amortisation requirements[40]

Sweden currently has two types of amortisation requirements, both applying to *new* mortgages. These requirements primarily work to curb

---

[39] Pass-through will depend on interest-rate fixation periods; the share of households with a variable rate in Sweden is around 50 percent.

[40] Amortisation requirements do not imply a need to repay the entire mortgage, since the requirements are no longer binding as soon as the LTV ratio and/or the LTI ratio drops below the required thresholds. Dropping below the threshold can be achieved either by reducing the mortgage debt burden through amortisations or it can be achieved by an increased market value of the property (the LTV ratio is reduced under a threshold), or by increases in household income (the LTI ratio drops below the threshold). In a market with increasing housing prices, the LTV ratio goes down and creates additional borrowing capacity.

mortgage lending by limiting the amount a household can afford to borrow.[41] The first amortisation requirement was introduced in 2016 (based on LTV) and the second in 2018 (based on LTI).

(1) LTV amortisation

The first requirement is based on the loan-to-value ratio that a household can achieve for a property they wish to purchase. The amortisation requirement is a percentage of the mortgage per year, and is set at

1 percent if LTV > 50 percent but LTV ≤ 70 percent,
2 percent if LTV is > 70 percent.

(2) Loan-to-income amortisation

The second amortisation requirement is based on a household's LTI ratio. *Loan* is defined as the total amount of *mortgage loans* a household has, i.e., not the total amount of debt which includes unsecured loans. Income is annual gross income for the household. The requirement is a percentage of the mortgage per year, and is set at

1 percent if LTI > 450 percent of the household's gross annual income.

These two requirements are additive and can thus add up to a maximum amortisation requirement of 3 percent of the mortgage per year, as long as the constraints are binding. The total amount that has to be amortised is summarised in Table 2.

Table 2. Total amortisation requirement in a discretionary income calculation.

Amortisation if:	LTV ≤ 50 percent	50 percent < LTV ≤ 70 percent	LTV > 70 percent
LTI ≤ 450 percent	0 percent	1 percent	2 percent
LTI > 450 percent	1 percent	2 percent	3 percent

---

[41] For example, they can afford to pay 2 percent amortisation but not 3 percent to pass the margin; that means they have to make sure that either the LTV goes below 70 percent or that their LTI-ratio stays below 450 percent. Or they are bounded by the nominal amount equal to 2 percent of amortisation to pass the banks' credit assessment.

5.2.2. Lender-based measures

In addition to macroprudential measures aimed at households, FI can introduce lender-based measures aimed directly at banks, such as capital requirements. Here we will briefly describe two such measures that FI has introduced. The first measure is a risk-weight floor for mortgage lending, i.e., a floor for how low the risk-weight can be set, when applied to mortgage lending. The second is CCyB.

Risk-weight floors were introduced as a response to the way Swedish banks calculated risk weights using internal risk-classification models based on historical data on loan losses. From an international perspective, these internal models generate very low risk weights for Swedish mortgages.[42] The low risk weights that Swedish banks applied to their lending was a cause for concern, since historical data did not always predict the future and we should not place too much confidence in models. The introduction of a floor was therefore highly justified, to prevent the combination of low risk weights and high leverage from the risk of becoming unsustainable. Risk-weight floors for mortgage lending were first set at 15 percent in 2013 and then raised to 25 percent in 2014.[43] This means that banks who apply internal risk-classification models have to use a little more of their own equity for mortgage lending.[44] These levels should be contrasted with the standardised approach for banks that do not use their own internal risk models, which is 35 percent.

A risk-weight floor is a good example of a macroprudential measure that requires reciprocity. At present, Denmark, Finland, Norway and Latvia

---

[42] See, e.g., FSR 2011:2 and FSR 2012:2.

[43] This measure imposes a credit institution-specific floor of 25 percent for average risk weights applied by banks using the internal ratings-based approach to the portfolio of retail exposures to obligors residing in Sweden secured by immovable property. The measure applies at the portfolio level to the average of the risk weights of the individual exposures weighted by the relevant exposure value.

[44] The risk-weight floors were introduced as a way to stop banks continuously lowering their internal estimates for risk weights, which came down from 0.5 for all mortgages when the internal risk models were first implemented to 0.05 before FI introduced the risk-weight floors.

are reciprocating the 25 percent risk-weight floor for mortgage lending, introduced by FI, while Estonia and Lithuania are not reciprocating, due to immaterial exposures.

Contrary to risk-weight floors, the reciprocation of the CCyB is mandatory in the EU up to a 2.5 percent requirement of CET 1 capital. The CcyB is designed to reduce the pro-cyclicality in the financial system, by requiring banks to accumulate capital when systemic risk is judged to be increasing. This thus dampens excessive credit growth in booming markets while at the same time creating buffers that can be used during periods of stress. The CcyB is set by FI each quarter and prior to the COVID-19 pandemic, between 2015 and 2019, the CCyB was increased from 1.0 percent to 2.5 percent.[45] At the onset of the COVID-19 pandemic, the FSA decided to reduce the buffer requirement to zero.

5.3. *Macroprudential policy actions taken in the Nordic–Baltic region*

Table 3 provides an overview of the implementation of macroprudential measures in the Nordic–Baltic countries. While it is beyond the scope of this chapter to discuss the various measures in detail, it can be noted that they focus on capital and liquidity requirements as well as borrower-based measures, such as LTV restrictions.[46] Tools targeting mortgage lending, such as amortisation requirements, debt-to-income or debt-service-to-income measures, are also used, but to a lesser extent. All the measures have gradually been implemented since 2010, as the respective countries have introduced the legal ability to implement them.

---

[45] Announced in/Implemented in: 2014/15, 1.0 percent; 2015/16, 1.5 percent; 2016/17, 2.0 percent; and 2018/19, 2.5 percent.

[46] In Sweden, FI, as both the micro- and the macroprudential supervisory authority, only categorises borrower-based measures as macroprudential. Lender-based requirements such as capital and liquidity requirements are not categorised as macroprudential, even if they fall under the category macroprudential for other countries.

Table 3. Overview of the implementation of macroprudential measures in the Nordic–Baltic countries.

	Loan-to-value Restriction	Debt-Service to Income Restriction	Increased Capital Requirements*	Liquidity Coverage Ratio	Net Stable Funding Ratio	Amortisation Requirements**
Denmark	X		X	X	X	
Estonia	X	X	X	X	X	X
Finland	X		X	X	X	
Iceland	X		X	X	X	
Latvia	X		X	X	X	
Lithuania	X	X	X	X	X	X
Norway	X	X	X	X		X
Sweden	X		X	X	X	X

Note: *Includes Counter-Cyclical Capital Buffer, Systemic Risk Buffer, Capital Conservation Buffer, Additional capital requirements for Systemically Important Institutions, Sector-Specific Risk-Weight Floor, Risk-Weight Floor. ** Or maximum loan maturity.
Source: Nordic-Baltic Macroprudential Forum (NBMF) (2021).

6. Limitations of macroprudential policy

It is difficult to identify what the "optimal" macroprudential policy should be in Sweden. Macroprudential policy is sometimes second-best, where first-best would be to address the fundamental causes of imbalances; in the case of household indebtedness the root causes mainly relate to housing and tax policy. In the absence of such action, macroprudential measures have therefore been needed. We will now look at the measures taken.

Starting with amortisation requirements in Sweden, they achieve three important goals. First, they increase safety margins for households, as they raise the level of expenditure a borrower has to be able to afford as part of a credit assessment.[47] Second, and linked to this, they should lead

---

[47] Amortisation requirements can temporarily be put on hold if a household should fall on hard times. This means that, during this period, the household can access the liquidity that was previously used for amortisation.

to a reduction of household debt over time. Third, house price increases due to increasing indebtedness are tempered by limiting the amount of debt households can take on.

However, as has been noted earlier, macroprudential measures alone cannot be much more than a sticking plaster if imbalances are caused by underlying structural problems. Furthermore, market participants will always try to find a way to circumvent regulation. Supervisors must remain vigilant and consider the risk in the system as a whole.

6.1. *Regulatory challenges*

A central challenge with regulation is that risk does not simply go away after you regulate an activity. It usually finds a new way. Therefore, it is imperative to monitor how banks and households respond to new regulation to guard against the potential emergence of any leakage into new types of lending or arbitrage techniques that may not meet the letter or spirit of the regulation.

This is a challenge *within* countries, when, e.g., new players on the mortgage market are competing with traditional banks for customers. The same tension also arises *between* countries with major cross-border banking activity, where it is important to ensure that countries that are supervisors for national branches honour reciprocity requests, to avoid regulatory arbitrage that undermines national regulation. A level playing field with robust regulation should help keep standards high, not low, avoiding a situation where competition leads to lowered regulatory standards in a race to the bottom.

6.1.1. *Potential leakage connected to borrower-based measures in Sweden*

The LTV limit, the LTV amortisation and the LTI amortisation are all requirements focussed on mortgage lending, and thus serve as a *mortgage* borrowing constraint for households. However, households can still borrow unsecured as long as they pass the bank's discretionary income assessment. This is why some of the lending may leak from mortgage lending into unsecured lending, when, e.g., households wish to get around the LTV limit. The same potential leakage could occur for a household that wishes to circumvent the LTV amortisations or the LTI amortisations.

How much a household is allowed to borrow from a bank is limited by the binding constraints created by borrower-based measures.[48] Banks have some flexibility in that they can adjust downwards other variables in their discretionary income calculations, to compensate for stricter amortisation requirements. This provides a way to create more room for lending when households are constrained from borrowing larger amounts of mortgage debt because of, e.g., amortisation requirements.

Potential leakages to unsecured loans need to be monitored closely. This is important because demand for both credit and housing is still very high.

6.1.2. Regulatory arbitrage and lender-based measures

For lender-based measures aimed at banks' mortgage lending, competition from new players in the mortgage market (i.e., non-banks) can create a risk for regulatory arbitrage.[49] For such cross-sectorial competition, it is important to consider what the regulatory requirements for the new players are.[50] If they are less strict, the new players could take advantage of their position, and thus undermine the purpose of the original regulation, and increase the risk and vulnerability of the system.

As banks lend money to pursue their aim of maximising return on equity, they still need to maintain sufficient capital to pass the capital requirements. Therefore, there is a temptation to increase the expected return by minimising the amount of equity the bank needs,

---

[48] Binding constraints will differ between households and the amount a bank will offer a given household will differ between banks.

[49] See the box "New players on the mortgage market" in FSR 2018:1 and Bertsch and Rosenvinge (2019).

[50] All borrower-based measures have applied for mortgage lending performed by new players on the mortgage market since 2019.

by lowering risk weights.[51] This type of incentive is always present, but it is amplified when banks have the ability to use internal risk models. In these cases, the banks use their internal assessments of risk as an input to the capital requirements. These assessments are, in turn, based on historical data and previous loss experience, and can result in excessively low risk weights. In such cases, risk-weight floors are motivated, to prevent the combination of low risk weights and high leverage from becoming unreasonable. For similar reasons, it is important to impose higher *unweighted* capital requirements on banks, in the form of higher leverage ratios. This ensures that banks have enough loss-absorbing capital, in the event realised losses significantly overshadow the model-implied losses.

To ensure the reciprocity of, e.g., risk-weight floors in the Nordic–Baltic region, coordination and cooperation are important and should be enforced through regular information-sharing and reporting.[52]

7. The pandemic has highlighted the importance of a resilient financial system

The pandemic has put the resilience of our economies to an unprecedented test and it is of interest to consider what lessons could be drawn from it.

In addition to the heavy toll in terms of illness and death, companies and households have had to cope with radically changing economic circumstances, with entire markets basically disappearing from one day to the next. Policymaking in such a situation is characterised by the most profound uncertainty. Authorities have had to engage in a wide spectrum of measures, sometimes merely hoping that they will have the intended effects. The Riksbank has deployed a battery of measures, making exceptional amounts of money available to weather the crisis, where many of the measures work as a kind of insurance. The measures are implemented to ensure that banks and companies have access to funding at a reasonable cost, primarily through a funding for lending

---

[51] See, e.g., Turk-Ariss (2017) and Ferri and Pesic (2016).
[52] Reciprocity within the Nordic–Baltic region has worked well, as described in Section 4.

scheme and QE. As far as we can see, the measures have had an effect; they have helped to keep interest rates low and maintain credit supply.

FI has, within its macroprudential mandate, acted to ensure that households who request it can temporarily pause amortisations.[53]

FI has also reduced the Swedish CCyB for banks from 2.5 percent to 0 percent to ensure that banks have sufficient capital to maintain lending and avoid a situation where lending is restricted because of insufficient capital. Related to this is also the relaxation of liquidity buffer requirements and recommendations on putting restrictions on dividend payments by banks; all aimed at ensuring the continued functioning of the banking system and the supply of credit through the pandemic.

The pandemic shows how quickly and unexpectedly the economic situation can change, and how important it is for the financial system to have good resilience to shocks. Earlier experiences also indicate that, in the long run, only well-capitalised banks have the capacity to supply the credit the economy needs. When the economic situation permits, the resilience of the financial system will therefore need to be reinforced again. If banks have used parts of their capital and liquidity buffers, they will need to gradually build up sufficient capital and liquidity again when the crisis is over.

During the pandemic, regulations have been temporarily eased both in Sweden and abroad, and there is a risk of these changes becoming permanent. If so, this would reduce the resilience of the financial system. The established regulations on banks' capital and liquidity should therefore be retained and not permanently undermined. In the next few years, Sweden, as well as other countries, should therefore introduce the internationally agreed new capital adequacy regulations based on Basel III.

8. Conclusions

In this chapter, we have used the Swedish and Nordic–Baltic experiences from macroprudential policymaking to try to distil some concrete conclusions of a more general nature. These conclusions are:

---

[53] This does not affect the discretionary income calculation where the requirement is still included. Households still have to pass the margin limits, even if they wish to pause their amortisations immediately after being approved for a mortgage.

- **Managing cross-border risks requires cross-border cooperation.** The integrated, cross border, nature of many financial systems, not least the Nordic–Baltic system, necessitates close cooperation between parties from several different jurisdictions. If there is no agreement between home and host supervisors to reciprocate macroprudential measures, macroprudential measures risk becoming less effective. This calls for regular contact to create a mutual understanding of the challenges each party faces. Creating platforms for regular interaction between relevant authorities in normal times is also key to building the personal trust needed to manage crises. The close Nordic–Baltic regulatory cooperation proved to be extremely useful in containing the fallout of the GFC and the Baltic crisis, as well as managing different idiosyncratic problems with a cross-border element.
- **Building resilience is a continuous struggle.** Financial systems are not stationary. Confirming the law of action and reaction, stability-oriented actions by authorities will always be met with reactions from the targeted parties, trying to circumvent them. The struggle to strengthen resilience of the financial system is therefore a continuous one, not a one-off experience.
- **Never waste a good crisis, but do not rely on it.** The value of a crisis to muster political momentum for reform is an old insight and still valid. The Swedish example during the 1990s is a good illustration of this, paving the way for far-reaching political decisions. However, it also shows that even in the direct aftermath of a crisis, momentum can falter and necessary reforms can fall by the wayside. For instance, in Sweden, we entered the GFC lacking proper crisis management capabilities, since the temporary legislation created to handle the 1990s crisis and the bank support agency had ceased to exist.
- **The institutional setup matters.** Macroprudential policy, microprudential supervision, monetary and even fiscal policies are all intertwined policy areas and the institutional setup affects the efficiency of the policy mix. The Swedish example shows the importance of establishing macroprudential authorities with clear mandates and independence, both from the political sphere and the financial sector. A delayed implementation of the macroprudential policy mandate, with a designated authority under the auspices of the

government, has not been enough to stop the increase of household indebtedness in Sweden, caused by the underlying structural problems in the housing market.
- **Macroprudential policy is not a panacea**. When there are deep-rooted structural issues behind stability problems, macroprudential measures may help but will always be second-best. In the Swedish case, a dysfunctional housing market, together with a tax system that incentivises leverage, hampers mobility and locks home-owners into unnecessarily large dwellings, has proven to be too politically difficult to address. International experience points to the importance of removing barriers to construction in preventing the build-up of macro-financial imbalances. In the absence of such structural reforms, other less effective measures have been deployed, the result of which will always be partial, temporary and insufficient to address the fundamental issues.
- **Building buffers in good times is key to enduring bad times**. The pandemic has illustrated the importance of resilience in the financial system. The regulatory reforms after the GFC have forced financial institutions to increase their resilience and soundness. This has permitted authorities to temporarily ease policy measures to contain the effects of the COVID pandemic on the real sector of the economy and avoid a financial crisis. Other contributing factors were the sound government finances and a broad monetary policy mandate that enabled the Swedish government and the Riksbank to respond forcefully to the economic challenges caused by the pandemic. Strengthened macroprudential requirements in good times have enabled FI to help households and banks by temporarily removing amortisation and buffer requirements during the pandemic. This is not to say that the requirements were strict enough, but that without them there would have been nothing to temporarily remove or relax. Buffers therefore need to be restored as soon as the situation permits, and established regulatory frameworks should be retained and not undermined.

References

Bentzel, R, A Lindbeck and I Ståhl (1963). Bostadsbristen — en studie av prisbildningen på bostadsmarknaden, IUI och Almqvist & Wiksell, Stockholm.

Bertsch, C and C-J Rosenvinge (2019). "FinTech Credit: Online Lending Platforms in Sweden and Beyond". *Riksbank, Economic Review* 2019: 2.

Englund, P (1999). "The Swedish Banking Crisis: Roots and Consequences", *Oxford Review of Economic Policy*, no. 3.

Ferri, G and V Pesic (2016). "Bank Regulatory Arbitrage via Risk Weighted Asset Dispersion", *Journal of Financial Stability*.

Ingves, S (2010). "The Crisis in the Baltic — The Riksbank's Measures, Assessments and Lessons Learned", February 2010.

Ingves, S, D Farelius and M Jonsson (2020). Financial Integration in the Nordic-Baltic Region vis-à-vis the EU: A Swedish Perspective".

Lindbeck, A (1967). "Rent Control as an Instrument of Housing Policy", in Nevitt, A A (ed), *The Economic Problems of Housing*, Macmillan, London.

Lindbeck, A (2016). "Hur avveckla hyreskontrollen?" Ekonomisk debatt.

Monetary Policy Report (2013). "Financial Imbalances in the Monetary Policy Assessment", archive.riksbank.se/Documents/Rapporter/PPR/2013/130703/rap_ppr_130703_eng.pdf

Riksbank (2020). "The Riksbank's Measures During the Global Financial Crisis 2007–2010", Riksbank Study, February.

Study Group of the Committee on the Global Financial System (2016). "Objective-Setting and Communication of Macroprudential Policies", CGFS Papers No. 57.

Swedish National Audit Office (2011). "Maintaining Financial Stability in Sweden: Experiences from the Swedish Banks' Expansion in the Baltics". https://www.riksrevisionen.se/download/18.78ae827d1605526e94b329e6/1518435435622/11-0345_RiR_2011_9_ENG.pdf

Turk-Ariss, R (2017). "Heterogeneity of Bank Risk Weights in the EU: Evidence by Asset Class and Country of Counterparty Exposure", IMF Working Paper.

Sweden's Experience of Deploying Monetary and Macroprudential Policies: A Discussion

Charles Bean

London School of Economics
UK Office for Budget Responsibility

The 2008–2009 Global Financial Crisis highlighted the potential value of pre-emptive policy action to reduce the risk of financial instability, as well as expanding the armoury of mitigating actions should such risks crystallise. This is now widely accepted and reflected in: the introduction of new instruments, such as the Basel III countercyclical capital buffer; the formalisation and deepening of the arrangements for the deployment of those instruments, such as the creation of financial policy committees; and the explosion of analytical work in central banks and academia to improve our understanding of those tools and how they interface with monetary and fiscal policies. However, we are still very much in the foothills and there is much to learn from each other's experiences. So comparative studies, like those in this volume, are of considerable value, especially as macroprudential policy architectures are quite heterogeneous, usually building on existing national arrangements rather than reflecting conscious design.

Ingves and Grip have provided a first-class contribution on the Swedish experience, including a useful overview of the policymaking architecture there and in the other Nordic–Baltic nations, together with an assessment of how effectively the macroprudential authorities have operated during and since the financial crisis. I cannot claim to be an expert on the Swedish model or experience, so in this contribution I shall pick up just a few issues that seem to me to have wider resonance.

My first relates to the Swedish (and Nordic–Baltic) institutional arrangements. In some countries, macroprudential responsibilities and powers are concentrated in one or two institutions. That is now the case in my own country, for instance, where the Bank of England has prime operational responsibility for banking supervision, macroprudential policy and monetary policy. Each has a separate committee in charge but there is considerable overlap in membership and the Bank's staff provide a common briefing basis.

In other countries, responsibilities and powers are spread across several institutions, though usually with some coordinating committee sitting on top. This is the case with the US, with its many regulators, brought together in the Financial Stability Oversight Committee. And it is necessarily the case also in the euro area, with the European Central Bank, constituent central banks and the European regulatory agencies brought together in the European Systemic Risk Board.

Although a medium-sized economy that is still outside the euro area, the Swedish arrangements seem to be a bit more towards the US end of the spectrum than the UK end, with Finansinspektionen (FI) in charge of the pre-emptive instruments, the Riksbank responsible for liquidity support and monetary policy, the Debt Office responsible for resolution, and the finance ministry sitting at the centre with key legislative responsibilities (including the implementation of borrower-based measures, acting on a recommendation of FI) and chairing the Financial Stability Council, which coordinates but does not decide.

Now a set-up like this can work fine but it also runs the risk of being confounded by disagreements or conflicting analyses between the various players, and of there being overlaps or underlaps. And the incentives that each faces can be quite different, as indeed is brought out by the discussion of the difficulty of restraining the growth in housing debt. The Financial Stability Council is presumably supposed to try to minimise these problems, but I would be interested to learn more as to how successfully the arrangements have proved in practice, from people who have seen it from the inside. Certainly, the UK had a set-up a bit like the Swedish model at the time of the global financial crisis. But that was found wanting when the crisis hit, which was why it was reengineered to concentrate more of the relevant powers in one agency.

A similar remark applies in respect of cross-border cooperation. Private financial institutions operate extensively across the national frontiers, leading to a need for active communication and information exchange and appropriate reciprocity in policy actions. However, the oversight architecture is quite heterogeneous across the Nordic–Baltic countries, with the designated macroprudential authority in some countries being the government, in others the financial supervisor, and yet in others the central bank.

Ingves and Grip believe that regional cooperation has worked pretty well, in large part because of the existence of long-standing networks. While it may indeed be the case that cooperation worked well, my expectation is that this international heterogeneity in macroprudential architecture would at least sometimes have resulted in frictions. On the basis that one learns more about the effectiveness and robustness of arrangements when things do not go so well, it would again have been valuable to read a more critical evaluation that brought out points of weakness and where there might be scope for improvement.

The second issue I will address is the role of borrower-based macroprudential measures. Ingves and Grip argue that while lender-based measures (such as raising risk weights and the countercyclical capital buffer) make banks more resilient, they are less effective at restraining a build-up of excessive debt when borrower-based measures (such as loan-to-value and amortisation requirements) may be more effective; though because they only affect new loans, the latter do need to be introduced early.

I have no problem at all with this analysis, but it is worth drawing out some of the political economy aspects around borrower-based measures. The public are likely to accept the imposition of lender-based measures as both necessary, and indeed desirable, to prevent banks having to seek public support should things go wrong. In most cases, the public will probably fail to grasp the link from tighter regulations on the banks through to a higher cost or reduced availability of credit. However, borrower-based measures impinge directly on a particular subset of the population, namely those about to take out loans, typically for house purchase. There is a strong likelihood that such potential borrowers will see themselves as being disadvantaged and that the policy is "unfair". Unavoidably then, it involves distributional considerations, which are generally better left at the door of elected politicians than unelected technocrats.

The Swedish set-up addresses this issue by giving FI the power to propose but the finance ministry the power to dispose. However, that opens up the possibility that the finance ministry will be unwilling to take the necessary action because it is worried about the political consequences. The alternative is to give the disposal power to the relevant macroprudential authority. That is now the case in the UK for instance, where the Bank of England's Financial Policy Committee has control of loan-to-value and debt-to-income limits on mortgages. But now there is a risk that their application will lack popular legitimacy unless there is already clear public support; this has yet to be tested in the UK context, I should add.

Finally, I will say a few words on the limitations of macroprudential policy. Ingves and Grip note the difficulty in applying macroprudential policy when the source of the problem is structural — in this case a dysfunctional housing market that favours high leverage and inhibits an expansion in the supply of housing. This is a problem that Sweden shares with the UK — indeed the UK housing market is probably even more badly distorted. However, politicians, instead of tackling the roots of the problem because it is politically too difficult, have instead preferred to introduce policies that merely tackle symptoms, such as providing tax breaks for first-time buyers, and which just serve to push prices and debt even higher.

The best the macroprudential authority may be able to do in such circumstances is to limit the collateral damage from such misguided structural policies. However, in such circumstances, it would take an especially brave macroprudential authority to introduce borrower-based measures to restrain lending (assuming it has the power to do so), as it would bring it into direct confrontation with the executive. This may ultimately result in the macroprudential authority finding limits imposed on its ability to act (including in other spheres of its responsibilities if it is the central bank) or even losing its powers altogether. In such circumstances, it may therefore be wiser to focus instead on building resilience through the imposition of lender-based measures, while at the same time advancing the case publicly for the implementation of more appropriate structural and fiscal policies.

CHAPTER 7

Chapter 7

The "Twin-Pillar" Framework of Monetary and Macroprudential Policies in China

Yiping Huang[*,†] and Tingting Lv[*,‡]

*National School of Development,
Peking University, China*
*‡PhD student,
Institute of South-South Cooperation and Development,
Peking University, China*

1. Introduction

China has not experienced a major financial crisis since the start of the economic reform at the end of 1970s. This was mainly attributable to two contributing factors — continuous rapid economic growth and the government's blanket guarantee. Serious financial problems did emerge from time to time during that period (Lardy, 1998). For instance, in 1992, the total amount of the so-called "triangular debts" or chain debts among companies was equivalent to one-third of total outstanding bank credit. In 1997, at the height of the Asian financial crisis, the average

---

[*] The views expressed in this chapter are those of the authors, not necessarily those of their affiliated institutions. The authors benefited from insightful comments by Yi Huang and other participants of the webinar jointly organised by the Monetary Authority of Singapore (MAS) and Bank for the International Settlement (BIS) in May 2021.

non-performing loan (NPL) ratio reached above 30 percent (Bonin and Huang, 2001). And in 2002, almost all the rural credit unions were technically insolvent. In all these cases, the government stepped in to help clean up the messes. The resultant financial burdens, such as the CNY1.4 trillion bad assets transferred from the four state-owned commercial banks (SOCBs) to their associated asset management companies in the second half of the 1990s, were gradually absorbed, thanks to continuous expansion of the economy.

In recent years, however, financial risks became more common. During the first half of 2015, the stock price indices in China declined sharply. Later that year, pressures of RMB depreciation and capital outflows suddenly escalated, following the reform of the central parity mechanism of the RMB exchange rate. In 2016, China's high leverage ratios, especially those of the non-financial corporations, which reached 160 percent of GDP, became an important global concern. In 2017, rapid expansion of shadow banking businesses, including wealth management products, led to the authorities adopting some new regulatory measures. In 2018, in order to rein in mushrooming liabilities at the local level, the National People's Congress (NPC) set a limit on the amount of local government debt outstanding at CNY18.29 trillion. In 2019, a large number of small banks, most notably Baoshang Bank, Hengfeng Bank and Jinzhou Bank, experienced severe balance sheet stresses. In 2020, the number of peer-to-peer lending platforms went down to 0 from the peak of 6,000 a few years ago. And, in 2021, financial difficulties experienced by a number of property developers, especially Evergrande, became a source of global concern. These incidents were the background for the policymakers' repeated warning against systemic financial risks in recent years (Zhou, 2017; Yi, 2020).

In 2017, the Chinese policymakers officially adopted the so-called "twin-pillar" framework of monetary and macroprudential policies, in order to achieve macroeconomic stability (Huang *et al.*, 2019; Li and Wu, 2019). After the 2007 global financial crisis, it became clear that monetary policy alone was not sufficient for ensuring financial stability. Here, financial stability may be defined as absence of disruption in provision of key financial services, especially provision of bank credit. Exploration of macroprudential policy started in 2009, with an aim to analyse both cross-time and cross-sectional spillovers of financial risks and to prevent or, at least, slow the build-up of such risks. According to the official design of the twin-pillar framework, the mandate of monetary policy is to achieve currency value stability, while that of macroprudential policy is to maintain financial stability, with appropriate coordination between the two. In February 2019, the People's Bank of China (PBC) created the Macroprudential Policy Bureau (MPB) within its institutional structure. The MPB is tasked to coordinate the design and implementation of the macroprudential policy framework and the related institutions.

This chapter attempts to provide a brief introduction and a preliminary assessment of China's twin-pillar policy framework, especially the new macroprudential measures. Why did financial risk incidents become more frequent recently? What was the rationale of creating the twin-pillar framework? What are the key macroprudential measures (MPMs) in China? Why are some of the MPMs different from those in advanced market economies? What are the outstanding hurdles for China to jump over in order to maintain financial stability? These are some of the key questions to be addressed in this chapter.

The main findings can be summarised as follows. First, China's gradual reform approach means that, while it moves steadily towards a free market system, a wide range of repressive financial policies continue during the transition period. The relatively high degree of financial repression did not prevent China from achieving economic growth and financial stability. This was probably because, when the financial markets and regulation were not well developed, repressive financial policies were able to play some useful roles by overcoming market failure and underpinning investor confidence. During the past decade or so, however, China's economic and financial performance deteriorated. In particular, the unique mechanism of relying on continuous economic growth and the government's blanket guarantee to ensure financial stability became increasingly less effective. From 2015, financial risks emerged in a wide range of areas, causing policymakers concerns about the risk of systemic financial crises.

Second, in 2017, the Chinese authorities officially established the "twin-pillar policy framework" to deal with macroeconomic instabilities, particularly systemic financial risks. The basic idea is for monetary policy to focus on price stability and for macroprudential policy to focus on financial stability, with appropriate cooperation between the two. The two pillars, both of which are still in the process of transition, are run by the PBC. Its monetary policy is transitioning from direct control to indirect regulation, and from quantitative tools to price instruments. The PBC started to explore ideas of macroprudential policy from 2009, although it incorporated differentiated and countercyclical policy instruments from 2003. China's current MPMs focus on three key areas of systemic importance: (1) the real estate sector; (2) cross-border capital flows; and (3) systemically important financial institutions (SIFIs), financial holding companies (FHCs) and important financial infrastructure.

Third, although it is too early to assess the effectiveness of this new policy framework, a preliminary look at the macroeconomic performance suggests that the monetary policy has been working quite well, judged by price and growth stability measures. The macroprudential policy has also helped defuse some major financial risks in recent years, although in some cases the government's blanket guarantee has continued to play important roles. It has yet to be seen if the macroprudential policy can independently fulfil its policy goals in the future, especially as China faces a series of grey rhino events, highlighted by a potential burst of property bubbles, inefficiency of high leverages and the consequences of massive capital outflows. One important criticism is that some of China's MPMs are not typical macroprudential instruments. These, however, should be viewed in the broad context of economic transition, as the "first-best" policy instruments are often difficult to formulate and sometimes do not work well in transition economies.

And, finally, preventing a systemic financial crisis requires a comprehensive set of policy actions, and the macroprudential policy is only one part of it. Some of the financial risks in China today are of systemic importance, others are more "local". But magnifying and transmitting "local" financial risks may also lead to systemic problems. More importantly, some financial risks, such as high leverages of the SOEs and local governments, are actually the results of the government's guarantee. The Chinese authorities should undertake the following four broad reform steps to control systemic financial risks. First, it is time to end the "dual-track" reform strategy and to achieve ownership neutrality.

While the government guarantee helped maintain financial stability in the past, it is now a part of the problem. Second, financial regulators need to play their roles in identifying and resolving risks. This should be done by clearly setting the policy objectives, equipping the regulators with needed authority, and introducing some degree of accountability. Third, there is also a need for a governance mechanism for operating the twin-pillar policy framework. The monetary and macroprudential policies should maintain separate decision processes and, at the same time, form proper ways of cooperation. One possibility is to establish the Financial Policy Committee for the macroprudential policy, alongside the Monetary Policy Committee, with overlapping members for the two committees. And, finally, it is important to further upgrade the macroprudential policy, by strengthening capabilities of evaluation and analyses of systemic financial risks. While the PBC should continue to work on introducing more conventional MPMs, as an emerging market economy, it should also remain open-minded in choosing policy tools. If CFMs are effective in controlling risks and preventing crises, then they should form parts of the MPMs. After all, "White or black, a cat is a good cat as long as it catches mice".[1]

The remainder of the chapter is structured as follows. The next section documents China's financial reform, including reform of the monetary policy, and assesses the changing impacts on economic growth and financial stability. In particular, it describes the rising financial risks in recent years. The third section introduces the "twin-pillar" policy framework, including the rationale behind this new construction, and outlines the evolution of both the monetary and the macroprudential policies — their objectives, key measures and institutional arrangements. The fourth section offers a preliminary assessment of the new policy framework and discusses some new challenges for achieving financial stability over the longer term. And the final section concludes the chapter by recommending a set of policies for preventing systemic financial crisis in China.

---

[1] This is a widely quoted phrase by the architect of China's economic reform policy, Deng Xiaoping.

2. Economic and financial performance during the reform period

China's reform period may be divided into two sub-periods according to economic and financial performance. Before the 2007–2009 global financial crisis (GFC), the Chinese economy achieved an average rate of growth of close to 10 percent, while the financial system remained largely stable. The pre-GFC economic performance was often described as the "China miracle" (Lin, Cai and Li, 1995). After the GFC, however, GDP growth slowed steadily, from above 10.6 percent in 2010 to 6.0 percent in the fourth quarter of 2019, right before the outbreak of the COVID-19. In the meantime, incidents of financial risks became more frequent and wide ranging. Concerns about high leverage ratios, property price bubbles, local government liabilities and banking sector problems caused worries about systemic financial crisis. The government had to devise a series of financial policies, such as the deleverageing policy adopted in 2016, to strengthen economic growth and to avert systemic financial crisis.

The changing pattern of economic and financial performance between before and after the GFC was probably related to the two distinctive features of the Chinese economy — it was both a developing country and a transition economy. When China started its economic reform in 1978, with GDP per capita at around US$200, it was one of the poorest countries in the world. In 2020, its GDP per capita reached US$11,000, literally a few steps away from the high-income level. Meanwhile, at the start of the reform, China had only one financial institution, the PBC, which served as the central bank, the financial regulator and a commercial bank. Over the following four decades, it re-built a new financial system, which may be characterised as "large in size of financial assets, extensive in government intervention and weak in financial regulation" (Huang and Ge, 2017). Quantitatively, China's financial system is already among the largest in the world. The top four SOCBs are identified as global systemically important banks (G-SIBs). Market capitalisation of both equity and bond markets is also ranked among the top three globally. China's broad money supply (M2) reached CNY218.7 trillion in 2020, equivalent to 215 percent of GDP. While this extremely high proportion mainly reflected China's bank-dominated financial system, it also led to unusually high leverage ratios.

Despite market-oriented reform, the government maintained extensive intervention in this gigantic financial system, including setting of banks' deposit and lending rates, intervention in exchange rates, allocation of bank credit, majority control of some large financial institutions and restrictions on cross-border capital flows (Huang and Wang, 2020). Estimates of the financial repression index (FRI), which measures the degree of government intervention, declined from 1.0 in 1980 to about 0.6 in 2018 (Figure 1). These confirm the trend of market-oriented financial reform during those years as the degree of government intervention decreased steadily. The same trend existed for other emerging market economies during that period, as a result of financial globalization. However, after more than forty years of financial reform, readings of the FRI for China were still significantly higher than those for other countries at similar stages of economic development. In fact, in 2018, China's FRI was still among the highest in the world.

Why did the Chinese government maintain high levels of financial repression while implementing market-oriented financial reform? One explanation relates to China's "dual-track" economic reform strategy. Unlike the former Soviet Union's "shock therapy" approach, the Chinese government proceeded with reform by creating more growth space for

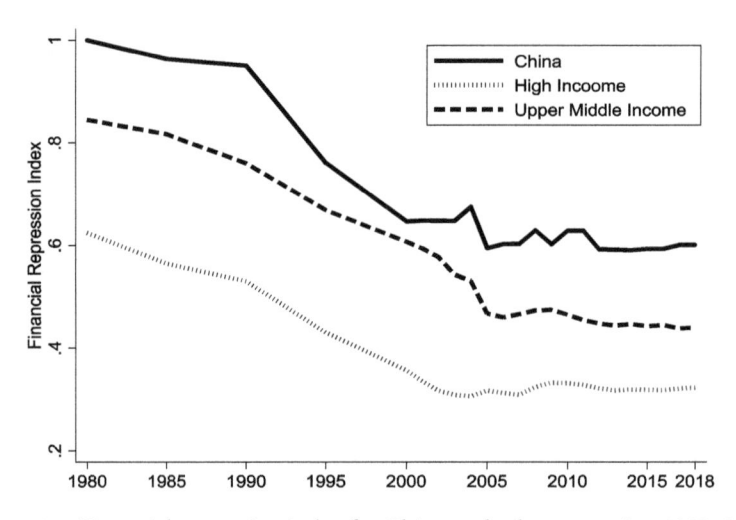

Figure 1. Financial repression index for China and other countries, 1980–2018. *Source*: Huang and Wang (2020).

the vibrant private sector, while protecting the relatively inefficient state-owned enterprises (SOEs) for economic and social stability purposes (Huang, 2010). In order to make this strategy work, there was a need for some subsidies to the SOEs. Unfortunately, it was not possible for the government to allocate additional fiscal resources for this purpose, as fiscal condition deteriorated sharply during the early stage of reform. Distortions in the factor markets, including markets for labor, capital, land and energy, were partly legacies of the centrally planned system and partly means to support the relatively inefficient SOEs. The repressive financial policies, such as allocation of cheap bank credit in favour of the SOEs, were implicit subsidies to those companies (Huang and Wang, 2017).

Surprisingly, the repressive financial policies did not prevent China from achieving rapid growth and financial stability. In fact, empirical analyses reveal positive contribution of financial repression to economic growth during the early decades of economic reform (Huang and Wang, 2011). While the common perception is that government intervention reduces efficiency of financial resource allocation and, therefore, is bad for growth (McKinnon, 1973), such a perception is based on an important assumption that the financial market functions efficiently. In countries where market mechanisms are not well developed, some degree of government intervention might be useful for correcting market failure problems (Stiglitz, 1994; Huang and Wang, 2017). In China, the SOCBs might not be the most efficient commercial banks, but they were quite effective in converting saving into investment. The government intervention also served as an important support for financial market confidence. In 1997, when the banking sector suffered from unusually high NPL ratios, there was no bank run. This was because depositors believed that the government would eventually step in to support the banks. If China completely liberalised its financial sector in 1978, it would probably have experienced a series of financial crises over the past decades.

During the past decade, however, economic and financial performance deteriorated visibly. Alongside continuous moderation of economic growth, there was a common complaint about weakening support for economic growth by the financial sector. The incremental capital–output ratio (ICOR), for instance, rose from 3.5 in 2007 to 6.3 in 2017, indicating a sharp decline in capital efficiency during that period. One of the most frequently discussed problems was the unusual difficulty for the small and medium-sized enterprises (SMEs) to obtain bank credit. Equally important but less discussed was the difficulty for households to find good investment channels for their gigantic amount of saving. At the same time, the frequency of financial risks also increased significantly, giving rise to systemic financial risk (Figure 2). The CNY4.0 trillion stimulus package adopted by the government during the GFC probably contributed to an accumulation of financial risks in the following years. But broad-based financial risks emerged in the forms of higher overall leverages, bad assets, asset bubbles, and unregulated shadow banking and digital financial businesses.

The sudden turn of economic and financial performance between before and after the GFC was, at least in part, caused by a change of the growth model. During the pre-GFC period, China enjoyed low-cost advantage, which underpinned the competitiveness of its labour-intensive exports. The financial system was probably not perfect, but it was quite effective in supporting the extensive input-driven growth model, since levels of uncertainty were relatively low in products, technology, management and markets at that time. After the GFC, however, China quickly reached the upper middle-income level. Many labour-intensive

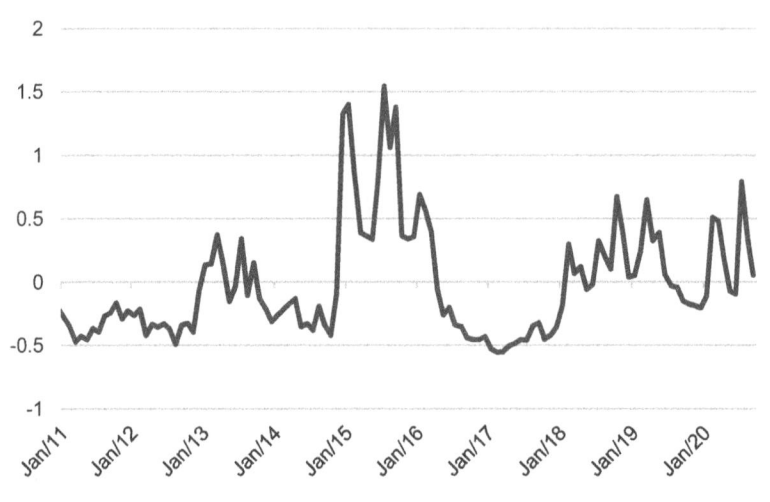

Figure 2. Systemic financial risk index for China, 2009–2020.
Source: Huang and Wang (2020).

manufacturers lost competitiveness. And they needed to upgrade their technology and products through innovation. This is the typical "middle-income challenge". Unfortunately, the financial system was not well suited to support innovation. In particular, the private sector, consisting mostly of SMEs, contributed about 60 percent of GDP growth, 70 percent of total corporate patents and 80 percent of urban jobs. But financial institutions often found it difficult to provide funding to SMEs due to difficulties of both accessing them and assessing their credit risks. Ownership discrimination in credit allocation and lack of market-based risk pricing, both of which were the results of repressive financial policies, created further barriers to SME funding. Therefore, financial efficiency declined over time, as illustrated by the steady rise of ICOR in the post-GFC period.

Similarly, the mechanism underpinning financial stability before the GFC, i.e., a combination of continuous rapid economic growth and government blanket guarantee, also became less effective in the post-GFC period. As GDP growth moderated steadily after 2010, it directly caused some financial problems, such as those associated with excess capacity and depressed investment returns. In the meantime, the prospect of absorbing financial messes through future rapid economic expansion became less likely. Under such a scenario, it became almost impossible for the government to continue to guarantee against any potential default or bankruptcy. Adding to this problem was the new financial innovation, as a response to insufficient funding for SMEs in the traditional financial industry. The rapid expansion of the shadow banking and digital financial transactions filled some supply gaps but also created new types of risks as most of these businesses were not properly regulated. From around 2017, systemic financial risks became a wide concern for both policymakers and market participants (Zhou, 2017).

Therefore, the change in the effectiveness of the financial system between before and after the GFC has been mainly triggered by the switch of the growth model from input- to innovation-driven. Repressive financial policies served the extensive growth model reasonably well before the GFC, due to relatively low production and market uncertainties. The post-GFC economic growth, however, has been a completely different story. The current financial system is not well suited for supporting innovation, particularly financing SMEs. At the same time, the old approach of relying on continuous rapid economic growth and the government's blanket guarantee have also become less effective in maintaining financial stability. During the past years, the Chinese government has devised three sets of financial reform policies to improve financial support for economic growth and to prevent systemic financial crisis. The first has been to better support economic innovation through financial reform and restructuring, including developing multi-layer capital markets, adopting new banking business models such as debt-equity combined financing and technology branch, and encouraging digital financial innovation such as Bigtech credit and digital supply chain financing. The second has been to further push ahead with the market-oriented financial reform. This could cover the achievement of ownership neutrality and market-based risk pricing. And the third has been to restructure the financial regulatory framework for dealing with financial risks.

3. Construction of the twin-pillar policy framework

The purpose of creating the twin-pillar framework of monetary and macroprudential policies in 2017 was to achieve overall economic and financial stability (Huang *et al.*, 2019; Li and Wu, 2019). This effort was related to three broad tasks of financial reforms outlined above, particularly the reform of financial regulation. But it went further by emphasising the importance of macroprudential policy for resolving systemic financial risks. Many of the financial risk factors that emerged during the past years, such as problems with shadow banking and small banks, could be addressed by financial regulation, as the prevailing regulatory regime was not sufficient for identifying and resolving financial risks. The right regulatory reform strategy should first clearly set the policy objectives, i.e., ensuring fair competition, protecting financial consumers and maintaining financial stability. Financial regulators should not be influenced by macroeconomic policy considerations. It might be useful for them to obtain a certain degree of regulatory independence and to be equipped with necessary regulatory tools. Proper regulatory reforms can go a long way in mitigating financial risks, but they might not be sufficient for containing systemic financial risks. This was the reason for the recent creation of the twin-pillar policy framework, especially the macroprudential policy.

Thinking about the twin-pillar policy framework may be traced back to mid-2009 when the PBC started to explore the concept of macroprudential policy. One of the most important lessons learned from the lead-up to the GFC was that monetary policy alone might not be adequate for controlling systemic financial risks. During the years before 2007, the Federal Reserve (Fed) chaired by Alan Greenspan maintained a relatively loose monetary policy, as inflation pressure remained muted and the Fed's mandate was to maintain price stability. The macroeconomic condition at that time was often characterised as the "great moderation" — strong growth, low inflation and low volatility of macroeconomic indicators. The subprime crisis that began in 2007, however, indicated that, while loose monetary policy conditions did not contribute to the rise of inflation, they fuelled accumulation of systemic financial risks, which eventually led to the GFC.

The basic idea of the twin-pillar framework is for monetary policy to focus primarily on price stability, or stability of the currency value, and for macroprudential policy to focus primarily on financial stability. Monetary and macroprudential policies may be made and implemented separately, and they may also form some ways for cooperation. The appropriate degree of separation between monetary and macroprudential policies is a subject of a heated debate, although almost everyone agrees that monetary policy decision should pay attention to financial stability. Caruana (2015) argued that the often-proposed separation principle for the two policies had an intuitive appeal, but was unconvincing as a general proposition. Meanwhile, Schularick *et al.* (2021) found that deploying discretionary leaning-against-the-wind monetary policy during credit and asset price booms was more likely to trigger crises than prevent them. In China, both policies are run by the PBC, which leaves some room for cooperation, although there is not yet a clear formal procedure on separation or cooperation between the two.

The twin-pillar framework is not yet a mature institution — not only was the framework only recently proposed, but both monetary and macroprudential policies are also still in the process of formulation or transition.

3.1. Transition of the monetary policy

During the pre-reform period, there was little room for monetary policy, as money supply and demand were literally set by the central plan. The post-reform evolution of the monetary policy could be characterised as a transition from direct control to indirect regulation, and from quantitative tools to price instruments. For instance, in the early years, the PBC directly determined the quantity of credit, at both the aggregate and bank levels. Lately, however, it has increasingly used interest rate measures, such as the 7-day collateralised repo rate (DR007) and the loan prime rate (LPR) to measure and regulate monetary policy conditions. Accordingly, the history of China's monetary policy may be divided into four periods: (1) credit plan in the central planned economy (1949–1978); (2) direct control based on management of total credit (1979–1997); (3) indirect control of aggregate money and credit (1998–2016); and (4) establishment of the modern central banking system (2017–now) (Huang *et al.*, 2020).

3.1.1. The period of the central credit plan

In the early 20th century, China's financial sector was actually pretty advanced. At that time, Shanghai was a major international financial center, with all types of financial institutions, including commercial banks, insurance companies and stock markets. And the financial system was also quite open and, at one point, there were more than 100 foreign currencies in circulation in the Shanghai market. China's financial sector, however, collapsed during the wars in the 1930s and the 1940s. The government quickly nationalised all the financial institutions from 1952 and shut down most of them from 1956, when the country started the movement of socialist transformation. The financial sector was effectively reduced to a mono-bank system, with the PBC affiliated to the MOF.

Under the newly established central planning system, the central credit plan was one part of the central plan. In fact, most of the financial intermediaries, operating under the investment plan, allocated long-term credit to priority sectors and projects selected by the governments. As the primary objective of the credit plan was to provide working capital for industry and commerce and to meet the requirements from the five-year development plans and the annual investment plans, the PBC and financial intermediation played only a limited role in controlling changes in money in circulation (Montes-Negret, 1995).

3.1.2. *The period of direct credit control*

At the start of 1978, the PBC was separated out from the MOF to act both as the central bank and a commercial bank. Meanwhile, the authorities also moved quickly to re-establish the financial system, commercial banks and insurance companies from the end of 1970s, and stock markets from the early 1990s. At the start of 1984, the original PBC was split into two institutions, with the commercial activities moved to the newly established Industry and Commercial Bank of China (ICBC) and the remaining forming the new central bank, PBC. The new PBC became a key player in monetary policymaking and financial regulation, although it functioned under direct instruction and supervision of the State Council.

In the meantime, the central credit plan evolved over time to suit the new financial and economic environment. The PBC formulated a direct regulatory framework for the management of bank credit, applying quotas for credit and cash. The central bank selected bank credit as its main intermediate policy target, in large part because of the administrative control it exercised over a very concentrated banking sector (Yi, 1994). The PBC dictated not only targets for annual growth of total bank credit but also allocation of credit to provinces and industries. In the meantime, the PBC also started to experiment with new methods of monetary policy, including compiling a money supply plan from 1987 and drawing the whole society's credit plan from 1989.

3.1.3. *The period of indirect control of money and credit*

In early 1995, the National People's Congress passed The People's Bank of China Law of the People's Republic of China (the PBC Law).[2] According

---

[2] The PBC Law was later revised in 2003.

to this Law, the PBC's responsibilities were, under the leadership of the State Council, to make and implement monetary policy, to prevent and resolve financial risks, and to maintain financial stability. One of the most important moves that the PBC undertook was to abolish the direct controls over bank credit at the start of 1998. Although the central bank still announced annual credit plans, it established an indirect management framework for money and credit, mainly using a set of new tools such as open market operations (OMOs), the reserve requirement ratio (RRR), and central bank relending and rediscount windows to regulate aggregate money supply and bank credit. Later on, the PBC created a number of new policy facilities for managing short-term liquidity conditions. As the relevance of M2 and new bank loans declined, the central bank compiled a new indicator, Aggregate Financing to the Real Economy (AFRE), in 2010 to gauge the financial sector's support to the real sector.

During this period, the PBC gradually focused more on interest rate instruments (Guo and Schipke, 2014). On the one hand, it pushed ahead with interest rate liberalization and granted commercial banks greater degrees of freedom in setting their deposit and lending rates by widening the allowed bands around the benchmark rates. By the end of 2015, the PBC had abolished all the restrictions on commercial banks' interest rates, although the practice of "window guidance" on deposit and lending rates continued in the following years. On the other hand, the central bank also paid more attention to the short-term market interest rates. The Shanghai Interbank offer rate (Shibor 1W) and the collateralised repo rate (DR007) became important indicators for measuring liquidity conditions in the interbank market.

3.1.4. *The period of the modern central banking system*

In 2017, the policymakers incorporated the concept of the "modern central banking system" in their financial reform program (Zhang, 2018). The modern central banking system, in essence, refers to a greater emphasis on price stability, interest rate policy tools, financial regulation and independence. This implied the continuation of monetary policy transition towards indirect regulation and interest rate policy tools.

The central bank gave up its direct control of credit quotas, although some influences continued under the Macroprudential Assessment framework. During this period, the PBC took two steps towards interest rate policy tools. One was the LPR, which was created in October 2013 and officially adopted as an operational policy target in August 2019. And the other was an interest rate corridor, focusing on DR007 or the reverse repo rate, with the interest rate on extra reserves as the floor and the short-term loan facility (SLF) overnight interest rate as the ceiling. But all these are still in the process of experimentation.

In addition, China's monetary policy framework is still in transition in several other ways. First, the final decision power of monetary policy belongs to the State Council, not the PBC. The draft revision of the PBC Law discussed in 2020 proposes that the PBC only needs to obtain prior approval from the State Council for interest rate and exchange rate policy adjustments and can decide on other monetary policy changes on its own.[3] Second, while the PBC Law states that the monetary policy objective is to achieve stable currency value, thereby supporting economic growth, in practice the monetary policy has four policy objectives — growth, employment, inflation and external account. Third, monetary policymaking in China follows a hybrid of interest rate and quantity rules, while the PBC still relies on some non-price policy tools (Figure 3).

Operational instruments	Operational targets	Intermediate targets	Policy objectives
• Quantity-based instruments. (e.g., RRR, CBBs, central bank lending, OMOs, etc.) • Price-based instruments (e.g., banks' base deposit and lending rates) • Window-guidance	• Non-borrowed reserves • Borrowed reserves • Short-term money market rate • Monetary base	• Money supply (narrow money supply M1 and broad money supply M2) • Bank credit (and also the total social financing) • Market interest rate (such as SHIBOR)	• Rapid economic growth • Full employment • Low and stable inflation • Balanced external account

Figure 3. China's current monetary policy framework.
Source: Huang et al. (2020).

---

[3] The PBC sought the public's opinion on the revision draft of the PBC Law on October 23, 2020 (http://www.pbc.gov.cn/goutongjiaoliu/113456/113469/4115077/index.html).

3.2. Evolution of the macroprudential policy

The other pillar, the macroprudential policy, is much younger and less well developed, although China was one of the earliest countries to explore and practise macroprudential policies (Zhou, 2011). The differentiated housing credit policy implemented and adopted from 2003 actually had the attributes of macroprudential management (Li and Wu, 2019). After the outbreak of the GFC, the PBC began studies on further enhancing macroprudential management (PBC, 2011). The 12th Five-Year Programme, released in 2010, described a counter-cyclical macroprudential management mechanism. In early 2011, the PBC introduced the differentiated and dynamic reserve adjustment mechanism. The purpose of designing this mechanism is to guide and incentivise financial institutions to maintain their own soundness and to adjust credit allocation counter-cyclically. This is done by linking credit allocation to the capital levels required for macroprudential purposes and taking into account the systemic importance and soundness of each financial institution as well as business cycles.

In 2016, the PBC upgraded the differentiated and dynamic reserve adjustment mechanism to a macroprudential assessment (MPA) system. The MPA system aims at guiding the behaviour of financial institutions in seven dimensions, including capital and leverage, assets and liabilities, liquidity, pricing behaviour, asset quality, cross-border risk exposure and implementation of credit policies (Table 1). The most important advantage of the MPA system, compared with the previous reserve adjustment mechanism, is its coverage of much broader areas. This was China's first more complete set of macroprudential policies, although many of the policy tools involved addressed individual institutions' financial risks more effectively than systemic financial risks.

The 19th National Party Congress held in the autumn of 2017 officially coined the term "twin-pillar framework of monetary and macroprudential policies" (Li and Wu, 2019). The Fifth National Financial Work Conference during the same year further emphasised the need to strengthen the macroprudential management for preventing a systemic financial crisis. The Conference also decided to establish the Financial Stability Development Committee of the State Council (FSDC) to strengthen

Table 1. Macroprudential assessment (MPA) system.

	Level 1 category	Level 2 category
1	Capital and leverage	Capital adequacy
		Leverage ratios
2	Assets and liabilities	Broadly defined credit
		Trusted loans
		Interbank liabilities/total liabilities
3	Liquidity	Liquidity coverage ratio
		Proportion of net stable fund
		Reserves
4	Pricing behaviour	Interest rate determination
5	Asset quality	Non-performing loan ratio
		Loan provision
6	Foreign debts	Stock of risk weighted foreign debts
7	Credit policy implementation	Compliance with credit policy
		Utilisation of central bank funds

Source: The PBC.

coordination of financial supervision. The office of the FSDC is located at the PBC, strengthening the PBC's responsibilities for macroprudential management and systemic risk prevention. The National People's Congress in early 2018 decided to merge the China Banking Regulatory Commission and the China Insurance Regulatory Commission into the new China Banking and Insurance Regulatory Commission (CBIRC) and enhanced the PBC's role in financial policymaking and coordination. In early 2019, the institutional reform programme approved by the Party Central Committee and the State Council further clarified the functions of the PBC in macroprudential management, including taking the lead in establishing a macroprudential management framework, and coordinating the supervision of systemically important financial institutions (SIFIs), financial holding companies (FHCs) and important financial infrastructure, and approved the creation of the Macroprudential Policy Bureau (MPB) within the PBC.

China's current macroprudential policy focuses on three main areas: the real estate market; cross-border capital flows; and supervision of commercial banks, SIFIs, FHCs and important financial infrastructures (Table 2).

Table 2. China's macroprudential policy framework.

	Instruments	Authority
Broad-based Tools	Leverage ratio	CBIRC
	Dynamic loan loss provisioning requirement	CBIRC
	Counter-cyclical Capital Buffer	PBC and CBIRC
	Macroprudential Assessment (MPA)	PBC
	The real estate loan concentration management system	PBC and CBIRC
Household Sector Tools	Maximum loan-to-value (LTV) ratio	PBC
Corporate Sector Tools	LTV limits on exposure to commercial real estate	PBC
	Macroprudential management for full coverage of cross-border financing (the corporate part)	PBC and SAFE
	Market access management and sustained regulation of FHCs	PBC
Liquidity Tools	Liquidity Coverage Ratio (LCR)	CBIRC
	Net Stable Funding Ratio (NSFR)	CBIRC
	Constraints on FX funding	PBC and SAFE
Structural Tools	Capital Surcharge on SIFIs	PBC

The first area concerns managing risks in the real estate sector. A property market bubble is one of the biggest concerns for financial stability in China. According to the usual criteria such as the ratio of the house price to household income or the ratio of rent to the house price, property prices in many major metropolitan cities in China are already quite high globally. Meanwhile, about 80 percent of Chinese households' wealth is held in the form of property. These have caused serious worries about the dire consequences of a property bubble bursting for households, financial institutions and the macroeconomy. The main macroprudential measure (MPM) that has been adopted by the PBC to deal with real estate risk is the maximum loan-to-value (LTV) ratio. From 2013, the PBC adjusted the LTV ratio requirement counter-cyclically several times to contain the risk of unsustainable real estate booms. In December 2020, the PBC and the CBIRC introduced the real estate loan concentration management system. Under this new system, the shares of Chinese banks' outstanding real estate loans and outstanding personal housing loans in total outstanding loans should not exceed the corresponding caps determined by the PBC and the CBIRC.

The second area involves the management of cross-border capital flows. Since the beginning of the economic reform, the Chinese government has been liberalising the capital account very slowly. The liberalisation policy has followed a general principle of "inflows first, and outflows second; equity investment first, and portfolio investment second; and long-term investment first, and short-term flows second". For at least the past two decades, the Chinese policymakers have been struggling to strike a balance between the need to liberalise the capital account and the desire to contain financial risks. If the macroprudential policy could help support financial stability even after liberalisation of the capital account, then the above struggle might become a non-issue. During the past years, the PBC devised a series of MPMs for this purpose, although there were controversies if such measures could all be regarded as macroprudential.

In September 2015, to curb excessive volatility in the foreign exchange market, the PBC implemented MPMs for forward sales of foreign exchange, requiring financial institutions to deposit 20 percent of the value of their forward sale contracts (including futures and swaps) as foreign-exchange risk reserves. The most recent adjustment was made in October 2020. In particular, the PBC decided to lower the foreign currency risk reserve ratio from 20 percent to zero, effective from 12 October 2020.

In December 2014, the PBC decided that offshore financial institutions' deposits in onshore financial institutions should be included in the categories of deposits that require deposit reserves. Initially, that required reserve ratio was set at zero. In January 2016, domestic financial institutions were required to set aside reserves at the normal reserve requirement ratio for deposits of offshore financial institutions, in order to inhibit the pro-cyclical behaviour of RMB's cross-border flows.

In 2016, the PBC established the full coverage of the macroprudential policy framework for cross-border financing. Enterprises and financial institutions were allowed to carry out cross-border financing business within the ceilings determined according to their capital conditions. The PBC could adjust the above financing activities counter-cyclically. Under this framework, FX funding was assigned a greater weight, when calculating the debt ceiling of an enterprise or a financial institution. This would, on balance, encourage enterprises or financial institutions to use more RMB funding than FX funding. For instance, the ceiling for financial institutions and enterprises was raised by 25 percent in March 2020 to support the recovery of the real economy and to combat the shocks from the pandemic. It was lowered to the previous level for financial institutions in December 2020 and for enterprises in January 2021.

And the third area is supervision of *commercial banks, SIFIs, FHCs and important financial infrastructures*. From 2011, drawing on Basel III, the CBIRC introduced a number of MPMs for commercial banks, including the leverage ratio, dynamic loan loss provisioning, the liquidity coverage ratio, the net stable funding ratio, etc. The mechanism of the counter-cyclical capital buffer was introduced by the PBC and the CBIRC in September 2020. The ratio for the counter-cyclical capital buffer was initially set at zero. The requirement for the counter-cyclical capital buffer will be re-evaluated and adjusted periodically to forestall systemic financial risks.

The banking sector holds an important place in China's financial system and the four largest banks have been included in the list of G-SIBs. In 2012, the CBIRC set a 1 percentage point higher capital surcharge for systemically important banks. In November 2018, the PBC, the CBIRC and the China Securities Regulatory Commission (CSRC) jointly published the "Guiding Opinions on Improving the Regulation of SIFIs", making clear the overall institutional framework for the assessment and identification, additional regulation, and recovery and resolution of SIFIs in China. In February 2021, the PBC and the CBIRC jointly released the "Measures for Assessment of Systemically Important Banks". The assessment indicator system of SIBs focuses on four dimensions: size, correlation, substitutability and complexity. Currently, the PBC is working with the CBIRC to formulate additional regulatory requirements for SIBs.

Regulation of FHCs is also a new policy issue. Since 1992, China has maintained the segregated financial regulatory regime, with individual financial regulators issuing licenses to financial institutions. However, a small number of institutions, such as Everbright Group, CITIC Group and Ping An Group, own multiple financial business licenses, including for commercial bank, investment bank, insurance, asset management, etc. During the past decade, several digital financial institutions, such as Tencent, Ant Financial and JD, obtained several financial licenses. As financial risks emerged in various areas in recent years, regulation of FHCs became an urgent task. From September 2020, in order to prevent cross-sector risk contagion, the PBC began to carry out market access management and sustained regulation of FHCs.

Finally, in February 2020, the PBC, the National Development and Reform Commission (NDRC), the MOF, the CBIRC, the CSRC and the State Administration of Foreign Exchange (SAFE) jointly released the "Work Plan for Coordinated Regulation of Financial Infrastructures". This coordinated regulation covers six types of financial facilities — financial asset registration and custody systems, clearing and settlement systems (central counterparties engaged in centralised clearing businesses included), trading facilities, trading report repositories, major payment systems and basic credit reporting systems, as well as their operators.

4. Challenges for the new policy framework

Formulation of the twin-pillar policy framework is still on-going, as the monetary policy is in transition and the macroprudential policy is also evolving. It is too early to tell how well this policy framework works for China, although recent macroeconomic performance should provide some indication about policy effectiveness. There are some important questions needing to be addressed to improve this twin-pillar framework. First, while there are separate decision-making processes for both the monetary policy and the macroprudential policy, to what extent and in what format should the two policies cooperate? Second, should the PBC's monetary policy framework converge with those of advanced market economies to focus on price stability, rely mainly on interest rate instruments and achieve a certain degree of independence? And, finally, what is the preferred decision-making process for the macroprudential policy and what are the appropriate prudential measures?

4.1. *Choices of appropriate MPMs*

The relative stability of real GDP growth and consumer price inflation during the past four decades provides some evidence of the effectiveness

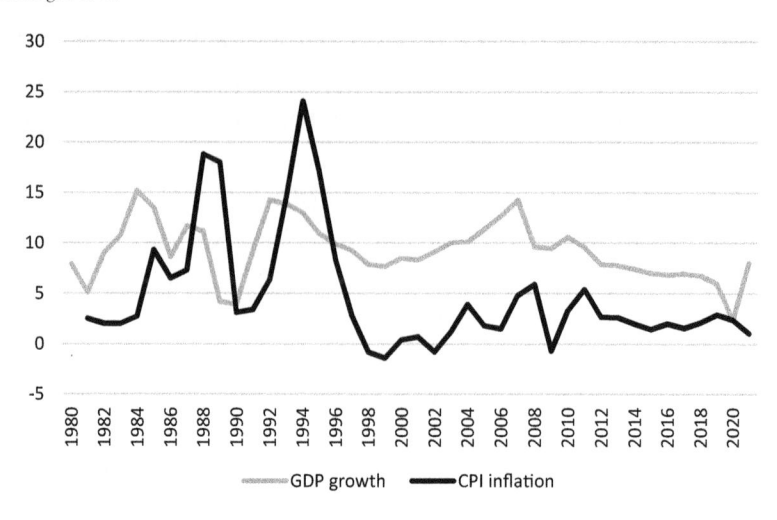

Figure 4. Real GDP growth and CPI inflation in China, 1980–2025.
Source: IMF.

of China's monetary policy (Figure 4). Although the monetary policy framework contained some unconventional policy elements, such as direct controls and quantitative tools, with the exceptions of two brief periods around 1988 and 1994, inflation pressure stayed largely modest, especially during the past two decades. GDP growth was also quite stable and strong, with the average rate of growth at above 9 percent during those four decades. Judged by the monetary policy objective specified by the PBC Law, "to maintain stability of the value of the currency and thereby promote economic growth", the monetary policy was quite successful. The current account, which is, in practice, also a part of the monetary policy objective, was less stable and the surplus stayed well above 5 percent of GDP during the 2005–2009 period. The persistent build-up of current account surplus was, at least partly, related to a lack of exchange rate flexibility and contributed to pressures for a currency appreciation and trade tensions with some major trading partners. After the GFC, however, the current account surplus stayed well below 3 percent of GDP.

An assessment of the macroprudential policy is more difficult since the policy is quite new. Whenever financial risks emerge, the government is often inclined to step in to stabilise the situation. This was evident when a certain number of small banks experienced balance sheet stresses in 2019 and when some bonds issued by SOEs or local investment vehicles suffered from default risks in 2020. Perhaps the most obvious case where the PBC policy effectively contained financial risk occurred between August 2015 and December 2016. On 11 August 2015, the PBC implemented an important reform of the mechanism for determining the central parity of the RMB exchange rate. Unfortunately, this positive move, allowing for a greater role of market forces in the formulation of the exchange rate, triggered widespread expectations of a currency depreciation and encouraged capital flight. These were compounded by the Fed's exit from its quantitative easing. The PBC quickly took a series of measures to stabilise the market condition by intervening in the foreign exchange markets and managing the cross-border capital flows. By the end of 2016, pressures for both currency depreciation and capital outflows were reversed (Figure 5).

Clearly, the PBC successfully averted a currency crisis in 2015–2016. But it is debatable whether this achievement is mainly attributable to the macroprudential policy for two reasons. First, the policy actions undertaken by the PBC then looked more like crisis-fighting than risk-preventing. A certain degree of investor panic was clearly evident in the markets following the "August 11, 2015" reform. In fact, despite the PBC's numerous policy actions, the RMB/USD bilateral exchange rate weakened

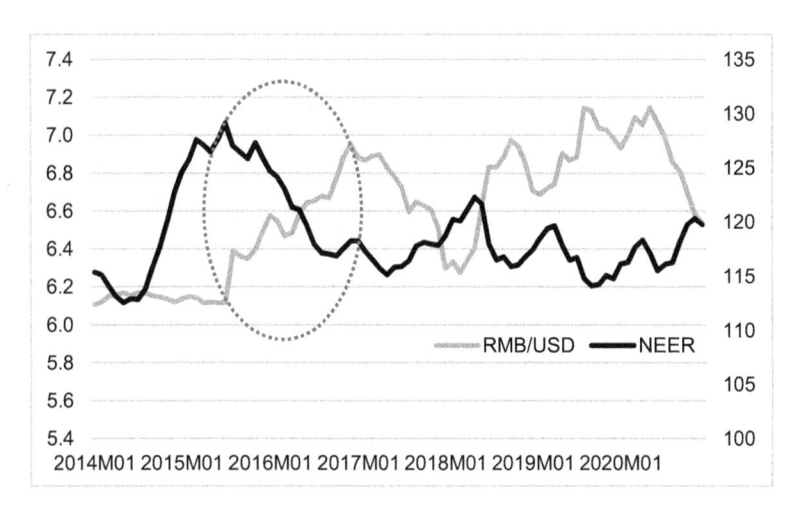

Figure 5. RMB/USD bilateral exchange rate and nominal effective exchange rate, January 2014–December 2020.
Source: IMF.

from 6.12 in July 2015 to 6.95 in December 2016. Second, most of the measures adopted by the PBC, such as intervention in foreign exchange markets and management of cross-border capital flows, were not typical MPMs.

This latter point raises a more general question: should cross-border capital flow management measures (CFMs) also form a part of the macroprudential policy? One common criticism of the Chinese macroprudential policy framework is that some of the measures concerning cross-border capital flows are more like capital account controls. Discussion of this issue has important implications for thinking about the design of macroprudential policy, especially for emerging market economies.

The Chinese experience provides a useful case study. First, it might be ideal for the PBC to eventually adopt some more "market-based" MPMs to slow the build-up of financial risks relating to external liabilities and the current account. But in its first steps of devising the policy framework, it might not be easy for the PBC to identify the threshold values for foreign borrowing or current account imbalances, let alone introduce appropriate market-based policy measures. In a way, some of the CFMs might be viewed as transitional policy tools.

Second, some of the CFMs are, in fact, consistent with the spirit of macroprudential management. The foreign currency risk reserve requirement introduced in September 2015, when capital outflow was a top challenge, was certainly in line with the idea of slowing the build-up of financial risks. In particular, this policy instrument contained an important feature of counter-cyclical adjustment. In October 2020 when capital inflows were quite strong, the PBC lowered the above reserve requirement from 20 percent to zero. This policy design is actually quite similar to the reserve requirement for commercial banks. It is also in the same spirit of the Tobin tax (Tobin, 1978).

And, third, perhaps the most controversial measure is setting of a debt ceiling or foreign debt ceiling for enterprises and financial institutions, as it looks like a central plan tool. However, before this policy was introduced, enterprises and financial institutions were required to obtain approval from the relevant authorities to have external borrowing within quota limits. Now the ceilings are calculated based on individual institutions' risk weighting and their capital conditions. This policy has made it easier for enterprises and financial institutions to raise funds from abroad, as it no longer requires approval for a borrowing quota. Indeed, the potential trouble with this measure might not be its "capital account control" style. Rather, it looks more "micro" than "macro" since the ceiling is applicable to individual enterprises and banks. However, such "micro" tools can only be replaced after more appropriate "macro" measures are well developed. Before that, they remain as the second-best options to control overall external borrowing. One lesson learned from China's experience of financial reform is that, before a market mechanism and financial regulation are well developed, a certain degree of repressive financial policies may be preferred, as they help overcome market failure and maintain financial stability. This principle should be also applicable to the design of macroprudential policy in emerging market economies.

Some CFMs might be useful generally for containing systemic financial risks, whether or not they are classified as MPMs. This is, in fact, in line with the Institutional View of the IMF (2012). Experiences of financial globalisation during the past four decades show that many emerging market economies were not able to withstand external financial shocks once their capital accounts were liberalised. Rey (2015) demonstrated that, with open capital account, most countries would lose a certain degree of monetary policy independence, regardless of exchange rate regimes. These do not imply that China and other emerging market economies should not pursue capital account liberalisation. Rather, they should pay particular attention to the proper sequencing of liberalisation, maintain certain restrictions on very volatile short-term capital flows and reserve the right to enforce cross-border capital flow management when financial stability is at risk.

4.2. Dealing with black swan or grey rhino risks

The Chinese policymakers recently made it a top priority to prevent a systemic financial crisis, as financial risks showed up in many areas. Some risks might be confined to local areas, while others could be of systemic influence. For instance, many of the digital financial problems, especially the messes created by the peer-to-peer lending industry, involved a large number of participants. But they were unlikely to pull down the entire financial system, at least in the short term. It is the individual financial regulators' responsibility to manage such "local" financial risks. Meanwhile, shadow banking transactions, the size of which was estimated as equivalent to 90 percent of total banking assets in 2017, had the potential of destabilising the entire banking sector. Although shadow banking transactions took place off the balance sheet, in practice, the banks still had to accept financial responsibilities should such transactions fail. The macroprudential policy's mandate is to mitigate such systemic financial risks.

There are at least two kinds of systemic risks: some could be unexpected (the black swan), while others might be anticipated (the grey rhino). By definition, it is hard to predict what kinds of black swan events would attack China. The only task that the regulators could embark on to prevent black swan events is to reduce overall economic rigidities and imbalances, such as high leverage ratios and large fiscal or current account deficits. In contrast, there already exist some easily perceivable grey rhino events in China today. One is a burst of the property bubble. The biggest problem is not high property prices or household leverage per se. The most important trigger for a property market crisis is a deterioration of the macroeconomic fundamentals. The property market experienced an extraordinary boom during the past two decades, thanks to strong economic growth, a high saving rate, limited investment channels, favourable demographic changes (the increasing number of new couples) and gradual urbanisation. Over the coming decades, all these macroeconomic factors, except urbanisation, are expected to move in the opposite direction. For instance, ageing of the population would raise the population dependency ratio from 42 percent in 2020 to 66 percent in 2050. These would inevitably cause an excess supply of properties, especially outside the major metropolitan cities.

Another anticipated risk is the inefficiency of high aggregate leverage ratios (Reinhart and Rogoff, 2014). China's non-financial sector leverages were equivalent to 160 percent of GDP in 2007. The stimulus policy implemented during the GFC quickly raised the leverage ratio to 240 percent of GDP in 2014. From 2016, seeing risks of a high leverage ratio, the government started to take de-leveraging policies. At the end of

2020, however, the leverage ratio increased to 270 percent of GDP, rising by more than 23 percentage points due to policies fighting COVID-19. This is more than 60 percentage points above the average of the emerging market economies. The high leverage ratio in China is attributable to at least two factors — one is the bank-dominated financial system and the other is the large number of zombie firms in the economy.

The other grey rhino event is the potential consequences of capital flight. So far, China's capital account has remained largely closed and the proportion of foreign assets in total households' financial assets has been insignificant. As the government liberalises the capital account, it is inevitable that Chinese households would diversify their investment to overseas financial markets. It deserves very close watching whether such outflows and the associated currency depreciation would become disorderly. This means that capital account liberalisation should be implemented with extra caution, in order to maintain financial stability.

5. How to prevent a systemic financial crisis?

What would a potential systemic financial crisis look like in China — the US-type dysfunctioning of the financial system, such as the subprime crisis during 2007–2009, or Japan-type growth stagnation, such as the lost decade in the 1990s? At least in the near future, the Japan scenario looks more plausible, because the government is still the most important player in overall financial intermediation and the external sector remains largely healthy. These suggest that a typical Minsky moment is unlikely to occur in China. But if financial efficiency continues to decline, the worst-case scenario is one of growth stagnation. The Japan-type crisis is by no means better than the US-type crisis, but it does generate less social and economic disruption and provides some time for the government to respond.

Preventing systemic financial crises is a comprehensive task. This is difficult by definition, but it is even more so in China, where many market and policy mechanisms are not yet well developed. In the past, China relied mainly on government guarantee to support financial stability, which, unfortunately, is no longer a sustainable option. Government guarantee will continue to play a role in managing financial risks in the foreseeable future, although its relative importance should decline steadily. This reflects the fact that China is a transition economy (Zhou, 2016). For China to be able to continuously maintain financial stability, it is vital to devise a set of institutions, in order to improve financial efficiency, enhance market discipline and mitigate financial risks. The macroprudential policy is an important part of those institutions. Other institutions, such as structural reforms and financial regulation, are equally important for preventing a systemic financial crisis.

First, it is time to consider ending the dual-track reform policy and to realise ownership neutrality. Protection of the relatively inefficient SOEs during the early years of reform was an important and useful transition strategy. But it did cause financial inefficiency and create risks. Some empirical analyses reveal that zombie firms were dominated by SOEs and that, on average, zombie firms had much higher debt/equity ratios than normal enterprises (Tan *et al.*, 2017). Today, SOEs and the local government investment vehicles also have much higher debt payment burden than private enterprises. This is, in fact, an important cause for the recent decline in financial efficiency and rise in financial risks. Given that it is not viable politically to completely let go of the SOEs, it might be advisable to leave them mainly in areas of upstream industries and public utilities. This way, they would not compete directly with private enterprises for financial services, and the government would be able to subsidise them in the form of service purchases. The bottom line is that, without forceful enforcement of market discipline, it is impossible to stop the decline in financial efficiency and accumulation of financial risks.

Second, it is also necessary to upgrade the capability of financial regulation in identifying and resolving financial risks. Since 1992, China has been developing a segregated financial regulatory regime and now has a complete set of regulatory rules and policy tools. However, the fact that financial risks emerged in a wide range of areas from 2015 suggests that financial regulation was not very effective. In the end, the government had to step in to clean up the mess. There might be many reasons why financial regulation did not work. All regulators had responsibilities for both regulation and development. That was why they were often tolerant of defaults or bankruptcy. Also, regulatory policies were often influenced by macroeconomic policy or even political factor. In some cases, the rules were simply not followed. Many city commercial banks ran into financial stresses a couple of years ago. One common problem was that they channelled large volumes of funds to enterprises related to their large shareholders. This was prohibited by regulatory rules but actually happened widely. Many of the financial risks occurred during the past years were actually not systemic risks. And most of them could be dealt with by more effective financial regulation. The necessary regulatory reform should contain at least the following three elements. First is to simplify the policy objectives for financial regulation — ensuring fair competition, protecting consumers and maintaining financial stability. The regulators should not be burdened with developmental or macroeconomic responsibilities. Second is to grant the regulators sufficient independence and authority. One of the main problems in the past was that punishment for improper or illegal behaviour was too light. Therefore, problems such as data fabrication were very popular. Once the regulatory rules are set, the regulators should be able to enforce them. And three is accountability of the regulators. If financial risks occur widely, it means that either no rule is set, such as the case of peer-to-peer lending industry before 2016, or rules are not enforced, such as the case of many city commercial banks in 2019. Regulators should take some responsibilities for both types of cases.

Third, it will be useful to set up a formal mechanism for division of labour and collaboration between monetary policy and macroprudential policy. These two pillars have their own respective policy objectives. Therefore, it is best that they maintain separate decision-making processes. But these two policies are also closely related. For instance, the monetary policy could affect financial stability, while the macroprudential policy might also influence inflation and growth. At the moment, as both policies are under the PBC, coordination should not be a problem. One possible working structure is to set up the Financial Policy Committee for officials and experts to deliberate on macroprudential policy, alongside the Monetary Policy Committee for monetary policy. Members of the two committees can overlap in order to ensure information sharing and policy coordination.

And, finally, developing the macroprudential policy framework will be an on-going process. As illustrated, the external debt ceilings for enterprises and financial institutions are probably still too "micro" but a big step forward from the previous requirement for quota approval. Despite the fact that some of China's macroprudential management measures are unconventional, the real test is if they work to reduce systemic financial risks. Again, taking cross-border capital flow management as an example, this might not be the ideal macroprudential policy measure for many emerging market economies, because capital controls reduce efficiency. For China, however, the difference between with and without capital account control is not about low efficiency versus high efficiency. It is about low versus high financial risk. Of course, China should make efforts to develop more market-friendly macroprudential measures. But as a transition economy and developing country, it should continue to devise some cross-border capital flow management tools for financial stability purposes. This is also in line with the views of the IMF (2012) that capital flow management and macroprudential measures overlap, especially if capital flows are a source of systemic financial risks.

References

Bonin, J. P. and Y. Huang. (2001). "Dealing with the bad loans of the Chinese banks." *Journal of Asian Economics*, 12(2), 197–214.

Caruana, J. (2015). "Revisiting monetary policy frameworks in the light of macroprudential policy." Panel remarks at the IMF seminar on "Revisiting monetary policy frameworks", 10 October 2015, Lima.

Guo, K. and A. Schipke. (2014). "New issues in monetary policy: International experience and relevance for China." PBC and IMF Joint Conference, Beijing.

Huang, Y. (2010). "Dissecting the China puzzle: Asymmetric liberalization and cost distortion." *Asia Economic Policy Review*, 5(2), 281–295.

Huang, Y., Y. Cho, K. Tao and C. Yu. (2019). "Monetary policy and macro-prudential policy collectively support macroeconomic stability." *Journal of Financial Research* (in Chinese), 474(12, 2019), 70–91.

Huang, Y. and T. Ge. (2019). "Assessing China's financial reform: Changing roles of repressive financial policies." *Cato Journal*, 39(1, Winter 2019), 65–85.

Huang, Y., T. Ge and C. Wang. (2020). "Monetary policy framework and transition mechanisms." In M. Amstad, G. Sun and W. Xiong (eds.), *The Handbook of China's Financial System*. Princeton: Princeton University Press.

Huang, Y. and X. Wang. (2011). "Does financial repression inhibit or facilitate economic growth: A case study of China's reform experience." *Oxford Bulletin of Economics and Statistics*, 73(6), 833–855.

Huang, Y. and X. Wang. (2017). "Building an efficient financial system in China: Need for stronger market discipline." *Asian Economic Policy Review*, 12(2), 188–205.

Huang, Y. and X. Wang. (2020). "Reform of China's financial sector: Progresses, challenges and future directions." Report prepared for the Asian Development Bank, Manila.

IMF. (2012). "The liberalization and management of capital flows — An institutional view." Policy Papers, International Monetary Fund, November 14, 2012, Washington DC.

Lardy, N. R. (1998). *China's Unfinished Economic Revolution*. Washington DC: The Brooking Institution.

Li, B. and H. Wu. (2019). "On intrinsic logic of the two-pillar macro-management framework of monetary policy and macroprudential policy." *Journal of Financial Research* (in Chinese), 474(12, 2019), 1–17.

Lin, J. Y., F. Cai and Z. Zhou. (1995). *The China Miracle: Development Strategy and Economic Reform*. Hong Kong: Chinese University of Hong Kong Press.

McKinnon, R. I. (1973). *Money and Capital in Economic Development*. Washington DC: The Brookings Institution.

Montes-Negret, F. (1995). "China's credit plan: An overview." *Oxford Review of Economic Policy*, 11(4), 25–42.

Reinhart, C. and K. Rogoff. (2014). "This time is different: A panoramic view of eight centuries of financial crises." *Annals of Economics and Finance*, 15(2), 1–60.

Rey, H. (2015). "Dilemma not trilemma: The global financial cycle and monetary policy independence." CEPR Discussion Papers 10591, London.

Schularick, M., L. Steege and F. Ward. (2021). "Leaning against the wind and the risk of financial crises." VoxEU, 12 January 2021.

Stiglitz, J. E. (1994). "The role of the state in financial markets." In Bruno, M. and Pleskovic, B. (eds.), *Proceeding of the World Bank Annual Conference on Development Economics, 1993: Supplement to the World Bank Economic Review and the World Bank Research Observer*. Washington DC.: World Bank.

Tan, Y., Z. Tan, Y. Huang and W. T. Woo. (2017). "Zombie firms squeezing out private investment: Evidence from Chinese industrial enterprises." *Economic Research Journal* (in Chinese), 5(2017), 177–190.

Tobin, J. (1978). "A proposal for international monetary reform." *Eastern Economic Journal*, (July/October, 1978), 4(3/4) 153–159.

Yi, G. (1994). *Money, Banking, and Financial Markets in China*. Beijing, China: Westview Press.

Yi, G. (2020). "Further on structure of China's financial assets and its policy implications." *Economic Research Journal* (in Chinese), 3(2020), 4–17.

Zhang, X. (2018). "Past and present of China's monetary policy framework." In Y. Chen and Y. Huang (eds.), *Views of China Finance 40 on Past 40 Years*. Beijing: CITIC Press.

Zhou, X. (2011). "On the response of financial policy to the financial crisis — Background, logic and main contents of prudential macroeconomic policy framework." *Journal of Financial Research* (in Chinese), 1, 1–14.

Zhou, X. (2016). "Managing multi-objective monetary policy: From the perspective of transitioning Chinese economy." *The 2016 Michel Camdessus Central Banking Lecture*, 24 June 2016, International Monetary Fund, Washington D.C.

Zhou, X. (2017). "Holding the bottom line of no systemic financial crisis." *People's Daily* (in Chinese), 22 November 2017.

The "Twin-Pillar" Framework of Monetary and Macroprudential Policies in China: A Discussion

Yi Huang

Fudan University and CEPR, China

Since the global financial crisis (GFC), macroprudential policy has been gradually adopted by policymakers and plays an increasingly important role in financial stability. Over the past four decades since the Chinese economic reform, the financial system has been rebuilt and is among the largest in the world quantitatively. Along with the frequent incidents of financial risks, high leverage ratios, property price bubbles, local government debt and banking sector issues, Chinese policymakers officially adopted the twin-pillar framework of monetary and macroprudential policies in 2017 to maintain inflation and financial stability. Thus, there is a growing body of literature on China's macroprudential policy, its relationship with monetary policy, its implementation and effectiveness.

Huang and Lv's (2021) is one of the most important and most recent studies on this topic and clearly illustrates the development of China's financial reform and the rationale of creating the twin-pillar framework. Since the beginning of economic reform, China's continuous rapid economic growth and the government's blanket guarantee have helped China avert financial crises even under a relatively high degree of financial repression, but this mechanism has become less effective along with the slower economic growth and high government leverage of the past decade. Hence, monetary policy alone is not sufficient anymore and the twin-pillar policy framework is created to deal with macroeconomic instabilities. China's current macroprudential measures (MPMs) mainly focus on three key sectors: the real estate sector, cross-border capital flows and supervision of commercial banks, systemically important financial institutions (SIFIs), financial holding companies (FHCs) and important financial infrastructures. The authors further assess the effectiveness of China's macroprudential policy and find that its independent effect is still ambiguous, and China is still faced with the challenges of policy spillovers for both China's and international-policy coordination, fiscal footprint, regional heterogeneity and monetary policy transmission and risk-takings. To deal with these challenges and more effectively prevent the systemic risks, they finally suggest ending the dual-track reform policy to realize ownership neutrality, increasing the capability of financial regulation, and setting up a formal mechanism for division of labor, and collaboration between the monetary and macroprudential policies to maintain separate decision processes aside from a certain degree of cooperation.

Moreover, China's monetary and macroprudential policies also attracted the attention of many international organizations. According to BIS "Macroprudential goals, implementation and cross-border communication", the People's Bank of China (PBC) leads China's joint conference on financial regulation and coordination, and has been exploring the innovation of macroprudential tools. The PBC has established the macroprudential assessment (MPA) system, including indicators for capital and leverage, asset and debt, liquidity, pricing, asset quality, risk of cross-border financing and the implementation of credit policy. Under the twin-pillar framework, macroprudential policy interacts closely and is coordinated with monetary policy, micro-prudential policy and fiscal policy, but these policies focus on different areas (McMahon et al., 2018). For instance, macroprudential policy is adopted to ensure financial stability, whereas monetary policy focuses on the overall economy, maintaining price stability and stimulating economic growth. However, their coordination is necessary and important since macroprudential policy affects the transmission of monetary policy. Moreover, in the era of globalisation, the domestic and international spillover impact of China's macroprudential policy is a challenge to the PBC, as mentioned previously by Huang and Lv (2021). Therefore, they emphasize the importance of cross-border capital flows which are a new factor in the global economy and some developing countries, including China. Since 2015, the PBC has enhanced the macroprudential management of cross-border capital flows, such as charging risk provisions for the forward sale of foreign exchange and increasing commission charges for speculative RMB trades, and extended its scope to all financial institutions and companies across the country.

Dr. Yi Gang, Governor of the People's Bank of China, provides more details about China's twin-pillar framework which aims to support the real economy and strike a balance between internal and external equilibrium (BIS Central Bank Speech 2019). Currently, China's monetary policy is gradually transitioning from quantity control to price control. However, price control sometimes is not efficient and thus in practice, macroprudential policy is implemented and has become increasingly important especially following the GFC. He emphasized that the twin-pillar framework should guard against four kinds of financial risks: abnormal market fluctuation and external shocks, credit risks, shadow banking risk and illegal financial activities.

From the previous studies, we clearly know the three main sectors China's macroprudential policy focuses on, but we need to investigate the connections among these sectors and how the connections influence the spillover effect of China's macroprudential tools. Huang, Pagano and Panizza (2020) find that local public debt crowded out the investment of private firms in corresponding cities by inducing banks to tighten credit supply to local firms, resulting in a credit reallocation from private enterprises to the local government. The local crowding-out of private investment in China is mainly due to the geographical segmentation and the limited scope for banks to reallocate funds due to the regulation on Chinese banks' lending volume. Hence, to maximize profits with limited credits, banks prefer lending to state-owned firms and tightening credit to riskier borrowers. What's more, Huang, Panizza and Portes (2018) find that risky firms with limited investment opportunities and funding may borrow abroad not to finance investment projects, but to boost profitability by engaging in speculative activities that operate as part of the shadow banking system, escaping the prudential regulation that limits risk-taking by leveraged financial firms. They further suggest that the rapid increase in the issuance of dollar bonds by risky firms was likely a result of regulatory reforms aimed at limiting risk-taking by this type of firms. Thus, the policymakers should take the link between regulation on banking sector and cross-border financing as well as the destination of cross-border inflows into consideration when designing macroprudential policy. There is also a strong link among the household, banking and real estate sectors, which should be considered by macroprudential policymakers. Van Bekkum et al. (2019) study the impact of macroprudential policy at the household level through the analysis of households' response to macroprudential lending limits. They find that the policy indeed induced households to reduce their mortgage debt when financing their first house, but that there is a liquidity-solvency trade-off for households in the sense that only low-liquidity households experienced financial health improvements. Moreover, a tightening of household-targeting macroprudential policy not only affects the households, but also leads banks to reallocate mortgage credit and lend more to riskier firms such as real-estate and construction firms (Epure et al., 2021; Acharya et al., 2021). The credit reallocation effects of macroprudential policies are stronger in booms, increasing the risk of a property bubble and reducing the available funding for other potential firms. Thus, policymakers should consider not only the benefits for household solvency, but also the costs associated with lower homeownership and the effect on the link between the banking and real estate sector.

As mentioned before, we can see that the banking sector plays a crucial role in the effectiveness of macroprudential policy. Thus, policymakers need to consider the banking sector's strong association with the real estate and cross-border financing, as well as its credit distributional effect. Galaasen et al. (2020) show a causal link between idiosyncratic firm shocks and banks' credit returns and the pass-on of shocks to granular borrowers and to banks' non-granular clients and finally the real economy. They also suggest that banks are subject not only to aggregate risk, but also to concentration risk which matters quantitatively. Hence, the concentration risk should be taken into account by policymakers.

References

Huang, Y. and Lv, T. (2021). "The "Twin-Pillar" Framework of Monetary and Macroprudential Policies in China".

Acharya, V. V., Bergant, K., Crosignani, M., Eisert, T., & McCann, F. J. (2021). "The Anatomy of The Transmission of Macroprudential Policies." Journal of Finance, Forthcoming.

The People's Bank of China (2017). "Macroprudential goals, implementation and cross-border communication," BIS Papers chapters, in: Bank for International Settlements (ed.), Macroprudential policy frameworks, implementation and relationships with other policies, volume 94, pages 99-102, Bank for International Settlements.

BIS (2019). "Yi Gang: China's monetary policy framework — supporting the real economy and striking a balance between internal and external equilibrium." Central Bank Speech, 30 January.

Epure, M., I. Mihai, C. Minoiu, and J. L. Peydró. (2021). "Global financial cycle, household credit, and macroprudential policies" (No. 1590).

Galaasen, S., R. Jamilov, R. Juelsrud, and H. Rey. (2020). "Granular credit risk" (No. w27994). National Bureau of Economic Research.

Huang, Y., M. Pagano and U. Panizza. (2020). "Local crowding-out in China." The Journal of Finance, 75(6), 2855–2898.

Huang, Y., U. Panizza and R. Portes. (2018). "Corporate foreign bond issuance and interfirm loans in China" (No. w24513). National Bureau of Economic Research.

McMahon, M., M. A. Schipke and X. Li. (2018). "China's monetary policy communication: Frameworks, impact, and recommendations." International Monetary Fund.

Van Bekkum, S., M. Gabarro, R. M. Irani and J. L. Peydró. (2019). "Take it to the limit? The effects of household leverage caps." The Effects of Household Leverage Caps, 11 December.

CHAPTER 8

© 2023 World Scientific Publishing Company
https://doi.org/10.1142/9789811259432_0016

Chapter 8

Timely, Sustained and Effective Macroprudential Policy: Exploring the Political Economy of Hong Kong's Prudential Standards in the 1990s*

Robert N McCauley[†,‡] and Catherine R Schenk[§]

[†]*Nonresident Senior Fellow,*
Global Development Policy Center,
Boston University
[‡]*Research Associate, Faculty of History,*
University of Oxford
[§]*Professor of Economic and Social History,*
University of Oxford

Abstract

The Hong Kong authorities oversaw a tightening of banks' mortgage lending standards in 1991 and subsequently reinforced them in the years before the property crash in 1997–98. That this wrenching crash did not result in a banking crisis requiring wholesale government support points to the success of this policy. This chapter analyses its political

---

*The authors thank, without implicating in any shortcomings, David Carse and Joseph Yam for interviews; Norah Barger, Jaime Caruana, Bill Coen, Hiroyuki Imai and Ilhyock Shim for discussion; Nelson Mann and Tony Suen for help with the HKMA archives and Zongyue Liu and Jimmy Shek for research assistance. The authors are especially grateful for access to the HSBC Asia Pacific Archive.

economy by drawing on contemporary explanations, archival evidence and interviews to identify the policy's motivations and management. Historically specific features of Hong Kong's economy and politics no doubt encouraged this innovation and contributed to its effectiveness. More broadly, we draw three lessons. First, the absence of an independent monetary policy in a very small, very open and very leveraged economy spurred the early use of direct macroprudential policy. Second, studies of such policy have neglected what we call "define, survey and inform" as a useful means for bank supervisors to provide market participants with the public good of information regarding the aggregate outcome of their decentralised credit decisions. Third, if new international standards for capital adequacy release bank capital, a policy response may be imperative to avoid ruinous competition among banks.

1. Introduction

Hong Kong's banking authorities oversaw the setting of mortgage lending standards from 1991 with unusual timeliness and sustained them in the face of attempts by banks to arbitrage the regulation. Ultimately, the standards passed the test of the property crash of 1997–1998 with flying colours: Hong Kong banks survived a wrenching property crash without wholesale government support.

This study differs from most studies of macroprudential policy of N cases over X years (Kuttner and Shim, 2013; Claessens, 2015; Morgan et al., 2015; Bruno et al., 2017; Cerutti et al., 2017; Richter et al., 2019). Instead, since macroprudential policy raises political economy issues, we draw on contemporary explanations, archival evidence and interviews to identify the policy's motivations and management. Was the interaction of Hong Kong's official supervisors and private bankers historically unique? Or can lessons be drawn for macroprudential policymakers elsewhere?

This study's strength, and its limitation, is that it interrogates one case for insights into how the policy originated and was sustained. Historically specific features of Hong Kong's economy and politics encouraged this innovation and contributed to its effectiveness. More broadly, the absence of an independent monetary policy in a (very) small open economy contributed to the early use of direct macroprudential policies. A more generalisable aspect was that, absent a policy response, new international standards for capital adequacy that released capital could have led to ruinous competition among Hong Kong's banks and a banking crisis. A further (generalisable) motivation was that banking supervisors made good use of a "light-touch" but worthy measure that is unfortunately not generally analysed among macroprudential measures, which we dub "define, survey and inform".

This case is of interest because the policy was joint, timely, sustained and effective.

(1) A *joint* policy: the Commissioner of Banking endorsed HSBC's public initiative in 1991 to limit the mortgage loan-to-value ratio (LTV) to 70 percent, and the successor Hong Kong Monetary Authority (HKMA) enforced it as bank supervisor. In 1994, supervisors additionally guided banks to keep property loans below 40 percent of local loans. In early 1997, the HKMA lowered the LTV to 60 percent for luxury properties and limited the mortgage debt service ratio to 50 percent to 60 percent (Wong et al., 2004; HKMA, 2011).

(2) A *timely* policy: it was implemented over five years before the peak of property prices.

(3) A *sustained* policy: property developers and some bankers called for a rise in the 70 percent LTV when property prices fell after the Federal Reserve (henceforth Fed) raised rates in 1994, but the government maintained the standard. The January 1997 LTV of 60 percent for luxury property tightened it. The sustained implementation compares favourably to the Spanish policy of forward-looking provisioning in the 2000s (Caruana, 2010; Saurina and Trucharte, 2017).

(4) An *effective* policy: residential mortgage lending slowed in relation to GDP, the response of bank credit growth to higher property prices downshifted, and banks proved remarkably resilient to the eventual 60 percent property price crash (McCauley et al., 1999; Gerlach and Peng, 2005). Unlike in Singapore, restraining property prices was not the primary goal (Rajan et al., 2022).

Section 2 highlights global forces bearing on Hong Kong in the early 1990s. Section 3 shows how these interacted with Hong Kong conditions and decisions. Section 4 asks whether the headline, "self-regulation victory" accurately summarised Hong Kong's introduction of the 70 percent LTV standard in 1991. Section 5 portrays the HKMA defending, extending and tightening the policy in the lead-up to the property crash. Section 6 assesses the policy's effectiveness. Section 7 seeks commonalities in Hong Kong, Singapore and Croatia. Section 8 concludes.

2. The global context

This section highlights global developments in finance and banking supervision that helped to shape prudential policy in Hong Kong in the early 1990s. By 1991, as political calm returned in China, low dollar interest rates, dollar depreciation and Basel I's halving of capital required to back mortgages conspired to boost Hong Kong's economy and to turbocharge its property market.

2.1. Fed ease and the dollar depreciation

In response to a range of domestic factors (McCauley *et al.*, 1999), the Fed reduced its policy rate from 8.25 percent in July 1990 to 5.75 percent in July 1991 and would lower it further to 3 percent by September 1992. Only in February 1994 did the Fed begin to lift its policy rate. Around the world, borrowers with loans based on the dollar London interbank offered rate (Libor) enjoyed stronger cash flows. Lower Fed rates propelled the dollar's decline in the early 1990s and any dollar-linked currency depreciated against its basket of trading partners' currencies.

These easy conditions threatened to destabilise any highly leveraged, highly open and dollar-linked economy outside the US border, such as that of Hong Kong.

2.2. Basel I and consideration of LTV standards in the UK and the US

In 1988, the internationally agreed Basel Accord set prudential capital requirements that favoured residential mortgages. The Bank of

England–Fed agreement that led to the Accord originally assigned a full weight to mortgages, treating them neutrally on par with business loans (Goodhart, 2011), but some European supervisors negotiated for their customary 50 percent weight.[1] This 50 percent weight on residential mortgages eased UK, US and Hong Kong bank capital requirements.[2]

Lower capital requirements led to more scrutiny of mortgage lending and mitigating risks to bank stability in the 1990s. The UK Treasury and Civil Service Committee of the House of Commons asked the Bank of England (April 1991) about setting a minimum LTV. Threadneedle Street replied in no uncertain terms:

> Controls are undesirable, not only because they are difficult to implement and enforce, but also because they interfere with the allocation of loans among borrowers that the lender feels is appropriate to the risk and return involved. They are an inferior policy instrument, *which would come under consideration only if interest rates could not achieve the desired result* [italics added to highlight clause relevant to Hong Kong].

The legislative history of the Federal Deposit Insurance Corporation Improvement Act (FDICIA) of 1991 made it clear that the US Congress wanted bank supervisors to set LTV standards to prevent unsound lending and bank losses (US Treasury et al., 1992). Nevertheless, in the face of industry resistance, supervisors did not set LTV ceilings for mortgages on owner-occupied houses or home equity loans, leaving them to banks' risk managers. Thus, while discussion of LTV measures was "in the air", neither of the main jurisdictions on which Hong Kong was modelled adopted them. Section 4 discusses how and why Hong Kong's response deviated from the US and UK approaches.

3. The Hong Kong context

Amid the calm in China, easy Fed policy, a depreciated dollar and Basel I combined to accelerate the rise of Hong Kong property prices.

---

[1] The authors are indebted to Norah Barger of the Board of Governors for this recollection.
[2] Quasi-government mortgage guarantees attenuated the effect in the US market.

Before sketching how international financial developments and capital standards played out in Hong Kong, this section highlights the colony's unusual institutional framework. A strong bankers' oligarchy with no central bank made a difference.

3.1. Hong Kong's institutional framework

Hong Kong's policy innovation arose within an unusual institutional framework. The colonial authorities did not establish a central bank, leaving important operational matters vested in the Banking Advisory Committee of prominent bankers. They also tolerated HSBC's considerable market power. The oligarchy of bankers provided credit to property developers, who built up land banks at public land auctions, and then set the pace of construction. Unlike in the US, no government-sponsored institution guaranteed mortgages and turned them into securities. As in Singapore, the Hong Kong government built public housing for a sizeable fraction of the population and by the early 1990s (as in the UK) the government began to sell state-owned apartments to tenants. The property market was divided into a large number of smaller, cheaper (often formerly state-owned) apartments and a growing number of newer, larger luxury property developments for upper-middle- and high-income earners.

3.2. Financial instability in Hong Kong

Global recession, international politics and bad banking had rocked Hong Kong's asset markets and banks in the 1980s. Strains in the negotiations between the People's Republic of China and the UK in the early 1980s piled political uncertainty on top of the damage done to the macroeconomy by high interest rates and weak international trade. In 1983–1986, political uncertainties, a collapse of property prices and reckless banking allowed by feeble supervision led to repeated runs on banks. Whereas the authorities had formerly responded to financial instability by cajoling leading banks to take over or otherwise support failing banks — notably HSBC had taken over its biggest rival Hang Seng Bank in 1965 — in the 1980s, the government repeatedly injected equity and assisted mergers after Standard Chartered withdrew its support for an ailing bank in 1983, prompting a banking crisis (Schenk, 2001, 2003).

In 1991, memories of financial instability were fresh. Eight years after taking over Hang Lung Bank in 1983, the government still owned it through the Exchange Fund. In June 1989, Hong Kong depositors reacted to the news from Tiananmen Square by running on the Bank of China and affiliates. In mid-1991, the global collapse of BCCI led uniquely to bank runs in Hong Kong. Run-prone[3] Hong Kong depositors even lined up at Citibank and Standard Chartered Bank branches. The latter run testifies strongly to the wrought nerves of Hong Kong depositors insofar as Standard Chartered Bank, then alongside HSBC and nowadays the Bank of China, was a note-issuing bank that could pay off depositors with its own notes out of the bales that were stored in the vault. Halfway between the 1984 political settlement and 1997 handover, in 1991 the colonial authorities looked to hand over a stable and prosperous territory. A property crash that wiped out local banks and led to bank runs was no recipe for financial or political stability.

3.3. *Hong Kong's linked exchange rate, private debt and the asset price cycle*

Through the exchange-rate link, the Fed's cheap money exerted a very strong and direct effect on Hong Kong. The link ensured that under normal circumstances the Hong Kong inter-bank offered rate (Hibor) tracked Libor closely. Figure 1 shows that US dollar market interest rates passed through to Hong Kong with rare exceptions, especially after the so-called "accounting measures" of July 1988. These deprived HSBC of its influence over the quantum of interbank liquidity, in effect giving the authorities control over the Hong Kong dollar monetary base (Greenwood, 2008, Chapter 11).

Despite significant public housing (40 percent of flats in 1991), Hong Kong's private debt, with almost 40 percent of bank loans property-related,

---

[3] In 1983, visiting Bank of England official Charles Goodhart and HM Treasury staffer David Peretz reported, with characteristic understatement, that runs in Hong Kong were "not uncommon" (James, 2020, p. 193). Recall that in 1983, no less than 117 years had passed since the last UK bank run (Shin, 2009).

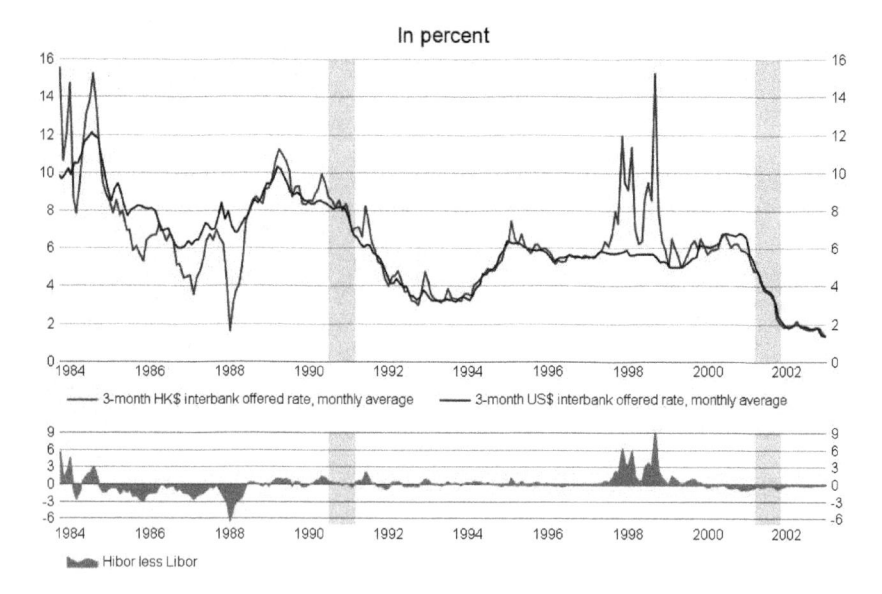

Figure 1. Hibor versus Libor, October 1983–2002.
Note: Shaded area denotes US recession.
Source: Refinitiv Datastream.

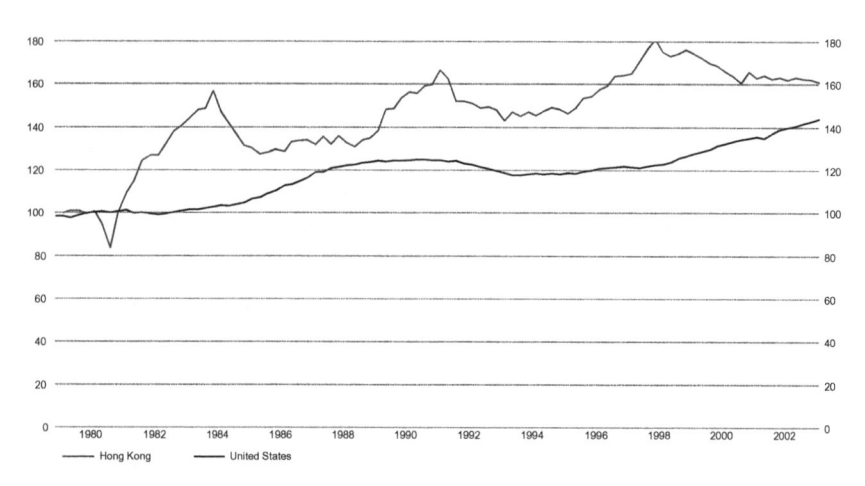

Figure 2. Hong Kong and US private debt to GDP ratios.
Source: Refinitiv Datastream.

had reached a high level by international standards. The territory's private debt to GDP ratio stood at 167 percent at the end of 1990, compared to the US ratio of 122 percent even after years of US corporate leveraging and booming property credit (Figure 2).

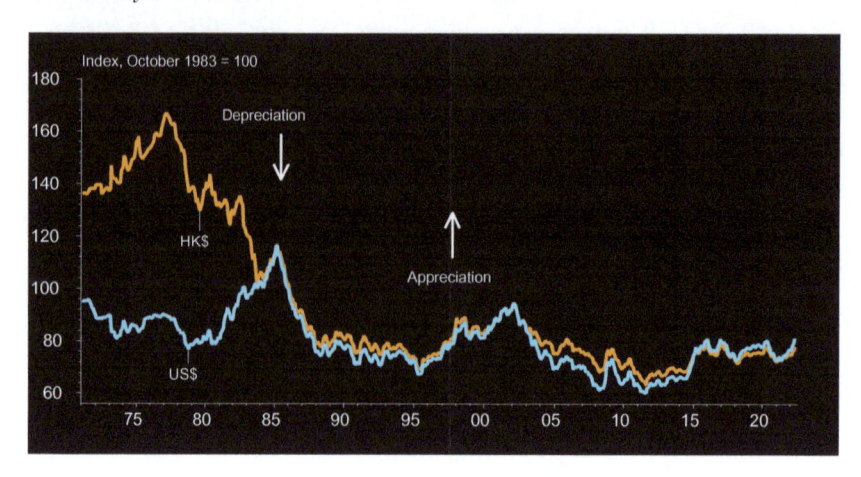

Figure 3. Hong Kong and US nominal effective exchange rates.
Note: BIS narrow indices.
Source: Refinitiv Datastream/Fathom Consulting; authors' calculations.

Moreover, almost all of Hong Kong's debt carried floating interest rates, whereas fixed-rate debt dominated US private credit (Borio, 1995). Thus, easy Fed policy turbocharged household and corporate cash flows in Hong Kong.[4]

A cheap dollar reinforced cheap money. In the decade after the onset of generalised floating exchange rates in 1973, the nominal effective exchange rate of the Hong Kong dollar bore no relationship to that of the US dollar. Indeed, in much of this period, the colonial authorities absent-mindedly neglected any anchor for the beleaguered Hong Kong dollar.[5] But after the link was re-established in October 1983, the two dollar currencies moved together closely. The Hong Kong dollar rode the US dollar's last leg up to early 1985. But then, when the US dollar lost 34 percent of its value from January 1985 to July 1991, the Hong Kong dollar effective rate declined by 30 percent, according to the BIS narrow indices (Figure 3). (See Section 7 on Singapore, which by contrast managed its nominal effective exchange rate.)

---

[4] Compared to Singapore, which set an 80 percent LTV ceiling in 1996 (Rajan *et al.*, 2022).
[5] As argued within the government by Deputy Secretary for Monetary Affairs Tony Latter (Greenwood, 2008, p. 104).

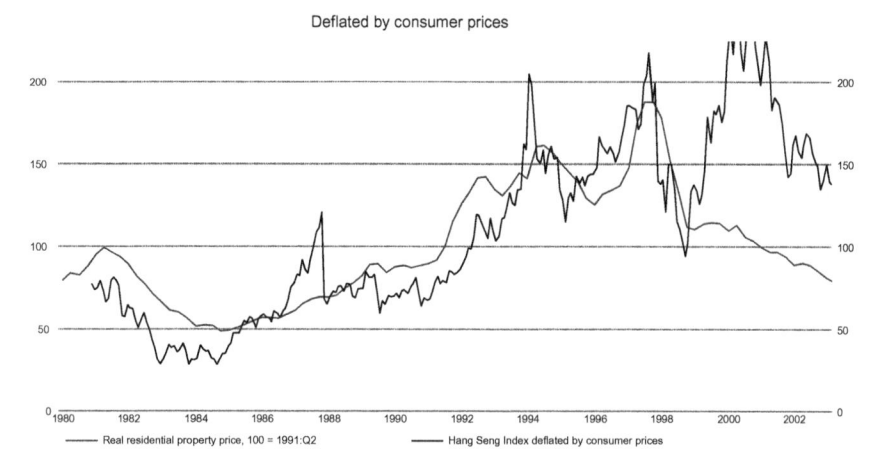

Figure 4. Hong Kong residential property prices and Hang Seng Index.
Source: Refinitiv Datastream.

Given the very open Hong Kong economy, the similar exchange rate outcome stimulated Hong Kong prices and activity more than US prices and activity. Imai (2010) calculates that traded goods and services amounted to fully one-half of Hong Kong's economy in 1991, with manufacturing still accounting for about 15 percent of GDP and traded services accounting for a larger 35 percent.[6] The openness of the US economy at the time, as measured by the manufacturing sector, fell short of half that level at 19 percent. Even if one adds service exports, it is clear that the Hong Kong economy was twice as open as the US economy. Openness magnified the effect of a shared currency depreciation on Hong Kong activity and prices.

Hong Kong's equity and property cycles (Borio and McGuire, 2004) seem to combine frequency and amplitude without parallel (Figure 4). A 50 percent crash in property prices was a memory less than a decade old in Hong Kong in 1991 (James, 2020). Ominously, rising prices drew in speculators and gangsters at a time when the government sought to

---

[6] Private communication with the authors. See Imai (2010).

sell off public-owned flats to owner-occupiers. What to do? The absence of the interest rate tool combined with repeated stimulus elicited a supervisory response.

3.4. *Basel I in Hong Kong: "Warts and all"*

Hong Kong's early adoption of Basel I left Hong Kong banks very well capitalised. Banking Commissioner Tony Nicolle resisted incorporating the 50 percent weight for residential mortgages into Hong Kong rules but faced stiff opposition. In May 1991, the *Far Eastern Economic Review*, citing a 32 percent rise in mortgage lending versus a 17 percent rise in overall lending, quoted him as saying of the 50 percent weight:

> It was one [that] I fundamentally disagreed with in Hongkong, and I tried to introduce the BIS requirements without it. But the banks protested — quite rightly I think — that if you are going to have international standards, [then] you have to have it [sic] warts and all. I think that we are now seeing the consequences (Taylor, 1991).

Just as a low US dollar Libor and a depreciated dollar particularly stimulated activity and stoked inflation in Hong Kong's very small, very open and very leveraged economy, so too the cut in the capital required to back residential mortgages particularly spurred mortgage market competition among banks there. This, in effect if not in intention, easing of macroprudential policy (outside the continent of Europe) exerted perhaps its greatest effect on this highly leveraged economy, releasing bank capital amounting to about 2 percent of GDP that could be leveraged 25 times with mortgages.

Just as the Hong Kong authorities had chosen to peg to the dollar and to permit free capital flows, so too they accepted the Basel I weight on mortgages, indeed against their better judgement. However, given the constraints imposed by these decisions, perhaps nowhere else in the world could some additional policy instrument do so much to reconcile monetary stability, international supervisory norms and financial stability.

4. Adopting the 70 percent LTV: "self-regulation victory"?

On 11 November 1991, HSBC announced that it had set a 70 percent norm for mortgage LTVs. Asked whether the move sought to head off government intervention, the bank's chair claimed that the initiative had lain with the bank. The *South China Morning Post* (SCMP) headline read, "Flat deposit decision a self-regulation victory for the banking industry".[7]

This section profiles the political economy of the adoption of the 70 percent LTV. Should one interpret this "industry initiative" (Yam, 2009) as a cover story for government regulation in a colony famous for its rule-based policy, even "positive non-interventionism"? After all, the later measures of 1994 (portfolio weight of 40 percent) and 1997 (60 percent LTV for luxury properties; the 50 percent to 60 percent debt service ratio) were *prima facie* supervisory initiatives. Or should one, following Kane (2020), interpret the banking authorities as enforcing the

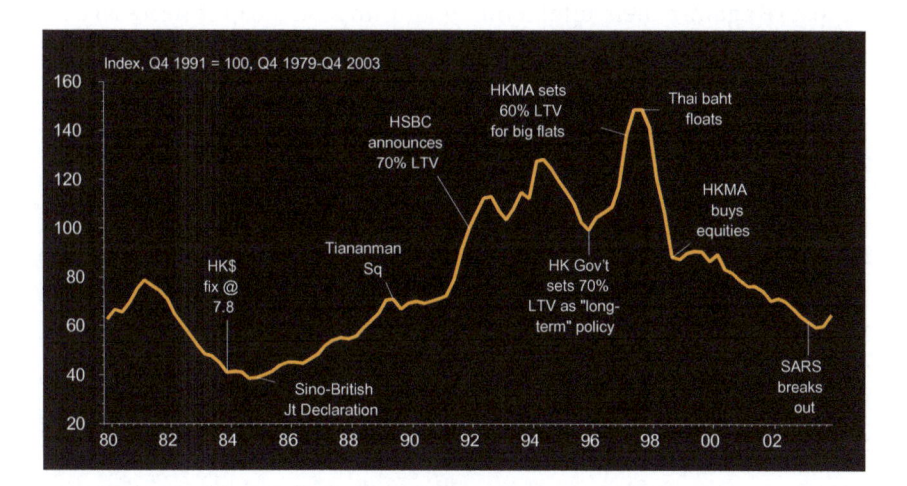

Figure 5. Hong Kong real property prices and LTV limit.
Note: Real property price is HK Statistics and Census Department all-dwellings index divided by CPI index.
Source: Refinitiv Datastream, BIS, authors' calculations.

---

[7] "Flat deposit decision a self-regulation victory for the banking industry", *South China Morning Post*, 13 November 1991.

will of leading banks on their competitors? There is certainly evidence that the government itself prompted a pre-emptive move by the banks.

In Hong Kong, the legal limit for residential mortgages was 90 percent LTV and banks routinely lent at 85 percent to 90 percent for existing customers. Banks set standard LTV limits according to the age of the property and the value of the property. Thus HSBC had lower LTV for properties over five years old and below HK$5 million. The residential mortgage market was also highly concentrated with the HSBC Group (including Wayfoong Finance and Hang Seng Bank) persistently accounting for about 40 percent of the market by value and number of loans. Figure 5 shows relevant policy changes and property prices.

The Banking Commissioner's campaign to tighten standards started at least seven months before HSBC lowered its LTV and proclaimed an industry standard. In April 1991, the outgoing Banking Commissioner Anthony Nicolle warned that banks should "weigh their mortgage exposure against their total lending and impose a cap if necessary".[8] Nicolle did not specify a ceiling on such loans because the prudent level could vary greatly according to the strategies and strengths of individual banks. He said that the level of exposure could be left to the discretion of bank management and praised the restraint showed by some institutions which had limited such business in the light of the sharp rise in home prices then.[9]

At the end of May 1991, Nicolle spoke out again about the need for banks to pay attention to their exposure, while noting that most banks had taken "extremely sensible" steps to scrutinise new home loans.[10] HSBC and Standard Chartered increased early repayment charges to push up the costs of speculation. Nicolle noted, "The leading players are already conscious of the need for caution … It's worthwhile making sure that the message is widely spread throughout the industry".

On 24 May 1991, Nicolle wrote to Ian R Wilson (of Standard Chartered), then chair of the Hong Kong Association of Banks (HKAB),

---

[8] Eva To, "Banks urged to cap mortgage exposure", *SCMP*, 30 April 1991.
[9] *Ibid.*
[10] Eva To, "Nicolle calls for lending prudence", *SCMP*, 28 May 1991.

to ask him to remind his members "of the need for prudence".[11] He noted that residential mortgage lending had increased by 7 percent from January–March 1991, which was slower than the final quarter of 1990 but still too quick for comfort. Prices were rising rapidly and Nicolle was "concerned that unrestrained growth could lead to an unsustainable level of property values". He also pointed out that mortgage lending was an increasing share of bank balance sheets. The delinquency rate was low, which supported the concessionary weight in the Basel capital requirement, but he offered the warning so familiar to financial advisers that "past experience may not be a reliable guide to the future". Over the next two months, the government began to prepare to tighten mortgage standards as property prices continued to surge.

By early August 1991 the government was ready to announce measures to try to stem speculation in the property market, especially for small and medium-sized flats. Banks were reported to be standing by to see if they would have to take additional steps if the government measures were inadequate. The context was the sale of flats in a new development at historically high prices.[12] Steve Martin, spokesman for HSBC, told journalists that:

> We are concerned about the rise in property prices and we want to control any speculative froth in the market and would therefore be prepared to both increase our rates and decrease the ratio of how much mortgage we give per property ... We will be looking at those (government) proposals with interest and deciding whether there is anything we can do to support them or react to them.[13]

Among the reactions in early August were changes to LTV norms. Standard Chartered reduced its LTV from 90 percent to 80 percent for properties over five years old (although they would continue to offer mortgages at 90 percent for newer properties) but not all banks followed.

---

[11] Nicolle (1991). HKMA Archives. He wrote on similar lines to the Deposit-Taking Corporation Association.
[12] Laguna City comprised 38 towers of waterfront luxury flats at Lam Tim developed by Cheung Kong Holdings and Hutchison Whampoa Property.
[13] *Reuters*, 7 August 1991.

A spokesman from the Bank of East Asia remarked that, "if market prices continue going up we will have some change in our lending policy".[14] In a survey of banks published by the *SCMP* on 3 August 1991, the banks in the Bank of China Group were reported to have reduced their LTV also to 80 percent to 85 percent.[15] In June 1991, Security Pacific Asian Bank had lowered its LTV norm from 90 percent to 80 percent for uncompleted flats and 85 percent for completed flats less than five years old. The senior vice president Alton Ng Ying-Chung noted that this change had not affected his bank's market share but that "We want our business to be safe and secure. Property prices have risen considerably within a short period of time… Obviously, it takes some time before we know whether the market can really support the present price of $2,800 a sq ft". Shanghai Commercial Bank also reported that it had imposed an 80 percent limit more than two months earlier, noting that "Speculation has been rife in the property market and we want to be more cautious". Nanyang Commercial Bank had introduced an 80 percent LTV on uncompleted flats and flats less than 5 years old at the end of July. The Bank of Communications reported that its advances were mainly at 80 percent over "the past few months" and that "Ninety per cent loans would only be extended on an individual basis". On the other hand, Overseas Trust Bank was still offering maximum mortgages at 80 percent to 90 percent. There was clearly a range of LTV deals on offer and a lack of consistency across banks in the market.

In response to the lack of consistent information, in early September, Albert Cheok, the Acting Commissioner of Banking, sent a questionnaire to 34 authorised institutions (both banks and deposit-taking corporations [DTCs]) about their residential lending practices and how they were changing in response to market conditions (and the Banking Commissioner's calls for prudence).[16] This group of institutions, all but six of which were banks, accounted for about 90 percent of

---

[14] *Ibid.*

[15] Connie Law, "Banks tighten mortgages as prices spiral", *SCMP*, 3 August 1991. The rest of the quotations in this paragraph are from this article.

[16] Letter Albert Cheok, Acting Commissioner of Banking to Ian Wilson, Chair of the Hong Association of Banks, 6 November 1991. HKMA Archives. 28 banks, 2 restricted licenced banks and 4 deposit-taking corporation (DTCs). For the relationship between banks and DTCs, see Schenk (2017).

residential mortgages. The survey, and its results, turned out to exert a galvanising effect on the leading banks in the market. It was reported in some detail in the local newspapers.

On 7 September 1991, the *SCMP* reported on the questionnaire.[17] It remarked that this was the first time a questionnaire on this topic had been circulated — it ran to five pages asking for financial information and details of each bank's mortgage lending policy. With respect to the latter, banks were asked how they calculated loan valuation ratios and the "income status of loan applicants".[18] Deputy Banking Commissioner Albert Cheok reassured the press that "the questionnaire was 'of no great matter'", denying it reflected heightened concerns about the residential property market. He also denied it was the first of its kind, but could not remember when the last such questionnaire was circulated. The latest exercise was simply part of the Commission's assessment of the banking industry conducted "from time to time", he said, "although naturally we are always concerned about all aspects of the banking business, that is our job". He admitted that the questionnaire had been issued against "a backdrop of the residential market being flavour of the month for a while" but clearly tried publicly to downplay its importance.[19]

On 16 September 1991, as the banks were filling in the survey, the so-called best lending rate (BLR) was lowered by 0.5 percent to 9 percent but the standard rate for mortgages was left at 10.75 percent, so the spread widened to 1.75 percent. Paul Selway-Swift, HSBC general manager, warned that the rise in property prices "is something that needs to be watched carefully. We may need to consider taking further action to calm it down a bit".[20] On 4 November 1991, the rate on new home loans was re-linked to BLR when the latter was reduced to 8.25 percent, but the spread stayed at 1.75 percent.[21]

Banks in Hong Kong thus took the opportunity presented by official concern over soaring flat prices amid buoyant credit growth to fatten

---

[17] Connie Law, "Regulator questions banks on mortgages", *SCMP*, 7 September 1991.
[18] *Ibid.*
[19] *Ibid.*
[20] Quoted in *SCMP*, 22 September 1991.
[21] Rosa Ocampo, "Banks tighten loans to balance rate cut", *SCMP*, 5 November 1991.

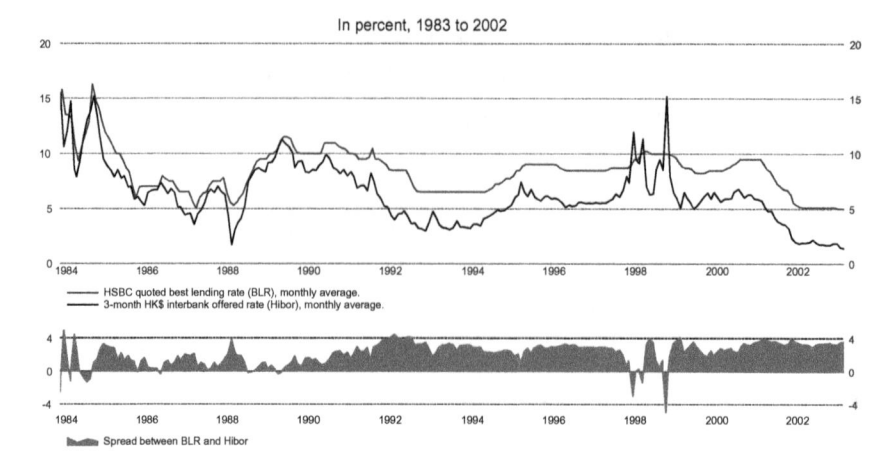

Figure 6. Hong Kong interest rates: HSBC best lending rate and Hibor. *Source*: Refinitiv Datastream.

their margins on the lending side. This mostly took the form of not passing through the decline in wholesale rates to administered lending rates (Gerlach and Peng, 2005). A wider spread between a market-set rate and an administered rate in a falling rate environment is par for the course, but, as the lower panel in Figure 6 shows, this widening proved persistent. Perhaps the banks anticipated the attack on their deposit rate cartel (Kwan, 2003), and sought to shift their net interest margin from the deposit side to the lending side.[22]

The banks returned the surveys by the end of September 1991, although the results were not shared with banks until early November. However, market leaders already seemed ready to take action. In mid-October the *SCMP* reported that "Standard Chartered Bank is urging Hongkong Bank [HSBC] and the Bank of China [BoC] to reduce their maximum mortgage loan amounts from 85 to 80 per cent of a flat's selling price in a bid to curb property speculation, banking sources say".[23] Standard

---

[22] Such a shift was observed in Switzerland when the Swiss National Bank moved to deeply negative policy rates and banks raised mortgage rates.

[23] Rosa Ocampo, "Chartered wants mortgage curbs", *SCMP*, 16 October 1991.

Chartered was considered more conservative than HSBC or BoC and had already been lending at 85 percent LTV for flats up to five years old when HSBC and BoC reduced their LTV from 90 percent to 85 percent earlier in October. Hang Seng Bank also trimmed its LTV to 80 percent earlier in October. Jardine subsidiary United Merchants Finance Ltd reduced its LTV to 70 percent for older properties and 80 percent for pre-sold flats, which M.K. Koo (manager for property financing) said "was basically in line with the ceiling fixed by other banks and financing firms".

In early October, officers at HSBC considered whether the rapid increase in home prices warranted a change in lending policy.[24] On the one hand, it was noted that mortgage loans were very profitable while delinquency rates were low and that this might warrant an increase in the bank's portfolio. On the other hand, it was concluded that while the increase in prices "does cause great concern and we should be on top of it all the time … no strategic revision is necessary at this stage".[25] At this point there was no consideration of adjusting LTV as part of this discussion.

By the end of October 1991, the surge in prices had not abated. On 22 October, the *Wah Kiu Yat Po* newspaper reported rumours that the largest lenders were preparing to reduce LTV to 70 percent.[26] Two days later the government released more land to try to reassure the market that there would be greater supply of residential units, but there were mixed views in the market about whether a crash like 1981–1982 was looming.[27] The rhetoric focused on prices rather than the scale of lending. "Our message is: 'Don't panic'" intoned Bowen Leung, the Deputy Secretary for Planning, Environment and Lands, during a press briefing. "There will be enough

---

[24] Memo Manager Retail Strategy and Development, to Assistant General Manager Retail Banking, 7 October 1991. HK139/58, HSBC Asia Pacific Archives [hereafter HSBC AP].
[25] *Ibid* — marginalia by Assistant General Manager Retail Banking, 12 October 1991. HK139/58 HSBC AP.
[26] *Wah Kiu Yat Po*, 22 October 1991. The article also reported rumours that the government was considering increasing capital gains tax on property. *WKYP* translates as *Overseas Chinese Daily News* and was the oldest Chinese language newspaper in Hong Kong. In late 1991, it was taken over from the Shum family by the *SCMP*. It ceased operations in 1995. It was considered politically neutral, or at least not pro-Beijing.
[27] Government land sales were watched closely in Beijing in advance of the handover in 1997.

land supply. There will be enough residential units".[28] The price surge seemed specific to Hong Kong: prices of high-end housing reportedly rose 8 percent in Singapore and 11 percent in Malaysia compared to 40 percent in Hong Kong in the first nine months of 1991. Some of this was speculative: "We've had people wander into our office and pick up two or three units as casually as if they were buying groceries", said an agent with View More Estate Agent Co. in Happy Valley. "On some days, we come close to running out of properties to sell".[29] Contemporary views were that the boom was caused partly by pent up demand after the Tiananmen Square Incident in June 1989 and the looming war in the Middle East in 1990. Prices began to lift once the Gulf War ended in March 1991, and in July the British and Chinese governments' agreement on construction of a new airport gave prices a fillip.[30] It is important to note that this was a time of inflation at 12 percent per annum, compared to the 4 percent interest that could be earned on deposits and the 10.25 percent standard rate on new mortgages. This gap created a strong incentive to shift deposits into down payments on flats. The drivers of demand were high savings from strong growth, low interest rates (especially on deposits) and inflation.

However, a collapse might loom: the ratio of mortgage servicing cost to median income reached about 74 percent in April 1991 and 90 percent in October. These levels were high compared to countries like the US where the ratio was about 25 percent, although still below Hong Kong's peak of 178 percent before the property market collapsed in 1982.[31] HSBC's chief economist Alan McLean remarked publicly that "It's premature to make that sort of judgment [crash looming] about the current market", he said. "But it looks like we may be quickly approaching that point".[32] At the end of October, Standard Chartered's analysis of the

---

[28] Quoted in Jesse Wong, "Hong Kong housing prices scale heights", *Wall Street Journal Asia*, 24 October 1991. Leung later became Private Secretary of the Government House from 1992 to 1995; and Secretary for Planning, Environment and Lands from 1995 to 1998. In November 1998, he was appointed Director of the Office of the Government of the Hong Kong SAR in Beijing until he retired in 2005.
[29] Quoted in Jesse Wong, *loc. cit.*
[30] *Ibid.*
[31] *Ibid.*
[32] *Ibid.*

property market suggested that, given that interest rate hikes could not be used to temper demand owing to the linked exchange rate, banks should exercise greater prudence in their mortgage lending to preclude the government's stepping in.[33]

In the first week of November 1991, the Government finally showed its hand and imposed a 2.75 percent stamp duty on all real estate transactions and Financial Secretary Hamish Macleod did not rule out a capital gains tax on property if the stamp duty measure did not dampen price rises.[34] The next weekend, the last before the stamp duty was effective, about 30,000 people queued for a lottery for 2000 flats in a Cheung Kong development (controlled by Li Ka-Shing), suggesting more froth.[35]

On 6 November 1991, Acting Commissioner of Banking Albert Cheok sent a letter to Ian Wilson, Chair of the HKAB, summarising the Commissioner's survey of 34 banks, DTCs and restricted licensed banks. It found that all but two of the institutions surveyed in September had tightened up their lending over the past four months. They employed a mix of reduced LTV or loan-to-income ratios, more conservative property valuations and shorter loan tenors.[36] An internal document showed that the largest lenders adjusted their policies in April and about 25 followed from June.[37] Before March 1991, most banks had lent for 16–20 years and this remained the modal tenor, but there were a few banks that reduced tenors to 11–15 years after March. All of the banks that had lent on a 21–25-year tenor reduced this to below 20 years. The survey revealed that banks had already considerably tightened their policies, but that less than a quarter intended to tighten any further over the next few months (all of which were locally incorporated). The internal document concluded that:

---

[33] Standard Chartered Hong Kong Economic Indicators, reported in *Wah Kiu Yat Po*, 30 October 1991.
[34] *Reuters*, 12 November 1991.
[35] "HK banks tighten up on mortgage lending", *Financial Times*, 12 November 1991.
[36] Letter from A. Cheok, Acting Commissioner of Banking to I. Wilson, Chair HKAB, 6 November 1991. HK139-232, HSBC AP.
[37] Overall findings from the survey on mortgage lending, 6 November 1991. HKMA Archives.

Fears of unabated escalation in property prices and unchecked speculation weakening borrowers' affordability yet further have led to the A[uthorised] I[nstitution]s' decisions to impose stricter rules on mortgage lending.[38]

While welcoming measures already taken, the Acting Commissioner of Banking pointed out to the HKAB that the pace of lending was actually accelerating (Q1: 5.4 percent; Q2: 9.3 percent; Q3: 9.3 percent) and that prices were still rising. He recommended that:

> the recent tightening needs to be further reinforced. Our survey indicates that some of the respondents are already seized of this need. Other institutions should think seriously about following suit. Loan-to-valuation and loan-to-income ratios, along with valuation policies, are clearly areas which need to be looked at critically and our survey indicates that institutions are well aware of this [see fn 36].

He thus offered a menu of alternatives and made clear that he expected further action. He did not go so far as to suggest that the Commission would act if the banks did not, but the Financial Secretary had already signalled the intention to intervene with the stamp duty.

The Banking Commissioner's survey threw light on changes in underwriting standards earlier in 1991. The internal document naming banks (redacted in the excerpt that the HKMA kindly provided to the authors of this paper) suggests the bilateral supervisory pressure brought to bear on outliers as part of the supervisors' "identify, survey and inform" strategy. Figure 7 shows that, while a few banks adjusted their mortgage underwriting policies in the Spring and Summer, most banks made adjustments in August 1991 when the government announced its intention to take action and sent out the questionnaire.

Figure 8 shows that the banks were mainly motivated by the rise in property prices and speculation rather than rebalancing their loan portfolios. At the same time, only one bank admitted to influence by government policy.

---

[38] *Ibid.*

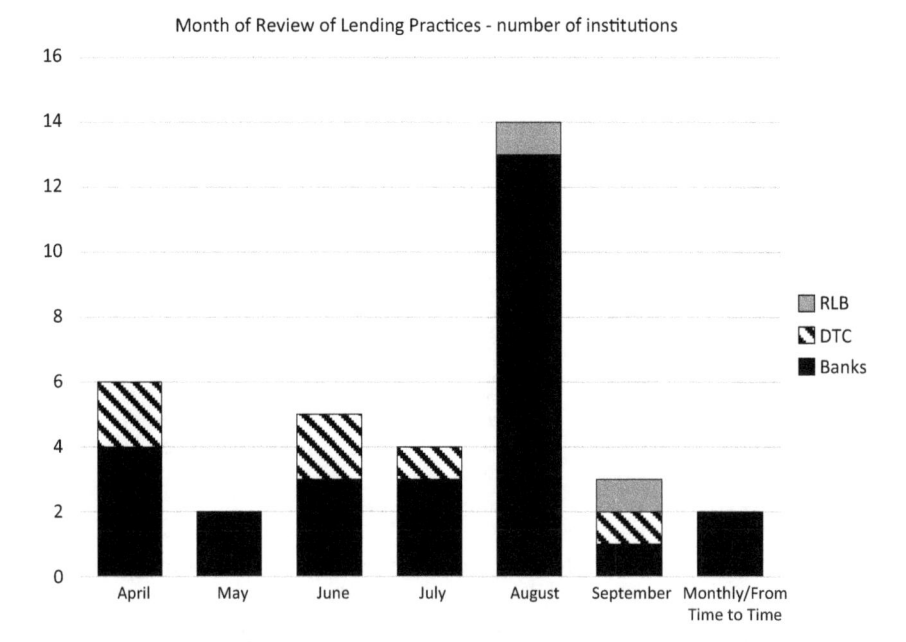

Figure 7. Month of review of mortgage lending practices, by number of reporting institutions.
Note: RLB = restricted license bank; DTC = deposit-taking corporation.
Source: Overall findings from the survey on mortgage lending, 6 November 1991. HKMA Archives.

Not surprisingly, almost all institutions expected to be increasing their mortgage lending by at least 10 percent in 1991, although not all to the same extent. One in five institutions expected to increase mortgage lending by over 40 percent compared with 1990 (Figure 9).

On 7 November 1991, the *SCMP* reported that bankers were relieved that Finance Secretary Hamish Macleod had not interfered further with mortgage lending policies despite his concern about banks' exposure. Roger Lacey, chief executive of Hongkong Chinese Bank (owned by Indonesian conglomerate Lippo, bankrupted in the Asian Financial Crisis) remarked, "Clearly, it is up to each bank to make its own judgement on how much of the balance sheet it wants to expose to the property sector."[39]

---

[39] Rosa Ocampo, "Relief as mortgage policies left alone", *SCMP*, 7 November 1991.

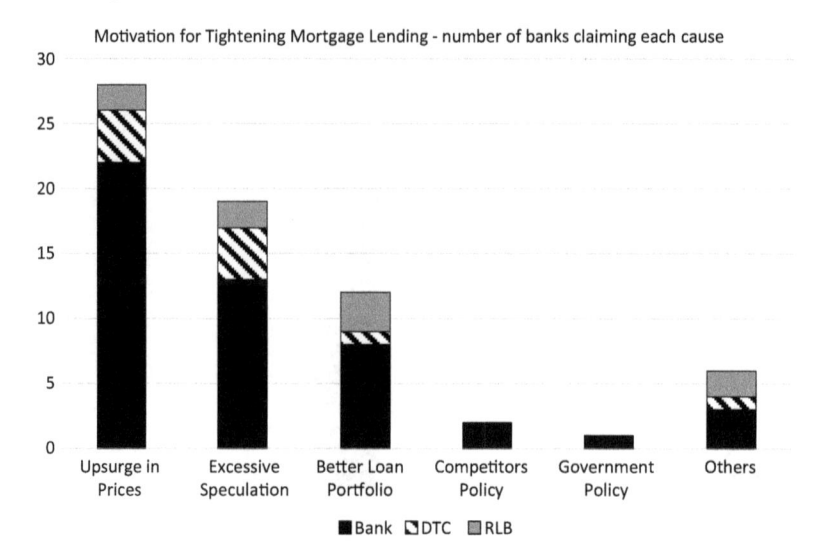

Figure 8. Motivation for tightening mortgage lending, by number of reporting institutions.
Note: DTC = deposit-taking company; RLB = restricted license bank.
Source: Overall findings from the survey on mortgage lending, 6 November 1991. HKMA Archives.

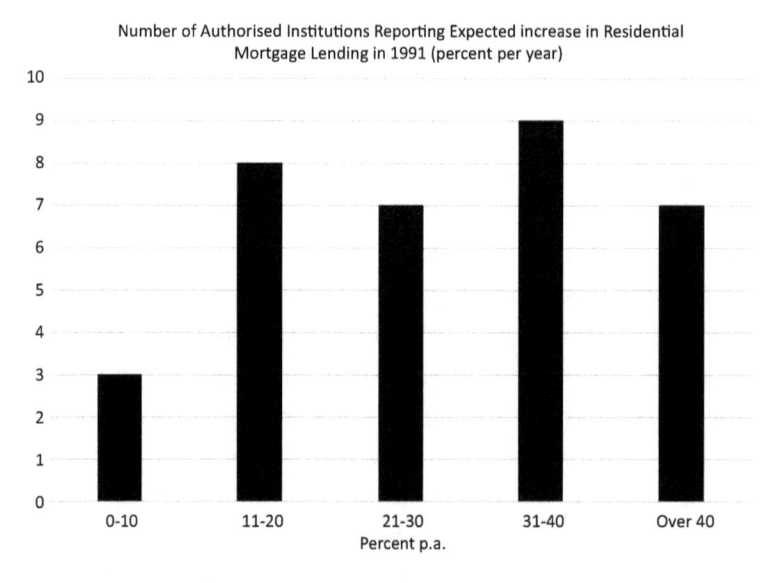

Figure 9. Number of institutions reporting expected rise in residential mortgage lending in 1991.
Source: Overall findings from the survey on mortgage lending, 6 November 1991. HKMA Archives.

Still, in his address to Legislative Council, Macleod urged banks to be more prudent and to review their lending policies. Mark Waller, CFO at Standard Chartered, and acting chairman of the HKAB, agreed that individual banks should set their own lending policies and went on to say that "the HKAB would take a stand on the 'deposit side', but would not ask the Government to limit loans for uncompleted flats to a certain percentage of the property value".[40] This seems to hint at an adjusted LTV (i.e., a larger down payment). Lacey remarked that the government could not use interest rates to cool the market because of the HKD's link to the USD and advocated changing the link from the USD to a link to a currency basket.[41] Derek Liu, corporate finance director at Hoare Govett, agreed.[42]

On 10 November 1991, the *SCMP* reported that HSBC and Standard Chartered were "urging the Government to impose a limit on pre-sale mortgages ... Both banking giants stressed that a united action on pre-sale mortgages could be highly effective in taking excessive heat out of the residential property market" by making it more difficult to speculate on units in new developments.[43] The article went on to note that "Hongkong Bank deputy general manager Mr Edwin Lau Chi-kit highlighted the importance of Government assistance because banks risked jeopardising business prospects with property developers if they acted on their own".[44] They hoped to lead a market-wide restraint on lending for pre-sale mortgages. *SCMP* reported that "Analysts said the warnings of the two banking giants suggested they were ready to take tougher action on pre-sale mortgages, but on the provision that rivals did the same".[45] However, action along this line was not in the end taken. Instead, HSBC acted independently the following day.

On 11 November 1991, HSBC announced it was reducing its standard LTV ratio from 80 percent to 70 percent, the second such reduction in

---

[40] *Ibid.*

[41] *Ibid.* See below regarding Singapore on whether a credible basket link yields an extra degree of freedom in monetary policymaking.

[42] *Ibid.*

[43] Eva To, "Standard Chartered Bank throws weight behind Hongkong Bank on pre-sale mortgage issue", *SCMP*, 10 November 1991. Pre-sale mortgages were for new build properties still under construction and were used by speculators who hoped to re-sell their properties at a higher price on completion of the building.

[44] *Ibid.*

[45] *Ibid.*

1991, to be effective on 13 November 1991. The new limit also applied at Hang Seng Bank (61.5 percent owned by HSBC). Throughout 1990 and 1991, HSBC Group and Hang Seng Group together accounted for about 38 percent of the residential housing market, an increase from about 33 percent in 1989.[46] The HSBC spokesman told the press that "…we are concerned that we should be doing everything we can to control overheating in the residential property sector".[47]

"Asked if the cut was a result of Carse's letter, the [HSBC] spokesman said 'It's not really, it's very much our own perception of the market'".[48] This was confirmed by HSBC chairman William Purves a few days later: "'No, this was a decision made by the bank', Mr Purves said when asked if the move was made to head off possible government intervention. 'We thought it was good for Hongkong, and what is good for Hongkong is good for us'".[49] He told reporters that the timing of the decision was prompted by 30,000 people queueing for a release of new flats in Tin Shui Wai, which convinced him that the market was overheated, "so on Monday the bank reduced the margin".[50] Alice Lam, director and general manager of Hang Seng Bank, also dismissed the idea that the new LTV policy was prompted by the government, telling *SCMP* that "We are constantly reviewing our lending policy, so this was not a direct result (of government entreaties), more of a coincidence".[51] The same article notes that Purves was flying to New York that day "to attend a board meeting of the beleaguered Marine Midland Bank which has been suffering heavy losses".[52] The lucrative Hong Kong mortgage business and net interest margins financed HSBC acquisitions and subsequent losses elsewhere. *Wah Kiu Yat Po* also published Hang Seng Bank's denial that the government had pressured the banks, although the bank's spokesperson acknowledged that the government had asked the banks to adjust their mortgage policies. Hang Seng Bank tightened its underwriting standards

---

[46] Reported in HK139/58, HSBC AP.
[47] *Reuters*, 11 November 1991.
[48] *Ibid.*
[49] G. Dalton, "Bank 'not pressured' on mortgages", *SCMP*, 15 November 1991.
[50] *Ibid.*
[51] Kenneth Ko, Peggy Sito and Catherine Beck, "Developers back new rules", *SCMP*, 13 November 1991.
[52] G. Dalton, "Bank 'not pressured' on mortgages", *SCMP*, 15 November 1991.

because surging prices made property less affordable and thus posed risk to banks.[53] The concern over the New Territories queues seems misplaced. Contemporary press accounts suggested that this episode was a "one-off" in anticipation of the incoming stamp duty.

Banks did not consistently apply the industry standard. Standard Chartered, Chase Manhattan, Hongkong Chinese Bank and First Pacific Bank followed a 70 percent LTV on 12 November but the BoC Group did not.[54] The Bank of East Asia (BEA) also did not adopt the new LTV — their limits were reported to be 80 percent to 85 percent. BEA spokesperson Rita Wong noted that, "Instead of just lowering the percentage of financing to home loans, we rather select our borrowers more carefully".[55] BEA headed the Chinese Hong Kong Bankers Association, having succeeded BoC.

The Hang Seng index fell sharply on the news from HSBC but soon recovered, partly because of the new limits' lack of credibility, or at least their flexibility. Property developers expressed their relief that banks had escaped externally imposed government controls and hoped that the limits would be lifted once the market cooled in the next two or three months.[56] William Phillips, managing director at Baring Securities, remarked that, "There's a bit of a perception that the public face of the banks saying they will not lend more than 70 pct is not entirely believed ... There's a general perception that there is flexibility in this policy".[57] Standard Chartered "softened the blow for customers with more than a year's savings history, letting them borrow at the concessional deposit level of 25 per cent" (i.e.,

---

[53] *Wah Kiu Yat Poi*, 12 November 1991, p. 1.

[54] "HK banks tighten up on mortgage lending", *Financial Times*, 12 November 1991; "More Hong Kong banks tighten their mortgage lending policies", *Wall Street Journal Asia*, 13 November 1991. Hong Kong Chinese Bank increased the share of mortgages in their local loan portfolio from "a negligible amount" to 20% in 1991. Henry Tse, HKCB's credit manager was quoted saying that "Lucrative returns and easy opportunities make mortgage lending attractive".

[55] "More Hong Kong banks tighten their mortgage lending policies", *Wall Street Journal Asia*, 13 November 1991.

[56] K. Ko, P. Sito and C. Beck, "Developers back new rules", *SCMP*, 13 November 1991. Robert Ng, chairman of Sino Land, is quoted at some length: "It's always good for the market to regulate itself. I think it's very healthy ... The less government interference, the better it is for the economy".

[57] V. McGlothern, "Hong Kong stocks end firmer in volatile trade", *Reuters*, 12 November 1991.

75 percent LTV rather than 70 percent).[58] There were also doubts about how long the measure would last. "Once property prices consolidate, the banks will raise the mortgage-lending ceiling again", said Andrew To, research director at Peregrine Brokerage Ltd.[59] This was supported by Alice Lam, director and general manager of Hang Seng Bank, who on 13 November 1991 was reported to remark "the bank would be lenient in its newly-imposed lending ceiling of 70 per cent for home mortgages", promising that if genuine end-users approached the bank with financial difficulties, "we would accommodate them".[60]

The new policy seemed to have an immediate impact, with HSBC and Standard Chartered reporting a sharp decline in mortgage applications in the weeks after the new LTV was imposed. HSBC general manager Paul Selway-Swift recorded a drop of 35 percent to 40 percent, bringing levels back to the first quarter of 1991. He remarked that

> A lot of genuine end users may not be able to afford to put up 30 percent out of their own pockets. The lower credit limit may be deterring some speculation, but we like to think we weren't getting too many speculators anyway because we vet all our loans carefully.[61]

Challenged with the idea that developers might lend instead of banks, Selway-Swift retorted that HSBC "would refuse to finance developers' lending activities, although he conceded most were already very cash rich". "So far they haven't approached us for loans, but I would like to make it known that if they did, they wouldn't get it [sic]".[62]

On the first anniversary of the 70 percent LTV threshold, Carse advised the press, "There are certainly no plans on our part to suggest to banks that they should lift or relax the 70 per cent ceiling at this stage." As to whether the limit might be eased or lifted during the first half of

---

[58] "Flat deposit decision a self-regulation victory for the banking industry", *SCMP*, 13 November 1991.

[59] "More Hong Kong banks tighten their mortgage lending policies", *Wall Street Journal Asia*, 13 November 1991. His opinion was backed up by others.

[60] K. Ko, P. Sito and C. Beck, "Developers back new rules", *SCMP*, 13 November 1991.

[61] Jane Hutchinson and Kennis Chu, "Banks see fall in housing loans business", *SCMP*, 24 November 1991.

[62] *Ibid.*

next year, Mr Carse said, "I can't say yes and I can't say no. It depends on the state of the market and the level of interest rates. We will take it as it comes."[63] The former Banking Commissioner Anthony Nicolle, who had moved to head Standard Chartered in Hong Kong, also cautioned against lifting the threshold to avoid speculation and to maintain affordability. Property values had come down in the wake of the restrictions and he suggested that any easing should be gradual "so the market doesn't go berserk".[64] This seems to reflect a strong belief in the calming nature of the limits. Carse could not confirm rumours that developers were circumventing the LTV limits by lending directly to their customers. With respect to banks, he claimed that "'broadly speaking the limit had held' but 'if we are given details of individual banks [circumventing the limits] we will certainly take it up with them'". He also drew attention to strains in the Japanese, US and UK property markets that reflected "over-gearing". The slowdown in the market from the highs in 1991 showed the success of Hong Kong's approach.[65]

The surveillance of the LTV limit was achieved through a policy we call "define, survey and inform". After the initial survey in September 1991, the Banking Commissioner conducted a follow-up survey in March 1992 to gauge the impact of the LTV limit.[66] The verdict was that "the results were encouraging" with a slowing in the growth of mortgage lending from 45 percent yoy in the quarter ending in September to 39 percent yoy in the final quarter of 1991 to December and to 30 percent yoy in the quarter to March 1992. Nevertheless, there was a surge by 70 percent in new loan approvals (not yet drawn down) in March compared to February so demand was still high and Carse advised banks to continue to exercise restraint. A month later, the survey revealed "fresh momentum" in loan growth so that "it would certainly be premature to consider any relaxation of existing lending criteria".[67] Carse also reflected on the lack of discipline, warning that "institutions should avoid making too many exceptions to

---

[63] Laura Tyson, "Call to ease loan rules rejected", *SCMP*, 16 November 1992.
[64] *Ibid.*
[65] *Ibid.*
[66] Letter from David Carse to Ian R. Wilson (Standard Chartered Bank) as Chair of HKAB, 15 April 1992. HK139-58 HSBC AP.
[67] Letter from David Carse to Ian R. Wilson, 9 June 1992. HK139-58 HSBC AP.

this rule [LTV], even for specially regarded customers". Thereafter, the Banking Commissioner undertook monthly surveys of the 30 or so banks and financial institutions with about 90 percent of the residential market. The results were sent to the HKAB for circulation among its members in a letter that tracked the number and value of new mortgages in graphs as well as setting out the monthly changes. Importantly, this is where the Banking Commissioner expressed his monthly view of the market and the stance that the banks should take in their lending. This advice varied slightly depending on market circumstances but consistently advised prudence and warned that there was no case to relax restrictions on lending.[68] In the reviews of the monthly surveys of banks in March, April and May 1993, Carse repeated the phrase "we continue to advise institutions to maintain the 70 percent loan to value guideline".[69]

Discipline was not complete. Notably, Standard Chartered, headed by the former Banking Commissioner Anthony Nicolle, broke the LTV most openly by offering easier terms of 75 percent LTV for established customers on the newest flats. In July 1992, they also reintroduced "decoration loans" to allow borrowers to increase LTV to 77 percent. This was described by Carse as "disingenuous".[70] A week later Carse reiterated in his monthly survey report (addressed to Ian Wilson, Chief Manager of Standard Chartered as chair of the HKAB) that "it would clearly be premature to relax the current 70 percent loan-to-value ratio. For this rule to be effective, it needs to be observed by all banks".[71] In September 1996, the HKMA (1996b) codified its proscription of the practice of advertising and extending personal loans in conjunction with residential mortgages.[72]

---

[68] The letters can be found in HSBC AP, HK139-232, HK139-233, HK139/58.

[69] David Carse to Paul Selway-Swift as chair of HKAB, 21 May 1993 and 21 April 1993, 23 March 1993. HK139/58, HSBC AP.

[70] Press clipping from *SCMP* 17 July 1992 and marginalia of a discussion with Carse. HK139-58, HSBC AP.

[71] Letter David Carse to I. R Wilson (Standard Chartered) Chair of HKAB, 24 July 1992. HK139-58, HSBC AP.

[72] Earlier, HKMA (1995c) proscribed deals described by the Secretary of Financial Services to the Hong Kong Government Legislative Council (1995) as follows: "Recently, a joint loan scheme has been introduced where the 'topping-up' element of a loan is provided by another bank in the form of personal loan with the property as security. We think that this arrangement has crossed the acceptable line".

Joint operations with property developers also challenged the 70 percent limit but banks faced pressure from the authorities to conform. HSBC did a deal with Henderson Land whereby HSBC advanced at a 70 percent LTV but then allowed Henderson Land to advance a further 20 percent against a second mortgage. According to internal HSBC documents, this "became the subject of criticism from the Financial Secretary and, for the time being, it is not politic for us to agree to additional similar deals".[73] In October 1993, Carse's monthly survey report specifically warned that "we would also advise banks against entering into arrangements with property developers which would result in borrowers being able to obtain financing in excess of 70 percent of property values".[74] Meanwhile, HSBC Group's dominant market share of about 38 percent seemed unaffected by the LTV limits.

In early March 1993 David Li, director and chief executive of Bank of East Asia, raised a question in the Legislative Council asking the administration to allow banks to relax their mortgage lending rates, given the decline in prices of since the LTV limits were introduced in November 1991.[75] This provoked a robust response from the Secretary for Monetary Affairs. He noted that the guideline had been "voluntarily adopted" but that the government "has since been urging all authorized institutions to adhere to the guideline" to enhance banking sector stability, stem price inflation and restrain speculation. On these three bases he deemed "the guideline has evidently been successful" but he cautioned against any relaxation given low real interest rates and the potential for another spike in prices, although "the situation will be kept under constant monitoring

---

[73] Memo from Senior Manager Corporate Banking to Assistant General Manager Corporate Banking, 26 February 1993. HSBC HK139/58, HSBC AP.

[74] Letter David Carse to Anthony Nicolle (Standard Chartered Bank) as chair of HKAB, 27 October 1992. HK139-58 HSBC AP. The Henderson Land deal was reported publicly in "Murmurs of discontent over mortgage limits", *SCMP*, 5 January 1993. On 3 March 1995, the HKMA (1995a) codified its guidance on mortgages extended in conjunction with loans by property developers. The bank mortgage would have to enjoy the first claim; the bank's risk assessment would have to include the developer's loan in the debt-to-income ratio; and the bank could not finance the property developer.

[75] Text of question and answer available in letter from David K.P. Li to the Secretary of the HKAB, 3 March 1993. HK139/58, HSBC AP. Li returned to the battle in May and July 1994 by challenging the LTV in Legislative Council.

and review". He also advised that "It can be safely assumed that relaxation in future, if any, will be cautiously controlled and will aim only at helping genuine end-users, and first-time buyers in particular. We believe that this position still commands general support among the banking sector". The authorities were surveying, monitoring and applying pressure for adherence to the LTV limit.

5. Guiding bank lending, formalising LTVs and setting affordability and a new LTV

This section profiles the subsequent elaboration of the policy before the peak of property prices in 1997. The HKMA both widened (Sections 5.1 and 5.3) and deepened its prudential measures on property lending (Sections 5.2 and 5.3).

5.1. *Guiding bank lending portfolios: Property loans at 40 percent of loans*

In February 1994, the HKMA (1994) widened its net from home mortgages to property exposures more generally. Home mortgages had grown in 1993 at much the same rate as nominal GDP, at about 15 percent, but other property loans had grown at a "less encouraging" rate of 25.8 percent. This left overall property exposures up 19.4 percent, noticeably larger in relation to GDP. As a result, property loans had increased their weight as a risk concentration, reaching 37.6 percent of loans for use in Hong Kong.

The supervisors rolled out a broad portfolio guide. They combined the comfortable approach of pressuring cross-sectional outliers with a less comfortable intention to restrain the aggregate over time. The supervisors guided banks to keep property loans to less than 40 percent of loans for use in Hong Kong, just above the industry average. Banks with ratios above this average were to adopt policies to stabilise the ratio or to bring it down. This was not a hard limit and the aggregate ratio crept higher.

Figure 10 shows that the ratio of residential mortgages alone to overall lending for use in Hong Kong had risen from 16 percent to 22 percent in

Loans to Individuals for Purchase of Private Residential Flats as a share of total loans and advances for use in Hong Kong (In %, 1978–1999)

Figure 10. Residential mortgage loans as a share of loans for use in Hong Kong.
Source: HKMA Quarterly Bulletin, Table 3.5.1.

the run up to the 1991 LTV intervention. The ratio then stabilised until just before the HKMA reduced the LTV on luxury flats in January 1997.

Figure 11 shows that the ratio was much closer to 40 percent for DTCs at the time of the new limit although they had a small share of the market compared to banks — approximately 10 percent compared to banks' 80 percent from 1990 onward. Figure 11 also shows that the 40 percent limit was breached by DTCs based on residential mortgage lending alone. Nevertheless, by 1997 they were losing market share to banks, including foreign banks, as the latter increased their exposure to residential mortgages.

Figure 12 shows that the benchmark ratio (total loans to the property sector) had peaked at 35 percent before the 1982 property crash with its destabilising effects on the banking system, but that this increase in exposure had mainly been vis-a-vis building and construction, property development and investment, rather than to residential mortgages. Also, by December 1994, the industry had hit the 40 percent mark but the portfolio concentration did not stop there.

Loans to Individuals for Purchase of Private Residential Flats as a share of total loans and advances for use in Hong Kong (In %, 1978–1999)

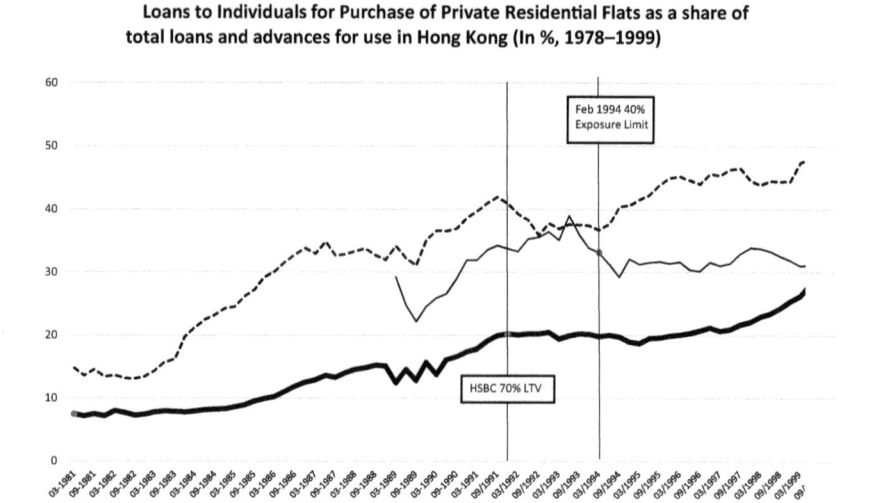

Figure 11. Residential mortgage loans as a share of loans for use in Hong Kong, by type of institution.
Source: HKMA Quarterly Bulletin, Table 3.5.1.

Nineteen months later, the HKMA (1995b) clarified its guidance. The 40 percent should not be interpreted as imposing a "upper limit", but rather served as a benchmark, especially since it did not distinguish between safer residential property and riskier commercial and development property exposures. Still, banks should have policies to cap such exposures, should respect the 70 percent LTV limit and should condition credit on the borrower's cash flow rather than the collateral value.

5.2. *Formalising the 70 percent LTV as government policy*

The *SCMP* reported that during the summer of 1993, the HKMA proposed that the 70 percent LTV replace the 90 percent limit in the definition of residential mortgages in the schedule of the Banking Act of 1986 covering mortgage lending. "By some mishap of information dissemination the proposal got leaked to the media. The way it was reported seemed to indicate the Government was ready to legislate

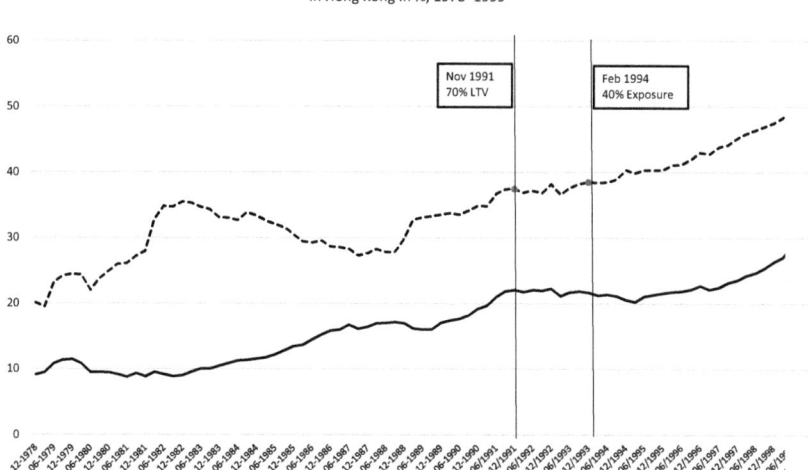

Total Property Lending (Development plus Residential Mortgages) as a Percent of All Lending for Use in Hong Kong In %, 1978–1999

Figure 12. Total property lending as a share of all lending for use in Hong Kong. Source: HKMA Quarterly Bulletin, Table 3.5.1.

limits on mortgage lending".[76] The formal schedule set the maximum 90 percent LTV for a loan to be treated as a residential mortgage qualifying for the 50 percent Basel weight; the HKMA insisted that banks would still be free to offer mortgages in excess of 70 percent LTV, albeit with double the required capital. The *SCMP* went on to report that

> The Monetary Authority emphasises the proposal was under consideration in the summer when it looked like things were getting so hot in the residential property sector that sterner action was going to be needed from the authority to stem the tide of property over-heating and speculation. In the wake of a tightening in bank lending policy it looks as though the Monetary Authority's plan would now prove unnecessary and as such it has now slipped off the agenda into a hold mode.[77]

---

[76] Gareth Hewett, "Loan ceiling stays but bankers must carry ball", *SCMP*, 17 November 1993.
[77] *Ibid.*

The banks had successfully resisted this move, but the HKMA reserved the right to return to the issue. In November 1994, Joseph Yam, as Chief Executive of the HKMA, suggested that the 70 percent LTV should be made permanent rather than "temporary" to enhance banking stability but this suggestion was not immediately taken up.[78]

At a Legislative Council meeting on 2 November 1995, the Hong Kong Government adopted the 70 percent LTV as a long-term policy (HKMA, 1996a). Secretary for Financial Services Rafael Hui marked the official transition from industry standard to government policy (Hong Kong Government, 1995):

> The guideline on the 70 percent mortgage ceiling is one of the important measures adopted by banks to control risks. One of the important principles of risk management is that bank loans should not be concentrated excessively on a certain trade or a certain market. In the case of Hong Kong, bank loans in relation to the property market is about 40 percent of the size of domestic loans offered by banks. The level is by international standard relatively high. ... although the proportion of bad debt in the market of residential property mortgage loans in Hong Kong is very low indeed, banks find it necessary to set a ceiling for property mortgage loans, with a view to cushioning the risks that may be incurred in case there is a drastic drop in property prices. In view of this, the Government supports that the 70 percent mortgage ceiling should continue to be adopted as a long-term policy. This policy is very important to maintaining the stability of our banking system. The relevant ceiling has been set out in the guideline issued by the HKMA to banks in respect of property loans. We believe that this guideline on the ceiling has been very useful to the management of risks by banks during peaks and troughs of the property market since 1991. Therefore, we should not lift or revise this ceiling casually in response to what may only be short-term market changes in a certain period.

---

[78] Speech by J. Yam reported in Banking World Hong Kong, clipping in HK139-233. HSBC AP.

5.3. *Setting affordability criterion and a lower LTV*

In the face of rapidly rising residential mortgage lending, the HKMA tweaked this "long-term policy" just months before the peak of the market. This was as clearly supervisory in initiative, as it was countercyclical in timing. In January 1997, the HKMA (1997a) issued a circular calling for a maximum 60 percent LTV for luxury properties, defined as those valued at more than HK$12 million, or over $1.5 million. The recital of facts included that property lending had increased by 18.9 percent in 1996 and that property lending as a share of loans for use in Hong Kong had breached 40 percent, rising from 39 percent at end-September 1995 to 40.7 percent at end-September 1996.

It also adopted an affordability criterion for the first time, limiting the mortgage debt service ratio to 50 percent to 60 percent (Wong *et al.*, 2004; HKMA, 2011). This guidance betrayed the height of property prices in Hong Kong in relation to income: the rule of thumb in most markets was one-third.

Noting 34 percent annualised growth in mortgage lending in the first half of 1997, HKMA (1997b) reminded banks of its full range of prudential measures and took a "serious view of non-compliance". This was in July, the month that the devaluation of the Thai baht marked the beginning of the Asian Financial Crisis.

6. Was the policy effective?

This question can be posed in two different ways. First, did the policy accomplish what its framers intended? And second, did market participants somehow end-run or arbitrage the policy and leave the goal unachieved in some broader sense? We take up the second question first, because it is the one posed in the most cited study of the 1991 LTV in Hong Kong.[79] We argue that the policy was effective viewed from either the broader or the more historic perspective.

---

[79] See also Wong *et al.* (2004, 2011, 2013). Gerlach and Peng (2005) shows 115 citations in RePEc, accessed 6 April 2021: https://econpapers.repec.org/article/eeejbfina/v_3a29_3ay_3a2005_3ai_3a2_3ap_3a461-481.htm

Writing from the Research Department of the HKMA, Gerlach and Peng (2005) provided strong evidence that the LTV policy succeeded in reducing bank lending in the territory ("loans for use in Hong Kong"), given the rise in property prices in the 1990s. Using a vector autoregressive analysis, they found that property prices led private credit growth, but not vice-versa. Splitting the sample in 1991, they found a significant drop in the parameter relating bank loans for use in Hong Kong to the official index of residential property prices. In particular, a 10 percent rise in real residential prices led to a 4 percent rise in real bank loans before, but only 1.3 percent after, the LTV change.

Two points are worth making about this result. First, our review of the 70 percent standard's adoption above suggests that it was not switched on like a light. The dummy that Gerlach and Peng (2005) used to represent the LTV standard was defined as a series of zeros until the break point and then a series of ones. The Banking Commissioner's survey (1991, p. 6) found that the banks with the largest market share tightened their standards in the second quarter, and that 91 percent by market share had tightened by end-September. If mortgage underwriting standards tightened in a less discontinuous fashion, the authors' estimated parameter may understate the effect (by the usual errors in variables analysis).

Second, Gerlach and Peng (2005) examined the entire stock of bank loans for use in Hong Kong, deflated by prices. They noted (*ibid.*, pp. 480–481) that doing so reduced the risk that the assessment was confounded by bank regulatory arbitrage that reclassified mortgage credit. As we have seen above, the banking authorities worked hard to prevent regulatory arbitrage in the form of the substitution of loans to developers and personal loans for high-leverage mortgages. Still, it is of interest to assess whether the 70 percent LTV standard hit its target as understood by the authorities at the time. That was, to reduce the growth of mortgage loans to that of nominal GDP.

Our contribution, then, is to assess the policy in a manner consistent with the intentions of the Commissioner of Banking and later HKMA Deputy Chief Executive. Here the record is very clear: the 70 percent LTV

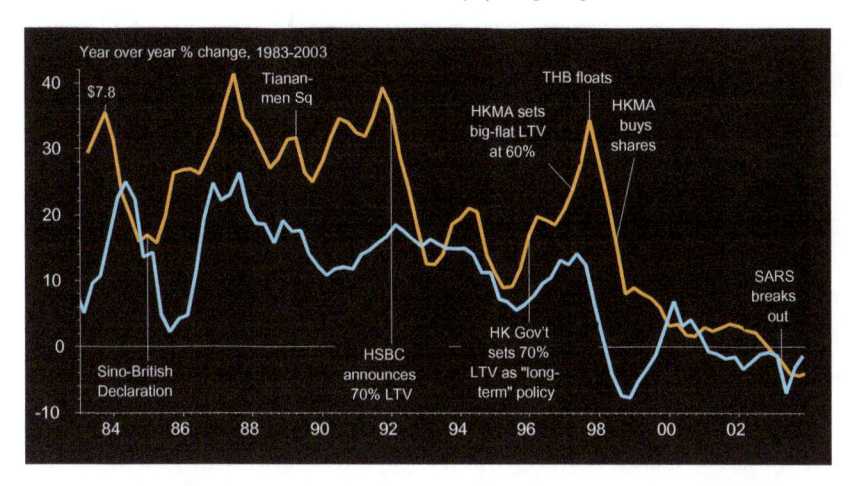

Figure 13. Growth of Hong Kong residential mortgages and nominal GDP.
Source: Refinitiv Datastream, HKMA, Hong Kong Statistics & Census Department, authors' calculations.

standard was associated with a very rapid drop of the growth rate of home mortgage lending to that of nominal GDP (Figure 13). The gap between the growth rate of home mortgage loans and that of GDP is wide in the third quarter of 1991, one quarter after the banks with the largest market share began to tighten their underwriting standards. By the fourth quarter of 1992, the growth rate of mortgages had fallen to that of nominal GDP. As HKMA (1994) suggested, "Without the 70% mortgage ceiling and other voluntary restrictions adopted by institutions, it is likely that the rise in lending would have been much greater."

7. Hong Kong, Singapore and Croatia

Before drawing conclusions, we cannot resist broadening the discussion to all three small open economy cases with open capital accounts, gathered in this volume. And all three have ceded the setting of their short-term interest rates to trading partners, albeit in different ways.

If "Hong Kong delegated the determination of its monetary policy to the Federal Reserve through its unilateral decision in 1983 to peg the

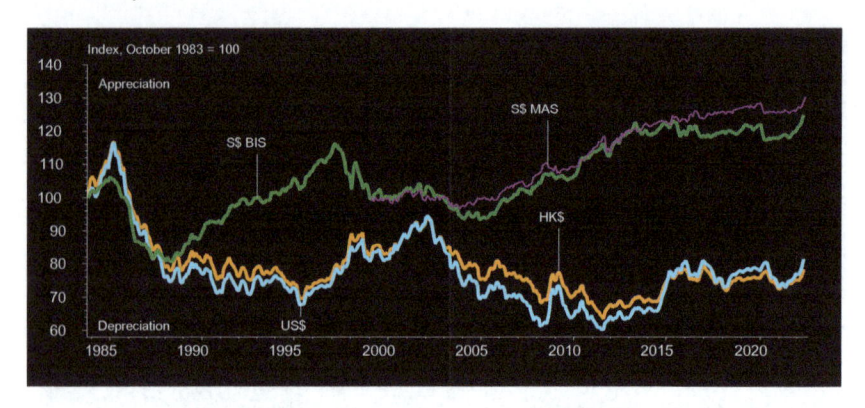

Figure 14. HK$, SG$ and US$ NEERs.

Note: BIS narrow indices.
Source: Refinitiv Datastream; BIS; MAS; authors' calculations.

Hong Kong dollar to the U.S. dollar" (Yellen, 2010), then Croatia did likewise through its peg to the euro. Less obviously, but no less surely, Singapore mostly delegated the determination of its interest rates to its trading partners. It did so by targeting a path of its nominal effective exchange rate in a so-called basket, band, crawl. Most of the time, the path has been upward by a percent or so per annum (Figure 14, especially the purple line showing the Monetary Authority of Singapore's calculation of the Singapore dollar nominal effective exchange rate [NEER]). Given open interest rate parity, which seems to hold in this case, Singapore's short-term interest rate has traded a percent or so below the average of its trading partners' policy rates.[80] In other words, by credibly targeting a crawl against the basket of its trading partners' currencies, Singapore's short-term interest rate is set by the combination of the rates of its trading partners and the crawl.

---

[80] See MAS (2000); Robinson (2001); McCauley (2001); Khor *et al.* (2004) and McCallum (2006). Singapore's approach can be seen as a Taylor Rule using the nominal effective exchange rate rather than the short-term interest rate as the left-hand side variable. It should not be confused with a floating exchange rate (Devereux, 2003) or a dollar peg (Ilzetski *et al.* (2019) vs. Ito and McCauley (2019).

Measures per year over the period covered

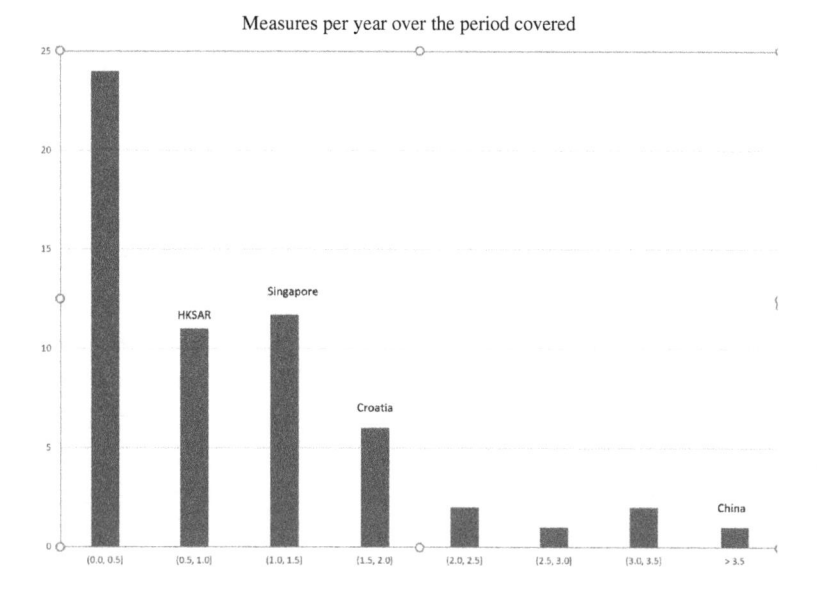

Figure 15. Frequency distribution of jurisdictions' use of macroprudential measures.
Note: Period of observation varies across jurisdictions.
Source: Kuttner and Shim (2016).

One way or another, having given up control over short-term interest rates, the authorities in Hong Kong, Singapore and Croatia have reached for macroprudential measures to stabilise their financial systems more than most. This is the message of Figure 15, which shows the frequency distribution of use of such measures. Not one of the three falls into the modal bucket, with an average of less than a half of a macroprudential measure per year.

8. Conclusion

How much of the political economy of prudential policy in Hong Kong in the 1990s is idiosyncratic or historically specific? Doubtless, historically specific features of Hong Kong's economic and political context encouraged this innovation and contributed to its effectiveness.

The case does provide take-aways for policymakers trying to use macroprudential policies outside the colonial context. First, studies of macroprudential policy have neglected what we call "define, survey and inform" as a useful means to provide market participants with the public good of information regarding the aggregate outcome of decentralised credit decisions. Second, clearly, the absence of an independent monetary policy in a (very) small open economy contributed to this early use of macroprudential policy, but so did a more leveraged private sector and so did greater reliance on short-term rates. Perhaps in their different ways, Croatia and Singapore make the same point. Third, if the transition to international standards for capital adequacy releases bank capital, a policy response may well be imperative.

References

Bank of England (1991): "Role and scope of mortgage limits", paper submitted to the Treasury and Civil Service Committee in April 1991, Bank of England *Quarterly Bulletin*, May, pp. 260–262.

Borio, C (1995): "The structure of credit to the non-government sector and the transmission mechanism of monetary policy: A cross-country comparison", *Financial structure and the monetary policy transmission mechanism*, BIS Papers no. 0, 15 March, pp. 59–105.

Borio, C and P McGuire (2004): "Twin peaks in equity and housing prices? *BIS Quarterly Review*, March, pp. 79–93.

Bruno, V, I Shim and H-S Shin (2017): "Comparative assessment of macroprudential policies", *Journal of Financial Stability*, **28**, pp. 183–202.

Caruana, J (2010): "The challenge of taking macroprudential decisions: Who will press which button(s)?" Speech to the 13th Annual International Banking Conference, Federal Reserve Bank of Chicago, with the IMF, Chicago, 24 September.

Cerutti, E, S Claessens and L Laeven (2017): "The use and effectiveness of macroprudential policies: New evidence", *Journal of Financial Stability*, **28**(C), pp. 203–224.

Claessens, S (2015): "An overview of macroprudential policy tools", *Annual Review of Financial Economics*, vol 7, pp. 397–422.

Devereux, M (2003): "A tale of two currencies: The Asian Crisis and the exchange rate regimes of Hong Kong and Singapore", *Review of International Economics*, **11**(1), pp. 38–54.

Gerlach, S and W Peng (2005): "Bank lending and property prices in Hong Kong", *Journal of Banking and Finance*, **29**(2), February, pp. 461–481.

Goodhart, C (2011): *The Basel Committee on Banking Supervision: A History of the Early Years 1974–1997*, Cambridge: Cambridge University Press.

Greenwood, J (2008): *Hong Kong's Link to the US Dollar: Origins and Evolution*, Hong Kong: Hong Kong University Press.

Hong Kong Government, Legislative Council (1992): *LegCo Sitting (Hansard)*, 6 May.

——— (1995): *LegCo Sitting (Hansard)*, 2 November.

Hong Kong Government (2008): Press release: LCQ1: "70% loan-to-value ratio cap for residential mortgage", LCQ1: 70% loan-to-value ratio cap for residential mortgage (info.gov.hk).

Hong Kong Monetary Authority (1994): "Property lending", 18 February https://www.hkma.gov.hk/eng/regulatory-resources/regulatory-guides/guidelines/1994/02/guide_59b/

——— (1995a): "The provision of mortgage finance to end users in conjunction with property developers", 3 March https://www.hkma.gov.hk/eng/regulatory-resources/regulatory-guides/by-subject-current/property-mortgage-lending/?&t=1610896373948.

——— (1995b): "Property lending", 13 September https://www.hkma.gov.hk/eng/regulatory-resources/regulatory-guides/guidelines/1995/09/guide_591b/.

——— (1995c): "Co-financing schemes in relation to residential mortgage lending", 30 October https://www.hkma.gov.hk/eng/regulatory-resources/regulatory-guides/guidelines/1995/10/guide_581b/, accessed 9 July, 2022.

——— (1996a): *Annual Report 1995*.

——— (1996b): "The use of personal loans to compete for residential mortgage business", 12 September https://www.hkma.gov.hk/eng/regulatory-resources/regulatory-guides/guidelines/1996/09/guide_592b/, accessed 9 July, 2022.

——— (1997a): "Criteria for property lending", 28 January https://www.hkma.gov.hk/eng/regulatory-resources/regulatory-guides/guidelines/1997/01/guide_593b/.

——— (1997b): "Property lending", 28 July https://www.hkma.gov.hk/eng/regulatory-resources/regulatory-guides/guidelines/1997/07/guide_594b/, accessed 9 July 2022.

——— (2011): "Loan-to-value ratio as a macroprudential tool - Hong Kong SAR's experience and cross-country evidence", *The influence of external factors on monetary policy frameworks and operations*, BIS Papers no 57, pp. 163–178.

Ilzetzki, E, C Reinhart and K Rogoff (2019); "Exchange rate arrangements entering the 21st Century: which anchor will hold?" *Quarterly Journal of Economics*, **134**(2), May, pp. 599–646.

Imai, H (2010): "Hong Kong's inflation and deflation under the US dollar peg: The Belassa-Samuelson effect or export price shocks?" *The Developing Economies*, **48**(3), September, pp. 319–344.

Ito, H and R McCauley (2019): "A key currency view of global imbalances", *Journal of International Money and Finance*, **95**, June, pp. 97–115.

James, H (2020): *Making a Modern Central Bank: The Bank of England 1979–2003*, Cambridge: Cambridge University Press.

Kane, E (2020): "Implicit and explicit norms and tools of safety net management", *China Finance Review International*, https://doi.org/10.1108/CFRI-12-2019-0163.

Khor, H, E Robinson and J Lee (2004): "Managed floating and intermediate exchange rate systems: the Singapore experience", Monetary Authority of Singapore, *MAS Staff Paper* No. 37.

Kuttner, K and I Shim (2016): "Can non-interest rate policies stabilise housing markets? Evidence from a panel of 57 economies", *Journal of Financial Stability*, **26**, October, pp. 31–44, originally BIS Working Papers no 2013.

Kwan, S (2003): "Impact of deposit rate deregulation in Hong Kong on the market value of commercial banks", *Journal of Banking and Finance*, **27**(12), December, pp. 2231–2248.

McCallum, B (2006): "Singapore's exchange rate-centered monetary policy regime and its relevance for China," Monetary Authority of Singapore, *MAS Staff Paper* No. 43.

McCauley, R (2001): "Setting monetary policy in East Asia: Goals, developments and institutions", *Future Directions for Monetary Policies in East Asia*, Sydney: Reserve Bank of Australia, pp. 7–55. (www.rba.gov.au/PublicationsAndResearch/Conferences/2001/mccauley.pdf).

McCauley, R, J Ruud and F Iacono (1999): *Dodging Bullets: Changing U.S. Corporate Capital Structure in the 1980s and 1990s*, Cambridge: MIT Press.

Monetary Authority of Singapore (2000): Financial market integration in Singapore: The narrow and broad views, *Occasional Paper* No 20.

Morgan, P, P Regis, and N Salike (2015): "Loan-to-value policy as a macroprudential tool: The case of residential mortgage loans in Asia", *Asian Development Bank Institute Working Paper* 528, May.

Nicolle, A (1991): "Mortgage lending", letter to I Wilson, Chairman, Hong Kong Association of Banks, 24 May.

Rajan, R, E Robinson and R Lim (2022): "Macroprudential policies and financial stability in a small and open economy: The case of Singapore", see Chapter 10 of this volume.

Richter, B, M Schularick, I Shim (2019): "The costs of macroprudential policy", *Journal of International Economics*, **118**, pp. 263–282.

Robinson, E (2001): "Discussion of Williamson's 'The case for a basket, band and crawl regime for East Asia'", in *Future Directions for Monetary Policies in East Asia*, Sydney: Reserve Bank of Australia.

Saurina, J and C Trucharte (2017): *The Countercyclical Provisions of the Banco de España, 2000–2016*, Madrid: Bank of Spain.

Schenk, C (2001): *Hong Kong as an International Financial Centre: Emergence and Development, 1945–1965*, London: Routledge.

——— (2003): "Banking crises and the evolution of the regulatory framework in Hong Kong 1945–70", *Australian Economic History Review*, **43**(2), July, pp. 140–154.

——— (2017): "Negotiating positive non-interventionism: Regulating Hong Kong's finance companies, 1976–1986", *The China Quarterly*, **230**, pp. 348–370.

Shin, H-S (2009): "Reflections on Northern Rock: The bank run that heralded the global financial crisis", *Journal of Economic Perspectives*, **23**(1), Winter, pp. 101–120.

Taylor, M (1991): "Low-rise apartments", *Far Eastern Economic Review*, 23 May, p. 63.

US Treasury, Office of the Comptroller of the Currency, Federal Reserve System, Federal Deposit Insurance Corporate, Office of Thrift Supervision (1992): "Real estate lending standards", 31 December.

Wong, E, T Fong, K Li and H Choi (2011): "Loan-to-value ratio as a macroprudential tool — Hong Kong's experience and cross-country evidence," *Hong Kong Monetary Authority Working Paper*, no 01/2011.

Wong, E, A Tsang, and S Kwong (2013): "How does loan-to-value policy strengthen banks' resilience to property price shocks — Evidence from Hong Kong," *Hong Kong Institute for Monetary Research Working Paper*, No. 03/2014.

Wong, J, L Fung, T Fong and A Sze (2004): "Residential mortgage risk and loan-to-value ratio", Hong Kong Monetary Authority *Quarterly Bulletin*, **4**, December, pp. 35–45.

Yam, J (2009): "Evolution of 70% loan-to-value policy", HKMA *inSight*, 4 June.

Yellen, J (2010): "Hong Kong and China and the global recession", *FRBSF Economic Letter*, 8 February.

Timely, Sustained and Effective Macroprudential Policy: Exploring the Political Economy of Hong Kong's Prudential Standards in the 1990s: A Discussion

Arthur Yuen

Deputy Chief Executive
Hong Kong Monetary Authority

It gives me great pleasure to share my views on Hong Kong's experience in the use of macroprudential measures to safeguard financial stability. I am grateful to Mr Robert McCauley and Professor Catherine Schenk for their research efforts, and their recognition of the effectiveness of the macroprudential measures implemented by the Hong Kong Monetary Authority (HKMA) since the 1990s.

The importance of macroprudential policies

The discussion on macroprudential policies is timely considering recent market developments. The accommodative monetary policies adopted by major economies in response to the COVID-19 public health crisis have provided renewed impetus to rising property and asset prices in many markets. How to rein in asset price inflation and prevent it from endangering financial stability in the event of an abrupt price adjustment is a topical issue within the central banking community.

As mentioned in Robert and Catherine chapter, the HKMA's macroprudential measures on mortgage lending were first introduced in 1991. They have helped Hong Kong weather several crises, including the Asian Financial Crisis, during which property prices plunged by as much as 70 percent between 1997 and 2003. Being an early adopter, the HKMA is encouraged to see that macroprudential measures have gained wider international acceptance after the Global Financial Crisis (GFC). Many jurisdictions have implemented macroprudential measures similar to those in Hong Kong, including loan-to-value ratio (LTV) caps and stress testing on the mortgagor's ability to cope with interest rate rises in terms of their repayment ability.

Challenges and mitigation: Calibration of macroprudential policies

I would like to share the HKMA's experience gained since the GFC in operating its macroprudential measures on mortgage lending. My remarks would focus on the "4Cs": Calibration, Competition dynamics, Cultural issues and Combating leakage.

Calibration: Driven by the low interest rate environment and limited housing supply, residential property prices in Hong Kong have continued to rise since the GFC. This has posed increasing risks to financial stability in Hong Kong. In response, the HKMA has implemented eight rounds of tightening of the macroprudential measures, from 2009 to 2017. Unlike monetary policies, there is a far more limited literature on how macroprudential measures should be calibrated with respect to changes in asset price levels. The complex dynamics underlying the property market in Hong Kong has made it very difficult, if at all possible, to develop an ex-ante framework governing how the HKMA should operate its macroprudential policies. So, what the HKMA has done is to tread extremely carefully in each round of adjustment. The HKMA has established a cross-departmental committee to regularly review whether the prevailing macroprudential measures would need to be adjusted, taking into account a host of factors including the property price trend, transaction volumes, domestic economic fundamentals and the external environment. The committee is chaired by the Chief Executive of the HKMA and comprises members from multiple functions including monetary management, banking supervision, research and macro-surveillance.

Some commentators have criticised the HKMA's macroprudential measures as being ineffective because they have not been able to arrest the rising trend of property prices. This is a misunderstanding of the objective of the HKMA's macroprudential measures. The objective of the HKMA's measures is not to tame property prices. Instead, they are aimed at strengthening the risk management of banks and thus safeguarding long-term banking stability. In this regard, it is worth noting that the average LTV ratio of new residential mortgage loans has been consistently lower than 60 percent while the average debt servicing ratio of new mortgages has been consistently lower than 40 percent, suggesting that the banking system has built-in buffers to safeguard its resilience.

Competition dynamics: Mortgage products in Hong Kong are homogeneous, in the sense that from the mortgagor's perspective it makes little difference which bank is offering the mortgage facility. There is, therefore, a strong tendency for banks to compete for the market share by lowering their underwriting standards. With the macroprudential measures in place, however, banks can compete for mortgage business only in terms of pricing (e.g., mortgage rate). Against a backdrop of rising property prices and a consistently low delinquency rate of mortgage loans, many banks have tried to outcompete their peers by pushing down the mortgage rate to record low levels. The HKMA has been concerned that the low mortgage rates that banks charge might not be adequate to cover the potential credit loss if property prices were to correct sharply in the future. The HKMA has, therefore, spent quite some time in ensuring that the mortgage pricing of banks is sustainable in the medium to long term.

Cultural issues: The chapter points out that the introduction of the 70 percent LTV guideline in 1991 was a joint initiative by the public and private sectors where both saw the need for a more prudent LTV standard. However, with banks increasingly focusing on short-term profit maximisation, the HKMA has seen instances where banks attempted to circumvent the macroprudential policies.

Some banks used their group entities outside Hong Kong to extend mortgage facilities exceeding the HKMA's limits to buyers of Hong Kong properties. These banks thought that they could bypass the HKMA's macroprudential measures through these "creative" cross-border arrangements. They were wrong. In all these cases, the HKMA made it clear to the banks that their activities were tantamount to regulatory arbitrage, which was unacceptable and which revealed a more fundamental problem about their corporate culture. If the senior management themselves did not comply with the regulatory requirements applicable to their institution, how can they expect their staff to observe the requirements of the bank? The HKMA shared its concerns with the relevant home supervisors and obtained their assistance to follow up on the issue at the group level. The banks were asked to put in place effective controls to prevent recurrence.

Combating leakage: The chapter has highlighted the challenge of policy leakage in the 1990s such as top-up loans in the form of a personal loan to finance the down-payment of property acquisitions. On this front, again, the market has moved on. These days, a major avenue of policy leakage is mortgage loans exceeding the HKMA's limits provided by non-bank institutions, such as finance companies and property developers. Both of them fall outside the HKMA's supervisory remit.

To address this, the HKMA requires banks to terminate credit relationships with finance companies offering mortgages that do not comply with its requirements. As for developers, higher risk weights are set for credit exposures to those property developers with significant exposures to high LTV mortgages. The HKMA recognises that these measures cannot completely stamp out the leakage. This brings up the question of whether there is a need to extend the regulatory perimeter to cover mortgage lending by non-bank institutions. It is noted that in some jurisdictions, residential mortgage loans provided by banks and non-bank institutions are subject to the same supervisory parameters.

Conclusion

I have shared our experience gained from the actual operation of the HKMA's macroprudential measures since the 1990s. Some are more practical, operational issues but some involve complex considerations deserving further analysis. I hope my sharing has provided some food for thought for the readers.

CHAPTER 9

© 2023 World Scientific Publishing Company
https://doi.org/10.1142/9789811259432_0018

Chapter 9

Macroprudential Policies for the External Sector: India's Approach and Experience*

Viral V Acharya

C V Starr Professor of Economics
Department of Finance
New York University Stern School of Business
vacharya@stern.nyu.edu

Abstract

This chapter provides a perspective on India's approach and experience in its macroprudential policies for the management of its external sector. Section 1 presents the empirical motivation and a conceptual framework for jointly deploying forex reserves and capital controls in the macroprudential policy of a "small"

---

*This chapter is based on the author's two co-authored pieces: (1) "Capital Flow Management with Multiple Instruments" (with Arvind Krishnamurthy), 2019, Central Banking, Analysis, and Economic Policies Book Series, in: Álvaro Aguirre & Markus Brunnermeier & Diego Saravia (ed.), *Monetary Policy and Financial Stability: Transmission Mechanisms and Policy Implications*, Edition 1, Volume 26, Chapter 6, pp. 169–203, Central Bank of Chile; and, (2) "Foreign Currency Borrowing of Corporations as Carry Trades: Evidence from India" (with Siddharth Vij), August 2018, Working Paper, New York University Stern School of Business. The piece benefited immensely from an insightful discussion by Dr Duvvuri Subbarao, former Governor of the Reserve Bank of India. The author is also grateful to Quirin Feckelstein for excellent research assistance.

open economy such as India, that is vulnerable to the risk of "sudden stops" in external capital flows. Section 2 discusses how macroprudential policies have been used in India to date, focusing on their recent evolution, particularly since the Global Financial Crisis (GFC). Section 3 provides an event-study analysis of the effectiveness of one specific macroprudential policy adopted by India in the aftermath of the "Taper Tantrum"[1] episode of 2013. Throughout, the focus is on external sector flows relating to fixed-income securities only, which come under the purview of the central bank in India (Reserve Bank of India [RBI]); equity investments in India are regulated by the securities exchange board and are largely perceived to be unrestricted except in the case of a few companies which have especially large foreign ownership.

1. Empirical motivation and conceptual framework

It is now well-recognised in academic, practitioner and policy circles alike that emerging markets (EMs) are affected by ebbs and flows of capital flows in a global financial cycle originating in developed economies (Rey, 2013). Managing this capital flow cycle is a central concern for EM governments and policymakers.

What exactly is the "global financial cycle"? As Rey (2013) explains, it is the cycle of financial conditions for EMs that are in one phase benign, possibly even frothy, but reverse sharply in another phase; typically, the switch in phases is triggered suddenly, i.e., as a "sudden stop" (Chang and Velasco, 2001; Kaminsky and Reinhart, 1999). For instance, an increase in the risk appetite of institutional investors in developed economies, possibly spurred by their central banks' easy monetary policy, leads to a surge in capital flows to EMs. These foreign capital flows, especially foreign portfolio investments (FPI) in debt and equity markets (as against the relatively illiquid foreign direct equity investments [FDI]), can reverse

---

[1] The Taper Tantrum of Summer 2013 was caused due to the US Federal Reserve announcements, indicating that the tapering of its post-GFC quantitative easing program was imminent. This led to a surge of capital outflows and asset price declines in EMEs.

quickly when monetary policy tightens in advanced economies or there is risk-aversion in their institutional investors, leading to a sudden stop for EMs and the risk of a sharp macroeconomic slowdown.

At the root of a recognition that EM governments and policymakers need to manage the capital flow cycle is the inevitability that they face the *Impossible Trinity* (see Obstfeld *et al.* (2005) for a review): they cannot simultaneously meet all three policy goals of an open capital account, a fixed exchange rate and an independent monetary policy. While most EMs seek an "interior solution", I will simplify the discussion in this chapter further by assuming that the EM government and policymakers seek to maintain some semblance of an independent monetary policy, which requires that, at a minimum, they manage capital flows in the lead-up to sudden stops and smooth, entirely market-based exchange-rate fluctuations (especially during sudden stops). Indeed, the Washington Consensus that capital controls are bad, always and everywhere, has given way to a more nuanced stand of the International Monetary Fund on the desirability of capital controls, given the experience of the EMs over the past three to four decades, ranging from external sector crises in Latin America and Southeast Asia, to those on a global scale.[2]

So, what makes India an interesting case study for the rest of the EMs as far as management of the capital flow cycle is concerned? Countries that are often found to be the most vulnerable to such a global financial cycle are the ones that have high "twin deficits", i.e., fiscal deficit and current account deficit. India by and large maintains twin deficits, barring rare exceptions when it registers a current account surplus due to a collapse of economic activity and imports (as witnessed during the lockdown-induced recession during the COVID-19 outbreak in 2020). In turn, India is often a candidate that is vulnerable to the global financial cycle. This point is evident in events of the last two decades for India on the external sector front.

Figure 1 plots, as an example, FDI and FPI flows into India over the period from 2004 to 2021. FPI flows (in orange) dropped sharply in the GFC period before rising in the post-crisis period, when developed

---

[2] "There be no presumption that full liberalization [of the capital account] is an appropriate goal for all countries at all times" (IMF, 2012).

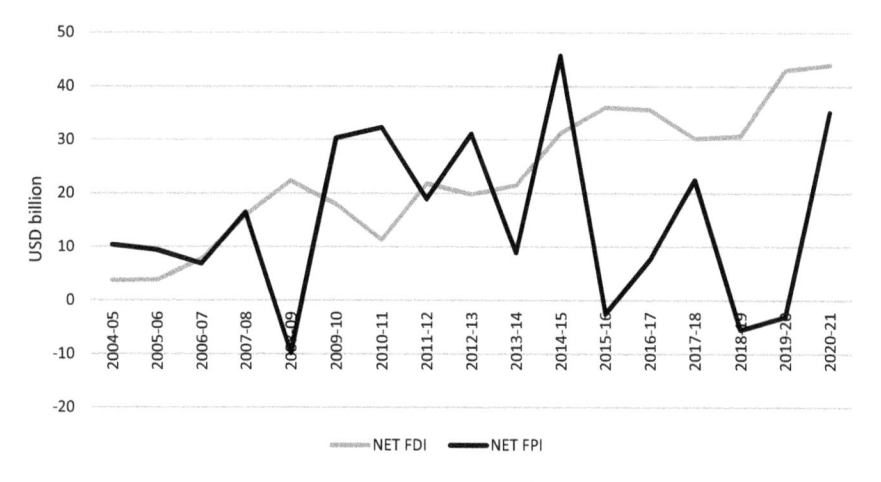

Figure 1. Volatility of FPI and FDI flows.
Note: Net Foreign Direct Investment (FDI) in blue and Net Portfolio Investment (FPI) in orange.
Source: RBI.

economy interest rates fell extraordinarily low. FPI flows reversed again during the Taper Tantrum" of 2013, when investors were surprised by the Federal Reserve announcement that it might tighten (taper off) its monetary policy (easing). When these fears eased in 2014, capital flows resumed before falling again in late 2015 as the Fed indeed raised rates. Similarly, the oil-price shock of April–October 2018, which coincided with the Federal Reserve interest rate hikes and its balance-sheet normalisation, led to FPI outflows. In striking contrast, Figure 1 shows that FDI flows into India are far more stable, including during the post–COVID-19 phase, which also resulted in sharp FPI outflows.

Throughout the chapter, the Taper Tantrum episode receives special attention as there is substantial time period before and after it for an analysis of macroprudential policies that were adopted post GFC, and then the Taper Tantrum. It is also the episode during which India stands out in the performance of its currency relative to other EMs on average. In particular, the capital flow reversal in the Taper Tantrum episode led to a sharp depreciation of the Indian rupee (INR). Figures 2 and 3 plot the exchange rate (red line) from 2004 to 2021, with the shaded region indicating the Taper Tantrum period. The rupee depreciated by over 30

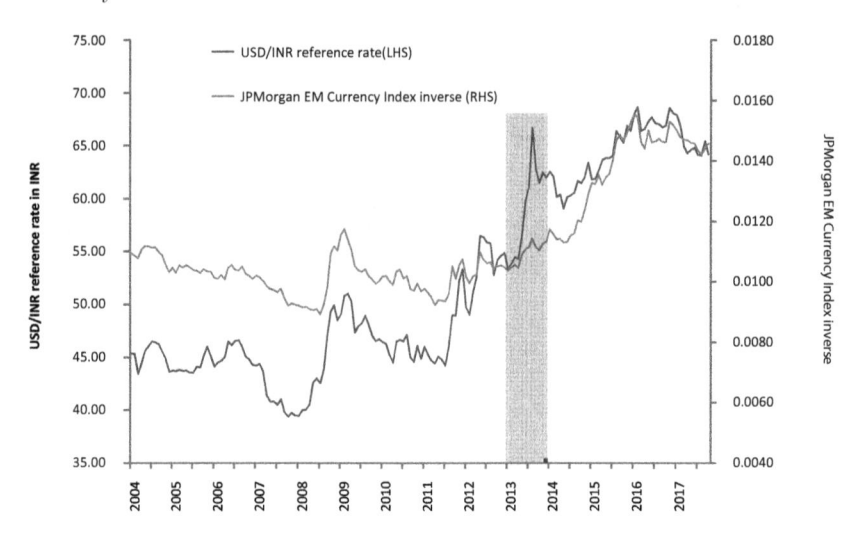

Figure 2. Exchange rate and 2013 Taper Tantrum — 2014–2017.
Source: Bloomberg, DBIE, RBI.

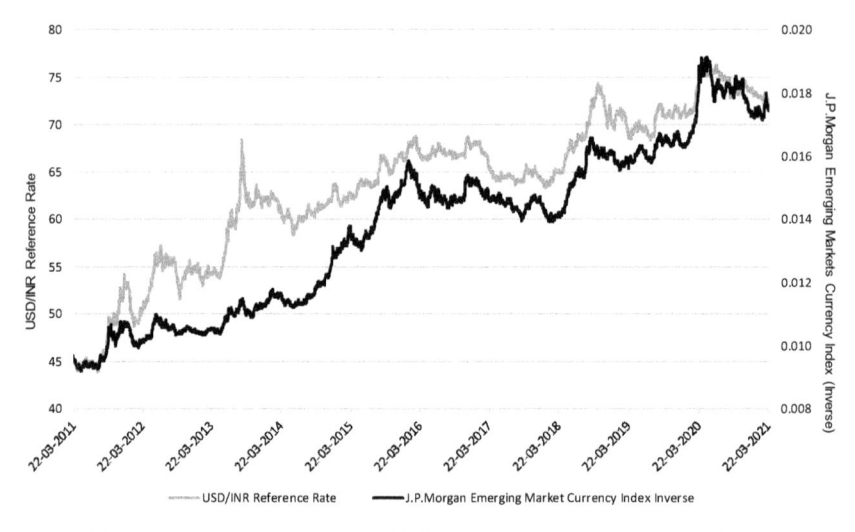

Figure 3. Exchange rate and 2013 Taper Tantrum — 2011–2021.
Source: Bloomberg, DBIEI.

percent against the US dollar in the summer of 2013, substantially more so than other EMs on average (blue line in graph).

A country's forex reserves are often considered a central form of defence against currency depreciations. A central bank can supply reserves during the downward spiral of currency depreciation and act as a buyer of last resort for the domestic currency. Figure 4 graphs India's forex reserves, showing that their level rose steadily after the GFC and until 2011, dipped slightly by 2012 and then remained relatively flat until the Taper Tantrum. In an absolute sense, India's reserves had accumulated by the 2013 Taper Tantrum to exceed the level in the crisis of 2008, thus suggesting greater external sector resilience. In 2019–2020, the level of reserves increased sharply, coincident with sharp inflows, especially in the form of FPI and FDI equity.

In spite of the accumulated level of reserves by the summer of 2013, the net capital outflow after the Federal Reserve's taper announcement led to a sharp depreciation in the exchange rate, as evident from Figures 2 and 3. This brings into focus the role of short-term external debt. While reserves can be considered a source of external sector strength, the extent of short-term debt that may come up for rollover can be considered a source of external sector vulnerability, and the two must be assessed relative to each other. The diagnosis of resilience of India's forex reserves in the summer of 2013 is reversed if one accounts for the build-up of India's external debt, especially its short-term component. Figure 5 plots the time series of India's external debt, which rose steadily and was at

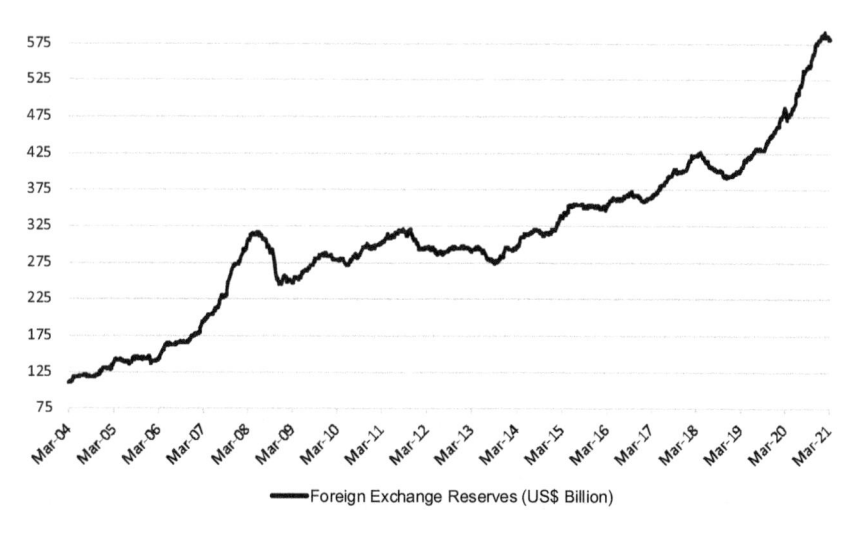

Figure 4. Foreign Exchange Reserves for India (USD Billion).
Source: RBI.

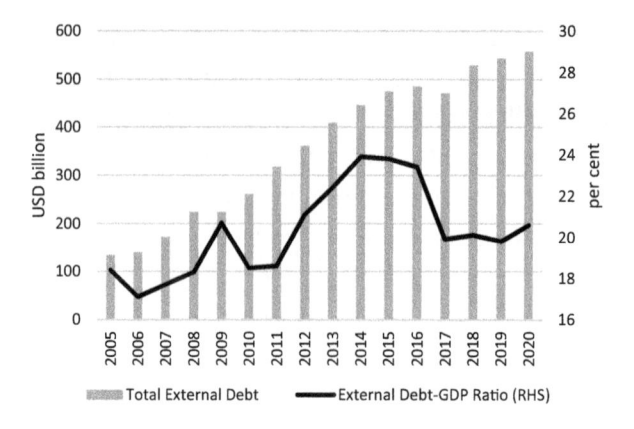

Figure 5. India's total external debt.

Source: RBI.

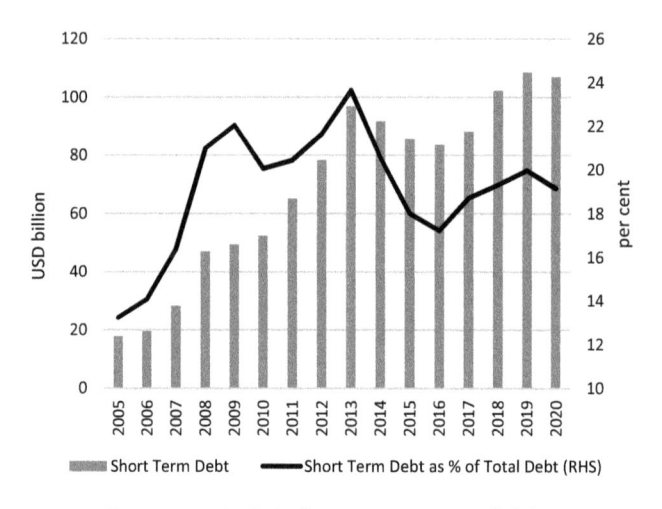

Figure 6. India's short-term external debt.

Source: RBI.

close to 25 percent relative to GDP around the Taper Tantrum. Equally important, the short-term component of this debt (with residual maturity of less than one year) is seen in Figure 6 to have also risen steadily (to around 20 percent short-term debt) by the 2013 Taper Tantrum.

To formalise the notion of how much reserves a central bank should hold, one approach is to consider the well-known Greenspan–Guidotti rule (Greenspan, 1999) that *a country's reserves should at least equal the short-term external debt*. Inspired by this, Acharya and Krishnamurthy

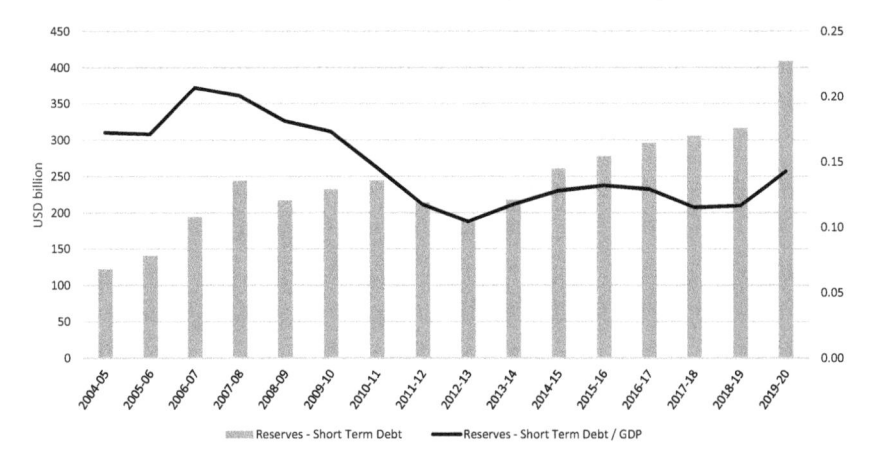

Figure 7. Country liquidity and reserves — Short-term external debt.
Source: World Bank, RBI, Ministry of Statistics & Program implementation.

(2019) define liquidity (or external-sector resilience) metric for a country i at time t as follows (the GDP merely serves to make the metric comparable across countries):

$$\text{Liquidity}_{i,t} = \frac{\text{Reserves}_{i,t} - \text{ST Debt}_{i,t}}{\text{GDP}_{i,t}} \quad (1)$$

Figure 7 shows that this liquidity measure had been steadily declining for India from a peak of above 20 percent prior to the GFC to a low of below 10 percent by the Taper Tantrum, thus more accurately capturing the possible loss of resilience as witnessed during the period from May–August 2013.[3] Interestingly, in spite of the record level of forex reserves in 2021 in an absolute sense, the liquidity measure is still short of its pre-GFC level due to the concomitant rise in short-term external debt.

To summarise, the case of India in the build-up to the Taper Tantrum suggests that forex reserves, *per se*, were not adequate in measuring external sector resilience against sudden stops. Reserve adequacy is contingent upon the quantity *and* quality of external debt and, in

---

[3] Acharya and Krishnamurthy (2019) document that this metric helps discriminate well among EMs in their exposure to the global financial cycle as evidenced in their asset price changes (equity, sovereign bond and foreign exchange) around the Taper Tantrum.

particular, the extent of short-term external debt. This observation then explains why, in response to capital flow volatility and attendant consequences on exchange rates, some EMs such as India have adopted two coincident policies as part of their macroprudential approach to the external sector: *accumulate foreign reserves and impose capital controls.*

Acharya and Krishnamurthy (2019) theoretically explain the interaction between foreign reserves policies and capital controls.[4] In practice as well as in much of the literature on capital flow management, capital controls and reserves management are cast as *alternative or substitute* instruments which can both reduce sudden-stop vulnerability. Their principal conceptual contribution is to explain that these policies interact and should in fact be seen by central banks as *complementary* instruments: Better capital controls enable more effective reserve management; likewise, a higher level of foreign reserves should be associated with stronger capital controls.

The intuition for their result is as follows. The sudden stop is a state of the world in which foreign creditors refuse to roll over both external (foreign currency) short-term debt and domestic (local currency) short-term debt. This can trigger both a currency crisis and a rollover/banking crisis. Borrowers with external debt will fire-sell domestic assets to convert to foreign currency, to repay foreign creditors. Foreign holders of domestic debt will convert repayments from this debt into foreign currency. The liquidation of domestic assets for foreign currency triggers a crisis in domestic currency. The rollover problem triggers defaults and potentially a banking crisis. In essence, what results is the twin-crisis during sudden stops in EMs.

The crisis is worsened if the aggregate amount of external and domestic short-term debt is higher, as this results in more fire-sales. *Ex post*, central bank reserves can be used to reduce currency depreciation as well as borrower defaults. Therefore, reserves reduce the magnitude of the fire-sale discount in prices, conditional on being in the sudden stop. However, *ex ante*, reserves induce greater undertaking of short-term liabilities by borrowers, a form of moral hazard from the insurance

---

[4] Their model builds on the seminal work of Caballero and Krishnamurthy (2001) and Caballero and Simsek (2016).

or "put option" effect of reserves in the case of sudden stops: the greater the reserves, the lower the anticipated fire-sale discount in prices, and in turn, the greater the undertaking of short-term liabilities. Hence, unless the build-up of reserves (insurance) is coincident with capital controls (restrictions) on the growth of short-term liabilities (the moral hazard), the insurance effect of reserves is undone by the private choice of short-term liabilities.

In other words, reserves and capital controls are complementary measures in the macroprudential toolkit. An important corollary, in the spirit of Pigouvian taxation of an externality, is that "taxes" on capital flows should be borrower-specific and depend on the fire-sale externality imposed by a given borrower. In particular, borrowers that are more likely to default at the time of a sudden stop should face greater capital controls in their ability to build up short-term debt. A version of this corollary also applies if capital controls are employed by the type of investors or investments: short-term horizon investors or short-term held investments should be subject to greater capital controls.

Finally, with capital flows into both foreign-currency- and domestic-currency-denominated assets, there arises a further complementarity. If capital controls can only be introduced on one margin, say foreign-currency debt, then they cannot be too tight. Otherwise, there is the prospect of arbitrage of capital controls between the two markets: short-term borrowing will switch to domestic-currency assets, even if domestic borrowing is costlier in a spread sense, as it enjoys weaker capital controls. Acharya and Krishnamurthy (2019) show that with an additional instrument, such as capital controls on domestic-currency debt, capital controls as a whole can be more effective, which then makes hoarding of forex reserves and their deployment during a currency crisis also more effective.

It turns out that much of India's macroprudential approach to the external sector, especially its calibrated capital control policy, can be understood in light of this conceptual framework. It should be noted that in the Indian context, monetary policy until 2013 was operated under a "multiple indicators" approach seeking to achieve balance between measures of inflation (consumer price inflation as well as wholesale price inflation) and financial stability (credit growth indicators). Since 2014, and officially since October 2016, monetary policy has been projected as managing consumer price inflation to a specific target level within a band, while paying attention to growth, via the choice of the central bank's repo rate, signalling a migration towards "flexible inflation targeting". Implicit in this chapter's focus on capital controls and reserves management is the (plausibly reasonable) assumption that an inflation-targeting central bank would wish to avoid, or risk external capital flight from, allowing its inflation credibility to erode by using monetary policy tools as an exchange-rate defence; in other words, it is assumed that its primary tools for exchange-rate management are capital controls in good times and reserves deployment in stressed times.[5]

2. India's approach to external sector resilience: Calibrated capital controls

India has over the past three decades (since the significant opening-up of its economy following the balance of payments crisis in 1991) deployed a range of macroprudential measures to contain the impact of sudden stops and reversals of foreign capital flows. Many of these measures had been in place prior to the Taper Tantrum; however, the Taper Tantrum led to a further revision of their nature, as explained below. This section discusses these measures through the conceptual framework presented in Section 1, on the optimal design of capital controls in macroprudential policy for the external sector.

An important point to note at the outset is that India does not borrow, other than occasionally from multilateral agencies, in the form of foreign-currency denominated sovereign debt (the so-called "original sin"); many of its state-owned banks and enterprises, however, do so.

---

[5] This view is consistent with the observation that during the "Taper Tantrum" of 2013, some interest-rate defence of India's exchange rate was undertaken by the central bank, whereas such defence was eschewed in October 2018 when oil prices surged globally from a threat of Iran sanctions in spite of a call from market participants to use interest rate policy by raising the repo rate to support the INR. Undertaking a joint analysis of capital controls, reserves management and monetary policy in assessing India's experience with the global financial cycle is a worthy goal for further analysis, but beyond the scope of the current chapter.

Given the devastating balance-of-payments problem of 1991, long-standing wisdom at the RBI, articulated by its top management in 1990s and 2000s, has been of allowing foreign capital in a (rough) pecking order — from direct equity investment (the most preferred) to foreign-currency sovereign bond (the least preferred).[6] Under this approach, foreign-currency-denominated Indian sovereign bonds have never been issued to external investors, even though the possibility of such issuance is routinely raised by the Government of India, to tap into ample external funds at low rates during the benign phase of the global financial cycle, and/or when its fiscal situation is stretched in terms of debt issuance relative to domestic savings.[7] By and large, the central bank's approach has been deemed well-founded, given the fragility of various kinds of flows under past sudden-stop scenarios, underscored especially by the taper tantrum episode of 2013.

India has three principal kinds of external debt once various forms of government debt from multilateral agencies, as well as non-resident Indian deposits, are excluded (the latter have usually been a source of stability for India during stress episodes): (1) FPI in domestic debt (in both Government of India securities at centre and state level, as well as corporate bonds); (2) external commercial borrowings (ECB), which are typically loans to Indian corporations, quasi-government entities or private firms, denominated in foreign currency; and, introduced most recently, (3) the rupee-denominated bonds (RDB) or "Masala bonds"

---

[6] The complete pecking order can be stated as: (1) direct equity investment (the most preferred); (2) portfolio equity flows; (3) portfolio flows in domestic-currency long-term corporate and government bonds; (4) long-term external commercial borrowings of corporates which are foreign-currency denominated; (5) portfolio flows in domestic-currency short-term corporate and government bonds; (6) short-term external commercial borrowings, and, finally, (7) foreign-currency sovereign bond (the least preferred).

[7] Two notable exceptions are (1) the Resurgent India Bonds which were issued by the State Bank of India as promissory notes in late 1990s (as India faced international sanctions relating to its nuclear capability tests), which were for all practical purposes deemed as a government of India offering, and (2) the Foreign Currency Non-Resident (FCNR) Deposits raised by banks immediately after the Taper Tantrum in 2013 with an exchange-rate guarantee from the RBI to issuing banks. Both forms of funding were raised mostly from non-resident Indians.

issued overseas, again by quasi-government entities or private firms, typically listed on the London Stock Exchange. Note that the Indian government does not directly borrow in foreign currency bond markets, even though it does borrow from multilateral agencies such as the World Bank in foreign currency; several government-owned enterprises — both financial and non-financial — do borrow in foreign currency bond markets and are considered as "corporations".

Net investments in these various segments of external debt are plotted over time in Figure 8 (stock in Panel A, flow in Panel B). The ECB contributed to the bulk of such external debt flows until the Taper Tantrum, after which time the FPI debt flows had overtaken as the most significant component in explaining the dynamics of total external debt. It is also worth pointing out the growth in the Masala bonds in 2017 as ECB borrowings fell. This switch in the nature of external debt is also reflected in Table 1 and Figure 9, which shows that the foreign-currency-denominated external debt has steadily declined since 2014 while the INR-denominated component has grown. Note, however, that there has again been a pickup in ECB issuance over the recent years (starting in 2018).

Macroprudential capital controls with regard to these different forms of external debt are briefly explained below, placing the various controls into broad categories so as to facilitate a possible interpretation in terms of the conceptual framework of Section 1.

2.1. Caps on exposure to global shocks

Restrictions on the level of external debt flows have been present in India in the form of absolute size limits on: (1) total FPI in domestic securities by asset class, with separate limits for Government of India securities (G-secs), State Development Loans (SDL) and Corporate bonds (amounting, e.g., in March 2021, to around $47 billion, $10 billion and $75 billion, respectively, or a total of about $132 billion across the three asset categories) and on (2) ECBs and Masala bonds (amounting together, e.g., in the last publicly available figure to a total of about $160 billion for 2018–2019).

Conceptually, the aggregate short-term external liability that cannot be rolled over relative to the forex reserves of the country is what matters for macroeconomic outcomes in the sudden-stop state. Moreover, the

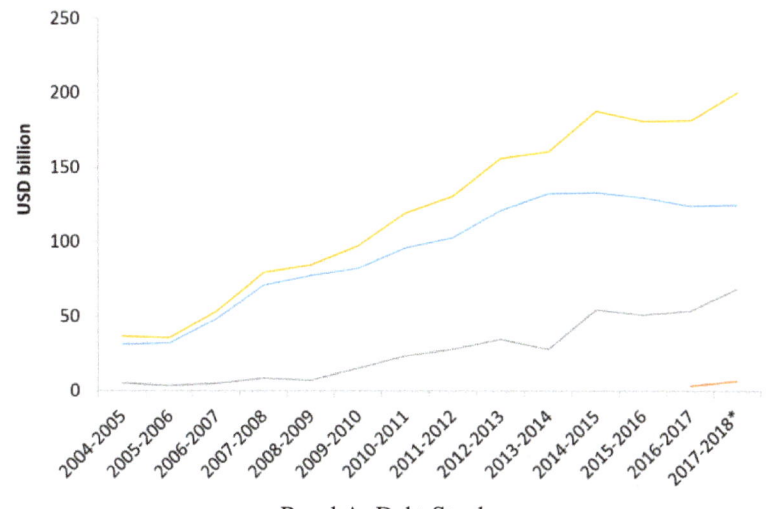

Panel A: Debt Stock

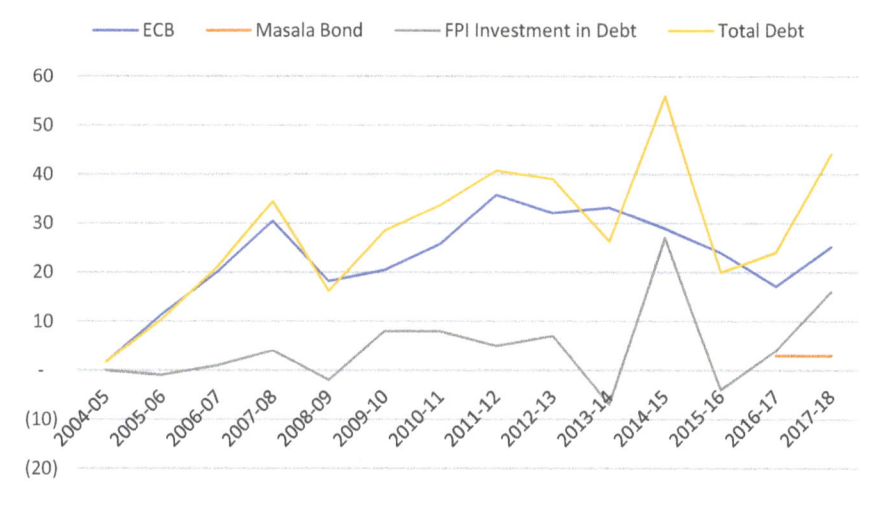

Panel B: Debt Flows

Figure 8. Debt stock and flows.
Source: RBI, NSDL and SEBI.

complementarity perspective indicates that borrowing limits should be closely tied to the central bank's holdings of foreign reserves and not just to the level of GDP (unless the reserves themselves are being maintained as a percentage of GDP). Furthermore, the limits should depend on *stocks*, rather than *flows*, of debt.

Table 1. Currency composition of external debt (%).

Currency	2011	2012	2013	2014	2015	2016	2017	2018	2019	2020
USD	55.3	56.9	59.1	61.1	58.3	57.1	52.1	49.3	50	52.9
INR	18.8	20.5	22.9	21.8	27.8	28.9	33.6	36.2	36.4	32.7
SDR	9.4	8.3	7.2	6.8	5.8	5.8	5.8	5.5	4.8	4.5
JPY	10.9	8.7	6.1	5	4	4.4	4.6	4.7	5	5.6
EUR	3.6	3.7	3.4	3.3	2.3	2.5	2.9	3.3	3.1	3.4
GBP	1.6	0.9	0.7	1.1	0.9	0.8	0.6	0.7	0.4	0.6
Others	0.4	1	0.6	0.9	0.9	0.5	0.4	0.3	0.3	0.4
Total (across rows)	100.0 %									

Source: RBI Bulletin, CEIC.

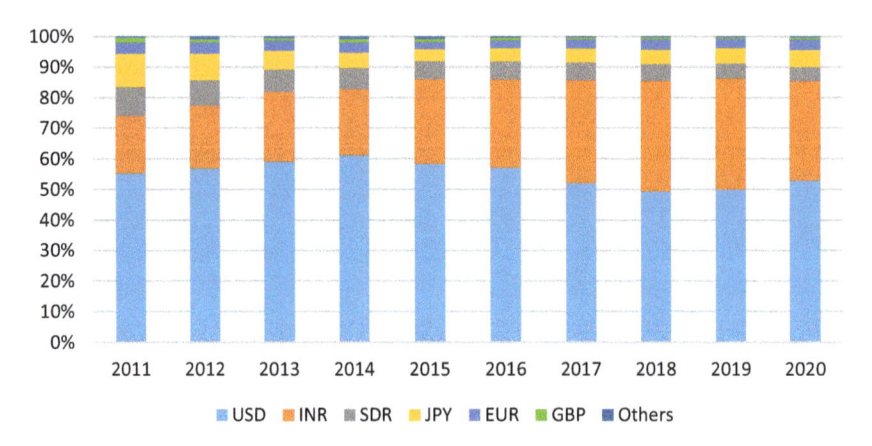

Figure 9. Currency composition of India's external debt.
Source: RBI Bulletin, CEIC.

In practice, the limits in India have either been set as a percentage of the underlying market size (as in the case of the G-sec and SDL limits as well as domestic corporate debt limits), or set as an absolute number (as in the case of external corporate debt limits but with some implicit connection to the level of GDP). These limits have been raised in a calibrated manner over time. For instance, Table 2 shows a snapshot for FPI limits in domestic-currency-denominated debt securities as of October 2017 (Panel A) and the progression from then to March 2021

Table 2. FPI limits (USD billion).

Panel A: 2017–2018 Q3.

Effective for Quarter	Central Government Securities			State Development Loans				Corporate Bonds			
	General	Long-Term	Total	General	Long-Term	Total	Effective for Quarter	Long-Term FPIs infrastructure	General	Total
2017–2018 Q3	29.29	9.31	38.60	4.63	1.44	6.07	2017–2018 Q3	1.47	33.64	35.10

Source: RBI, DBIE.

Panel B: 2017 Q4–2021 Q1 (USD Billion).

Period	G-Sec-General	G-Sec-Long Term	SDL-General	SDL-Long Term	Corporate Bonds	Total Debt
FPI limit for the HY Oct 2020–Mar 2021	32.34	14.28	9.33	0.98	74.67	131.60
FPI limit for the HY Apr–Sept 2020	32.34	14.28	8.88	0.98	59.19	115.67
FPI Limit for the HY Oct 2019–March 2020	33.94	15.87	8.44	0.98	43.71	102.94
FPI Limit for the HY Apr–Sept 2019	32.37	14.30	6.85	0.98	41.80	96.30
FPI Limit for the HY Oct 2018–March 2019	30.79	12.73	5.25	0.98	39.87	89.62
FPI limit for the HY Apr–Sept 2018	28.59	10.85	4.80	0.98	36.78	82.00
FPI limit for the HY Oct 2017–Mar 2018	26.38	8.98	4.34	1.88	33.69	75.27

Source: RBI.

(Panel B). In the case of foreign-currency debt, there is a rule-based dynamic limit for outstanding stock of ECBs at 6.5 percent of GDP. In both cases, roll-out of the limits has been gradual, presumably based on implications of capital inflows on the exchange rate.

An important recent exception to capital controls has been the Fully Accessible Route (FAR) for investment by non-residents in securities issued by the Government of India, that was introduced on March 30, 2020. Under this route, non-residents or foreign investors are eligible to invest in "specified securities" without any limit or restriction. All new issuances of government securities of 5-year, 10-year and 30-year tenors are eligible for investment under the FAR. The intention here has been to pave the way for the inclusion of Indian government securities in international indices, in order to attract (passive) indexed flows; such index inclusion by and large requires full convertibility on the capital account (i.e., no capital controls whatsoever), however eliminating capital controls in specific securities is being viewed as an intermediate step.

As explained below, there are several other aspects to these limits which conform to the conceptual framework, even though not all do. In particular, there are limits by investor-type and by borrower- or issuer-type, as well as restrictions on the nature of the debt. These aspects have evolved over time given India's experience with external sector vulnerability, as well as in a state-contingent manner based on overall borrowing needs relative to the size of domestic savings.

2.2. Restrictions on investors by their horizon of investment

Within FPI limits for G-secs, SDLs and corporate bonds, there have been at times sub-limits by investor type as shown in Panel A of Table 2, in particular, for Long-Term versus General investors, where Long-Term includes Insurance firms, Endowments and Pension Funds, Sovereign Wealth Funds, Central Banks and Multilateral Agencies, whereas General covers all other qualified institutional investors. The Long-Term category was added to the corporate bonds limit in October 2017. Prior to July 2017, the unutilised portion of the Long-Term category was transferred to the General category, a feature that was then removed. However, since April 2018, all the existing sub-categories under the category of corporate bonds have been discontinued and there is only a single limit as shown in Panel B of Table 2.

Overall, the investor-specific investment restrictions can be understood as limits that are type-dependent, where type refers to investor horizon since the immediacy demanded by short-term investors (typically carry traders) creates a fire-sale externality in the sudden-stop state.

Interestingly, FPI restrictions in the 90's also included sub-limits for 100 percent debt funds as against minimum 70:30 equity-debt investment ratio funds. In addition, there were minimum lock-in periods of up to three years on investors once they purchased Indian debt securities. While such restrictions would also find conceptual support as ways to limit the type of short-term external debt, these were over time replaced entirely by investor categories based on horizon (Long-Term vs General) and/or minimum maturity restrictions (as explained below).

Somewhat surprisingly, long-term investors such as pension funds, insurance companies and sovereign wealth funds were not allowed by India to be eligible lenders in ECBs until 2015. There was, however, an indirect policy attempt to ensure that the sudden-stop risk did not directly affect the domestic banks (who had significant deposit liabilities), achieved by disallowing the refinancing of ECBs by Indian banks as well as preventing the underlying ECB exposure from being guaranteed by Indian banks, financial institutions or non-bank financial companies (NBFCs). This latter approach presumably recognised that banks might be high liquidity demanders if they were hit by the sudden-stop risk.[8]

2.3. *Restrictions on maturity of the underlying investment*

Until November 2013, there was a carve-out for FPI investments in short-dated debt instruments, viz., Treasury Bills and CP, as shown in Table 3. Exit of FPIs from these investments was swift during the Taper Tantrum and contributed to the downward spiral of currency depreciation. Hence, FPIs were then disallowed altogether from investing in liquid short-term money-market debt instruments such

---

[8] These restrictions on domestic financial institutions were in part also to avoid the ever-greening of non-performing loans using foreign capital.

Table 3. Debt investment restrictions.

Type of securities	April-2013 $ bn	Jun-2013 $ bn	Nov-2013 $ bn
1. Government debt	25	30	30
a. T-Bills within overall limit	5.5	5.5	5.5
b. Carved out limit for SWFs & other LT FIIs	—	5	5
2. Corporate bond	51	51	51
a. CPs within overall limit	3.5	3.5	3.5
b. Credit enhancement bonds within overall limit	—	—	5
3. Total Limit (1 + 2)	76	81	81

Source: DBIE, RBI.

as Treasury Bills (T-Bills) or commercial paper (CP). In fact, India introduced even tighter restrictions in the form of residual maturity restrictions of investments by FPIs in debt holdings to be of minimum three years of maturity at origination or purchase. These restrictions were potentially effective ways of limiting short-term external debt in case such a sudden-stop state materialised.[9]

Some of these restrictions on maturity of investment have since been relaxed. As of March 2021, FPIs are permitted to invest in G-secs, including in T-Bills, and SDLs without any minimum residual maturity requirement, subject to the condition that short-term investments by an FPI under either category shall not exceed 30 percent of the total investment of that FPI in that category. FPIs are also permitted to invest in corporate bonds with minimum residual maturity of above one year, subject to the condition that short-term investments in corporate bonds by an FPI shall not exceed 30 percent of the total investment of that FPI in corporate bonds.

A similar rationale for limiting the maturity of underlying external debt has existed in India for ECBs. Following the Taper Tantrum, policies

---

[9] Another possible rationale for requiring FPIs to hold longer-dated instruments is that it exposes them to greater interest-rate risk, which could deter excessive presence of short-term investors looking for "carry" by arbitraging interest-rate differentials with an early exit.

were revised in November 2015 to require that a borrower could undertake an ECB of up to $50 million (foreign-currency-denominated under the so-called Track-I of ECB, or INR-denominated under Track-III of ECB) with a minimum average maturity of three years; or up to $50 million if the maturity is five years. In contrast, no borrowing limit within the overall ECB limit was imposed for borrowings meeting a minimum average maturity of 10 years (for foreign-currency-denominated borrowing under Track-II of ECB). These maturity restrictions were not as onerous prior to the Taper Tantrum. Since January 2019, the minimum maturity is three years for all ECBs, foreign-currency- or rupee-denominated, with certain exceptions.[10]

2.4. *Voluntary retention route for FPIs*

An elegant alternative to identifying specific types of investors as Long-Term or to restricting the maturity of individual investments is to have investors themselves *commit* to maintaining the funds they bring into a country as long-term investments. India has recently adopted such an approach to encourage long-term investments in government and corporate debt by creating a separate route for FPI investment called the "Voluntary Retention Route" (VRR), which was introduced on 1 March 2019. FPI investments through the VRR are free of the macroprudential and other regulatory prescriptions applicable to FPI investments in debt markets, provided FPIs voluntarily commit to retain a required minimum percentage of their investments in India for a period of their choice greater than a prescribed minimum.

In particular, FPIs can voluntarily participate in VRR and commit to remain invested for a Committed Portfolio Size (CPS) for a committed retention period (presently a minimum period of three years but as decided by the RBI from time to time). FPIs have the flexibility to modulate with inflows and outflows of their investments between 75 percent and

---

[10] For ECBs raised from a foreign equity holder and utilised for specific purposes, the minimum maturity is five years; and, for ECBs up to US$50 million per financial year raised by the manufacturing sector, which has been given a special dispensation, the minimum maturity is only one year.

100 percent of CPS. FPIs can exit before the committed retention period by selling their investments, fully or partly, to other FPI(s) which would need to abide by the same terms and conditions.[11]

FPIs opting for the VRR investment are in turn provided wider facilities and exempted from certain macroprudential measures: (1) VRR investments are exempt from minimum residual maturity requirement,[12] concentration limit[13] and issue-wise limits[14] that those under the general FPI route are subjected to; (2) Participating FPIs in VRR can undertake repo/reverse repo transactions for cash management and use any currency or interest rate derivates to hedge currency or interest rate risks, which are not available to the general FPI route; and, (3) FPIs can invest the income from their VRR investments at their discretion, and such investments are permitted even in excess of the CPS.

The investment limit under the VRR is around $21 billion as of March 2021 and is available "on tap" for allotment. Figure 10 shows that the scheme has been reasonably successful, with steady inflow of funds, reaching a cumulative sum of around $15 billion by March 2021; other details specific to the nature of individual investments are not yet publicly available. The success of the scheme suggests that capital controls can be calibrated to have restrictions but with "carrot" thrown in to FPIs in the form of exemption from restrictions, for committing to a longer investment horizon.

---

[11] At the end of retention period, an FPI may (1) liquidate its portfolio and exit, or (2) continue its investment under VRR for an identical retention period, or (3) shift its investment to the general FPI route subject to availability of limits therein, or (4) hold its investments until its date of maturity or sale, whichever is earlier.

[12] (As described in Section 2.3) Minimum residual maturity requirement for non-VRR FPI: FPIs shall not invest in corporate bonds with residual maturity less than one-year at the time of investment; and short-term investments by an FPI in any debt portfolio, *viz.*, G-Sec or SDL or corporate bonds, shall not exceed 30 percent of the respective portfolio.

[13] Concentration limit for non-VRR FPI: No FPI (including related FPIs) shall invest for more than 10 percent of the investment limits in any category of debt, *viz.*, G-secs, SDLs and corporate debt. For long-term FPIs, however, the said limit is 15 percent.

[14] Issue-wise limit for non-VRR FPI: Investment by any FPI, including investments by related FPIs, shall not exceed 50 percent of any issue of a corporate bond.

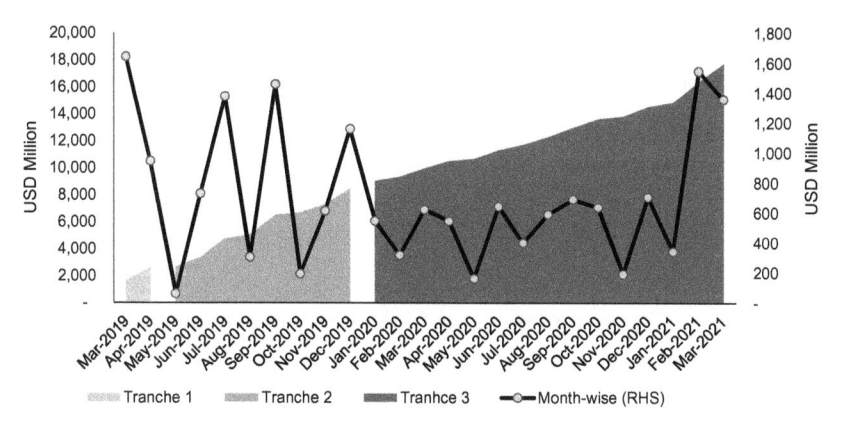

Tranche 1: Mar 11, 2019 to Apr 30, 2019; Tranche - 2 May 27, 2019 to Dec 31, 2020; Tanhce - 3: From Jan 24, 2021 till exhaustion of limits.

Figure 10. Allotment of investment limits under Voluntary Retention Route (Cumulative and Month-wise).
Source: Reserve Bank of India.

2.5. Regulatory arbitrage between domestic and overseas corporate external debt

India permitted "Masala bonds" or ECBs denominated in rupees (the so-called Track III) in September 2014. For macroprudential reasons and as ECBs were envisioned as bilateral loan arrangements, the issuance of ECBs faced various tenor and all-in-cost constraints, end-use requirements, eligibility requirements on borrowers and lenders and the like, as explained above. Borrowings under Track III were, however, not subject to cost caps that applied to other ECBs, as the borrowing in INR was considered as not subject to exchange rate risk. However, borrowing in INR funded by foreign lenders is still subject to the sudden-stop risk on rollover of such rupee-denominated borrowings. Nevertheless, the scope of eligible borrowers and lenders remained similarly restrictive as for dollar ECBs.

To widen the international investor base for corporates, an additional route of RDB, or Masala bonds, was introduced in September 2015. Since these were intended to be bonds issued under market discipline, they were subject to a more relaxed regulatory regime. Most important of these was the much wider scope of eligible borrowers (any corporate or body corporate including real estate investment trusts, or REITs, and infrastructure investment trusts, or InvITs), eligible investors (any investor from FATF-compliant jurisdictions) and end-use (no restrictions except for a small negative list). Masala bonds also had an advantage *vis-à-vis* the FPI route in domestic bonds insofar as investors in Masala bonds did not have to register in India and the bonds were issued in international finance centres such as London with well-established financial and legal infrastructure. Further, there was no listing requirement for Masala bonds. FPI investments were subsequently allowed in unlisted instruments, but were subjected to a cap.

As noted, at the inception of this market, Masala bonds were viewed by regulators as bond-market borrowings similar to other FPI investments. They received a liberal regulatory treatment under the presumption that these bonds would have transparent pricing and other forms of market discipline. In actual practice, many Masala bond issuances were essentially bilateral loans issued as bonds, often to related entities. Coupon rates in many instances had no linkage with market-borrowing rates and varied from extremely low rates (related party transactions to circumvent ECB and FDI restrictions) to high rates (to circumvent the all-in-cost ceilings under the ECB route). Complicated structures using Masala bonds were also used to bypass the ECB cost caps. The overall evidence from issuances suggested that many entities were exploiting the relaxed regulatory treatment of Masala bonds to bypass ECB norms on bilateral funding arrangements.

Recognising this regulatory arbitrage between ECB and Masala bonds, and that both were vulnerable to sudden stops because the source of capital was foreign creditors, India chose to harmonise their regulations. In June 2017, the RBI prescribed cost caps (Treasury yield + 300 bps) as well as minimum maturity period for Masala bonds (three or five years, depending on the issue size). The minimum maturity period also harmonised the Masala bond investments by foreign creditors to the restrictions on FPI in domestically issued debt. Masala bonds were also not allowed to be issued to related entities. Finally, in January 2019, there was a complete harmonisation of foreign-currency-denominated ECBs with the rupee-denominated ECBs (merging of Tracks I, II and III), with issuer eligibility extended to all corporates eligible to receive FDI, but with issuance for all maturities subjected to the cost cap of 450 bps over six-month LIBOR/swap rate.

Such harmonisation, in response to the observed regulatory arbitrage by issuers and investors in the pre-harmonisation period, reinforces the importance of setting capital flow management policy based on the entirety of an EM's debt spectrum.

2.6. *Restricting high liquidity demanders in external corporate debt*

In the spirit of a Pigouvian form of taxation, wherein borrowers who contribute more to the fire-sale externality in the sudden-stop state are charged a greater "tax" for taking on short-term external debt, Indian capital controls seek to ensure that only relatively high credit quality borrowers tap into ECBs by (1) imposing coupon ceilings by debt issue, (2) carving out sub-limits on investments in risky instruments such as unlisted corporate bonds and security receipts (a form of distressed asset resolution instrument) and (3) ruling out excessive correlated liquidations by having investment sub-limits by sector. Sub-limits (1) and (3) are no longer applicable as the eligible borrower list was liberalised in 2019 to include all Indian entities eligible to receive FDI.

Notably, restriction (1) limits ECBs to high-rated borrowers. In particular, there are the all-in-cost (AIC) issuance cost ceilings for ECBs, which prescribe that borrowers in the three- to five-year range cannot issue ECBs at a coupon of six-month LIBOR+ceiling or higher as indicated in Table 4. A higher ceiling applies for issuances greater than five-year maturity. These ceilings have evolved over time in a somewhat counter-cyclical manner relative to the evolution of six-month Libor (Figure 11) — as global interest rates eased post the GFC, the coupon ceilings were raised, and with global rates tightening since 2015, the ceilings were lowered. However, this form of differential taxation does not exist for domestic debt issuances purchased by the FPIs, except to the extent that the current market-practice in the domestic corporate debt market is to fund only relatively high-rated investment-grade borrowers.

Acharya and Vij (2018) study the efficacy of the 2015 change in AIC issuance cost ceilings, a specific instance of macroprudential regulation of the external sector in India targeted at the foreign currency borrowing of non-financial corporations, which is discussed next.

Table 4. Evolution of AIC spread over Libor-6 month/Swap.

Minimum average maturity	3-year to 5-year (in bps)	More than 5 years (in bps)
2004–2005	200	350
2007–2008	150	250
2008–2009	200	350
2009–2010	300	500
2011–2012	350	500
2015–2016	300	450
2016–2017	450	450
2017–2018	450	450
2018–2019	450	450
2019–2020	450	450

Source: DBIE, RBI.

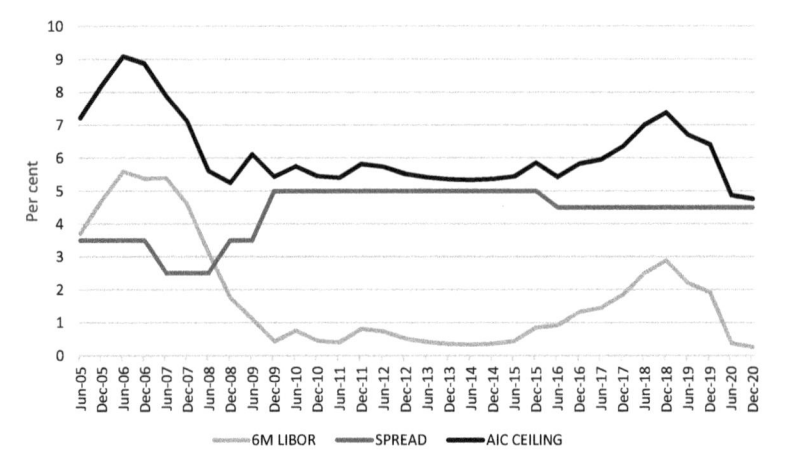

Figure 11. All-in-Cost for ECBs with five-year minimum maturity.
Source: RBI.

3. An event study of India's capital control change around the Taper Tantrum

Figure 12 shows the total amount of India's outstanding foreign currency debt and the USD–INR foreign exchange rate during 2004–2019. Although the INR steadily depreciated against the USD, the outstanding stock of dollar debt steadily increased.

As discussed in Section 2.6, the RBI lowered in 2015 the maximum permitted interest rate at which Indian corporate borrowers could borrow

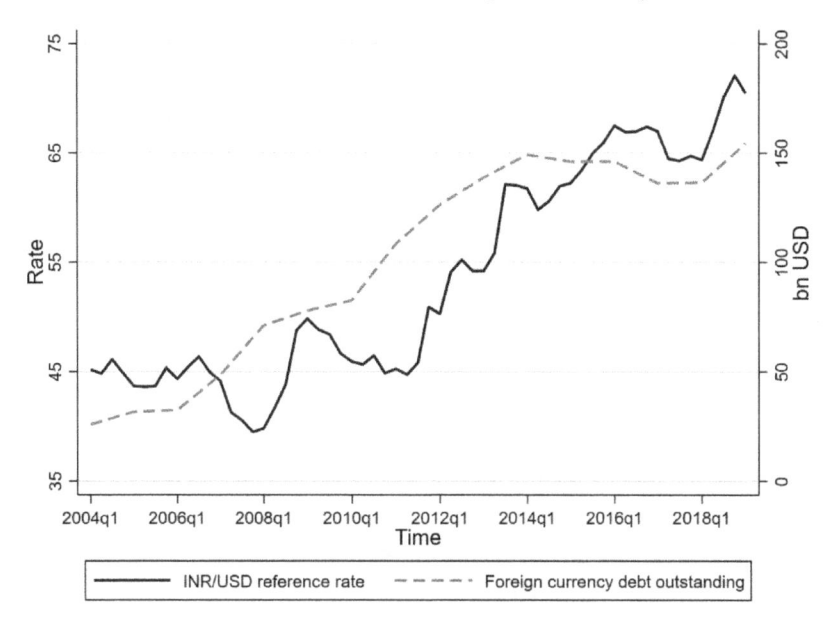

Figure 12. Foreign currency corporate debt and INR/USD exchange rate.
Note: The figure shows the evolution of the INR/USD exchange rate and the stock of foreign currency debt outstanding from March 2004 to March 2019.
Source: Acharya and Vij (2018).

in foreign currency debt markets. This move was in the aftermath of Taper Tantrum of May–August 2013 in which India faced significant capital outflows and currency depreciation. The aim of reducing these interest-rate caps for foreign currency debt was to restrict access to only those firms that could borrow at relatively low interest rates, presumably higher-quality and lower-risk borrowers, as these borrowers would be less likely to face rollover problems in a sudden stop.

To examine the effects of this specific change in macroprudential regulation and the induced dynamics of corporate foreign-currency borrowing, Acharya and Vij (2018) construct a detailed data set of Indian firms that borrow abroad, including data on every instance of foreign debt issuance (amount, maturity and debt type), matched to accounting and stock market data of borrowing firms. The final sample consists of 1,786 firms that, on average, borrowed twice during our sample period of 2004–2019, with 5 percent of the firms borrowing more than 10 times.

Consider some factors that might explain corporate borrowing in external markets: (1) exporters can naturally hedge their foreign currency borrowing through their revenues; (2) firms investing in foreign assets (e.g., oil and gas companies) may want to finance those assets in the same currency and (3) firms may have incentives to borrow abroad at a cheaper interest rate and invest it locally at higher interest rates. The third reason is a corporate "carry trade" (Bruno and Shin, 2017, 2020) that is profitable if the firm can unwind the trade before the currency depreciates and/or if the central bank steps in by deploying its forex reserves to prevent currency depreciation.

Empirical analysis undertaken by Acharya and Vij (2018) shows that the carry trade motive plays an important role in foreign currency borrowing by Indian corporates, particularly in the period of low US interest rates following the GFC. To proxy for the profitability of the carry trade, a Sharpe Ratio-like measure is defined, which is the difference of short-term interest rates between India and the US, normalised by the implied volatility of the exchange rate backed out from foreign exchange options. Figure 13 shows that this carry trade measure is positively correlated with the aggregate foreign currency debt issuance in the period following the GFC. Econometric results show that the *same* firm (i.e., after controlling for firm fixed effects in the tests) is more likely to borrow in foreign currency when the carry trade is more profitable in the post-crisis period. The carry trade does not explain borrowing in the period before the GFC pointing to the importance of US monetary policy easing in explaining global financial flows (Rey, 2013).

Furthermore, stock market data show that the returns of Indian foreign currency borrowers become more sensitive to movements in the USD–INR exchange rate as they borrow more. This indicates that the borrowers are likely not fully hedging the foreign exchange risk that comes from the new external debt. Firms that are more likely to borrow abroad when the carry trade is more profitable see the most increase in stock return sensitivity to the exchange rate. Event studies around the Taper Tantrum indicate that these firms experience significantly larger equity market declines following the announcement of the Federal Reserve hinting at imminent normalisation of its post-GFC quantitative easing program (Figure 14).

Focusing on the RBI's reduction in 2015 of the maximum interest rate at which firms could borrow abroad, the authors find that this

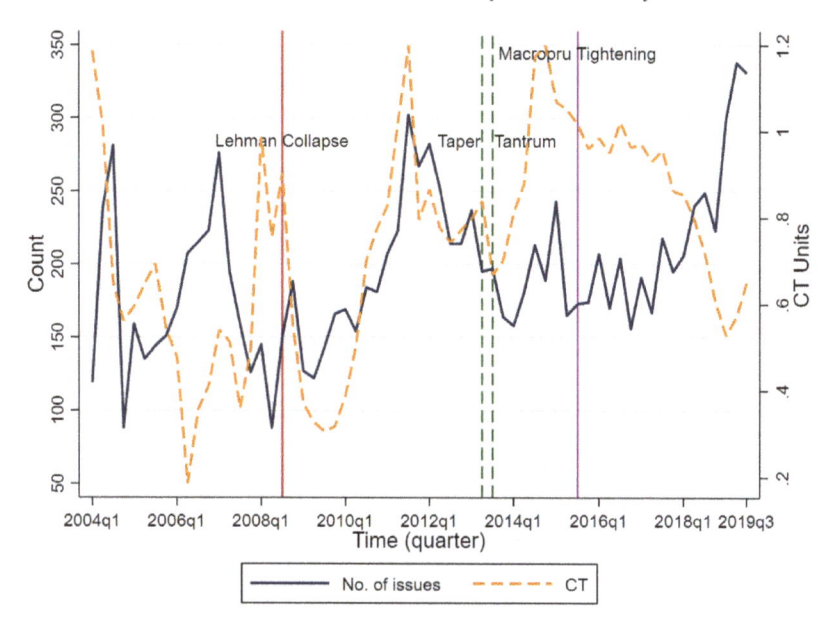

Figure 13. Foreign currency debt issuance and the carry trade.
Note: The figure plots the total number of foreign currency debt issues each quarter against CT, a proxy for the profitability of the dollar carry trade. CT is the difference in three-month interest rates between India and the US scaled by the implied volatility of three-month FX options. The sample period is from January 2004 to September 2019.
Source: Acharya and Vij (2018).

macroprudential policy action had significant effects on carry trade borrowing. Following the reduction in the interest-rate cap, the carry trade profitability no longer significantly explained foreign currency borrowing. Also, following the policy change, firms with higher interest expenses and those with a higher import share of raw materials were the ones most affected in terms of reduction in external borrowing. This shows that the regulation worked as intended by preventing from borrowing in foreign currency the *ex ante* riskiest borrowers — in terms of credit quality as well as exposure to currency depreciation.

Finally, the period of market stress at the beginning of the COVID-19 pandemic (March 2020) was characterised for the EMEs by unprecedented portfolio outflows and tightening of financing conditions. Tests analogous to the Taper Tantrum analysis confirm that carry trade borrowers did not do any worse during the COVID-19 crisis compared to other borrowers.

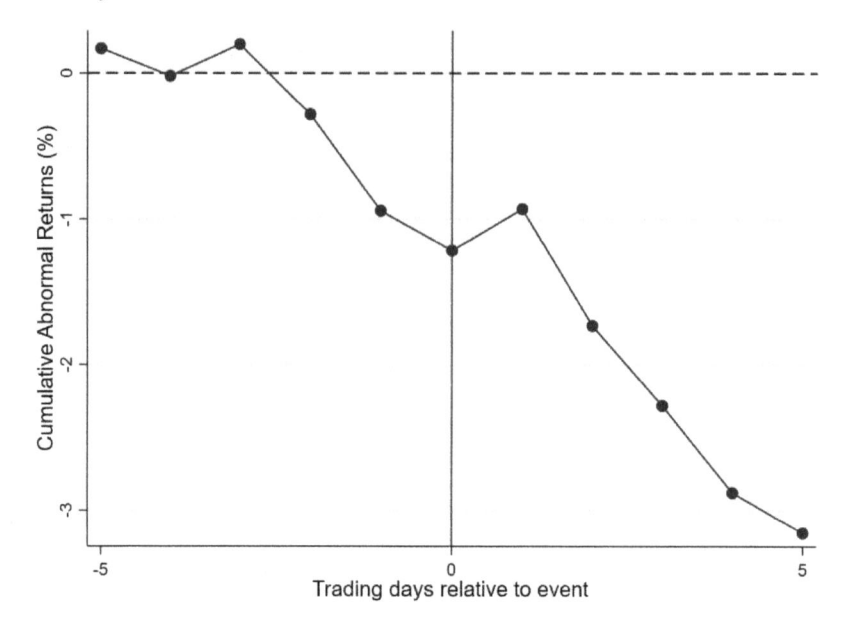

Figure 14. Taper tantrum event study.

Note: The figure shows the cumulative abnormal return (CAR) for stocks of foreign currency borrowers that borrow when the carry trade is more profitable relative to other foreign currency borrowers. The event date is 19 June 2013, a date on which Chairman Ben Bernanke of the US Federal Reserve indicated that tapering of quantitative easing would commence later in 2013. A multivariate market model is used for estimating abnormal returns with the NIFTY return proxying for the market return while INR/USD return proxies for FX return. The estimation window is 180 calendar days and ends five trading days before the event date.
Source: Acharya and Vij (2018).

This suggests that under the new macroprudential regime since 2015, the risks arising from carry trade borrowing by Indian corporates have been substantially mitigated.

In summary, this evidence is supportive of the inference that macroprudential controls limiting capital flows can curb risks arising from foreign currency borrowing by corporates in EMs. Firm-level data show that Indian firms issue more foreign currency debt when the interest rate differential between India and the US is higher. This "carry trade" relationship breaks down once regulators institute more stringent interest-rate caps on borrowing; riskier borrowers cut issuance the most. Stock price exposure of issuers to currency risk rises after issuance, a source of vulnerability during the "Taper Tantrum" episode of 2013, which macroprudential controls subsequently nullified, as confirmed during the outbreak of the COVID-19 pandemic.

4. Conclusion

Are there lessons from this Indian experience for the ongoing external sector headwinds faced by the EMs? As the global economy entered a new cycle of US monetary policy easing post April 2020, foreign currency borrowing accelerated along with its attendant risks. This cycle is turning swiftly in 2021 with a sharp, even if inequitable, economic rebound and persistent supply-chain disruptions that have raised price levels in the short run, with a risk of even higher inflation over the medium term, as reflected in the firming up of the US long-term interest rates. In such ebbing phase of the global financial cycle, excessively risky foreign borrowing by corporates and sovereigns in EMs might hurt domestic growth and financial stability down the line, as global capital flows have started retrenching after a relatively short benign phase. India's experience suggests that a calibrated targeting of capital controls in macroprudential regulation of the external sector can play an important role in reducing such a vulnerability.

Equally importantly, that the global financial cycle is in part caused by interest-rate and liquidity-management policies of developed economy central banks, implies that global coordination in managing capital flows remains an important issue for international policy agenda. The Federal Reserve reacted with alacrity during the outbreak of COVID-19 pandemic in being a "global lender of last resort" through a timely provision of dollar swap lines to foreign central banks; there seems an equally strong imperative to put in place an institutional arrangement for such swap lines when the Federal Reserve normalises interest rates and the size of its balance sheet, to limit avoidable stress on the external front for EMs such as India (see Mishra and Rajan (2016) and Patel (2018)).

References

Acharya, V V and A Krishanmurthy (2019). "Capital Flow Management with Multiple Instruments", Central Banking, Analysis, and Economic Policies Book Series, in: Álvaro Aguirre & Markus Brunnermeier & Diego Saravia (ed.),

Monetary Policy and Financial Stability: Transmission Mechanisms and Policy Implications, Edition 1, Volume 26, Chapter 6, pp. 169–203, Central Bank of Chile.

Acharya, V V and S Vij (2018). "Foreign Currency Borrowing of Corporations as Carry Trades: Evidence from India", August, Working Paper, New York University Stern School of Business.

Bruno, Valentina, and Hyun Song Shin (2017). "Global Dollar Credit and Carry Trades: A Firm-Level Analysis." *The Review of Financial Studies*, **30**(3): 703–749.

Bruno, Valentina, and Hyun Song Shin (2020). "Currency Depreciation and Emerging Market Corporate Distress." *Management Science*, **66**(5): 1935–1961.

Caballero, R J and A Krishnamurthy (2001). "International and Domestic Collateral Constraints in a Model of Emerging Market Crises." *Journal of Monetary Economics*, **48**(3): 513–548.

Caballero, R J and A Simsek (2016). "A Model of Fickle Capital Flows and Retrenchment." Technical Report, National Bureau of Economic Research.

Chang, R and A Velasco (2001). "A Model of Financial Crises in Emerging Markets." *Quarterly Journal of Economics*, **116**(2): 489–517.

Greenspan, A (1999). "Currency Reserves and Debt." Remarks Before the World Bank Conference on Recent Trends in Reserves Management, Washington, D.C., 29 April 1999.

IMF (2012). "The Liberalization and Management of Capital Flows: An Institutional View". IMF Policy Paper (November 2012).

Kaminsky, G L and C M Reinhart (1999). "The Twin Crises: The Causes of Banking and Balance-of-Payments Problems." *American Economic Review*, **89**(3), 473–500.

Mishra, P and R G Rajan (2016). "International Rules of the Monetary Game," in: John H. Cochrane, Kyle Palermo and John B. Taylor (eds.), *Currencies, Capital, and Central Bank Balances*, pp. 3–52, Hoover Institution Press.

Obstfeld, M, J C Shambaugh and A M Taylor (2005). "The Trilemma in History: Trade-offs Among Exchange Rates, Monetary Policies, and Capital Mobility". *Review of Economics and Statistics*, **87**(3): 423–443.

Patel, U (2018). "Emerging Markets Face a Dollar Double Whammy: The Fed must Adjust its Balance Sheet Shrinkage to Limit the Effects of Less Liquidity", *Financial Times* , 3 June 2013.

Rey, H (2013). "Dilemma not Trilemma: The Global Cycle and Monetary Policy Independence." *Proceedings, Economic Policy Symposium*, August 2013, Jackson Hole, pp. 1–2.

Macroprudential Policies for the External Sector: India's Approach and Experience: A Discussion

Duvvuri Subbarao

Former Governor, Reserve Bank of India

Volatile capital flows have exacerbated the policy challenges for emerging market central banks. Indeed, every emerging market economy (EME) crisis over the last four decades — be it the series of crises in Latin America in the 1980s, the Tequila Crisis of Mexico and the East Asan Financial Crisis in the 1990s or individual country crises in Turkey, Russia or Argentina in the 2000s — has been a consequence of sharp surge, sudden stop and abrupt reversal of capital flows.

Over the last three decades, India too experienced bouts of volatile capital flows almost every time the global financial cycle turned abruptly, and at each time the country's macroeconomic and financial stability had become hostage to the vagaries of capital flows, taking a heavy toll on growth and welfare.

Intellectual shift on capital flow management policies

The cumulative experience of emerging markets in managing volatile capita flows over the last three decades has engendered a remarkable intellectual shift in the world view on capital flow management. The old view, driven by the Washington Consensus, was that capital controls are bad, always and everywhere. That orthodoxy has since yielded to a more nuanced position — that in the face of large and volatile flows, capital controls are not only necessary but even desirable to defend the economy against financial instability.

Viral Acharya's paper draws from the experience of India to highlight the challenges of calibrating capital controls. From a practical policy perspective, there are two takeaways from the chapter.

- "Keep it simple" is in general a good guide to policy. However, it is exceedingly difficult to keep capital control policies simple given the complexity of the problem — the variety of flows, the variety of players in home and host countries and the variety of situations that the controls have to respond to.
- "Keep it stable" is in general a good guide to policy. Frequent tweaking of policy erodes efficiency and credibility. However, it is exceedingly difficult to keep capital control policies stable given the all-too-frequent and abrupt turns in the global financial cycle, rapid changes in the home macroeconomic context, quickly changing market dynamics and the constant race between the regulators and the regulatees to keep ahead.

With that preface, by way of discussion, I want to raise five policy issues that India and EMEs have to deal with in managing capital flows.

First issue: Appropriate choices under the Impossible Trinity Trilemma

The challenge that a typical EME faces in capital account management is best understood in terms of the "Impossible Trinity" argument which asserts that at any given time, a country can at best secure only two of the three policy goals of an open capital account, a fixed exchange rate and an independent monetary policy.[1]

Countries have made different choices under the Impossible Trinity Trilemma. The most common case, typical across advanced economies, is to give up on a fixed exchange rate so as to run an open economy with

---

[1] See Obstfeld *et al.* for a discussion of the history of the Impossible Trinity.

an independent monetary policy. On the other hand, economies that adopt a hard peg — that is opt for a fixed exchange rate — give up on an independence of monetary policy. Examples include the currency boards set up by Hong Kong and, for a time, Argentina.

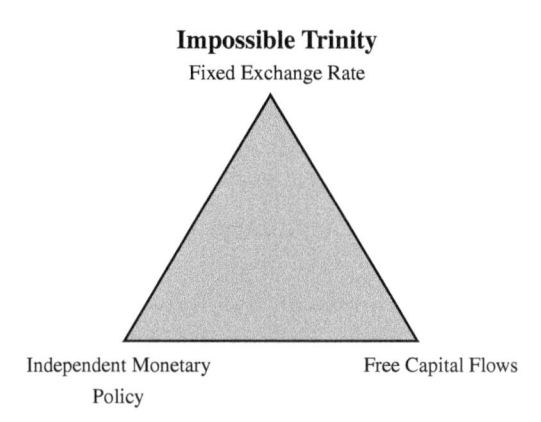

Impossible Trinity
Fixed Exchange Rate

Independent Monetary Policy   Free Capital Flows

In contrast to advanced economies which opt for corner solutions, EMEs have typically opted for middle solutions, giving up on some flexibility on each of the variables to maximise overall macroeconomic advantage. The contours of this middle solution are typically the following: (1) let the exchange rate be largely market determined but intervene in the market to smooth excess volatility; (2) run an open capital account but institute some controls on the types of flows and their entry and exit; (3) because of partial liberalisation of the exchange rate and the capital account, sacrifice some monetary policy independence.

Questions: A few important questions triggered by the trilemma. Are the middle solutions adopted by EMEs efficient? Do they inspire confidence in times of shocks? Unlike corner solutions of which there are only three possibilities, several variants of the middle solutions are possible. What, if any, should be the guidelines for EMEs to calibrate their policy stance across these variants without sacrificing efficiency and credibility?

Second issue: Monetary policy to defend the exchange rate

In some influential research work, Hélene Rey (2015) of the London Business School argues that when the global financial cycle turns abruptly, the trilemma of the Impossible Trinity actually degenerates into a dilemma in that a country that is open to capital flows and allows its currency to float still loses some monetary autonomy. Such sudden turns in financial cycles, as she explains, are usually associated with abrupt changes in the global risk appetite caused by shifts in the policy direction of the US Federal Reserve by virtue of the fact that the dollar is effectively the global reserve currency.

The practical implication for EMEs like India of Rey's research is that in the face of volatile capital flows, the exchange rate cannot be depended upon to bear the full brunt of adjustment. In other words, even if they allow the exchange rate to fully float in response to capital flows, contrary to what the Impossible Trinity will have us believe, they still will still forfeit some monetary policy independence unless they manage their capital accounts.

Whether Rey's thesis is valid depends on how the trilemma is interpreted. The trilemma does not say that monetary autonomy provides full insulation against global shocks. All it says is that there is more scope for addressing shocks with monetary policy in a country with floating exchange rates — or with strong controls on international capital flows — than for a country with a pegged currency and open capital markets.

Questions: Does India's experience validate Rey's research? Therein lies a bigger question. When is it appropriate to invoke monetary policy to defend the exchange rate? This is not just a theoretical issue. India faced this dilemma during the taper tantrums in 2013 when, along with capital controls, macroprudential polices and forex intervention, it also had to raise the interest rate to stem capital outflows. Will the use of monetary policy to safeguard the currency erode the inflation targeting credentials of the central bank?

Third issue: Sovereign borrowing in foreign currency — Original sin?

India's government has largely refrained from borrowing in foreign currencies. It is not as if it does not borrow from foreign lenders; foreign portfolio investors are allowed, albeit within some limits, to buy the government's onshore rupee bonds where the currency risk is borne by the lender. India has often shown off this prudence as a badge of honour, especially as some EMEs with sovereign exposure to foreign currencies had seen their external sector shocks amplified.

Given this context, when the Indian government announced in 2019 that it will raise a modest amount of its total borrowing requirements in foreign currency in foreign markets, critics panned the decision as needless adventurism.

From a purely objective point of view, a persuasive case can be made for the "dollar bonds". By far the biggest benefit is the intangible impact of the government signalling its confidence about opening up the economy. For a country that has an unsavoury reputation of being excessively cautious in liberalising its external sector, the positive externalities of this bold decision can be significant. The economy will attract not just larger foreign portfolio flows but, in time, also larger foreign direct investment.

The policy shift can also be expected to pave the way for Indian bonds entering global indices which will draw in index-tracking funds and reduce yields overall. Further, a dollar bond will enable India's risk premium to be more accurately estimated, potentially leading to a rating upgrade.

As against these putative benefits, there are formidable concerns. The biggest fear is that this adventurism will make India hostage to the wild swings of global sentiment. Investors are, after all, fair weather friends; they lend liberally when the going is good, but swiftly back out at the slightest hint of trouble, exposing the country to volatile exchange rates and ruthless market turmoil. For a country that had a devastating external payments crisis in 1991 and a near crisis during the taper tantrums of 2013, these are dire warnings.

Critics have also contended that issuing debt in foreign currencies is a route followed by countries which are unable to issue debt in their own currency. India is certainly not in that category. If the idea is to attract more foreign inflows, it could be done by raising the ceiling for foreigners into onshore rupee bonds.

Another argument against the proposal is that sovereign borrowing in foreign currency may not raise overall foreign funding. Many investors who are now buying rupee bonds in the domestic market will happily pass on the currency risk to the government and switch to dollar bonds in the external market.

By far the biggest and possibly clinching argument against moving forward is the peril of the "original sin" which has brought many emerging markets to grief. Experience shows that governments start off believing that they will remain prudent, open their doors wider and soon become so addicted to foreign money they would not stop until a crisis hits them. To believe that markets can discipline governments is a stretch. The stories of Argentina and Turkey are telling examples.

Questions: What is it about sovereign borrowing in foreign currencies that makes it more risky than other types of capital flows? Given these pros and cons and India's own difficult experience with volatile capital flows, is sovereign borrowing in foreign currency net positive for EMEs?

Fourth issue: IMF's institutional view on capital account management

For a long time, the IMF used to sermonise emerging markets on the benefits of full capital account opening. However, with the experience of the Global Financial Crisis and in what is a remarkable example of candour and transparency, the IMF admitted that "there be no presumption that full liberalization [of the capital account] is an appropriate goal for all countries at all times" (IMF, 2012).

The IMF's revised position was such a sharp departure from prior orthodoxy that it considered it fit to embark on a rather unusual measure — issue a board-approved Institutional View on capital flow management to guide Fund assessment of member countries. At the heart of the Institutional View was the acknowledgement that "Capital flow liberalization is generally more beneficial and less risky if countries have reached certain levels or — thresholds — of financial and institutional development. [However], liberalization needs to be well planned, timed, and sequenced in order to ensure that its benefits outweigh the costs, as it could have significant domestic and multilateral effects".

The change in IMF's stance was a welcome departure from its earlier rigid stance, but it failed to quell the debate. Emerging markets were irritated by how heavily the Institutional View was caveated, and raised many objections.

First, who is to decide whether capital flows are excessive or volatile? Second, the revised view stipulates that capital controls should not discriminate between residents and non-residents. How is this tenable when it is non-residents who flee at the first sign of trouble and thereby exacerbate the problem?

Third, the revised view stipulates that all other measures should be exhausted before capital controls are invoked. Why indeed has the IMF ruled out circumstances where capital controls may have to be the first line of defence to deal with destabilising capital flows? In his influential book on Depression Economics, Nobel Laureate Paul Krugman says that leading into the Asian Financial Crisis in the 1990s, Australia, a rich country, and the Asian economies, all of them emerging markets, had a similar risk build-up. However, the markets allowed Australia to make a smooth adjustment and avert a crisis, even as they denied a similar privilege to the Asian economies and pushed them into a devastating crisis (Krugman, 2009).

Question: Does the IMF Institutional View accord sufficient flexibility to EMEs in a crisis situation? Given the outsized power of market perceptions, should EMEs be allowed greater flexibility in managing a crisis response?

Fifth issue: Currency wars — Sharing of the burden of adjustment between advanced economies and EMEs?

The anguish and frustration of EMEs about the pain of managing capital flows assumed centre stage during the Quantitative Easing (QE) years (2010–2012) following the Global Financial Crisis. "Currency Wars" figured prominently on the agenda of virtually every G-20 meeting, with the battles lines clearly drawn between advanced economies and EMEs.

The consistent refrain of EMEs at the G-20 meetings used to be that the unconventional monetary policies of advanced economies were taking a heavy toll on their economies and that advanced economies must factor in this spill over impact in formulating their domestic policies. They argued that these cross-border capital flows were a consequence of globalisation — maintaining open borders for trade and finance. Both sides, advanced and EMEs, have benefitted from emerging markets opening up, and so both sides also must share the costs of globalisation; it is unfair to abandon the entire burden of adjustment to emerging markets.

Advanced economies, led by the US, were largely dismissive of these grievances. Their mandate, they would argue, is entirely domestic — promoting growth and preserving stability at home. It is not possible to subordinate that domestic mandate to international obligations. They did not deny the existence of spillovers but would contend that such spillovers were an inevitable by-product of their policy effort to revive their domestic economies.

Moreover, the argument went, advanced economy recovery is an international public good inasmuch as emerging markets too would benefit if advanced economies recovered soon, as that would increase demand for emerging economy exports. Their counter to emerging markets would typically end with the homily that the latter should set their own houses in order to cope with the forces of globalisation rather than scapegoat the domestic policies of advanced economies

In the context of this debate, here is what former Federal Reserve Chairman Bernanke wrote in his book, *The Courage to Act*, on what he said at the G-20 meeting in South Korea in October 2010:

> I argued that because we are an important trading partner for many countries, the rest of the world would benefit from a stronger US recovery. I said that countries with sound monetary, budget and trade policies could better withstand any short-term disruptions from our easing (Bernanke, 2015).

Question: To what extent are advanced economies obliged to factor in spill over effects into their policy calculations? Can there be any objective rules of the game in this regard?

References

Bernenke, Ben S. (2015): *The Courage to Act: A Memoir of a Crisis and Its Aftermath*, W. W. Norton & Company.
IMF (2012): The Liberalization and Management of Capital Flows: An Institutional View; November 2012.

Krugman, Paul (2008): *The Return of Depression Economics*, W. W. Norton & Company.

Mishra, Prachi and Rajan, Raghuram G. (2016): "Rules of the Monetary Game," Working Papers id:10533, eSocialSciences.

Obstfeld, Maurice, Shambaugh, Jay C. and Taylor, Alan M. (2005): "The Trilemma in History: Trade-offs Among Exchange Rates, Monetary Policies, and Capital Mobility", *Review of Economics and Statistics*, **87**(3): 423–443.

Rey, Hélène (2015): Dilemma not Trilemma: The Global Financial Cycle and Monetary Policy Independence, NBER Working Paper No. 21162, May, Revised February 2018.

CHAPTER 10

Chapter 10

Legacy of Early Crisis and Incomplete Institutional Reforms on the Financial Sector in Indonesia[*]

M. Chatib Basri[†] and Reza Y. Siregar[‡,§]

[†]*Senior Lecturer, Department of Economics,*
University of Indonesia
[‡]*Special Advisor,*
Coordinating Ministry for Economic Affairs,
Republic of Indonesia
[§]*Faculty Member, Bank Indonesia Institute*

Abstract

The collapse of an economy and the meltdown of its financial system often unveil the weakness of the regulatory and the supervisory institutions and lead to adjustments or even evolution of the functions and responsibilities of the relevant institutions, including the central bank. The COVID-19 pandemic crisis is no exception. The reforms that have taken place following the past crises, especially the 1997 East Asian

---

[*] The first draft of this chapter was presented at the Asian Monetary Policy Forum 2021 Special Edition and MAS-BIS Conference on "Macro-financial Stability Policy in a Globalised World: Lessons from International Experience", 26–28 May 2021. The authors wish to thank the Governor of Bank Indonesia, Perry Warjiyo, for the insightful comments on the early draft of the chapter. The views expressed are of the authors and do not necessarily represent the institutions that they are associated with.

crisis, have profoundly shaped the modern central bank, the financial supervisory institutions and the coordination among the members of the Financial System Stability Forum (FSSF) in Indonesia. The changes have positively strengthened the country's financial sector. However, many old questions or debates remain or resurface. Moreover, this study argues that the past reforms and their executions have left lasting impacts undermining the effectiveness of the policies of the relevant institutions today, including the coordination among them.

1. Background and objective

The legacy of the 1997 East Asian crisis lives on, shaping up the landscapes of monetary policy and financial regulatory institutions in Indonesia. The Central Bank Act No. 23/1999, which was enacted in May 1999 and replaced the Central Bank Act 1968, explicitly states that Bank Indonesia is "an independent national institution, which is free from the intervention of the government". Around the same period, the IMF proposed the establishment of the Financial Service Authority (FSA) with the task of supervising and regulating four financial sectors: banking, security market, insurance and pension funds. The initial target date for the formation of the FSA was 2002, but the FSA was eventually established only in 2010.

Globally, debates among academics and policymakers following the 1997 crisis have led to three major contesting viewpoints. First is that monetary policy should maintain a relatively narrow mandate of price stability, leaving the financial stability mandate to prudential authorities. The second view is to "lean against the wind", i.e., price stability may not be sufficient for financial stability. Therefore, the central bank must act to "lean against" the emergence of financial imbalances. The third view is that financial stability is price stability. The proponents of this view argue that financial stability and price stability are so intertwined that they often cannot be distinguished. The second and third views have arguably become the principal guidance of Bank Indonesia's policy frameworks.

While price stability is the anchor of Bank Indonesia's Inflation Targeting Framework, as stipulated in the Central Bank Act No. 23/1999, macroprudential policy measures have been actively deployed to mitigate the build-up of systemic risks to financial stability as well to achieve price stability under the central bank's policy-mix strategy, particularly since 2010. Striking the balance between maintaining financial stability and enhancing the contribution of the financial system to economic growth has been the primary aim of the macroprudential policy measures. Capital flow management measures have also complemented the central bank's policy mix.

This chapter demonstrates the challenges and the dilemma facing Bank Indonesia in its efforts to manage the multiple objectives of price stability, financial stability and growth contribution of the financial sector, including during the period of the COVID-19 pandemic crisis. In Section 2, we introduce the policy mix carried out by Bank Indonesia in recent years to mitigate the impacts of COVID-19 on the domestic economy.

Section 3 further elaborates the challenges for Indonesia, a country facing twin deficits (budget and current account), in navigating the Impossible Trinity since early 2000s. The key message here is that while a well-orchestrated central bank policy mix of monetary policy, macroprudential policy and capital flow management measures is vital, a well-designed coordination between monetary and fiscal policies is a pre-requisite for Indonesia to successfully navigate the Unholy Trinity policy constraints.

In Section 4, we revisit key events that have shaped the coordination between the central bank and the relevant regulatory and supervisory institutions. We will argue that one needs to comprehend the landscapes of the monetary, supervisory and regulatory institutions and to appreciate their evolutions in order to exhaustively assess the dynamics, intricacies and effectiveness of policy coordination between these institutions in Indonesia. Section 5 provides brief concluding remarks to end the chapter.

2. Bank Indonesia's policy mix and the role of macroprudential policies

The phrase "policy mix" appeared in the economic policy literature in the 1960s, and the term has long been attributed to the Nobel Economics Prize winner, Robert Mundell (Mundell, 1962, 1963, 1971). The term "policy mix" implies a focus on the interactions and interdependencies between different policies/instruments as they affect the extent to which intended policy outcomes are achieved. It is now well argued that global financial crises, including the COVID-19 pandemic crisis, warrant the role of policy-mix measures to address the multiple challenges, domestic and external, facing the economy.

In normal times, central banks would typically focus on inflation. However, in an abnormal situation, such as in a state of severe economic crisis, a single policy direction and conventional economic policies may prove insufficient to achieve the objectives of stabilising the domestic economic condition. Central banks worldwide, aware of the conditions that the new global economic conjuncture necessitates, have complemented and reformed their existing conventional monetary policy frameworks by enhancing other policies such as macroprudential policy, capital flow management policy, fiscal policy coordination and structural adjustment stimulus.

The adoption of credible policy mix by Bank Indonesia, particularly since 2010, has largely been responsible for its success in preserving price and financial stability while supporting economic growth through close coordination with the fiscal authority. Siregar and Goo (2010) demonstrate that the policy-mix approach has solidified the credibility of Bank Indonesia's Inflation Target anchor. Their study demonstrates that the flexibility of the policy-mix instruments facilitates the balancing between the central bank's primary target of price stability with that of exchange rate stability, while keeping support for the growth momentum.

Past experiences of Bank Indonesia have also underscored the important role of macroprudential policies in the Bank's overall macroeconomic policy-mix management. IMF (2013) and Siregar (2011) have further argued that achieving the objective of financial stability requires dedicated macroprudential policies. In line with that argument, Agung *et al.* (2016) and Warjiyo (2017) highlight the prominent role of macroprudential policies in Bank Indonesia's efforts to balance the trade-offs between monetary policy autonomy and stable exchange rates, prices and capital flows under the central bank's flexible Inflation Targeting Framework.

In 2020, Bank Indonesia maintained an accommodative macroprudential policy stance with a focus on two aspects, namely maintaining financial system resilience to mitigate the impact of COVID-19 on the financial sector, as well as accelerating the economic recovery by expanding the role of financing. IMF (2021) claims that timely adjustments of Bank Indonesia's policy mix eased the monetary condition and anchored financial stability at the early stage of the COVID-19 outbreak in Indonesia in March 2020. On the foreign exchange front, Bank Indonesia carried out triple interventions in the spot market, the domestic non-deliverable forward (DNDF) market, and the secondary market of government bonds in April 2020. The primary aim of these measures was to support and stabilise the local currency amidst the unprecedented shock caused by the outbreak of the COVID-19 pandemic in Indonesia, particularly during the first half of 2020.

To ensure adequate liquidity in the forex market, Bank Indonesia increased the auction frequencies from three days per week to daily, starting from March 2020. In March 2020, the US Federal Reserve launched the Foreign and International Monetary Authorities (FIMA) repo facility. Until 30 September 2021, international monetary authorities with accounts at the Federal Reserve Bank of New York were eligible to use the facility. It allowed, for the first time, international institutions to raise dollar cash by posting their US Treasuries to the Fed's System Open Market Account. On 9 April 2020, Bank Indonesia secured access to FIMA through a $60 billion repurchase agreement line. It stands ready for use if required, to add US dollar liquidity as another backstop.

On the policy rate front, Bank Indonesia had aggressively cut its seven-day Repo Rate from 5 percent in early 2020 to 3.5 percent by February 2021. In line with the expansionary monetary policy and the objectives of liquidity support and incentive provision for targeted sector financing, macroprudential measures had also been implemented. In particular, Bank Indonesia lowered the foreign currency reserve requirement ratio for conventional commercial banks from 8 percent to 4 percent in March 2020. At the same time, the rupiah reserve requirement ratio was cut by 50 bps for banks that were engaged in export–import financing, as well as financing of the micro-, small- and medium-sized enterprises and other priority sectors.

Adjustments to the Macroprudential Intermediation Ratio (MIR) and the Macroprudential Liquidity Buffer were carried out to encourage the intermediation function to support economic growth during the COVID-19 pandemic crisis while maintaining prudence. The MIR is a ratio of the loans and securities owned to the deposits and securities issued. The upper and lower bounds of the MIR are regularly adjusted to affect credit growth in the financial system. With the rise of government bond issuance to support the fiscal stimulus, commercial banks in Indonesia have steadily accumulated a larger share of their assets in the form of sovereign bonds. By the end of 2020, the banking sector of Indonesia parked over 17 percent of their assets in government bonds, a rise from around 13 percent in December 2019. To boost the falling credit growth, Bank Indonesia enforces and monitors the MIR range closely.

Another frequently employed macroprudential policy instrument to boost the demand in the domestic economy is the loan-to-value ratio. In March 2021, Bank Indonesia relaxed the down-payment regulations to boost property and automotive sales. At the same time, the loan-to-asset value ratio was increased to 100 percent from the previous range of 85 percent–95 percent, depending on the property type.

Following the outbreak of the COVID-19 pandemic crisis, Bank Indonesia has also been called to support fiscal financing. In a bid to boost higher public spending, the Indonesian government temporarily suspended the 3 percent of GDP ceiling on the budget deficit until 2022. Additionally, the Government Regulation in Lieu of Law No. 1 of 2020 removed the ban on central bank purchases of longer-term government bonds in the primary market. In July 2020, the central bank agreed to directly purchase government bonds worth around 397.56 trillion rupiah ($27.6 billion) in a burden-sharing scheme. The government's budget deficit rose to 5.7 percent of GDP in 2020, up from 2.2 percent in 2019. The 2021 budget deficit (as percent of GDP) is expected to stay around the same level reported in 2020.

The role of Bank Indonesia is vital, not only in providing the financing need for the fiscal deficit, but also in anchoring stability in the debt market. Amidst the rise in economic uncertainty, the share of non-resident holdings of rupiah-denominated government bonds declined from 38 percent of the total stock at the end of 2019 to 27 percent at end-September 2020. Over the same period, Bank Indonesia's share of rupiah-denominated bonds increased from 10 percent to 20 percent of the total. Section 3 revisits the recent episodes of policy coordination between the fiscal authority and the central bank and reviews the implications for the country's management of external accounts.

3. Navigating the unholy trinity in Indonesia

Indonesia's high dependence on portfolio inflows to finance the country's twin deficits, namely the current account and budget deficits, has become a prominent source of macroeconomic and financial sector vulnerabilities. The type of financing of these deficits matters greatly, especially for the debt sustainability and the financial sector stability of the country. In recent years, foreign direct investments (FDIs) have not recorded the much-needed surge. Instead, portfolio investment, especially in the country's sovereign debts, has attracted a high share of foreign ownership.

Under the global environment of short-term and highly volatile financial cycles, Rey (2013) argues that independent monetary policy is possible if and only if the capital account is managed. Recent studies have further claimed that under a highly open financial account system, the traditional impossible policy trilemma has turned into a "dilemma". As we learnt from our own experiences in Indonesia during the post-2007 Global Financial Crisis period, the well-orchestrated central bank policy mix of monetary policy, macroprudential policy and capital flow management measures along with the close coordination between monetary and fiscal policies are pre-requisites for Indonesia to successfully navigate the Unholy Trinity policy constraints. Juhro *et al.* (2021) claim that the emerging economies' policymakers can enhance the effectiveness of monetary policy in dealing with inflation deviation or sharpen the effectiveness of exchange rate stability by placing more weights on macroprudential policies.

In 2009, the US Fed enacted an unprecedented monetary policy, namely Quantitative Easing (QE), to overcome the sub-prime financial crisis. This policy was largely responsible for the capital inflow surge to Emerging Markets (EMs), which in turn led to appreciations in the exchange rates of the EM countries, including Indonesia. Around the same period, the prices of several key commodities rose. Indonesia, Brazil and

South Africa benefited from the combination of the commodity boom and capital inflows. During this period, local currencies strengthened due to the positive terms of trade effect and capital inflows. Basri (2016) shows that the Indonesian rupiah appreciated against the US dollar from the Fed's adoption of the QE policy at the start of 2009, and the trend continued through the second quarter of 2011.

As well documented in early studies, portfolio investment, other investment (banking) and FDI inflows often surge in a synchronised manner during periods of relatively strong economic growth across the globe (Siregar and Choy, 2010). A pick-up in the trading activities of goods and services and in FDIs accompanied the strong inflows of other investment (banking) and portfolio investment into Indonesia from 2004 to 2012. Over the window of almost a decade, the FDI flows to Indonesia had primarily targeted natural resources and domestic consumption rather than manufacturing exports. The rapid and robust domestic economic growth of 5 percent–6 percent per annum stimulated more investment, leading to upsurges in imports. As expected, the current account deficit widened considerably. This was not unique to Indonesia, but similar patterns emerged in many other growing economies.

On the back of the widened current account deficit, the Indonesian rupiah began to show signs of weakening from the second half of 2011. Instead of increasing interest rates to soften the deterioration of the current account deficit, Bank Indonesia decreased interest rates and intervened heavily in the foreign exchange market to defend the rupiah, resulting in the misalignments of the rupiah and inviting speculative attacks on the local currency. The government's refusal to cut energy subsidies further widened the budget deficit and worsened the overall situation in the foreign exchange market.

What can we learn from the experiences above? As foresaw by the Unholy Trinity, under Bank Indonesia's commitment to maintain free capital flows and its independent monetary policy, the strong capital inflows would drive a sharp appreciation in the rupiah's exchange rate. Consequently, as discussed above, the current account deficit will deteriorate and expose the country's balance of payment position to the risks associated with the swings in portfolio investment. When Bank Indonesia tried to alleviate the appreciation pressure on the rupiah, the cost would rise along with the widening spread of the Fed Funds Rate and the Bank Indonesia rate.

Basri (2016) argues that the government should have tightened its fiscal policy to reduce the financing need and therefore the pressure on the rupiah. At the same time, Bank Indonesia can balance its policy mix of allowing the rupiah to strengthen, by adopting capital flow management measures and employing macroprudential measures to limit the risk exposures arising from capital flows on the banking and other relevant sectors of the economy. However, applying a tight fiscal policy during economic boom periods is not politically easy.

The reverse occurred during the 2013 Taper Tantrum. In May 2013, Bernanke hinted at the possibility of ending the QE policy (tapering its securities purchases). The intention became clear when Bernanke testified to the Congress on 22 May 2013. The news directly impacted the EM markets. The EM stock market indices fell and the currencies depreciated. Aizenman *et al.* (2014) claim that the immediate impact of Bernanke's announcement was especially felt in the EM countries with current account surpluses, high international reserves and low debt. However, over time, the cumulative impact of Bernanke's tapering news significantly affected stock prices and credit default swap (CDS) spreads in countries seen as fragile.

Indonesia was confronted with the same impact. The rupiah weakened, bond yields rose and the stock market gains eroded (Figures 1 and 2). Meanwhile, challenging debates regarding revisions to the 2013 budget were ongoing in the parliament. Market uncertainty loomed. Efforts by the government and Bank Indonesia to calm the markets were not helping as no immediate concrete steps were taken. As previously discussed, the main problem facing Indonesia was the current account deficit resulting from the investment boom triggered by capital inflows (Figure 3). At the same time, the budget deficit rose due to the pressure from fuel subsidies, albeit still under 3 percent of GDP and less than those reported by the other Fragile Five countries.[1]

---

[1] By law, the budget deficit must be below 3% (a consolidation of the central and regional government budget deficits). As a rule of thumb, the regional government deficit is set at 0.5%, while the central government deficit at 2.5%.

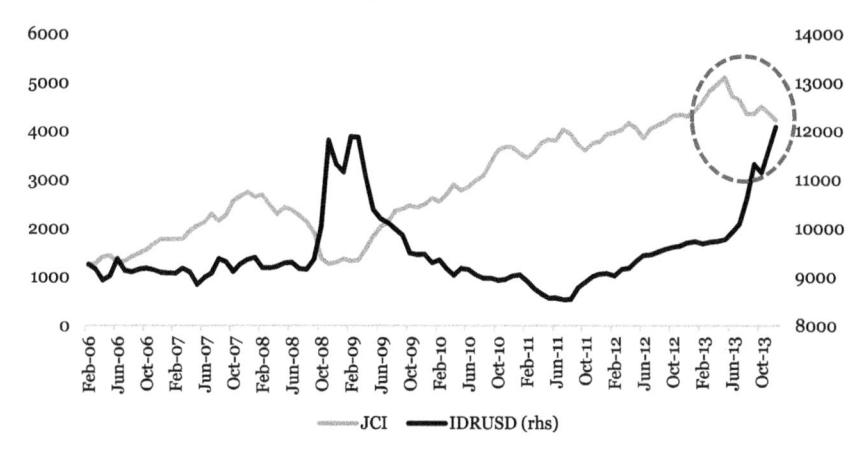

Figure 1. Weaker rupiah along with losses in stock exchange.
Source: CEIC.

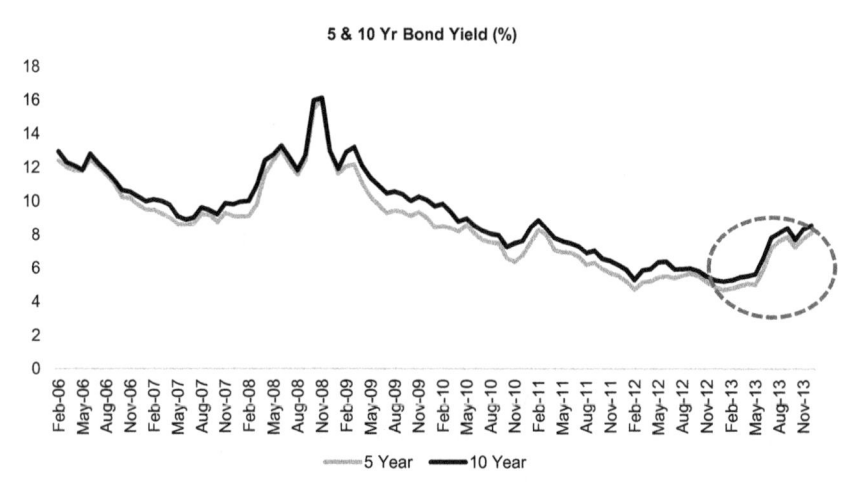

Figure 2. Cost of budget financing rose.
Source: CEIC.

A combination of expenditure-reducing and expenditure-switching policies with continuous market guidance was the appropriate move to handle the current account deficit at the time in Indonesia. An expenditure-reducing policy by tightening fiscal, monetary and macroprudential policies, coupled with an expenditure-switching policy, by allowing exchange rate adjustments, was warranted (Caves *et al.*, 2006). For Indonesia, a right mix of policies, instead of relying only on one policy,

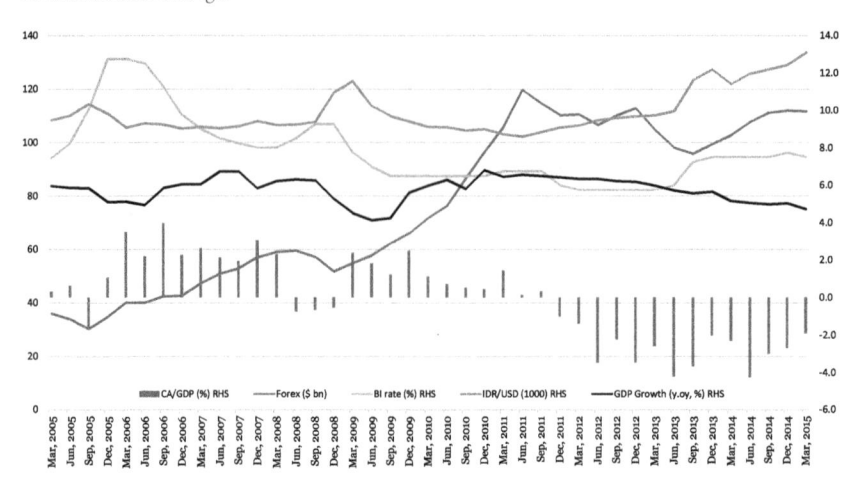

Figure 3. Macroeconomic landscape during and post–2013 Taper Tantrum. Source: CEIC.

was necessary. Too high interest rates may undermine the quality of bank loans which in turn would encourage capital outflows. Overly tight fiscal policy will, on the other hand, disrupt welfare programs and stall economic growth, potentially putting significant depreciation pressures on the local currency, as reported during the 1998 Asian Financial Crisis. Triggering such a trauma would result in a self-fulfilling prophecy, fuelling a panic.

To further curb capital outflows, the Indonesian government should have applied what is known as a Reverse Tobin Tax. In the case of the *Tobin Tax*, short-term capital inflows are taxed. With the *Reverse Tobin Tax,* the government gives tax incentives to those investors who do not repatriate earnings, but rather reinvest profits. Why not just apply the Tobin Tax, but provide incentives rather than penalties? The answer: Indonesia is a country with an open capital account regime, and thus any regulations to limit capital flows require that changes be made through amendments to prevailing laws, involving a tedious political parliamentary process. If this happens, investors would have ample time to leave Indonesia before the Tobin Tax could be applied. Given this reality, incentives like the Reverse Tobin Tax are far more feasible than the Tobin Tax. The Indonesian government adopts this measure in its Sovereign Wealth Fund draft, in which if a foreign tax subject does not repatriate its earnings, but instead re-invests in Indonesia, it will not be taxed. Another alternative is to enhance and deepen the country's financial market instruments or products, so that Indonesians, or Indonesian exporters, have the option to invest in foreign currencies in Indonesia (*onshore*), and hence increase the supply of dollars domestically.

4. Milestones in Indonesia's institutional overhauls and unintended consequences

To comprehensively assess the dynamics and the intricacies of monetary policy and macroprudential policy in Indonesia, one needs to first comprehend the landscapes of the monetary, supervisory and regulatory institutions and to appreciate their evolutions. Economic theory provides theoretical foundations behind reforms, and global experiences unveil guidelines for best practices. However, facing the constraints of the political environment and institutional weaknesses in emerging markets, even sound theories and best global practices often fall short in ensuring workable and effective institutional reforms to achieve policy targets.

Fostering prudential regulatory and supervisory institutions to work closely with the Central Bank and the Fiscal Authority is a recipe to manage economic growth and financial stability, but the success of the efforts does not only depend on the policy framework. In fact, Indonesia's experiences demonstrate that the institutional set-up and political situation weigh heavily on the overall outcomes of the policy efforts. Like the experiences of many emerging markets globally, the policymakers in Indonesia do not have the luxury of working in a vacuum where they can ignore political factors and institutional constraints. The euphoria of a much greater democratic political system following the 1997 East Asian crisis has arguably contributed to the sub-optimal transformations in the policy and regulatory executions.

One of the milestone reforms in the financial sector following the 1997 East Asian crisis in Indonesia was inarguably the establishment of an independent and integrated financial Supervisory Authority (*Otoritas Jasa Keuangan* or OJK) in 2011. The OJK is an independent institution with the task and the authority to integrate the supervision and microprudential regulation of the financial sector in Indonesia. Prior to the OJK's establishment, Indonesia had multiple supervisors and regulators of its financial sector. The Bapepam-LK regulated and supervised the country's capital markets. Bank Indonesia was responsible for the tasks of regulating and supervising the banking sector. The Ministry of Finance was in charge of the regulation and supervision of the insurance sector.

Many viewed the need for a full integration of the financial supervisors in Indonesia following the financial sector collapse in 1997–1998 (Taylor and Fleming, 1999; Siregar and James, 2006). Indonesia experienced a rapid rise in the role of financial conglomerates and bancassurance in early 2000s. Major commercial banks in Indonesia already offered multiple investment assets to their customers, in addition to the standard banking services. It is estimated that around 85 percent of mutual fund products in Indonesia were sold via banking institutions by mid-2000s. The 1997 East Asian crisis demonstrated well that the fragmented supervisory bodies were inept in forming an overall risk assessment of a financial conglomerate due partly to the ranges of financial risks.[2]

From the very beginning, the pros and cons of independent and integrated supervisory and prudential agencies have been heavily contested for the developed and developing economies (Grenville, 2005; Goodhart, 2001). For the developing economies, the separation of the banking supervisory function from the central bank, in particular, continues to be heavily debated, including in Indonesia. Goodhart (2001) posits that in the case of emerging economies:

> "a combination of anecdote and experience (admittedly mostly observed through a central banking prism) does suggest that banking supervision in developing countries has been rather better done if taken under the wing of a central bank."

Grenville (2005) further claims that handling a banking crisis will be far easier if supervisory functions remain under the Central Bank.

---

[2] Taylor and Fleming (1999), for instance, argue that while the supervision of the banking and securities sectors tends to focus on the risks associated with the asset side of the balance sheet (such as the size of the non-performing loans), the financial risk for the insurance company occurs mostly from the liability side of the balance sheet.

This is because the initial signals of a banking problem will be seen in the payments system and the short-term money market, for which the Central Bank has better information.

In addition, good governance and accountability are critical in the overall success and legitimacy of independent supervision and regulation (Hupkes et al., 2005). The experiences of many countries have also emphasised that the separations of supervision, prudential and macroeconomic policies (fiscal and monetary) place a strong emphasis on the importance of coordination among the relevant institutions. Particularly, the role of the Central Bank as the *Lender of Last Resort* (LoLR) and the roles of the Deposit Insurance authority and the Ministry of Finance need to be clearly spelled out. Next, we will touch on several past events in which the institutional set-ups, historical experience/stigma and political situations continue to test the effectiveness and the credibility of the current prudential and supervisory institutions in the country, including policy coordination among them.

4.1. Bank Indonesia's Liquidity Support (BLBI) of 1998

The policy decision by Bank Indonesia to extend liquidity support for the troubled banking system following the outbreak of the 1997 East Asian financial crisis has left a profound impact and a stigma for future policymaking decisions. The large lump-sum figure spent on Bank Indonesia's Liquidity Support initiative and the eventual steep rise in public debt posed macroeconomic policy challenges to the country for many years to come. There were wide probes against corruption allegations involving several bankers and officials from Bank Indonesia. This controversy eventually unfolded on the ownership of the policy. Djiwandono (2004) claims that the liquidity policy support was a step taken by Bank Indonesia to prevent the collapse of the banking sector and payments system. However, the decision was made based on instructions from the President to Bank Indonesia (at the time, Bank Indonesia was not yet independent) to assist banks experiencing liquidity issues. Djiwandono (2004) therefore argues that the government (President) had the ownership of the policy. However, after the liquidity support turned into a political divide, Bank Indonesia was seen as the responsible party. On this incident, Djiwandono (2004) writes:

> "In such circumstances, straight and clean officials can be accused and found guilty of corruption, even in the absence of evidence to support such accusations. The champions of justice in their fight against corruption have tended to overlook the plight of such officials, forgetting that a corrupt legal system (widely defined) can be used not only to protect wrongdoers but also to attack the innocent."

4.2. The case of Bank Century

Another policy decision that did have political implications was the government's decision to rescue Bank Century during the early stage of the 2008 Global Financial Crisis. The Financial System Stability Committee (KSSK), set up by the Finance Minister and the Governor of Bank Indonesia, had determined that the collapse of Bank Century posed a systemic risk towards the entire domestic banking system. The government and Bank Indonesia were of the opinion that the economic situation was relatively fragile at that time, as reflected by the 30 percent fall of the Indonesian rupiah against the US dollar in late 2008. Under this circumstance, the collapse of a bank or a financial institution could result in a market panic. Even though Bank Century was relatively small, with low interconnectedness to the rest of the financial sector and the economy, the government and Bank Indonesia considered the psychological factor of market players as extremely important. Bank Indonesia's argument was based on Indonesia's experiences in the 1997–1998 crisis, when the closure of 16 banks — which only controlled 2.3 percent of total banking assets — had a very negative effect on the financial markets. This had resulted in large cash withdrawals by depositors in the banking sector, fuelling a much wider economic and financial crisis in the country.

Unlike in other countries such as Singapore, Australia and Malaysia, the Government of Indonesia did not adopt a blanket guarantee system in late 2008. The Vice President at the time, Jusuf Kalla, rejected the proposed idea of a blanket guarantee due to a concern over moral hazards.

The government and Bank Indonesia ended up only raising the guarantee on deposits from Rp100 million to Rp2 billion (Saheruddin, 2017). This led to a risk of potential migration of banking funds from Indonesia to countries where blanket guarantees were in force. With a relatively small guarantee, the fear over systemic risk from the banking sector to the entire financial sector escalated and led to the eventual bailout of Bank Century in November 2008. The decision to bail out Bank Century had political implications, especially when the President and Vice President-elect (SBY-Boediono) started to form their cabinet in August 2009. The ensuing political pressure continued when the cabinet was appointed in October 2009, with protesters demanding the resignation of both Sri Mulyani (the Minister of Finance at that time) and Boediono (then the Vice President) almost every day and for the Anti-Corruption Committee (KPK) to investigate the case. One Deputy Governor of Bank Indonesia was eventually convicted of corruption. Until today, the case has not been fully resolved, and legal uncertainties, as in the case of BLBI above, have continued to undermine the decision-making process of banking supervision and regulation, including coordination between relevant parties, in Indonesia.

4.3. Coordination between OJK and Bank Indonesia

Under a stable economic condition, coordination should not lead to problems. However, the coordination process will become increasingly difficult during a banking crisis or when the banking sector is under pressure. The Financial Safety Net Law states that to prevent a financial system crisis in the banking sector, OJK must coordinate with Bank Indonesia in determining a Systemic Bank case. The OJK must also coordinate with Bank Indonesia to update the Systemic Bank list every six months. The problem is that, as anyone knows, changes can happen in mere days in the financial sector (including banking). Thus, there is the risk that the information will not be timely or up-to-date. Yet, on the other hand, the Law regulates that a Systemic Bank facing liquidity problems can submit a request to Bank Indonesia for a short-term liquidity loan. The procedure is as follows. OJK conducts an assessment on the solvency requirements and health of the Systemic Bank. Based on the results from the OJK's assessment, Bank Indonesia will then have to decide whether to provide a short-term liquidity loan or short-term liquidity financing. One can easily imagine asymmetrical information problems that could arise here. OJK provides the supervision and assessment on solvency, while Bank Indonesia provides the liquidity. Under normal conditions, this coordination should be relatively easy, but because the risk and responsibility lay with Bank Indonesia, it is understandably not clear-cut for Bank Indonesia to provide liquidity solely based on a recommendation from OJK. The situation is further complicated by the lingering legal issues and stigmas from the previously discussed 1998 BLBI and Bank Century cases. It makes perfect sense that Bank Indonesia would be incredibly cautious, and that the coordination process is far more complicated than it would seem at first glance.

4.4. *Decision-making process in the FSSF*

The same issue arises in the decision-making process for the insolvent Systemic Banks. The Law regulates that in such cases, OJK will request a meeting of the FSSF. The members of the FSSF include the Ministry of Finance, Bank Indonesia, OJK and the Deposit Insurance authority. Decisions on the follow-up steps for the insolvent systemic bank must be reached through deliberation and consensus in the FSSF. If a decision is not reached, the case will be rejected, but it can be re-submitted within 24 hours after which the decision will be based on a majority vote. Although the mechanism for resolution exists, coming up with a consensus decision is nevertheless difficult, as the supervision is performed by OJK, but the FSSF members must decide. One of the underlying and classical challenges here is again with the issue of asymmetrical information. Mishkin (1999) argues that different aspects of asymmetric information contributed to the coordination issue among the supervisory and regulatory institutions in different episodes of financial crises globally, including of the 1997 East Asian crisis.

The lingering stigmas from BLBI and Bank Century, as well as the complexity of the coordination process under the FSSF, complicate regulation and supervision of the banking sector, especially in times of crises. Djiwandono (2004) points to the concerns policymakers have about making decisions, particularly in banking cases. This is why, following the outbreak of the COVID-19 pandemic, the Government Regulation in Lieu of Law no. 1 of 2020 on COVID-19 management and national economic recovery, passed on 31 March 2020, included a specific article which states that the costs arising to save the economy are economic costs and not losses, and that policymakers cannot be convicted so long as they follow the law and act in good faith. The very existence of this article reflects the uncertainty facing policymakers, which can be directly linked to the traumas of the BLBI 1998 and Bank Century cases.

4.5. Regulatory forbearance

It is generally understood that regulatory forbearance should be phased out timely. Studies show that a weak banking sector can lead to a banking crisis and eventually a debt crisis. Reinhart and Rogoff (2011) examine how the mounting private debt resulting from banking crises becomes public debt. Thus, conceptually, regulatory forbearance needs to be removed, so that a banking sector crunch can be identified early. However, the reality is not always so simple, with several factors complicating the process. There are reasons other than banking technicalities which make reducing regulatory forbearance difficult, including the function of development agents, political considerations and vested interests. There are also economic reasons during economic slowdowns. For example, in 2020, OJK implemented a policy of relaxing the lending standards for credits to be considered as current. As a result, the non-performing loans (NPLs) seem to be relatively small and manageable. However, loans at-risk are relatively high. The OJK policy will be in effect through March 2023, after which the true NLP figures will be revealed. At that time, those banks which have not built adequate loan provisions will likely be exposed to trouble loans.

While regulatory forbearance does increase risk, the banking sector would be under incredible pressure without the OJK's loan standard relaxation measure. Any rushed attempt to reduce regulatory forbearance, on the other hand, poses the risk of bank closures and its systemic consequences. As discussed, the painful experiences of the 1998 Asian Financial Crisis have left lingering impacts, including the closures of 16 banks at the recommendation of the IMF. Indonesian regulators have been further traumatised by the Bank Century bailout, which resulted in intense legal and political issues.

5. Brief concluding remarks

The breakdown of an economy and the meltdown of its financial system often unveil the weakness of the current stage of the regulatory and the supervisory institutions and often lead to adjustments or even the evolution of the functions and responsibilities of the relevant institutions, including the central bank (Goodhart, 1998; Bordo, 2007a, 2007b). The COVID-19 pandemic crisis is no exception. The reforms which took place following the past crises, especially the 1997 East Asian crisis, have profoundly shaped the laws regulating the modern central bank, the financial sector supervisory institutions and the other members of the FSSF in Indonesia. The changes have positively strengthened the country's financial sector. However, as illustrated earlier, many questions or debates remain or resurface. Moreover, this study argues that the evolution of the past reforms and their sub-optimal executions have left a lasting impact or legacy undermining the effectiveness of the policy implementation by the relevant institutions, including the coordination between them.

In particular, two lingering issues arose again during the outbreak of the COVID-19 pandemic crisis. The first is the debate on the need to establish an integrated financial sector supervisor and to separate the banking supervisor from the central bank. The need to have a closer and improved coordination between Bank Indonesia and the Ministry of Finance is another on-going debate. Balancing between policy coordination and independence of the central bank was tested again during the COVID-19 pandemic crisis. Handling of the banking sector bailout measures during the 1997 crisis and the case of Bank Century in 2008 has left a stigma on the current crisis management protocol and the decision-making process at the FSSF in Indonesia.

With a widening of functions and responsibilities, especially following recent economic and financial crises, central banks around the world, including Bank Indonesia, need to adapt. History suggests that there is no constancy in the practice of central banking, and that the function of the central bank needs to change (Mohan, 2012). Regulatory reviews, however, should not only affect the Central Bank Act, but also the laws on the rest of the FSSF members in Indonesia.

References

Agung, J, S M Juhro, and T Harmanta (2016): "Managing Monetary and Financial Stability in a Dynamic Global Environment: Bank Indonesia's Policy Perspectives", *BIS Papers*, no. 88.

Aizenman, J, M Binici and M M Hutchison (2014): "The Transmission of Federal Reserve Tapering News to Emerging Financial Markets", *NBER Working Paper*, no. 19980, March.

Basri, M C (2016): "The Fed's Tapering Talk: A Short Statement's Long Impact on Indonesia", *Ash Centre Occasional Papers*, Harvard Kennedy School, Harvard University, June.

Bordo, M D (2007a): "A History of Monetary Policy", in *The New Palgrave Dictionary of Economics*, second edition, London, U.K.: Springer.

Bordo, M D (2007b): A brief history of central banks, *Federal Reserve Bank of Cleveland Economic Commentary*, December.

Caves, R, J Frankel and R Jones (2006): *World Trade and Payments: An Introduction*, New York, NY: Pearson.

Djiwandono, S (2004): "Liquidity Support to Banks during Indonesia's Financial Crisis", *Bulletin of Indonesian Economic Studies*, **40**, 1, pp. 59–75.

Grenville, S (2005): "Financial Sector Supervision What We Have Learned So Far", Paper Prepared for the OECD Roundtable, Tokyo, 27–28 October.

Goodhart, C (1998): *The Evolution of Central Banks*, Cambridge, MA: The MIT Press.

—— (2001): "The Organizational Structure of Banking Supervision", *FSI Occasional Papers*, no. 1, Financial Stability Institute, Basel, Switzerland.

Hupkes, E M Quintyn and M W Taylor (2005): "The Accountability of Financial Sector Supervisors: Principles and Practice", *IMF Working Paper*, WP/05/51.

IMF (2013): "Key Aspects of Macroprudential Policies".

IMF (2021): "IMF Country Report No.21/46", March.

Juhro, S M, K P Prabheesh and A Lubis (2021): "The Effectiveness of Trilemma Policy Choice in the Presence of Macroprudential Policies: Evidence from Emerging Economies", *The Singapore Economic Review*, online publication, May 18.

Mishkin, F S (1999): "Lessons from the Asian Crisis", *NBER Working Paper*, no. 7102, April.

Mohan, R (2012): "Diversity to Combat Groupthink", *OMFIF Bulletin*, May, pp. 6–7.

Mundell, R (1962): "The Appropriate Use of Monetary and Fiscal Policy for Internal and External Stability," *IMF Staff Papers*, **9**, 70–79.

Mundell, R (1963): "Capital Mobility and Stabilization Policy under Fixed and Flexible Exchange Rates", *Canadian Journal of Economics*, **29**, 475–485.

Mundell, R (1971): "The Dollar and the Policy Mix," *Essays in International Finance*, no 85.

Reinhart, C, and K Rogoff (2011): "From Financial Crash to Debt Crisis", *American Economic Review*, **101**(5), pp. 1676–1706.

Rey, H (2013): "Dilemma not Trilemma: The Global Financial Cycle and Monetary Policy independence", paper presented at the Jackson Hole Symposium, August.

Saheruddin, H (2017): "Explicit Deposit Insurance Coverage, Ownership, and Risk Taking: Evidence from a Natural Experiment", *Indonesia Deposit Insurance Corporation Research Working Paper*, November.

Siregar, R Y and W E James (2006): "Designing an Integrated Financial Supervisory Agency", *ASEAN Economic Bulletin*, Vol. 23, No. 1, pp. 98–113.

Siregar, R Y and K M Choy (2010): "Determinants of International Bank Lending from the Developed World to East Asia", *IMF Staff Paper*, Vol. 57, Issue 2, pp. 484–516.

Siregar, R Y and S W Goo (2010): "Effectiveness and Commitment to Inflation Targeting Policy: Evidences from Indonesia and Thailand", *Journal of Asian Economics*, Vo. 21, Issue 2.

Siregar, R Y (2011): "Macroprudential Approaches to Banking Regulation: Perspectives of Selected Asian Central Banks", *ADBI Working Paper Series*, No. 325, November.

Taylor, M and A Fleming (1999): "Integrated Financial Supervision: Lessons of Northern European Experience", *Policy Research Working Paper* No. 2223, World Bank, Washington, DC.

Warjiyo, P (2017): "New Framework of Central Bank Policy Mix", Lcture given at the *Workshop on Central Bank Policy Mix: Issues, Challenges, and Policies*, organized by Bank Indonesia Institute, Jakarta, 25–28 April 2017.

© 2023 World Scientific Publishing Company
https://doi.org/10.1142/9789811259432_0021

Legacy of Early Crisis and Incomplete Institutional Reforms on the Financial Sector in Indonesia: A Discussion

Perry Warjiyo

Governor, Bank Indonesia

This chapter is very well-written, addressing a critical issue in the institutional setting between monetary authority, financial system regulatory and supervisory authority and fiscal authority. It is important to define the precise role and responsibility of each institution: the fiscal policy by the Ministry of Finance, the monetary and macroprudential policies by the Central Bank (Bank Indonesia) and the individual (microprudential) supervision by the Financial Supervisory Authority (*Otoritas Jasa Keuangan* [OJK]) as well as the Deposit Insurance Corporation (*Lembaga Penjamin Simpanan* [LPS]). The key is to have independent institutions in the context of interdependence and policy coordination among the aforementioned institutions.

The central bank cannot be the only game in town. The question is: how to strengthen the coordination with other authorities? This will be the focus of my comments which will cover two aspects: the central bank policy mix and the coordination in executing the financial system stability mandate.

The central bank policy mix

Bank Indonesia is one of the pioneers in implementing the central bank policy mix: it started developing and implementing policy mix in 2010. Currently, there are many developments of policy-mix framework such as the ones in the IMF (Integrated Policy Framework), BIS and a few other central banks in emerging market economies. I am honoured to have a chance to offer Bank Indonesia's views on this matter.

We view the central bank policy mix as an extension of the Flexible Inflation Targeting Framework (FITF) for formulating and implementing monetary policy in small open economies. The monetary policy aims to achieve price stability and manage external stability through a mix of interest rate policy and foreign exchange (FX) intervention. In Indonesia, for instance, excessive volatility of exchange rates and portfolio flows poses serious risks to the inflation target and financial stability through its effect on the balance sheet of banks and corporates. Bank Indonesia intervenes in the FX market when its assessment shows that its inflation forecast is outside the target range due to exchange rate dynamics or when it aims to smooth out large exchange rate volatility due to sudden shocks to capital flows from global spillovers. The goal of the intervention is to achieve the level of exchange rates that is in line with fundamentals and market mechanisms. As mentioned in the paper, Bank Indonesia has successfully navigated various global spillovers, including taper tantrums, using the combination of interest rate policy and FX intervention.

Under the central bank policy mix, the FITF is extended further with the addition of macroprudential policy to support financial stability. The objective of macroprudential policy is to manage the procyclicality of the financial sector, achieve balanced intermediation and manage cross-section systemic risks coming from macro-financial linkages. In Indonesia, financial stability relates highly to the procyclicality of bank credits, which is linked to commodity, property and external debt cycles.

The experience in Indonesia shows that implementing the central bank policy mix suits Bank Indonesia's objectives of maintaining price stability and exchange rate stability and supporting financial system stability. This includes Bank Indonesia' experience at the beginning of the COVID-19 pandemic when it cut the policy rate, conducted FX intervention and relaxed macroprudential policy. The relaxation of the macroprudential policy is supported by the fact that the financial cycle is still below the long-run trend, hence the relaxation helps to support financial system stability. Bank Indonesia is very proud of the achievements of implementing the policy mix. I have documented Bank Indonesia's experience in my book titled *Central Bank Policy: Theory and Practice*, published in 2019.

Coordination in achieving financial stability

Now, let me turn to the second issue: strengthening the coordination and defining the clear role and responsibility of independent institutions in the context of interdependence and policy coordination among the relevant institutions. In Indonesia, financial stability is a shared responsibility under the Financial System Stability Committee (*Komite Stabilitas Sistem Keuangan* [KSSK]), which consists of Ministry of Finance with the fiscal policy mandate, Bank Indonesia with the monetary and macroprudential policy mandates, OJK with the microprudential supervision mandate and LPS with the deposit insurance function.

Let me address the three questions outlined in Section 4 of the chapter (Milestones in Indonesia's Institutional Overhauls and Unintended Consequences). The first question is regarding the role of Bank Indonesia as the lender of last resort. We have to be clear that the central bank's role as the lender of last resort is for short-term liquidity support for solvent banks and not for insolvent banks. However, in Indonesia, there is no clear mechanism for the resolution of insolvent banks, which may include closure, new investors or early intervention. The issue is not about the coordination between Bank Indonesia and OJK, but the unclear early resolution mechanism between OJK and LPS. There should be an expansion of LPS' mandates to give an early intervention power and mechanism to deal with insolvent banks (early resolution). With the new mandate, the role and responsibility of LPS will be clear and would allow them to address the problem with insolvent banks.

The second question is on the coordination between Bank Indonesia and OJK. Under the current arrangements, the coordination between Bank Indonesia and OJK has been significantly improved through regular meetings and a clear mechanism of macroprudential and microprudential supervisions for systemic and non-systemic banks. In the case of systemic banks, coordination on determining the list is already set out clearly by the Law. The resolution approach is also clear under the KSSK: bail-in rather than bailout. In the case of a bailout, there will be government bond issuance which the central bank can purchase. The issue is on insolvent non-systemic banks, and one solution is giving the early resolution mandate to LPS.

The last question is on the KKSK decision-making process. There are two possible options: consensus-based or giving veto rights to the Minister of Finance. The first option is the existing decision-making process which usually takes more time but will allow for checks and balances and shared responsibility and accountability among the members. The second option of giving the Minister of Finance veto rights expedites the decision-making process but reduces the checks and balances. Giving the Minister of Finance veto rights also means that the Minister will assume the sole responsibility, which may not be preferable under the current political arrangements.

Final remarks

The chapter is well written and highlights lessons that can be drawn from Indonesia's experience as Bank Indonesia reforms its policy mix and institutional arrangements related to financial system stability, especially related to the independence of institutions in the context of interdependence and policy coordination among institutions.

References

Gopinath, Gita. 2019. "A Case for An Integrated Policy Framework", Remarks at the Overview Panel of the Jackson Hole Economic Policy Symposium. Available at https://www.kansascityfed.org/documents/6966/GopinathPaper_JH2019.pdf

Warjiyo, Perry and Solikin M. Juhro. 2019. *Central Bank Policy: Theory and Practice*. Emerald Publishing.

CHAPTER 11

Chapter 11

Lessons from Macro-Financial Policy in Korea*

Hyun Song Shin and Kwanho Shin

Bank for International Settlements
Korea University

1. Introduction

The goal of macroprudential frameworks is to moderate the procyclicality of the financial system and thereby secure resilience and stability of the financial system as a whole. The experience of Korea since the Great Financial Crisis (GFC) of 2008 provides an informative window on both the theory and the practice of macroprudential frameworks, and how such frameworks have been adapted in the light of shifting vulnerabilities. These shifting vulnerabilities in turn reflect underlying shifts in the pattern of financial intermediation. In this chapter, we will review the recent experience of Korea in the implementation of macroprudential policies and draw major lessons from it.

Korea is a useful backdrop to study two themes that run through the recent global experience. The first theme is the changing patterns of financial intermediation from banks to capital markets, and the changes in the way that procyclicality of financial conditions manifests itself. The

---

*The authors are grateful to Ilhyock Shim, Hwanseok Lee and other conference participants for their comments. The authors thank Hyein Han and Jongwon Kim for their excellent research assistance. Kwanho Shin gratefully acknowledges financial support from the Bank for International Settlements.

crises of 1997 and 2008 were centred on wholesale funding of the banking sector, especially the dollar-denominated, short-term, non-core liabilities of the banking sector. However, the period following the GFC has seen a moderation of the banking sector fluctuations. The focus has increasingly moved to the bond market, especially the local-currency-denominated segment of government bonds. At the same time, Korea's relationship with the rest of the global financial system has seen a notable shift. Increasingly, the external fixed income assets of Korean residents through pension funds and life insurance companies and the associated FX-hedging activities through the FX swap market have changed the way that dollar-funding pressures become visible during times of financial stress. The widening of the FX basis vis-à-vis the US dollar during the March 2020 COVID-19 stress period was especially notable in the case of the Korean won.

This leads naturally to the second theme that runs throughout our chapter, which is the role played by external financial conditions and the impact of exchange rate fluctuations on domestic financial conditions. The 1997 crisis in Korea underscored the vulnerabilities of the "twin mismatch" of currency and maturity mismatches on the balance sheet. Dollar funding pressures were amplified by this twin mismatch. The development of a deep and liquid local currency sovereign bond market was motivated by the objective of reducing or eliminating the twin mismatch by issuing bonds in domestic currency and by borrowing in long maturities. However, the participation of global investors in the local currency bond market has meant that a tightening of global financial conditions is reflected in the exit or ex post hedging by such investors, such that issuing domestic currency instruments has not proved to be sufficient to insulate the borrower from fluctuations in global financial conditions. Carstens and Shin (2019) have dubbed this migration of the currency risk from the borrower's balance sheet to the investor's balance sheet as "Original Sin Redux".

Korea's local currency bond market has grown in size and depth from local investor participation, such that foreign investors form a relatively small proportion of the total holdings, compared to major emerging market economies (EMEs). Instead, the growing heft of the domestic institutional investor base has meant that dollar funding pressures have increasingly exhibited themselves through deviations from covered interest parity — where the dollar interest rate implicit in forward exchange rates indicate greater dollar funding needs relative to money market rates. The sharp widening of the FX basis in the USD–KRW swap market gives a vivid lesson on the changes that have taken place in the FX market. The dollar funding pressures were exacerbated by the spike in dollar demand on the part of securities firms that were under pressure to meet increased margins. The hedging demand for dollars by issuers of retail structured products in the equity market — the so-called equity-linked securities (ELS) — was important.

The FX-hedging demand for foreign bonds by Korean institutional investors and the margin adjustments associated with ELS illustrate the changing role of Korea as increasingly being a creditor to the rest of the world. Nevertheless, the dollar funding stresses that appeared in March 2020 have underlined the importance of a macroprudential mindset, and the continual updating of the tools and policies of central banks and policy authorities, to meet the new challenges ahead.

2. Macro-financial landscape

We begin by summarising a few salient features of the macro-financial landscape in Korea, as reflected in a number of key aggregate time series and their time series properties. Following the band-pass filtering methods of Christiano and Fitzgerald (2003) allows us to focus on a few notable features that anticipate some of the key themes in our chapter. Drehmann *et al.* (2012) and Borio (2014) have popularised the use of the band-pass filter method for financial cycles. Aikman *et al.* (2015) is another example of the application of such methods for slow-moving credit aggregates in the economy.

We apply the band-pass method to four series: (1) non-core liabilities of the banking sector as percentage of M2 (non-core/M2), (2) credit to GDP ratio (credit/GDP), (3) stock price index deflated by CPI (equity) and (4) housing price index deflated by CPI (housing price).

Following Shin and Shin (2011), we calculate non-core liabilities of the banking sector by summing up foreign borrowing, debt securities, repos, promissory notes and certificate of deposits. Hahm *et al.* (2013) find that non-core banking sector liabilities serve as a good indicator of the vulnerability to a crisis in EMEs. The sample period is from 1991Q1 to 2020Q4. Following Aikman et al. (2015), we examine two frequencies. Medium-term cycles capture fluctuations within 8–20 years, while short-term cycles comprise fluctuations within the two- to eight-year range. The short-term frequency matches the focus relevant to typical business cycle fluctuations, while the medium-term cycles are aimed at slower-moving series that are typical of credit and funding aggregates.

Table 1 reports the summary statistics of the four financial series before the band-pass filter is applied. We report them for both the full sample period and a sub-sample period that starts from 2010Q3. We consider the sub-sample period from 2010Q3 to focus attention on the post-GFC experience, as well as to take account of the introduction of major macroprudential policy initiatives in Korea in 2010Q2, to be described below. Overall, the mean growth rate of financial variables is lower than that of real GDP. We calculate time differences, instead of growth rates, for non-core/M2 and credit/GDP.

However, the standard deviation of financial variables is generally higher than that of real GDP. In the sub-sample period, the standard deviation of both financial and real variables is lowered.[1] As far as

Table 1. Summary statistics of financial indices and real GDP.

Variables	Whole Sample (1991Q1–2020Q4)					2010Q3–2020Q4				
	Count	Mean	SD	Min	Max	Count	Mean	SD	Min	Max
Non-core/M2	119	0.004	1.28	−4.14	3.39	42	−0.34	0.68	−2.06	1.77
Credit/GDP	118	0.83	2.30	−8.30	6.42	41	0.99	1.55	−1.63	5.87
Real House prices	118	−0.14	2.31	−9.82	7.03	41	0.00	0.95	−1.78	1.66
Real KOSPI	118	0.30	12.49	−51.42	38.14	41	0.38	5.36	−12.13	11.96
Real GDP	119	1.16	1.35	−6.80	4.40	41	0.63	0.82	−3.20	2.10

Note: We calculate quarterly time-differences for non-core/M2 and credit/GDP and quarterly growth rates for housing price index (for Seoul), KOSPI index and real GDP. The whole sample period is from 1991Q1 to 2020Q4.
Source: Authors' calculations.

---

[1] Except for the period of the Asian Financial Crisis in 1997–1998, the macroeconomic stability of Korea has continued to improve since 1970, resulting in a gradual decline in the volatility of the economic growth rate and inflation (Lee, 2009).

non-core/M2, credit/GDP and real GDP are concerned, even their mean growth rates are lowered in the sub-sample period.

Figures 1 and 2 plot short-term and medium-term cycles, respectively, of the four financial variables and real GDP. We also apply the same band-pass filter to derive short-term frequency (business cycles) and medium-term frequency fluctuations of real GDP. The vertical lines represent financial crises in 1997 and 2008, respectively. In both Figures 1 and 2, we can clearly see that the volatility of financial cycles is much higher than that of real GDP. In both figures, we notice that the volatility of both financial and real cycles is lowered after the 2008 crisis. In Figure 1, which

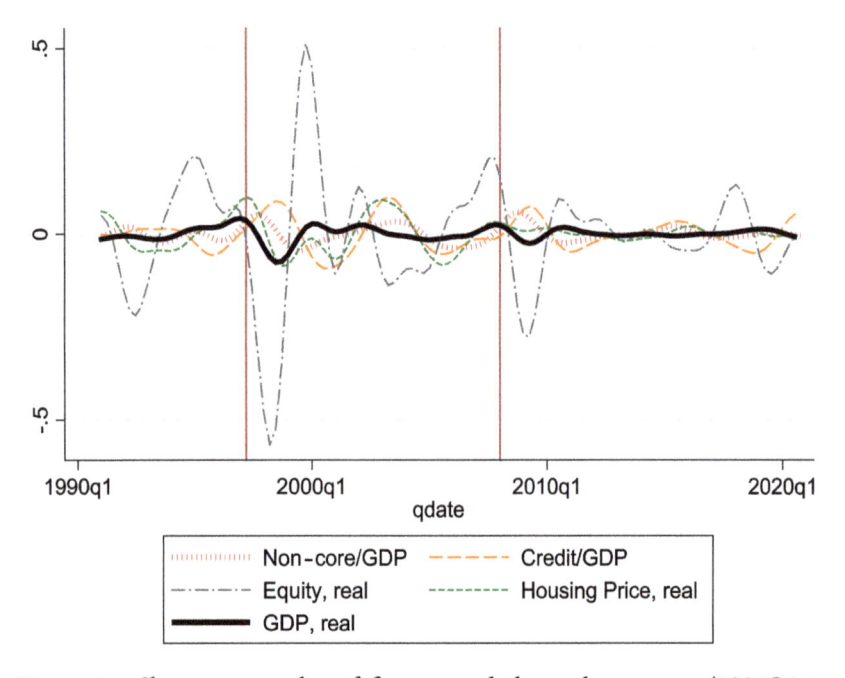

Figure 1. Short-term cycles of finance and the real economy (1991Q1 to 2020Q4).

Note: Following Shin and Shin (2011), we calculate non-core liabilities of the banking sector by summing up foreign borrowing, debt securities, repos, promissory notes and certificate of deposits. Credit refers to the sum of household and corporate. Equity is Kospi index. Housing price refers to housing purchasing price index for Seoul provided by KB Kookmin Bank. We apply a bad-pass filter developed by Christiano and Fitzgerald (2003). Following Aikman *et al.* (2015), short-term cycles comprise fluctuations within the two- to eight-year range. The two vertical lines correspond to the 1997 and 2008 crises.
Source: Authors' calculations.

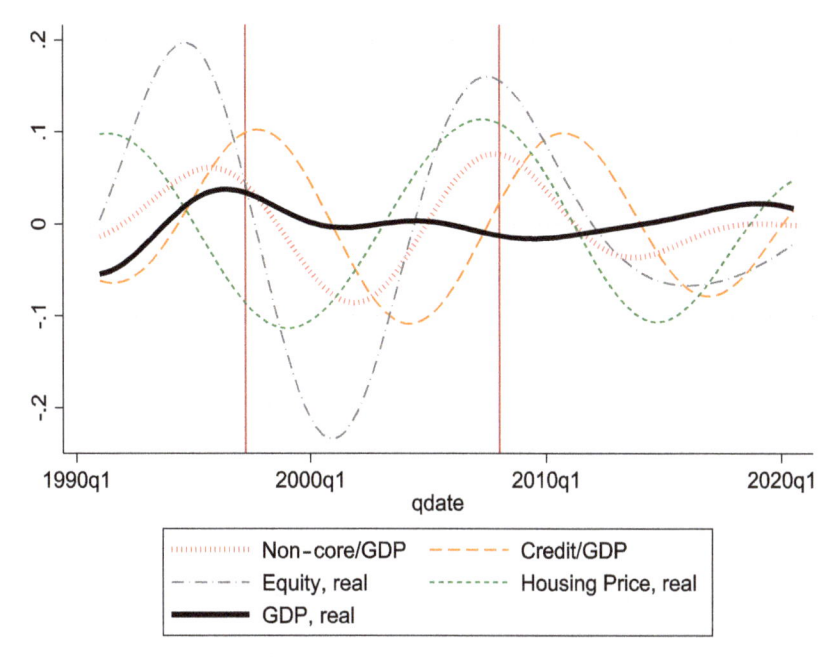

Figure 2. Medium-term cycles of finance and the real economy (1991Q1–2020Q4).

Note: We apply a bad-pass filter developed by Christiano and Fitzgerald (2003). Following Aikman *et al.* (2015), medium-term cycles comprise fluctuations within the 8- to 20-year range. The two vertical lines correspond to the 1997 and 2008 crises. For others, see notes for Figure 1.

Source: Authors' calculations.

shows short-term cycles, we do not find financial booms before the two financial crises except for a boom of housing price before the 1997 crisis and a boom of equity before the 2008 crisis.

In contrast, Figure 2, which shows medium-term cycles, exhibits financial booms that are almost always found around the two financial crises. In this sense, we provide support for the hypothesis that medium-term financial cycles are more closely associated with the financial crisis and the resulting downturn in the real economy. In particular, the peak of the non-core/M2 cycle is most closely located to the start of both financial crises. The peak of the credit/GDP cycle is also informative, although it is lagging the financial crises. While the peaks of equity and housing price cycles are located close to the start of 2008 crisis, they preceded the 1997 crisis for years.

Table 2. Characteristics of short-term and medium-term cycles of financial variables and real GDP (1991Q1–2020Q4).

Short-term Cycles	Volatility	Amplitude Expansion	Amplitude Contraction	Duration Expansion	Duration Contraction	Cycles
Noncore/M2	0.022	0.058	−0.043	10.00	7.00	19.00
Credit/GDP	0.043	0.117	−0.123	10.50	9.00	22.00
Real House prices	0.041	0.12	−0.05	11.00	6.00	21.00
Real KOSPI	0.161	0.344	−0.265	6.00	6.00	15.00
Real GDP	0.019	0.043	−0.043	11.00	6.00	21.50
Medium-term Cycles						
Non-core/M2	0.044	0.100	−0.113	22.50	24.00	46.50
Credit/GDP	0.067	0.167	−0.194	25.00	25.50	45.50
Real House prices	0.076	0.191	−0.216	28.00	30.50	58.50
Real KOSPI	0.119	0.394	−0.329	26.00	29.50	51.00
Real GDP	0.019	0.023	−0.031	25.00	20.00	45.00

Note: Medium- and short-term cycles are derived from a bad-pass filter developed by Christiano and Fitzgerald (2003) that comprise fluctuations within the 8- to 20-year and 2- to 8-year ranges, respectively.
Source: Authors' calculations.

In Table 2, we report the median volatility, amplitude and duration of both short-term and medium-term cycles of financial variables and real GDP. The volatility is measured by the standard deviation of the cyclical component. To calculate the amplitude and duration of cycles, we identify peaks and troughs that are defined as local maxima and minima. The amplitudes of expansion and contraction are defined as differences in the variable from a trough to the next peak and from a peak to the next trough, respectively. The duration of cycles is defined as the period from a peak to the next peak or from a trough to the next trough.

For short-term cycles, the volatility of other financial variables is approximately twice the volatility of real GDP, but the volatility of non-core/M2 is comparable to that of real GDP. The volatility of the Equity series is much larger than that of real GDP. The duration of financial variables and real GDP is approximately the same.

In the medium-term cycles, the volatility of financial variables is much larger than that of real GDP. Even without including Equity, whose volatility is the largest, the average volatility of financial variables is about three times as large as that of real GDP. The average amplitude of financial variables is even larger: their average is, without including Equity, about six times as large as that of real GDP. In contrast, the duration of financial variables is marginally longer than that of real GDP.

Fluctuations in capital flows have been an important element of past financial stresses in Korea. Figure 3 presents gross and net capital inflows, and the exchange rate against the US dollar. A sharp depreciation of the Korean won (a sharp increase in the exchange rate series) is associated with sudden reversals in capital inflows. Capital inflows have been associated with domestic credit expansions (IMF, 2017), and provide a point of contact between external financial conditions and domestic credit growth.

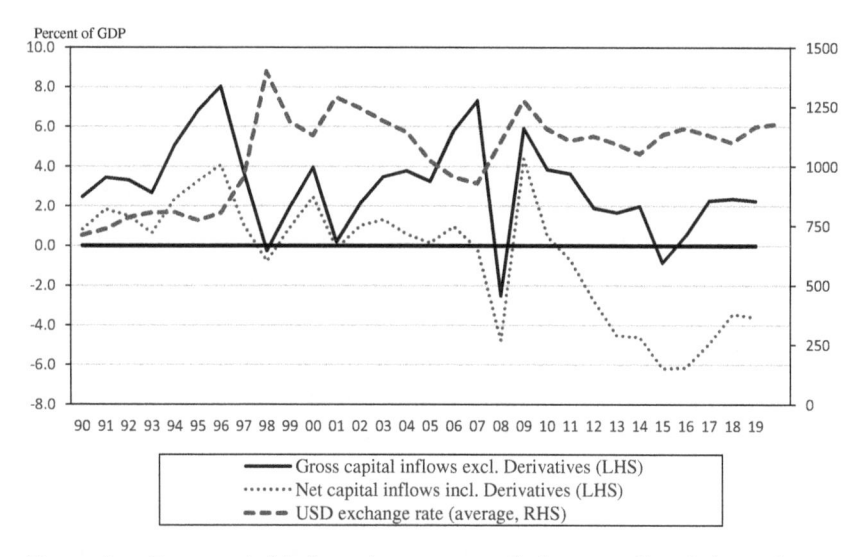

Figure 3. Gross capital inflows (percentage of gdp, annual) and the exchange rate (1990–2019).
Note: Gross (net) capital inflows are divided by nominal GDP to calculate percentage of GDP. The exchange rate is against the U.S dollar averaged over year.
Source: Authors' calculations based on the Bank of Korea database.

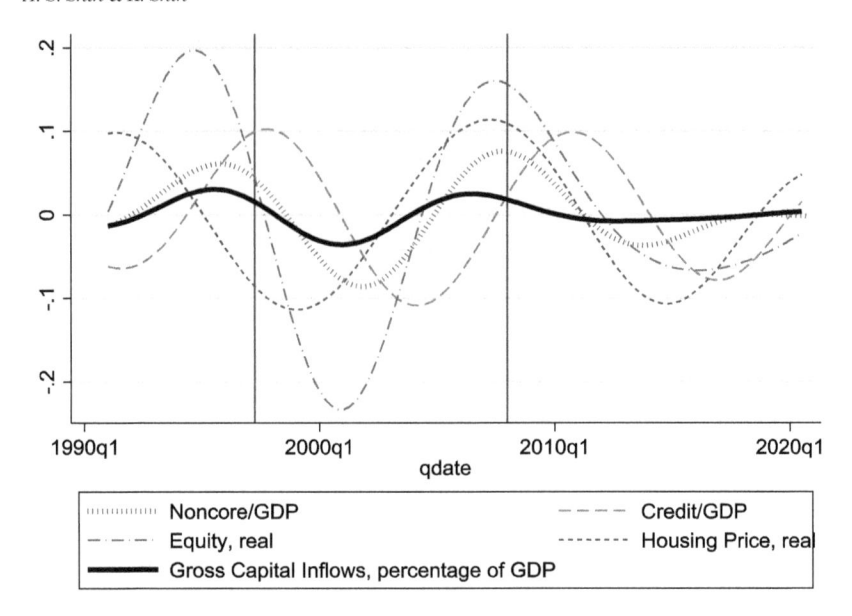

Figure 4. Medium-term cycles of finance and gross capital inflows (1991Q1–2020Q4).
Note: We apply a bad-pass filter developed by Christiano and Fitzgerald (2003). Following Aikman *et al.* (2015), medium-term cycles comprise fluctuations within the 8- to 20-year range. The two vertical lines correspond to the 1997 and 2008 crises. For others, see notes for Figure 1.
Source: Authors' calculations.

In Figure 4, we present medium-term cycles of gross capital inflows along with other financial series at the same medium-term frequency. In Figure 4, we find that at least before the 2008 crisis, gross capital inflows and other financial variables tended to co-move over the medium-term cycles. Hence there is a possibility that gross capital inflows are a major factor driving medium-term financial cycles. Like other financial cycles, though, the volatility of gross capital inflows was lowered after the 2008 crisis.

In Table 3, we report the time series properties of our financial series by examining the dynamic cross-correlations between gross capital inflows and other financial variables over the medium-term frequency, up to five-quarter lags and leads. Non-core/M2 is highly correlated with both lags and leads of gross capital inflows, with the correlation ranging from 0.52 to 0.95. It is more highly correlated with lags than leads of gross capital

Table 3. Dynamic correlations between financial variables and gross capital inflows over medium-term cycles.

(a) Whole sample, 1991Q1–2020Q4

	Correlation with Gross Capital Inflow/GDP$_t$										
	$t-5$	$t-4$	$t-3$	$t-2$	$t-1$	t	$t+1$	$t+2$	$t+3$	$t+4$	$t+5$
Noncore/M2	0.92	0.94	0.95	0.95	0.93	0.89	0.84	0.78	0.70	0.61	0.52
Credit/GDP	0.55	0.47	0.38	0.28	0.18	0.07	−0.04	−0.15	−0.25	−0.35	−0.45
Housing Price	0.24	0.30	0.36	0.41	0.46	0.51	0.55	0.60	0.63	0.66	0.68
Equity	0.72	0.78	0.83	0.87	0.90	0.91	0.91	0.89	0.86	0.81	0.76

Note: We report the dynamic cross-correlations between gross capital inflows and other financial variables over medium-term frequency up to five-quarter lags and leads during the whole sample period from 1991Q1–2020Q4.
Source: Authors' calculations.

(b) Sub-sample, 2010Q3–2020Q4

	Correlation with Gross Capital Inflow/GDP$_t$										
	$t-5$	$t-4$	$t-3$	$t-2$	$t-1$	t	$t+1$	$t+2$	$t+3$	$t+4$	$t+5$
Non-core/M2	0.53	0.59	0.64	0.68	0.71	0.73	0.66	0.59	0.52	0.45	0.39
Credit/GDP	0.11	0.04	−0.03	−0.11	−0.20	−0.29	−0.42	−0.53	−0.62	−0.69	−0.75
Housing Price	0.66	0.70	0.74	0.77	0.79	0.80	0.68	0.56	0.44	0.33	0.23
Equity	0.25	0.21	0.17	0.11	0.05	−0.03	−0.17	−0.30	−0.40	−0.48	−0.55

Note: We report the dynamic cross-correlations between gross capital inflows and other financial variables over medium-term frequency up to five-quarter lags and leads during the sub-sample period from 2010Q3–2020Q4.
Source: Authors' calculations

inflows, suggesting that capital inflows drive cycles of non-core/M2, not vice versa. Credit/GDP is also quite highly correlated, but with only lags of gross capital inflows, with the correlation value ranging from 0.18 to 0.55. Housing price and Equity are also highly correlated with both lags and leads of gross capital inflows, with the correlation value ranging from 0.24 to 0.68 and from 0.72 to 0.91, respectively. In the sub-sample period of 2012Q3–2020Q4, the correlations between financial variables and gross capital inflows are generally still positive, at least for lagged values, but much lowered except for housing price, for which the correlation is approximately the same.

3. Monetary and macroprudential policy framework

A key aim of macroprudential policy is to moderate the procyclicality of the financial system and it does so by influencing the financial intermediation process; it operates on the assets, liabilities and leverage of intermediaries. In this respect, macroprudential policy and monetary policy share some common themes (Figure 5).

For instance, both policies affect the *demand for credit* by reallocating spending over time, by either postponing spending (i.e., by inducing consumers and firms to borrow less) or bringing forward spending (i.e., by inducing them to borrow more). Both policies affect the *supply of credit* by influencing the funding cost of the intermediary. Macroprudential policies aim to reduce risk-taking by constraining leverage, both of borrowers and of financial intermediaries. Even here, the parallels with monetary policy turn out to be closer than may be appreciated at first glance. The so-called "risk-taking channel" of monetary policy points to monetary policy working through intermediary leverage and risk-taking more generally.[2]

However, there are two important differences between monetary policy and macroprudential policy. The first difference is that macroprudential policy is aimed at specific sectors or practices. In some respects, macroprudential policy harks back to the directed credit policies used by many advanced economies up to the 1970s, although these were used

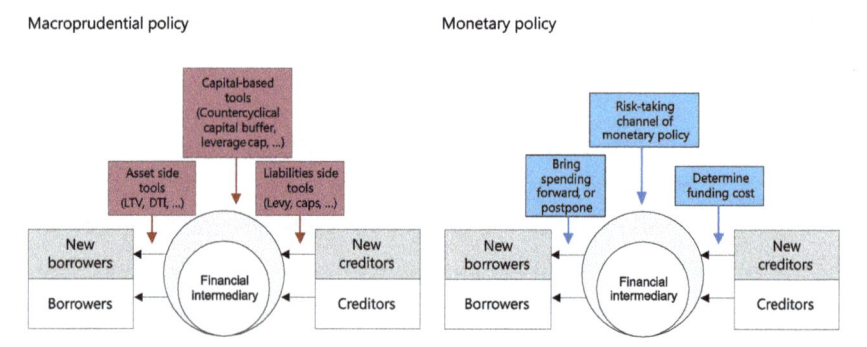

Figure 5. Comparison of macroprudential policy with monetary policy.

---

[2] The term "risk-taking channel" was coined in Borio and Zhu (2012). Empirical studies have pointed to monetary policy shocks being a key determinant of intermediary leverage. See Bruno and Shin (2015).

to channel credit to favoured sectors, as well as to constrain credit. In contrast, monetary policy influences risk-taking more broadly, both within the domestic financial system but also across borders, and is harder to circumvent.

On the other hand, the broader impact of monetary policy cuts both ways; domestic monetary policy is constrained by global conditions. This is the second difference between monetary policy and macroprudential policy. Korea's experience illustrates well how the exchange rate and global financial conditions are relevant for macroeconomic fluctuations.

The monetary policy framework in Korea was shaped in the aftermath of the Asian Financial Crisis of 1997, through an amendment of the Bank of Korea Act in 1998 that spelled out the mandate of the Bank of Korea in terms of price stability.

The Bank of Korea adopted the framework of inflation targeting, with the target being 3 percent initially but then lowered to 2 percent in 2016. However, inflation realisations have been low. Since 2012, the inflation rate has undershot the target, even after the inflation target was lowered to 2 percent in 2016. CPI inflation rate was rarely above the new target of 2 percent and stayed much lower. In August 2019, the headline CPI inflation rate was –0.04 percent, the first negative reading in history.

In Figure 6, we plot the policy rate along with the CPI inflation rate and its targets. As the CPI inflation rate quickly declined in 2012, the Bank of Korea began to gradually lower the policy rate, but the financial stability implications posed a conundrum. Figure 6 illustrates how the Bank of Korea has been pulled in two different directions in the conduct of monetary policy. During the period denoted with a circle, the Bank of Korea raised the policy rate twice despite of the continuous decline in the inflation rate.

Figure 7 presents the growth rate of household debt and its share as a percentage of disposable income. The growth rate peaked at 11.6 percent in the fourth quarter of 2016 and remained above 10 percent until the second quarter of 2017. The share of household debt as a percentage of disposable income also rapidly increased in 2016 and 2017. According to Figure 4, housing price cycles hit a bottom in 2015 and started to rise rapidly from 2016. Figure 8 also shows that housing price, which had been stagnating for a long time, began to rise again in 2015. All of these

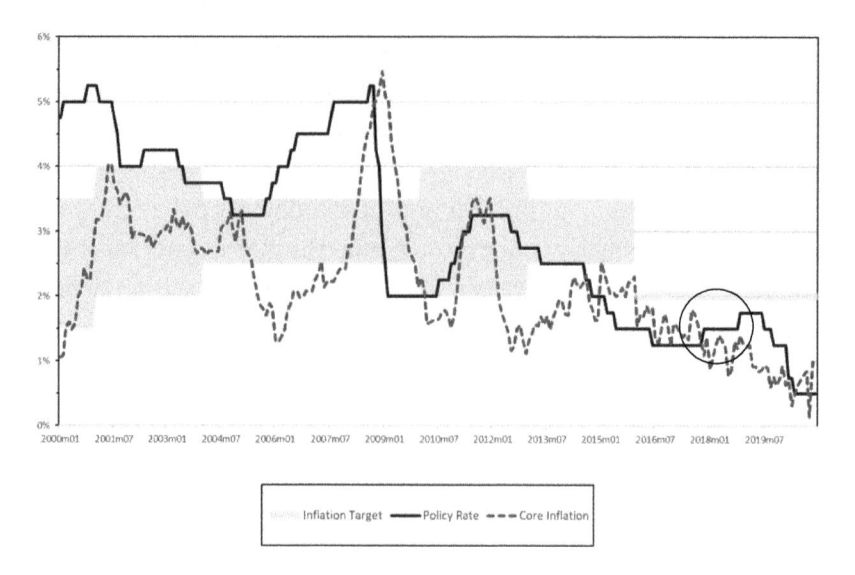

Figure 6. CPI inflation and policy rate (2000M1–2020M12).
Note: CPI inflation rate is year on year changes. The inflation target was a 1 percent or 2 percent range but changed to a single point in 2016.
Source: The Bank of Korea.

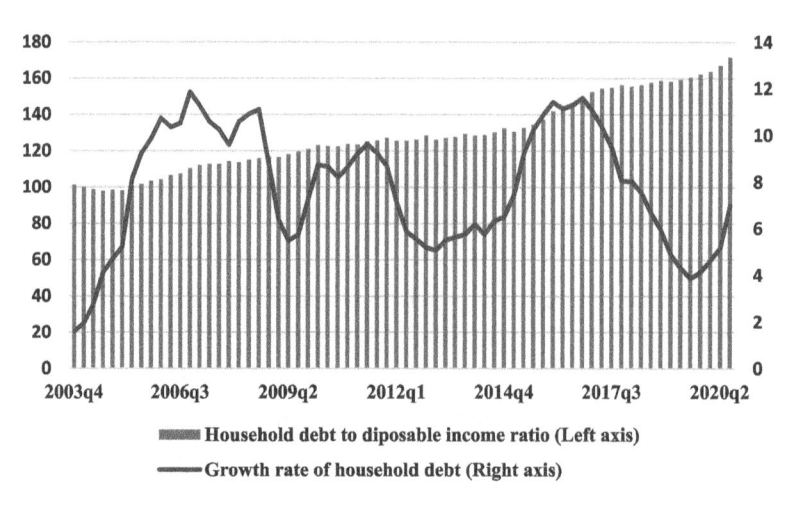

Figure 7. Household debt growth and its share as percentage of disposable income.
Source: The Bank of Korea.

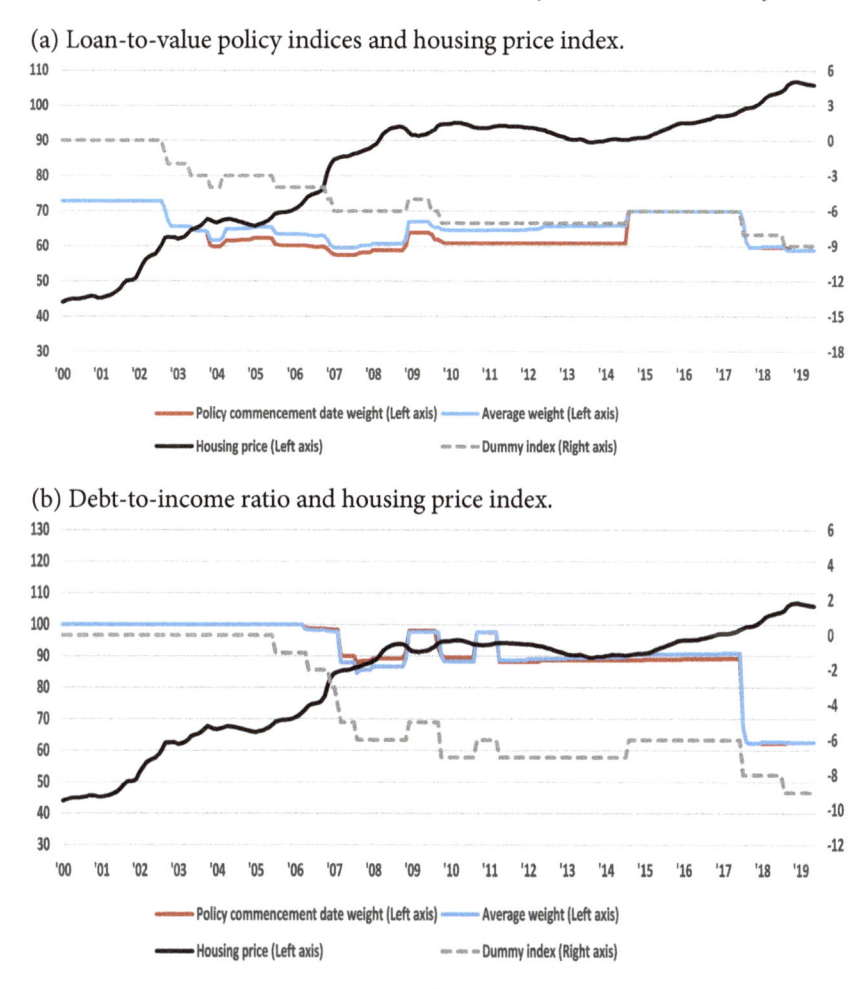

(a) Loan-to-value policy indices and housing price index.

(b) Debt-to-income ratio and housing price index.

Figure 8. Macroprudential policies of loan to value and debt-to-income ratio (2000M01–2019M05).
Source: Kim and Oh (2020) and the Bank of Korea.

combined meant an indication of financial instability, and made it difficult for the Bank of Korea to actively respond to lowered inflation rate.

The focus of the monetary policy mandate on inflation targeting was also reflected in the changes in the institutional arrangements, where the banking supervision function was carved out of the Bank of Korea. The amendment to the Bank of Korea Act in 1998 enhanced the independence of the Bank of Korea but transferred the supervisory office to a new entity, Financial Supervisory Commission (FSC) that was placed in charge of overseeing all financial institutions, including commercial banks, securities firms and insurance companies.

The amendment of the Bank of Korea Act in 2011 incorporated financial stability as a secondary objective of the Bank of Korea. Monetary policy was seen as affecting risk-taking and financial stability, but the primary mandate remained the inflation objective. The conventional approach (for instance, Bernanke [2011]) has been to allocate roles to monetary policy and financial supervision such that monetary policy focuses on macroeconomic objectives and macroprudential tools are used to address risks to financial stability.

In line with this approach, the macroprudential tools to achieve financial stability have not been assigned to the Bank of Korea. Currently, the Financial Supervisory Service (the front-line supervisory agency, renamed from Financial Supervisory Commission) and the Financial Services Commission (a separate oversight body) are jointly responsible for macroprudential as well as microprudential policies for financial stability.

A coordinating committee (Macroeconomic and Financial Policy Meeting) that convened the Finance Ministry, the Financial Services Commission, Financial Supervisory Service and Korea Deposit Insurance Corporation was established in 2012. However, meetings were intermittent until 2018. The COVID-19 pandemic has injected urgency into more meaningful coordination of policies. From November 2020, the committee has adopted regular monthly meetings with the goal of monitoring macroprudential soundness, and to efficiently and systematically carry out cooperation among related organisations.[3]

One main issue has been how the Bank of Korea coordinates with other prudential regulators in the conduct of macroprudential policies. The most important concern is that despite the addition of a financial stability objective to the goals of the central bank, the Bank of Korea has no tools in place (other than monetary policy) to address financial stability objectives. For example, in 2014, the regulations on the real estate market were loosened by the government to boost the economy,

---

[3] See regulations on the establishment and operation of Macroeconomic and Financial Policy Meeting under Presidential Decree No. 429.

and the Bank of Korea also lowered its policy rate following its price stability mandate, resulting in a surge in household debt. The reluctance to lower interest rates in response to the decline in inflation reflects the tension that, while the Bank of Korea has a financial stability mandate as a secondary objective, it lacks the tools to pursue that goal, other than monetary policy itself.

Although the conventional approach is to follow the division of roles whereby macroprudential policy focuses on financial stability, while monetary policy is devoted to price and economic stability, Kim and Mehrotra (2018) show that monetary and macroprudential policies both affect financial and real variables in similar ways. To the extent that monetary policy and macroprudential policy have similar effects on financial stability as well as macroeconomic aggregates such as real GDP and the price level, a clean division of the roles will prove challenging. However, the mandate of the Bank of Korea is clear — its primary mandate is to focus on its inflation objectives.

Some evidence points to complementarity between monetary and macroprudential policies when considering their impact on constraining credit growth, although results vary by type of shock.[4] Bruno *et al.* (2017) show that when macroprudential tools are actually employed in practice, they tend to be employed in the same direction as monetary policy.[5] In other words, a tightening of macroprudential instruments tend to go hand-in-hand with a tighter monetary policy stance. In any event, there is little dispute that the central bank is best-placed in providing the overall picture of macro-developments. Beyond this, the absence of a formal role in macroprudential policymaking can be seen as a gap in the current institutional arrangements.[6]

---

[4] See IMF (2013), Cerutti *et al.* (2015), Kuttner and Shim (2016) and Akinci and Olmstead-Rumsey (2018).

[5] See also Chapter 15 in this volume that show interactions between monetary policy and macroprudential regulation.

[6] See Kim *et al.* (2016) for suggestions on cooperation between the Bank of Korea and other authorities. Osiński *et al.* (2013) stress that the clarification of respective mandates, functions and toolkits maximises synergies and limits the potentially negative consequences among policymakers involved.

4. Experience of macroprudential policymaking in Korea

Macroprudential policy in Korea before the GFC was aimed at slowing the housing market and household mortgages. The most frequently used policies were (1) loan-to-value (LTV), (2) debt service-to-income (DTI), (3) real estate tax and (4) risk-weights and provisioning (IMF, 2017). Korea is one of the few countries where LTV and DTI measures were regularly used before the GFC. IMF (2019a) finds that these macroprudential measures have been effective in mitigating credit growth and housing cycles in Korea.[7]

Figure 8 illustrates how LTV and DTI indices along with the housing index have evolved over time.[8] In Figure 8(a), three indices of LTV, constructed by Kim and Oh (2020), are presented. The dummy index represents adding 1 or subtracting 1 depending on whether a newly implemented LTV measure is tightening or loosening conditions, without incorporating the intensity of the measure. They also constructed two more LTV indices that used weights on the coverage of policies. The first weighted index (policy commencement date weight) used the intensity of the measure on the commencement date, while the second one (average weight) used the average intensity during the sample period. Figure 8(a) shows that an LTV measure was introduced as early as September 2002 in Korea. After that, LTV measures were used quite actively. Figure 8(b) illustrates three similarly constructed, indices of DTI. The DTI measure began to take effect in July 2005, somewhat later than the LTV measure, but has been also used regularly since then.

There have been many studies that investigate the impact of LTV and DTI measures based on the experiences of Korea, and they have come to similar conclusions — that the policies indeed had some traction. An evaluation of the LTV and DTI measures in Korea was made by Choongsoo Kim (2013), a former governor of the Bank of Korea. According to the study, the two measures (LTV and DTI) were adjusted in a broadly countercyclical manner, quite successfully containing financial risks in the housing market. IMF (2019b) also confirms that tightening LTV and DTI

---

[7] As pointed out by Kim and Oh (2020), however, these policies have limitations that they were also used not only for financial stability purpose but also to stimulate the economy.
[8] We thank Soyoung Kim for sharing the data.

regulations in Korea enhanced the banking system's resilience to house price and income shocks by dampening the procyclicality of the housing price. Jung and Lee (2017) find that DTI measures were more effective than LTV measures in stabilizing house prices in Korea. Kim and Oh (2020) also show that LTV and DTI measures have significant effects on house prices and household bank loans, particularly when both policies are implemented together.

We now turn to the external dimension. The external dimension of macroprudential frameworks associated with capital flows has been important in Korea, and it is this aspect that has attracted the most attention after the GFC. Korea has built on the lessons from the crises of 1997 and then again in 2008 to pioneer new approaches to macroprudential policies aimed at mitigating risks from the external sector and episodes of capital flow booms and subsequent reversals.

Following the 1997 Asian Financial Crisis, the Bank of Korea moved to an inflation-targeting regime with floating exchange rates.[9] However, the role of the exchange rate in the monetary policy framework has taken on added significance due to the financial channel of exchange rates, as discussed in the BIS Annual Economic Report of 2019 (BIS, 2019, Chapter II). The main complicating factor is that exchange rate fluctuations can influence economic activity through real and financial channels. The trade competitiveness channel operates through net exports. This channel is well-known and standard in open-economy macro models. In contrast, the financial channel operates through exchange rate fluctuations which trigger valuation changes, balance-sheet adjustments and shifts in risk-taking, both in financial and real assets, with an impact on the real economy. Although the financial channel of exchange rates has historically been less prominent than the net exports channel, it has become more important with the greater integration of the global financial system in recent years.

Crucially, the financial channel of exchange rate fluctuations often operates in the opposite direction relative to the net exports channel.

---

[9] According to the *de jure* classifications, Korea moved from the market average exchange rate system to the floating exchange rate system in December 1997. However, according to the IMF, Korea adopted a managed floating regime before the 1997 crisis and moved to a floating exchange rate regime afterwards. However, Reinhart and Rogoff (2004) classify Korea's exchange rate regime before the 1997 crisis as a crawling peg regime.

Under the net exports channel, it is when the domestic currency *depreciates* that real economic activity picks up. In contrast, the financial channel operates through the easing of global financial conditions that accompanies a weaker dollar. During these episodes, there is a broad strengthening of emerging market currencies, such that a stronger domestic currency is associated with easier domestic financial conditions and stronger real activity (Bruno and Shin, 2015).

Given its history, a major focus of macroprudential policy in Korea has been on mitigating risks from the external sector, including using capital flow management measures.[10] To address the twin mismatches of currency and maturity mismatches that were identified in the 1997 crisis, the Korean government introduced regulations on the liquidity ratio and the gap ratio for foreign currency.[11] Despite these regulations, the Korean economy experienced again financial vulnerability during the GFC in 2008. As argued by Park and Shin (2020) and Shim and Shin (2021), an interconnected global financial system brings issues of spillovers to the fore. The interconnected nature of global banking and the wholesale dollar funding associated with it were important channels that transmitted the shocks hitting advanced economy banking systems to other connected financial systems. As a manifestation of these channels, short-term cross-border bank borrowing increased rapidly in Korea, fuelled by interoffice funding from headquarters to branches operating in Korea, which turned out to be the most important factor causing financial instability when the flows reversed.

Macroprudential measures were introduced after the GFC, aimed at curbing the reliance of the banking sector on short-term wholesale funding denominated in foreign currency. Bruno and Shin (2014) examine the impact of these macroprudential tools. The toolkit consisted of (1) a leverage cap on the notional value of foreign exchange derivatives contracts; (2) a levy on the non-core liabilities of the banks and (3) a normalisation of tax exemptions for foreign investors. Bruno and Shin (2014) find that these measures were effective in lowering the sensitivity of bank capital flows to shifts in global conditions. Additional liquidity measures such as liquidity coverage ratio of both domestic and foreign

---

[10] See IMF (2019b) for various interpretations of capital flow management measures.
[11] See Lee (2013) for details.

currencies were introduced in 2015. Kim and Lee (2017) also find that these macroprudential tools were effective in curbing excessive capital inflows to Korea. As noted in Section 2, the amplitude of the financial cycle has substantially decreased since the third quarter of 2010, suggesting that these measures are working properly.

Figure 9 shows gross capital inflows by type along with the exchange rate against the US dollar for each year from 1990 to 2019. It is evident that the sharp depreciation of the Korean won is closely associated with the sudden reversal in capital inflows. Decomposing capital inflows into FDI, portfolio equity, portfolio debt and bank borrowings shows that bank borrowings are most closely related to the exchange rate movement. This was the reason externally oriented macroprudential measures in Korea were focused on controlling bank borrowings. Since short-term borrowings were easily reversed, the key goal of capital flow management measures was to reduce their procyclical tendencies. Figure 10(a) shows that short-term borrowings declined drastically in the run-up to the GFC, causing sharp depreciation of the exchange rate. They remained stable

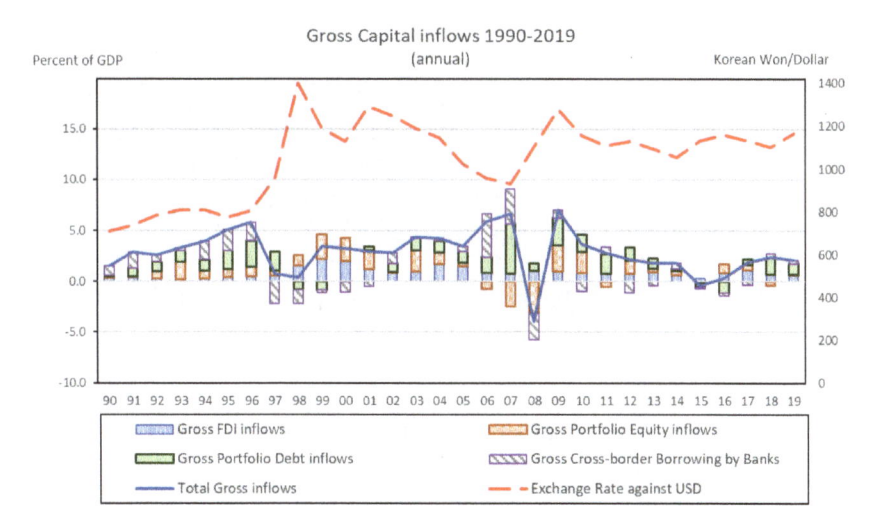

Figure 9. Gross capital inflows by type (Percentage of GDP, Annual 1990–2019).
Note: Gross capital inflows are calculated by summing up gross FDI, gross portfolio equity, gross portfolio debt and gross cross-bordering borrowing by banks. Other inflows (except for those for banks) are not included.
Source: Authors' calculations based on the Bank of Korea database.

(a) Cross-border borrowings by banks.

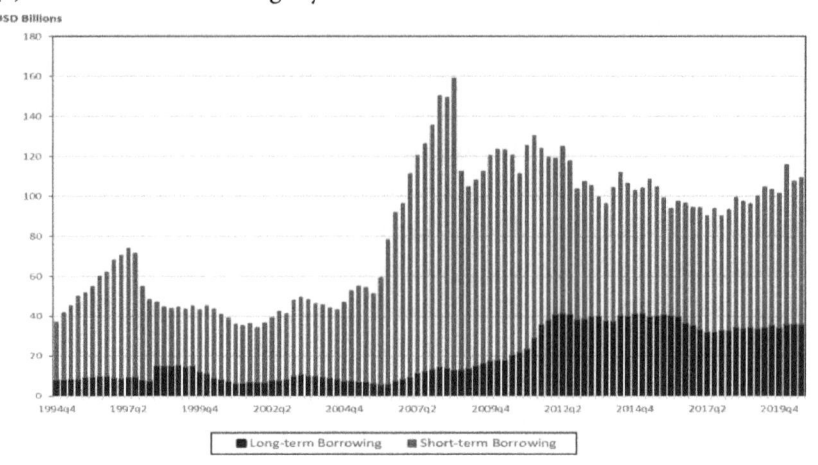

(b) Cross-border bond liabilities of banks.

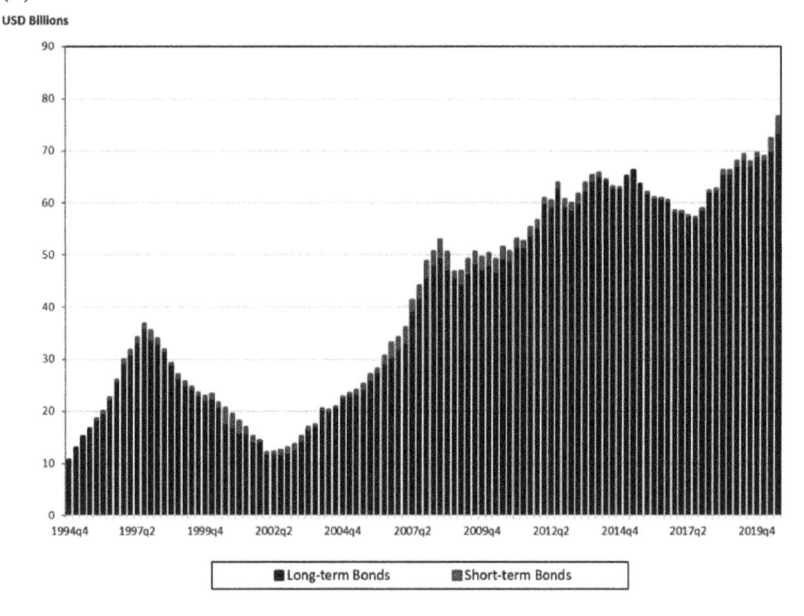

Figure 10. Cross-border bank liabilities (1994Q4–2020Q3).
Note: Cross-border debt securities liabilities of banks are obtained from the international investment position.
Source: The Bank of Korea database.

afterwards, and then gradually declined as capital flow management measures began to take effect in 2010. On the other hand, long-term borrowings increased even after the GFC, but the increase was small compared to the decline in short-term borrowings.

5. Changing patterns of financial intermediation and the bond market

The decline in short-term borrowing by Korean banks coincided with a general deleveraging of the global banks after the GFC. On the other hand, the bond market was relatively unaffected and continued to expand, even after the GFC. Figure 10(b) shows cross-border debt securities liabilities of Korean banks. While the amount of short-term bonds continued to be minimal, long-term bonds continued to grow after the GFC. This occurred despite the introduction of bank-funding–oriented macroprudential measures.

The broad shift from banks to bond markets was also due to non-bank borrowers. Figures 11(a) and 11(b) show gross cross-border liabilities of the government and corporates. Again, while cross-border borrowings declined after the GFC (Figure 11(a)), cross-border bond liabilities of both the government and corporates continued to increase even after the GFC (Figure 11(b)). Shin (2013) has dubbed the shift in the pattern of borrowing from banks to bond markets the "second phase of global liquidity".

A key theme in the post-GFC period has been the development of local currency bond markets in EMEs. The main lesson of the financial crises of the 1990s in EMEs was that the combination of currency mismatch and maturity mismatch (the "twin mismatches") was a key source of vulnerability or financial instability. Building on these lessons, many EMEs fostered the development of local currency bond markets, especially the government bond market. Korea was no exception.

Figure 12 provides several snapshots of the growth of the Korean won sovereign bond market in recent years. The growth of the local currency bond market was part of a general trend toward overcoming the "original sin" of not being able to borrow externally in domestic currency. However, due to the less-developed domestic institutional investor base,

(a) Cross-Border borrowings.

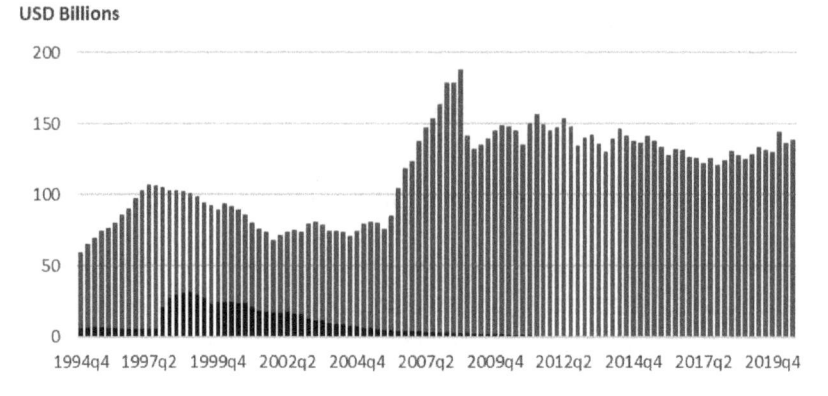

USD Billions

1994q4 1997q2 1999q4 2002q2 2004q4 2007q2 2009q4 2012q2 2014q4 2017q2 2019q4

■ Government   ■ Corporate

(b) Cross-Border bond liabilities

USD Billions

1994q4 1997q2 1999q4 2002q2 2004q4 2007q2 2009q4 2012q2 2014q4 2017q2 2019q4

■ Government   ■ Corporate

Figure 11.   Gross cross-border liabilities (1994Q4–2020Q3).
Note: Cross-border bond liabilities of the government and corporations are obtained from the international investment position.
Source: The Bank of Korea.

foreign investors have played an important role in EME local currency bond markets, giving rise to an "original sin redux" (Carstens and Shin, 2019; BIS, 2019).

The exchange rate plays an important amplifying role in the portfolio adjustment of global investors. The core mechanism is the financial

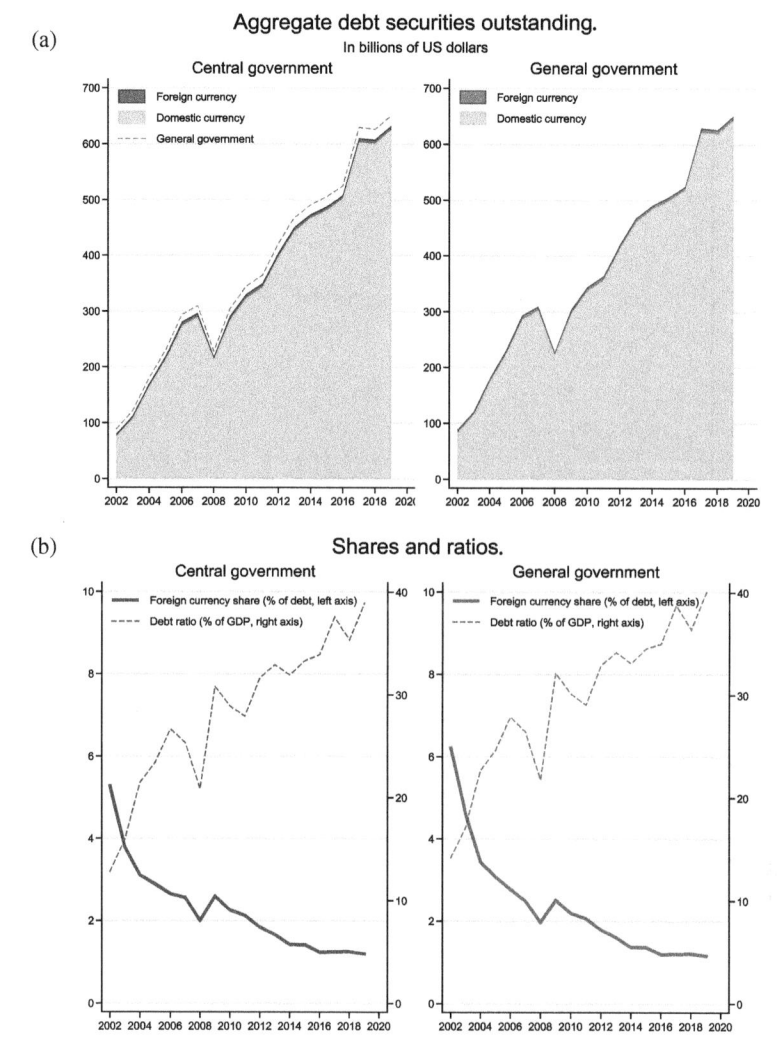

Note: CG and GG debt outstanding in domestic currency, face value, domestic market; for CG and GG debt in foreign currencies, all maturities IDS growth rates are applied pre-2018.

Figure 12.   Government debt securities outstanding — Korea.
Source: National data and BIS international debt statistics.

(c) **External holdings of GG debt securities.**

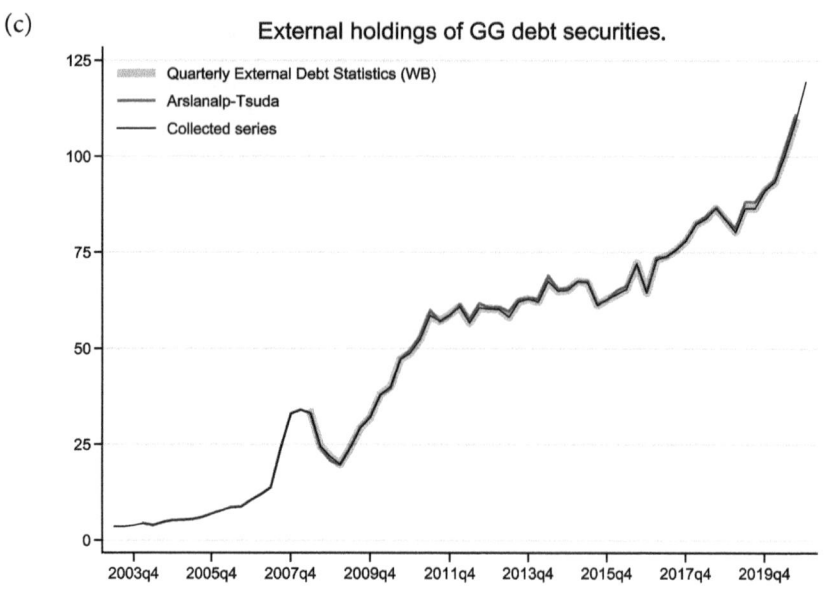

Note: These are quarterly external debt holdings, general government, face value, including both long and short-term. The holdings series likely include GG debt in all currencies, since it coincides with Korean QEDS data (which do not break out foreign holdings by currency).

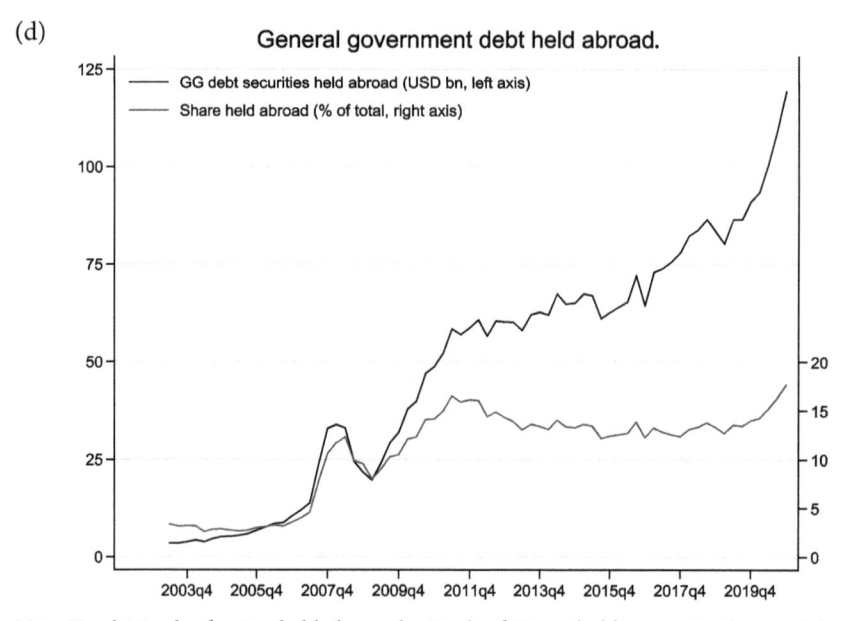

(d) **General government debt held abroad.**

Note: To obtain the foreign held share, the Bank of Korea holdings series (quarterly) were matched to total GG debt outstanding (interpolated to quarterly frequency, and extrapolated into 2020).

Figure 12. (*Continued*)

channel of the exchange rate. In the presence of currency mismatches on borrower balance sheets as a consequence of borrowing in foreign currency (original sin), a weaker exchange rate hampers borrower balance sheets. Borrowing in local currency from foreign lenders does not eliminate this problem, but rather shifts it to lender balance sheets as these now have assets in foreign currency and liabilities in their domestic currency (original sin redux). A weaker EME currency lowers the value of local currency assets in foreign investors' home currency terms, tightening their value-at-risk constraints. This triggers portfolio outflows from EMEs, pushing up their bond spreads by raising the credit risk premium. The same mechanism plays out in reverse when EME exchange rates appreciate (Hofmann et al., 2020). Indeed, during the acute stress period of March 2020, those EMEs with higher shares of foreign ownership in their local currency bond markets experienced somewhat larger increases in their local currency bond spreads.

6. Dollar funding and FX hedging of outward bond investment

During the acute phase of the March 2020 financial stress, indicators of dollar funding costs in foreign exchange markets rose sharply. Especially notable was the FX swap basis. The FX swap basis is the difference between the dollar interest rate in the money market and the implied dollar interest rate from the FX swap market, where someone borrows dollars by pledging another currency as collateral.[12] A negative basis means that borrowing dollars through FX swaps is more expensive than borrowing in the dollar money market.

Normally, the basis is close to zero, as an arbitrageur can exploit the basis and supply dollars in the FX swap market in order to exploit the price difference. However, during periods when bank balance sheet capacity is scarce, the funding constraints can be reflected in a non-zero basis. In particular, a large negative basis reflects a scarcity of dollar funding.

---

[12] For example, an investor sells euros for dollars, while simultaneously entering into a forward agreement to buy back the euros at a pre-agreed exchange rate at a fixed date in the future. This pre-agreed exchange rate is called the "forward rate", and defines an implicit interest rate on the dollar relative to that in euros given the current spot exchange rate.

Figure 13 plots the FX basis for major currencies against the US dollar during the acute phase of the crisis, taken from Avdjiev *et al.* (2020). The widening of the basis had been evident especially at short maturities. At the height of the stress, three-month basis widened to as much as −144 bp for the Japanese yen, −85 bp for the euro, −107 bp for the Swiss franc and −62 bp for the pound sterling (Figure 13, left-hand panel). The FX basis for the Korean won widened even further, reaching −270 bp at its height (Figure 13, right-hand panel) before the announcement of central bank dollar swap lines quelled the stress in the FX swap market.

To understand the stresses in the FX swap market, it is important to consider both sides of the FX swap market — those wishing to obtain dollars and those willing to supply them. On the demand side, institutional investors (insurers, pension funds and other portfolio asset managers) play a key role. Such investors have obligations in domestic currency, but they hold a globally diversified portfolio, with a substantial portion denominated in the US dollar. To finance the purchase of dollar assets, they swap domestic currency into dollars, thereby gaining access to dollar funding on a currency-hedged basis. Their portfolios have grown substantially since the GFC, giving rise to greater hedging needs.

Figure 14, taken from the BIS data on swaps and forwards, shows the outstanding amounts of contracts that has the Korean won on one side

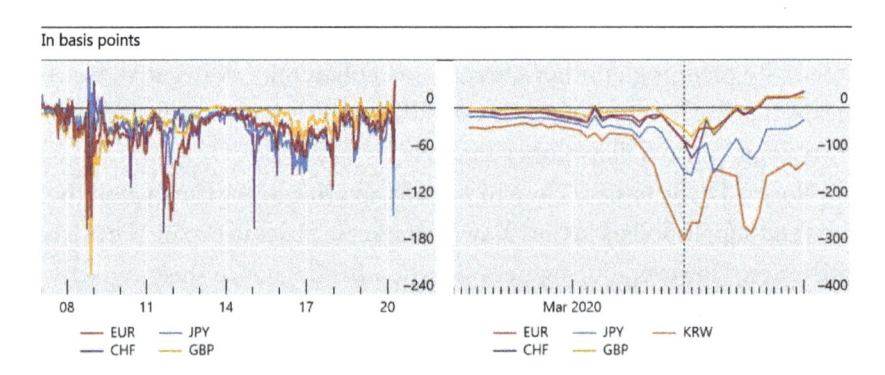

Figure 13. Three-month FX swap basis against the US dollar.
Note: Calculated exploiting the covered interest parity condition as the spread between three-month US dollar Libor and three-month FX swap-implied US dollar rates. The vertical dashed line in the right-hand panel indicates 15 March 2020 (the announcement of the enhancement of swap lines between the Federal Reserve and five central banks).
Source: Bloomberg; authors' calculations.

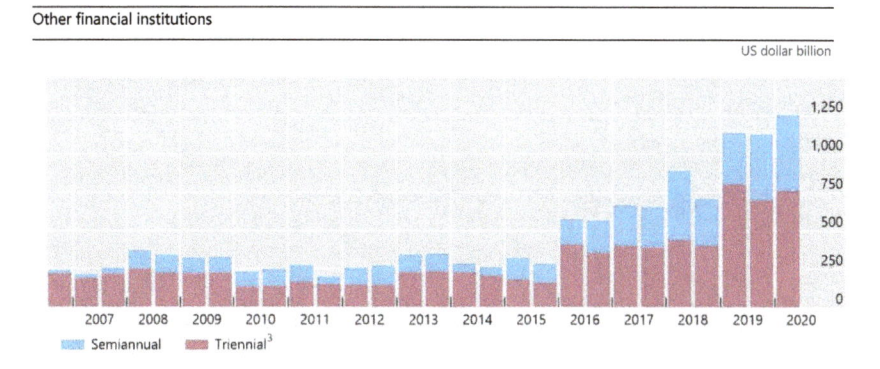

Figure 14. FX forwards and swaps, Korean Won.

Note: Korean won on one side of the contracts. Excluding banks classified as reporting dealers. Estimated triennial aggregates are adjusted for growth rates from semi-annual aggregates between the two Triennial surveys. Last Triennial Central Bank Survey of Foreign Exchange and OTC Derivatives Markets was conducted in 2019. The amounts combine the OTC Derivatives data, reported semi-annually, and the Triennial Survey (outstanding), reported every three years. Here the levels between the two Triennials are adjusted for semi-annual growth rates. Twelve countries report the OTCD and 54 report the Triennial. For the global market, the Triennial survey amounts add relatively little. But, for non-major currencies (eg KRW), the amounts collected in the Triennial can be substantial. The jumps in the graph in 2010, 2013, 2016 and 2019 are mainly due to Triennial reporting by reporting dealers in Korea.
Source: BIS OTC derivatives statistics.

of the contract, which are mostly vis-à-vis the US dollar. The outstanding amounts have increased sharply in recent years, reflecting the rapid increase in the outward fixed income investments of Korean institutional investors.

Financial turbulence in March 2020 led to a sharp decline in the supply of hedging services by banks. In addition, banks experienced drawdowns of credit lines from corporate borrowers, which crowded out other forms of lending by banks. Together, the pullback in the supply of dollars from banks and market-based intermediaries (even as dollar demand remained high) resulted in the sharp increase in indicators of dollar funding costs.

The experience in March 2020 reiterates the lesson that the dollar exchange rate takes on the attributes of a risk capacity indicator for the

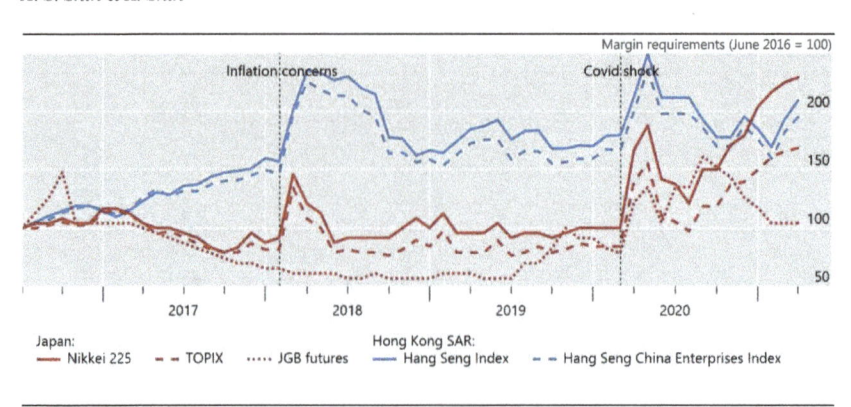

Figure 15. Procyclicality of Margining — Asian CCPs.
Note: Monthly averages. JGB = 10-year Japanese government bond.
Source: HKFE Clearing Corporation Limited (HKCC); Japan Securities Clearing Corporation; authors' calculations.

banking sector. This reflects the tendency for an appreciating US dollar to dampen dealer banks' intermediation capacity. For this reason, the dollar exchange rate and dollar funding costs tend to move in lock-step, as they did during the market turbulence in March 2020.

Another element in dollar funding stress in Korea during the acute phase of the COVID-19 pandemic was the role of securities firms that were under pressure to meet increased margins associated with their equity derivative positions. These securities firms were at the centre of hedging demand for dollars as issuers of retail structured products in the equity market — the so-called equity-linked securities (ELS) — were important.

Figure 15 shows the time series of margins associated with the Nikkei 225 index and the Hang Seng index. The sharp increase in margins in March 2020 is notable. The FX-hedging demand for foreign bonds by Korean institutional investors and the margin adjustments associated with ELS illustrate the changing role of Korea as increasingly being a creditor to the rest of the world. Nevertheless, the dollar funding stresses that appeared in March 2020 have underlined the importance of a macroprudential mindset, and the continual updating of the tools and policies of central banks and policy authorities, to meet the new challenges ahead.

A special report (2021) issued by the Korean authorities identified four factors that contributed to vulnerability of the Korean financial markets.[13] First, in the non-bank financial institutions, the exposure to foreign exchange risk was growing and the problem of currency and maturity mismatches was aggravated, but the resulting risks had not been properly managed. The increased weight of Korean institutional investors had been especially important. They expanded investment outside Korea where the securities firms were the main intermediaries. Securities firms' foreign assets and liabilities grew 267 percent and 478 percent, respectively, from the end of 2016 to the end of 2019. These figures far exceeded the growth rates of banks' foreign assets and liabilities, which were 16 percent and 19 percent, respectively. However, the Korean authorities' report cited lack of oversight of the foreign exchange risk of these financial institutions.[14]

Second, the existing regulations and monitoring system were mainly centred on the banking sector, and the current regulatory system had limitations in overseeing the risks of non-banking sectors. Currently, a monitoring system and stress test requirements related to foreign currency liquidity were in place only for banks.

Third, since the authorities in charge of foreign exchange soundness were dispersed, effective monitoring of, and swift response to, instability in the foreign exchange market were not possible. As already pointed out above, macroprudential supervision is being exercised separately by the Bank of Korea, the Financial Services Commission and the Financial Supervisory Service in Korea, and close cooperation among them has not been achieved.

Finally, the private sector was heavily dependent on the government's foreign reserves, but in the case of an emergency, the government was not able to properly supply foreign exchange liquidity. The supply of foreign

---

[13] The special report was prepared by the Ministry of Economy and Finance (2021) in collaborations with the Financial Services Commission, the Financial Supervisory Service and the Bank of Korea.

[14] As the global stock market was hit by the COVID-19 pandemic, Korean securities firms fell into a severe dollar shortage mainly due to margin calls related to structured products that are linked to overseas stock markets such as equity-linked securities (ELS), equity-linked bonds (ELB), derivative-linked securities (DLS) and derivative-linked bonds (DLB).

currency liquidity, such as foreign currency loans, were available mainly for banks, and such liquidity was not sufficiently delivered to non-bank financial institutions or corporations, which were the main end users.[15]

7. Conclusion: Lessons learned and challenges ahead

Korea's experience with the use of macroprudential tools underlines several important lessons. Foremost among them is the importance of having a coherent overall macro-financial policy framework that incorporates monetary policy as part of the overall framework. The discussion associated with the development of monetary policy frameworks in EMEs (see BIS [2019, Chapter II]) as well as the IMF's Integrated Policy Framework (IPF)) reflects the increased awareness of the importance of monetary and macroprudential policies being employed in a coherent way, especially when external sector considerations and the exchange rate are considered.

The institutional arrangements underpinning the macro-financial policy framework have continued to evolve with the advances in thinking on the nature of the policy challenges. The role of the central bank that has an explicit financial stability mandate (as is the case for the Bank of Korea) needs to be further clarified, with a view to reconciling the mandate with the appropriate tools.

Macroprudential measures imposed on the banking sector have been mostly effective in contributing to the desired objectives of policy. In this respect, the early roll-out of LTV and DTI regulation before the GFC aimed at the housing market stands out. The externally oriented macroprudential measures aimed at the vulnerabilities associated with short-term funding instruments of banks have also seen some success.

However, the experience of the financial stresses during the COVID-19 crisis of March 2020 highlights the challenges that are still ahead. While macroprudential policies have so far been aimed mainly at the banking sector, the experience in March 2020 has shown the limitations of an

---

[15] Banks were reluctant to provide foreign exchange liquidity to non-bank financial institutions and corporations because they lack in proper collateral or were of low credit ratings.

approach that focuses exclusively on the banking sector alone. The role of non-bank financial intermediaries will need to be incorporated more effectively into the overall design and management of macroprudential frameworks. This imperative places the additional onus on effective coordination between public authorities. While Korea is not unique in this regard, its rapidly evolving place in the global financial system and its changing role as increasingly being a creditor and investor in global markets mean that policy will need to evolve with the changing landscape.

References

Aikman, D, A Haldane and B Nelson (2015): "Curving the credit cycle", *Economic Journal*, **125**(585), 1072–1109.

Akinci, O and J Olmstead-Rumsey (2018): "How effective are macroprudential policies? An empirical investigation" *Journal of Financial Intermediation*, **33**, 33–57.

Avdjiev, S, E Eren and P McGuire (2020): Dollar funding costs during the Covid-19 crisis through the lens of the FX swap market (No. 1). *BIS Bulletin*, no 1.

Bernanke, B (2011): "The effects of the great recession on central bank doctrine and practice," Remarks at the *56th Economic Conference*, Federal Reserve Bank of Boston, 18 October 2011.

BIS (2019): "Monetary policy frameworks in EMES: Inflation targeting, the exchange rate and financial stability", Chapter II, Annual Economic Report 2019, June.

Borio, C (2014): "The financial cycle and macroeconomics: What have we learnt?" *Journal of Banking & Finance*, **45**(C), 182–198.

Borio, C and H Zhu (2012): "Capital regulation, risk-taking and monetary policy: A missing link in the transmission mechanism?" *Journal of Financial Stability*, **8**(4), 236–251.

Bruno, I, J Kim, S Kim, S Kim and K Shin (2016): "Financial stability, macroprudential policy tools and the role of the Bank of Korea," (in Korean), *Korean Economy Analyses*, **23**(1), 185–272.

Bruno, V and H S Shin (2014): "Assessing macroprudential policies: Case of South Korea", *The Scandinavian Journal of Economics*, **116**(1), 128–157, January.

_____ (2015): "Capital flows and the risk-taking channel of monetary policy", *Journal of Monetary Economics*, **71**, 119–132.

Bruno, V, I Shim and H S Shin (2017): "Comparative assessment of macroprudential policies", *Journal of Financial Stability*, **28**, 183–202.

Carstens, A and H S Shin (2019): "Emerging markets aren't out of the woods yet", *Foreign Affairs*, 15 March 2019.

Cerutti, E, S Claessens and L Laeven (2015): "Macroprudential policies: Analysing a new database", Paper presented at the DNB-EBC Conference in Amsterdam, the Netherlands, on "Macroprudential regulation: From theory to implementation", 29–30 January.

Christiano, L and T Fitzgerald (2003): "The band pass filter", *International Economic Review*, **44**(2), 435–465.

Drehmann, M, C Borio and K Tsatsaronis (2012): Characterising the financial cycle: Don't lose sight of the medium term! *BIS Working Papers*.

Hahm, J H, H S Shin and K Shin (2013): "Non-core bank liabilities and financial vulnerability", *Journal of Money, Credit and Banking*, **45**(s1), 3–36.

Hofmann, B, I Shim and H S Shin (2020): "Bond risk premia and the exchange rate." *Journal of Money, Credit and Banking*, **52**(S2), 497–520.

IMF (2013): "The interaction of monetary and macroprudential policies", Washington: International Monetary Fund.

IMF (2017): Increasing resilience to large and volatile capital flows: The role of macroprudential policies — case studies, IMF Policy Paper.

IMF (2019a): "Republic of Korea: Selected Issues", IMF Country Report No. 19/133.

IMF (2019b): "The IMF's View on Capital Flows in Practice", Prepared by Staff of the International Monetary Fund for Group Institutional of Twenty.

Jung, H and J Lee (2017): "The effects of macroprudential policies on house prices: Evidence from an event study using Korean real transaction data", *Journal of Financial Stability*, **31**, 167–185

Kim, C (2013): "Macroprudential Policies: Korea's Experiences", Paper presented at the *Rethinking Macro Policy II: First Steps and Early Lessons Conference*, IMF, Washington, D.C., 16–17 April 2013.

Kim, K and J Y Lee (2017): Estimating the effects of FX-related macroprudential policies in Korea. *International Review of Economics & Finance*, **50**, 23–48.

Kim, S and A Mehrotra (2018): "Effects of monetary and macroprudential policies — Evidence from four inflation targeting economies", *Journal of Money, Credit and Banking*, **50**(5) August, 967–992.

Kim, S and J Oh (2020): "Macroeconomic effects of macroprudential policies: Evidence from LTV and DTI policies in Korea", *Japan and the World Economy*, **53**(March), 100997.

Kuttner K and I Shim (2016): "Can non-interest rate policies stabilize housing markets? Evidence from a panel of 57 economies", *Journal of Financial Stability*, **26**, 31–44.

Lee, J J (2009): "Changes in the business cycle of the Korean Economy: Evidence and explanations", (in Korean) *KDI Journal of Economic Policy*, **31**(2) December, 47–85.

Lee, J K (2013): "The operation of macro prudential policy measures: The case of Korea in the 2000s", World Bank, https://doi.org/10.1596/978-1-4648-0002-3_ch7.

Ministry of Economy and Finance (2021): "A special report on liquidity management and backstop of foreign currency liquidity", mimeo.

Osiński, J, K Seal and L Hoogduin (2013): "Macroprudential and microprudential policies: Towards cohabitation", IMF Staff Discussion Note.

Park, C-Y. and K Shin (2020): "Contagion through national and regional exposures to foreign banks during the Global Financial Crisis", *Journal of Financial Stability*, **46**(100721), February.

Reinhart, C M and K S Rogoff (2004): "The modern history of exchange rate arrangements: A reinterpretation", *The Quarterly Journal of Economics*, **119**(1), 1–48.

Shim, I and K Shin (2021): "Financial stress in lender countries and capital outflows from emerging market economies", *Journal of International Money and Finance*, **113**, 102356.

Shin, H S (2013): Second phase of global liquidity and its impact on emerging economies. Keynote speech at Federal Reserve Bank of San Francisco Asia Economic Policy Conference, 4 November 2013.

Shin, H and K Shin (2011): Procyclicality and monetary aggregates, *NBER Working Papers* 16836, National Bureau of Economic Research.

Lessons from Macro-Financial Policy in Korea: A Discussion

Hwanseok Lee

Bank of Korea

Korea's experience of the past several decades shows that the transmission channel of external shocks continually shifts along with the sectors where financial regulation is weak. At first, during the Asian Financial Crisis, the channel ran through the currency and maturity mismatches on firm and bank balance sheets, and it later shifted to banks' excessive short-term external borrowing during the global financial crisis. The COVID-19 shock in 2020 shows that the vulnerability is now located in non-bank financial institutions (NBFIs) and their foreign portfolio investment. In the aftermath of each crisis, the Bank of Korea and the Korean government made efforts to improve the macro-financial policy framework; thus, the current framework can be best understood as the historical result of these continuous responses against shifting vulnerabilities.

The chapter by Hyun Song Shin and Kwanho Shin (Shin and Shin, 2021) provides a comprehensive overview and assessment of Korea's monetary and macroprudential policy framework by reviewing its macro-financial vulnerabilities over the last 25 years. Importantly, it evaluates the external shock Korea faced during the COVID-19 crisis and identifies the new vulnerability formed around the rapid growth of foreign portfolio investment led by NBFIs. Through an in-depth assessment of the Korean financial markets, the chapter provides the important implication that policy coordination is becoming ever more critical, particularly among the many authorities whose roles and responsibilities intersect with NBFI activities.

The purpose of this note is to support and complement the evaluation of Korea's policy framework by Shin and Shin (2021). It provides some additional information related to Korea's capital flows/macroprudential policy and offers a complementary perspective on the characteristics of the dollar liquidity shortage in Korea caused by the COVID-19 shock. The note concludes by drawing attention to new potential vulnerabilities and emphasising the importance of sound economic fundamentals.

Original sin redux: The Korean case

Opening up the capital account in the 1990s gave emerging market economies (EMEs) the opportunity to fund domestic investment from abroad. They were, however, not able to borrow in their own currency in the long term ("original sin"; Eichengreen and Hausmann, 1999). The "twin" currency and maturity mismatches amplified the disruption in EMEs during the Asian financial crisis, and Korea was not an exception. Since then, EMEs have developed local currency bond markets, which seems to have alleviated the problem of not being able to borrow abroad in local currency, by strengthening domestic borrowing ability. Shin and Shin (2021), however, emphasise that this merely transplanted the currency mismatch problem from borrowers' balance sheets to lenders' ("original sin redux"; Carstens and Shin, 2019). During the most recent crisis, foreign investors' flight from EM local currency bond markets was exacerbated by their losses from exchange rate depreciation (Hofmann *et al.*, 2020).

When we take a look at the Korean case, this effect of the exchange rate was seen in foreigners' equity investment rather than foreigners' bond investment. The Korean bond market has grown significantly since the Asian financial crisis,[1] but the participation of foreign investors is not large

---

[1] Bond market capitalisation grew from 56.5 percent of GDP in 1998 to 119.2 percent in 2020.

compared to other EMEs,[2] as Shin and Shin also note. Furthermore, more than half of foreigners' bond investment is made by public entities like central banks or sovereign wealth funds. These intrinsically long-term investors continued to inject funds into the Korean bond market even during the peak of the COVID-19 crisis.

That said, the insight that exchange rate fluctuations make foreigners' portfolio investment more volatile for EMEs, is valid and important also for Korea. The exchange rate tends to fluctuate cyclically with global risk appetite, amplifying the volatility of foreigners' equity investment. It is known in the market that equity investors tend not to hedge against FX risk, especially in comparison with bond investors. Foreign equity investors in Korea have shown the tendency to increase their investment during times of won appreciation and decrease it during depreciation (Figure 1(b)). In addition, as the foreign ownership share is as high as 30 percent in the equity market, the strategic complementarity among foreign investors intensifies their synchronised movement.

During the initial COVID-19 shock, severe capital outflows happened mainly through the stock market in Korea (Figure 1(a)). The outflow

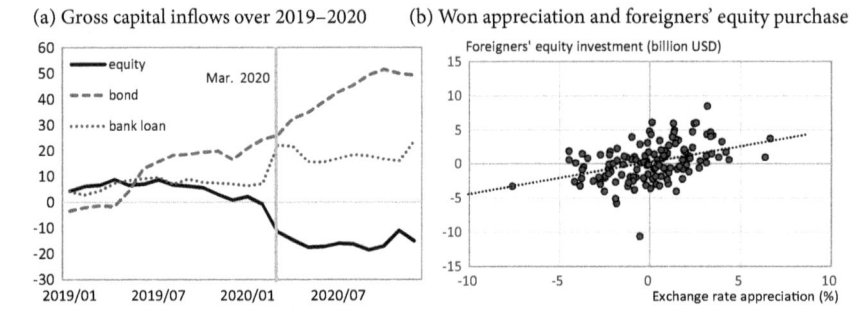

Figure 1. Gross capital inflows and correlation between exchange rates and equity inflows.

Note: Panel (a) shows cumulative flows from January 2019 (billion USD, sourced from Balance of Payments, Bank of Korea). Panel (b) shows the scatter plot of the monthly Korean won appreciation rate against the US dollar and foreigners' equity investment from Jan. 2010 to Mar. 2021.

---

[2] Foreign investors account for 15.9 percent in Korea's government bond market as of the end of December 2020. To compare with other Asian EMEs, the ratios for Indonesia, Malaysia, and Thailand are 25.2 percent, 25.2 percent and 13.6 percent, respectively (sourced from the ADB).

during March 2020 amounted to $11 billion, and it continued through April ($3 billion) and May ($3 billion). This was mainly attributable to the increased financial market uncertainty, but the exchange rate might also have played a significant role in amplifying the outflows. The acute depreciation of the Korean won around this time was probably one of the factors driving foreign investors' loss-cut transactions.

FX-related macroprudential policy: Limitation and the need for further development

Banks' excessive short-term FX borrowing was where the vulnerability lay during the global financial crisis. After the crisis, Korea introduced a series of FX-related macroprudential policies, as explained in the chapter. The reforms are, in general, evaluated to have had a positive impact by mitigating the FX vulnerabilities formed around banks' external borrowing. In line with the previous studies, Shin and Shin's analysis of the macro-aggregates concludes that the tools have helped to reduce macro-financial volatility.

The FX-related macroprudential measures introduced in Korea are valuable tools that can alleviate the burden of monetary and FX policy, as having an additional point of leverage that influences financial institutions' behaviour can help to achieve multiple policy goals. Korea has been actively adjusting these measures in accordance with the business cycle, and it did so also during the COVID-19 shock.[3]

However, as heterogeneous market participants adapt to the regulatory changes, attempts at circumvention or regulatory arbitrage appear. This can be seen more clearly from the micro-level data. For instance, it is argued that the lengthening of banks' external borrowing maturities is driven mainly by foreign bank branches' borrowing from their parent banks (Ahn *et al.*, 2020). Though nominally long-term, these are internal transactions within each global banking group, and some raise doubts

---

[3] The ceilings on the FX derivative positions of banks were raised by 25 percent on 18 March 2020. The bank levy on non-deposit FX liabilities was waived for three months, from April to June. The FX liquidity coverage ratio was lowered temporarily to 70 percent, down from 80 percent.

about the financial stability implications of the lengthened maturities (e.g., Ahn *et al.* [2020] and Yun [2021]).

In this regard, the set of macroprudential policies is something that we need to develop further as our experiences accumulate, rather than a master solution that should remain invariant. In this process, close coordination among policy authorities will be of utmost importance, as Shin and Shin (2021) argue.

Foreign portfolio investment and NBFIs: Qualitative improvements needed

The most recent crisis revealed a new vulnerability that had been built up through the rapid expansion of foreign portfolio investment. Shin and Shin (2021) describe the problem in detail and summarise that "the margin adjustments associated with ELS illustrate the changing role of Korea as increasingly being a creditor to the rest of the world". This is indeed a formerly unseen type of financial instability in Korea, and is related to the rapid increase of its foreign investment. The foreign portfolio investment of Korean pension funds, insurance companies and securities firms increased explosively after the global financial crisis due mainly to population ageing, and Korea's role in the global financial market changed from a net debtor to a net creditor in 2014. Figure 2(a) shows the rapid increase in foreign bond holdings by Korean residents over the past six years, mainly driven by NBFIs.

We have noticed a positive change in capital flows since becoming a net creditor in the world capital market. It appears that the increased amount outstanding of overseas investment is helping to make our FX market more resilient. In times of high uncertainty, local investors tend to withdraw their foreign investment. For example, Korean NBFIs' net foreign bond investment was reduced by $5.2 billion during the period between February and April 2020 (Figure 2(b)). This pattern of retrenchment offsets the disruptive effects from the sudden departures of foreign investors, by reducing the volatility of net capital flows and the exchange rate. The scale of retrenchment has increased recently (Yun, 2020), and some have gone further to note that recent capital flow patterns in Korea show safe-haven-like characteristics (e.g., Hansen and Krogstrup

(a)

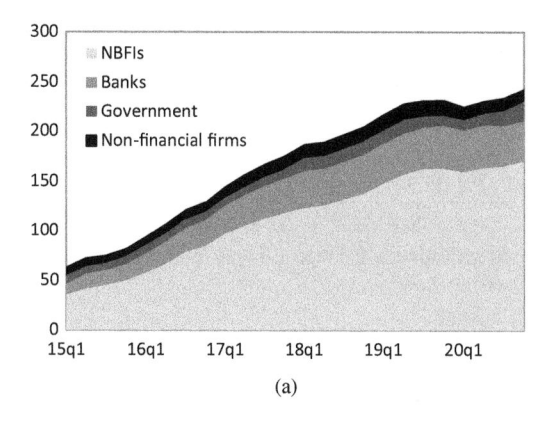

	2018	2019	2020	Feb-Apr 2020
NBFIs	21.0	16.2	-3.2	-5.2
Banks	5.1	2.3	-3.4	0.9
Government	4.0	-3.5	9.5	0.3
Misc.	3.0	2.0	-0.7	-0.6
Total	33.2	17.0	2.2	-4.6

(b)

Figure 2. Gross portfolio outflows (bond).
Note: The unit is billion USD.
Source: Balance of Payments and international investment position statistics of the Bank of Korea.

[2019]). In this sense, it is an important observation of Shin and Shin that being a world creditor has implications for FX market stability.

That being said, the severity of the dollar liquidity shortage in Korea during the COVID-19 shock was different from the other risk-off episodes it went through recently. Also, it is important to notice that not all global creditors experienced a dollar liquidity shortage of a similar magnitude to what Korea experienced during the shock. This is related to a couple of unique weaknesses of Korean financial institutions that should be considered together with Shin and Shin's observation.

First, despite having grown significantly, NBFIs have not kept pace in terms of the development of their investment practices and techniques, which tend to exhibit herd behaviour and lack of diversity. For instance,

Table 1. Currency-related derivatives outstanding by types of financial institutions.

	Total	Banks	Securities Firms	Insurance	Mutual Funds
Short-term	64.0	64.1	65.9	34.7	88.7
Long-term	36.0	35.9	34.1	65.3	11.3

Note: As of September 2020. "Short-term" means derivatives with less than one-year maturity, and "Long-term" means derivatives with longer than one-year maturity. The unit is percentage.
Source: Financial Supervisory Service.

securities firms increased their size significantly by selling so-called equity-linked and derivative-linked securities (ELS and DLS) which became popular because they can offer marginally higher returns in normal times.[4] They were very successful in attracting yield-sensitive retirement funds. The tragedy was that these products performed badly in tail events like the COVID-19 shock.

Second, the short-term FX hedging practice of NBFIs also played an important role by exacerbating the extreme liquidity shortage in the swap market. Long-term investors including insurance firms commonly hedged their overseas investment through short-term FX swaps. About 64 percent of financial institutions' currency-related derivative contracts were with maturity of less than a year (Table 1). FX swaps were popular mostly because they were cheaper than long-term contracts. By relying on short-term hedging, however, institutional investors exposed themselves to roll-over risk, and that worsened the situation in March 2020.

Concluding remarks: New vulnerabilities and the importance of fundamentals

Perhaps the most important lesson to be taken from this discussion is that while macro-financial vulnerability changes in form and location, it does not disappear. That is why policymakers must always keep a close eye on the latest market developments. One such example is the recent digital transformation of the financial sector. FinTech and BigTech companies are expanding the boundary of NBFIs and the

---

[4] The size of these auto-callable funds (or structured retail products) increased five-fold over the last 10 years (from 22.4 trillion won in 2010 to 108.2 trillion won in 2019).

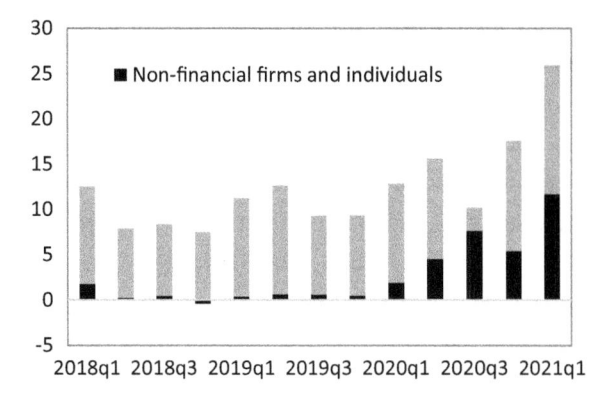

Figure 3. Korean residents' foreign equity investment.
Note: The unit is billion USD.
Source: Balance of Payments, Bank of Korea.

financial services they offer. Although the economic benefits generated by these new entrants in the financial sector is increasing, potential systemic risk may also be accumulating through regulatory arbitrage (Frost *et al.*, 2019).

Another example in Korea is the rapid growth of individual investor platforms. Foreign stock investment became increasingly popular in 2020. The share of retail investors in total foreign equity investment was negligible up until 2019, but it began to spike in 2020 (Figure 3). During the first quarter of 2021, 45 percent of foreign equity purchases were made by individuals (and non-financial firms). This can be understood as a result of investors' portfolio diversification in the environment of low domestic interest rates, but another important driver was the retail investor platforms which made overseas investment much easier for individuals.

These platforms are likely to continue growing in size and significance along with other NBFIs. Close examination is needed on how this development would affect domestic FX and financial markets in the event of another episode of instability in the international financial market, because a degree of herd behaviour is being observed, similar to that of the ELS/DLS crisis. More than half of individuals' foreign equity investment is in US stocks, and NASDAQ-traded shares in particular.

Last but not least, the lesson that shifting vulnerabilities cannot be perfectly eliminated emphasises the importance of having strong macro-fundamentals that can make the economy resilient to various shocks. The Bank of Korea and the Korean government have acted promptly to restructure financial regulations and the policy framework over the last 30 years, and in so doing have been able to avoid making the same mistakes twice. However, the point of vulnerability repeatedly changed in form and reappeared elsewhere, and each time it was Korea's sound economic fundamentals that eventually helped us overcome the crisis. Korea's strong manufacturing base in particular has been a boon for the domestic economy, especially during the past year. Pandemic-induced behavioural changes have increased global demand for Korean goods, which in turn has helped continue to drive foreign liquidity into the Korean FX market.

References

Ahn, JaeBin, Young-ju Kim, and Hyunjoon Lim (2020). "For whom the levy tolls: the case of a macroprudential stability levy in South Korea", mimeo.

Carstens, Agustín, and Hyun Song Shin (2019). "Emerging markets aren't out of the woods yet-how they can manage the risks". *Foreign Affairs*, March 15.

Eichengreen, Barry, and Ricardo Hausmann (1999). "Exchange rates and financial fragility". *National Bureau of Economic Research Working Paper*, No. w7418.

Frost, Jon, Leonardo Gambacorta, Yi Huang, Hyun Song Shin, and Pablo Zbinden (2019). "BigTech and the changing structure of financial intermediation". *Economic Policy* 34, No. 100, pp. 761–799.

Hansen, Niels-Jakob, and Signe Krogstrup (2019). "Recent shifts in capital flow patterns in Korea: An investor base perspective". *IMF Working Paper*, No. 19/262.

Hofmann, Boris, Ilhyock Shim, and Hyun Song Shin (2020). "Emerging market economy exchange rates and local currency bond markets amid the Covid-19 pandemic." *BIS Bulletin*, No. 5.

Shin, Hyun Song, and Kwanho Shin (2021). "Lessons from macro-financial policy in Korea". *Macro-financial Stability Policy in a Globalised World: Lessons from International Experience*, Asian Monetary Policy Forum 2021 Special edition and MAS-BIS conference.

Yun, Youngjin (2020). "Post-crisis changes in the pattern of capital flows-The case of Korea." *Economics Bulletin*, 40, No. 1, pp. 601–611.

Yun, Youngjin (2021). "Cross-border bank flows through foreign branches and the effect of a macroprudential policy", *Pacific Economic Review*, forthcoming.

CHAPTER 12

Chapter 12

Macroprudential Policies and Financial Stability in a Small and Open Economy: The Case of Singapore[*]

Ramkishen S. Rajan,[†] Edward S. Robinson[‡] and Rosemary Lim[§]

[†]*Yong Pung How Professor, Lee Kuan Yew School of Public Policy,*
National University of Singapore
[‡]*Deputy Managing Director (Economic Policy) and Chief Economist,*
Monetary Authority of Singapore
[§]*Executive Director, Macroprudential Surveillance Department,*
Monetary Authority of Singapore

Abstract

Singapore has successfully harnessed financial globalisation to promote rapid growth and development, but it has concomitantly been highly exposed to the vagaries of the global financial markets, making it susceptible to macro-financial risks. Singapore has proactively utilised macroprudential

---

[*] The authors appreciate detailed and helpful comments from the discussant to this chapter, Deng Yongheng as well as MAS colleagues: Choy Keen Meng, Aloysius Lim, Wong Siang Leng, Andrew Tan, Cyrene Chew, Tan Boon Heng, Brian Lee and Lily Chan as well as valuable research assistance from Sasidaran Gopalan, Nimeesha Takalkar and Ruijie Cheng. The usual disclaimer applies.

policies (MaPPs) which are primarily targeted at the property market to manage domestic financial stability on a system-wide basis. This chapter describes the set of property-related MaPPs used by Singapore over the last two decades. It then goes on to examine the extent to which housing price growth in Singapore co-moves with global housing prices and whether MaPPs can insulate the domestic housing market from fluctuations in global financial conditions. The empirical analysis offers strong evidence to suggest that Singapore's MaPPs as a whole have produced a dampening impact on the growth of the country's property prices. The results also show that the use of a multiple set of instruments to maintain property market stability may be more effective than relying on a single instrument, possibly due to the fact that there may be multiple sources of disequilibria impacting the market. The chapter discusses some possible lessons from the Singapore experience and highlights ongoing challenges in the conduct of MaPPs.

1. Introduction

Singapore has been among the most ardent supporters of trade and investment globalisation. As of 2018, Singapore's trade in goods and services as a proportion of Gross Domestic Product (GDP) was over 320 percent, making it one of the most trade-dependent economies in the world.[1] Similarly, Singapore's stock of inward FDI stood at US$1.5 trillion in 2018 (410 percent of GDP), making it the fourth largest in the world in aggregate terms and second largest (behind Hong Kong) as a share of GDP.[2]

Singapore's approach to financial globalisation has been nuanced and well-sequenced (Rajan, 2016). To be sure, financial globalisation can be thought of as constituting two distinct components, viz. the

---
[1] Data from World Bank's World Development Indicators.
[2] Data from UNCTAD.

degree of internationalisation of the financial sector and the extent of capital flows. Singapore moved from being an offshore financial centre in the 1970s to a regional financial centre in the 1980s and 1990s and is now among the top global financial centres (along with New York, London, Hong Kong and Tokyo), with the financial sector constituting a significant share of domestic economic activity. By 2019, the financial services sector on the whole accounted for about 13 percent of the country's GDP, 14 percent of its services exports and 6 percent of its employment and it has consistently been a significant growth driver of the Singapore economy (Figure 1). In addition, Singapore has an exceptionally large stock of external liabilities and assets (averaging 17 times its GDP since 2000), emphasising its openness to capital flows (Figure 2). However, embracing all aspects of financial globalisation has made Singapore susceptible to disruptions caused by surges and sudden stops in gross capital flows, which in turn has made macroeconomic management a complex and challenging task, as it has in small and highly open economies more generally.

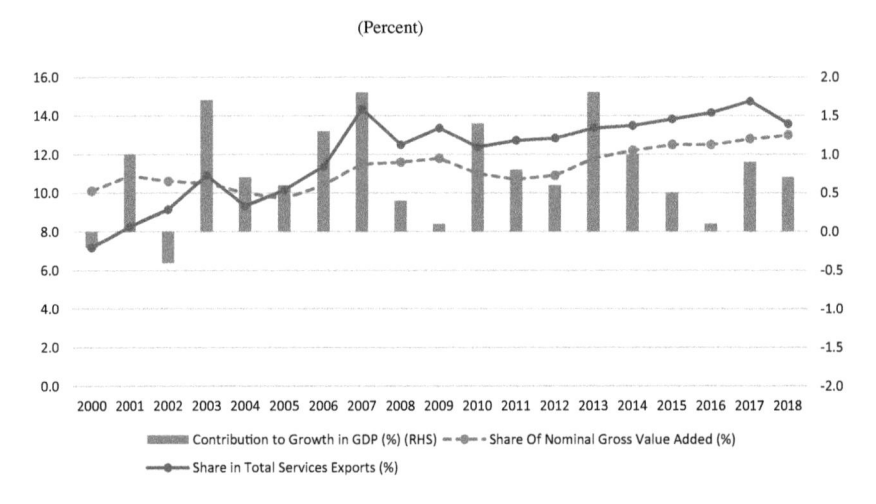

Figure 1. Significance of financial sector in Singapore.
Source: Based on data from Singapore Department of Statistics.

(Percent of GDP)

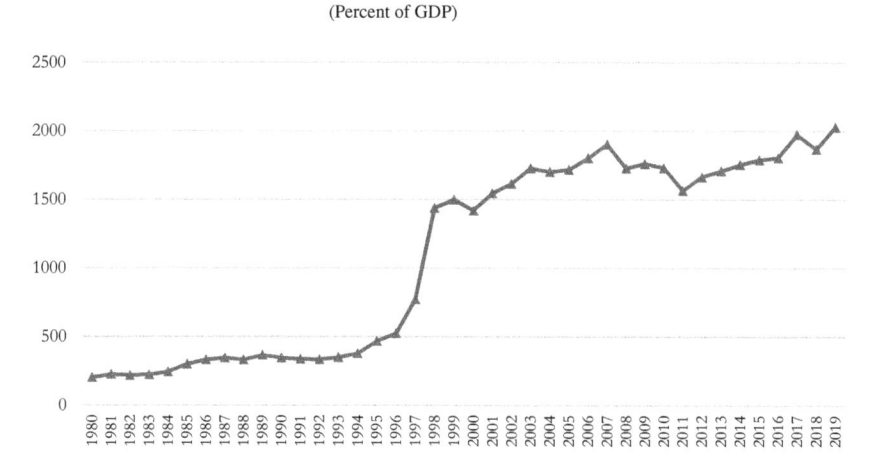

Figure 2. Stock of external assets and liabilities in Singapore.
Source: Based on data from Lane and Milesi-Ferretti (2017) and updates from ADB.

Conventional wisdom suggests that as countries "learn to float", greater exchange rate flexibility should shield the domestic economy from external shocks and afford it enhanced monetary autonomy. However, this view was challenged by Hélène Rey, who emphasised that the global financial cycle and global liquidity driven by US dollar funding have undermined the ability of central banks in emerging economies to manage their own monetary conditions regardless of the exchange rate regime (Rey, 2013, 2016; Passari and Rey, 2015).[3]

Singapore recognised the limits of the insulating powers of flexible exchange rates early on, and consequently adopted a monetary policy framework centred on the exchange rate as an ideal intermediate target of

---

[3] There have been a number of critiques of and nuances to Rey's Dilemma hypothesis. Obstfeld *et al.* (2019) and Klein and Shambaugh (2015) argue that the conventional wisdom regarding the Impossible Trilemma remains relevant (i.e., exchange rate flexibility does have insulation powers). Cheng and Rajan (2020) and Han and Wei (2018) suggest that there may exist a 2.5 lemma between the Dilemma and Trilemma. This issue remains an area of ongoing debate.

monetary policy for medium-term price stability.[4] Since the early 1980s, the Monetary Authority of Singapore (MAS) has operated a Band, Basket and Crawl (BBC) regime. The Singapore dollar is managed against an undisclosed basket of currencies (trade-weighted exchange rate) rather than a single currency. Recognising the importance of ensuring some degree of flexibility to accommodate global and regional shocks, the currency is managed within an undisclosed band. MAS intervenes in the foreign exchange market when the trade-weighted currency index is about to reach the edges of the policy band or occasionally within the band if there are concerns about "excessive" volatility.

There is evidence to suggest that under Singapore's exchange rate policy regime, the nominal effective exchange rate (NEER) has been adjusted to stabilise inflation and output, especially the former (Cavoli and Rajan, 2007; McCallum, 2014; Parrado, 2004). In other words, while the level of Singapore's real effective exchange rate is anchored by the country's underlying fundamentals in the long term, MAS has also used the exchange rate as a countercyclical tool in the short term.[5] Of particular significance is that while there has been a willingness to allow for a faster rate of appreciation of the Singapore dollar during boom periods to curb inflation, MAS policy has generally kept the domestic currency relatively stable on a trade-weighted basis in the event of a moderate downturn.

---

[4] As noted by Ong (2013):

"(T)he structure of the Singapore economy reduces the scope for using interest rates as a monetary policy tool. First, the corporate sector is dominated by multinational corporations (MNCs), which rely on funding from their head offices (typically in developed economies) rather than on local banking systems or debt markets. Second, Singapore's role as an international financial centre has led to a large offshore banking centre that deals primarily in the G3 currencies, and it is one where assets denominated in those currencies far exceed those of the domestic banking system. As there is no control on capital flows between the offshore (foreign currency) and domestic (Singapore dollars) banking systems, small changes in interest rate differentials can lead to large and rapid movements of capital. As a result, it is difficult to target interest rates in Singapore as any attempt by MAS to raise or lower domestic interest rates would be foiled by a shift of funds into or out of the domestic financial system."

[5] Specifically, one can estimate a monetary policy reaction function in which the policy instrument is the NEER rather than the interest rate.

Singapore's steadfast commitment to fiscal prudence has afforded it the policy space to use countercyclical fiscal policy to manage output gaps (along with specific supply-side measures) when needed during periods of severe downturns (such as during the Global Financial Crisis [GFC] and more recently during the COVID-19 pandemic when the government unveiled four Budgets from February to May 2020 amounting to 19.2 percent of GDP).[6] However, periods of more moderate downturns have historically been viewed as opportunities to facilitate necessary economic restructuring and skills upgrading, cleansing the economy of inefficiencies and facilitating resource reallocation, rather than artificially stimulating the demand side of the economy, i.e., a sort of Schumpeterian view of the world (need for creative entry and destruction).[7]

Beyond macro-stability, the GFC has made apparent the role of macro-financial linkages in amplifying shocks and building up systemic risks. Since then, there has been a rife debate in many countries about whether central banks should explicitly recognise the role of the financial cycle during the boom period and include financial stability as a secondary objective when deciding its interest rate policy stance, versus just dealing with the aftermath of any possible market crash (Borio, 2013). However, this "Lean versus Clean" debate has been somewhat less germane to Singapore given its exchange rate-centred monetary policy, which implies that domestic interest rates largely follow foreign interest rates (adjusted for expected future movements in the Singapore dollar).[8]

Instead, Singapore has used macroprudential policies (MaPPs) to manage financial stability concerns, specifically to tackle the accumulation of systemic risks that might not be adequately dealt with by microprudential supervision and regulation. While MaPPs have become part of the toolkit of policymakers worldwide since the GFC (IMF, 2020), Singapore has been using them since the mid-1990s as a means of safeguarding financial stability and encouraging financial prudence among households. Even in

---

[6] https://www.singaporebudget.gov.sg/budget_2020/budget-measures
[7] See Caballero and Hammour (1994) for a theoretical examination of the cleansing impact of recessions.
[8] However, MAS does have some degree of control over domestic liquidity conditions via sterilisation operations as well as the fact that it allows some flexibility in the exchange rate (within the band).

Singapore though, macroprudential activism has intensified only over the last decade as the extended period of ultra-accommodative monetary policy implemented by larger advanced economies unleashed a monetary tsunami which threatened to compromise financial and macroeconomic stability in economies with open capital accounts.

As part of its macroprudential framework, the MAS has expanded its toolkit to include the countercyclical capital buffer (CCyB) since January 2016 (currently set at zero) and has had an established framework to manage domestic systemically important banks (D-SIBs),[9] which have been subject to additional regulatory measures since 2015.[10] However, as will be discussed, most of the MaPPs in Singapore have been focussed on the property market, which is closely linked to the balance sheets of households and banks as well as the overall macroeconomy. The overarching aim of MaPPs in Singapore is to contain the build-up of financial stability risks through measures to reduce the volatility of property prices and dampen spurts of excessive price appreciation.[11] Apart from a cap on banks' property-related exposures (at 35 percent of their total exposures), the vast majority of the MaPPs are aimed at the borrower side, such as ceilings on the loan-to-value (LTV) ratio, caps on the total debt servicing ratio (TDSR) and limits on the loan tenure. These MaPPs have been complemented with various fiscal measures on property transactions such as additional buyer's stamp duties (ABSD), seller's stamp duties (SSD) as well as supply-side measures in the form of government land sales.

---

[9] Foreign banks can also be D-SIBs. If identified, one of the requirements is to subsidiarise if they have significant retail presence.

[10] Seven institutions have been classified as being D-SIBs, viz. three local banks and four foreign banks.

[11] While Singapore is not unique in predominantly imposing housing-related MaPPs, it has also used prudential measures to instil household financial prudence in the motor vehicle market, although these loans account for a smaller share of household debt compared to housing loans. Specifically, MAS re-introduced financing restrictions on motor vehicles granted by financial institutions in 2013, imposing LTV ceilings (50%–60%) for motor vehicle loans (excluding commercial vehicles and motorcycles) as well as capping the maximum tenure of a motor vehicle loan at five years. These measures were adjusted in 2016, to LTVs of 60%–70% and a maximum loan tenure of seven years.

This chapter describes the set of property-related MaPPs used by Singapore over the last two decades (especially the last decade), evaluates their effectiveness and draws lessons from the country's experience. The remainder of the chapter is organised as follows. Section 2 outlines the governance structure of MaPPs in Singapore, discusses the types and frequency of use of MaPPs and offers some indication of their possible impact. Section 3 reviews the available literature analysing aspects of the effectiveness of MaPPs in Singapore. Section 4 undertakes an empirical exercise to examine the extent to which Singapore's house prices are synchronised with global house prices and if, and to what extent, property-based MaPPs help to decouple the two. Section 5 offers a few lessons from Singapore's experience and highlights general areas of concern regarding the use of MaPPs. Section 6 concludes the chapter.

2. MaPPs in Singapore[12]

As Singapore's central bank and integrated financial supervisor, MAS is the macroprudential authority responsible for financial stability and oversight of the financial system. In exercising this mandate, MAS deploys MaPPs to insulate the financial system and real economy from risks associated with systemically important nodes, risk concentrations and unsustainable dynamics in financial and asset markets. While MaPPs have a longer history in Singapore than many other advanced economies, they were used rather sparingly between 1997 and 2005.[13] However, they have been used with far greater frequency since 2009 in response to risks arising from the property market. Table 1 summarises the set of MaPPs utilised by Singapore, including policy measures under MAS' purview as well as instruments under the charge of other relevant agencies, particularly with respect to the property market. While some of the MaPPs are more broad-based (such as CCyB), it is apparent that Singapore has targeted the property market as the key source of systemic risk.

---

[12] This and the next section are informed by IMF (2019a, 2019b), FSB (2018) and various MAS Financial Stability Reports, accessible from: https://www.mas.gov.sg/publications?content_type=Financial%20Stability%20Reviews.&page=1&content_type=Financial%20Stability%20Reviews

[13] A set of MaPPs were introduced in May 1996. See Section 2.2.

Table 1. Singapore: List of demand-related macroprudential measures in use.

Measures	Current Calibration	Last Change
Broad-based Tools Applied to the Banking Sector		
Countercyclical capital buffer (CCyB)	MAS implements, since January 1st, 2016, a CCyB framework (including reciprocity requirements) consistent with the Basel Committee on Banking Supervision (BCBS) framework. CCyB decisions are pre-announced by up to 12 months and at least annually in MAS Financial Stability Review (FSR). The CCyB is currently set at 0 percent.	January 2016
Capital conservation buffer	In line with the requirements and phase-in arrangements set out under the Basel III framework, MAS has implemented the requirement for a capital conservation buffer (CCB) for Singapore-incorporated banks. From 1 January 2019, Singapore-incorporated banks need to meet a CCB of 2.5 percent (increased from 1.875 percent) of CET1.	January 2019
Liquidity Tools Applied to the Banking Sector		
Liquidity Coverage Ratio/ Minimum Liquid Asset Requirement	All D-SIBs are required to comply with the Liquidity Coverage Ratio (LCR) requirement, both on an all-currency level and a Singapore Dollar (SGD) level. All other banks in Singapore may elect to comply with the LCR requirement or the Minimum Liquid Assets (MLA) framework, similarly both on an all-currency level and an SGD level. For the three local banking groups which cover all internationally active banks in Singapore, the all-currency LCR requirement stated at 60 percent on 1 January 2015 and increased 10 percent annually to reach 100 percent on 1 January 2019. These banks are also subject to an SGD LCR requirement of 100 percent from 1 January 2015. For other D-SIBs as well as non-D-SIBs that elect to comply with the LCR framework, they are subject to an all-currency LCR requirement of 50 percent and an SGD LCR requirement of 100 percent from 1 January 2016.	January 2015

Table 1. (*Continued*)

Measures	Current Calibration	Last Change
	For banks complying with the MLA requirement, they are required to hold liquid assets denominated in any currency of at least 16 percent of its qualifying liabilities (a subset of the banks' liabilities) in all currencies from 1 January 2016. They are also required to hold liquid assets denominated in SGD of at least 16 percent of its SGD qualifying liabilities.	
Net Stable Funding Ratio	All D-SIBs are required to meet the Net Stable Funding Ratio (NSFR) requirement on an all-currency level from 1 January 2018. For the three local banking groups which cover all internationally active banks in Singapore, the all-currency NSFR requirement is 100 percent. For other D-SIBs, the all-currency NSFR requirement is 50 percent.	January 2018
Tools applied to the Household Sector		
Maximum LTV on loans granted by financial institutions[14]	Individual borrowers: First Housing Loan: 75 percent; or 55 percent if the loan tenure is more than 30 years (25 years where the property purchased is an HDB flat) or extends past age 65. Second Housing Loan: 45 percent; or 25 percent if the loan tenure is more than 30 years (25 years where the property purchased is an HDB flat) or extends past age 65. From Third Housing Loan: 35 percent; or 15 percent if the loan tenure is more than 30 years (25 years where the property purchased is an HDB flat) or extends past age 65. Non-individual borrowers: 15 percent.	July 2018
Total Debt Servicing Ratio (TDSR) on loans granted by financial institutions	60 percent maximum ratio applicable to all loans, except to mortgage equity withdrawal loans with LTV ratios of 50 percent and below.	March 2017

(*Continued*)

---

[14] In addition to LTVs, there exists a Minimum Cash Down Payment imposed since January 2013: First Housing Loan: 5%; or 10% if the loan tenure is more than 30 years or extends past age 65. From Second Housing Loan: 25%.

Table 1. (Continued)

Measures	Current Calibration	Last Change
Mortgage Servicing Ratio (MSR) for HDB flats and Executive Condominiums (ECs)	MSR limits for housing loans granted by financial institutions for all HDB flats as well as EC units where the minimum occupation period has not expired, is capped at 30 percent of a borrower's gross monthly income. MSR limit for housing loans granted by HDB for all HDB flats is capped at 30 percent of a borrower's income.	December 2013
Elimination of interest-only mortgages on loans granted by financial institutions	Interest-only housing loans and loans in which the developer absorbs interest payments on behalf of the borrower for a period of time are disallowed.	September 2009
Maximum tenure for private properties	Absolute limit of 35 years on the tenure of housing loans granted by financial institutions	October 2012
Maximum tenure for HDB properties	Maximum tenure for housing loans granted by HDB at 25 years and for loans granted by financial institutions for the purchase of an HDB flat at 30 years	August 2013
Seller's Stamp Duty (SSD)	SSD on holding periods of up to three years with rates ranging from 4 percent (for properties sold in the third year) to 12 percent (for those sold within the first year)	March 2017
Additional Buyer's Stamp Duty (ABSD)	12 percent for Singapore Citizens (SCs) buying their second residential property; 15 percent for SCs buying their third and subsequent residential property; 5 percent for Singapore Permanent Residents (SPRs) buying their first residential property; 15 percent for SPRs buying their second and subsequent residential property; 20 percent for foreigners; 25 percent for entities; 30 percent for housing developers (with 25 percent remittable, subject to conditions).	July 2018
Tools applied to the Corporate Sector		
Lending to particular industries or sectors	Total property-related exposure of a bank is capped at 35 percent of total eligible assets.	

Source: IMF (2019a, 2019b).

With over 90 percent of Singaporeans owning their homes, property is a significant component of households' balance sheets. Housing constitutes almost 50 percent of total household assets and almost 75 percent of total household liabilities, making home-owners and housing-related borrowers rather susceptible to potential risks in the housing sector. Equally important are housing-market-related risks to Singapore's financial sector as property-related loans account for 25 percent–30 percent of total loans, with the bulk of them extended to the private housing sector. Thus, stability in Singapore's property market is critical to ensure the resilience of households and financial institutions against shocks, consequently enhancing the country's overall macroeconomic and financial sector stability.[15] In addition, given that home ownership has been a long-standing national policy of the Singapore government, home affordability is an issue of particular significance, though it is not explicitly used as an indicator for monitoring systemic risks.[16,17] The macro-financial linkages between the housing market, financial system and the real economy are summarised in Figure 3.

2.1. *Governance structure of MaPPs*

MAS is the sole public institution in Singapore with a MaPP mandate and has powers under various legislations to apply MaPPs independently. MAS has a tiered governance structure for MaPPs, with major policy decisions on the financial regulation framework (including MaPPs) being made by the Board-level Chairman's Meeting and implemented by two management-level committees, viz. the Management Financial

---

[15] Singapore's home ownership is distributed between public housing at 80% and private housing at 20%. About 80% of housing loans (in value terms) are extended by financial institutions, of which, 85% are for private housing and 15% for public housing. The remaining 20% of housing loans is extended by the Housing and Development Board (HDB), all of which are for public housing.

[16] The main policy tool addressing home affordability is the supply of partially subsidised public flats from the HDB, which dominates housing supply.

[17] Of course, the flip side of the affordability argument is that MaPPs could themselves have an adverse impact on affordability by raising the cost of credit and adversely impact broader economic activity and income growth.

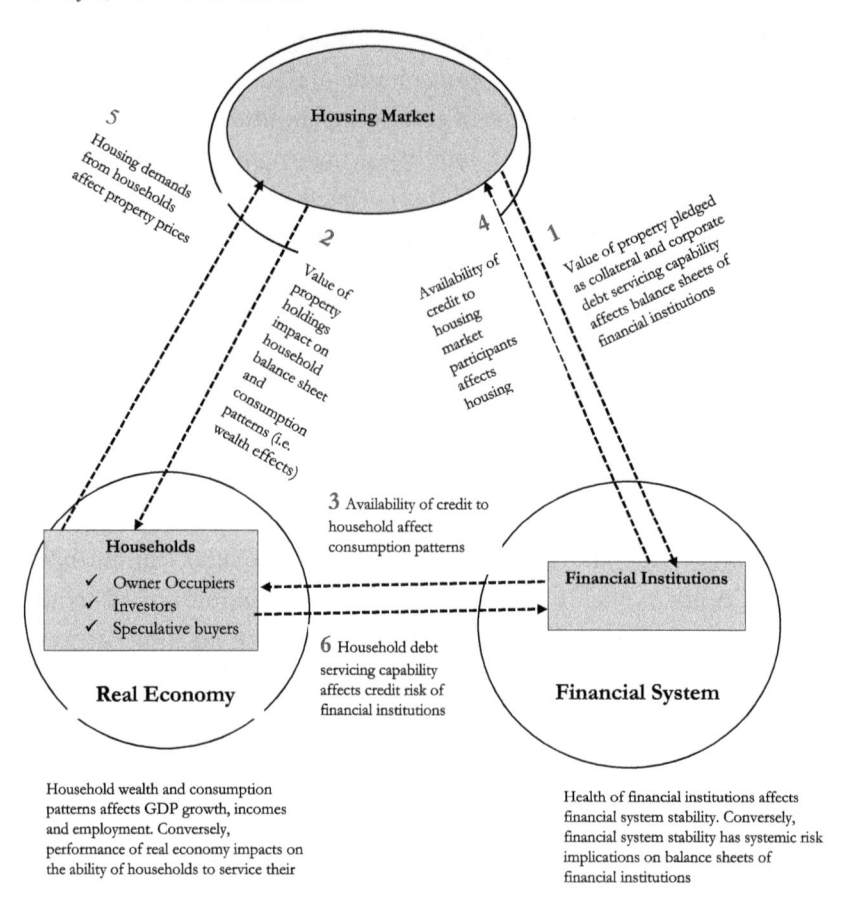

Figure 3. Systematic linkages between the housing market, the financial system and the real economy.
Source: MAS (2011).

Stability Committee (FSC) and the Management Financial Supervision Committee (MFSC). FSC, which meets on a quarterly basis, is chaired by the MAS Managing Director and is in charge of financial stability, including the formulation and communication of MaPPs to the general public.[18] MFSC is chaired by the Deputy Managing Director

---

[18] The FSC is supported by the Macroprudential Surveillance Department (MSD) within the Economic Policy Group which is responsible for coordinating surveillance over risks and vulnerabilities in the financial system and analyses of macroprudential policy and financial stability issues.

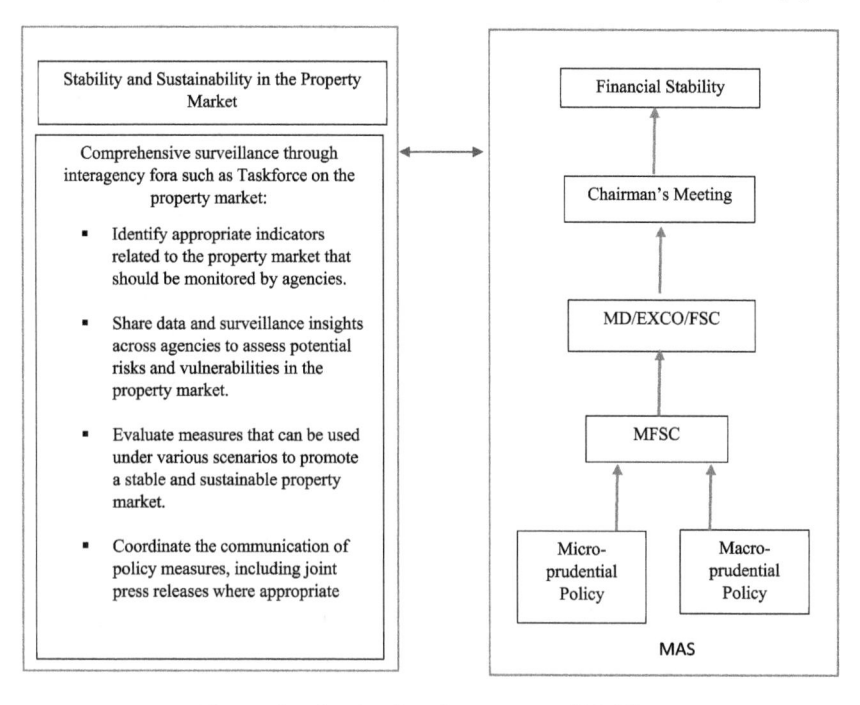

Figure 4. Institutional structure of MaPPs.

Note: Matters with implications for financial stability will be appropriately referred up to Chairman's Meeting. MD stands for Managing Director, EXCO for Executive Committee, FSC for Management Financial Stability Committee, MFSC for Management Financial Supervision Committee.

Source: IMF (2019a, 2019b).

(Financial Supervision) and is responsible for supervision of financial institutions. For the property market specifically, MAS coordinates MaPP measures with the Ministry of Finance and the Ministry of National Development as part of an interagency taskforce on the property market (Figure 4). While MAS implements credit-based MaPP tools, the Ministry of Finance is in charge of fiscal measures in the form of SSD and ABSD, and the Ministry of National Development is responsible for supply-side measures such as the Government Land Sales programme and project completion timelines.

2.2. Types and evolution of property-related MaPPs in Singapore[19]

Singapore's use of housing-related policy measures dates back to the policy package announced in May 1996 in response to the tripling of the private residential property price index (PPI) between 1990Q1 and 1996Q2 (Figure 5). This initial package of measures included a mix of housing-credit MaPPs such as a limit on the LTV ratio of 80 percent and disallowing foreigners from taking Singapore dollar-denominated housing loans; fiscal measures included SSD and capital gains taxes (on properties sold within three years of purchase) which were levied to discourage speculation, typically characterised by shorter holding periods of housing property; and supply-side measures involving adjustment in the timing of government land sales.

The PPI peaked in 1996Q2 just after the measures were imposed but fell sharply with the onset of the Asian Financial Crisis (AFC). In November 1997, the SSD was suspended.[20] By 1998Q4 the PPI had lost 45 percent of its value from its peak in 1996Q2. While the property market did bounce back, it proved short-lived as the Dot-com crash, Avian flu and other factors exerted downward pressure again on asset prices. In October 2001, capital gains taxes were suspended (and have been eschewed since then) and foreigners' access to Singapore dollar-denominated housing loans was reinstated while the government slowed down its planned land sales. The PPI during this period remained rather stagnant.

In July 2005, the LTV requirement was eased from 80 percent to 90 percent and the minimum cash down-payment requirement was also lowered from 10 percent to 5 percent. Buyer stamp duty concessions were withdrawn in December 2006.[21] A recovery in property prices took place between 2006 and 2007, followed by a sharp run-up in prices and

---

[19] This section draws partly on the timeline available at the MAS website: https://www.mas.gov.sg/publications/macroprudential-policies-in-singapore

[20] Additionally, buyers were allowed to defer payments until the completion of their housing units under the Deferred Payment Scheme (DPS). The lacklustre order books meant that developers were given more time to complete their projects. The DPS was withdrawn in October 2007.

[21] In Singapore, the buyer's stamp duty was previously treated by policymakers as a fiscal tool instead of a macroprudential measure. However, it is included for comprehensiveness given that it could have had similar macroprudential effects before 2009.

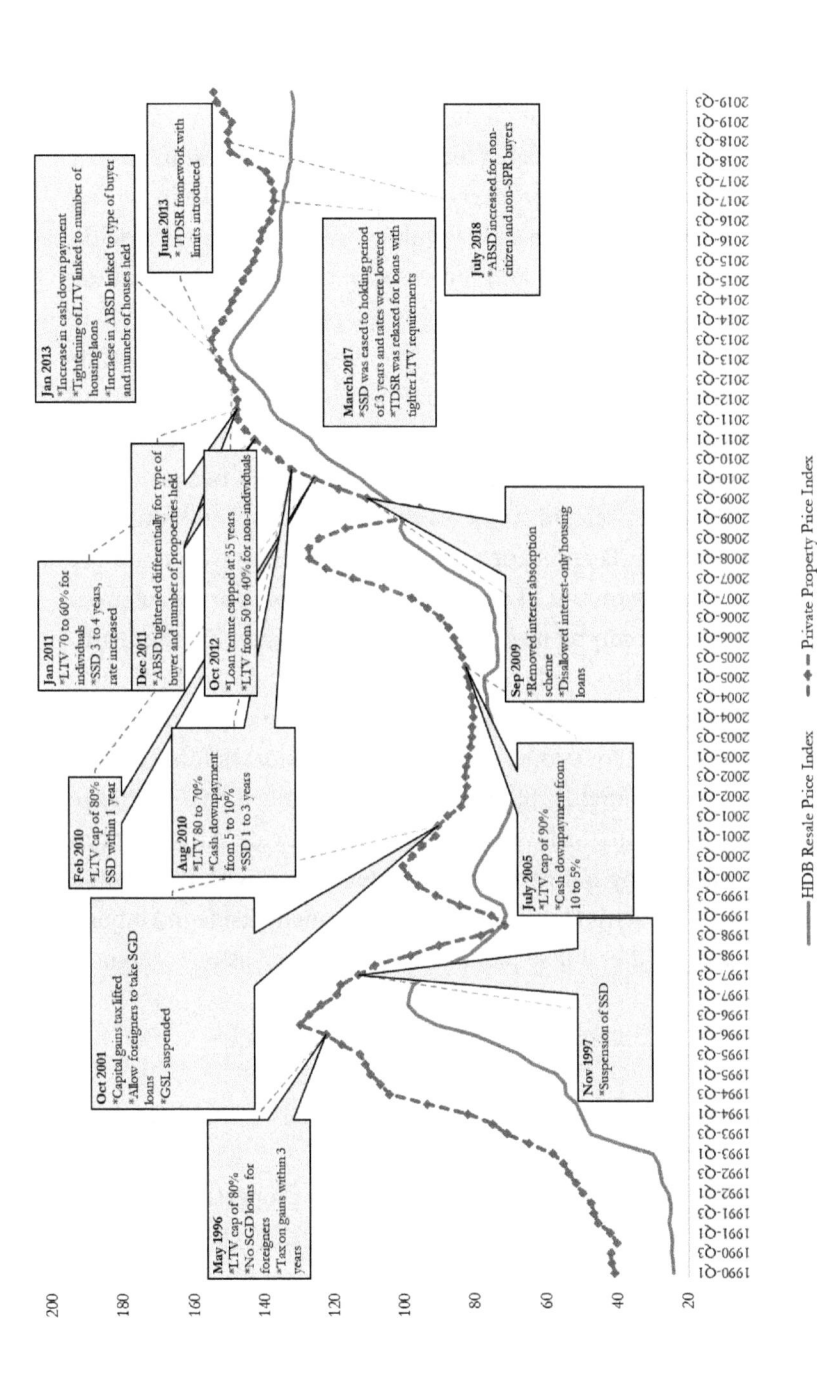

Figure 5. Property-related macroprudential measures.

Source: Updated based on Robinson (2019).

transactions between 2007 and 2008. By 2008Q2 the PPI had reached its pre-AFC peak. The onset of the GFC subsequently caused private housing prices in Singapore to plummet. Between 2008Q3 and 2009Q2, the PPI corrected by 25 percent alongside a fall in transaction volumes. Government land sales were suspended given the sluggishness in uptake.

By mid-2009, Singapore's property market recovery began in earnest due to a combination of foreign capital inflows in search of higher yields, benign domestic interest rates and increases in the resident population (Chow and Xie, 2016). The PPI rose by over 60 percent from 2009Q2 to 2013Q3. It was also during this period that Singapore experienced its most aggressive use of MaPPs. In particular, between September 2009 and December 2013, Singapore undertook eight rounds of policy measures to rein in the booming private housing market which had reached new highs by early 2013. Housing-related credit was tightened via several rounds of reductions in LTV limits and capping of loan tenures, as well as via the imposition of a ceiling on the TDSR, which caps the proportion of gross monthly income that can be used for servicing all loans. Concurrently, fiscal measures were also used to raise the transaction costs of property transactions that posed more significant risks to the market. In particular, the SSD was reinstated for properties sold within a short holding period after purchase. Subsequently, SSD levy rates were hiked twice and the holding period subject to the levy was also extended twice. An ABSD was introduced, followed by increases in ABSD levy rates, with differential rates imposed on residents (i.e., citizens and permanent residents) buying their second and third or subsequent properties as well as on foreigners and corporates.

The specific chronology of policy actions was as follows:

- September 2009: interest-only housing loans and interest-absorption scheme[22] loans were disallowed.
- February 2010: SSD was reinstated on housing properties that were bought and sold within a year. Simultaneously, LTV was reduced to 80 percent.

---

[22] These are loans in which the developer absorbed interest payments on behalf of the borrower for a period of time.

- August 2010: SSD was extended to all residential properties bought and sold within three years, but with a stepped reduction as the holding period increased; LTV on borrowings from financial institutions was furthered lowered to 70 percent; and the required cash down-payment for purchases was increased from 5 percent to 10 percent.
- January 2011: the period for which SSD was levied was extended to four years and rates of SSD were increased. Simultaneously, LTV for existing borrowers taking up their second and subsequent housing loans was brought down to 60 percent for individuals and 50 percent for other borrowers.
- December 2011: an ABSD was levied for the first time. Foreigners and corporates were levied at a much higher rate of 10 percent; whereas residents were charged 3 percent for third and subsequent property purchases.[23]
- October 2012: maximum tenure on loans from financial institutions was capped at 35 years. LTV for individuals with loan tenure beyond 30 years and loan period extending beyond the retirement age of 65 years was lowered to 40 percent, if they had outstanding housing loans at the time of borrowing, while the 60 percent limit applied only to borrowers with no outstanding housing loans.
- January 2013: LTV rules were further tightened for borrowers applying for second or subsequent housing loans. Cash down-payment requirement was raised to 25 percent for individuals applying for second or subsequent housing loans. ABSD was increased on the second and third or subsequent property for permanent residents and citizens respectively. ABSD was also levied on permanent residents for the first home purchase, while ABSD for foreigners was raised to 15 percent.[24]

---

[23] Permanent residents (PRs) buying the second and subsequent property will pay an ABSD of 3%. Singapore citizens buying the third and subsequent property will also pay an ABSD of 3%.

[24] ABSD was levied on the purchase of residential property, with revised rates as follows: 15% on foreigners and corporates; 5% on permanent residents buying the first residential property and 10% on buying a second or subsequent residential property; and 7% on citizens buying a second residential property and 10% on buying a third or subsequent property.

- June 2013: TDSR framework was introduced, requiring financial institutions to compute debt servicing ratios using a standardised methodology, and a headline threshold of 60 percent. Along with LTV and cash down-payment requirements, the TDSR framework was intended to augment the quality of housing credit and rein in excessive leverage in the housing market.[25]

The period 2013–2017 saw stagnant transaction volumes and a gradual correction in prices in Singapore's private housing sector. Subsequently, on the back of a strong global economic recovery, the PPI witnessed an upswing of almost 10 percent from 2017Q2 to 2018Q2. In July 2018, housing-related credit was once again tightened as the LTV ratio was lowered from 80 percent to 75 percent. Fiscal measures were also tightened via higher ABSD rates for resident buyers of a second or subsequent private residential housing property (from 7 percent to 12 percent and 10 percent to 15 percent, respectively) as well as for non-resident buyers (from 15 to 20 percent), who could obtain loans from overseas and were unlikely to be impacted by the tightening of domestic credit measures. Property developers were disincentivised from hoarding land by the requirement to complete the development and sale of all their housing units within five years of purchasing the land, failing which they would not be eligible for the remission of an ABSD of 25 percent on the purchase price of the land paid upfront.[26]

The period immediately after the GFC saw a rapid growth in housing loans. Housing loans from financial institutions recorded an average annual increase of 10.8 percent Y-o-Y between 2010 and 2013 (Figure 6). The imposition of credit tightening measures noted above coincided with a steady decline in the growth rate of mortgage loans from financial institutions. With a further round of LTV tightening in 2018, mortgage loan growth turned negative. Revealingly, after the implementation of LTVs in 2010–2011, the share of new mortgage loan borrowers with one

---

[25] Given the run-up in public housing prices, the government also levied the Mortgage Servicing Ratio (MSR) for the repayment of housing loans for HDB flat purchases, capped at 30% of gross monthly income (see Table 1).

[26] The authorities also imposed a non-remittable 5% ABSD on developers buying residential properties for housing development (primarily as a means of encouraging prudent land sales activity).

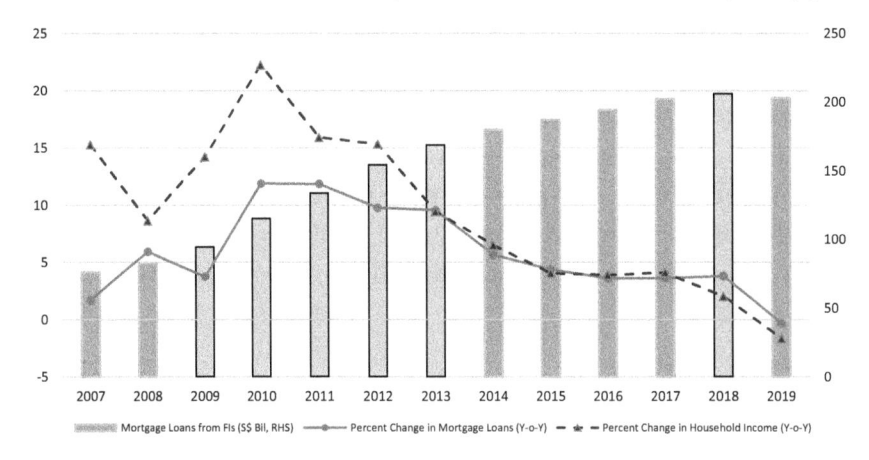

Figure 6. Mortgage loans and from financial institutions and household income.
Source: Data from MAS.

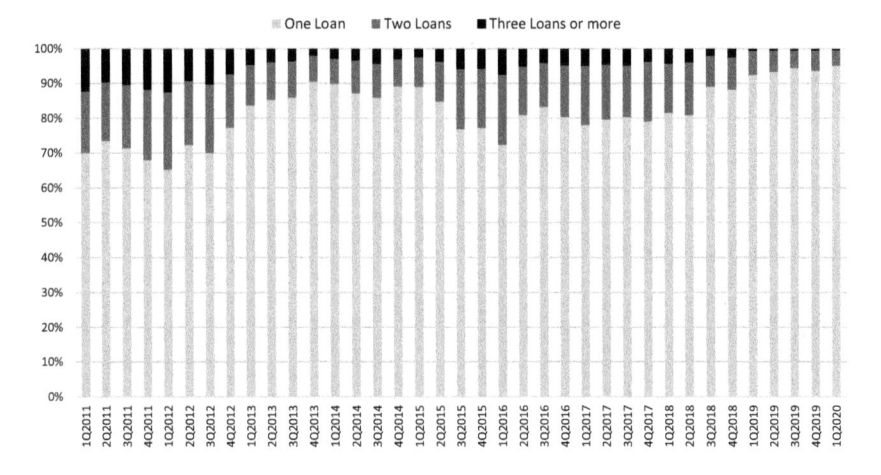

Figure 7. Share of new mortgage loan borrowers by number of loans.
Source: Data from MAS.

loan increased relative to those with two or more loans, suggesting the positive impact of a gradation in LTV requirements based on the number of properties purchased (Figure 7).

Mortgage loans as a share of GDP, which had grown steadily since 2007 from 46 percent to just around 54 percent by 2013–2014, stabilised and has been on a decline since then. Consistent with this, household debt as a share of GDP that peaked at around 74 percent of GDP in 2014 gradually declined since then, with the corresponding share at 63 percent of GDP in 2019 (Figure 8).

Consistent with the tightening of credit-related measures, there was a reduction in the purchases of new private housing properties by Singapore residents between late 2009 and early 2014. However, transaction volumes of foreigners continued to rise until late 2011 as they were presumably less hindered by the credit-related measures (Figure 9). To be sure, the share of

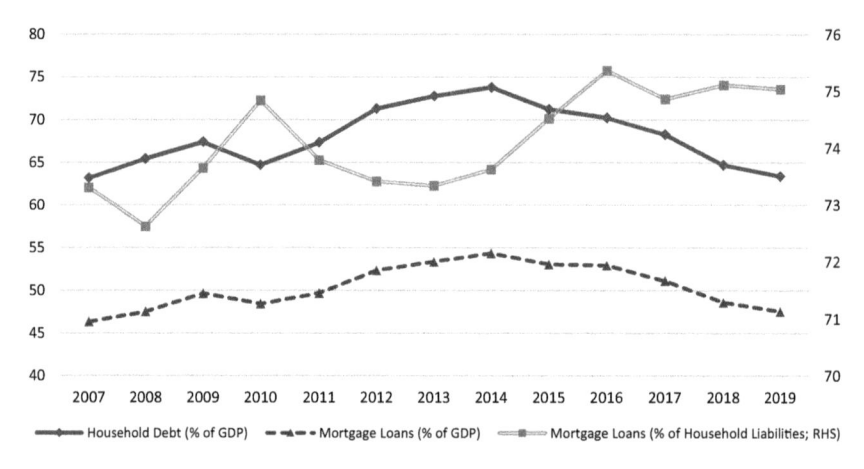

Figure 8. Household debt and mortgage loans.
Source: Data from MAS.

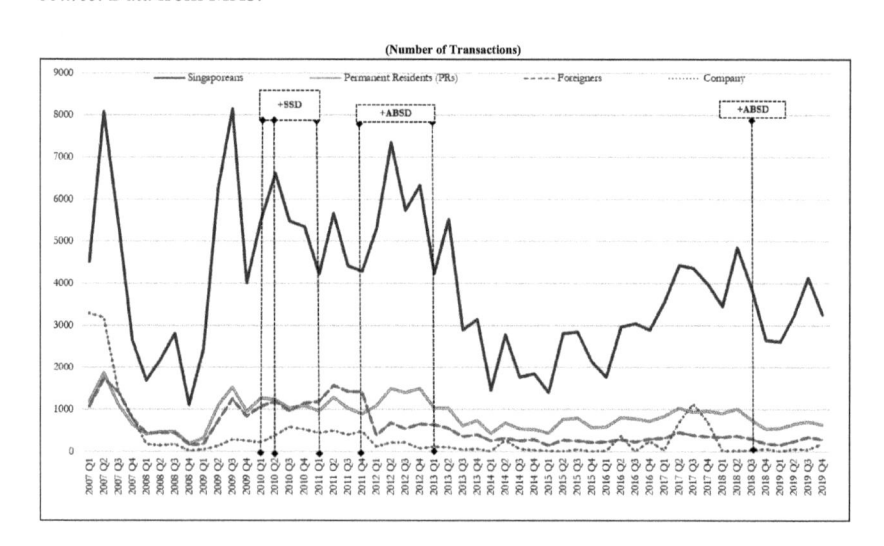

Figure 9. Purchasers of private property in Singapore by type.
Source: Based on transactions data from MAS.

(Percent Share of Total Transactions)

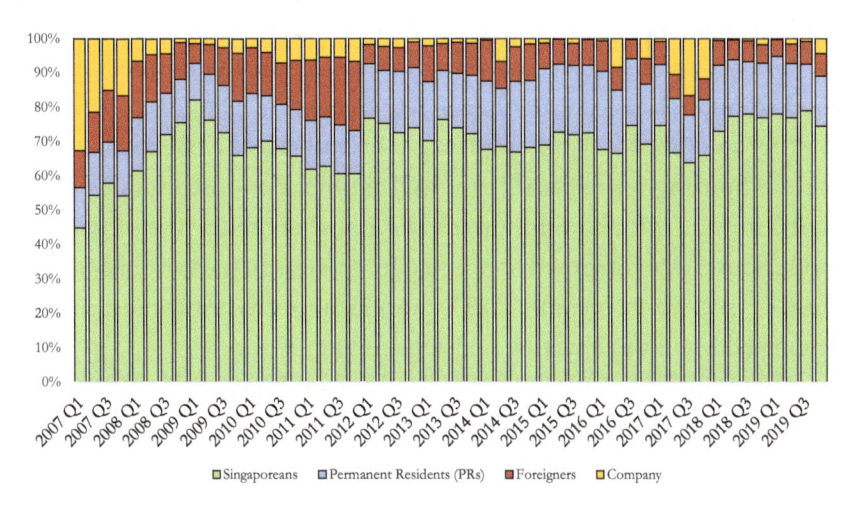

Figure 10. Purchasers of private property in Singapore by type.
Source: Based on transactions data from MAS.

foreign purchases which averaged about 11 percent of total purchases in 2009 and 2010 started rising sharply and reached a peak of 20 percent of all sales by late 2011, before falling back sharply and averaging 7 percent from then on, with the tightening of ABSD, especially on foreigners (Figure 10).[27]

Overall, as is apparent, Singapore has deployed various types of policy measures in an attempt to pre-emptively address the build-up of systemic risks by reining in sharp property price appreciations.

3. Literature review

There has been a growing body of literature that uses panel studies to assess the effectiveness of MaPPs especially in terms of managing credit booms (IMF, 2020). However, given the importance of the property market in impacting financial and macroeconomic cycles in Singapore,

---

[27] While the share of foreign purchases by individuals remained subdued, there was a notable spike in corporate purchases in 2017, buoyed by a surge in collective sales for redevelopments.

most of the MaPPs are buyer-based measures aimed at enhancing resilience of households as well as financial institutions.

Using quarterly data for 57 countries (comprising both emerging markets and advanced economies) over the period 1980Q1 to 2011Q4, Kuttner and Shim (2016) empirically investigate the effectiveness of various housing-related MaPPs (as well as other non-interest rate policy tools) in moderating house prices and housing credit. They find that while housing credit growth is affected by changes in the various MaPPs, the debt-service-to-income (DSTI) ratio turns out to be the most robust among all MaPPs in affecting housing credit growth.

Extending Shim *et al.*'s (2013) database on housing market policy actions, Richter *et al.* (2018) introduce a novel dataset on changes in maximum LTV ratios that are both exogenous and adjusted for intensity, for a sample of advanced and emerging market economies. Using quarterly data for 56 countries from 1990Q1 to 2012Q2, they investigate the effects of changes in maximum LTV ratios on output and inflation. Their empirical results suggest that changes in maximum LTV ratios have only modest effects on output as well as inflation. However, they find robust evidence of asymmetry in that LTV tightening (relative to loosening) produces sizeable effects on output and that these results tend to be stronger for emerging markets than advanced economies. While the effects of changes in maximum LTV ratios on inflation are found to be negligible, the comparable effects on credit growth and house prices appear to be substantial.

Alam *et al.* (2019) introduce the IMF's integrated macroprudential policy (iMaPP) database. Two features of the database stand out in relation to the other existing cross-country databases on MaPPs. The first relates to the wider coverage in terms of the sample countries and time period. The information on MaPPs is compiled for 134 countries on a monthly basis from 1990M1 to 2016M12.[28] The second pertains to the coverage of instruments. The database offers indices (of a binary nature) for 17 types of instruments (dummy indices) along with the specification of whether the policy actions were tightened or loosened in each instance.[29] The empirical analysis undertaken in this study focuses on which of the

---

[28] The tightening by Singapore in 2017–2018 is not captured by the iMaPP database.
[29] Further, it provides information on the average regulatory limit on the LTV ratios.

MaPP instruments have significant effects in dampening household credit growth as well as housing prices. To do so, the study estimates panel regressions for 63 countries (including advanced and emerging markets) over the period from 1991Q1 to 2016Q4. Overall, the results show that loan-related MaPPs such as DSTI and LTV limits significantly dampen household credit growth, while the effects on housing prices are found to be relatively weaker. Further, the results also provide evidence of non-linearity in how LTV changes affect household credit, with the effect per percentage point of LTV tightening tending to diminish with the size of adjustment. Finally, their results also show a non-linear effect of tightening of LTV limits on consumption in that the effect of additional tightening under already tight conditions tends to be larger.

McDonald (2015) empirically examines whether the effectiveness of tightening versus loosening MaPPs depends on the phase of the "housing cycle" during which they are implemented. Focusing on 100 policy adjustments in LTV and debt-to-income (DTI) limits across 17 countries from 1990Q1 to 2013Q4,[30] the results show that tightening measures tend to produce sizeable effects during phases of credit expansion and when house prices are relatively more expensive (high house price-to-income ratio). In comparison, the results suggest that loosening measures have relatively smaller effects. That said, during downturns (with weak credit growth and cheaper housing prices), the observed differences between the impact of tightening and loosening on levels of housing credit are quite small.

While there have been a number of empirical studies on the effectiveness of MaPPs at a country level using time series data (see for instance, Jacome and Mitra (2015)), the literature specifically on Singapore is rather limited. The handful of empirical studies that have focussed on Singapore are discussed below.

Deng *et al.* (2019) evaluate the net effects of cooling measures in Singapore using the regression discontinuity method on house transaction data over the period from September 2009 to December 2013. The study

---

[30] The sample includes Australia, China, Taiwan ROC, Hong Kong SAR, Japan, Korea, Malaysia, New Zealand, Philippines, Singapore, Thailand, Denmark, Canada, Sweden, Latvia and Norway.

finds that the MaPPs have succeeded in both ensuring affordability as well as preventing price speculation, with housing prices falling by 10 percent–15 percent without generating any notable side-effects.

An MAS study (Wong et al., 2015) estimates relationships between key variables in Singapore's private property market using quarterly data between 2002Q3 and 2014Q2. This study also attempts to disentangle the effects of credit, fiscal and supply-side policies and finds that the tax-based measures have had a larger impact on property transactions and property prices than the conventional credit-based MaPPs which limit the amount of mortgage loans. Further, the results suggest that the signalling role of supply-side measures in the form of announcements of government land sales also seems to have been effective in dampening price appreciations.

Using a bounds testing approach to measure the effectiveness of housing policies introduced between June 1981 and December 2013 in maintaining price stability, Lee and Xie (2015) identify the LTV ratio as a housing policy in Singapore that is effective in the short run, alongside the capital gains tax and Central Provident Fund (CPF) measures, while debt-to-income ratios are effective in the long run. Across time horizons, Singapore's housing policy is found to impact property prices and transaction volumes in a countercyclical manner.

In an empirical analysis of 10 Asian countries, Lee et al. (2015) examine the effectiveness of different MaPPs in dampening credit growth, leverage growth and housing price appreciation, using a qualitative vector autoregressive (Qual VAR) model which allows MaPPs to be defined in a continuous form rather than as a binary variable. The empirical results specific to Singapore spanning a sample period from 2000Q1 to 2013Q4 reveal that the imposition of MaPPs has been relatively successful in producing a dampening effect on housing prices and credit expansion, while their impact on leverage growth has been minimal.

Finally, IMF (2019b) undertakes an empirical analysis of the impact of MaPPs in Singapore on residential housing prices using a three-dimensional panel (quarter, region and property types). The study uses quarterly data on residential prices and rents across different property types (data on private non-landed residential properties are available from 2004, while data on public housing units are available from 2007Q2) and regions in Singapore. The study suggests that it takes six quarters after policy implementation for a particular MaPP to reach its peak impact on residential prices, of about a 7 percent decline in prices. The analysis also finds that the private residential prices of the Core Central Region appear to be relatively more impacted by stamp duties as the region tends to attract relatively more purchases from foreigners and corporates, which engender greater speculative activity.

4. Effectiveness of MaPPs in Singapore: An empirical investigation

As is apparent from the review of the literature, the handful of studies on Singapore find MaPPs to be effective in managing the property cycle. Since the post-GFC period of easy money but also the period before that, the global financial cycle has heightened the degree of house price synchronisation across economies (Cesa-Bianchi et al., 2015; Duca, 2020; Hirata et al., 2013; IMF, 2018a; Katagiri, 2018). At times, this has influenced domestic housing price dynamics in ways that might otherwise not be warranted by domestic fundamentals, an issue of particular concern to a highly globalised country like Singapore. Given that the private residential property market has systemic implications for the financial system[31] and tends to have larger interconnectedness and linkages to global spillover channels, this section will focus on understanding the extent to which price growth for private housing in Singapore co-moves with global house prices and whether MaPPs can insulate the domestic housing market from global fluctuations.[32]

4.1. *Data and methodology*

The generic estimating equation will take the following form:

$$gr\_RPPI_{jt} = \delta_j + \beta_1 gr\_GHPI_t + \gamma X_{jt} + \rho_t + u_{it} \qquad (1)$$

---

[31] The private housing market has systemic implications for the financial system given its larger banking exposures. About two-thirds of housing loans extended by financial institutions are to borrowers purchasing private residential properties.

[32] A study by the IMF (2019b) has noted that house price growth in Singapore had been synchronised with global house prices until end-2013 after which there appeared to have been some decoupling following the implementation of a series of MaPPs.

where:

gr_RPPI_{jt} is the growth rate of the property price index of non-landed private residential properties in each region j within Singapore at time t;

gr_GHPI_t is the growth rate of the average global housing price index (GHPI) (across 57 countries) at time t taken from the IMF[33];

X_{jt} is a vector of the economic determinants of housing prices in Singapore drawn from the literature that includes the following:

$$X_{jt} = \begin{Bmatrix} \text{Real Gross Domestic Product (GDP) Growth} \\ \text{Real Interest Rate (RIR)} \\ \text{Pipeline Supply} \\ \text{Real Effective Exchange Rate (REER)} \\ \text{Regional Population} \end{Bmatrix}$$

δ_j and ρ_t denote region- and time-fixed effects;

and u_{jt} is the idiosyncratic error term.

A priori, since Singapore is a global city with no capital controls, we would expect a close positive co-movement between growth in global house prices and Singapore's house prices, implying a positive coefficient for β_1. With regard to the determinants of housing prices, we expect higher real GDP growth and a larger regional population to induce greater housing demand, which will consequently result in a rise in property prices. As for real interest rates (RIR), a higher RIR implies higher costs of borrowing which would likely dampen housing prices. The nexus between changes in REER and house prices is not quite straightforward. On the one hand, REER appreciation may lead to a rise in domestic property prices if consumers or firms spend more as a result of a rise in

---

[33] On the basis of house price changes between 2013 and 2017, the IMF (2017) places countries into three clusters, viz. gloom, bust and boom. Singapore is listed in the gloom category along with Brazil (Rio de Janeiro); China (Shanghai); Croatia (Zagreb); Cyprus (Nicosia); Finland (Helsinki); France (Paris); Greece (Athens); Macedonia (Skopje); Netherlands (Amsterdam); Russia (Moscow); Slovenia (Ljubljana); and Spain (Madrid). While this clustering is interesting, it is rather ad hoc and would obviously change based on the time period considered (the time period of our analysis is 2004–2019). We therefore use the full set of countries in the IMF sample. The study also confirms robustness by considering another database on real residential property prices by the BIS. The details are discussed further in this section.

the value of their assets (i.e., wealth effect). On the other hand, a stronger currency in the form of an appreciation of the Singapore dollar (in real trade-weighted terms) could drive down foreign demand for Singapore's assets, which would translate into a lowering of house prices in Singapore, implying a negative relationship. Finally, higher pipeline supply or higher availability of land supply in general should effectively contribute to lower house prices.[34]

Next, we explicitly include the role of MaPPs in the baseline specification. The aim is to understand empirically the impact of MaPPs on house price synchronicity between Singapore and the world,[35] while factoring in regional variations in property prices within Singapore. To that end we augment Equation (1) as follows:

$$gr\_RPPI_{jt} = \delta_j + \beta_1 gr\_GHPI_t + \beta_2 MaPPs_t \\ + \beta_3 gr\_GHPI_t * MaPPs_t + \gamma X_{jt} + \rho_t + u_{jt} \quad (2)$$

β_2 captures the effectiveness of MaPPs on house price growth in Singapore (i.e., dampening impact) and we would expect it to be negative as their intended effect is to dampen the growth in regional property prices. In contrast, β_3 will be the key parameter of interest that

---

[34] While our focus is on non-landed private residential properties, there is clearly a linkage between public and private housing in that a wealth effect resulting in an "upgrading" demand for housing accounts for almost two-thirds of the annual demand for private housing, from owners of public housing (IMF, 2019a). In addition, rising private property prices invariably raise land and related construction costs which in turn impact public house prices (the housing subsidy for the first-time purchase of public housing takes the form of a flat grant). While HDB resale prices are generally less volatile compared to private housing prices, there is some empirical evidence to suggest that the prices of these two components of housing have been fairly correlated in the past (Chia et al., 2017). Any relevant effects from HDB resale prices could be picked up by drivers such as GDP growth and population, which appear in the control variable X_{jt} in the empirical model. Nonetheless, there are material differences in buyer profiles in the public and private housing markets, given that foreigners and households above a certain income threshold are restricted from purchasing HDB flats and would only purchase private properties.

[35] MaPP measures such as ABSD, LTV ratios, Sellers' Stamp Duty and the Total Debt Service Ratio (TDSR) considered in this study are primarily targeted at the private residential property market.

enables us to test the effectiveness of MaPPs on decoupling specifically. We hypothesise the interaction term β_3 between selected MaPPs and global house price growth to be negative and statistically significant, implying that MaPPs facilitate the decoupling of Singapore's property market from global factors.

Given the regional panel data setting, we estimate Equations (1) and (2) using a conventional panel fixed effects estimation procedure incorporating both regional and time (quarterly) fixed effects, thus controlling for both unobserved region-specific fixed characteristics as well as time-fixed effects that might affect regional property prices in Singapore.[36] We make use of the heterogeneity within Singapore based on available regional data on the property price index of non-landed residential properties in the core central region (CCR), the rest of the central region (RCR) and outside the central region (OCR). This allows us to capture panel variations across Singapore in terms of property prices.

With regard to the imposition of MaPPs, we first make use of a composite MaPP index (MPI) constructed by MAS based on the following instruments: Buyer's Stamp Duty; ABSD for foreigners and domestic buyers; LTV ratios for first, second and third housing loans, respectively, and SSD. When a tightening (loosening) of a MaPP measure in the index is implemented, the index will increase (decrease) by 1. For example, tightening the LTV limits for the first and second housing loan are taken as separate measures and hence raises the MPI by 2 (Figure 11).[37] This method of aggregating individual measures is similar to those in the literature, such as Kim and Mehrotra (2017).

As the composite MPI does not differentiate between the various types of MaPP instruments or take into account their intensity, we also make use of the individual MaPP levers to assess their effectiveness in decoupling

---

[36] We recognise that the fixed effects estimates will remain robust only if there is no endogeneity arising from the correlation between the time-invariant component of the error term and the regressor of interest. We also undertake GMM estimation subsequently to check for robustness.

[37] For consistency in interpretation, we invert the original measurement of LTV so that an increase in LTV would indicate tightening.

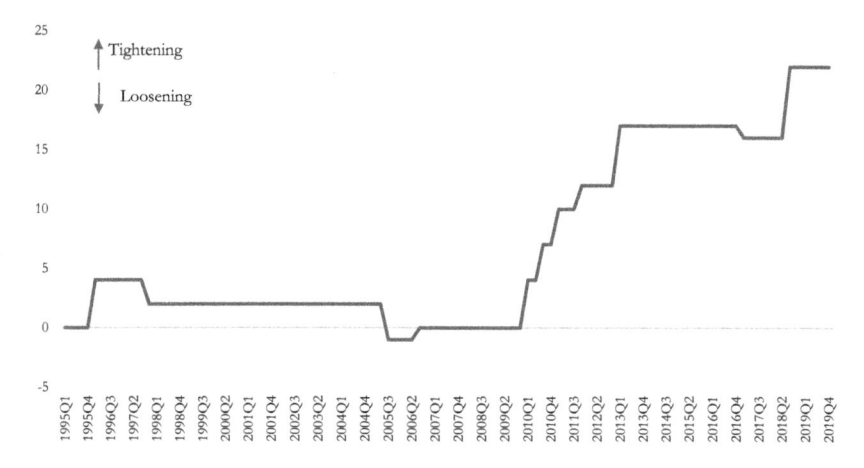

Figure 11. Composite Macroprudential Index (MPI).
Source: Based on data from MAS.

Singapore's property prices from global prices.[38] The data sample is on a quarterly basis from 2004Q1 to 2019Q4, which corresponds to the availability of Singapore's regional price index of non-landed residential properties. Table A1 provides the definitions and sources of the data used in the empirical exercise.

4.2. *Empirical results*

Our benchmark results for the full sample are summarised in Table 2. Column (1) presents the results of estimating Equation (2), which indicate the effectiveness of the composite MPI in dampening regional

---

[38] An additional instrument in the form of Total Debt Servicing Ratio (TDSR), which is a structural rather than cyclical MaPP introduced in 2013Q2, was excluded from the construction of the aggregate MPI index but is used individually. When used separately, TDSR is coded as a dummy variable, which takes the value 2 for the full year of its introduction in 2013Q2 until 2014Q4, after which it takes the value 1 for the remainder of the sample period, broadly capturing a decaying effect. In the earlier period following the introduction of TDSR (i.e., quarter it was implemented and the three subsequent quarters), its effects on prices were assumed to be larger as borrowers and the banking system required some time to adapt to the newly introduced measure. The reason for this decaying effect is that buyers likely had to re-evaluate their property purchases while banks had to adjust their credit administrative functions, after which these factors were more likely to have been priced in.

Table 2. Benchmark results: Impact of MaPPs on housing price growth.

	(1) Aggregate MPI	(2) ABSD & SSD	(3) LTV Avg (Inverted)	(4) ABSD Foreign	(5) TDSR
GHPI	2.345***	2.293**	3.031**	2.188**	3.353
	(0.307)	(0.242)	(0.424)	(0.257)	(1.367)
Pipeline Supply	−0.067	−0.054**	−0.049*	−0.0557*	−0.0534**
	(0.048)	(0.012)	(0.011)	(0.015)	(0.005)
RIR	−1.275***	−1.125***	−1.369***	−0.857***	−0.631**
	(0.305)	(0.078)	(0.102)	(0.062)	(0.145)
Real GDP Growth	0.495***	0.453***	0.472***	0.469***	0.636***
	(0.126)	(0.011)	(0.010)	(0.029)	(0.024)
REER	−0.158	0.021	−0.138	0.0223	0.391**
	(0.244)	(0.069)	(0.097)	(0.098)	(0.054)
Regional Pop	0.497***	0.466**	0.427**	0.402**	0.0472
	(0.097)	(0.055)	(0.067)	(0.087)	(0.030)
MPI	−0.326***				
	(0.062)				
MPI*GHPI	−0.090*				
	(0.053)				
ABSD&SSD		−0.368**			
		(0.069)			
ABSD&SSD*GHPI		−0.116*			
		(0.038)			
LTV Avg (Inv)			−0.158**		
			(0.038)		
LTV Avg*GHPI			−0.0528*		
			(0.016)		
ABSD Foreign				−0.240*	
				(0.081)	
ABSD Foreign*GHPI				−0.126**	
				(0.031)	
TDSR					−0.740***
					(0.066)
TDSR*GHPI					−1.706
					(0.984)
Observations	162	162	162	162	162
R-Squared	0.499	0.479	0.501	0.451	0.374
Number of Regions	3	3	3	3	3
Fixed Effects	Yes	Yes	Yes	Yes	Yes

Note: The three regions in Singapore are Core Central Region (CCR), Rest of the Central Region (RCR) and Outside Central Region (OCR). More details on the regional classification are available from Urban Redevelopment Authority, Singapore. Robust standard errors in parentheses. *** $p < 0.01$, ** $p < 0.05$, * $p < 0.1$.

property prices as well as the presence of decoupling effects. Columns (2) through (5) evaluate the effectiveness of individual MaPP instruments.

Focusing on Column (1), we observe that all the determinants of regional property prices carry the expected signs and most of them turn out to be statistically significant. For instance, higher growth in global house prices tends to increase Singapore's regional property prices as expected, while a higher cost of borrowing captured by an increase in RIR strongly deters the growth of property prices. Furthermore, consistent with our priors, both higher growth of domestic output and a larger regional population tend to be positively associated with regional property prices and the estimated coefficients are highly statistically significant at the 1 percent level. While an increase in pipeline supply seems to have the appropriate negative sign, suggesting that a higher availability of land supply dampens growth in regional property prices, the variable is not statistically significant, possibly because its effects are longer-term in nature.[39] A rise in the REER (appreciation) enters the regression with a negative sign but is statistically insignificant, suggesting the tension between the wealth and price effects as discussed previously.

With regard to the impact of the MPI which is our primary interest, Column (1) shows strong evidence that Singapore's MaPPs as a whole have produced a dampening impact on the growth of the country's regional property prices, as captured by the negative and highly statistically significant coefficient of β_2. In terms of its economic significance, we note that every additional tightening measure (that translates into an increase of MPI by 1) seems to be associated with a 0.33-percentage-point reduction in Singapore's regional property price index. Furthermore, as noted, we test the decoupling hypothesis by introducing the interaction term (β_3) between the MPI and growth in global housing prices. Our results reveal that the interaction term turns out to be both statistically significant and has the correct negative sign, thus lending support to the decoupling impact of MaPPs.

---

[39] Alternatively, using uncompleted private residential units launched for sale as a proxy for land supply also tends to produce the correct negative sign and the coefficient remains statistically insignificant in this specification.

In the next four columns we make use of the individual MaPPs to check for variations in the effectiveness across different MaPP levers.[40] In terms of the dampening effects of MaPPs on domestic property prices, we find consistent results for all instruments, i.e., ABSD and SSD, LTV caps, ABSD levies on foreigners and TDSR tend to achieve the desired goal of dampening regional property prices. In terms of decoupling, we once again find that the impact of the interaction terms between global house price growth and individual MaPP levers are comparable and consistent with that of the composite MPI, with the impact of the ABSD imposed on foreign buyers being especially significant. Overall, our results seem to provide broad evidence in support of the robustness of the different MaPP instruments in effecting a decoupling of Singapore's property prices from global price movements as well as dampening the growth in regional property prices within the country.[41]

4.3. Robustness

By way of robustness, we do three things. First, we re-run our regressions focusing only on the central region of Singapore where there is likely to be a relatively higher concentration of property purchases by foreigners (individuals as well as corporates). Second, we re-run the benchmark regressions using a dynamic panel estimation procedure. We recognise that one of the empirical challenges in estimating Equation (2) could be reverse causality. Property-cooling measures may likely be imposed during periods of high credit growth and price appreciation. Similarly, the expectation of imposition of MaPPs may lead to a surge in prices and subsequent decline post-implementation.

---

[40] The sum of the impact across different MaPP levers does not equal to the results for the composite MPI reported in column (1) as the structures of the MaPP levers and the MPI are different. Further, there could be interactions amongst the MaPP levers that are not considered in the individual regressions of the different MaPP levers.

[41] It should be noted also that while the TDSR does not seem to have any insulating effect, it clearly has strong direct effects in reducing housing price growth.

In the absence of credible instruments, an alternative is to make use of the Blundell–Bond (1998) system-GMM estimator to mitigate potential reverse causality concerns to a reasonable extent. System GMM is also a common way to overcome possible biases of applying fixed effects to dynamic panels.[42] Third, we re-estimate our baseline model with an alternative real residential property price index compiled by the Bank for International Settlements (BIS).[43]

As can be seen in Table 3, the basic results remain largely robust when limiting the sample to the central region, and notably, the decoupling hypothesis tends to be supported even more strongly in the case of ABSD imposed on foreigners. In addition, the introduction of the TDSR framework not only dampens regional property prices but also seems to have insulating properties.[44]

Table 4 summarises the results of the GMM estimation. It is useful to note that if the estimated coefficient on the lagged dependent variable is closer to zero, it denotes weak persistence but with a high speed of adjustment, while a coefficient closer to one would imply persistence but with a slower speed of adjustment. As the results clearly show, the magnitude of the coefficient on the lagged dependent variable across

---

[42] Note that this estimator uses lagged levels of the series as instruments for the endogenous variables in the equation in first differences and lagged differences of the dependent variable as instruments for the equation in levels. While this serves as a useful robustness exercise, a caveat to bear in mind is that this estimator is best suited for a "small T-large N" setting, which does not apply to the data employed in the estimation here (i.e., it has a relatively larger T compared to N).

[43] The BIS real residential property price index (RPPI) database contains data for 59 countries including both advanced and emerging markets. While the IMF's global house price index is a simple average of real house prices for 57 countries, the BIS series is a weighted average of real residential property prices. For more details, see https://www.bis.org/statistics/pp_residential_2011.htm and https://www.bis.org/statistics/pp.htm?m=6%7C288%7C640 (last accessed on 7 June 2021).

It is also worth noting that the correlation between the growth rate of IMF's real GHPI and BIS' real RPPI series is 0.84.

[44] On the other hand, LTV's own effect becomes marginally insignificant. This might be a reflection of the close complementarity between these two policy variables as elaborated upon in the next section.

Table 3. Benchmark results for central region: Impact of MaPPs on housing price growth.

	(1) Aggregate MPI	(2) ABSD&SSD	(3) LTV Avg (Inverted)	(4) ABSD Foreign	(5) TDSR
GHPI	2.610***	2.504**	3.646**	2.417***	4.694***
	(0.371)	(0.0975)	(0.148)	(0.375)	(0.0702)
Pipeline Supply	−3.286	−2.050	−7.587	−3.209	−0.0561*
	(6.852)	(6.367)	(4.538)	(7.182)	(0.00507)
RIR	−1.302***	−1.177**	−1.475**	−0.916**	−0.700
	(0.373)	(0.0800)	(0.101)	(0.359)	(0.170)
Real GDP Growth	0.499***	0.468***	0.479**	0.492***	0.638**
	(0.156)	(0.00427)	(0.0111)	(0.164)	(0.0408)
REER	−0.0349	0.0830	−0.114	0.103	0.435*
	(0.302)	(0.108)	(0.141)	(0.306)	(0.0359)
Regional Pop	0.538***	0.495**	0.418**	0.420***	0.0696
	(0.126)	(0.0140)	(0.0153)	(0.133)	(0.0808)
MPI	−0.310***				
	(0.0754)				
MPI*GHPI	−0.121*				
	(0.0731)				
ABSD&SSD		−0.345*			
		(0.0551)			
ABSD&SSD*GHPI		−0.140*			
		(0.0219)			
LTV Avg (Inv)			−0.146		
			(0.0295)		
LTV Avg*GHPI			−0.0798*		
			(0.0117)		
ABSD Foreign				−0.213**	
				(0.0828)	
ABSD Foreign*GHPI				−0.162*	
				(0.0900)	
TDSR					−0.682*
					(0.0763)
TDSR*GHPI					−2.677**
					(0.129)
Observations	110	110	110	110	108
R-squared	0.519	0.500	0.523	0.474	0.423
Number of regions	2	2	2	2	2

Note: The three regions in Singapore are Core Central Region (CCR), Rest of the Central Region (RCR) and Outside Central Region (OCR). More details on the regional classification are available from Urban Redevelopment Authority, Singapore. Robust standard errors in parentheses. *** $p < 0.01$, ** $p < 0.05$, * $p < 0.1$.

Table 4. System-GMM results for full sample.

	(1) Aggregate MPI	(2) ABSD&SSD	(3) LTV Avg (Inverted)	(4) ABSD Foreign	(5) TDSR
Lagged DV	0.341***	0.331***	0.324***	0.091**	0.265***
	(0.030)	(0.035)	(0.023)	(0.040)	(0.052)
GHPI	1.107***	1.019***	2.134***	1.838***	0.871*
	(0.075)	(0.117)	(0.114)	(0.272)	(0.521)
Pipeline Supply	0.178***	0.211***	0.166***	−0.264	0.186***
	(0.023)	(0.018)	(0.023)	(4.207)	(0.029)
RIR	−0.018	−0.079	−0.094	−0.622***	−0.468***
	(0.139)	(0.148)	(0.161)	(0.129)	(0.108)
Real GDP Growth	0.486***	0.582***	0.443***	0.566***	0.494***
	(0.111)	(0.094)	(0.104)	(0.107)	(0.131)
REER	−0.309**	−0.361***	−0.372***	−0.801***	−0.290***
	(0.144)	(0.110)	(0.140)	(0.091)	(0.108)
Regional Pop	0.137	0.259	0.0919	0.665***	0.544***
	(0.141)	(0.169)	(0.153)	(0.084)	(0.189)
Aggregate MPI	−0.404***				
	(0.118)				
MPI*GHPI	−0.134***				
	(0.00637)				
ABSD&SSD		−0.011			
		(0.027)			
ABSD&SSD*GHPI		−0.198***			
		(0.009)			
LTV Avg (Inv)			−0.233***		
			(0.039)		
LTV Avg*GHPI			−0.074***		
			(0.003)		
ABSD Foreign				−0.310**	
				(0.158)	
ABSD Foreign*GHPI				−0.289***	
				(0.003)	
TDSR					−4.748***
					(0.360)
TDSR*GHPI					0.135
					(0.389)
Observations	159	159	159	159	159
Number of Regions	3	3	3	3	3

Note: The three regions in Singapore are Core Central Region (CCR), Rest of the Central Region (RCR) and Outside Central Region (OCR). More details on the regional classification are available from Urban Redevelopment Authority, Singapore. Robust standard errors in parentheses. *** $p < 0.01$, ** $p < 0.05$, * $p < 0.1$.

all specifications is rather small and closer to zero especially in the case of column 4. This is suggestive of weak persistence and higher speed of adjustment, which also implies that our original baseline estimation using panel fixed effects is not inappropriate. Further, we also observe that the dynamic panel estimates align closely with the fixed effects estimates, suggesting that endogeneity bias may not be a problem. Focusing specifically on the effects of MaPPs, the system-GMM results support the broad conclusions established above regarding the decoupling and direct effects of MPI which are now even more statistically and economically significant. In addition, it is noteworthy that the effects of the composite MPI on real property prices are more economically significant than those of the individual MaPPs (column 1 vs columns 2–4).[45] This offers some preliminary evidence that the use of multiple instruments may be more effective than the use of a single one to maintain property market stability, possibly due to the fact that there may be several sources of disequilibria impacting the market including foreign demand, domestic speculation (at the initial stages), investment purchases, etc.

The final robustness check using BIS' real residential property price index is summarised in Table 5. Consistent with our benchmark results, we find that the overall MPI is clearly quite effective in terms of both dampening Singapore's house price and decoupling it from global house prices, as captured by the statistical and economic significance of both β_2 and β_3 coefficients. The individual MaPPs (i.e., ABSD and SSD, LTV caps, ABSD levies on foreigners) too are effective tools, with the TDSR's effectiveness limited primarily to moderating house price growth.

---

[45] As noted, TDSR is not part of the composite MPI index and therefore not directly comparable.

Table 5. Benchmark results using BIS Residential Property Price Index (RPPI).

	(1) Agg MPI	(2) ABSD & SSD	(3) LTV Avg (Inverted)	(4) ABSD Foreign	(5) TDSR
RPPI	1.581***	1.061***	2.285***	1.111***	0.278
	(0.296)	(0.258)	(0.414)	(0.265)	(0.450)
Pipeline Supply	−0.0769	−0.0507	−0.0716	−0.0322	−0.0178
	(0.0806)	(0.0845)	(0.0789)	(0.0835)	(0.0376)
RIR	0.854	0.698	0.921*	0.827	0.301
	(0.540)	(0.566)	(0.537)	(0.576)	(0.228)
Real GDP Growth	0.486***	0.649***	0.449**	0.519***	0.943**
	(0.180)	(0.182)	(0.178)	(0.188)	(0.139)
REER	−0.0529	0.105	−0.0590	0.209	0.303
	(0.327)	(0.341)	(0.321)	(0.322)	(0.139)
Regional Pop	0.0223	−0.0579	0.0432	−0.0672	−0.206
	(0.148)	(0.154)	(0.146)	(0.159)	(0.121)
MPI	**−0.328***				
	(0.0916)				
MPI*RPPI	**−0.0918***				
	(0.0253)				
ABSD&SSD		−0.189*			
		(0.0970)			
ABSD&SSD*RPPI		**−0.0855***			
		(0.0317)			
LTV Avg (Inv)			**−0.190***		
			(0.0466)		
LTV Avg*RPPI			**−0.0525***		
			(0.0127)		
ABSD Foreign				−0.192*	
				(0.103)	
ABSD Foreign*RPPI				−0.0605*	
				(0.0305)	
TDSR					−2.195**
					(0.376)
TDSR*RPPI					0.186
					(0.307)
Observations	111	111	111	111	111
R-squared	0.507	0.455	0.522	0.377	0.404
Number of regions	3	3	3	3	3
Fixed Effects	Yes	Yes	Yes	Yes	Yes

Note: Robust Standard errors in parentheses. *** $p < 0.01$, ** $p < 0.05$, * $p < 0.1$.

5. Lessons and implications from the Singapore experience

This section discusses some possible lessons that might be useful to highlight from the Singapore experience. The evidence offered in the previous section suggests that MaPPs have been effective in insulating Singapore from global housing price fluctuations. Apart from the insulating properties of MaPPs (i.e., decoupling), the empirical exercise offers evidence that they have a direct effect in moderating house price growth (i.e., dampening).[46] While there is certainly a need for a more careful assessment of the direct and indirect impacts of MaPPs in Singapore using more granular data, this section highlights some possible lessons that might be useful to highlight from the Singapore experience.[47]

Whole of government approach: Singapore's approach to MaPPs is based on a multi-pronged strategy that necessitates close coordination between different parts of the government. This "whole-of-government" approach (IMF, 2019a, 2019b) involves close coordination and information sharing between MAS and other government agencies such as the Ministry of Finance (for fiscal measures) as well as the Ministry of National Development (for supply side measures such as land sales), through an inter-agency property market task force that meets at least once every quarter. This ensures that property related risks to financial institutions and household balance sheets can be assessed and tackled in a systematic and pre-emptive manner to maximise the effectiveness of MaPPs by minimising regulatory arbitrage as well as clearly signalling policy intent.

Coordination between microprudential and macroprudential regulation: There is close coordination within MAS between microprudential

---

[46] Annex 1 provides further evidence from a SINGVAR model maintained by MAS. The SINGVAR-MPP model is one of MAS' suite of models and is a multi-variate vector autoregressive (VAR) model for Singapore aimed at analysing how the macroeconomy interacts with the domestic banking system. This model builds on the SINGVAR-Financial model described in di Mauro and Galesi (2017) and is augmented with a composite MaPP index (the MPI) and a TDSR dummy. The results from the model corroborate the above findings that MaPPs are effective in dampening house price growth: one-unit tightening in the composite MPI (corresponding to a single change in any MAPP measure) leads to a 0.42% decline in real house prices on average over the first year of the shock.

[47] Of as much concern as cross-border leakages is that Singapore's use of sector-specific MaPPs may have a domestic impact in the form of cross-asset substitution.

supervision and the formulation and implementation of MaPPs at all stages, involving the macroprudential surveillance, prudential policy and banking supervision departments. Thus, MAS is not hampered by concerns about MaPP implementation that may be caused by fragmented institutional arrangements. Rather, the coordinated approach has been instrumental both in ensuring the effective enforcement of MaPPs and in highlighting any potential loopholes or new risks emerging within financial institutions.[48] A specific example of the importance of this coordination has been highlighted by Robinson (2019):

> "The implementation of the TDSR framework in 2013 demonstrated how microprudential and macroprudential measures can be complementary in addressing risks from mortgage loans. Microprudential surveillance by the banking supervisors revealed that lenders employed uneven practices when computing and evaluating debt-service-to income ratios of mortgage loan applicants. On the macroprudential surveillance front, detailed household credit data suggested increasing systemic risks from rising household indebtedness, corroborating evidence from the microprudential perspective. The TDSR framework we introduced thus aligned the best lending practices, improving risk management at the individual bank level, but also address the build-up of broader systemic risks."

Incrementalism and multiplicity in instruments: Singapore has consciously used a broad set of instruments to tackle financial stability risks and concerns, especially those emanating from the property market. While this multi-pronged policy strategy appears to have been effective in moderating the rate of price appreciations (Annex 1), the partial elasticity of each instrument remains somewhat unclear. A pragmatic approach to policy therefore has involved relying on several levers. Indeed, as noted in the empirical section, there is some evidence that the aggregate MaPP index has an economically more significant overall impact on the property market than individual MaPPs. This also illustrates the strong signalling effects of the combined set of instruments, especially when individual MaPPs are announced and implemented as a package, capturing the

---

[48] Empirical analysis by Masciandaro and Volpicella (2016) suggests that central banks can do their job in macroprudential management more effectively when they are also responsible for microprudential supervision.

common intent and coordination among relevant government agencies. Beyond the use of a variety of demand-side MaPPs, Singapore is rather unique in being able to implement supply-side measures by varying supply via the government land sales programme. This has been important not only as a signalling tool to manage price growth expectations but also to help ensure that housing supply over time (taking into account construction lags) is closely matched with the fundamental drivers of housing demand, including income and population growth.[49]

Constant vigilance and re-calibration of policies: In light of the fact that the transmission channels of MaPPs are still not fully clear and that there is potential scope for regulatory arbitrage, MAS has remained alert to the need to fine-tune existing policies in order to enhance their effectiveness. For example, the impact of LTVs has likely been strengthened by the TDSR which in turn has been made more effective[50] by setting loan term limits (i.e., limiting circumvention possibilities arising from extension of loan tenures to reduce repayments). Similarly, the sudden and rapid spread of COVID-19 saw the government providing temporary relief measures, which allowed more time to meet ABSD remission requirements for property developers and individuals that might have been affected by disruptions to construction timelines and sales of housing units.

Interactions between monetary policy and MaPPs: Absent the divine coincidence, the Tinbergen (1952) principle states that there must be at least as many independent policy tools as there are policy objectives. To be sure, the so-called "assignment problem" suggests that in the event there are policy trade-offs, inflation should be the remit of monetary policy (exchange rate policy) while the goal of financial stability can be assigned to MaPPs which are designed to limit systemic vulnerabilities by focusing on the entire financial system. It is commonplace to argue that monetary and macroprudential authorities should consider each

---

[49] As noted, the signalling and longer-term impacts of land supply are not adequately captured by the empirical model in Section 4, which failed to find statistical or economic significance on price growth.

[50] DSTI and LTV changes are usually coordinated (Kuttner and Shim, 2016) as they serve different but complementary purposes. While LTV limits are meant to guard against house price shocks, ceilings on DSTI ratios are aimed at protecting against interest rate and income shocks (Jacome and Mitra, 2015).

other's actions when making decisions (Nier and Kang, 2016). However, there may not always be such policy trade-offs. In such a scenario, there is scope instead to exploit complementarity between the two policies. The logic behind limiting the focus of each policy to a specific objective is to minimise uncertainty and confusion among the public as to the rationale for a particular policy stance and the ultimate policy objectives. For instance, the use of MaPPs to manage property price inflation in the absence of systemic risks and financial stability concerns may be viewed as triggering false alarms which, if done often enough, may possibly erode the credibility of the authority and could ultimately call into question the consistency of the entire macroeconomic policy framework.

In Singapore, insofar as accommodation costs (i.e., housing and utilities) constitute slightly more than one-fifth of the consumer price index (CPI), the relevant question that has sometimes been posed is whether there is a role for sectoral-based MaPPs in helping to manage inflationary concerns, in the absence of systemic risks.[51] Conversely, if a run-up in property prices is driven by capital flows and there are concerns about systemic risks without any obvious inflationary concerns, is there then a role for an exchange rate appreciation along with a tightening of MaPPs to manage such risks, or is it more desirable to limit the latter's focus to financial stability (see Figure 12)?[52] In practice, the approach to coordination in Singapore has been a pragmatic one, with MAS recognising that both macroeconomic and financial stability need to be pursued jointly over a medium-term horizon. Since MAS has the mandate for both monetary and macroprudential policies, there is room to explore and exploit complementarities between the two policies. However, MAS has found it efficient to assign monetary policy to price stability and macroprudential policy to financial stability.[53] Under most scenarios,

---

[51] For instance, Singapore's inflation rate between 2010 and 2012 spiked (4% on average) primarily due to escalating house and auto prices.

[52] The argument made above is distinct from the "Lean versus Clean" debate which focuses on whether monetary policy should lean against the build-up of financial imbalances even if inflation remains within target.

[53] Empirically, it has been shown that monetary policy has a larger impact on aggregate demand (and subsequently prices) than macroprudential policy, and macroprudential policy has a larger impact on bank credit (and on the property market) than on overall aggregate demand and general price movements.

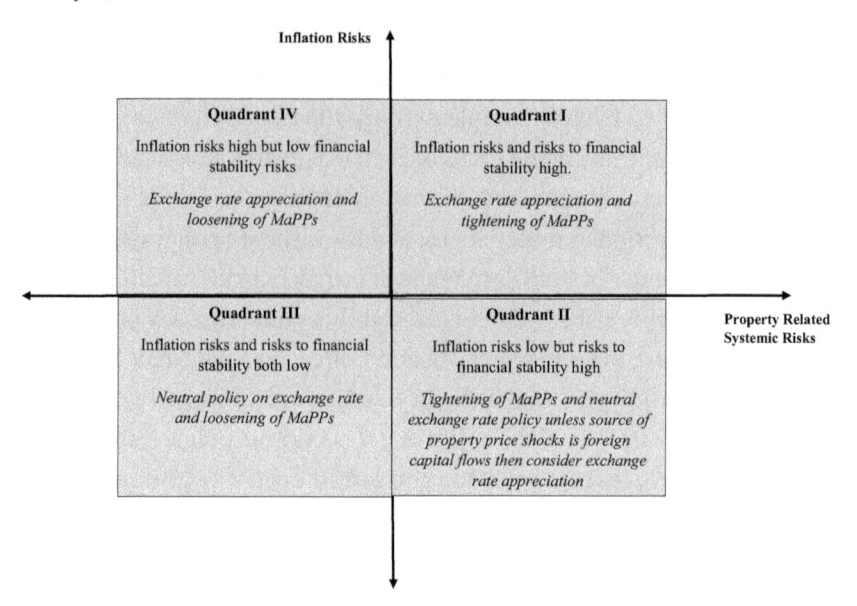

```
                    Inflation Risks ↑
        ┌─────────────────────────┬─────────────────────────┐
        │      Quadrant IV        │      Quadrant I         │
        │ Inflation risks high but│ Inflation risks and     │
        │ low financial           │ risks to financial      │
        │ stability risks         │ stability high.         │
        │                         │                         │
        │ Exchange rate           │ Exchange rate           │
        │ appreciation and        │ appreciation and        │
        │ loosening of MaPPs      │ tightening of MaPPs     │
        ├─────────────────────────┼─────────────────────────┤
        │      Quadrant III       │      Quadrant II        │
        │ Inflation risks and     │ Inflation risks low but │
        │ risks to financial      │ risks to financial      │
        │ stability both low      │ stability high          │
        │                         │                         │
        │ Neutral policy on       │ Tightening of MaPPs and │
        │ exchange rate and       │ neutral exchange rate   │
        │ loosening of MaPPs      │ policy unless source of │
        │                         │ property price shocks is│
        │                         │ foreign capital flows   │
        │                         │ then consider exchange  │
        │                         │ rate appreciation       │
        └─────────────────────────┴─────────────────────────┘
```
→ Property Related Systemic Risks

Figure 12. Trade-offs and options for monetary policy and MaPPs in managing risks.
Source: Authors' illustration.

there is no conflict between these two policies, and thus there has not been any need for pro-active coordination in the setting of monetary and macroprudential policies.[54] While information exchange has to date been sufficient to allow policy objectives to be achieved efficiently, there is certainly scope for holistically optimising the mix of monetary and macroprudential policies within the domestic economy to exploit the complementarity of instruments for a better outcome.[55]

The external dimension: While most countries define MaPPs to involve only financial-related regulations aimed at managing systemic risks, Singapore has taken a more broad-based interpretation of MaPPs. For instance, the IMF (2019b,c) has opined that because of the differentiated rates on the ABSD on locals versus foreigners, it is assessed as both a capital flow management measure (CFM) and a macroprudential

---

[54] Equivalent to the adoption of a non-cooperative Nash strategy, which takes the other policy setting as given.
[55] However, a careful analysis of the pockets of disequilibrium in the economy and asset markets will need to be conducted jointly, together with their spillover effects.

measure, according to the IMF's Institutional View (IMF, 2018b).[56] However, such concerns about labelling have not deterred MAS which takes a pragmatic view and looks to employ the best set of policies that will be effective in managing financial stability.[57] Thus, in the case of stamp duties, the evidence suggests that there was heavy foreign interest in the local property market given the availability of cheap funds overseas (IMF, 2019b). Policies aimed at limiting domestic credit to households would thus be insufficient to stem property market surges. In fact, given that Singapore chose not to impose wider CFM measures to mitigate financial stability risks associated with capital flows, the differentiated stamp duties helped to "level the playing field" between residents, who may have been constrained in raising funds domestically for property purchases, and foreigners, who may have been able to borrow elsewhere and bypass domestic credit intermediation.[58] Further, the differentiated (higher) ABSD was also imposed on domestic investors (i.e., those looking to purchase second and third properties). Viewed in this light, the ABSD was more of a policy aimed at curbing speculative and investment demand, whether by foreigners or locals, to help ensure housing remained affordable for residents' consumption (i.e., own dwelling) purposes.[59]

---

[56] Other economies, including Hong Kong SAR, Australia, Canada and New Zealand, have also applied property-related measures that are differentiated between residents and non-residents.

[57] Indeed, IMF (2020, Chapter 3) focuses specifically on how emerging economies can use MaPPs to manage external shocks and enhance resilience against such shocks.

[58] In addition, international (property) investors have their own risk-reward trade-off, one that is premised on an international calculus of cost of funds and alternative investments which are quite different from considerations confronting the domestic consumers of housing services for own-residence purposes.

[59] However, the possibility of agents looking for regulatory loopholes remains a general concern for such MaPPs, as is the case with any kind of regulation. For instance, cash-rich local investors in property could create trusts to purchase another property on behalf of their children, hence avoiding the ABSD on multiple properties. Couples could also transfer one spouse's part share to the other spouse (i.e., "decoupling"). Similarly, developers could create associate companies that effectively "purchase" unsold units so that they are not penalised for unsold units. Policymakers hence need to keep abreast of such strategies and balance the need to fine tune regulations versus the very real concern over regulatory creep.

Beyond labelling issues, another important external dimension about MaPPs of potential concern is whether measures implemented to mitigate systemic risk on a particular entity or sector merely end up causing a migration of activity and risks to other jurisdictions, hence undermining their overall effectiveness. Being an international financial centre, Singapore is especially susceptible to such cross-border regulatory leakages stemming from internationally active banks, especially with regard to capital-based macroprudential policy tools such as the CCyB.[60] To minimise the possibility of this boundary problem of financial regulation *a la* Goodhart (2008), MAS is involved in regular information exchange on issues relating to financial stability with its regional and international counterparts and also takes part in various multilateral and bilateral central bank meetings and fora.[61] Certain segments of property can be seen as an investment asset class and Singapore is benchmarked against other global cities in this regard. Thus, developments in the Singapore market could be influenced by broader demand conditions including those induced by the introduction of property-related MaPPs elsewhere in the region. These cross-border demand and policy spillovers remain a concern for Singapore and other regional economies. Viewed through the lens of the Financial Trilemma *a la* Schoenmaker (2011), Singapore and other regional economies have to date chosen financial autonomy and financial stability at the expense of greater financial integration in specific asset classes.

Unintended consequences: Policymakers need to be concerned about the unintended consequences of their policies. For instance, in the case of Singapore, an argument has been made in some quarters that while the policy of disincentivising developers from hoarding property helps to promote a better demand-supply outcome, requiring the units to be developed and sold within a certain time frame could have partly

---

[60] Buch and Goldberg (2017) find that compared with adjustments to capital requirements, changes to LTV ratios and liquidity instruments have a higher likelihood of impacting cross-border bank credit.

[61] According to MAS, a tightening of MaPPs could dampen portfolio investment and other investment inflows while reducing the volatility of capital flows into Asia in the subsequent quarter (MAS, 2017a, 2017b).

contributed to the sharp price appreciation in 2018. In particular, as developers had to develop and sell off landbanks that had been purchased five years ago, they ran out of land and had to bid aggressively for land as property prices were recovering, leading to a sharp escalation in land prices and increased activity in the private residential property market.[62] MAS and the government agencies in charge of land sales and urban planning in Singapore (Ministry of National Development and Urban Redevelopment Authority, respectively) have regular dialogue sessions with market participants and consultants to gather market intelligence that would be useful for policy surveillance and hence policymaking, including managing any possible unintended consequences.

Unwinding: While much work has been done on examining the effectiveness of tightening controls to cool property price appreciation, relatively less work has been done on the best strategy to return to a neutral macroprudential stance. If the unwinding of MaPPs is done too hastily or prematurely, that could itself be a cause for a further build-up of financial excesses by releasing pent-up demand.[63] Beyond using judgement and discretion, it is not clear whether there is a set of best practices or principles that can guide these loosening strategies especially given that downcycles tend to be much more short-lived and sharper than upturns.[64] The challenge for policymakers is to manage the stance on MaPPs in such a way that the price dynamics consistent with sustainable conditions in the housing market are in line with the long-term drivers of property demand, including demographics, income growth and interest rates.

Communication Strategy: Unlike monetary exchange rate policies, in which the policy and communication frameworks are well-developed and instruments are clear and rather limited, MaPPs entail a wide range

---

[62] https://www.straitstimes.com/business/property/singapore-property-glut-tied-to-official-curbs-cdl-says

[63] Of course, some MaPPs that are structural in nature will remain regardless of the financial cycle. The issue is how to recalibrate the MaPPs that are cyclical.

[64] For instance, the unwinding of MaPPs and the buyer's stamp duties in mid-2005 to late 2006 in Singapore coincided with a surge in property prices and transactions, which came to an end with the onset of the GFC.

of tools to deal with the multi-dimensional nature of systemic risk.[65] In addition, implementation of MaPPs is often viewed as being rather ad hoc, discretionary and can have significant and sudden distributional effects and adjustment costs (on banks and households),[66] with the ultimate objectives not always clear to the public, especially as their effects take time to fully materialise (Forbes, 2019). This suggests the need to improve the clarity and transparency of communication of MaPPs as well as to educate the public on the role, rationale and expected objectives and impacts of such policies. MAS has attempted to enhance communication via the publication of a comprehensive *Financial Stability Review* which is issued annually.[67,68] Nonetheless, efforts to enhance communication of financial risks and vulnerabilities as well as macroprudential frameworks and policy stances to the broader public remain an ongoing endeavour in Singapore as it does more generally elsewhere.[69]

6. Concluding remarks

Overall, while Singapore today has a dynamic and extremely internationalised financial sector, its approach towards financial globalisation has been carefully calibrated over the years, dictated by pragmatism rather than ideology, and there has been a willingness to

---

[65] Conversely, this large variety of macroprudential instruments allows policymakers to use specific instruments to address systemic risks that originate from specific sectors, rather than a single blunt instrument such as monetary policy or exchange rates.

[66] Of course, monetary policy too has distributional consequences, as do periods of prolonged high inflation or deflation. However, the impacts of MaPPs — especially housing-related ones — can be rather sudden and immediate. Frost and van Stralen (2018) examine the impacts of alternative types of MaPPs on income inequality.

[67] https://www.mas.gov.sg/publications?content_type=Financial%20Stability%20Reviews.&page=1&content_type=Financial%20Stability%20Reviews. The FSR used to be a semi-annual publication until 2006.

[68] The focus has generally been on an ex-post communication strategy. There is an issue with ex-ante communication, i.e., announcing a planned tightening could lead to buyers bringing forward their house purchases, leading to a further surge in house prices.

[69] This said, the major property market measures are announced via joint press releases with other government agencies. Also, there are other communication channels employed by MAS such as speeches by MAS senior management and the MAS Annual Report.

alter policy direction if and when the need has arisen. This in turn has ensured that the country has been able to reap the benefits of having a large and dynamic financial sector without being faced with overly disruptive booms and busts that have afflicted many other small and open economies. Singapore's decision to fully embrace all dimensions of financial globalisation has been of enormous benefit to the country, though it has also become much more exposed to the vagaries of the global financial markets and far more susceptible to macro-financial risks. In addition, the exchange-rate–centred monetary policy and limited interest rate autonomy in Singapore could — depending on global monetary conditions — at times give rise to strong incentives for risk-taking. The post-GFC period is a particularly stark case in point. Given all these, Singapore has utilised MaPPs — which are primarily targeted at the property market — to manage domestic financial stability on a system-wide basis.

Singapore's approach to managing financial stability by ensuring a stable and sustainable property market has been well articulated by Singapore's then Minister for National Development, Lawrence Wong and is worth reproducing here:

> "Basically, we have concluded that the government cannot take a hands-off attitude to the property cycle and allow bubbles to develop — this is not what a responsible government should do. Our aim is not to bring prices down but to steady the cycle and to stabilise the market — to have a steady and sustained property market, moving broadly in line with income growth…So this is our approach now with regard to the property market. It is a shift from the past where we tended to be more laissez-faire and hands-off…..We have not quite moved to the extent of what Central Banks do with monetary policies and the business cycle. There you have a long history of intervention and a lot of literature about what works and what doesn't work, what instruments to use, and how monetary policies can be effective at stabilising the business cycle. We are learning from our own experiences and what other countries have done" (Wong, 2019).

To sum up, the quest to: (1) design an appropriate policy mix (types of MaPPs and accompanying fiscal, land sales and monetary policy); (2) enhance the transparency and effectiveness of the public communication strategies and (3) better understand and manage possible leakages and unintended consequences of MaPPs, remain key challenges for Singapore, as they do for other countries that actively use such tools, to safeguard overall financial stability.

References

Alam, Z., A. Alter, J. Eiseman, G. Gelos and H. Kang (2019). "Digging Deeper—Evidence on the Effects of Macroprudential Policies from a New Database," Working Paper No. 19/66, IMF, March.

Blundell, R. and S. Bond (1998). "Initial Conditions and Moment Restrictions in Dynamic Panel Data Models," *Journal of Econometrics*, **87**(1), 115-143.

Borio, C. (2013). "Macroeconomics and the Financial Cycle: Hamlet without the Prince?" VoxEU.org, 2 February.

Buch, C.M. and L.S. Goldberg (2017). "Cross-Border Prudential Policy Spillovers: How Much? How Important? Evidence from the International Banking Research Network," *International Journal of Central Banking*, **13**, 5-54.

Caballero, R.J. and M.L. Hammour (1994). "The Cleansing Effect of Recessions," *American Economic Review*, **84**, 1350-1368.

Cavoli, T. and R.S. Rajan (2007). "Managing in the Middle: Characterizing Singapore's Exchange Rate Policy," *Asian Economic Journal*, **21**, 321-342.

Cesa-Bianchi, A., L.F. Cespedes and A. Rebucci (2015). "Global Liquidity, House Prices, and the Macroeconomy: Evidence from Advanced and Emerging Economies," *Journal of Money, Credit and Banking*, **47**(S1), 301-335.

Cheng, R. and R.S. Rajan (2020). "Monetary Trilemma, Dilemma, or Something in Between?" *International Finance*, **23**(2), 257-260.

Chia, W.M., M. Li and Y. Tang (2017). "Public and Private Housing Market Dynamics in Singapore: The Role of Fundamentals," *Journal of Housing Economics*, **36**, 44-61.

Chow, H.K. and T. Xie (2016). "Are House Prices Driven by Capital Flows? Evidence from Singapore," *Journal of International Commerce, Economics and Policy*, **7**(1), 1-21.

Deng, Y., J. Gyourko and T. Li (2019). "Singapore's Cooling Measures and its Housing Market," *Journal of Housing Economics*, **45**, 1051-1064.

Duca, J.V. (2020). "Making Sense of Increased Synchronization in Global House Prices," *Journal of European Real Estate Research*, **13**(1), 5-16.

di Mauro, F. and A. Galesi (2017). "Macro-Financial Modelling of the Singapore Economy: A GVAR Approach", *MAS Macroeconomic Review*, **16**(2), 80–89.

Financial Stability Board (FSB) (2018). Peer Review of Singapore Review Report February.

Forbes, K.J. (2019). "Macroprudential Policy: What We've Learned, Don't Know, and Need to Do," *AEA Papers and Proceedings*, **109**, 470–475.

Frost, J. and R. van Stralen (2018). "Macroprudential Policy and Income Inequality," Working Paper No. 598, De Nederlandsche Bank NV, May.

Goodhart, C. (2008). "Boundary Problem in Financial Regulation," *National Institute Economic Review*, **206**, 48–55.

Han, X., and S.J. Wei (2018). "International Transmissions of Monetary Shocks: Between a Trilemma and a Dilemma," *Journal of International Economics*, **110**, 205–219.

Hirata, H., A. Kose, C. Otrok and M. Terrones. (2013). "Global House Price Fluctuations: Synchronization and Determinants," Working Paper No. 13/38, IMF, February.

IMF (2018a). "Global Financial Stability Report, April 2018: A Bumpy Road Ahead," IMF, April

IMF (2018b). "The IMF's Institutional View on Capital Flows in Practice," Report prepared for Group of Twenty meeting, July.

IMF (2019a). "Singapore: Financial System Stability Assessment," IMF Country Report No. 19/224, July.

IMF (2019b). "Singapore: Financial Sector Assessment Program Technical Note — Macroprudential Policy," IMF Country Report No. 19/227, July.

IMF (2019c). "Singapore: 2019 Article IV Consultation — Press Release Staff Report; and Statement by the Executive Director for Singapore," IMF Country Report No. 19/233, July.

IMF (2020). Wold Economic Outlook, April 2020: The Great Lockdown, IMF.

IMF (2017). "Chart of the Week: Global House Prices—Where Is the Boom?" March 27 https://blogs.imf.org/2017/03/27/chart-of-the-week-global-house-prices-where-is-the-boom/

Jacome, H.L.I. and S. Mitra (2015). "LTV and DTI Limits—Going Granular," IMF Working Paper 15/54, July.

Katagiri, M. (2018). House Price Synchronization and Financial Openness: A Dynamic Factor Model Approach, Working Paper No. 18/209, IMF, September.

Kim, S and A. Mehrotra (2017). "Effects of Monetary and Macro-prudential Policies — Evidence from Inflation Targeting Economies in the Asia-Pacific

Region and Potential Implications for China," BOFIT Discussion Paper No. 4/2017, Helsinki.

Klein, M.W. and J.C. Shambaugh (2015). "Rounding the Corners of the Policy Trilemma: Sources of Monetary Policy Autonomy," *American Economic Journal: Macroeconomics*, **7**, 33–66.

Kuttner, K.N. and I. Shim (2016). "Can Non-interest Rate Policies Stabilise Housing Markets? Evidence from a Panel of 57 Economies," *Journal of Financial Stability*, **26**, 31–44.

Lane, P.R. and G.M. Milesi-Ferretti (2017). "International Financial Integration in the Aftermath of the Global Financial Crisis," IMF Working Paper No. 2017/115. https://www.imf.org/en/Publications/WP/Issues/2017/05/10/International-Financial-Integration-in-the-Aftermath-of-the-Global-Financial-Crisis-44906.

Lee, D.K. and T. Xie. (2015). "Evaluating Singapore's Housing Policies: A Bounds Testing Approach," Research Collection Lee Kong Chian School Of Business.

Lee, M., R.C. Asuncion and J. Kim (2015). "Effectiveness of Macroprudential Policies in Developing Asia: An Empirical Analysis," ADB Working Paper No. 439. https://www.adb.org/sites/default/files/publication/162311/ewp-439.pdf

Masciandaro, D. and A. Volpicella (2016). "Macro Prudential Governance and Central Banks: Facts and Drivers," *Journal of International Money and Finance*, **61**, 101–119.

McCallum, B. (2014). "Monetary Policy in a Very Open Economy: Some Major Analytical Issues," *Pacific Economic Review*, **19**, 27–60.

McDonald, C. (2015). "When is Macroprudential Policy Effective?" BIS Working Paper No. 496, April.

Monetary Authority of Singapore (MAS) (2011). "MAS Financial Stability Review," November.

Monetary Authority of Singapore (MAS) (2017a). "MAS Financial Stability Review," November.

Monetary Authority of Singapore (MAS) (2017b). "Macroprudential Policies: A Singapore case study," in Macroprudential Frameworks, Implementation and Relationship with other Policies, BIS Papers No 94, December.

Nier, E. and H. Kang (2016). "Monetary and Macroprudential Policies-Exploring Interactions," BIS Papers No. 86

Obstfeld, M., J.D. Ostry and M.S. Qureshi (2019). "A Tie That Binds: Revisiting the Trilemma in Emerging Market Economies," *The Review of Economics and Statistics*, **101**, 279–293.

Ong, C.T. (2013). "An Exchange-Rate-Centred Monetary Policy System: Singapore's Experience," Market Volatility and Foreign Exchange Intervention in EMEs: What Has Changed? BIS Papers No. 73, October.

Parrado, E. (2004). "Singapore's Unique Monetary Policy: How Does it Work?" Working Paper No. 04/10, IMF, January.

Passari, E. and H. Rey (2015). "Financial Flows and the International Monetary System," *Economic Journal*, **125**, 675–698.

Pesaran, M.H., T. Schuermann and S.M. Weiner (2004). "Modeling Regional Interdependencies using a Global Error-correcting Macroeconometric Model," *Journal of Business and Economic Statistics*, **22**, 129–162.

Phang, S.Y. (2004). "House Prices and Aggregate Consumption: Do They Move Together? Evidence from Singapore," *Journal of Housing Economics*, **13**, 101–119.

Rajan, R.S. (2016). "Singapore's Unique Tack on Financial Globalisation," *Business Times*, November 24.

Rey, H. (2013). "Dilemma not Trilemma: The Global Financial Cycle and Monetary Policy Independence," Proceedings Federal Reserve Bank of Kansas City Economic Policy Symposium, Jackson Hole, pp. 285–333.

Rey, H. (2016). "International Channels of Transmission of Monetary Policy and the Mundellian Trilemma," *IMF Economic Review*, **64**, 6–35.

Richter, B., M. Schularick and I. Shim (2018)." The Macroeconomic Effects of Macroprudential Policy," Working Paper No. 740, BIS, August.

Robinson, E. (2019). "Nexus Between Monetary and Macroprudential Policy," Joint BOT-IMF High-level Conference, November.

Schoenmaker, D. (2011). "The Financial Trilemma," *Economics Letters*, **111**, 57–59.

Shim, I., B. Bogdanova, J. Shek and A. Subelyte. (2013). "Database for Policy Actions on Housing Markets," *BIS Quarterly Review*, 83–95.

Tan, Y.H. (2019). "The Monetary Authority of Singapore's Macroprudential Policy Toolkit," Case-study, Lee Kuan Yew School of Public Policy. Singapore: National University of Singapore. https://doi.org/10.25818/2q4v-bw24

Tinbergen, J. (1952). *On the Theory of Economic Policy*. Books (Jan Tinbergen). North-Holland: Amsterdam.

Wong, N.S., A. Lim and S.L. Wong (2015). "Using Macroprudential Tools to Address Systemic Risks in the Property Sector in Singapore." *SEACEN Financial Stability Journal*, **4**, 27–41.

Wong, L. (2019). Speech by Minister Lawrence Wong at the Institute of Real Estate and Urban Studies (IREUS) Conference on 'Real Estate and Urban Studies', Singapore, May 24. https://www.mnd.gov.sg/newsroom/speeches/

view/speech-by-minister-lawrence-wong-at-the-institute-of-real-estate-and-urban-studies-(ireus)-conference-on-real-estate-and-urban-studies

Annex 1: MAS' SINGVAR Model Introduction

In this Annex, a variant of the SINGVAR model, part of MAS' suite of macroeconomic models, is used to analyse the impact of macroprudential policy in Singapore on housing prices as well as the credit market. The SINGVAR is a multivariate time series vector autoregressive model, consisting of two blocks that captures in a reduced form the macro-financial linkages in the Singapore economy: the first block represents the real (or macro) sector while the second consists of the domestic banking system.

The macro block[70] contains the key aggregate macroeconomic variables of the Singapore economy which interacts with other countries at the global level via the Global Vector Autoregression model (GVAR), first developed by Pesaran *et al.* (2004). This allows the international transmission of economic and financial shocks originating from abroad to flow through to the SINGVAR. Meanwhile, the financial block explicitly models the heterogeneity of individual banks in Singapore and allows interaction amongst themselves, as well as with the real sector of the economy. The financial block thus incorporates basic information on the structure of the balance sheets of individual financial institutions in Singapore. These variables take into account asset composition (nominal bank credit divided into housing and non-housing loans), profitability (net interest margin) and financial fragility (non-performing loan ratio). The number of variables in the SINGVAR are kept to a minimum, to avoid the

---

[70] In the latest version of the SINGVAR model, variables in this macro block consists of real GDP, real private consumption, real house price, headline CPI inflation, MPI, TDSR dummy, nominal effective exchange rate (NEER), SIBOR, 10-year Singapore government bond yield and the NODX-weighted foreign GDP.

Annex 1: (*Continued*)

"curse of dimensionality", which would render robust empirical estimation unfeasible. The macro block of SINGVAR is estimated over 1996Q1–2019Q4 while the estimation period of the financial block is from 2004Q2–2019Q4. More information about the model can be found in di Mauro and Galesi (2017).

Modified SINGVAR Model

For the purpose of analysing macroprudential policy effects in Singapore, further development was undertaken to augment the model above with a macroprudential policy lever and a binary TDSR variable.

The macroprudential policy lever is a composite index of macroprudential policy measures, as described in Section 4.1 of this chapter. Essentially, the MPI is a simple count measure of various macroprudential measures implemented in Singapore. When a tightening (loosening) of a macroprudential policy measure in the index is implemented, the index will increase (decrease) by 1 unit. The TDSR is included as a time dummy taking the value of 1 in all periods following the introduction of TDSR in Q2 2013 and 0 otherwise.

With these additions, the augmented model can be utilised to analyse the potential macroeconomic and financial impact of macroprudential policy. The effects of a change in the composite MPI will affect the real economy and be transmitted to the banking sector, which are then amplified by interbank linkages and subsequently feed back to the real economy.

The Effects of a Macroprudential Policy Tightening in the Model

Based on this model, Figures A-1 and A-2 show the impulse responses from an increase in the MPI by 1 percent (equivalent to a *single* instance of macroprudential policy tightening). The results indicate that a tightening of one macroprudential measure is associated with a 0.42 percent decline in real house prices on average over the first year after the shock. (Figure A-1; dashed

(*Continued*)

Annex 1: (*Continued*)

lines represent 90 percent confidence bands) Despite this, private consumption declines only marginally by an average of 0.03 percent during the first year, and

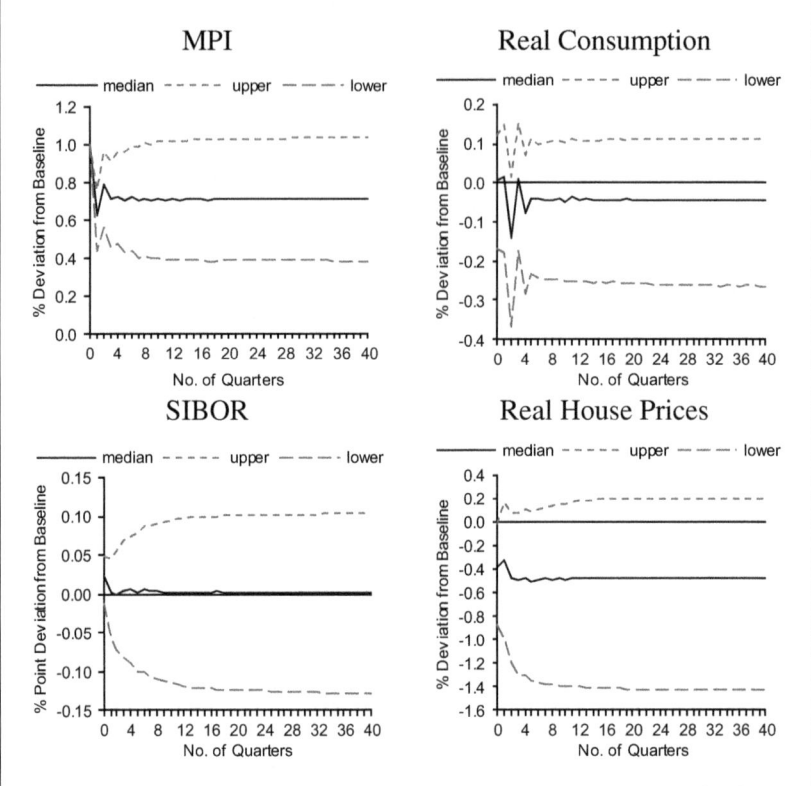

Figure A-1. Macroeconomic impulse responses to a shock in macroprudential policy index (MPI).[71]

the long-run impact on consumption remains marginal. This is consistent with studies such as Phang (2004), which find no evidence that house price increases have produced either wealth or collateral enhancement effects on aggregate consumption in Singapore. The impact on SIBOR is expectedly indiscernible

---

[71] The figure for each variable shows the median estimate and its accompanying bootstrap upper and lower error bands.

Annex 1: (*Continued*)

as interest rates in Singapore are largely determined by global interest rates. Over the long run, the impact on the level of the real house price is a decline of 0.48 percent, but in growth rate terms, real house prices revert to baseline.

On the financial side of the economy, the tighter macroprudential policy leads to lower demand for new housing loans and subsequently, the total stock of nominal housing credit declines, albeit by only 0.12 percent in the first year (Figure A-2). An increase in the stock of nominal non-housing credit is also observed, suggesting that there is a reallocation of funds on banks' loan books.

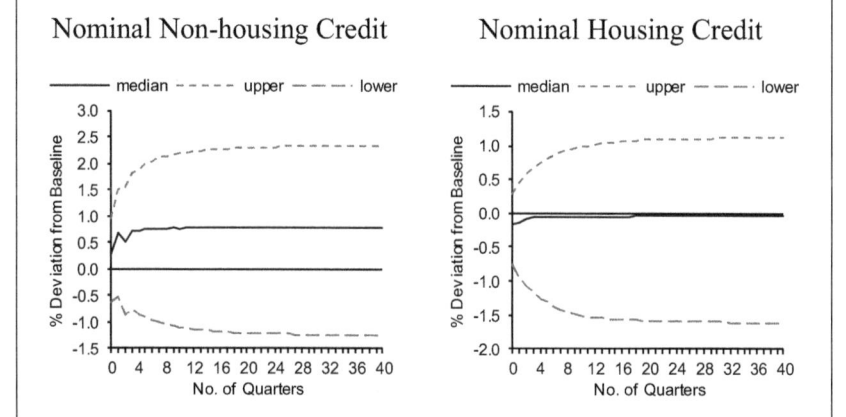

Figure A-2. Financial impulse responses to a shock in macroprudential policy index (MPP).[72]

(*Continued*)

---

[72] The figure for each variable shows the median estimate and its accompanying bootstrap upper and lower error bands.

Annex 1: (*Continued*)

Table A1. Definitions and sources.

Variable	Source and Definition
Real Regional Property Price Index (PPI)	Quarterly Nominal Regional PPI sourced from Urban Redevelopment Authority (URA), Singapore, accessible from: https://www.ura.gov.sg/Corporate/Property/Property-Data Deflated using consumer price index (CPI) to obtain Real regional PPI.
Global House Price Index (GHPI) (Growth Rates)	Real GHPI across 57 countries sourced from International Monetary Fund (IMF), accessible from: https://www.imf.org/external/research/housing/
BIS Real Residential Property Price Index (RPPI)	Real RPPI across 59 countries sourced from BIS, accessible from: https://www.bis.org/statistics/pp.htm?m=6%7C288%7C640
Pipeline Supply	Pipeline supply for Singapore sourced from URA, accessible from: https://www.ura.gov.sg/Corporate/Property/Property-Data
Real Interest Rate (%)	Computed as the difference between money market rates and inflation, sourced from IMF
Real GDP Growth (%)	Quarterly real GDP growth from IMF's World Economic Outlook
REER Index	Quarterly broad series sourced from Bank for International Settlements (BIS)
Regional Population	Regional population sourced from https://data.gov.sg/dataset/resident-population-by-planning-area-subzone-and-type-of-dwelling-2015
MPI and components	MAS data
TDSR	Constructed based on MAS data

# Macroprudential Policies and Financial Stability in a Small and Open Economy: The Case of Singapore: A Discussion

Yongheng Deng

John P. Morgridge Distinguished Chair Professor in Business
Wisconsin School of Business
University of Wisconsin-Madison

The property market is an essential driver of Singapore's economy as well as many economies in Asia and worldwide. Governments worldwide have tried to use macroprudential policies (MaPPs) to stabilise property prices and their economies as well. However, the global financial cycle and global liquidity driven by US dollar funding have undermined the ability of central banks in emerging economies to manage their own monetary conditions.

In this chapter, Ramkishen Rajan, Edward Robinson, and Rosemary Lim examine the extent to which housing price growth in Singapore is correlated with global housing prices and whether MaPPs can insulate the domestic housing market from global fluctuations.

Summary

Ramkishen, Edward, and Rosemary find that Singapore's approach to implementing MaPPs, as a whole, has produced a cooling impact on the excessive appreciation of the country's property prices.

The chapter documents that using multiple instruments (MaPPs, microprudential supervision and regulation, monetary policy) to maintain property market stability is more effective than a single one due to various sources of disequilibria impacting the market.

The authors also delve into lessons from Singapore's experience in implementing the MaPPs, including

- Singapore adopts a whole-of-government approach to implement MaPPs. Therefore, it depends on close coordination and information sharing between different government agencies, such as MAS, Ministry of Finance, MND, URA, etc.
- The close coordination between microprudential and macroprudential regulations ensures the effective enforcement of MaPPs but also helps to draw attention to potential loopholes and new risks arising within financial institutions.
- Interactions between monetary policy and MaPPs allow the Singapore government to exploit the complementarity of instruments to achieve overlapping objectives.
- Singapore adopts a pragmatic approach involving incrementalism and multiplicity to MaPPs instruments, which offers an economically more significant impact on the property market.
- Constant re-calibration of policies allows MAS to fine-tune existing policies to stop possible "loopholes" as needed and enhance their effectiveness.
- Unintended consequences are always something that policymakers need to be concerned about. For example, an argument has been made against the policy of disincentivising developers from hoarding landbank. The critics worry that developers have to develop and sell off landbanks within the five-year period. As a result, they may run out of land and bid aggressively for land when the property market is recovering. Consequently, it may push up the land prices in the market. Therefore, MAS, MND and URA have regular dialogue sessions with market participants to gather market intelligence, which helps manage any possible unintended consequences.

- Unwinding strategy to ensure that the property price dynamics consistent with sustainable conditions in the housing market align with the long-term drivers of housing demand, including demographics, income growth, and interest rates.
- Communication strategy to improve the clarity and transparency of MaPPs, including educating the public on the role, rationale, expected objectives and impacts of such policies.

The global financial cycle and global liquidity driven by US dollar funding have created challenges for the central banks in emerging economies to manage their monetary conditions. Singapore has proactively utilised MaPPs to achieve domestic financial stability on a system-wide basis. Most of the Singapore government's MaPPs have been focused on the property market to contain the build-up of financial stability risks through measures to reduce the volatility of property prices and dampen the surges of excessive price appreciation.

Singapore's MaPPs instruments include

- A cap on banks' property-related exposures
- MaPPs aiming at the borrower side
  - Ceilings on the loan-to-value (LTV) ratio,
  - Caps on the total debt servicing ratio (TDSR),
  - Limits on loan tenure.
- Fiscal measures on property transactions
  - Additional buyer's stamp duties (ABSD),
  - Seller's stamp duties (SSD).
- Supply-side measures such as control through government land sales.

Figure 5 in Chapter 12 shows using a multiple set of MaPPs instruments, as a whole, has produced a cooling impact on the excessive appreciation of the country's property prices.

Figure 9 in Chapter 12 shows that the fiscal measures on property transactions, such as imposing the seller's stamp duties (SSD) and additional buyer's stamp duties (ABSD), have effectively dampened the private residential property transaction volume.

Comments

My comments will focus mainly on the empirical part of the analysis.

The chapter focuses on the impacts of the MaPPs on the private residential property sector (see, for example, Chapter 12, Section 2, Figures 5 and 9). The empirical analysis in Section 4 focuses on examining the extent to which house price growth in Singapore is correlated with global house prices and whether MaPPs can insulate the domestic housing market from global fluctuations. It is not clear to me whether the property price index of non-landed residential properties, RPPI, in Section 4, measures the Singapore domestic housing price growth (HDB + private) or the private residential property sector only.

If RPPI covers only the private residential property sector, given that 80 percent of Singapore's residential property market is under the public sector, I would suggest also controlling for HDB PPI in the empirical specifications.

The empirical model specified in Section 4 regresses the growth rate of the property price index of Singapore's non-landed residential property, RPPI, to the growth rate of the average global housing price index across 57 countries compiled by IMF, GHPI plus a set of the economic determinants of housing prices in Singapore. The underlying assumption is that the global housing prices are homogenously synchronised across countries. However, the IMFBlog article reports that a closer look at the global house index reveals three tracks. Singapore, China, Brazil, France, Italy, etc., are 18 countries in the gloom cluster (the dotted line) distinctively different from the rest of the countries (the red and blue lines) (see Figure 1).

The IMF report also quotes Deng *et al.* (2019), noting that not only are there differences across countries, but the situation differs even within countries.

I would suggest running a robustness test by replacing the current GHPI (average of 57 countries HPIs from IMF) with the IMF cluster HPIs (average of HPIs from the 18 countries in the IMF gloom cluster).

Finally, it is always challenging to identify the transmission channel of multiple sources of disequilibria that impact Singapore's property market. It is not an easy task to develop a clean identification strategy to pin down the effectiveness of the MaPPs to insulate the domestic housing market from global fluctuations. I would suggest that authors consider using

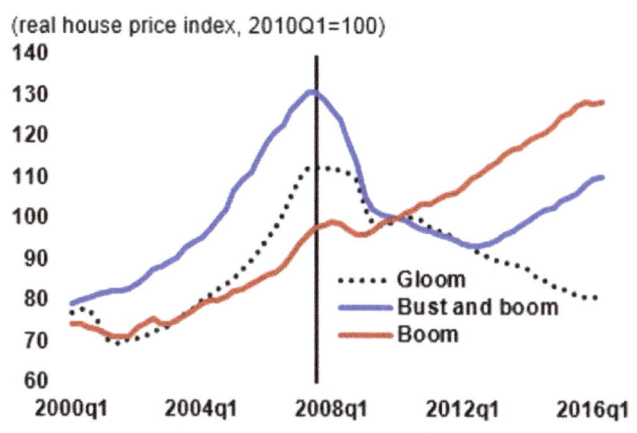

(real house price index, 2010Q1=100)

Figure 1. Real house price.
Source: Ahir and Loungani (2016).

Sources: Bank for International Settlements; European Central Bank; Federal Reserve Bank of Dallas; Savills; and national sources.
Note: Boom = Australia, Austria, Belgium, Canada, Chile, Colombia, Czech Republic, Hong Kong SAR, India, Israel, Kazakhstan, Korea, Malaysia, Mexico, Norway, Peru, Philippines, Slovak Republic, Sweden, Switzerland, and Taiwan POC.
Bust and boom = Bulgaria, Denmark, Estonia, Germany, Hungary, Iceland, Indonesia, Ireland, Japan, Latvia, Lithuania, Malta, New Zealand, Portugal, South Africa, Thailand, United Kingdom, and United States.
Gloom = Brazil, China, Croatia, Cyprus, Finland, France, Greece, Italy, Macedonia, Morocco, Netherlands, Poland, Russia, Serbia, Singapore, Slovenia, Spain, and Ukraine.

the Pearson correlation test to examine the global and local correlations between global house prices and Singapore private PPI. The authors may also consider using Time Lagged Cross Correlation test (such as the Granger causality test) to study the potential leader–follower pattern of the global house prices movements and Singapore private PPI.

In conclusion, this is a very important policy paper. I strongly encourage academics and policymakers to read it if you have not done so.

References

Ahir, Hites and Prakash Loungani, (2016). "Global House Prices: Time to Worry Again?" IMFBlog, 8 December 2016.

Deng, Yongheng, Joseph Gyourko, and Teng Li, (2019). "Singapore's Cooling Measures and Its Housing Market," *Journal of Housing Economics*, **45**, 101573.

CHAPTER 13

© 2023 World Scientific Publishing Company
https://doi.org/10.1142/9789811259432_0026

Chapter 13

Monetary Policy Frameworks in Latin America: Evolution, Resilience and Future Challenges*

Ana Aguilar, Alexandre Tombini and Fabrizio Zampolli

Representative Office for the Americas
Bank for International Settlements

Abstract

Since the adoption of inflation targeting and flexible exchange rates, central banks in Latin America have had to cope with large and persistent capital inflows and currency appreciation, occasionally interrupted by shorter period of capital outflows and elevated exchange rate volatility. Despite these difficult conditions, central bank frameworks have proved generally resilient, including during the COVID-19 crisis. This chapter examines how central banks' policy frameworks have evolved over the past two decades and what challenges lie ahead.

---

*The views expressed in this chapter are those of the authors and do not necessarily represent those of the BIS. We are grateful to Enrique Mendoza and participants at the MAS-BIS conference on "Macro-financial Stability Policy in a Globalised World: Lessons from International Experience", 26–28 May 2021, for their comments and suggestions. Rafael Guerra provided excellent research assistance.

1. Introduction

Over the past few decades, central banking in Latin America went through a profound transformation. In the late 1990s, after the severe disruptions caused by frequent balance of payment and public debt crises in 1970s and 1980s, a strong consensus for sweeping reforms aimed at ensuring macro-financial stability finally emerged. Most central banks in the region abandoned fixed exchange rates for inflation targeting as their main nominal anchor. At the same time, authorities took measures to consolidate public finances, build resilience into their banking systems and make their economies more open to trade and finance.

Along with the tailwinds of lower global inflation, this change in regime was key to achieving lower and more stable inflation in the region. Since then, the policy framework of central banks — how central banks use their policy tools to achieve their objectives — have continued to evolve and adapt. Two periods, in particular, have been key to shaping the way central banks operate in Latin America. The first is the commodity super cycle of 2005–2008, which followed the entry of China into the World Trade Organization (WTO) in 2001. Improved terms of trade and better growth prospects drew large foreign direct investment (FDI) and portfolio flows in several Latin American economies. However, these inflows were also increasing vulnerabilities through debt accumulation. Central banks in the region realised that to reduce these vulnerabilities and build safety margins against possible capital flow reversal, they had to implement FX intervention and macroprudential policies alongside strict monetary policy instruments.

The second period is the aftermath of the Great Financial Crisis (GFC), during which bank deleveraging and unconventional monetary policy (UMP) in advanced economies led to a new wave of capital, which coincided with a greater relevance of market-based finance. Not only did the region's central banks continue to use multiple instruments but they also expanded their toolkit and made their pursuit of financial stability more explicit. Moreover, by this time, the continued refinement of inflation targeting and central bank communication had also helped to anchor inflation expectations more firmly and to reduce the exchange rate pass-through. Domestic financial markets had also become deeper, thanks to institutional reforms and greater stability.

It is by no accident that most Latin American economies went through periods of global financial turbulence such as the GFC in 2008–2009 and the Taper Tantrum in 2013 relatively unscathed. Several economies suffered a sudden stop in capital and a sharp tightening in domestic financial conditions, but none suffered the types of deep crises experienced in the past, with widespread bank failures, large contractions in economic activity and high inflation. Besides, smaller vulnerabilities and greater buffers had reduced the "fear of floating", allowing greater scope for floating exchange rates to act as shock absorbers. Indeed, currency depreciations were a key factor facilitating the reduction of the large current account deficits that arose after the sharp drop in commodity prices in 2014–2015. More recently, in the COVID-19 crisis, the toolkit that Latin American central banks developed over the previous years allowed them to respond aggressively and timely to the unprecedented drop in economic activity.

This chapter describes how monetary policy frameworks have evolved in the five major Latin American economies (Brazil, Chile, Colombia, Peru and Mexico) that have consistently implemented inflation targeting since its adoption in the late 1990s and early 2000s.[1] Section 2 highlights how the adoption of inflation targeting crucially coincided with wide-ranging reforms, which strengthened macroeconomic fundamentals. Section 3 turns to the major episodes of inflows and outflows in Latin America, illustrating how different external shocks influenced the economy and how authorities responded. Section 4 assesses how central banks' policy frameworks coped during the COVID-19 crisis. Finally, Section 5 concludes with the main lessons learnt so far and the future challenges.

2. Strengthening macro-financial fundamentals

During the 1980s, Latin America experienced large macroeconomic imbalances, often culminating in currency, banking and sovereign crises. Massive capital outflows, large output losses and slow growth resulted,

---

[1] In the rest of the Chapter, Latin America and Latin American economies generally refer to these five economies.

making the 1990s a "lost decade" (Ocampo, 2014; Ramos-Francia et al., 2014). It took about a decade to see again large, sustained inflows of foreign capital into the region and growth return to healthier levels.

The strengthening of macro-financial fundamentals contributed to such fortunes. A fundamental step, as of mid-1990s, was the granting of independence (de jure or de facto) to central banks. Coupled with prohibitions on monetising public debt and deficits, this allowed most central banks to focus on the primary objective of controlling inflation.[2] At the same time or soon after, following a global trend, most central banks in Latin America opted for inflation targeting and flexible exchange rates, which helped consolidate the expectations of low inflation among the public.[3]

First, countries pursued fiscal consolidation and strengthened their fiscal positions, after having suffered the adverse consequences of fiscal crises such as high inflation, sharp budget adjustments and contraction in economic activity (Figure 1). These efforts included successful debt renegotiations and the privatisation of public enterprises. However, a major improvement was the strengthening of fiscal institutions with the implementation of fiscal responsibility laws to improve fiscal consolidation (Chile in 1990, Brazil in 2000, Colombia and Peru in 2003 and Mexico in 2006).[4]

---

[2] For example, the Bank of Mexico was granted autonomy in 1993 along with the prohibition to provide direct credit to the government. The Central Reserve Bank of Peru was given strict limits to the amount of governments bonds it could purchase in secondary markets. The Central Bank of Chile was until the outbreak of the COVID-19 pandemic prohibited to provide any credit to the public sector. And the Central Bank of Brazil was granted by parliament full autonomy in February 2021. In 2000 and 2006, respectively, Brazil and Mexico passed legislation that imposed limits to spending and debt. See, e.g., Gutiérrez (2003).

[3] Brazil, Chile and Colombia adopted inflation targeting in 1999, and Mexico and Peru in 2000. For the adoption of inflation targeting in Latin America and changes in institutional processes see, e.g., Carstens and Werner (1999); Bogdanski et al. (2000); Armas and Grippa (2005) and Cespedes and Soto (2006).

[4] For example, in 2000, Brazil's congress approved a fiscal responsibility law to improve fiscal transparency and encourage continued fiscal consolidation at all levels of government. Peru introduced a fiscal law in 1999 and in 2003, which helped reduce Peru's fiscal deficit. Colombia has also introduced fiscal responsibility laws in 2003. See, e.g., Singh et al. (2005) and Hausmann (2002).

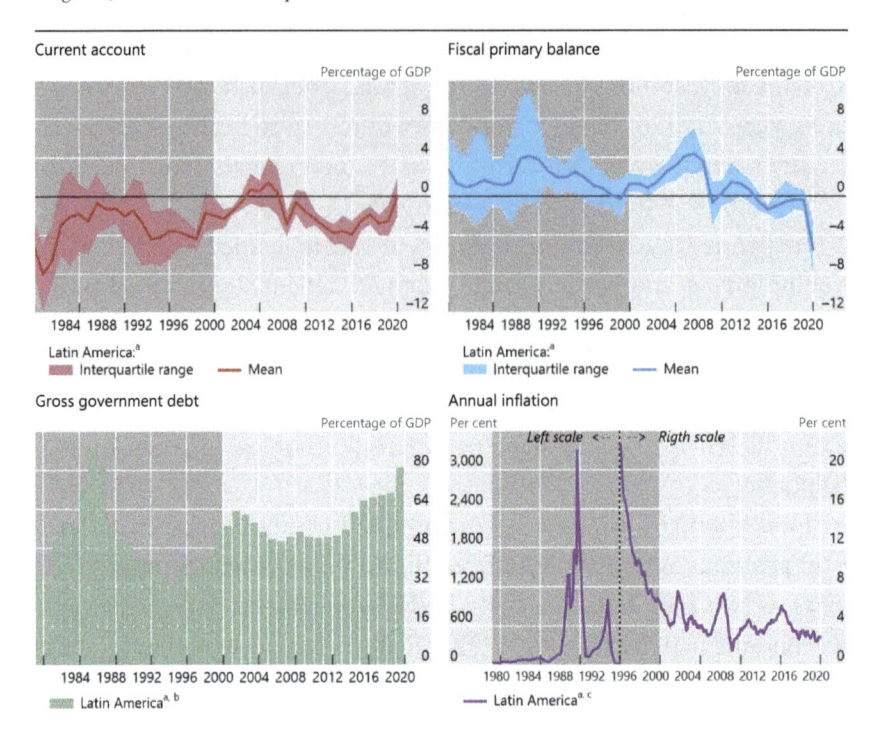

Figure 1. Economic fundamentals strengthened before inflation targeting in Latin America.

Note: Shaded area indicates period before Inflation Targeting regimes were implemented in the region.

[a]Latin America include Brazil, Chile, Colombia, Mexico, and Peru.
[b]Third quartile reported.
[c]Simple average of the annual inflation rate. Hyperinflation episodes are included in the simple average.

Source: Global Financial Data; IMF, *World Economic Outlook*; national data; authors' calculation.

Second, countries concluded several trade agreements (e.g., Mexico, NAFTA in 1994; in South America, Mercosur in 1991, Andean Community in 1969, and a number of other agreements under the umbrella of LAFTA [Latin American Free Trade Association] and then LAIA [Latin American Integration Association] in the 1990s).[5] These agreements boosted

---

[5] Foreign Trade Information System, Organization of American States, http://www.sice.oas.org.

competition and provided a legal framework that attracted and protected foreign investment, which in turn helped modernise production and improve productivity (e.g., Laird and Messerlin [2002] and Dingemans and Ross [2012]).

Third, important reforms to pension systems helped not only to reduce the future fiscal burden but also to develop domestic capital markets.[6] The creation of private pension funds generated an extra stable flow of resources that funded government debt, including at the longer end of the yield curve. Indeed, governments were generally able to lengthen the maturity of their securities.[7]

Finally, countries implemented various structural reforms aimed at increasing productivity, including tax reforms and privatisation as well as institutional changes to labour markets and the financial sector. Such reforms were beneficial but economic performance and income distribution did not improve as much as expected in the late 1990s.[8]

Along with the tailwinds of favourable global conditions, changes in the central banks' policy frameworks and structural reforms were accompanied by a significant reduction in inflation and interest rates. Inflation expectations became better anchored around targets and inflation risk premia narrowed. Eventually, the exchange rate became the financial variable that absorbed financial volatility, instead of interest rates, which were highly volatile before the adoption of inflation targeting (Figure 2).

Furthermore, for most economies, with lower public financial requirements, external financing needs greatly diminished, leading to more manageable current account deficits. Country credit risk diminished,

---

[6] For example, Chile was the first Latin American country to reform its pension system by introducing a private, defined-contribution scheme in 1981. Later on, in 1993, in Mexico, the public system was replaced with a private one. Colombia and Peru modified the public system and added a new private tier. In addition, Brazil offered supplementary pensions. See, e.g., Singh *et al.* (2005) and Mesa-Lago (2002).

[7] In Mexico the average public debt maturity increased from 0.7 years in 1993 to 7.2 years in 2010. This became a valuable reference for the private bond market and for longer-term mortgages.

[8] The evidence in Lora and Barrera (1997) suggests that the reforms implemented during the 1990s had a substantial effect on productivity, investment and growth. However, more recent studies indicate that early estimates may have overstated the benefits of the reforms; see, e.g., Lora (2001) and Goldfajn *et al.* (2021).

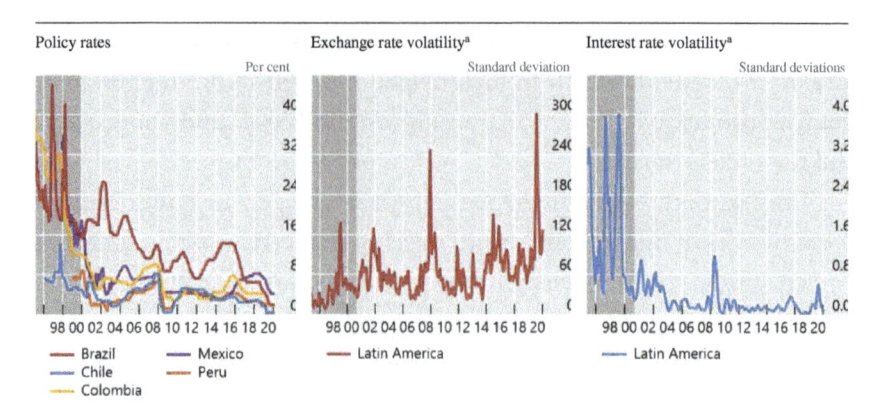

Figure 2. Interest rates as monetary policy instruments and FX flexibility.
Note: Shaded area indicates period before Inflation Targeting regimes were implemented in the region.
[a] Simple average for Latin American countries. Latin America include Brazil, Chile, Colombia, Mexico, and Peru. Volatility is the standard deviation estimated using a three-month window for the bilateral exchange rates and a four-month window for the policy rates.
Source: National data; authors' calculation.

and significant swaths of sovereign and corporate debt obtained investment grade from international rating agencies.

All these changes improved foreign investors' confidence. As a result of this and the uncertainty caused by the East Asian Financial Crisis, in the late 1990s Latin America was attracting a higher share of FDI flows than other emerging economies regions.[9] For example, in 1997, net FDI inflows to Latin America increased by 28.3 percent compared with an increase of 8.6 percent in Asia and a decline of 2.4 percent in Africa. As a result, Latin America's share of developing countries' FDI rose from 33.7 percent in 1996 to 37.6 percent in 1997, while other developing regions' were decreasing. Within Latin America, Brazil and Mexico were leading destinations.[10]

---

[9] That said, during the Asian Financial Crisis, Latin American economies were not insulated from global market turbulences. The increased interlinkages of financial markets contributed to greater volatility of capital flows during 1997–1998 unrelated to domestic markets' fundamentals (Calvo and Mendoza, 2000).

[10] During 1997, Brazil received approximately 29 percent of total FDI inflows into Latin America, while Mexico, Colombia, Chile, and Peru received 21.5 percent, 9.6 percent, 4.3 percent and 3.6 percent, respectively (UNCTAD, 1998).

3. Strengthening the monetary policy frameworks

3.1. *The pre-GFC commodity boom*

At the time that Latin American economies adopted inflation targeting and strengthened their macroeconomic fundamentals, China was admitted to the WTO in 2001. Since then, China's growth took off, reaching double digit for several years, leading to the onset of a commodity super cycle that lasted until 2014–2015 (Figure 3, left-hand panel) and to a reduction in global manufacturing prices relative to commodity ones.

These changes affected Latin American economies differently. Commodity exporters such as Brazil, Colombia, Chile and Peru experienced an improvement in their terms of trade (Figure 3, centre panel) as well as large and persistent currency appreciations (Figure 3, right-hand panel), which coincided with stronger growth in investment, output and domestic credit (Figure 4).[11] In contrast, manufacturing exporters such as Mexico lost an important share of US imports to China and suffered a deterioration in their terms of trade. Several productions in Mexico and other countries were based on the abundance of low skilled

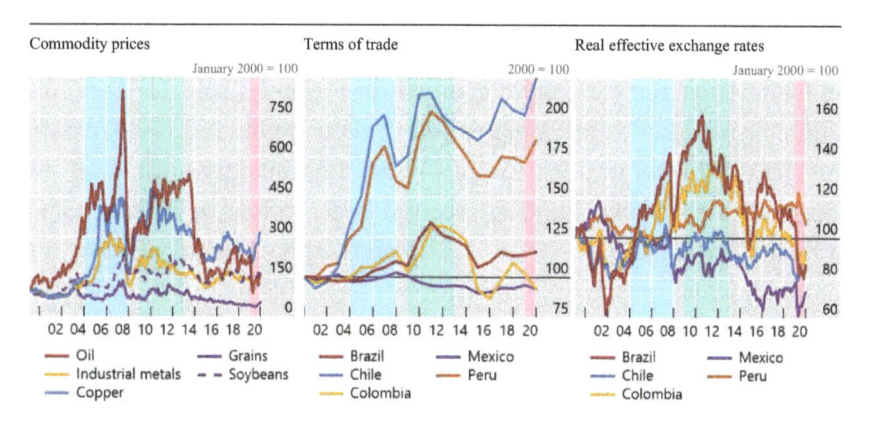

Figure 3. Impact on Latin America of commodity price boom since 2000.
Note: Shaded areas represent the boom on commodity prices (blue), the period after the GFC but before the Taper Tantrum (green) and the COVID-19 pandemic (red).
Source: IMF, World Economic Outlook; national data.

---

[11] An important positive side effect in these countries was the significant reduction in poverty and inequality; see e.g., IMF (2021).

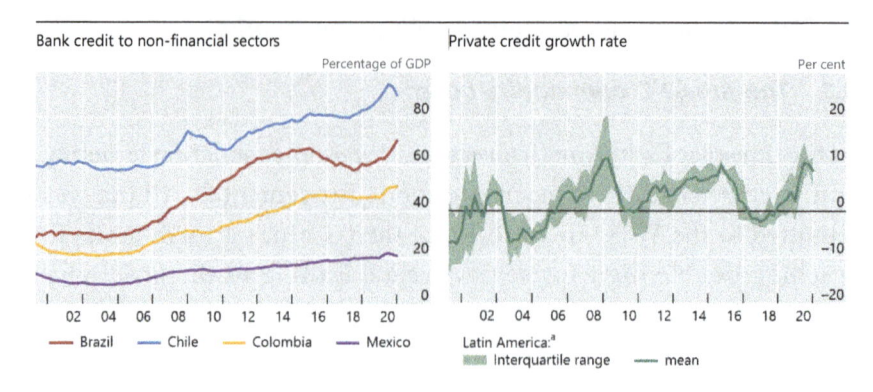

Figure 4. Credit developments.
[a]Latin America includes Brazil, Chile, Colombia and Mexico.
Source: National data; authors' calculation.

labour but even so, were not able to compete with the much lower costs of similar productions in China (Amoroso *et al.*, 2008). For example, Mexico's textile exports to the US were decimated. The economy kept its manufacturing capacity but had to go through a deep reorganisation that shifted resources towards the automotive industry and other less labour-intensive productions.

The different impact of China's emergence as a global economic power on Latin American economies and growth prospects coincided with a different magnitude and composition of their capital inflows. During the 2005–2008 commodity boom — and subsequently until 2015 — commodity exporting countries received larger inflows as a percentage of their GDP than in previous years. Importantly, a significant part of the additional flows was accounted for by non-resident portfolio inflows, which were short-term and more volatile (Figure 5, left-hand panel). In comparison, during the same period, Mexico received a smaller share of overall flows than the commodity exporters. Yet it was also receiving a larger share of portfolios flows than in the past (Figure 5, right-hand panel).

In economies experiencing large inflows and stronger growth, like the Latin American commodity exporters during the period 2005–2008, the use of strict monetary policy instruments poses at least two challenges. First, if inflation is already close to target, inflation-targeting central

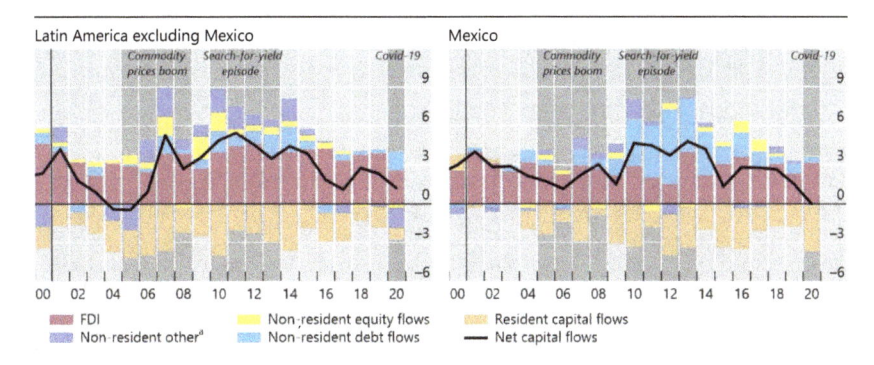

Figure 5. Capital flows composition: commodity vs manufacturing economies (as a percentage of GDP).
Note: Vertical line represents the year China was included into the WTO (2001).
^aOther is a residual category that includes non-resident flows other than those included in FDI, equity and debt flows.
Source: IMF, International Financial Statistics; authors' calculation.

banks have less room to hike rates to cool domestic demand and slow debt accumulation. Second, an increase in short-term interest rates may even exacerbate exchange rate appreciation, which in turn could attract additional capital flows and further ease domestic financial conditions. That is, the financial effects of the exchange rate can significantly dampen its cooling impact on trade and output, while debt and other financial vulnerability continue to accumulate.[12] Furthermore, the sole use of interest policy is generally insufficient to build the buffers needed to withstand possible episodes of capital stop or reversal (BIS, 2019a).

The same forces can work in the opposite direction when the currency depreciates. In the presence of low economic growth, the central banks may want to lower interest rates to boost economic activity, but this could lead to further currency depreciation, higher inflation, and a further

---

[12] The strength of these effects depends on the size of foreign-currency-denominated debt and how large is the presence of foreign investors in local currency markets. In the presence of foreign-currency-denominated debt, an appreciation of the exchange rate can improve the balance sheet of borrowers and lenders, leading to greater credit availability and narrower credit spreads. Similarly, an appreciating currency normally makes local currency bonds more attractive to foreign investors. See, e.g., BIS (2019a); Hofmann *et al.* (2020); and Carstens and Shin (2019).

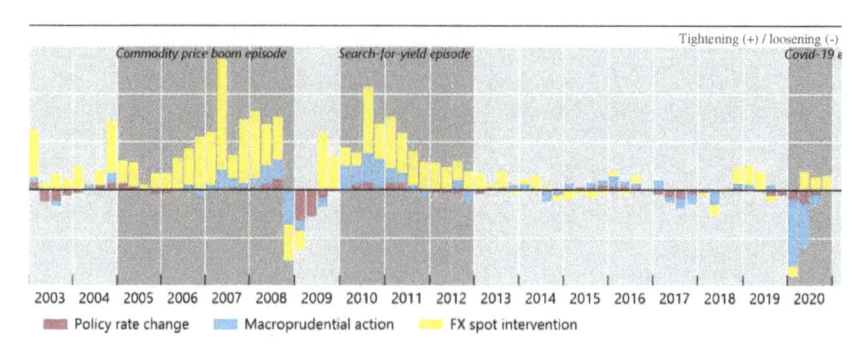

Figure 6. Use of multiple instruments by Latin America economies.
Note: BR, CL, CO, MX and PE. Policy rate change = average quarterly change in the policy rate in percentage points across the five countries divided by 50 basis points; macroprudential action = average number of the sum of tightening (+1) or loosening (−1) actions by a country across the countries; FX spot intervention = average value of the percentage change in total FX reserve assets in US dollars excluding gold across the five countries normalised by its standard deviation, where a positive value means purchasing foreign currency and selling local currency and a negative value selling foreign currency and purchasing local currency.
Source: Budnik and Kleibl (2018); Reinhardt and Sowerbutts (2016); Shim *et al.* (2013); FSB Covid-19 policy action database; IMF, *Integrated Macroprudential Policy (iMaPP) Database*, originally constructed by Alam *et al.* (2019); IMF, *International Financial Statistics*; Datastream; national data; authors' calculations.

tightening of domestic financial conditions through the financial channel of the exchange rate. In the 2005–2008 period, Mexico's central bank was facing such a dilemma: its ability to cut policy rates was constrained by the need to support the exchange rate and to limit its impact on inflation as well as to prevent risk premia from widening.

In the Latin American economies facing appreciating currencies and capital inflows, central banks and other authorities adopted additional instruments besides interest rate policy. Using multiple instruments was not new to them — having been employed also in the early stages of inflation targeting — but it increased in intensity over the commodity boom (Figure 6).

Specifically, FX intervention played an important role. All central banks intervened with two main motives in mind: to increase international reserves and to smooth excess exchange rate volatility

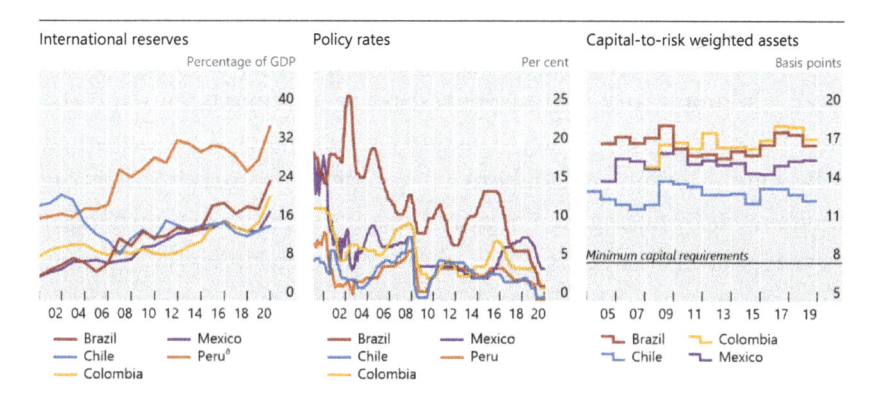

Figure 7. Building buffers to mitigate risks and complementing policy rates.
ᵃ 2020's observation from the Central Reserve Bank of Peru.
Source: IMF, *World Economic Outlook*; Institute of International Finance; national data.

(Figure 7, left-hand panel).[13] For example, building buffers was particularly important in Brazil, Colombia and Peru. Even in Chile, where FX intervention had been extremely infrequent, the central bank intervened in 2008 — as it did in the early 2000s — to boost international reserves as these were at relatively low levels compared to other emerging market economies (EMEs). Limiting exchange rate volatility (or slowing the rate of currency appreciation) for macroprudential purposes was also relevant in some countries due to the strong appreciation and domestic credit increase.

FX intervention was complemented by macroprudential measures, generally aimed at reducing financial institutions' exposures to the exchange rate and fast-growing segments of the domestic credit market. These tools were used not only to improve the resilience of the financial

---

[13] International reserves constitute an important backstop that contributes to improve investors' confidence and reduce both the probability and the adverse effects of a sharp tightening in external financial conditions. Cecchetti *et al.* (2011) and Berkmen *et al.* (2012) indicate that larger exchange reserves at the outset of the GFC improved macroeconomic performance in its aftermath. Borio *et al.* (2020) shows that larger foreign exchange reserves along with higher bank capital reduce the fiscal cost of banking crises.

system but, in some cases, also in an attempt to contain or smooth financial booms.[14] The tools most frequently deployed, especially in Brazil, Colombia and Peru, were reserve requirements on deposits, often differentiated according to maturity and currency. As documented by Brei and Moreno (2019), banks responded to increases in reserve requirements by raising loan rates and keeping deposit rates unchanged or even lowering them during periods of large capital inflows.[15] This was unlike the response of banks to a hike in the policy rate, which tended to increase both loan and deposit rates. Thus, besides increasing the resilience of financial institutions, reserve requirements contributed to weakening the link between capital flows and domestic liquidity and provided more leeway for policy rate increases (Figure 7, centre panel). In addition to reserve requirements, other frequently used tools during the commodity boom included limits to currency mismatches and loss provisioning.

3.2. The GFC and the challenges arising in its aftermath

Thanks to the measures taken by central banks and other authorities, a favourable cyclical position and well capitalised banking sectors (Figure 7, right-hand panel), no countries in Latin America had any major financial imbalances at the outset of the GFC. Latin America commodity exporters had been able to accumulate significant international reserves pre-crisis and had strengthened their fiscal positions. And, after the crisis burst, they could count on a rapid recovery of commodity prices and a positive medium-term growth outlook in the wake of the extraordinary monetary and fiscal expansionary measures enacted by G20 countries, and China in particular. As a result, when the GFC struck, these economies experienced only a mild and short output contraction followed by a quick rebound.[16]

---

[14] There is overwhelming evidence that macroprudential policy measures improve the resilience of the financial system. Evidence that macroprudential tools also help to restrain significantly financial booms is more mixed. See, e.g., BIS (2018).

[15] See also Montoro and Moreno (2011).

[16] As stressed, e.g., by De Gregorio (2013), an external observer who only knew about their history of financial crises in Latin America would have been amazed at the fact that Latin American economies did not suffer any major crisis during the GFC.

Even Mexico, which in 2009 suffered one of the largest GDP contractions among EMEs (-7.7 percent GDP), did not suffer a major crisis, partly owing to international credit arrangements. While the country had a sound financial system and low private sector debt levels, it had until then experienced low growth for several years and had low levels of foreign exchange reserves relative to its peers, making it vulnerable to a loss of investors' confidence. A crucial stabilising factor was the concession by the IMF of a Flexible Credit Line (FCL) designed to allow countries access to financial resources without the stigma associated with a traditional IMF programme.[17]

Having weathered the GFC, major Latin American economies had to face the challenge of a new wave of capital inflows generated by advanced economies' unconventional monetary policy measures (IMF, 2014). This time, capital flows were larger and more volatile than in the wave experienced prior to the GFC. Their composition had also changed. The share of portfolio investment increased further during 2010-2015 for commodity exporters, but even more in Mexico, where FDI flows declined as a share of both GDP and total inflows (Figure 5, blue bars). Moreover, portfolio flows became more varied by type of investors as well as geographically. In particular, cross-border banking diminished, especially from North American banks, while the role of asset managers, investment funds and other non-bank financial intermediaries increased (CGFS, 2021). As the latter were not regulated as strictly as banks, these changes created new challenges for authorities.[18]

Another important change was the development of local currency markets, especially for sovereign debt, and the increased participation of foreign investors (Figure 8, left-hand panel). Along with greater international risk appetite, institutional developments played an important role. The latter comprised removing administrative barriers for investors to enter and exit local markets, including to FX markets,

---

[17] The IMF approved a programme of USD 47 billion to Mexico during the GFC. Indeed, the FCL facility became a useful external financing backstop for several countries, including for Colombia, Chile and Peru during the COVID-19 crisis.

[18] Also see, e.g., Lane and Milesi-Ferreti (2017), Avdjiev *et al.* (2018); BIS (2019b) and Alfaro *et al.* (2020).

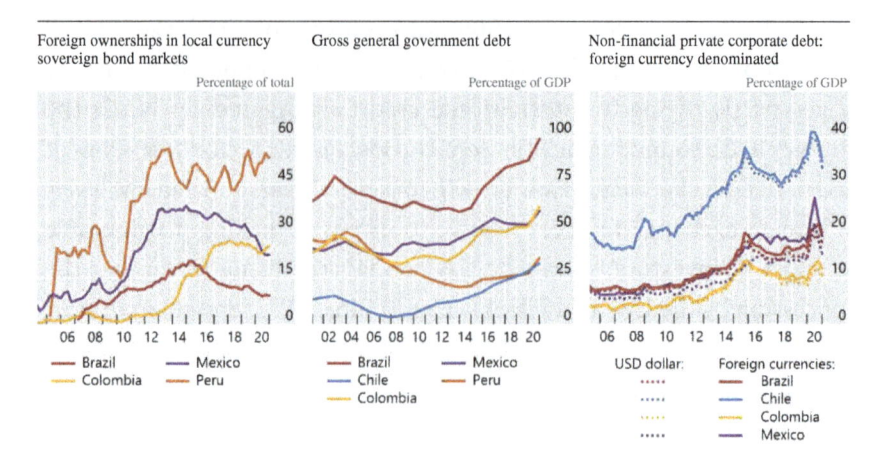

Figure 8. Financial vulnerabilities have increased.
Source: IMF, World Economic Outlook; Institute of International Finance.

and the development of derivatives markets to allow the possibility of hedging positions. In several cases, greater accessibility was rewarded with the inclusion of a country's bonds into a global bond index, which helped draw further investment from abroad.[19]

The greater diversification of capital flows represented a positive development overall as it helped deepen local financial markets and reduce the currency mismatches that amplified previous crises. At the same time, however, the greater presence of portfolio investors exposed EMEs to new risks. Passive investment strategies and other practices by asset managers can lead to herding behaviour and contagion. In addition, the larger share of domestic currency debt owned by foreign investors did not fully eliminate currency risk but shifted it to lenders, who may not be hedged. Unhedged investment may give rise to adverse feedback loops between yields and exchange rates and exacerbate global shock transmission ("Original Sin Redux") (BIS, 2019a; Hoffman et al., 2020; Carstens and Shin, 2019).[20] Indeed, there is some evidence that the sensitivity of capital flows in Latin America to global financial conditions has increased since the GFC.[21]

---

[19] For an analysis of the role of benchmark driven investments in EM local bond markets see Arslanalp et al. (2020). See also Jeanneau and Tovar (2006).
[20] For a recent assessment of the benefits and costs of capital flows, see CGFS (2021).
[21] See, e.g., Ahmed (2017), Gonçalves et al. (2019) and CGFS (2021).

Large capital inflows and the accompanying strengthening of their currencies were leading in several economies to an undesired relaxation in domestic financial conditions as well as the build-up of financial vulnerabilities. Both public debt — largely financed in local currency and with the increasing participation of foreign investors — and foreign-currency-denominated corporate debt increased substantially post-GFC (Figure 8, centre and right-hand panels). Furthermore, a significant share of the flows that had financed those debts was expected, at some point, to reverse with the unwinding of unconventional monetary policy measures in major economies. A major concern was that such a reversal could also occur unexpectedly and abruptly, and be potentially amplified by the greater relevance of non-bank finance.

3.3. *The post-crisis evolution of policy frameworks*

The response of central banks and other authorities to the challenges created by the post-GFC developments consisted of actions on multiple fronts.

First, although the objectives pursued by central banks did not change, the organisation of central banks was generally modified to reflect their greater emphasis on monitoring financial stability risks as well as on ensuring that measures regarding financial stability were made and communicated to the public more effectively. Hence, financial stability committees and divisions were created or strengthened. Financial stability reports were introduced or became more analytical. And, in several countries, inter-agency arrangements between the central bank, other financial authorities and relevant government ministries were established to improve the coordination of policy decisions (Table 1).

Second, following the post-GFC regulatory reform process, new prudential regulation was introduced to strengthen the resilience of the financial sector. This new regulation went beyond what were required by Basel III standards and fit to each country's needs (Table 2). For example, both Brazil and Mexico introduced guidelines for reporting derivatives positions of corporations after the GFC. Stress tests were also revamped and used more systematically in several central banks.

Table 1. Macroprudential frameworks: Objectives decisions and coordination

	Brazil	Chile	Colombia	Mexico	Peru
Central banks' financial stability objectives					
Financial stability objective	Efficient, solid financial system	Normal functioning of internal and external payments	To promote financial stability	To promote a healthy development of financial system	To regulate credit in the financial system
Statutory mandate	No	Yes	No	No	Yes
Source of mandate	Central bank's mission statement	Central bank charter	Central bank charter	Central bank charter	Constitution
Macroprudential objectives	Yes, narrow objective	No[a]	No	No	No
Inter-agency arrangements in financial stability frameworks					
Chair		Minister of finance	Minister of finance	Minister of finance	Minister of finance
Inter-agency forum	National Monetary Council	Financial Stability Council	Coordination committee	Consejo de Estabilidad del Sistema Financiero	There is no inter-agency body[b]

[a] The central bank has the power to accommodate it under its mandate.
[b] The banking supervisor is invited to the central bank board meeting quarterly.
Source: Villar (2017).

Table 2. Instruments in macroprudential frameworks.

	Brazil	Chile	Colombia	Mexico	Peru
Countercyclical capital buffers	√		√	√	√
Dynamic provisions			√		√
Sectoral capital requirements	√		√		√
Countercyclical capital requirements	√		√		√
Margins and haircuts	√		√		√
LTV ratios	√	√	√	√	
Debt-to-income ratios	√	√	√		
Limits on currency mismatches	√	√	√	√	√

Note: Table has been adjusted with the latest information.
Source: BIS (2021) and Villar (2017).

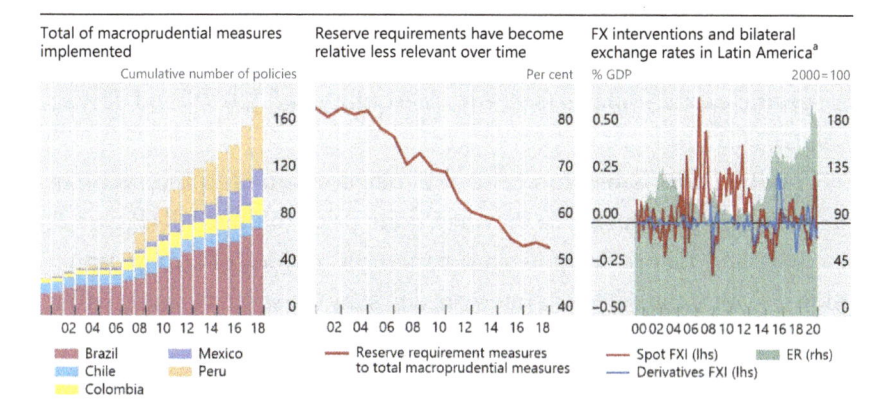

Figure 9. Macroprudential policies and FX interventions in Latin America.
Note: An increase of the exchange rate denotes a depreciation. Reported proxies of FX interventions, measures as a percentage of GDP (Adler *et al.*, 2021).
[a] Latin America represents the three-months moving average of Brazil, Chile, Colombia, Mexico and Peru. Positive values denote FX buying and negative values a FX selling.
Source: Adler *et al.* (2021); IMF, *Integrated Macroprudential Policy (iMaPP) Database*, originally constructed by Alam *et al.* (2019); authors' calculations.

Third, compared to the pre-GFC period, Latin American central banks made greater use of macroprudential policy. This is evident from the continuous increase in the number of macroprudential measures taken after the GFC, especially in Brazil, Mexico and Peru (Figure 9, left-hand panel). Furthermore, such an increase corresponded to the adoption and/or more frequent use of a wider range of macroprudential policy measures. As a result, while reserve requirements remained an important tool, their relative importance over this period continued to decline (Figure 9, centre panel).

Countries also differed in terms of the frequency and the range of tools deployed (Table 2). In Brazil and Peru, where macroprudential policy was more active, a wide range of tools was used except for dynamic provisioning (Brazil) and limits on borrowing (Peru). In Colombia too, authorities made use of all major categories of macroprudential policies, albeit less frequently than in other countries. Limits on currency mismatches continued to be key in all countries. Some central banks also used capital flow management tools during exceptional circumstances.

For example, in addition to implementing reserve requirements on banks' short FX spot positions after the GFC, authorities in Brazil imposed taxes on specific capital inflows (see, e.g., Mesquita *et al.* [2010] and Terrier *et al.* [2011]).[22]

Finally, Latin American central banks continued to intervene in foreign exchange markets as they had done prior to the GFC (Figure 6, blue bars and Figure 9, right-hand panel). In periods of strong capital inflows, several central banks intervened to slow the speed of appreciation and to accumulate additional international reserves. In periods of market turbulence, as during the Taper Tantrum episode in 2013 and later after the end of the commodity super-cycle in 2014–2015, FX interventions aimed to eliminate market disruptions or lack of liquidity, or to ensure that markets remained orderly, rather than to improve competitiveness or to pursue an exchange rate objective.[23] An important change in FX operations post-GFC was the increasing intervention by most central banks in FX derivatives markets, which reflected the developments of these markets in the region and the significant increase in the demand for hedges, especially in the non-financial corporate sector.

With the more frequent and intense use of multiple instruments, decision-making has become potentially more complicated. In this regard, central banks have generally followed a decision-making approach close to the Tinbergen principle of one instrument, one objective: that is,

---

[22] Latin American authorities were particularly active in their use of macroprudential policy in the early post-GFC years. For instance, in Colombia in 2011 concerns about rising household leverage led authorities to raise loan loss provisions on consumer loans at banks with historically high non-performing loans (Vargas *et al.*, 2017). The Central Bank of Brazil raised the regulatory capital requirement for auto loans due to the rapid growth in the auto loan market during 2009–2010 (Costa de Moura *et al.*, 2017). At end of 2010 and in 2011, the countercyclical buffer was increased to smooth rapid credit growth (Pereira da Silva *et al.*, 2012).

[23] The motives for intervening in FX markets have generally been quite stable over time (BIS, 2013). Among them, restoring orderly market functioning is the most important (BIS, 2021). Both the size and type of intervention were generally adopted after a careful diagnosis of the source of the pressure in the foreign exchange market (e.g., a particular market segment) and adapted to the specific type of investor or flows associated with it. For temporary or seasonal needs of liquidity in foreign exchange, for example, central banks used repo operations, while for more permanent changes in foreign exchange liquidity, they favoured outright sales in the spot market.

interest rate policy as the main instrument for achieving price stability; FX intervention for addressing excessive exchange rate volatility and liquidity shortages and macroprudential policy measures as the main instruments for reducing financial stability risks. This arrangement is shown to be optimal in theory and generally facilitates communication with the public (Carrillo *et al.*, 2021). That said, central banks are mindful of the possible interaction between instruments and the fact that the same instrument can contribute to multiple objectives.

Overall, the use of multiple instruments allowed Latin American economies to maintain the benefits of a flexible exchange rate regime. As the adverse effects of large swings in the exchange rates on the financial system and on inflation were reduced, exchange rates could play their traditional stabilising role through their impact on trade and output. This was the case, for example, after the bust of commodity prices in 2014–2015, which led to a large widening of current account deficits in Latin American commodity exporters. Their currencies depreciated significantly, contributing over time to reducing these deficits without leading to any financial stress or sharp tightening of domestic financial conditions.

4. The COVID-19 pandemic

The contraction following the onset of the COVID-19 pandemic constituted one of the most difficult tests for central banks' policy frameworks over the past two decades. As of March 2020, lockdowns and mobility restrictions led to the shutdown of large parts of the economies, an unprecedented sharp drop in output and a large increase in unemployment, depriving many families and firms of vital liquidity and causing major disruptions in financial markets. Even the safest segments of global financial markets, such as the US Treasury markets, were close to a seizure in March (BIS, 2020a).

The key to restoring market confidence was the prompt response by the US Federal Reserve and other major central banks in slashing interest rates and providing liquidity. Yet Latin American central banks also played an important role in stabilising local market conditions and minimising the impact of the shock on domestic economic activity. Indeed, there was no sudden stop from external financing as the ones suffered during the crises before the new century.

The response from Latin American central banks involved the use of a wide range of instruments, yet without requiring significant changes to their policy frameworks.

First, most central banks were able to make effective use of their standard interest rate policy, cutting policy rates in the early stage of the crisis (Aguilar and Cantú, 2020). Compared with other EMEs, central banks in Latin America generally cut rates by a larger margin (Figure 10, left-hand panel). That central banks could do that was not, at

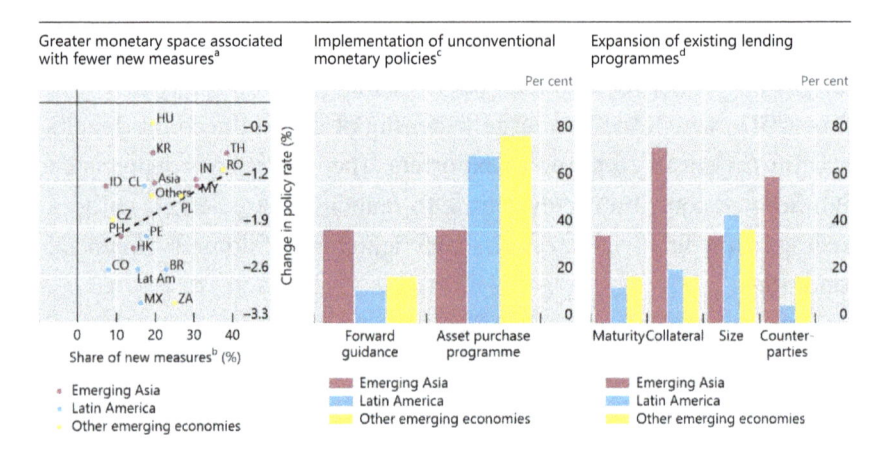

Figure 10. Differences in monetary policy expansion across EMEs during COVID-19.

Note: Measures implemented during the 2020. BR = Brazil; CL = Chile; CN = China; CO = Colombia; CZ = Czech Republic; HK = Hong Kong; HU = Hungary; ID = Indonesia; IN = India; KR = Korea; MY; Malaysia; MX = Mexico; PE = Peru; PH = the Philippines; PL; = Poland; RO = Romania; TH = Thailand; ZA= South Africa.

[a] Latin America = BR, CL, CO, MX and PE. Emerging Asia = HK, ID, IN, KR, MY, PH, and TH. Other emerging economies = CZ, HU, PL, RO, and ZA.

[b] Share represents the percentage of new measures to the sum of interest rate, reserve policy, lending and repo operations, foreign exchange and asset purchases measures during the 2020.

[c] Each bar represents the percentage of countries relative to their region/group of countries.

[d] Expressed as a share of all expansions to existing programmes pre-COVID-19 crisis; a single programme can be adjusted in multiple dimensions.

Source: Cantú *et al.* (2021); central bank websites; national data; authors' calculation.

the start of the crisis, a sure thing. In previous episodes of rapid currency depreciation — most recently in a number of countries after the collapse of commodity prices in 2014–2015 — central banks in the region were compelled to raise policy rates to prevent further currency depreciation and fend off increases in inflation (see, e.g., Végh et al. [2017]). In contrast, at the start of the outbreak, they could benefit — in addition to a wide output gap — from the actions they had taken after the GFC, which reduced the exposure of their economies to large swings in the exchange rate and strengthened their inflation fighting credibility.

Second, besides cutting policy rates, Latin American central banks implemented a wide range of exceptional operations (Figure 10, centre panel). The lion's share of these measures consisted in lending operations to financial institutions. Central banks expanded the eligibility of securities as collateral for liquidity facilities and the corresponding counterparties. They also adapted existing liquidity facilities to support bank credit targeted at small and medium-sized enterprises (SMEs). Importantly, these measures were complemented, except in Mexico, by government credit guarantees, which gave financial institutions the incentive to use the thus-obtained liquidity to increase lending to the non-financial sectors of the economy.

Third, several central banks also acted as "market makers of last resort" in several markets. Their intervention was largely in FX markets, but in some cases also included purchases of government and/or corporate bonds. Unlike in advanced economies post-GFC, the goal of asset purchases was limited to restoring market functioning rather than compressing yields. Given a history of fiscal dominance and high inflation, most Latin American central banks are prohibited or severely restricted in their ability to purchase sovereign bonds; and those that can intervene in these markets are generally reluctant to do so. This explains why Latin American central banks have generally not used asset purchases as intensively as advanced economies and EMEs in other regions (Figure 10, centre and right-hand panels).[24]

---

[24] The central banks of Chile and Colombia bought bonds amounting to 2.1 percent and 1.1 percent of GDP, respectively, well below the purchase of other EMEs such as, e.g., the Philippines (5.7 percent), Croatia (4.9 percent) and Poland (4.5 percent). The central banks of Brazil and Chile obtained changes to their legal mandate to extend the range of assets they could buy, even if they have not as yet used these new powers. Brazil and Mexico also conducted swap operations to change the maturity of outstanding public debt.

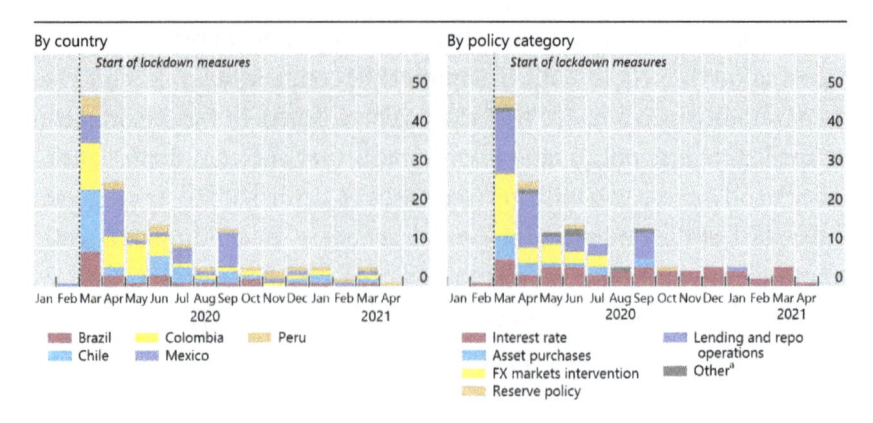

Figure 11. During the COVID-19 pandemic policy response was prompt.
Note: Measures up to 6 April 2021.
[a] Other category includes loan guarantee programs, technical changes to facilities and changes to central bank's law.
Source: Cantú *et al.* (2001); national data; authors' calculation.

Finally, an important innovation has been the introduction of forward guidance in a number of countries where policy rates reached a near zero level or their historical low. In economies that are more volatile than advanced economies, the effectiveness of forward guidance is still to be proven.

Most of the tools used by Latin American central banks during the COVID-19 crisis were not qualitatively new, but their scale and scope were much larger, consistent with the size and unique nature of the shock. Most interventions were concentrated between March and April 2020, soon after the start of the global pandemic (Figure 11). That central banks were able to implement so many measures so rapidly owed to the fact that most measures had been used previously. Except for some changes, their playbook was already available. Furthermore, the use of new measures was smaller in Latin America and inversely related to the initial monetary policy space (Figure 11, left-hand panel). The need to introduce new measures, especially asset purchase programmes (centre panel), seems to have been reduced by the ability of cutting policy rates sharply at the start of the crisis. Importantly, any new measures did not require changes in the legal mandate of the central bank, with a few exceptions in which central banks sought and obtained the permission such as to conduct purchases of sovereign bonds. Yet, the need to conduct these operations did not arise, as liquidity provisions to the financial sector proved effective to channel credit to those in need in the private sector.[25]

While the COVID-19 crisis has not led to major changes in the toolkits of Latin American central banks, it has brought about some changes in some of the operational aspects of their frameworks (BIS, 2020b; BIS, 2021). Specifically, in terms of policy analysis, models, projections and scenarios have been adapted in the initial quarters of the COVID-19 crisis to incorporate the unique features of the shock, including the higher degree of uncertainty. For example, the Bank of Mexico temporarily adopted a set of scenarios for growth and inflation in replacement of baseline forecasts. In terms of communicating to the public, challenges went beyond the need to acknowledge greater uncertainty. The wider array of tools has also made communication more complex. And the rapid evolution of the crisis increased the frequency of announcements and press releases. In some cases, monetary policy decisions and communications regarding liquidity and lending facilities were made instantaneously, outside scheduled meetings, announcements or press conferences. In addition, several central banks teamed up with the ministry of finance and other financial authorities to convey the message of a coordinated response.

To sum up, Latin American monetary policy frameworks worked well before and during the pandemic. Before the pandemic, especially in the aftermath of the GFC, those frameworks had allowed central banks to build buffers and reduce the exposure of the economy to external financial conditions. During the pandemic, frameworks have allowed central banks to respond effectively, without requiring major changes or additions to their toolkit and their modus operandi. Thanks to the actions taken before and during the COVID-19 crisis, flexible exchange rates have continued to work as shock absorbers, except in the early stages of the outbreak.

---

[25] In Chile, the constitution was changed to allow the central bank to purchase government bonds in the secondary market for financial stability purposes only and with the vote of at least four of the five members of the central bank's board. In Brazil, the central bank obtained the legal authorisation to purchase private bonds in the domestic secondary market.

Notably, large depreciations during the outbreak did not undermine confidence as in previous episodes of financial stress.[26]

5. Conclusions and challenges ahead

Over the past two decades, the policy frameworks of the main Latin American central banks have successfully evolved and expanded to deal with larger and more volatile capital flows driven by developments in commodity markets and unconventional monetary policies in major economies. So far, these frameworks have proven fit for purpose, allowing the economies to weather the GFC, period of financial turmoil such as the Taper Tantrum and, more recently, the consequences of the COVID-19 outbreak. However, while the COVID-19 crisis may have passed its most acute phase, it is not over yet. Policy frameworks may have to continue evolving in the face of new challenges. There are several.

A first major challenge for the region's central banks is to decide the appropriate sequence and pace of the phasing-out of crisis measures. Indeed, at the time of writing, Latin American central banks had already begun to withdraw monetary policy accommodation in the face of rising inflationary pressures. Although the latter are expected to be transitory, the size of the increase and its persistence have already surprised several central banks. Central banks face difficult choices. On the one hand, a slower tightening pace could help smooth post-pandemic structural adjustments, reduce the risk of insolvencies for highly indebted but otherwise viable firms and reduce pressures on fiscal accounts. On the other hand, it may raise the risks of capital outflows and of inflation expectations becoming unanchored. Stronger policy frameworks and greater credibility should give central banks greater room for manoeuvre,

---

[26] BIS (2021) mentions the impact of large depreciations on uncertainty as a potential important mechanism that could amplify output contractions. This channel may be especially relevant in countries with a history of persistent fiscal imbalances and frequent balance of payments crises, in which a severe drop in economic activity and high inflation often accompanied past sharp depreciations (and exits from fixed exchange rate regimes).

but higher public and private debt levels and pandemic-induced structural changes complicate their decisions.

A second related challenge for central banks is how monetary policy should interact with fiscal policy. So far, monetary and fiscal policies have supported each other. By lowering risk premia and improving macroeconomic stability, a strong monetary policy framework has helped increase fiscal sustainability. In turn, a strong fiscal framework, including fiscal rules, has helped increase monetary policy space and made monetary policy more effective (e.g., Barthsch *et al.* [2020]). Going forward, the legacy of higher public debt post-pandemic and the difficulty to find socially acceptable ways to consolidate public finances may make it more difficult to preserve this virtuous complementarity.

This difficulty has at least two important implications. First, central banks need to be protected from short-term political pressures. Several central banks in the region already have effective rules, including those governing the appointments of senior officials and explicit restrictions on the purchases of sovereign bonds. However, autonomy can be further strengthened, as is the case of the law that granted greater operational autonomy to the Central Bank of Brazil in February 2021. Second, history has clearly taught us that no monetary policy framework, however good, can be ultimately viable if fiscal sustainability is not guaranteed. Any efforts to improve monetary policy frameworks should therefore be complemented by efforts to consolidate public finances post-pandemic.

A third important challenge is how to improve the use of multiple instruments and the related problem of communicating their use effectively to the public. Having more instruments to deploy makes it more difficult to explain the central bank reaction function to the public. Following an approach close to the Tinbergen principle of one instrument per objective may help simplify communication, but it is not satisfactory. Instruments interact with each other and the same instrument can influence other objectives. In this regard, theory is still lagging behind practice (BIS, 2019a). Developing realistic models for policy analysis as well as conducting empirical studies may help improve the understanding those interactions and make the trade-offs faced by central banks more precise and easier to relay to the public.

References

Adler, G, K S Chang, R C Mano and Y Shao (2021): "Foreign exchange Intervention: a dataset of public data and proxies", *IMF Working Paper*, no 21/47, February.

Aguilar, A and C Cantú (2020): "Monetary policy response in emerging market economies: why was it different this time?" *BIS Bulletin*, no 32, November.

Ahmed, S, B Coulibaly and A Zlate (2017): "International financial spillovers to emerging market economies: How important are economic fundamentals?" *Journal of International Money and Finance*, vol 76, pp 133–152.

Alam, Z, A Alter, J Eiseman, G Gelos, H Kang, M Narita, E Nier and N Wang (2019): "Digging Deeper — Evidence on the effects of macroprudential policies from a new database", *IMF Working Paper*, no 19/66, March.

Alfaro, L, E Faia, R Judson and T Schmidt-Eisenlohr (2020): "Elusive safety: the new geography of capital flows and risk", *NBER Working Paper Series*, no 27048, April.

Arslanalp, S, D Drakopoulos, R Goel, and R Koepke (2020): "Benchmark-driven investments in emerging market bond markets: taking stock", *IMF Working Paper*, no 20/192, September.

Amoroso, N, D Chiquiar, N Quella, and M Ramos-Francia (2008): "Determinants of Mexico's comparative advantages and of the performance of its manufacturing exports during 1996–2005", *Bank of Mexico Working Paper*, no 2008-01, February.

Armas, A and F Grippa (2005): "Targeting inflation in a dollarized economy: the Peruvian experience", *IDB Research Department Working Paper*, no 538, September.

Avdjiev, S, B Hardy, S Kalemli-Özcan and L Servén (2018): "Gross capital flows by banks, corporates and sovereigns", *BIS Working Papers*, no 760, December.

Barthsch, E, A Benassy-Quere, G Corsetti and X Debrun (2020): "It is all in the mix: how can monetary and fiscal policies work or fail together", *Geneva Reports on the World Economy*, no 23, December.

Berkmen, S P, G Gelos, R Rennhack and J P Walsh (2012): "The global financial crisis: explaining cross-country differences in the output impact", *Journal of International Money and Finance*, vol 31, no 1, pp 42–59.

Bank for International Settlements (2013): "Market volatility and foreign exchange intervention in EMEs: what has changed?" *BIS Papers*, no 73, October.

――― (2018): "Moving forward with macroprudential frameworks", *Chapter IV, Annual Economic Report*, June.

―――― (2019a): "Monetary policy frameworks in EMEs: inflation targeting, the exchange rate and financial stability", *Chapter II, Annual Economic Report*, June.

―――― (2019b): "BIS triennial central bank survey of foreign exchange and over-the-counter (OTC) derivatives markets", December.

―――― (2020a): "A global sudden stop", *Chapter I, Annual Economic Report*, June.

―――― (2020b): "A monetary lifeline: central banks' crisis response", *Chapter II, Annual Economic Report*, June.

―――― (2021): "Capital flows, exchange rates and monetary policy frameworks in Latin American and other economies", *A report by a group of central banks including members of the Consultative Council for the Americas and the central banks of South Africa and Turkey*, 15 April.

Bogdanski, J, A Tombini and S R da Costa (2000) "Implementing Inflation Targeting in Brazil", *Central Bank of Brazil Working Papers Series,* no 1, July.

Borio, C, J Contreras and F Zampolli (2020): "Assessing the fiscal implications of banking crises", *BIS Working Papers*, no 893, October.

Brei, M and R Moreno (2019): "Reserve requirements and capital flows in Latin America", *Journal of International Money and Finance*, vol 99, 102079, December.

Budnik, K and J Kleibl (2018): "Macroprudential regulation in the European Union in 1995–2014: introducing a new data set on policy actions of a macroprudential nature", *ECB Working Paper Series*, no 2123, January.

Cantú, C, P Cavallino, F De Fiore and J Yetman (2021): "A global database on central banks' monetary responses to Covid-19", *BIS Working Papers*, no 934, March.

Calvo, G and E Mendoza (2000): "Contagion, globalization, and the volatility of capital flows", in *Capital Flows and the Emerging Economies: Theory, Evidence, and Controversies*, Edwards S (ed.), National Bureau of Economic Research, pp. 15–41.

Carrillo, J, E Mendoza, V Nuger and J Roldán-Peña (2021): "Tight money-tight credit: coordination failure in the conduct of monetary and financial policies", *American Economic Journal: Macroeconomics*, vol 13, no 3, July, pp. 37–73.

Carstens, A and A Werner (1999): "Mexico's monetary policy framework under a floating exchange rate regime", *Bank of Mexico Working Paper,* no 9905, May.

Carstens, A and H S Shin (2019): "Emerging market aren't out of the woods yet: how they can manage the risks", *Foreign Affairs*, 15 March.

Cespedes, L and C Soto (2006): "Credibility and inflation targeting in Chile", *Central Bank of Chile Working Paper,* no 408, December.

Cecchetti, S, M R King, and J Yetman (2011): "Weathering the financial crisis: good policy or good luck?" *BIS Working Papers,* no 351, August.

Committee on the Global Financial System (CGFS) (2021): Changing patterns of capital flows, *GFCS Papers,* no 66, May.

Costa de Moura, M and F Martins (2017): "Macroprudential policy in Brazil", in "Macroprudential frameworks, implementation and relationship with other policies", *BIS Papers,* no 94, December, pp 77–86.

De Gregorio, J (2013): "Resilience in Latin America: lessons from macroeconomic management and financial policies", *IMF Working paper,* no 13/259, December.

Dingemans, A and C Ross (2012): "Free trade agreements in Latin America since 1990: an evaluation of export diversification", *Cepal Review,* no 108, December, pp 27–48.

Goldfajn, I, L Martinez and R. Valdes (2021): "Washington consensus in Latin America: from raw model to straw man", *Journal of Economic Perspectives,* vol 35, no 3, pp 109–132.

Gonçalves, C, A David and S Pienknagura (2019): "Capital flows to Latin America in the aftermath of the commodities super-cycle", in "Regional Economic Outlook, Western Hemisphere: stunted by uncertainty, October 2019", International Monetary Fund, October.

Gutiérrez, E (2003): "Inflation performance and constitutional central bank independence: evidence from Latin America and the Caribbean," *IMF Working Paper,* no 03/53, March.

Hausmann, R (2002): "Unrewarded good fiscal behavior: the role of debt structure", presented at the IMF/WB Conference on Rules-based Fiscal Policy in Emerging Market Economies, Oaxaca, February 14–16.

Hofmann, B, I Shim and H S Shin (2020): "Emerging market economy exchange rates and local currency bond markets amid the Covid-19 pandemic", *BIS Bulletins,* no 5, April.

International Monetary Fund (IMF) (2014): *Managing Economic Volatility in Latin America,* G Gelos and A Werner (eds.), IMF.

⎯⎯⎯ (2021): "Commodity cycles, inequality, and poverty in Latin America", *Western Hemisphere Department,* IMF.

Jeanneau, S and C Tovar (2006): "Latin America's local currency bond markets: an overview", in "New financing trend in Latin America: a bumpy road towards stability", *BIS papers,* no 36, December, pp 46–64.

Laird, S and P Messerlin (2002): "Trade policy regimes and development strategies: a comparative study," *LAEBA working papers,* no 7, December.

Lane, P and G Milesi-Ferretti (2017): "International financial integration in the aftermath of the global financial crisis", IMF Working Papers, no 17/115, May.

Lora, E (2001): "Structural reforms in Latin America: what has been reformed and how to measure It", *IDB Working Paper*, no 466, December.

Lora, E and F Barrera (1997): "El crecimiento económico en América Latina después de una década de reformas estructurales", *Coyuntura Económica: Investigación Económica y Social*, vol 27, no 3, September.

Mesa-Lago, C (2002): "Myth and reality of pension reform: the Latin American evidence," *World Development*, vol 30, no 8, pp 1309–1321.

Mesquita, M and T Torós (2010): "Brazil and the 2008 panic", in "The global crisis and financial intermediation in emerging market economies", *BIS papers*, no 54, December, pp 113–120.

Montoro, C and Moreno R (2011): "The use of reserve requirements as a policy instrument in Latin America", *BIS Quarterly Review*, March, pp 53–65.

Ocampo, J (2014) "The Latin American debt crisis in historical perspective", in "Life after debt: the origins and resolution of debt crisis", ed by Stiglitz, J and D Heymann, pp 87–115.

Pereira Da Silva, L and R Harris (2012): "Sailing through the global financial storm: Brazil's recent experience with monetary and macroprudential policies to lean against the financial cycle and deal with systemic risks", *Central Bank of Brazil Working Paper*, no 290, August.

Ramos-Francia, M, A Aguilar, S García, and G Cuadra (2014): "Heading into trouble: a comparison of Latin American crises and the Euro Area's current crisis", Bank of Mexico *Working Paper*, no 2014-17, August.

Reinhardt, D and R Sowerbutts (2015): "Regulatory arbitrage in action: evidence from banking flows and macroprudential policy", *Bank of England Working Paper*, no 546, September.

Shim, I, B Bogdanova, J Shek and A Subelyte (2013): "Database for policy actions on housing markets", *BIS Quarterly Review*, September, pp 83–95.

Singh, A, A Belaisch, C Collyns, P De Masi, R Krieger, G Meredith and R Rennhack (2005): "Stabilization and reform in Latin America: a macroeconomic perspective on the experience since the early 1990s", *IMF Occasional Papers,* no 238.

Terrier, G, R Valdés, C Tovar, J Chan-Lau, C Fernández-Valdovinos, M García-Escribano, C Medeiros, M-K Tang, M Vera and C Walker (2011): "Policy instruments to lean against the wind in Latin America", *IMF working paper*, no 11/159, July.

United Nations Conference on Trade and Development (1998): "World investment report, 1998: trends and determinants", *United Nations Publications,* no E.98.II.D.5.

Vargas, H, P Cardozo and A Murcia (2017): "The macroprudential policy framework in Colombia", in "Macroprudential frameworks, implementation and relationship with other policies", *BIS papers,* no 94, December, pp 103–128.

Végh, C, L Morano, D Friedheim and D Rojas (2017): "Between a rock and a hard place: the monetary policy dilemma in Latin America and then Caribbean", *WB LAC Semiannual Report*, October.

Villar, A (2017): "Macroprudential frameworks: objectives decisions and policy interactions", in "Macroprudential frameworks, implementation and relationship with other policies", *BIS papers,* no 94, December, pp 7–24.

© 2023 World Scientific Publishing Company
https://doi.org/10.1142/9789811259432_0027

Monetary Policy Frameworks in Latin America: Evolution, Resilience and Future Challenges: A Discussion

Enrique G. Mendoza

University of Pennsylvania

NBER

This chapter provides an interesting and detailed narrative of the monetary policy frameworks (MPFs) that Latin American countries have implemented since the 1990s, studying their past performance and their response to the COVID-19 pandemic. The authors characterise accurately the history of high inflation and unsustainable fiscal and exchange rate policies that led to the widespread adoption of inflation targeting and flexible exchange rates in the region. They also narrate carefully how the frameworks evolved and responded to external conditions, particularly the waves of large capital inflows followed by Sudden Stop episodes, fluctuations in the terms of trade and a prolonged period of low global inflation and high liquidity. In particular, the authors discuss the introduction of financial stability considerations into the MPFs. In addition, they highlight important differences across countries or groups of countries in how they have been affected by external conditions and responded to shocks, particularly for countries that are commodity exporters vis-à-vis those that are exporters of manufactures. The authors conclude that overall, the MPFs have proven resilient in the face of these challenges and the ongoing COVID-19 pandemic.

I am in broad agreement with the description of both the history that led to the adoption of the existing MPFs and the characterisation of their core elements at present (namely inflation targeting in an environment of exchange rate flexibility and supplemented by sound fiscal and financial policies). My comments focus on four issues that the authors do mention but that I see as playing a more significant role.

Good policies and good luck

The external environment since the late 1990s contributed to taming of inflation and keeping it subdued, because of the overall deflationary forces at work in the world economy and the surges in global liquidity, and also in some countries at particular times because of the favourable strong winds from commodity prices. About 20 years ago, in a paper for a World Bank conference, Guillermo Calvo and I posed a similar hypothesis for the taming of inflation in Chile, the first country in Latin America to adopt the new MPF based on inflation targeting (Calvo and Mendoza, 1999). Our argument was not that monetary policy had not contributed to bringing inflation under control. Indeed, Latin America's economic history was plagued with examples where *bad* monetary policy caused major economic disasters, so just by not doing the *wrong* thing, Chile was doing the *right* thing. However, our argument was that the Chilean monetary policy in the 1990s benefitted a lot from a mix of high copper prices, low energy prices and large capital inflows, along the lines of some of the external transmission mechanisms that this chapter documents. We used the recursively identified VAR methodology that was popular then and showed that a strong real appreciation fuelled by the favourable external factors was an important driver of the taming of inflation in Chile, even after controlling for the policy instrument of the central bank.

The world has changed a lot since then. The surges of global liquidity and the global deflationary pressures that have marked the first two decades of the 21st century dwarf the capital inflows and moderate inflation of the early 1990s. Until this year, very high liquidity and very low global inflation were the norm. In several advanced economies, very low inflation became a problem and even turned into deflation. There was also the commodity supercycle that the authors described. These observations put together suggest that what Guillermo and I examined for Chile as a case study may also apply to other countries in the region, particularly commodity exporters, but also for exporters of manufactures.

Take a stance on the "New" MPF for financial stability

The chapter discusses the post-2008 evolution of MPFs to incorporate financial stability considerations, which in fact started earlier in Latin America than in advanced economies, in the aftermath of the 1990s Sudden Stops. While the chapter acknowledges that traditional monetary policy is insufficient from this perspective, it could take a stronger stance on whether it favours enriching the apparatus used to conduct monetary policy (namely, the Taylor rule or variations thereof) with some financial target, and if so which one, or whether it favours separating monetary policy from financial/macroprudential policy altogether. Analytically, it seems to make sense to split the two, because of Tinbergen's principle: it is always best to use two instruments to target two policy goals. Indeed, in my work with Julio Carrillo, Victoria Nuguer and Jessica Roldan, which started when the three of them were at the Bank of Mexico, we show using a standard Neo-Keynesian model that a policy regime with dual rules, a Taylor rule that targets inflation and a financial rule that targets financial spreads or credit ratios, dominates by large margins both a regime that uses only a standard Taylor rule and one in which the Taylor rule is expanded to include targeting spreads (Carrillo et al., 2021). The rationale is that there are two distortions at work in the economy: nominal rigidities that justify monetary policy intervention and a financial friction (costly state verification by lenders) that justifies financial policy intervention. Reading through this chapter, it seems that what most countries are doing is more in line with the dual-rules regime, but the study could be more explicit about this point and make a stronger case for why it is the best regime.

On a related vein, it is worth considering the evolution that has occurred in the thinking and structuring of the conduct of monetary policy inside central banks, to integrate financial stability considerations. In many central banks, this has implied restructuring of the departments involved in monetary and financial policies, which used to exist as separate entities with separated tasks. Now, there is a wide intersection where the expertise of the two areas is combined. This has also affected macroeconomic modelling. In most central banks, this has implied directing resources to the development of richer models that could tackle financial frictions, and could speak to the effects of financial policies and the interaction of monetary and financial or macroprudential policies.

Another key point related to this issue is the extent to which Basel III has been implemented, particularly the countercyclical capital buffer (CCyB). Basel III is a radical change from its predecessors because of the emphasis it puts on the macro-implications of financial regulation. But the implementation of this new form of regulation has meant that central banks and the broader structure of financial regulation (which, in most countries, has key players outside the central bank) have had to change, along the lines I described above. The chapter does provide some valuable information and history on the evolution of financial regulation and macroprudential policies, and the type of instruments being used and to what degree, across the region. It would be very helpful, however, to add a description of where countries are in terms of the design and implementation of the CCyB, and how they differ in terms of its management. For instance, in Chile, there is a complex arrangement such that the central bank is in charge of modelling and making recommendations for the management of the CCyB but another super-regulator (the Financial Markets Commission) has veto power; for other aspects of macroprudential policy, their roles are reversed.

The approach countries are taking to the design and implementation of the CCyB is also worth surveying and discussing. Take again the example of Chile. The BIS recommends activating the CCyB when the credit gap exceeds 2 percent, and then tightening linearly to a maximum where the gap reaches 10 percent. The BIS defines the credit gap as the deviation from trend in the credit-to-GDP ratio for the broadest measure of credit available, constructed with a one-sided Hodrick — Prescott filter with the smoothing parameter set to 400,000 (based on the assumption that financial cycles last 20 years).[1] Country authorities have the discretion, however, to design their own CCyB guidance system. Chile adopted a

---

[1] Annex 1 in *Guidance for National Authorities Operating the Countercyclical Capital Buffer*, BIS, (2010).

strategy that combined a model of early warning indicators to assess the likelihood of financial crises, a stress-testing model to quantify the effects of a crisis on individual banks, and a Neo-Keynesian DSGE model with financial frictions to quantify the macro-effects of the CCyB. They opted for this approach because their research showed several problems with the proposed BIS guidance applied to Chile: (1) detrending the credit–GDP ratio was not desirable (since credit and GDP displayed different trends); (2) the high smoothing parameter exaggerated the duration of the credit cycle and hence resulted in the CCyB being active for too long and at levels higher than needed, even during recessions; (3) the activation and maximum thresholds should be higher (2 percent and 10 percent thresholds were too restrictive given the higher volatility of credit, which was a common feature in emerging markets); and (4) the BIS credit gap retained low-frequency movements in the credit–GDP ratio, making it difficult to separate "over-borrowing" situations from normal credit cycles and benign low-frequency credit movements (e.g., financial development).

The Central Bank of Chile found that, because of these limitations, the CCyB would have been active at its maximum from late 1995 to end-2002, including during the recession triggered by the 1990s Sudden Stop. The CCyB would also have been active in late 2013 and at its maximum in 2014, but the Bank documented that credit growth during this period was due to FDI-related loans and overseas corporate bond issues matched with overseas investments, both of which they did not regard as signs of vulnerability. They also found that a measure of the credit gap using only bank credit performed better than a measure using bank and non-bank credit. The former did not have the "false positives" calling for activating the CCyB in 1998 and 2014, and predicted better their financial crises events since the 1980s. In addition, they found that real bank credit, instead of bank credit-to-GDP, performed better in terms of signalling crises.

The Chilean experience suggests that we are likely to find that other countries in the region are also adopting their own CCyB guidance, and it would be very interesting to have a cross-country comparison of what is being done. This is very important for the MPFs given the new approach to supplement them with financial stability considerations. The CCyB is one of the core new instruments of macro-financial policy, and it interacts (or interferes) with the transmission mechanism of monetary policy. It is also important for assessing what we can expect going forward, because it is a new instrument that has yet to be "tested by fire".

Synchronicity of policy and politics

Perhaps the most significant economic policy challenge for Latin America, looking beyond the COVID-19 crisis, is the seismic shift that has occurred in the synchronicity of economic policies, and between these policies and political regimes. The taming of inflation in Latin America had a lot to do not just with the change to a much better MPF and better international conditions, but also with the fact that this was part of a comprehensive change in which populist dogma was discarded, seemingly forever. Well-articulated, coordinated efforts in fiscal, monetary, financial, trade and structural reform policies were implemented and in relative harmony with political systems that generally supported radical policy changes from two or three decades of failed policies. While I agree with the authors' argument that the MPFs have been resilient and served us well, a key challenge looking ahead is whether they can remain resilient now that external conditions are more inflation-prone and that central banks are the last bastion of sensible economic policymaking in various parts of Latin America. The changes that have taken place in Argentina, Brazil, Mexico, Peru, Venezuela and even in Chile and Colombia, suggest that in the coming years, central banks will be under serious pressures, not just in day-to-day practice of monetary policy and financial regulation, but in deeper structural issues like the desirability of central bank independence, restrictions of central bank financing to the government, and even control of the central bank's international reserves.

Where Latin America failed with COVID-19

The chapter makes an excellent point in noting that the COVID-19 pandemic hit Latin America when central banks were in a strong position and able to respond with both conventional and unconventional policies. It is worth emphasising, as the chapter does to some extent, but more forcefully that this position of strength was a by-product of the merits of two decades of practising sound monetary and financial policies under the MPFs. This is my previous point, that indeed we had both good luck and good policies. Monetary policy played a key role, in a precautionary sense, because thanks to the sound MPFs and favourable external conditions, countries were able to accumulate reserves, strengthen financial systems and build credibility, all of which supported the monetary policy responses to COVID-19.

This is all good and a major improvement over what would have happened in the past, if COVID-19 had hit, say, in the early 1980s. However, we should not congratulate ourselves. COVID-19 has been very difficult everywhere, but its amplification into a major human tragedy in Latin America and other emerging and developing countries is a self-made disaster. This has a lot to do with incoherent, inept health policies; dilapidated, inefficient health systems and very limited fiscal space. In stark contrast with how two decades of strong monetary policy and favourable external conditions have prepared Latin American countries to be able to respond to COVID-19 in the monetary and financial sphere, the disastrous management of the health sector pre-COVID-19 and the inept practices at handling lockdowns, health resource allocation and now vaccines in many countries of the region, have meant that COVID-19 hit like strong wind and thunder on bone-dry wood. Moreover, a weakening fiscal stance and growing public debt in recent years mean that fiscal policy could not do what monetary policy did.

Central bank actions to respond to COVID-19 have been of comparable (relative) scope and size in Latin America as in advanced economies. In contrast, the immediate response of fiscal policy through August 2020, in terms of "above-the-line" expenditures, ranged from barely at par (Brazil 8.3 percent of GDP, Chile 8.4 percent) to weak (Argentina 3.9 percent, Peru 6.6 percent) to dismal (Colombia 2.7 percent, Mexico 0.6 percent). The same applied to emerging and developing countries worldwide, where the average increases were 3.3 percent and 2.4 percent, respectively. These compared with 12.5 percent in Canada or 11.8 percent in the US, and an average of 7.4 percent for all advanced economies. By March 2021, fiscal policy response to COVID-19 in the US reached 25.5 percent of GDP while that in Argentina, Brazil, Chile and Mexico remained about the same.[2] This is not a call for unsustainable fiscal profligacy. It is intended to make the point that if the region ever needed fiscal space, it was in 2020, to provide massive transfers to the large population affected by lockdowns and pay for surging health expenditures. However, the countries in the region had little fiscal space, so they could not afford the war-like fiscal deficit blow-out that the health crisis called for, and their populations suffered as a result. Moreover, lacking strong fiscal support and despite *de jure* mandates, lockdowns tended to be weaker *de facto*, as indicated by the –0.2 correlation between the Google business mobility index and log income per-capita. This added to the severity and persistence of the pandemic in emerging and less developed countries.

The net outcome of the disparity in fiscal responses has been that surging private saving-investment gaps have coincided with mild declines in public saving-investment gaps in Latin America, resulting in sizable *increases* in current account balances between the first and third quarters of 2020 (in Brazil, 4 percentage points; in Mexico, 5.5; in Chile, 4.5), while the current account deficit of the US has widened by 1.5 percentage points of GDP.[3] COVID-19 surges during winter of 2021 in South America, coupled with delays in vaccination and widespread use of vaccines with low efficacy rates (e.g., Chile, Mexico, Uruguay), suggest that the region will take longer to recover from the COVID-19 crisis. But by then, the global winds may change and, as the paper warns, Latin America may find itself having to tighten monetary policies to keep pace with potential tightening in the US and other advanced economies.

References

Carrillo, Julio, Enrique G. Mendoza, Victoria Nuguer, and Jessica Roldan, "Tight Money-Tight Credit: Coordination Failure in the Conduct of Monetary and Financial Policies," *American Economic Journal: Macroeconomics*, Vol. 13, no. 3, July 2021, pp. 37–73.

Calvo, Guillermo A. and Enrique G. Mendoza, "Empirical Puzzles of Chilean Stabilization Policy" in *Chile: Recent Policy Lessons and Emerging Challenges*, G. Perry and D. M. Leipziger (eds.), World Bank, 1999.

---

[2] Data up to August 2020 from IMF *Fiscal Monitor*, October 2020 and up to March 2021 from IMF *Fiscal Monitor*, April 2021.

[3] *Source*: OECD Data (https://data.oecd.org/trade/current-account-balance.htm)

CHAPTER 14

© 2023 World Scientific Publishing Company
https://doi.org/10.1142/9789811259432_0028

Chapter 14

Leave No Stone Unturned — Macroprudential Policy in Croatia Between the Global Financial Crisis and COVID-19*

Boris Vujčić,[†,¶] Mirna Dumičić Jemrić[‡,**] and Lana Ivičić[§,††]

[†]*Governor of the Croatian National Bank*
[‡]*Chief Advisor, Croatian National Bank*
[§]*Senior Advisor, Croatian National Bank*
[¶]*boris.vujcic@hnb.hr*
[**]*mirna.dumicic@hnb.hr*
[††]*lana.ivicic@hnb.hr*

Abstract

This chapter describes the Croatian National Bank's activities aimed at managing systemic risks and strengthening the system's resilience to potential shocks in the dynamic five-and-a-half years of post-Global Financial Crisis recovery until the pandemic crisis, from 2015 to mid-2020. Special focus is put on the optimal timing for the activation of countercyclical capital buffer (CCyB), consumer protection issues, developments in the real estate market and limitations of macroprudential policy in dealing with systemic risks arising from that market, as well as on the CNB's measures taken in response to the COVID-19

---

*The authors thank Vedran Šošić for valuable comments and suggestions.

pandemic. This experience has further contributed to a better understanding of certain systemic risks, as well as the reach and effects of macroprudential policy instruments.

1. Introduction

Croatia has been known as one of the pioneers in the use of macroprudential policy. A complex policy setup has well predated the 2008 Global Financial Crisis, reducing macroeconomic imbalances in the run-up and enhancing resilience of the financial system throughout the crisis. While this experience is well documented (Vujčić and Dumičić, 2016; Dumičić and Šošić, 2015), this chapter looks into a more recent period of economic expansion starting from 2015 and ending with the COVID-19 pandemic crisis.

From 2015 to the outbreak of the COVID-19 pandemic crisis, Croatia went through a period of favourable macroeconomic developments, which supported the unwinding of most vulnerabilities in the real and financial sectors. However, while risks in general have been declining, pockets of vulnerability have continued to emerge, particularly those arising from the interconnectedness of large corporates, as well as those related to the strong growth of residential real estate prices and strong consumer lending.

In the observed period, the Croatian National Bank (CNB) continuously recalibrated measures to preserve financial stability and mitigate systemic risks, which proved to be crucial for supporting the stability of the financial system when COVID-19 struck.

Following the introduction, Section 2 presents the most important macroeconomic and financial developments from 2015 to mid-2020 as well as the evolution of vulnerabilities. Section 3 describes the CNB's activities aimed at managing systemic risks and strengthening the system's resilience to potential shocks. Special focus is put on the optimal timing for the activation of countercyclical capital buffer (CCyB), consumer protection issues, developments in the real estate market and, in particular, limitations of macroprudential policy in dealing with systemic risks arising from that market and finally an overview of CNB's measures taken in response to the COVID-19 pandemic. The conclusion draws main lessons from Croatian experience in this relatively short, but very dynamic, period for the macroprudential policy.

2. Systemic risk developments in Croatia from 2015 to 2020

The macroeconomic situation in Croatia from 2015 to the escalation of the COVID-19 pandemic was marked by favourable developments in export demand, particularly for tourism services, investments and household consumption (Figure 1). This, combined with an accommodative monetary policy stance and favourable financing conditions, eased the process of unwinding accumulated internal and external imbalances.

Strong fiscal adjustments put the ratio of general government debt to GDP on a firmly downward path. Coupled with deleveraging of the private sector and strong growth of exports, fiscal adjustments gave way to the substantial surplus in the current and capital account, which facilitated robust external deleveraging (Figures 2 and 3). Nevertheless, elevated external indebtedness was still making the country vulnerable to a potential significant deterioration of international financing conditions and volatility of capital flows.

Drying-up of capital inflows, triggered by the Global Financial Crisis, in the face of a weak external position has fuelled depreciation pressures on the exchange rate, which has marked much of the period since 2008. As Croatia emerged from the crises in 2015, depreciation pressures

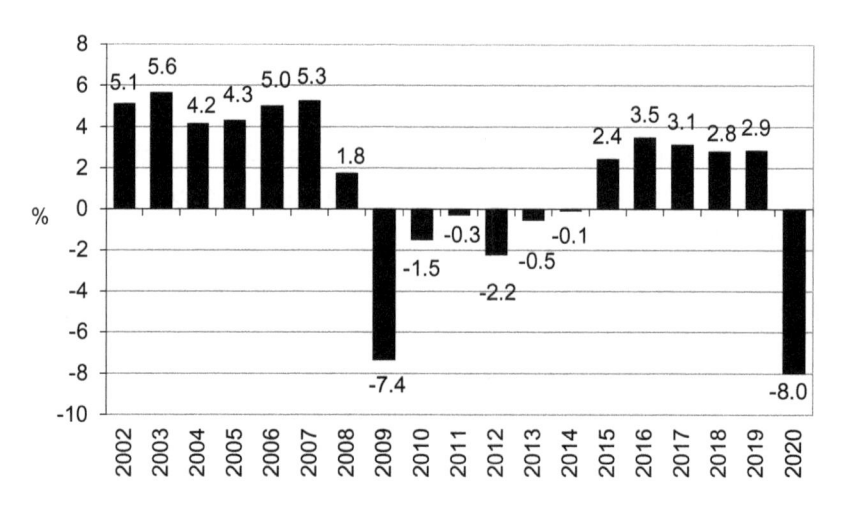

Figure 1. Real GDP, rates of change.

Source: CBS.

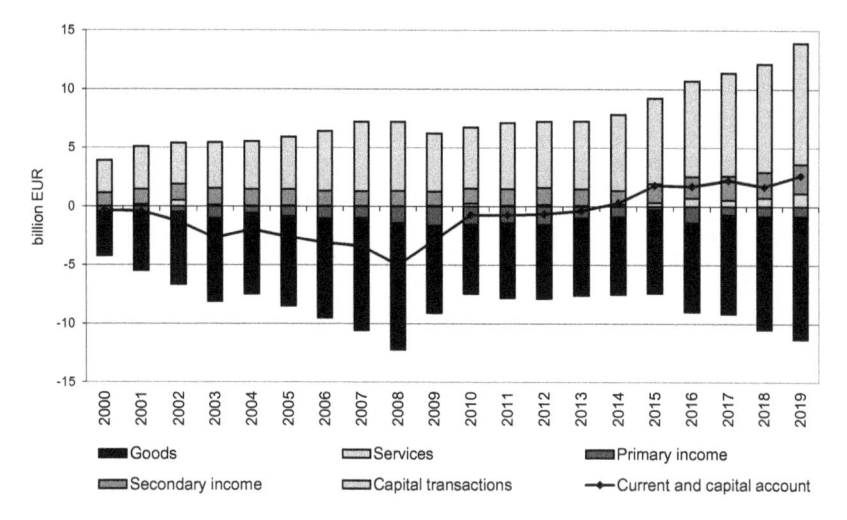

Figure 2. Structure of the current and capital account balance.
Note: Negative values of FDI liabilities indicate inflow of FDI.
Source: CNB.

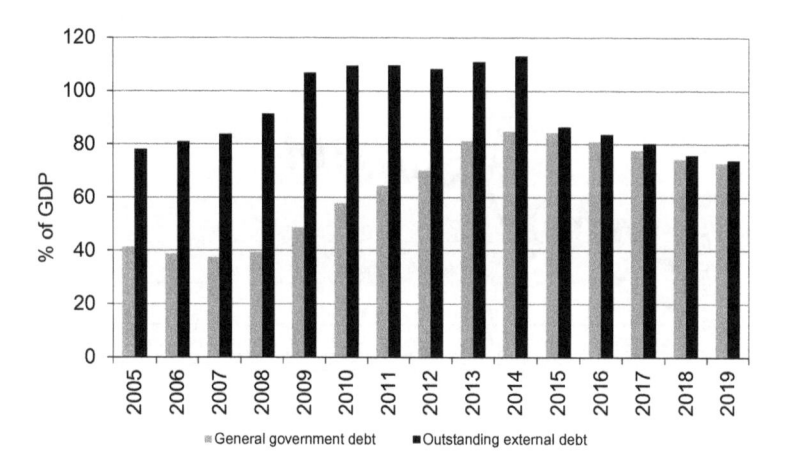

Figure 3. Public and external debt.
Source: Eurostat and CNB.

turned into appreciation pressures (Figure 4). This time around, the source of appreciation pressures was much healthier, rising receipts in the current (exports of goods and services and EU funds) and capital (EU funds) accounts, rather than debt-generating capital inflows as was

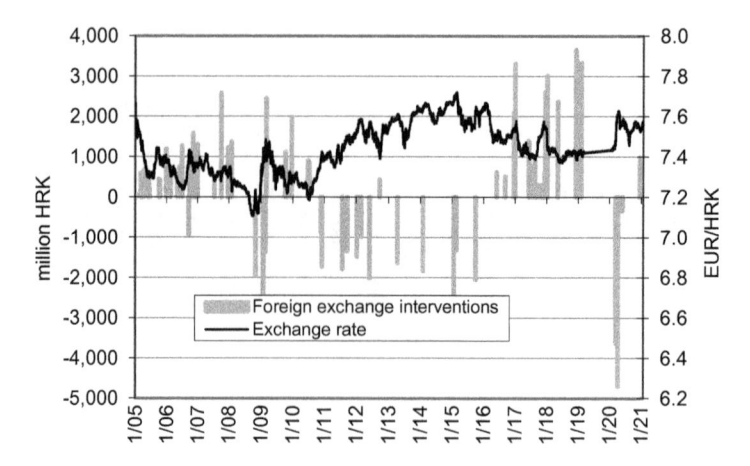

Figure 4. Foreign exchange interventions and exchange rate.
Source: CNB.

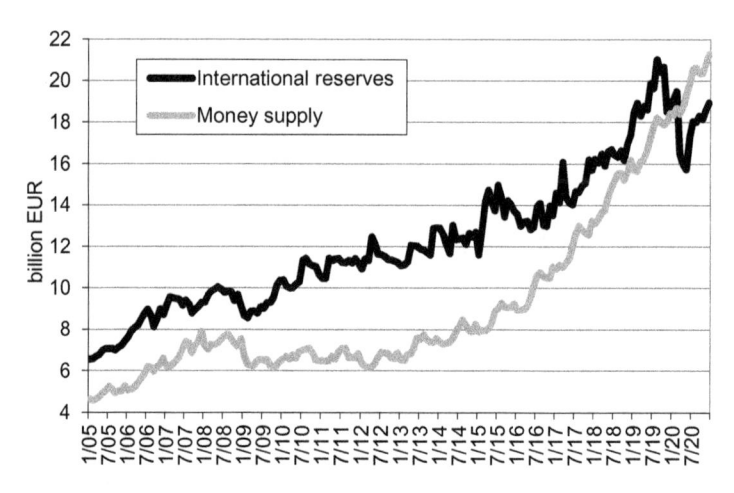

Figure 5. CNB's international reserves and money supply.
Source: CNB.

the case before the Global Financial Crisis. Those surpluses have not only facilitated deleveraging of the private sector but also pushed up the level of international reserves and supported monetary accommodation (Figure 5). In the environment of low inflation, moderate credit growth and current and capital account surplus, such monetary policy loosening was appropriate. It further improved financing conditions and supported

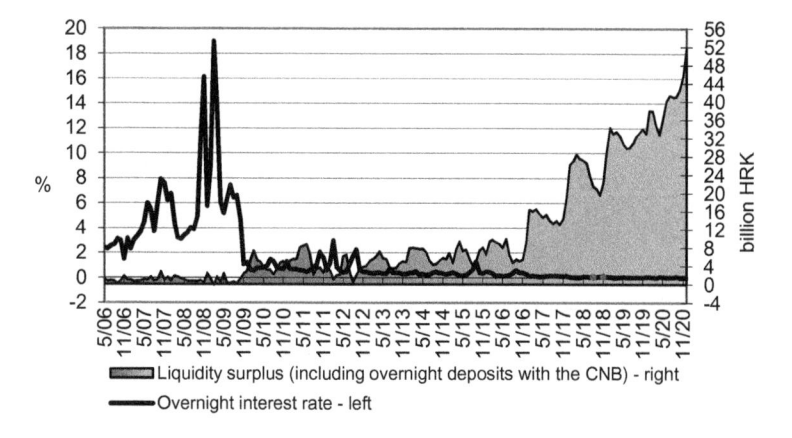

Figure 6. Liquidity surplus and overnight interest rate.
Source: CNB.

economic recovery, while never pushing it into the overheating territory (Figure 6). Moreover, the rise of international reserves additionally strengthened the country's overall resilience to potential shocks, which proved to be especially important in the turmoil following the outbreak of the COVID-19 pandemic (Figure 5).

In addition to a favourable macroeconomic environment, several developments in the financial sector were conducive to a strengthening of the banking sector's capacity to absorb potential shocks. First, banks continued to accumulate capital, while liquidity buffers remained ample (Figure 7). Further on, pervasive euroisation, a well-entrenched weakness of the financial system, had been gradually declining. Moreover, borrowers started to lock in historically low interest rates by increasingly switching to fixed rates, stemming the interest-induced credit risk. The growth of disposable income and employment, as well as the growing shares of domestic currency loans and loans with a fixed interest rate reduced the exposure of households to currency and interest rate risks. Despite the sustained reduction of corporate foreign currency indebtedness, total exposure of the non-financial corporate sector to currency risk remained elevated. Still, good financial results and low interest rates have improved debt sustainability metrics and corporate resilience to shocks. Deleveraging achieved during the period of subdued lending has reduced the banking sector's dependence on cross-border wholesale funding

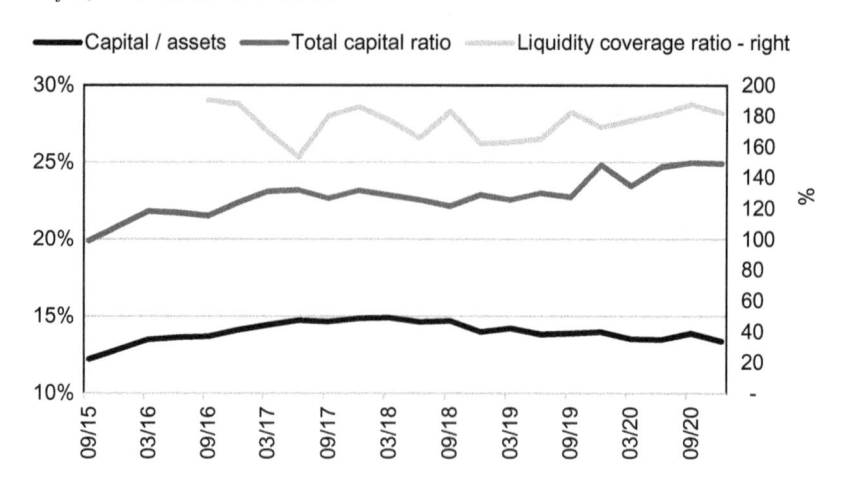

Figure 7. Banking sector capitalisation and liquidity.
Source: CNB.

while strengthening stable domestic sources of finance. Favourable macroeconomic trends also helped banks to deal with the legacy stock of non-performing loans, supporting the recovery of borrowers and easing the sale of impaired assets. Nevertheless, some risks continued to lurk, such as high and rising concentration in the banking system and strong interdependence between the banks and the sovereign. Also, some new risks started to emerge, adding to challenges for the macroprudential policy.

3. Financial stability challenges since 2015

The CNB has continuously focused on preserving financial stability since the early 2000s, but the financial stability mandate has been formally strengthened only in the post–Global Financial Crisis period. This has taken place after Croatia entered the EU in mid-2013, as part of the pan-European regulatory and institutional overhaul following the introduction of Basel III and the establishment of the European Systemic Risk Board. Following on a prudent approach of pushing banks into creating ample capital buffers, which have been substantially above the Basel prescribed minimum requirements, the CNB adopted a new capital regulation in a way that warrants preservation of the existing capital buffers by means of replacing some of the previously used measures with new instruments. All new capital buffers have been introduced between 2014 and 2015, immediately upon the adoption of the new regulation, without a phase-in period. Such an approach was feasible as the Croatian banking sector was well capitalised before the new regulation came into force, with substantial excess capital above the regulatory requirements.

3.1. *CCyB — Rules vs. discretion*

On top of the minimum own fund requirements, since 2014 credit institutions in Croatia have been required to maintain combined capital buffers. It encompassed capital conservation buffer (CCB) of 2.5 percent for all credit institutions and systemic risk buffer (SRB) of 1.5 percent or 3 percent on top of CCB. SRB depended on the size and importance of the credit institution, with large institutions required to maintain the higher rate. CCyB was initially set to zero and was never increased. Finally, systemically important credit institutions (O-SIIs) were designated, but appropriately assigned buffers for O-SIIs under the new Capital Requirement Directive IV overlapped with the structural systemic risk buffer, so in practice it was ineffective before the new Capital Requirement Directive (CRD V) started to apply.[1] However, O-SII status made these institutions eligible for recovery within the resolution procedure, which implied the establishment and maintenance of appropriate minimum requirement for own funds and eligible liabilities (MREL) requirements,[2] as well as more stringent reporting requirements and more frequent on-site supervision. Under the CRD V, transposed into the national Act on Credit Institutions that came into force at the end-2020, these two buffers became additive. As previous systemic risk buffer also covered

---

[1] As systemic risk buffer applies to all exposures, each systemically important credit institution needed to apply only the higher between its systemic risk buffer rate and its systemically important institutions buffer rate.

[2] Minimum requirements for own funds and eligible liabilities as laid down in the Bank Recovery and Resolution Directive (BRRD).

some risks stemming from the market and exposure concentration in the banking sector that were accounted for in the higher buffer rate for large banks (3 percent), in order to avoid double counting of risks, the systemic risk buffer rate was recalibrated before the two buffers became cumulative. From end-December 2020, it amounted to 1.5 percent for all credit institutions.

CCyB in Croatia was set at zero upon its introduction in 2015 (with implementation from 2016) and has remained at the same level since then. Recovery of the Croatian economy was late compared to other EU Member States, and the same was the case with credit developments. When credit finally took off in 2017–2018, it was concentrated in the household sector while corporate loans continued to stagnate or even declined. However, even household credit growth never reached the levels calling for macroprudential action, except the action targeted specifically at the segment of consumer loans. CCyB, as a broad-based instrument targeting excessive growth of overall credit, was not deemed appropriate to target this specific market segment. Instead, other measures were used to mitigate risk arising from excessive consumer lending. For all these reasons, CCyB remained effectively inactive throughout the observed period.

Although wider credit developments warranted maintenance of CCyB at the zero level, methodological issues regarding the calibration of the buffer deserved a closer inspection. Basel credit-to-GDP gap, which served as an analytical basis for the activation of the buffer, remained deeply in the negative territory when the recovery of credit activity started and would reach the trend line only after several years of rapid credit growth (Figure 8).

Historical circumstances that are not likely to repeat themselves — rapid financial deepening following the privatisation and internalisation of the financial system and liberalisation of capital flows against the background of benign international financial environment of the early 2000s — make the credit-to-GDP gap infer an unrealistically high equilibrium level of credit to GDP. The main weakness of Basel credit-to-GDP gap is a requirement of long data series without major structural breaks in order to properly estimate the trend value. Basel credit gap is likely to lag much behind credit booms in emerging economies similar

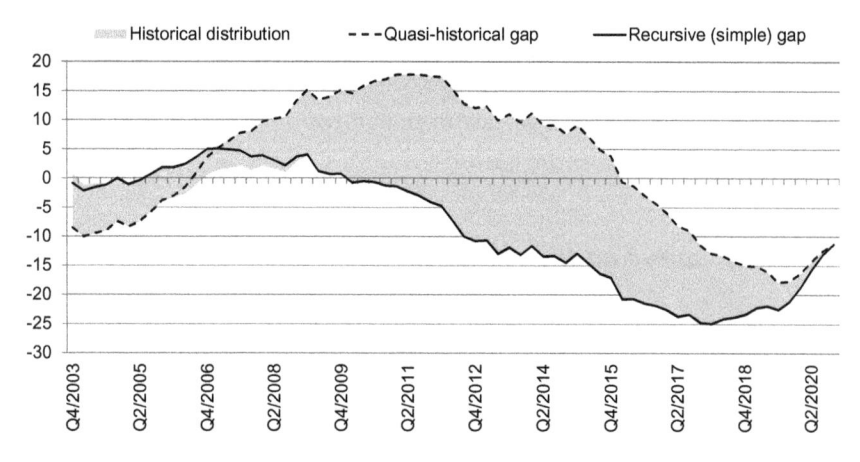

Figure 8. Standardised credit-to-GDP gap.

Note: Calculations are made on a sample as of 2000. The quasi-historical gap is calculated on the entire sample, while the recursive gap is calculated on the right-hand side moving sample (of available data for each quarter), with the last observations being always the same for both gap indicators. The historical distribution of the calculated gap is the area between the lowest and the highest value of the gap calculated by moving the sample to the right.

Source: Croatian Bureau of Statistics (original series of nominal GDP, seasonally adjusted by the CNB); CNB (tables D1, D5 and H15 for time series of credit); time series are subject to revision and available on the CNB website.

to Croatia. When calibrating the CCyB, it is therefore important to keep in mind that the credit-to-GDP gap may not be an adequate early warning indicator — and it needs to be complemented with a broader set of variables that might signal the build-up of systemic risks related to excessive credit growth in the financial system.

Finally, the unprecedented shock to the global economy posed by the COVID-19 pandemic highlighted a weakness of starting to build the CCyB only in the upswing phase of the financial cycle. In the event of a crisis triggered by external factors to the domestic economy, such as a health crisis or a global economic disturbance, zero buffer rate withholds a policy lever. When an economy enters into a downturn with zero CCyB rate, even ample buffers for structural systemic risk and systematically important institutions may not adequately support lending in the crisis as these buffers should in principle be invariant to the cycle. Therefore, it is worth considering to set CCyB at above zero when already close to the neutral zone of the financial cycle (so-called "positive neutral" strategy), which would enable capital release even in downturns that do not follow the overheating phase of the cycle.

3.2. *Keep an eye on the consumer*

Financial regulators traditionally used to assume that consumers borrowed in a rational manner. Of course, various unforeseen circumstances, such as adverse health conditions or losing one's job, can make it hard for consumers to service their debt. However, such individual hardship was not expected to have systemic consequences. Regulators used to restrict their actions to ensuring the transparency of information on lending conditions, while abstaining from attempts to nudge consumers towards, or away, from any particular financial product or service. However, as two recent examples painfully demonstrated — subprime crisis in the US and CHF-indexed mortgage loans in Central and Southeast Europe — household borrowing under overly optimistic scenarios, or simply not taking into account reasonable downside risks, can permeate the financial system with systemic risk. Even if the financial system discloses all the necessary information and regulators keep an eye on systemic risks arising from household over-indebtedness, unforeseen economic developments have a potential to trigger consumer distress and unearth a potential for litigations and conduct risk, as witnessed in many jurisdictions across Europe. Therefore, macroprudential measures aimed at consumers are not only necessary to enhance consumer protection and borrowers' resilience but also to safeguard the stability of the financial sector.

With these considerations in mind, CNB recently enacted several types of measures in order to reduce risks arising from household borrowing and to further build resilience into the banking system. The overarching principle of regulating household borrowing was to reduce exposure of consumers to different risks and increase their debt-servicing capacity. That, in turn, reduced the potential losses for credit institutions related to the risk of borrowers defaulting on their loans. Two specific risks have been identified recently — a large build-up of exposure to interest rate risk in the household sector and overly loose lending standards for consumer borrowing — and remedial action has been taken in order to stem excessive risk-taking behaviour.

Interest rates in Croatia followed a downward trend over the past three decades, except for a relatively short uptick following the outbreak of the Global Financial Crisis (CNB, 2017). Therefore, interest rates have never been perceived as a major source of risk by the households, who have traditionally taken substantial interest rate exposures. As interest rates worldwide gradually converged to their historic lows, the potential for an increase of interest rates greatly outweighed any possibility of further declines, particularly over the course of a typical mortgage which on average ran over 20 and sometimes even up to 30 years of maturity. With the share of outstanding variable-rate mortgages exceeding 80 percent, CNB moved on to increase awareness of interest rate risk and supply of options to hedge the risk (Rosan, 2017).

In late 2017, the CNB recommended to credit institutions to make it easier for consumers to hedge interest rate risk. The CNB also recommended to banks to enhance their supply of fixed interest rate loans, while providing the option for existing customers to lock in historically low levels of interest rates. Simultaneously, the CNB issued an information list with an overview of basic properties for several standard types of loans for each single bank that lent to households, including options to hedge interest and exchange rate risks. It was assumed that consumers often lacked information on interest rate risk as well as knowledge on potential actions to mitigate it. On the other hand, banks were well-informed market participants who were able to purchase wholesale hedging for their interest rate exposures at a moderate cost. Intervention was framed in a market-friendly manner, promoting transparency and competition between the credit institutions, and further supported by the public information campaign (Figure 9).

In the post-2015 period, the Croatian National Bank relied on monetary accommodation to support the lending activity and recovery of the economy. While loans to the corporate sector had been decreasing throughout most of the observed period (Figure 10), consumer lending started to rapidly accelerate from 2017 (Figure 11). Rising employment, income and consumer optimism coupled with a prolonged decline in

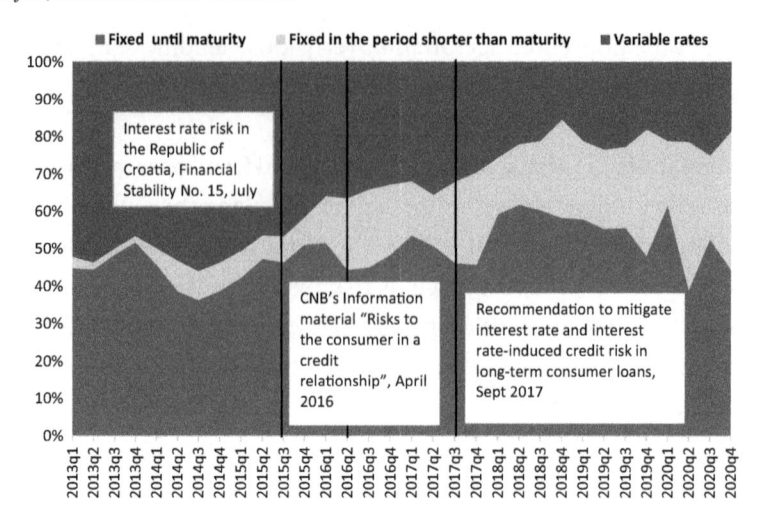

Figure 9. Newly granted loans to households by the type of interest rate.
Source: CNB.

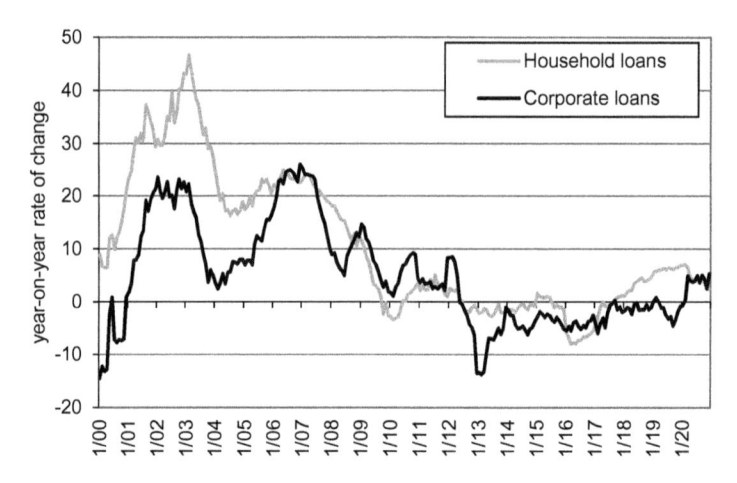

Figure 10. Loans to households and corporate sector.
Source: CNB.

interest rates and the release of pent-up demand for consumer durables spurred the demand for loans. On the supply side, banks found consumer lending more attractive because relatively higher interest rates on consumer loans boosted their battered interest margins.

Consumer lending additionally accelerated in 2018 after a tightening of lending standards for housing loans. Interaction of European Banking

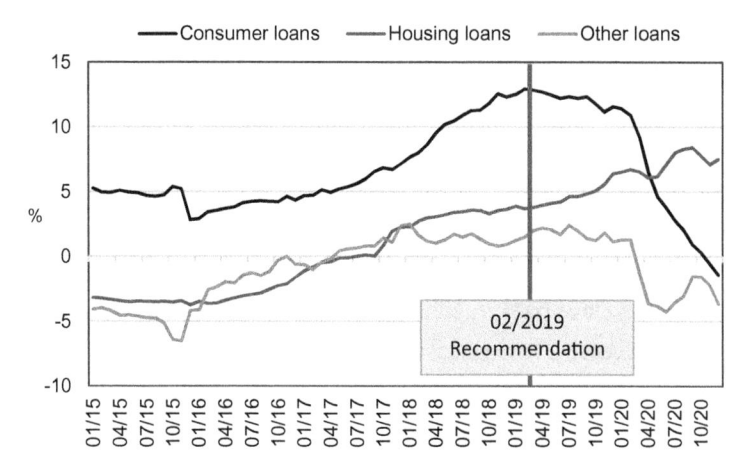

Figure 11. Loans to households.

Source: CNB.

Authority (EBA) guidelines on creditworthiness assessment and local rules on forced debt collection significantly reduced the supply of housing loans compared to banks' previous internal rules. The CNB's decision of implementing the EBA guidelines restricted the amount of monthly instalment for a housing loan to the level of consumer income eligible for seizure. This introduced an indirect limit on the amount of housing loans relative to consumer income. The consumers and the banks turned instead to consumer lending, which remained subject to more lenient regulatory criteria for creditworthiness assessment. In response to growing demand, banks substantially increased the maximum amounts of consumer loans, and loans with maturities of 10 years became a norm rather than an exception. Still, even consumer loans of high amounts and with long maturities required little paperwork and no collateral, with the whole process of granting a loan often taking place through digital channels within less than 24 hours.

The simple and rapid manner in which these loans were granted, and a further relaxation of lending standards against longer initial maturities and larger loan amounts, drew an increasing number of borrowers and further accelerated consumer lending. For all the mentioned reasons — simple and fast procedures, lenient lending standards, often sizeable loan amounts and long maturities — this particular market segment was identified as a potential source of systemic risk.

In response to a potential rise in credit risk associated with the rapid growth in consumer loans, the CNB in February 2019 recommended to credit institutions to harmonise lending standards for consumer loans with original maturity equal to or longer than 60 months, with the standards applied for housing lending. In addition, the CNB used supervisory powers to request banks to specifically include potential losses arising from consumer loans in their internal assessments of capital requirements and to include claw-back mechanisms in their compensation plans in the event of excessive losses arising from such placements. The purpose of the recommendation was to harmonise the criteria for assessing creditworthiness between housing loans and consumer loans with a longer initial maturity, encourage prudent borrowing and thus strengthen household and bank resilience to possible unfavourable economic and financial developments. In addition, potential room for regulatory arbitrage has been curbed by closing the gap in lending standards for housing loans and for consumer loans with long maturities.

Consumer lending started to gradually decelerate as banks implemented the recommendation over the course of 2019, but the annual growth rate of these loans remained above 10 percent until February 2020. However, with the outbreak of the pandemic in 2020, consumer lending completely stalled as income stagnated and consumer optimism tanked. On the other hand, housing loans continued to accelerate despite the pandemic, on the back of the government subsidy program. Two major types of household lending completely decoupled (Figure 11). An expected fall in employment and disposable income of households largely increased the probability that risks accumulated during the period of accelerated growth in consumer lending will materialise. The increase in loan renegotiations over the following months suggests that households could see difficulties in debt repayment. As fiscal support and loan moratoria mitigate corporate bankruptcies as well as the corresponding rise of non-performing loans, the process of risk materialisation in the segment of consumer loans could only be at an early stage. With many employees in vulnerable sectors facing uncertain prospects, increased labour market churning could harm the quality of consumer loans even against the background of relatively stable aggregate employment figures.

Although the CNB was aware that the recommendation would not have the same effect as a binding regulation, this choice was a justified course of action for two reasons. The first reason referred to the lack of an adequate legal basis for enacting binding borrower-based measures, and the second to the insufficient data available that prevented effective calibration of a binding regulation. The first issue was solved through recent changes of the regulatory setup within the framework of entering the European Exchange Rate Mechanism II (ERM II) and joining the close cooperation with the Banking Union. Since then, the CNB has been explicitly empowered to implement borrower-based measures. The design and supervision of such measures require individual data on lending standards, which have so far not been systematically collected by the CNB. For that reason, in 2020, the CNB introduced a new reporting system for credit institutions on consumer lending standards, which included monthly reporting on a granular basis (at the level of the individual loan) on all newly-granted consumer loans.

3.3. Real estate market — Dark corners of macroprudential policy

Following the strong expansion in the run-up to the Global Financial Crises, the Croatian housing market underwent a prolonged period of falling prices and contracting turnover, which lasted from 2008 to 2015 (Figures 12 and 13). Activity in the real estate market bottomed out in 2016 and started to recover only in 2017. Yet, the pace of increase in residential real estate (RRE) prices rapidly accelerated and by early 2020, average prices reached the pre-crisis level and were once again showing signs of overvaluation. The real estate market proved resilient in the first year of the COVID-19 crisis, as RRE prices continued to rise to historically high levels, departing further from fundamentals, while the decline in the number of transactions was fairly modest.

The main factors contributing to the RRE price increase included historically low interest rates, favourable labour market trends in tandem with high consumer optimism regarding the acquisition of RRE and a release of pent-up demand accumulated during the immediate post–Global Financial Crisis period, as well as the implementation of

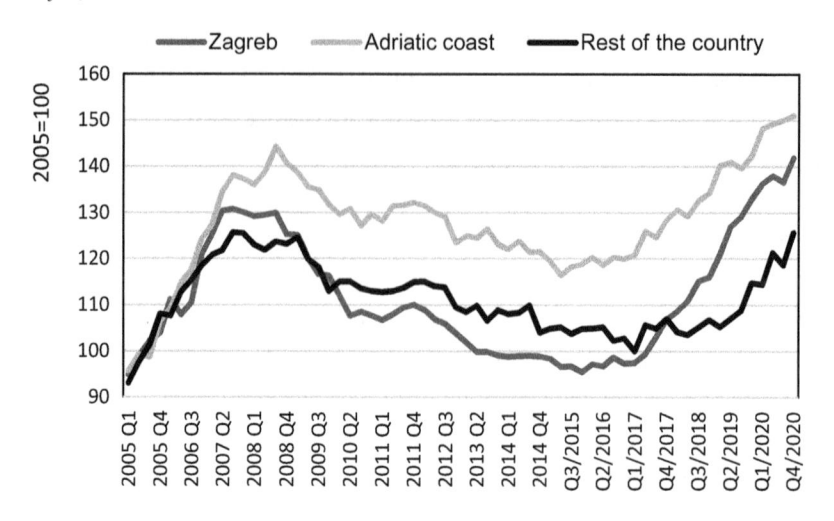

Figure 12. RRE prices in Croatia.
Source: CBS.

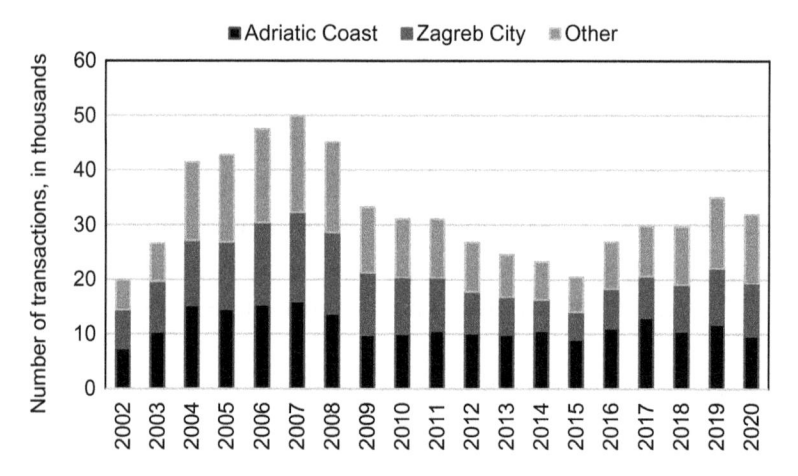

Figure 13. Real estate market activity — number of transactions.
Source: CBS and CNB calculations.

a government housing loan subsidy program. The RRE prices on the Adriatic coast and in the City of Zagreb were also influenced by the further rise of the tourism sector (which increased the demand for daily and weekly rentals) as well as strong demand by foreign investors. The traditional preference of Croatian citizens towards investing in real estate combined with record low interest rates in the domestic banking market and volatility in the capital market, encouraged households to divert their assets from bank deposits or securities into RRE. Finally, a further small push to prices came from the reduction of the real estate transaction tax rate from 4 percent to 3 percent as of the beginning of 2019.

Unlike in the previous pre-crisis period, the push to RRE price increase did not come from excessive lending. The contribution of mortgage lending to the RRE market was in part limited by the tightening regulation on loan enforcement in mid-2017, in conjunction with the microprudential regulation[3] that indirectly introduced strict limits on debt-service-to-income (DSTI) ratios for mortgages. Since indirect restrictions on DSTI ratios became one of the strictest in Europe,[4] de facto excluding many potential borrowers from the real estate market, it made little sense to reduce them even further by means of further tightening prudential regulation of mortgages.

The CNB nevertheless acted to prevent potential regulatory arbitrage arising from increasing volumes of consumer lending under more lenient standards. Still, such an action did not decelerate in any meaningful way the pace of RRE price increases.

Although there is no reliable data on the breakdown of real-estate transactions between those financed by cash or by a loan, according to the anecdotal evidence the expansion was partly driven by the cash

---

[3] EBA Guidelines EBA/GL/2015/11 and EBA/GL/2015/12, as implemented in CNB Decision on the additional criteria for the assessment of consumer creditworthiness and on the procedure for the collection of arrears and voluntary foreclosure (Official Gazette 107/2017).

[4] After credit institutions complied with the CNB Decision and the provision that the amounts required for the legally determined minimum costs of living cannot be used for loan repayments, for debtors with below average net salary the highest permitted DSTI ratio has been indirectly limited to 25 percent. For debtors with above average net salary, the part of the salary exempt from seizure is fixed at two-thirds of the average salary in the Republic of Croatia so the maximum permitted DSTI ratio rises as their net salary rises. Although these regulations protect consumers from excessive borrowing and enable the banks to collect their claims in case of foreclosure, at the same time they restrict consumer's ability to take on new loans. In comparison with other EU member states, the implicit limit on the DSTI ratio of 25 percent for debtors with a below average income puts Croatia in the group of countries with very restrictive standards (for more information, please see CNB (2019).

transactions. It is important to notice that not only lending rates were low, but deposit rates were at zero or might even turn negative. After observing that trend for a few years, part of the depositors decided to diversify their deposits into real estate. Along with the low interest rates, the contribution of investors with cash available at hand, including foreign investors, to the RRE boom, while loan growth remained muted until recently, rendered standard macroprudential policy much less effective, with only a limited impact on price developments. Recent acceleration of mortgage lending was in large part backed by the expanded government subsidy program, that in 2020 was almost twice as large as in the previous year (estimated subsidies amounted to HRK 4.5 billion or approximately 7 percent of the total mortgage loans outstanding in 2020 vs. HRK 2.3 billion or approximately 4 percent of total housing loans outstanding in 2019), contributing further to the rising RRE prices. That is a good example of a situation in which macroprudential policy cannot mend the cracks opened by monetary or fiscal policy. Consequently, this leads to the conclusion that some other policies might be more efficient in preventing such trends.

3.4. *Do not forget the granularity — The Croatian Parmalat*

The Agrokor Group was the largest Croatian company in terms of revenue and employment. It was a vertically integrated company operating in agriculture and food processing with major retail operations, both within Croatia and neighbouring countries, and the scope of its activities started to spill over into other areas, such as construction, tourism and health. Despite the fact that many companies from the Agrokor Group were listed on the stock exchange, concerns were present about the transparency of the group's finances. These concerns were gradually mounting and they culminated in Moody's downgrade of Agrokor's outlook from stable to negative within the B3 credit rating category in early 2017, and one of the largest creditors[5] accused the company's management of manipulating financial statements. At that moment, with deteriorating credit ratings, the largest creditors unwilling to refinance

---

[5] Russian VTB Bank.

the debt and thousands of suppliers rushing for the exit to collect their claims based on extended trade credits ahead of others, the company became unable to pay incoming bills.

The company employing about 2 percent of the workforce in the country (and as many abroad) was considered to be too big to fail. However, the large potential cost of state intervention was a reason to avoid bailout as the audit uncovered unreported losses (amending the reports for 2015 and 2016) amounting to 4 percent of Croatian GDP on the balance sheet, that exceeded 15 percent of the Croatian GDP in 2016. Existing insolvency legislation had never been tested on such a large and complex case, with debtors ranging from a large base of suppliers to domestic financial institutions, international banks and bondholders. In April 2017, a special law on receivership — Act on Extraordinary Administration Procedure in Companies of Systemic Importance for the Republic of Croatia — was enacted as a solution to the problem. Also in April 2017, the Extraordinary Commissioner was appointed, with a mandate to guide a long and complex process of reaching an agreement with the creditors on partial debt cancellation and restructuring of the remaining debt, while restructuring the ownership structure of the company along the way. All these had to be done while maintaining regular business operations of the large and complex holding company.

For a long time, the financing needs of Agrokor were of a special concern for the CNB. Already some five years before the financial collapse of the company, the CNB had been continuously limiting the exposure of domestic banks to what was defined as a single risk. As the balance sheet of the conglomerate grew too large to obtain finance from domestic sources alone, and the CNB limited the exposure of domestic banks, the company increasingly started to rely on international financial markets to fund growth and expansion. However, as the moment of collapse got near and a number of banks were reluctant to increase exposure towards a company, a complex web of financial flows originating from suppliers and non-bank financial institutions started to emerge. As both suppliers and non-banks financing the company relied on bank funding, this exacerbated the threat of contagion to the banking system. The CNB therefore had to continuously monitor indirect exposures of the banking system to the Agrokor Group and adapt the regulatory perimeter to include the likes of factoring and leasing companies as well as a growing number of non-financial entities. As these suppliers and financial institutions were identified as highly exposed to Agrokor, banks were immediately, upon identification, requested to consolidate those exposures within the calculations of large exposure to Agrokor.

The approach taken by CNB in the process of identification of connected clients in the Agrokor case followed the basic idea of identification of potential domino effects between clients, regardless of the type of connection. Information on all entities likely to take a serious hit when contagion kicked in was collected from various sources (on-site bank supervision, media, news, internal bank reports, etc.). Every individual transaction or product extended by a bank to potentially connected enterprises were investigated on a case-by-case basis and cross-referenced through the entire banking system, with every entity identified in one bank as connected with the group triggering immediate checks through all banks. Such a comprehensive approach, encompassing business interconnectedness, credit dependency, implicit support and structured transactions, enabled the identification of common patterns of economic interdependence and the adjustment of the perimeter of supervisory actions aimed at limiting systemic risks stemming from exposures of the banking/financial sector to the Agrokor group.

Despite the huge systemic relevance of Agrokor for the real and financial sectors, the crisis and the subsequent restructuring of the Agrokor Group affected the economy and banking sector only to a small extent. Thanks to the consistent regulatory policy of high capitalisation and liquidity levels, as well as the CNB's timely activities to limit the banking system's exposure to risk identified as connected to the Agrokor Group, the banking system was able to withstand the costs arising from the restructuring of the group and some of its suppliers without a major hit to income and capital.

Also, the Agrokor crisis erupted against a background of favourable macroeconomic conditions. It made the crisis easier to handle, but also left a reminder that not all shocks have macroeconomic origin. Rather, the opposite may be true, with the spillover of idiosyncratic shocks onto macroeconomic fluctuations and/or financial stability. Increasing risk of granularity to our economies has important ramifications for macroeconomic management and financial system regulation, including the way we think about financial stability and macroprudential policy (Ebeke and Eklou, 2017). Small countries may be particularly vulnerable to the risk of granularity, with some of the largest corporates exceeding the capacity of the financial system to provide funding and absorb potential losses. Such exposures need to be monitored on a continuous basis with authorities performing regular stress tests which also include the risk of spillovers between the corporate members of large conglomerates.

3.5. *Real time stress test — COVID-19 pandemic*

The escalation of the COVID-19 pandemic in early 2020, combined with the epidemiological measures and uncertainty about the duration of the pandemic, have had a strong negative impact on real and financial developments (Figure 14). Yet again, the Croatian banking system met the crisis with high levels of capital and liquidity (at end 2019, the total capital ratio for the banking sector was 23.2 percent while the liquidity coverage ratio amounted to 173 percent), providing once again a pillar of stability as the economy got caught in the global turmoil.

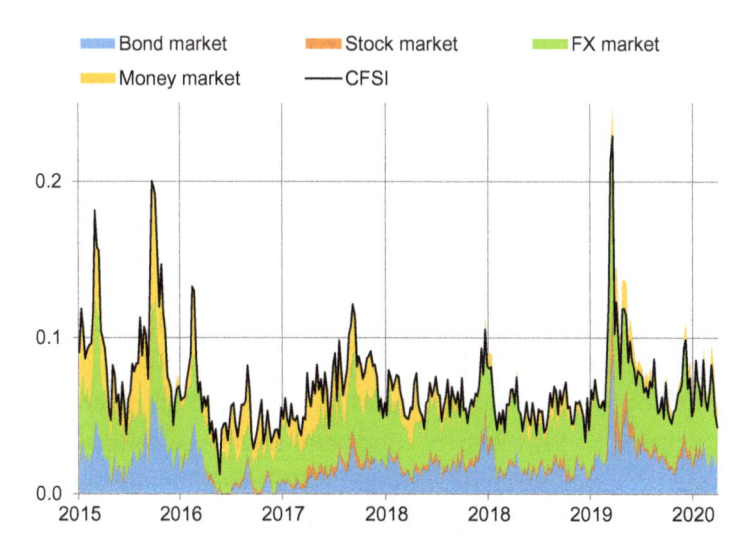

Figure 14. Financial stress index.

Source: Bloomberg, ZSE, CNB.

The temporary tightening of financial market conditions was reflected in the high level and the increased volatility of the financial stress index (Figure 14). The value of the CROBEX stock index strongly declined, while yields in the bond market surged against significant liquidity problems in the investment fund industry. However, from the financial stability point of view, the most important shock was the depreciation pressures on kuna against the euro.

As a response to these shocks, the CNB had acted quickly, combining a set of monetary and supervisory measures. The main goal of the measures was to ensure unhindered capital flows to the real sector, with different instruments used to preserve the exchange rate stability, providing kuna and foreign currency liquidity to the domestic financial system and maintain stability in the government securities market. Such a setup had proven to be sufficient to deal with the shock, so there was no need to use traditional macroprudential instruments beyond restrictions on dividend distributions.

In order to preserve the stability of the domestic currency's exchange rate against the euro, the CNB intervened in the foreign exchange market. In a series of large interventions, a total of 2.5 billion euros (approximately 5 percent of GDP) was sold to domestic banks in March and April 2020. In addition, the CNB had agreed with the European Central Bank (ECB) on a currency swap arrangement to the tune of two billion euros. At the same time, in order to stabilise the government securities market, which was under a sell-off pressure due to redemption-induced demand of investment funds, the CNB initiated an asset purchase program and started to buy government bonds on the secondary market in addition to maintaining standard open market operations and reducing the general reserve requirement ratio from 12 percent to 9 percent. In order to provide liquidity where it was needed the most rather than simply boosting excess reserves of the banking system, the CNB expanded the list of eligible participants in securities purchase and sale operations by adding pension and investment funds and insurance companies. The CNB used the asset purchase program (APP) to maintain stability of the bond market and preserve financing conditions for all sectors. These actions were inconsistent with preserving the stability of the exchange rate, which was equally under pressure, in particular given the significant size of the APP of 5.5 percent of the GDP, the second largest among emerging markets. The dilemma of supporting the exchange rate stability versus injecting liquidity into the domestic financial system is typical for a small, open emerging market central bank in a time of a global distress. Amongst others, two things were particularly helpful, namely the size of the foreign exchange reserves and the fact that the CNB had agreed on a swap arrangement with the ECB in April. That eased the pressure in the FX market and allowed for a smooth continuation of the APP to ease the financing conditions.

By using supervisory measures to preserve financial stability, the CNB provided space for the optimal use of monetary policy instruments. Temporarily allowing banks to use a liquidity coverage ratio (LCR) below the prescribed minimum of 100 percent directly supported the liquidity of the domestic economy, which also eased funding conditions in the domestic market and helped maintain the stability of the kuna exchange rate against the euro. However, there was no need for banks to use this option.

In addition, the CNB temporarily permitted more flexible use of supervisory rules on the classification of placements, by allowing credit institutions to keep favourable regulatory treatment of exposures to clients affected by the COVID-19 outbreak that were assessed as not risky at the end of 2019, and which will now be granted payment deferrals or other restructuring measures, as well as new financing directed at mitigating the effects of the COVID-19 pandemic on their operations. This measure eased both the pressure on banks and the corporate sector, allowing the uncertainty to dissipate, before banks are pushed to make potentially massive credit risk downgrades with a large possible impact on corporate access to finance. At the same time, in order to preserve solvency and liquidity, credit institutions were ordered to maintain the profit realized in 2019 and to adjust the payments of variable remuneration accordingly.

Given the supervisory and monetary policy measures taken and the relatively high surplus of capital compared to regulatory requirements, there was no need for a change in the macroprudential policy instruments beyond restrictions on dividend distributions. Moreover, applicable capital buffers (capital conservation buffer and systemic risk buffer) were by definition intended to address structural systemic risks by increasing the resilience of banks, so their reduction should be related to the decrease in systemic risks. On the contrary, the countercyclical buffer of capital, which should be gradually built up in periods of strong credit growth and high cyclical pressures, and which was meant to be released in the downward phase of the financial cycle, was applied at 0 percent before the COVID-19 outbreak crisis, as explained in Chapter 3.

4. What should we learn?

The dynamic five-and-a-half years of post–Global Financial Crisis recovery until the pandemic crisis, have definitely further contributed to a better understanding of certain systemic risks, as well as the reach and effects of macroprudential policy instruments.

The Agrokor Group crisis pointed out the dangers of a high concentration of banks' exposure to related parties, but also of mutual exposures of companies, especially in small countries. However, despite the huge systemic relevance of Agrokor for the real and financial sector, the effects of this crisis remained limited. The reason why this crisis ultimately had relatively small consequences in relation to the huge importance of Agrokor in the domestic economy was the CNB's timely implementation of regulations that limited the exposure of domestic banks to the Agrokor risk. This had ensured that the corporate insolvency shock did not spill over into a systemic banking crisis. This indicated the importance of timely identification of systemic risks and their adequate addressing. In this concrete case, supervisory measures that were consistently implemented for many individual banks had an effect on the financial stability of the system as a whole.

An analysis of the underlying factors behind strong RRE price growth shows that the reach of macroprudential policy in mitigating related systemic risks is limited. This implies that some other polices might be more efficient in preventing an accumulation of such risks, such as fiscal policy or even taking such risks into account when setting monetary policy. There are many ways in which fiscal policy could affect the real estate market, from tax reliefs to various forms of subsidies. The latest example in Croatia refers to the state program of subsidising housing loans. As confirmed by Kunovac and Žilić (2020), after its initiation in 2017 until the outbreak of the pandemic, it further contributed to the strengthening of real estate demand and rising prices, thus having a procyclical effect on the RRE market. While the most recent round of the program launched in autumn 2020 supported the market faced with a negative shock, it further widened the gap between prices and economic fundamentals and magnified risks associated with a potential future drop in RRE prices.

The recent COVID-19 crisis stressed once again the need for maintaining a high level of capital and liquidity buffers in good times in order to preserve financial stability in bad times. The sudden outbreak of the crisis also brought attention to the importance of an early application of macroprudential instruments in order to build buffers in time. Buffers that credit institutions accumulated during the normal and upswing phase of the real and financial cycle have proven essential to mitigate the initial shock and to enable supporting measures extended to households and non-financial corporations. Although the Croatian banking sector was in general well capitalised and liquid and there had been no need for additional capital relief measures, the fact that countercyclical buffer was applied with 0 percent rate could be seen as a potential limitation in a situation of an unexpected shock such as the COVID-19 pandemic. As other capital buffers in application are covering structural systemic risks, the existence of a capital buffer aimed to cover cyclical systemic risks would provide the CNB with an additional tool that could be used if necessary. In addition, a message that the release of countercyclical buffer conveys to the public strengthens the confidence in the central bank and its capability and determination to support the banking sector and credit activity. Experience with the sudden COVID-19–induced crisis provides empirical evidence of the usefulness of the so called "positive neutral" strategy of holding a non-zero countercyclical buffer rate as a neutral rate in normal times.

Due to the extremely strong turbulence in the financial markets and the panic that prevailed, the COVID-19 crisis pointed to the importance of decisive, fast and well-communicated policy actions, but also on the readiness to think and act "out of the box". In the Croatian case, this especially referred to the stabilisation of the exchange rate, but also the domestic bond market, which at one point was practically frozen. In addition, the exceptional situation resulted in extraordinary reactions, which referred to a set of unprecedented measures that ensured the liquidity of the overall financial system. As the APP in Croatia was highly successful in stabilising the financial shockwaves which originated from the pandemic, it is worth to mention the preconditions for its success. The first and foremost requirement for success of the APP was the institutional track record and credibility accumulated by the CNB, as the implicit condition built into the APP in general was the central bank's independence and its ability and willingness to reverse the course at any point in time if it perceived that risks were starting to exceed the benefits of the program. The second key ingredient for success of the APP was the more robust overall policy setup and stronger fundamentals (in particular the size of international reserves) than in recent history. Monetary policy does not operate in a vacuum. Structural, financial and fiscal policy need to be attuned to provide scope for supportive monetary policy — which is no mean feat even in some advanced economies. Finally, the APP played out in a benign financial environment. As central banks of the world's major economies pushed "pedal to the metal", such an exceptionally accommodative stance stabilised global capital flows and reduced the risk of sudden stops and capital flow reversals, which would inevitably tighten domestic financing conditions. In the case of Croatia, entering into a currency swap arrangement with the ECB and the subsequent ERM II accession also helped to stabilise the markets and make the APP a success.

References

CNB, 2017, Macroprudential Diagnostics No. 1, Analytical Annex: The issue of interest rate risk — a review of the results of the Interest rate survey, February.

CNB, 2019, Macroprudential Diagnostics No. 8, Box 1: Indirect limit on the amount of loan repayment relative to debtor's income.

CNB, 2020, Macroprudential diagnostics, May.

Dumičić, M. and Šošić, V., 2014, Credit cycles and central bank policy in Croatia: lessons from the 2000s, Chapter 7 in Nowotny, E., Ritzberger-Grünwald, D. and Backé, P. (eds). *Financial Cycles and the Real Economy. Lessons for CESEE Countries*. Edward Elgar, Cheltenham, UK, Northampton, MA., pp. 96–113.

Ebeke, C. and Eklou, K.M., 2017, The granular origins of macroeconomic fluctuations in Europe, IMF Working Paper WP/17/229, November.

Kunovac, D. and Žilić, I., 2020, Home sweet home: The effects of housing loan subsidies on the housing market in Croatia, CNB Working Paper W-60, October.

Rosan, M., 2017, Exposure of the private non-financial sector to interest rate risk: Analysis of results of the survey on interest rate variability, CNB Surveys S-24, October

Vujčić, B. and Dumičić, M., 2016, Managing systemic risks in the Croatian economy, macroprudential Policy, BIS Papers no. 86, September.

Leave no Stone Unturned — Macroprudential Policy in Croatia Between the Global Financial Crisis and COVID-19: A Discussion*

Tuomas Peltonen

Deputy Head of Secretariat
European Systemic Risk Board

Introduction

Boris Vujčić, Mirna Dumičić Jemrić and Lana Ivičić present interesting insights of the Croatian macroprudential policy making between the Global Financial Crisis and the COVID-19 crisis. In fact, Croatia has been one of the European countries that has actively used macroprudential policy in managing systemic risk. Their analysis not only presents some interesting country-specific features but also common challenges for a small open economy in managing financial stability risks. Based on the Croatian experience, some key findings can be presented:

- There is a need for more granular data for systemic risk monitoring;
- It is crucial to analyse and understand interconnectedness beyond banking and cross-border;

---

* The views expressed here are those of the author and do not necessarily represent the views of the European Systemic Risk Board or the European Central Bank.

- Interactions and coordination of policies are important and there are limits for macroprudential policy; and
- COVID-19 experience provides some important reflections for adjustments to the macroprudential policy frameworks and tools.

The following sections will elaborate these points further.

Need for granular and timely data and tools for systemic risk analysis

The COVID-19 shock, Agrokor Group crisis and developments in household borrowing in Croatia teach us some important lessons, in particular, the need for granular data to monitor systemic risk. This includes data on:

- Soundness of borrowers (non-financial corporations [NFCs] and households [HHs]);
- Large and concentrated exposures; and
- Interconnectedness of the financial system and the real economy.

The COVID-19 crisis illustrates well why granular and timely data is so important for policymakers. Specifically, it shows the need to account for significant sectoral heterogeneity in the impact of the COVID-19 shock to the real economy (i.e., some sectors such as travel and gastronomy are more significantly hit by the shock than others) in risk identification. In fact, the COVID-19 shock has illustrated very clearly also the need for information of the soundness of the borrowers as well as the lenders. Of particular importance are distributions of lending standards and information about the balance sheet indicators of the borrowers. It also illustrates the need to strengthen the cross-sectoral and cross-border dimensions of the analysis. All of these points were also highlighted in the Croatian Agrokor Group crisis, where granular information was needed on market-based financial intermediation that can often be cross-border.

Pure data will not suffice as granular data also requires specific skills and systemic risk analytic tools, so that different types of interconnections and interdependences can be discovered and used for systemic risk analysis.

Crucial to understand interconnections beyond banking

At the height of the COVID-19 turmoil, broad-based repricing of risk with the need to make payments led to an imbalance in the demand for and supply of highly liquid assets (so called "dash for cash"). This also affected non-bank financial entities such as insurers and asset managers. This illustrated well the nexus between market liquidity and funding liquidity, which is very complex.

In Croatia, the Croatian National Bank (CNB) initiated an asset purchase programme to stabilise the Croatian government securities market that was under sell-off pressures due to the redemption-induced demand of investment funds during the COVID-19 crisis.

Another example is the Agrokor Group crisis in Croatia, during which the CNB monitored indirect exposures to the group as suppliers and non-banks financing the group relied on instead of bank funding. This followed the fact that the CNB had limited data on domestic banks' direct exposures to the group.

Both of the above examples illustrate the need to understand interactions beyond the traditional banking sector for financial stability analysis.

Policy interactions and coordination are important

As highlighted by the authors, there are several examples of the Croatian economic situation where coordination of various policies has been important. Prior to the COVID-19 shock, coordination between monetary, fiscal and macroprudential policies was used to address issues related to foreign exchange borrowing of NFCs and HHs, surges in consumer loans and surges in house prices and lending for house purchases.

While the Croatian experience shows successful and coordinated policy actions to mitigate systemic risk, it also illustrates some limitations of macroprudential policy in a small open economy, which is also subject to capital in- and outflows (see also ESRB [2020]).

Another example of close policy coordination highlighted by the authors relates to the COVID-19 response by the Croatian authorities, when they countered a significant economic and financial shock, the depreciation of the currency and bond market illiquidity. In this occasion, policies ranging from fiscal and monetary policies to micro- and macroprudential policies were in place to mitigate the impact of the COVID-19 shock to the real economy and the financial system. An important lesson from this event is the consistency of communication and coordination of various policy actions in order to achieve the desired policy outcome.

Issues for reflection for macroprudential policymakers

The analysis of the Croatian macroprudential policy experience by the authors and their broader observations provide some early reflections for macroprudential policymakers following the COVID-19 turmoil.

Regarding data and financial stability analysis, the following questions arise:

- How to exploit (and potentially collect new) granular data on the balance sheet and leverage of borrowers?
- How to strengthen the cross-sectoral and cross-border dimensions of the analysis?
- How to better monitor market-based financial intermediation?

Moreover, regarding macroprudential policy and instruments, the following aspects would deserve further discussion:

- The need for more macroprudential space, i.e., releasable buffers;
- The availability of tools to address risks in NFCs (borrower-based measures);
- The role of dividend restrictions in the macroprudential toolkit; and
- The role of policy coordination and communication at the national and international levels

By considering these reflections, macroprudential policy frameworks could be further improved in order to be better prepared for future financial crises.

Reference

European Systemic Risk Board (ESRB) (2020): "The global dimensions of macroprudential policy", Reports of the Advisory Scientific Committee, no 10, February: https://www.esrb.europa.eu/pub/pdf/asc/esrb.asc200211_globaldimensionsmacroprudentialpolicy~93059069e3.en.pdf

CHAPTER 15

© 2023 World Scientific Publishing Company
https://doi.org/10.1142/9789811259432_0030

Chapter 15

Towards a New Monetary-Macroprudential Policy Framework: Perspectives on Integrated Inflation Targeting*

Pierre-Richard Agénor[†] and Luiz A. Pereira da Silva[‡]

[†]*Hallsworth Professor of International Macroeconomics and Development Economics, University of Manchester, UK*
[‡]*Deputy General Manager, Bank for International Settlements (BIS), Switzerland*

Abstract

Bank-dependent, middle-income countries (MICs) continue to be confronted with significant challenges to achieve price and financial stability. This chapter discusses how Integrated Inflation Targeting (IIT) can help to address them. Section 2 provides a brief overview of the performance of inflation targeting regimes in MICs since the Global Financial Crisis. Section 3 defines the characteristics of IIT, with a focus on interactions between monetary policy and macroprudential regulation, possibly supplemented by other policies (namely, foreign exchange intervention and temporary capital controls) that central banks

---

*The authors are grateful to several BIS colleagues, as well as Barry Eichengreen and conference participants, for discussions and comments on an earlier draft. The views expressed in this chapter are those of the authors and do not necessarily reflect those of the BIS.

and regulators may need to rely on to promote economic stability. The "mechanics" of IIT and the operational challenges that it faces (including the need for international coordination of macroprudential policies) are then discussed in Sections 4 and 5. Section 6 argues that IIT itself should be part of a broader Integrated Macro-Financial Policy Framework (IMFPF), which blends together IIT with a fiscal policy framework that involves the combination of fiscal rules and a stabilisation fund — even in MICs that are not highly exposed to commodity price shocks — to provide the fiscal space needed for fiscal policy to regain its countercyclical role.

1. Introduction

Since the early 1990s, a number of countries have adopted inflation targeting (IT) as their regime of choice for conducting monetary policy. But in the aftermath of the Global Financial Crisis (GFC) the performance of IT has come under greater scrutiny. Some observers have drawn attention to the fact that IT — even in the flexible form in which it has been applied at the outset by most countries — could pose significant risks to economic stability if central banks ignore interactions between monetary and macroprudential policies, and how these policies affect macroeconomic and financial stability. These concerns have led to a number of contributions in recent years with respect to the design of macroeconomic policy frameworks in general, and central bank mandates in particular, in the post-GFC world. One of these contributions (Agénor and Pereira da Silva, 2019), relates to a new perspective on IT, labeled *Integrated Inflation Targeting* (IIT). Its focus has been on the policy challenges that are specific to bank-dependent, middle-income countries (MICs) — most importantly, managing capital flows, through not only monetary and macroprudential policies but also through (sterilised) foreign exchange market intervention and temporary capital controls.

This chapter goes deeper into some of the key features of IIT, by focusing on a series of issues that were only briefly, or incompletely, addressed in our previous contributions. It proceeds as follows. Section 2 provides a brief overview of the performance of IT regimes in the past two decades, and discussed some of the challenges that these regimes are confronted with. Key among these challenges are: (1) building and maintaining policy credibility; (2) mitigating exchange rate volatility, and the reasons for doing so and (3) potential trade-offs between price stability and financial stability. Section 3 discusses the characteristics of IIT. It begins by taking stock of the debate on whether monetary policy and macroprudential regulation are complements or substitutes. It then defines and discusses the key features of IIT, namely, (1) the joint calibration of monetary and macroprudential policy instruments; (2) an explicit and contingent financial stability mandate delegated to the central bank, acting in coordination with macroprudential regulators, under various institutional arrangements; (3) the need for foreign exchange intervention and possibly temporary capital controls as additional instruments and (4) the enhanced need for transparency and communication.

Section 4 focuses on the "mechanics" of IIT regimes, i.e., the use of integrated macroeconomic models to understand and calibrate jointly monetary and macroprudential policies. It begins with the presentation of a simple integrated model of a closed economy, amenable to graphical analysis, to stress the need for basic intuition about the role of banks, financial frictions and the transmission mechanism of monetary and macroprudential policies. It also illustrates how these policies can be combined to respond to an adverse shock and return the economy to its initial equilibrium. It then discusses the use of more advanced open-economy dynamic stochastic general equilibrium (DSGE) models for integrated policy analysis, and provides some recent examples focusing on policy challenges faced by bank-dependent MICs. The use of these models to evaluate the performance of countercyclical policy rules and calculate the gains from policy coordination is also examined.

Section 5 identifies some operational challenges associated with the implementation of IIT. It discusses some of the practical changes to central bank mandates (with respect, in particular, to an explicit financial stability mandate and the use of policy interest rates to address financial stability concerns) and the need for an integrated report that highlights potential interactions between monetary and macroprudential policies. The implementation of integrated quantitative models in central banks is also briefly examined. Finally, the role of international policy coordination in the area of macroprudential policy, and its implications for the performance of an IIT regime, are explored as well. Section 6 provides concluding remarks. It argues, in particular, that IIT should itself be part of a broader Integrated Macro-Financial Policy Framework (IMFPF), which blends together IIT with a fiscal policy framework that involves the combination of fiscal rules with a stabilisation fund — even in MICs that are not directly exposed to commodity price shocks — in order to create fiscal space and allow fiscal policy to regain a countercyclical role in normal times.

2. IT: Brief overview of performance and challenges

As of May 2021, 36 countries (including Indonesia, South Korea, and Thailand) claimed to operate an explicit IT regime. Figure 1 provides a list of these countries and shows that large differences in initial inflation prevailed at the time the regime was formally adopted. Most of these countries practice *flexible IT*, which involves not only maintaining price stability as the main goal of monetary policy but also, to some extent, mitigating output fluctuations and (as discussed later) exchange rate volatility.

2.1. *Main features of IT regimes*

A conventional IT regime is characterised by three main features. The first is a public announcement of an inflation target (in the form of either single points or bands, symmetric or asymmetric) to be reached

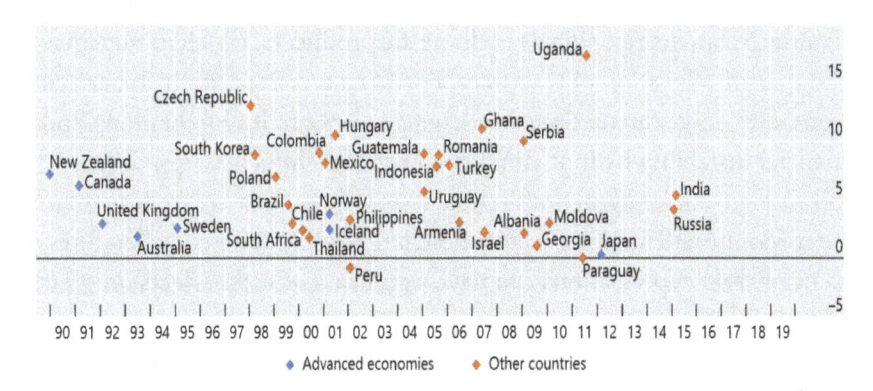

Figure 1. Countries operating an IT regime, 1990–2021.
Source: Central bank data; Datastream; national data.

at a specified horizon or maintained permanently. The second is an explicit policy decision framework to achieve the inflation target, and the third is a high degree of transparency, and an effective communication strategy, regarding the course of action planned by the central bank. Transparency is an essential component of IT as it helps to anchor expectations. Communication is also critical because even when the inflation target is well publicised, uncertainty about the horizon at which the target is expected to be achieved can destabilise expectations and may translate into higher inflation volatility. In fact, since its inception IT has been thought of by many advocates as a policy framework whose main characteristic is to enhance the transparency and coherence of monetary policy.

The early literature highlighted the absence of a *de facto* targeting of the nominal exchange rate as a key requirement for implementing an IT regime (see Agénor, 2002). However, in many of the developing countries that adopted IT, monetary authorities have continued to pay considerable attention to the value of the domestic currency — often adopting a de facto target path or band. There are various reasons for the central bank to be concerned with nominal exchange rate movements. In particular, the exchange rate has a direct impact on inflation and plays a key role in transmitting monetary policy shocks to prices. If the passthrough effect is high, the central bank may be tempted to intervene on the foreign exchange market to limit currency fluctuations. A high degree of nominal exchange rate instability may also be of concern if it translates into a high degree of variability in the real exchange rate and distorted relative price signals to domestic producers, which in turn may lead to a misallocation of resources. Furthermore, in partially dollarised economies, large fluctuations in exchange rates can lead to banking and financial instability by inducing large portfolio shifts between domestic and foreign-currency-denominated assets. Finally, in countries where the corporate and banking sectors hold large foreign-currency liabilities, exchange rate depreciations can have significant adverse effects on their balance sheets.

In an IT regime, the central bank reacts to an inflation forecast, because of the typical lag that exists between the change in the policy instrument and its actual impact on inflation. Thus, the credibility of monetary policy depends not on achieving a publicly observable, intermediate target that is viewed as a leading indicator of future inflation (as is the case under monetary or exchange rate targeting), but rather on the credibility of a *promise* to reach the inflation target in the future. This, in turn, depends on whether the public believes that the central bank will indeed stick to the objective of price stability. Credibility — and, by extension, the reputation of the monetary authority — therefore plays a crucial role in stabilising inflation expectations under IT and inducing them to be more forward-looking. In turn, if expectations are firmly anchored by the inflation target, a one-off shock to the price level would have only a transitory effect on the inflation rate. Conversely, in an IT regime in which the central bank lacks credibility, inflation would likely be persistently above target — without any benefits in terms of higher output and employment.[1]

At the same time, because performance can only be observed ex post, the need for transparency and accountability becomes more acute under this regime, in order to help the public to assess the stance of monetary policy and determine whether deviations from target are due to unpredictable shocks rather than policy mistakes. Thus, in order for IT to be a credible commitment, the public must be informed of (and understand) the policy actions the central bank plans to take and must believe that these actions are consistent with achieving the inflation target. However, accountability is difficult if performance must be assessed on the basis of inflation outcomes only. Indeed, the lag between policy actions and their impact on the economy makes it possible (or tempting) for the central bank to blame unforeseen or totally unpredictable events for inadequate performance, instead of taking responsibility for policy mistakes. To mitigate this risk, central banks in IT countries are usually required to justify their policy decisions and publicly explain differences between actual outcomes and inflation targets, through the regular

---

[1] Under imperfect credibility of an IT regime, inflation expectations can be viewed as a weighted average of past inflation and the inflation target. If the degree of inertia (the weight attached to past inflation in the formation of inflation expectations) is a function of how long actual inflation deviates from the target (as noted earlier), a longer convergence period could also weaken credibility and impart greater inertia to inflation.

publication of an *Inflation Report*, by providing public explanations of why the rate of inflation has deviated from the target, how long these deviations are expected to persist, and what policies the central bank intends to implement to bring inflation back to target. As discussed later on, however, the new challenges that central banks face in an IIT regime require a rethinking of strategies to achieve transparency and accountability.

2.2. Performance of IT regimes

Figure 2 shows the evolution of actual inflation, expected inflation and the target band for three Asian countries, Indonesia, South Korea and Thailand. Figures 3 and 4 complement that information by showing, respectively, deviations of inflation from target (defined as the midpoint of the band), and deviations of actual inflation from expected inflation. In addition, Figure 5 shows the volatility (or degree of dispersion) of inflation expectations.

Taken together, these figures suggest that in all three countries deviations of actual inflation from the target value (within the band) have been fairly small at times, but relatively large also at other times. The same outcomes can be observed in the larger sample of IT-MICs considered by Agénor and Pereira da Silva (2019). Proximate causes for these results

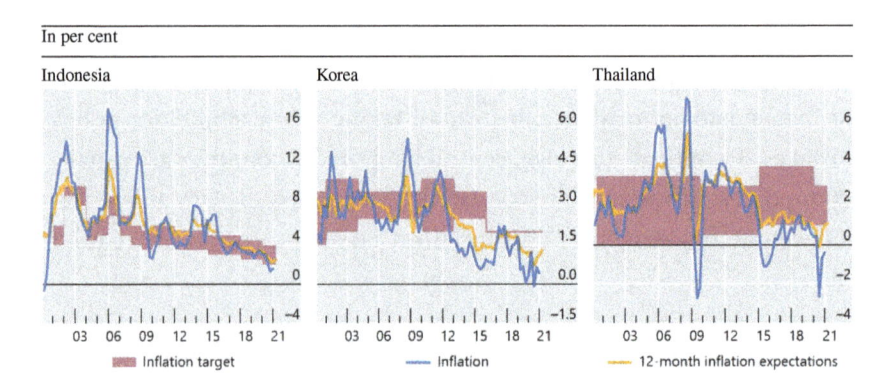

Figure 2. Asian IT countries: Actual inflation, expected inflation, and target band, 2000–2021.
Source: Consensus economics; national data; authors' calculations.

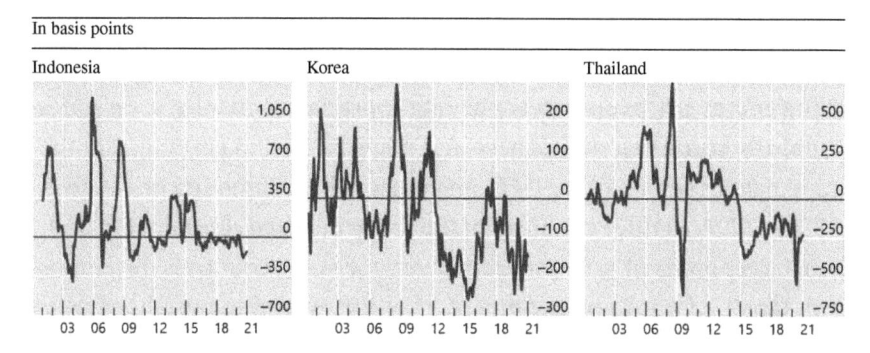

Figure 3. Asian IT countries: Deviations of inflation from target, 2000–2021.
Source: National data; authors' calculations.

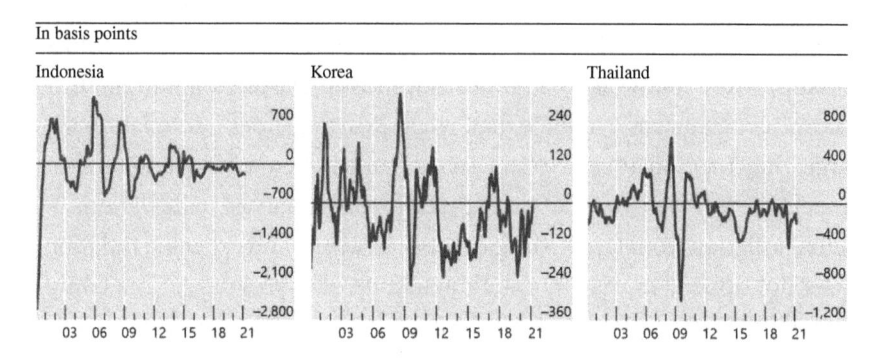

Figure 4. Asian IT countries: Deviations of actual inflation from expected inflation, 2000–2021.
Source: Consensus economics; national data; authors' calculations.

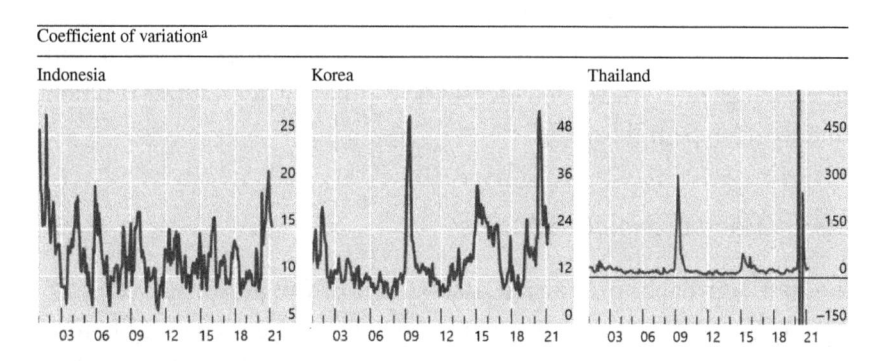

Figure 5. Selected IT-MICs: dispersion of inflation expectations, 2000–2021.
Note: [a]Coefficients of variation multiplied by 100.
Source: Consensus economics; authors' calculations.

vary across countries and include food price increases, domestic demand expansion and exchange rate depreciation in some cases, as well as falling energy prices and exchange rate appreciation in others. Episodes of globally correlated shocks have also played a role; in particular, in the immediate aftermath of the GFC, and during the commodity price shock of 2008–2009, all three countries in the group deviated substantially from their target levels of inflation. Moreover, for some countries deviations from target appear to be asymmetric: countries tend to overshoot their inflation target more often than they undershoot. This is the case for Indonesia, for instance. In South Korea, the dispersion of inflation expectations also increased sharply in the aftermath of the GFC.

In addition, even though inflation expectations have been less volatile than actual inflation, there are periods when large increases in headline inflation were followed by significant jumps in expected inflation. This may be construed as evidence that, when positive shocks to inflation are large, they have an adverse effect on central bank credibility and tend to impart more inertia to inflation expectations. In contrast to deviations in actual inflation from target, the gap between actual and expected inflation does not appear to display much evidence of asymmetry. This could perhaps reflect the fact that, in these countries, inflation expectations have been well anchored to the inflation target.

A more formal analysis of the performance of IT regimes, relative to non-IT regimes, has been conducted in a number of empirical studies. These studies have generally followed one of two approaches. The first measures the effects (or lack thereof) of IT on the level and volatility of inflation, as well as other macroeconomic variables, including output and the exchange rate. The second focuses on estimating interest rate reaction functions for central banks.

2.2.1. Macroeconomic outcomes

The first approach to a formal assessment of the performance of IT regimes consists of comparing macroeconomic outcomes (1) before and after the adoption of IT in individual countries; (2) in IT countries, compared to a control group of non-IT countries. To a significant extent, the focus of this literature has been on whether the adoption of IT has contributed to significant declines in average inflation, lower inflation volatility and macroeconomic stability in general, compared to before its adoption in a particular country or relative to countries that have maintained a different monetary policy regime. A key issue in that context is the extent to which, as noted earlier, increased credibility of the monetary policy commitment to low and stable inflation translates into reduced volatility of inflation expectations. In addition to the level and volatility of (actual and expected) inflation, some studies have also discussed the implications of IT for the level and volatility of output, the magnitude of the exchange rate pass-through, and the volatility of nominal and real exchange rates.

The review of the evidence provided by Agénor and Pereira da Silva (2019) shows that a key result of these empirical studies is that IT regimes in MICs have been fairly successful in achieving price stability — even more so, in many regards, than advanced economies (AEs). One reason for this could simply be that, to begin with, AEs did not suffer to the same extent from severe or highly volatile inflation and benefited from higher central bank transparency. Another is the possibility that the adoption of IT was more effective in countries where initially the central bank's reputation was weak and monetary policy lacked credibility. In addition, the level of expected inflation fell in many IT-MICs (relative to the control group), and both the variability of expected inflation and the average absolute forecast error (controlling for the level and variability of past inflation) fell significantly. Inflation persistence declined as well — a result that is consistent with the view that IT was successful in making inflation expectations more forward-looking, thereby reducing the degree of inflation inertia. However, empirical studies provide mixed evidence on whether IT has contributed to a reduction in output volatility and exchange rate volatility.

2.2.2. Central bank policy response

The second empirical approach to evaluating the performance of IT regimes has focused on estimating central bank interest rate reaction functions under IT and non-IT regimes. The key issue is the extent to which the adoption of IT has altered central bank operating behaviour, not only with respect to traditional objectives (inflation deviations from target and output gaps), but also with respect to exchange rate changes, fluctuations in asset prices, indicators of monetary conditions and so on. In most cases, the methodology has involved estimating country-specific simple and augmented Taylor-type rules and testing for statistical significance of the coefficients of the additional variables in the regressions.

As discussed in detail in Agénor and Pereira da Silva (2019), the evidence based on estimated policy reaction functions largely corroborates the results based on macroeconomic outcomes. It suggests that, in many MICs, IT central banks became over time more responsive to deviations in actual (or expected) inflation from target — improving, in so doing, prospects for macroeconomic stability. From that perspective, the fact that some (although not all) studies find a positive effect of exchange rates in Taylor rules does not necessarily reflect a deliberate attempt to target the exchange rate, but rather an indirect response to the impact that it has on aggregate demand. It may also be evidence in favour of *fear of floating*, which may itself (as discussed next) result from various considerations. It is also important to note that the fact that some studies are unable to detect a *systematic* effect of exchange rate changes on policy rates does not preclude the possibility that central banks react *episodically* to these changes.[2]

In sum, regardless of the methodology used, recent studies reach similar conclusions: the adoption of an IT regime in MICs has led to lower average inflation rates and reduced inflation volatility compared to a control group of non-IT countries, and possibly a lower exchange rate pass-through. At the same time, the volatility and persistence of inflation expectations have fallen (substantially in some cases) over time. However, credibility has remained a "work in progress" in some countries. A possible reason for that, as discussed further later, is the fact that central banks may confuse markets at times by signalling a stronger preference

---

[2] Indeed, these studies (which are usually based on linear regression techniques) do not capture the fact that policy response may be non-linear, in the sense that it occurs only when, for instance, the (cumulative) change in the exchange rate is relatively large compared to a norm set by the central bank, or when that change is in one direction only (appreciation).

for output or exchange rate stability, relative to price stability. As a result of this perceived shift in preferences, credibility can be lost quickly, and restoring it takes time. As discussed later on, this has implications for adding a financial stability mandate to central banks.

2.3. Challenges to conventional IT regimes

Despite performing well during the past two decades (especially in MICs, as documented earlier), conventional IT regimes in MICs continue to face a number of challenges — old and new. In what follows we focus on three of them: the difficulty of building and maintaining policy credibility; the role of exchange rate volatility and fear of floating and the potential trade-offs between price stability and financial stability.[3]

2.3.1. Building and maintaining credibility

As noted earlier, the credibility of an IT regime depends on the credibility of a *promise* to reach the inflation target in the future. However, in many countries, establishing credibility has proved elusive, with adverse effects on inflation expectations and actual inflation. In countries where central banks are perceived to have a high preference for output stability or exchange rate stability (which may lead to the so-called *exchange rate dominance*), the credibility of an announced inflation target may be significantly undermined. In turn, as noted earlier, lack of credibility may contribute to inflation persistence. In addition, credibility depends not only on the extent to which the *level* of inflation deviates from its target, but also on *how long* these deviations last. Adopting a target band, instead of a point target, does not, by itself, solve the problem.[4] Although the adoption of an IT regime may itself help to improve the credibility of the policy regime when initially there is uncertainty about the central bank's policy preferences, in practice improving credibility requires

---

[3] Agénor and Pereira da Silva (2019, Chapters 4 and 5) provide a broader discussion.
[4] The reason is that there is a trade-off between credibility and flexibility in the choice of the target band: the wider the bands are, the more likely it is that the point target (or the midpoint of the band) will be achieved, but the less credible the target becomes.

delivering consistently over time rates of inflation that do not depart significantly and systematically from preannounced targets. To need to strengthen credibility is an important consideration when discussing the possibility of extending central banks' mandate to explicitly account for financial stability considerations.

2.3.2. Mitigating exchange rate volatility

As noted earlier, in principle the adoption of an IT regime requires the absence of any commitment to a particular value of the exchange rate. However, rather than allowing the currency to float freely, in practice central banks in IT-MICs have often intervened heavily in foreign exchange markets. In fact, the scale of foreign exchange market intervention, in either the spot or the forward market, has increased massively since the GFC (see Gadanecz *et al.*, 2014; Frankel, 2019; and Bank for International Settlements, 2020).[5]

There are various reasons for this *fear of floating* (Calvo and Reinhart, 2002). First, the exchange rate has a direct impact on inflation and plays a key role in transmitting monetary policy and exogenous shocks to prices. If the pass-through effect is high, the central bank may be tempted to intervene on the foreign exchange market to limit currency fluctuations. Second, a high degree of nominal exchange rate volatility may be of concern if it translates into a high degree of variability in the real exchange rate, which may distort relative price signals and lead to a misallocation of resources. Third, especially in dollarised IT-MICs, large fluctuations in exchange rates can lead to banking and financial instability, as well as large fluctuations in asset prices, by inducing large portfolio shifts between domestic and foreign currency-denominated assets.

The evidence suggests that this last rationale for *fear of floating* — mitigating adverse effects of currency fluctuations on balance sheets and their impact on domestic financial markets, especially in dollarised

---

[5] Foreign exchange market intervention has taken a variety of forms, including, for instance, outright foreign exchange transactions in the spot or futures foreign exchange markets using non-deliverable forward contracts (NDFCs), where the central bank pays counterparties the equivalent in domestic currency. See Garcia and Volpon (2014), Domanski *et al.* (2016) and Gonzalez *et al.* (2018).

countries — has become increasingly important rationale for foreign exchange intervention in recent years.[6] From that perspective, foreign exchange market intervention can be viewed as complementing macroprudential regulation or as a bona fide macroprudential policy instrument in its own right, in addition to contributing to exchange rate stability — as documented in empirical studies (see Fratzscher *et al.*, 2019). However, as discussed next, much depends on the extent to which intervention is sterilised, and whether sterilisation itself may contribute to macroeconomic volatility through expansionary effects.

2.3.3. Price stability and financial stability

As noted in Section 1, the role of monetary and macroprudential policies in achieving macroeconomic and financial stability has been the subject of an extensive debate since the GFC. Two issues have dominated this debate. The first relates to the extent to which central banks, in addition to pursuing a price stability objective, should also respond directly to measures of financial fragility. The reason, according to some observers, is that an IT central bank focusing exclusively on its standard macroeconomic objectives may neglect information about the build-up of financial imbalances that do not translate immediately into headline inflation. As a result, policy interest rates may not rise sufficiently, or rapidly enough, to prevent the build-up of financial imbalances.

The second issue relates to how best to combine monetary policy and macroprudential regulation, given that both policies influence each other's transmission process to the economy. Indeed, the credit and business cycle effects of macroprudential policy may influence price developments and monetary policy decisions, whereas changes in monetary policy, even when they are motivated solely by price stability considerations, may affect systemic financial risks through their impact on the cost and availability of credit, as well as their effect on asset prices. These linkages create potential trade-offs in the use of these policies with respect to achieving

---

[6] See Adler and Tovar (2014) and Patel and Cavallino (2019). Another motive for foreign exchange intervention is the need to build up foreign exchange reserves as self-insurance against external shocks.

simultaneously macroeconomic and financial stability. Addressing these two issues is at the core of the IIT regime discussed next.

2.3.4. Monetary and macroprudential policies: Complements or substitutes?

As noted earlier, two issues that have dominated the debate on the design of IT regimes in the post-GFC world relate to the extent to which central banks, in addition to pursuing a price stability objective, should also respond to systemic financial risks, and how best to combine monetary policy and macroprudential regulation, given that both policies influence each other's transmission process to the economy. Indeed, there is now a large amount of evidence to suggest that monetary policy may affect not only price stability but also financial stability, through various channels — including a risk-taking channel, as discussed by Borio and Zhu (2012). Indeed, changes in interest rates affect not only aggregate demand and supply but also financial conditions through intermediation costs, asset prices, borrowing and collateral constraints, banks' balance sheets and risk-taking behaviour, and default risks as well as capital flows and exchange rates. Conversely, it is also now well established that macroprudential policy regimes can affect the monetary transmission mechanism (Agénor, 2020, Chapters 2 and 3). These interactions have led to an ongoing debate on whether monetary and macroprudential policies are complements or substitutes in achieving macroeconomic and financial stability.[7] In what follows we examine the various arguments for and against complementarity and provide an overall assessment of the state of this debate.[8]

2.3.4.1. Tinbergen's rule and the nature of shocks

A broad interpretation of complementarity in this context is that both policy interest rate and a (representative) macroprudential instrument

---

[7] For a more detailed discussion of the issue of complementarity or substitutability between macroprudential and monetary policies, see Adrian and Liang (2018), Carrillo et al. (2017) and Agénor and Flamini (2022), and the references therein.

[8] The issue of what monetary policy should react to, given that there is no consensus on what "financial stability" means, is discussed later on.

are needed to achieve both objectives of price and financial stability — in line with Tinbergen's rule.[9] This allows the central bank to achieve exactly, and continuously (in the absence of temporary shocks and if dynamic rules are sued) its targets. Complementarity can occur in two ways: (1) each instrument mitigates the other's adverse side-effects; and (2) both instruments reinforce each other's benefits.

However, in practice, central banks typically aim to minimise deviations from targets, rather than achieving them exactly and continuously. If so, each instrument may affect both targets in the same direction (reducing volatility, for instance). They may therefore be substitutes at times, depending on the shock and on which instrument can be deployed. Indeed, substitutability means that the use of either one of the two instruments helps to mitigate macroeconomic (in)stability and financial (in)stability. Put differently, instruments can be (partial) substitutes once we depart from the view that the two targets have to be achieved exactly. For instance, consider the case of a massive inflow of capital (or *sudden flood*, as referred to by Agénor et al. (2014, 2018)). As is well-known, in such conditions there are side effects of monetary policy that limit its use. Macroprudential policy — or another instrument, such as temporary capital controls — may be a (partial) substitute (see Agénor and Pereira da Silva (2021)). Thus, if both are used to some degree, relying more on one allows policymakers to rely less on the other.

At the same time, depending on the origin of shocks, a trade-off may emerge between the two objectives when a single instrument is used. Consider, for instance, a negative demand shock. Either policy can be used to lower interest rates, to sustain credit expansion and output and prevent deflation. A reduction in policy interest rates lowers the cost of borrowing and stimulates lending. However, if credit expands too rapidly, financial vulnerabilities can be exacerbated; a potential conflict between macroeconomic stability and financial stability objectives may emerge. A macroprudential policy tightening may be needed to mitigate the initial

---

[9] Strictly speaking, Tinbergen's principle is concerned with the existence of a solution to the dynamic system of equations driving the economy; it does not assert that any given set of policy responses will, in effect, lead to that solution. To make that assertion, it is necessary to investigate the stability properties of that system.

drop in the loan rate. The policies are adjusted in opposite directions, but they fundamentally complement each other.

Alternatively, consider a positive supply shock, which raises output and reduces inflation. In response to lower inflation, the central bank lowers the policy rate, which again stimulates lending. To dampen the increase in credit and mitigate financial stability risks, the macroprudential regulator needs again to tighten its policy, in order to attenuate the initial drop in the loan rate. Policies are adjusted in opposite directions, but once again they are fundamentally complementary. In other words, there is no difference between a (negative) demand shock and a (positive) supply shock, if monetary policy responds primarily to inflation.

However, if the tightening of macroprudential policy is too aggressive, the result could be a contraction in investment and aggregate demand. This could magnify downward pressure on inflation — which would, in turn, call for the central bank to reduce further the policy interest rate, and so on. Monetary and macroprudential policies would be in conflict and partially offset each other. Lower inflation requires a more accommodative monetary policy, but credit expansion necessitates a tightening of macroprudential policy. However, by solving *jointly* for the two policies, the trade-off between objectives can be internalised — regardless of the nature of the coordination arrangement that exists between policy authorities.

Finally, consider a financial shock, in the form of a drop in in the bank markup over the marginal cost of funds, i.e., the policy rate. The shock lowers the loan rate and stimulates credit and output, while raising inflation. In response, the central bank must tighten the policy rate, which raises the cost of credit. The regulator also tightens macroprudential policy in response to credit growth. There is no conflict between objectives and this time complementarity implies that instruments are adjusted in the same direction to address risks to macroeconomic and financial stability.

2.3.4.2. Should monetary policy lean against the wind?

The next issue to address is whether monetary policy should be used to *lean against the wind* of financial vulnerabilities. There are four main arguments for doing so: a short implementation lag; the fact that monetary policy can mitigate financial system procyclicality; the fact that it is a blunt instrument, which "gets through all the cracks" and the fact that it is generally (although not always) less subject to political pressures.

First, monetary policy decisions are typically implemented quickly, whereas the time needed to deploy or some macroprudential policy instruments can be significant. For instance, when countercyclical capital buffers are adjusted, banks are typically given up to a year to adjust their capital ratios. The goal is to mitigate the risk of a credit crunch. The decision to use monetary policy should therefore be time-contingent and should depend not only on the availability of other macroprudential tools but also on how quickly these tools can be deployed. Second, monetary policy may be quite effective in terms of mitigating the inherent procyclicality of the financial system, which tends to amplify shocks occurring elsewhere in the economy. This may be due to overly optimistic expectations and the tendency to underprice risks in good times, as well as overreaction in bad times. By leaning against the financial cycle, a more active monetary policy may mitigate procyclicality, while at the same time contributing to stabilise conventional macroeconomic targets, namely, output and inflation. Third, monetary policy gets through "all the cracks", because it affects funding costs for all. It is difficult to escape its reach through (domestic and international) regulatory arbitrage, as may occur when macroprudential instruments are deployed. Finally, macroprudential policy is more subject to lobbying and political pressure — as illustrated, for instance, by the reaction of financial sector operators to higher capital requirements when Basel III was introduced — compared to monetary policy. The overall implication is that monetary policy should be tightened more during booms (even if inflation appears to be stable in the near term) and eased less aggressively during busts. Tightening during booms helps to restrain the build-up of financial imbalances.

There are also several arguments *against* the use of monetary policy to respond to risks to financial stability. These arguments relate to the fact that monetary policy itself may be a source of financial instability; the policy rate can be too blunt an instrument; concerns with financial stability may weaken the credibility of the central bank and hamper its ability to achieve price stability and the use of monetary policy may be subject to constraints in an open economy.

First, monetary policy itself may induce boom-bust cycles in asset prices; this is because low interest rates may promote a search for yield and excessive risk-taking (Borio and Zhu, 2012). Some observers have argued that, in advanced economies, monetary policy was too loose prior to the GFC and that it contributed to growing financial imbalances. However, there is no evidence that monetary policy is a systematic cause of boom-bust cycles in MICs. In fact, given the prevalence of non-competitive credit markets in these countries, low policy rates may mean higher spreads, higher profits and possibly *less* systemic risk to the financial system.

Second, while the bluntness of the policy rate can be an advantage (as noted earlier), it may also be a drawback. By affecting funding costs for all, it may have adverse supply-side effects if working capital needs, for instance, are financed to a significant extent by bank credit. If excessive credit growth occurs in specific sectors (such as real estate), strengthening countercyclical sectoral macroprudential tools, such as the debt-to-income (DTI) ratio, the loan-to-value (LTV) ratio and the debt-service-to-income (DSTI) ratio, is more appropriate. Targeted countercyclical tools, such as capital buffers, liquidity requirements, and dynamic (or, more correctly, cyclically-adjusted) provisions, may also prove more effective, not only in terms of dampening credit growth and reducing risk-taking in these sectors but also, and more generally, in terms of increasing the resilience of the financial system. At the same time, it is also important to note that there is mixed evidence on the effectiveness of some of these tools. In comprehensive reviews, the Bank for International Settlements (2018) and Borio *et al.* (2022) noted that macroprudential policy measures have indeed been generally successful in terms of strengthening the financial system's resilience. By construction, capital and liquidity requirements increase buffers available to banks, and naturally contribute to a more resilient and stable financial system. Some sectoral macroprudential tools, such as LTV and DSTI limits, have also helped to moderate credit growth and house price booms. Evidence to that effect has been provided by Zhang and Zoli (2016) and Kim and Mehrotra (2018) for Asia, and by Akinci and Olmstead-Rumsey (2018) for a broader group of countries.

However, overall, their restraining impact has not always been sufficient to prevent the emergence, or the amplification, of financial imbalances. Indeed, several studies, summarised in Agénor and Pereira da Silva (2019), show that macroprudential policies did not prevent rapid credit growth in a number of MICs.[10] A possible reason for that is possible implementation problems. With respect to countercyclical capital buffers, for instance, if it is costly for banks to raise capital in a recession, they may choose to cut lending immediately — thereby worsening the recession. The use of this instrument also faces serious operational challenges — even in a strong supervisory environment. In particular, the Basel III recommendation is to use the gap between the credit-to-GDP ratio and its trend as a guide in adjusting capital buffers (see Drehman and Tsatsaronis (2014)). However, the credit-to-GDP ratio is a noisy indicator; if this ratio rises because of a fall in the denominator (GDP) rather than an increase in the numerator (credit) — as tends to occur in the early stages of a recession — its mechanical use would then produce unintended effects. This may help to explain why few countries have activated this tool since it was introduced.

Alternatively, some observers have suggested that a larger set of indicators should be used for systemic risk assessment, including asset prices, leverage ratios, changes in lending standards, measures of balance sheet stretch and so on (Behn *et al.*, 2013; IMF, 2013). The problem, however, is the risk of conflicting signals, which implies that a hierarchical monitoring system may still be necessary. Finally, the issue of how macroprudential tools interact is not yet fully understood. For instance, do capital buffers and loan loss provisions, whose goal is to address unexpected and expected loan losses, respectively, generate different market signals? Do they have different effect on banks' risk-taking incentives over the cycle?

Third, if the central bank lacks credibility, adding a financial stability objective to monetary policy may weaken the public's perception of its commitment to price stability and possibly destabilise expectations, making it more difficult to achieve low and stable inflation. To illustrate the issue at stake, consider once again the case of a negative demand

---

[10] There is also evidence of asymmetry in the effects of some macroprudential tools; they seem to help to manage the expansionary phase of financial cycles, but work less well in busts. See Claessens *et al.* (2013), Cerutti *et al.* (2017), Altunbas *et al.* (2018) and Borio *et al.* (2022).

shock, which lowers both output and inflation. In a standard IT regime, because there is no trade-off between price stability and output stability, the appropriate response is to lower the policy rate. This reduces the loan rate, which stimulates lending and raises aggregate demand and prices. However, if the shock is persistent and low rates for too long promote a *search for yield*, there may be a conflict between macroeconomic (price and output) stability and financial stability.

A proposed response by some in this case is to keep interest rates higher than required and lengthen the horizon for achieving the inflation target. However, concerns about systemic risk may be difficult to convey to agents, partly because in practice there is no consensus (yet) on defining "financial stability". If so, lengthening the target horizon could have adverse effects on expectations and monetary policy credibility. The key reason is that even though a more gradual policy response may help to maintain both macroeconomic and financial stability, there is no credibility gain from eliminating or avoiding a hypothetical event, i.e., an episode of severe financial volatility. Thus, if, to begin with, the central bank lacks credibility, adding a financial stability objective to monetary policy may well have an adverse impact on price expectations — thereby making it more difficult to achieve and maintain low inflation. In such conditions, there may be a *stabilisation cost* associated with using monetary policy to address financial stability concerns. Yet, it is important also to realise that a financial stability objective may not always adversely affect central bank credibility; this depends also on initial conditions. If initially inflation is above target, a rise in the policy rate motivated by systemic risk concerns may also be beneficial from the perspective of macroeconomic stability.

Fourth, depending on the nature of shocks, the scope for using monetary policy may be limited. This is the case when countries are faced with a *sudden flood* of capital, triggered by lower world interest rates (Agénor et al., 2014, 2018). These inflows are often associated with real exchange rate appreciation, widening current account deficits, a domestic boom characterised by a credit expansion, asset price pressures, increases in aggregate demand, an expansion in output and — often over time only, given the initial appreciation — inflationary pressures. In such conditions, the scope for adjusting interest rates to respond to macroeconomic and financial risks is limited, because higher domestic interest rates may exacerbate capital inflows. This creates a role for macroprudential policy — as well as other measures, such as sterilised intervention and temporary capital controls, as discussed later — to manage capital inflows and mitigate their destabilising effects on the domestic economy.

The foregoing discussion suggests that depending on shocks, and assumptions about how the economy operates, monetary and macroprudential policies are generally complementary.[11] This does not mean that these policies should operate in the same direction — only that both are needed, to avoid conflicts when a single tool is used. Under some circumstances, they can operate as (partial) substitutes. In particular, *leaning against the wind* may contribute to promoting financial stability when *all hands on deck* are needed. The fact that there may be a "credibility problem" created by bestowing a financial stability objective to the monetary authority means that there are new challenges for central banks in terms of the design of their institutional mandates (and more generally the division of tasks between policy authorities), the degree of transparency and communication of their policy decisions, and accountability. As discussed next, these are indeed some of the key issues that an IIT regime must address. In particular, because the concept of "financial stability" has proved elusive, it is important to adopt an *operational* approach and define it in terms of an *intermediate financial target*, to avoid confusing the public.

3. IIT: Definition and key features

From the perspective of MICs, IIT can be defined as a flexible IT regime with four characteristics:

(1) Monetary and macroprudential policies are calibrated jointly to achieve macroeconomic and financial stability;
(2) The central bank is bestowed an explicit but contingent financial stability mandate, and the scope — depending, in particular,

---

[11] Evidence that macroprudential and monetary policies are complements in achieving price and financial stability is provided by Bruno *et al.* (2017), in a study focusing on Asian economies. In the same vein, Gambacorta and Murcia (2017) find that macroprudential policies that are used as complements of monetary policy have larger negative effects on credit growth than other types of measures.

on the nature and persistence of shocks, and on how quickly macroprudential tools can be deployed — for using policy interest rates to respond to financial imbalances;
(3) The policy toolkit includes foreign exchange intervention and possibly temporary capital controls, which should be combined with monetary and macroprudential tools — as needed, and in ways that depend on the economy's structural characteristics, the nature of the shock that policymakers must respond to, and the speed (or frequency) with which each instrument can deployed; and
(4) Greater transparency and communication, through integrated, and systematic, policy assessments.

3.1. *Joint calibration of policy instruments*

Under an IIT regime, monetary and macroprudential policies should be calibrated jointly to achieve macroeconomic and financial stability. The key reason is that the transmission mechanisms of these policies are closely intertwined and operate largely through the same channels — the credit market, which continues to play a critical role MICs, and asset prices. Both policies affect the cost at which the public borrows, either directly or indirectly. As a result, they both affect credit growth — a variable that has been linked consistently to financial instability and asset price bubbles (see Agénor and Montiel (2015) and Agénor (2020)). Indeed, excessively rapid credit growth tends to be accompanied by a weakening of lending standards and credit quality, which tends to increase financial fragility in a downturn. There is also robust evidence to suggest that credit booms significantly raise the likelihood of an asset price bust or a financial crisis in MICs.

It is also important to note that a joint calibration is necessary whether monetary and macroprudential policies are complementary or not, and regardless of whether the CB *leans against the wind* — given the growing consensus (discussed earlier) that macroprudential policy may not be sufficient to address financial stability concerns. Thus, it does not depend on the exact nature of the institutional mandate bestowed to each authority, as long as there is a framework for coordination.

Naturally, for this joint calibration to be done effectively, policymakers must use models where the financial system, and financial frictions, are explicitly accounted for, and interactions between the transmission mechanisms of monetary and macroprudential policies are well captured. This would also allow an evaluation of the gains from policy coordination, which depend not only on the model but also the nature of the policy objective functions and the policy rules. These operational implications are discussed further in the next section.

3.2. *Explicit but contingent financial stability mandate*

A second feature of IIT is the emphasis on the fact that the financial stability mandate must be *explicit*. Otherwise, should the central bank raise interest rates for financial stability considerations, it could destabilise markets and foster volatility. This risk is all the more serious if, to begin with, the central bank's credibility is weak. An explicit mandate avoids uncertainty about policy preferences and promotes transparency; but because financial stability (as a final goal) is difficult to define, the mandate should be carefully worded, to avoid confusing markets. In particular, the financial stability goal should be defined in terms of an intermediate target — such as excessive credit growth, or a broader set of indicators, including, for instance, asset prices, as discussed earlier. There are three reasons for that: (1) the fact that monetary policy has a short implementation lag, compared to some macroprudential policies — even those (such as capital buffers or cyclically adjusted loan-loss provisions) that are explicitly countercyclical in nature; (2) the fact that macroprudential policy, while it has helped to increase financial system resilience, has (so far) been less successful at mitigating credit growth; and (3) there are circumstances under which macroprudential tools cannot be deployed, or are deemed insufficiently powerful, to mitigate credit growth and an across-the-board adjustment in policy rates is warranted. Moreover, the possibility of using policy interest rates to address financial stability concerns, either by themselves or possibly in coordination with macroprudential instruments, if and when needed, must also be stated explicitly. At the present time, this is not the case, even in countries where the central bank's mandate has already been extended to account explicitly for financial stability considerations (Archer, 2017).

At the same time, the central bank's financial stability mandate, and the decision to use monetary policy to respond to financial risks, must be *state contingent*. Indeed, the expanded mandate should state explicitly that there are "exceptional circumstances" that may warrant the use of monetary policy to promote financial stability. These "exceptional circumstances" need to be clearly explained when they occur. The reason is the need to recognise and measure, in real time, excessive credit growth (a robust predictor of financial instability for MICs) or destabilising changes in a broader set of indicators (which, as noted earlier, is more difficult).

The use of the policy interest rate must be *time contingent* as well, because of the need to act in timely fashion. This is difficult because of the standard problem of control lags — related not only to the impact of changes in policy instruments on market rates but also the impact of changes in market rates on private behavior. A time-contingent use of monetary policy is important also because of the need to determine when *all hands on deck* are required. Indeed, there is a need to assess why existing macroprudential tools are not sufficient and/or why they cannot be deployed quickly. This may be difficult in real time. As noted earlier, the counter cyclical capital buffer is generally subject to a long implementation lag; banks are typically given up to a year to comply with an increase in capital ratios. Thus, the impact on the cost of borrowing, and thus credit growth, can be delayed; (cyclically-adjusted) loan-loss provisions may also be subject to the same problem.

A key issue in this context is whether financial system vulnerabilities build up gradually in response to credit booms. If that is the case, implementation lag is less of a concern. If not, there is a rationale for getting monetary policy to contribute to mitigating financial imbalances, and/or for using other macroprudential instruments that can be deployed quickly (such as reserve requirements in MICs). If monetary policy is called upon to react, it is important to ensure that this is done in a timely fashion. Delays in recognising the need for action (i.e., the point at which macroprudential measures alone are deemed insufficient) could make the central bank's intervention too late to be effective. From that perspective, and given that control lags exist for all tools, it is important for the central bank to react *expected* credit market developments — just as it reacts to *expected* price developments in a standard IT regime.

3.3. *Foreign exchange intervention and capital controls*

A third feature of IIT is that while central banks should maintain a flexible exchange rate regime, to mitigate excessive volatility and promote macroeconomic and financial stability they may need to supplement, and combine, monetary and macroprudential policies with foreign exchange market intervention and/or temporary capital controls. The extent to which these instruments should be deployed depends in general on the economy's structural characteristics (including the depth of the foreign exchange market) and the nature of the shocks impinging on the economy.

3.3.1. Foreign exchange intervention

There is significant evidence that, in recent years, in many MICs — even among those operating an IT regime — central banks have consistently reacted to foreign exchange market pressure with frequent intervention.[12] Moreover, there is evidence that the decision to intervene has been increasingly driven by the goal of limiting exchange rate volatility, rather than concerns about competitiveness, the degree of exchange rate pass-through, currency and maturity mismatches or the need to build foreign-currency reserves for precautionary reasons (Adler and Tovar, 2014; Patel and Cavallino, 2019). The focus on mitigating exchange rate volatility — rather than on a particular exchange rate level — has itself reflected concerns with the potential impact of such volatility on price expectations and price stability (especially with a high pass-through) and on financial stability (as a result of balance-sheet mismatches,

---

[12] In practice, foreign exchange intervention has often been asymmetric — through the spot market with large inflows, and through the forward market with large outflows (as is the case for Brazil), the latter reflecting a fear of losing reserves. See Adler *et al.* (2020) for a discussion.

for instance). In that sense, foreign exchange intervention has also a macroprudential dimension, which is being increasingly recognised.[13]

There has also been greater recognition that sterilised foreign exchange intervention, by inducing an increase in credit and aggregate demand, may be expansionary.[14] In Agénor et al. (2020) and Agénor and Pereira da Silva (2021), for instance, sterilised intervention, in the presence of economies of scope in banking, creates a direct financial channel through which exchange rate fluctuations may amplify credit market fluctuations. This financial channel operates separately from the conventional channel through which the exchange rate can affect domestic financial conditions — according to which an appreciation, induced by capital inflows, puts downward pressure on prices, thereby resulting in lower policy and market interest rates and an expansion in investment. If credit is already growing at a significant pace, this may exacerbate financial stability risks. Although the evidence that foreign exchange market intervention may weaken the central bank's ability to stabilise output and prices remains limited and far from robust, it implies that the macroeconomic effects of intervention depend importantly on the monetary and macroprudential policy responses that are being implemented at the same time, i.e., on the overall policy mix.

3.3.2. Temporary capital controls

In an IIT regime, it is also important for central banks to have access in their policy toolkit to temporary capital controls — in the form of taxes on foreign borrowing, taxes on fixed income and equity inflows, and so on — particularly in response to external financial shocks which may have a large effect on capital flows. Such controls may not only be able to mitigate the macroeconomic effects of capital flows (as discussed earlier) but also, to the extent that they may help to mitigate credit growth and exchange rate volatility associated with these flows, they may also have a financial stability objective. Thus, just like foreign exchange rate intervention, temporary capital controls may also have a

---

[13] See Agénor et al. (2020), who also discussed the evidence.
[14] See Garcia (2011), Agénor et al. (2020), as well as the references therein.

macroprudential dimension. This is particularly the case if they relate to the ability of domestic banks to borrow abroad.

It is also worth noting that, in general, the evidence regarding the effectiveness of capital controls in terms of their impact on the *volume* (as opposed to the *composition*) of capital flows, and macroeconomic stability, remains mixed.[15] However, there is only scant evidence on whether *temporary* (or countercyclical) capital controls, as opposed to structural (or permanent) controls, have contributed to greater macroeconomic and financial stability.[16] Temporary effectiveness is all that is needed when faced with sudden floods and neither monetary policy nor macroprudential policy can respond quickly and effectively. At the same time, it is important for policymakers to understand that, even when imposed on a temporary basis, capital controls may have adverse signaling effects (with respect notably to the country's commitment to open capital markets), which may destabilise expectations and exacerbate macroeconomic and financial volatility. These adverse effects should be factored into the decision to activate this instrument in the first place.

3.4. *Transparency and communication*

Under an IIT regime, transparency and communication must be improved significantly. Key reasons, as noted earlier, are the need to explain to the public what policy authorities mean by "financial stability" (an elusive concept, as noted earlier), what the "contingent" nature of the financial stability mandate of the central bank signifies, and why joint calibration of policy instruments is necessary in the presence of several objectives. From that perspective, it is important for central banks to publish an *integrated report* on macroeconomic and financial stability. Separate narratives, as most IT countries do at the present time (i.e., the publication of separate inflation or monetary policy reports, and financial stability reports, often at different time

---

[15] See Agénor and Pereira da Silva (2019) and the references therein.
[16] Indeed, as noted by Eichengreen and Rose (2014), historically capital controls have often taken a permanent form.

intervals, and with the latter only rarely focusing on cyclical risks to the financial system) may confuse markets and make inflation expectations more volatile.

4. The mechanics of IIT regimes

A key feature of IIT, as noted earlier, is that the joint calibration of monetary and macroprudential policies should be conducted in macroeconomic models that properly account for (1) the role of banks and financial market imperfections; and (2) the fact that macroprudential regimes may alter the monetary transmission mechanism, whereas monetary policy may affect key operational targets for financial stability, such as credit growth, interest rate spreads and asset prices.

There is by now a large literature on macroeconomic models with both types of characteristics. The development of these models has been spurred in part by the renewed emphasis in macroeconomics, since the GFC, on the role of the financial system in transmitting and amplifying shocks occurring elsewhere in the economy. This literature is large and has been reviewed in a number of contributions.[17] In the present case, to illustrate the issue at stake, we begin with a simple macroeconomic model of a bank-dependent closed economy with credit market frictions in which both monetary policy and macroprudential regulation can be analysed.[18] This model is simple enough to be solved analytically and for its properties to be illustrated graphically. It provides intuition for some of the results that can be gauged from more advanced, quantitative models. Of course, there are a number of issues that simple models (by design) cannot address; we therefore consider next a related class of more advanced quantitative models and discuss how these models can be put to use in an IIT regime.

---

[17] See Agénor (2020, Chapter 1) and the references therein.
[18] The model is essentially an extension of the closed-economy framework developed in Agénor (2020, Chapter 2), in which house prices and their impact on collateral values are considered explicitly.

4.1. A simple integrated macro model

Following a description of the structure of the model, the macroeconomic equilibrium is characterised. The macroeconomic effects of monetary and macroprudential policies, both individually and jointly, are then analysed.

4.1.1. Model structure

Consider a closed economy producing a single homogeneous good. There are six categories of agents: firms, households, commercial banks, the government, the central bank and the financial regulator. Their behaviour is briefly considered in turn, before market-clearing conditions are specified.

4.1.1.1. Firms

Firms pay a fraction $\psi^W \in (0,1)$ of their wage bill in advance and to do so borrow from banks. Working capital loans are not subject to default risk and are therefore made at a rate that reflects the cost of borrowing from the central bank, i.e., the refinance rate, i^R. Thus, if W denote the nominal wage and N the quantity of labour employed, the wage bill, inclusive of borrowing costs, is defined as $(1+\psi^W i^R) W \cdot N$.

The production function takes a Cobb–Douglas form,

$$Y = N^\alpha (K_0)^{1-\alpha} \qquad (1)$$

where K_0 is the beginning-of-period stock of capital and $\alpha \in (0,1)$.

The nominal wage, is rigid at $\underline{W}$. Profit maximisation yields therefore

$$\underline{Y^s} = Y^s(P; i^R), \quad \partial Y^s/\partial P > 0, \quad \partial Y^s/\partial i^R < 0 \qquad (2)$$

which shows that higher prices, or a lower cost of borrowing, lead to an increase in output.

Investment is given by

$$I = I(i^L - \pi^e), \quad I' < 0 \qquad (3)$$

where i^L is the loan rate and π^e the expected inflation rate, assumed constant. Thus, investment is inversely related to the real loan rate.

4.1.1.2. Households

Household labor supply is perfectly elastic at the going wage.[19] They hold two categories of financial assets: currency (M, which bears no interest) and bank deposits, D. Household financial wealth, F, is thus defined as:

$$F = M + D \qquad (4)$$

Assets are imperfect substitutes. The deposit-cash ratio is defined as

$$D/M = \nu(i^D), \qquad (5)$$

where i^D is the deposit rate and $\nu' > 0$. An increase in the deposit rate raises the share of deposits relative to cash. Combining (4) and (5) yields

$$D/F = d(i^D) \qquad (6)$$

where $d' > 0$.

Total household wealth, A^H, is defined as

$$A = F + P^H \underline{H} \qquad (7)$$

where $\underline{H}$ is the (constant) quantity of housing and P^H its nominal price, which is fully flexible and adjusts instantaneously to equilibrate supply and demand.

The real demand for housing is given by

$$H/P = h(i^D - \pi^e, \pi^{H,e}, Y^s) \qquad (8)$$

where $\pi^{H,e}$ is the expected rate of increase in house prices, and with $\partial h/\partial(i^D - \pi^e) < 0$, $\partial h/\partial \pi^{H,e} > 0$, and $\partial h/\partial Y^s > 0$. Thus, an increase in the real deposit rate lowers the demand for housing, whereas an increase in expected housing inflation, or in income, tends to raise it. The first

---

[19] This assumption (which implies that effort provides no disutility) helps to simplify the analysis by avoiding the case where, given that the nominal wage is exogenous, unemployment emerges in equilibrium.

two effects are standard portfolio effects, whereas the third captures a positive correlation (or procyclical relationship) between house prices and economic activity.[20]

Household spending, C, depends (1) positively on income, Y^s; (2) negatively on the real deposit rate, $i^D - \pi^e$; and (3) positively on beginning-of-period real financial wealth:

$$C = \alpha_1 Y^s - \alpha_2(i^D - \pi^e) + \alpha_3(F_0/P) \qquad (9)$$

where $\alpha_1 \in (0,1)$ is the marginal propensity to consume and $\alpha_2, \alpha_3 > 0$.

The positive effect of income on consumption is consistent with the evidence on liquidity constraints on households in MICs (Agénor and Montiel, 2015, Chapter 2). The negative effect of the real deposit rate captures an intertemporal substitution effect. The positive effect of real financial wealth on consumption captures the fact that individuals tend to spend more when the real value of their financial assets increases — a well-documented fact.[21]

4.1.1.3. Commercial banks

Bank assets consist of loans to firms (to finance both working capital needs and investment), L, and reserves held at the central bank, RR. Their liabilities consist of deposits, D, and borrowing from the central bank, L^B. The balance sheet of the banking system is thus

$$L + RR = D + L^B \qquad (10)$$

Reserves do not pay interest and are determined by:

$$RR = \mu D \qquad (11)$$

where $\mu \in (0,1)$ is the required reserve ratio.

---

[20] Evidence that house prices are procyclical is provided, for instance, by Cesa-Bianchi et al. (2015).
[21] For simplicity, it is assumed that interest on deposits is paid, and profits are distributed, at the end of each period and do not affect current consumption. In addition, capital gains and losses due to changes in house prices are assumed to affect savings only, not consumption.

The deposit market is competitive, and banks view deposits and central bank loans as perfect substitutes. Thus, the return on these deposits is equal to the cost of borrowing from the central bank, corrected for the (implicit) cost of holding unremunerated reserves:

$$i^D = (1 - \mu)i^R \qquad (12)$$

The interest rate on investment loans, i^L, is the sum of the marginal cost of funds, i^R, a premium that reflects the possibility of default, θ, and a macroprudential tax, τ^L, which captures the cost effect of prudential instruments such as capital requirements and loan-loss provisions:

$$i^L = i^R + \theta + \gamma \tau^L \qquad (13)$$

where $\gamma > 0$.

Households own all firms, and they make their housing assets available to the firm they own at no cost for use as collateral for loans. The premium that banks impose is therefore inversely related to collateralisable net worth, i.e., the difference between the value of real estate assets, $P^H \underline{H}$, minus their liabilities, the beginning-of-period borrowing for investment, L_0:

$$\theta = \theta(\kappa P^H \underline{H} - L_0) \qquad (14)$$

where $\kappa \in (0, 1)$ is the proportion of real estate assets that can effectively be used or pledged as collateral and $\theta' < 0$. Thus, the higher the value of the collateralisable real assets that firms can pledge, relative to initial liabilities, the lower the premium and the cost of borrowing. Because both $\underline{H}$ and L_0 are predetermined, the premium varies inversely with house prices, P^H.

Given that the supply of deposits, and thus required reserves (for μ given), are determined by households, and that the outstanding stock of loans is determined by firms' demand for credit, Equation (10) implies that borrowing from the central bank is determined residually:

$$LB = L + RR - D \qquad (15)$$

4.1.1.4. Central bank and regulator

The central bank supplies liquidity to commercial banks through a standing facility at the prevailing refinance rate, i^R. Its balance sheet consists, on the asset side, of loans to commercial banks, L^B, and, on the liability side, of the monetary base, given by the sum of currency in circulation, M, and required reserves, RR:

$$L^B = M + RR \qquad (16)$$

The regulator sets both the required reserve ratio, μ, and the tax rate on loans, τ^L.

To highlight the role of reserve requirements, suppose that the composition of bank liabilities affects the cost of borrowing from the central bank. Thus, the refinance rate is defined as the sum of a constant base policy rate, i^T, and a penalty rate, which is increasing in the ratio of central bank borrowing to deposits:

$$i^R = i^T + \upsilon(L_0^B/D) \qquad (17)$$

where $\upsilon' \geq 0$.[22] From Equations (6) and (12), $D = d(i^D)F_0 = d[(1-\mu)i^R]F_0$. Thus, a higher required reserve ratio reduces the deposit rate, which lowers deposits and raises the central bank borrowing-deposit ratio, L_0^B/D. From Equation (17), this in turn leads to an increase in the penalty and refinance rates, and consequently the loan rate. Equation (17) captures in a simple way the assumption of imperfect substitutability between deposits and central bank borrowing, from the perspective of the monetary authority.

4.1.1.5. Market-clearing conditions

There are six equilibrium conditions to consider: four for financial markets (cash, deposits, loans to firms, and central bank loans to commercial banks), one for the housing market and one for the goods market.

---

[22] To simplify matters, in Equation (17), central bank borrowing is measured at the beginning of the period.

At the prevailing deposit, loan, and refinance rates, the markets for deposits, investment loans and central bank credit adjust through quantities. The equilibrium condition of the housing market is given by

$$H/P = P^H \underline{H}/P \tag{18}$$

which, using Equation (8), can be solved for the real price of housing, p^H:

$$p^H = P^H/P = h(i^D - \pi^e, \pi^{H,e}, Y^s) \tag{19}$$

i.e., using Equations (2) and (12) to substitute out for Y^s and i^D,

$$p^H = p^H(P;\, i^R,\, \mu) \tag{20}$$

where

$$\partial p^H/\partial P = (\partial h/\partial Y^s)(\partial Y^s/\partial P) > 0,$$
$$\partial p^H/\partial i^R = (1-\mu)(\partial h/\partial i^D) + (\partial h/\partial Y^s)(\partial Y^s/\partial i^R) < 0,$$
$$\partial p^H/\partial \mu = -\, i^R(\partial h/\partial i^D) > 0.$$

Thus, an increase in prices, by reducing real wages and raising output and income, raises real house prices. An increase in the refinance rate, by reducing output and raising the deposit rate, lowers them. An increase in the required reserve ratio, by reducing the deposit rate, raises the demand for houses as well as their price.

The goods market equilibrium condition is

$$Y^s = C + I \tag{21}$$

The last equilibrium condition relates to the market for cash. However, it is not an independent condition and can be eliminated.[23]

4.1.2. Macroeconomic equilibrium

To establish macroeconomic equilibrium, there are three conditions to consider, related to the financial market, the housing market and the

---

[23] See Agénor (2020, Chapter 2). Recall that consumption depends on beginning-of-period nominal financial wealth, so changes in cash holdings have no direct effect on the equilibrium.

goods market. In solving the model, expected inflation rates are assumed constant and normalised to zero.

Consider first the housing and financial market equilibrium conditions. Substituting Equations (12) and (20) in Equation (13), and noting that $P^H = Pp^H$, yields

$$i^L = i^R + \theta[(\kappa Pp^H(P; i^R,\mu) \cdot \underline{H} - L_0] + \gamma \tau^L \tag{22}$$

i.e.,

$$i^L = FF(P; i^R, \mu, \tau^L)$$

where, given that $\partial h/\partial P > 0$, $\partial h/\partial i^R < 0$, and $\partial h/\partial \mu > 0$,

$$\partial FF/\partial P = \kappa \underline{H}[p^H + P(\partial p^H/\partial P)]\theta' < 0, \quad \partial FF/\partial i^R = 1 + \kappa \underline{H}P(\partial p^H/\partial i^R)\theta' > 0,$$
$$\partial FF/\partial \mu = \kappa \underline{H}P(\partial p^H/\partial \mu)\theta' < 0, \quad \partial FF/\partial \tau^L = \gamma > 0$$

Equation (22) defines the equilibrium condition of the financial sector and the housing market. An increase in the price of goods, P, raises output, income and the demand for real assets; as a result, house prices increase, and so do collateral values. The premium therefore falls, and so does the loan rate. This negative effect, as discussed next, is the key source of the financial accelerator effect. An increase in the refinance rate, i^R, has both a direct, one-to-one effect on the loan rate, but also an indirect effect: by raising the deposit rate it lowers the demand for housing, which puts downward pressure on house prices. As a result, the value of collateral falls, and the loan rate increases. An increase in the required reserve ratio, μ, lowers the deposit rate and raises the demand for housing; this raises house prices, and thus collateral values, thereby lowering the loan rate. An increase in the macroprudential tax, τ^L, raises the loan rate.

Consider now the equilibrium condition of the domestic goods market. Substituting the supply Equation (2) and the investment function (3), together with the consumption function (9), after substituting (12) for the deposit rate, in condition (20), and setting $\pi^e = \pi^{H,e} = 0$, gives

$$Y^s(P; i^R) = \alpha_1 Y^s - \alpha_2(1-\mu)i^R + \alpha_3(F_0/P) + I(i^L) + G.$$

Differentiating totally this expression and re-arranging yields

$$i^L = GG(P; i^R, \mu) \tag{23}$$

where

$$\partial GG/\partial P = [(1 - \alpha_1)(\partial Y^s/\partial P) + \alpha_3(F_0/P^2)]/I' < 0,$$

$$\partial GG/\partial i^R = [(1 - \alpha_1)(\partial Y^s/\partial i^R) + \alpha_2(1-\mu)]/I' \lessgtr 0, \partial GG/\partial \mu = -\alpha_2 i^R/I' < 0.$$

An increase in the goods price, P, lowers aggregate demand through a negative wealth effect on consumption. At the same time, it also boosts aggregate supply, by reducing the real wage, and raises consumption, as a result of an income effect. Because $1 - \alpha_1 > 1$, the net effect is excess supply, which requires a fall in the loan rate to increase investment and restore equilibrium. An increase in the refinance rate, i^R, has in general an ambiguous effect on the equilibrium loan rate, because it leads to a contraction in both aggregate supply and aggregate demand. It lowers output supply, as well as consumption (by reducing income and increasing incentives to save). Thus, if the supply-side effect is strong, the model can reproduce a *stagflationary effect* of contractionary monetary policy. In what follows, the focus will be on the case where ψ^W, the proportion of the wage bill financed by bank borrowing, is low enough to ensure that the supply-side effect is dominated by the demand-side effect. As a result, there is excess supply (at the initial level of prices) and this requires a reduction in the loan rate to boost demand. Consequently, $\partial GG/\partial i^R > 0$. An increase in the required reserve ratio, μ, lowers the deposit rate and mitigates incentives to save; by raising current consumption, it creates excess demand at the initial level of prices. The loan rate must fall to restore equilibrium.

Equations (22) and (23) determine the equilibrium values of the two key endogenous variables in the model: the loan rate, i^L, and the price of goods, P. Figure 6 presents the determination of macroeconomic equilibrium, in terms of the FF and GG curves. The equilibrium obtains at point E, where the two curves intersect.[24]

4.1.3 Monetary and macroprudential policies

To illustrate the functioning of the model, we consider three independent experiments: an increase in the refinance rate, an increase in the

---

[24] Based on dynamic stability considerations, it can be established that curve GG must be steeper than FF. See Agénor (2020, Chapter 2).

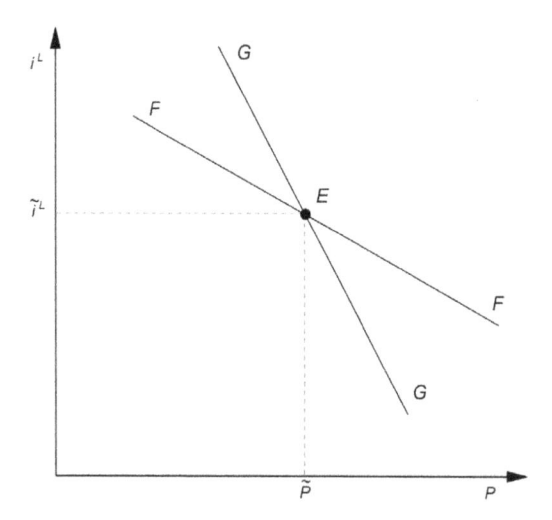

Figure 6. Macroeconomic equilibrium.
Source: Agénor (2020, Chapter 2).

macroprudential tax rate, and a rise in the required reserve ratio. For clarity, we assume in the first two cases that the liability composition effect is absent, so that $v' = 0$ in Equation (17).

Consider first an increase in the refinance rate, i^R. Macroeconomic effects are illustrated in Figure 7. The immediate impact of the policy (the marginal cost of funds for banks), it is "passed on" directly, and fully, to borrowers, thereby inducing a contraction in investment. Curve FF shifts upward, to F′ F′. On the goods market, the higher refinance rate raises directly the deposit rate, thereby lowering consumption as a result of the intertemporal substitution effect. This reduces aggregate demand; holding prices (and thus the supply of goods) constant, restoring equilibrium would require a fall in the loan rate to stimulate investment. Curve GG shifts therefore downward. The new equilibrium point, as shown in Figure 7, is at point E′.

On impact, the loan rate jumps from the initial equilibrium at point E to point B, which reflects the direct effect of a higher refinance rate. At the initial level of prices, the contraction in investment and consumption puts downward pressure on prices. During the transition, the drop in prices reduces output (by raising the real wage), income, and house prices, and the value of collateral; the rise in the premium tends to increase the loan rate. Thus, following its initial jump from E to B, the loan rate continues

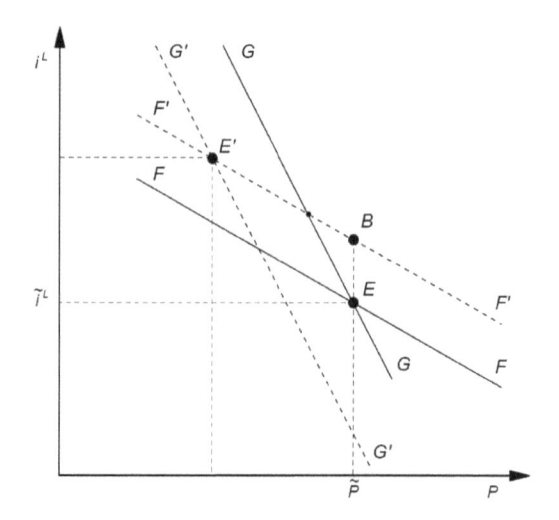

Figure 7. Increase in the refinance rate.

to increase from B to the new equilibrium point E′, corresponding to the intersection of F′ F′ and G′ G′, as prices fall to restore equilibrium in the goods market. The movement from B to E′ corresponds to the *financial accelerator effect*. It therefore exacerbates the countercyclical movement in loan rates.[25]

Next, consider an increase in the tax rate on loans, τ^L. The results are illustrated in Figure 8. A higher τ^L leads to an outward shift in FF, with no change in GG. The new equilibrium of the economy obtains at point E′. The increase in the loan rate is associated with a contraction in credit and investment, as well as a fall in prices; in turn, the fall in prices raises the real wage, which leads to a contraction in output. The reduction in income leads to lower house prices and a fall in collateral values. A financial accelerator effect is once again at play: after the jump in the loan rate from point E to point B, there is excess supply of goods (at the initial level of prices) due to the contraction in investment. As prices fall, and collateral values drop, the premium rises, thereby inducing (as before)

---

[25] At the new equilibrium E′, investment is definitely lower, given that it depends only on the loan rate. For consumption, while a higher refinance rate tends to lower spending initially, the reduction in goods prices tends to raise it, through the wealth effect. Because lower prices also lead to a contraction in output, the net effect on consumption is in general ambiguous.

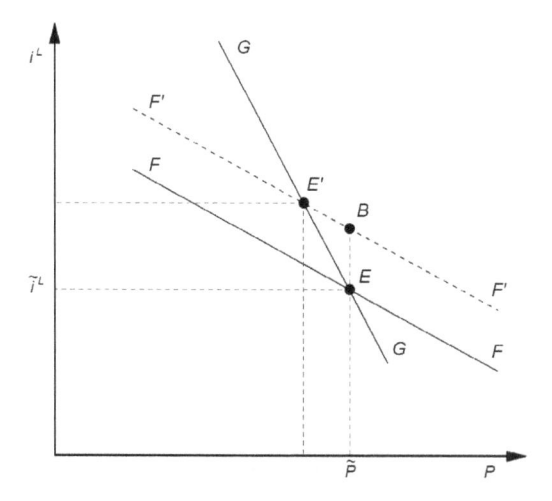

Figure 8. Increase in the tax rate on loans.

a further increase in the loan rate from B to E′. The fundamental reason why the financial accelerator effect operates is because an increase in the tax on loans, just like a rise in the refinance rate, raises, on impact, the cost of borrowing and initiates a gradual drop in prices that lowers collateral values and raises the premium during the adjustment process. The key difference between the two instruments is that because the tax on loans has no effect on the deposit rate (unlike the refinance rate), the contraction in aggregate demand at the initial level of prices results solely from a drop in investment, rather than from both consumption and investment.

The results of an increase in the required reserve ratio, μ, are reported in Figure 9, in the two cases where $\upsilon = 0$ and $\upsilon > 0$ in Equation (17). As can be inferred from Equation (12), the immediate effect of the policy is to lower the deposit rate, which reduces the incentive to save and stimulates current consumption. Suppose first that there is no liability composition effect, so that, $\upsilon = 0$. At the initial level of prices, the increase in aggregate demand requires a higher loan rate to clear the goods market; thus, GG shifts unambiguously upwards to G′ G′. In that case, the increase in the required reserve ratio has no direct effect on the loan rate, which implies that FF does not shift. The new equilibrium is at point E″; characterised by higher goods prices and a lower loan rate. Higher goods prices raise output and income, and thus house prices, which increases collateral values and lowers the loan rate. Moreover, the lower deposit rate raises the demand for real assets, which further raises house prices and lowers the cost of borrowing for firms. Put differently, in this case an increase in the required reserve ratio is *expansionary* — both because of higher consumption and investment.

However, suppose now that $v' > 0$. The fall in the deposit rate, by reducing the demand for deposits, also raises the ratio of central bank borrowing to deposits, and therefore the penalty and refinance rates, as can be inferred from Equation (17). Consumption depends as before on the deposit rate, which is given by Equation (12) as $i^D = (1 - \mu)i^R$. However, because both μ and i^R increase, the net effect on the deposit rate is now in general ambiguous; thus, in contrast to the case where $v' = 0$, curve GG could shift upwards or downwards. In Figure 9, GG is assumed to shift upwards when $v' > 0$, to facilitate the comparison between the two cases. In addition, the increase in the refinance rate implies now that FF shifts upwards. The outcome illustrated in Figure 9 corresponds to the case where v' is high enough to ensure that the shift in FF is large relative to the shift in GG, so that the new equilibrium at E' is characterised now by *lower* prices and a higher loan rate. Once again there is an accelerator effect; after jumping from E to B in response to the higher required reserve ratio, the loan rate continues to increase between B and E', as prices and collateral values fall. Put differently, the policy is now contractionary, in contrast to the case where $v' = 0$.

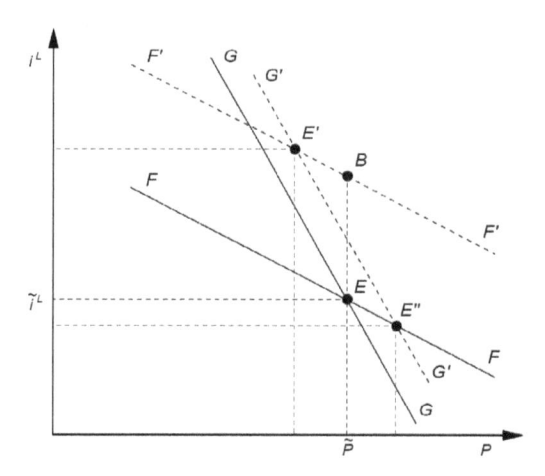

Figure 9. Increase in the required reserve ratio.

Perspectives on Integrated Inflation Targeting 659

This simple model can also be used to illustrate the benefits of combining monetary and macroprudential policies. Suppose that the initial equilibrium of the economy is at E^0, corresponding to the intersection of F^0F^0 and G^0G^0. Suppose also that there is an arbitrary shock to the housing market — an autonomous increase in demand, which leads to higher house prices (and thus higher collateral values, a lower premium, and an expansion in investment), while at the same time there is a discretionary increase in consumption. Graphically, as shown in Figure 10, curve GG shifts upwards (or to the right) from G^0G^0 to G^1G^1, whereas curve FF shifts downwards (or the right) from F^0F^0 to F^1F^1. The adjustment process is by now familiar: holding goods prices constant, the loan rate drops from E^0 to B, stimulating further investment; excess demand leads to higher goods and house prices, leading to a further drop in the loan rate during the transition, as collateral values go up. The equilibrium shifts from E^0 to E^1, the point at which F^1F^1 and G^1G^1 intersect. The accelerator effect corresponds again to the movement from B to E^1: the shock is amplified by the endogenous response of banks to changes in collateral values.

Now, suppose that the policy authorities would like to bring the economy back to the initial equilibrium point E^0, and suppose that to do so they want to increase the refinance rate. As shown in Figure 10, and

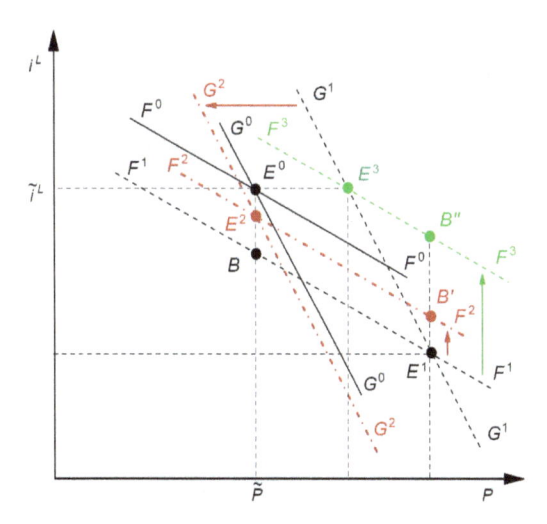

Figure 10.   Positive shock to house prices: Policy combinations.

similar to Figure 7, curve FF would shift further up, from F^1F^1 to F^2F^2, and GG would shift down, from G^1G^1 to G^2G^2, which is located beyond G^0G^0. The adjustment process would be similar to Figure 7 — an upward jump in the loan rate from E^1 to B' and a subsequent increase from B' to the new equilibrium point E^2. However, at E^2, although the central bank has been able to restore prices to their initial value, the loan rate is below its initial value; thus credit (investment loans) is too high — which may be a concern from a financial stability viewpoint. Put differently, with one instrument, the central bank can achieve only one target exactly, the price level in this case.[26]

Suppose that, instead, the macroprudential tax is increased. The adjustment process is then as in Figure 8: curve F^1F^1 shifts upward to F^3F^3, whereas GG remains at G^1G^1 does not change. In Figure 10, the increase in the tax, and thus the shift in the financial equilibrium curve, are large enough to ensure that the loan rate jumps up from E^1 to B'', and the new equilibrium is reached at E^3. At that point, the policy has restored the loan rate to its initial value; however, prices are too high, and this may create concerns from a macroeconomic stability viewpoint. Put differently, once again, with one instrument only one objective can be achieved. Both results are consistent with a literal application of Tinbergen's rule, as discussed earlier.

Now, it may be that an equilibrium at E^2 or E^3 is not a major concern for the policy authorities; in the first case, they are willing to accept a higher amount of credit to the economy than prevailed initially, whereas in the second they are willing to accept a higher level of prices than originally achieved. However, they can also use the instruments discussed earlier *in combination*, in order to restore exactly the initial equilibrium. Indeed,

---

[26] Of course, it is possible that the increase in the refinance rate induces an upward shift in FF (due to the direct effect of the policy rate on borrowing costs on impact) that happens to be large enough to take it all the way back to its initial position, while at the same time generating a downward shift in GG (due to the direct effect of i^R on consumption, through intertemporal substitution) that takes it all the way back to its initial position — in which case the economy would return exactly to point E^0. However, given the arbitrary nature of the initial shock, this is highly unlikely; the change in the policy rate can be calibrated, in general, only with respect to one target — either the price level or the loan rate — but not both.

this can be achieved by, first, calibrating the increase in the policy rate in such a way that GG returns exactly to its initial position G¹G¹, which would imply that FF, despite shifting up, would remain beneath its original position F⁰F⁰.[27] Second, the macroprudential tax can be increased in such a way that FF is shifted up further to its original position. In a sense, monetary policy is adjusted primarily to eliminate the excess demand for goods, and its impact on prices, whereas macroprudential policy is used primarily to raise borrowing costs and reduce the demand for loans. This "policy assignment" is consistent with the practical policy advice that one would expect when a shock originates fundamentally in the credit market. Moreover, the policies are adjusted in the same direction (tightening) and are fundamentally complementary — they are both needed to restore macroeconomic stability and financial stability.[28] A similar exercise can be performed to illustrate how changes in the base policy interest rate, i^T, and the required reserve ratio, μ, can be combined to bring the economy back to its initial equilibrium position, when the liability composition effect discussed earlier holds (i.e., $v' > 0$).

These experiments illustrate fairly well how a simple integrated macroeconomic model that captures some key features of MICs can be used for policy analysis. Of course, to enhance its usefulness, the analysis should be extended to an open-economy setting, to account, in particular, for foreign exchange intervention and capital controls, in line with our previous discussion about the range of policy tools that central banks should consider in an IIT regime. This is done in Agénor and Pereira da Silva (2021), who also illustrate how this broader set of policy instruments can be combined in response to capital inflows induced by a reduction in the world interest rate.

---

[27] The FF curve will necessarily remain below its original position F⁰F⁰ curve, because the increase in the refinance rate needed to restore GG to its initial position is *smaller* than the increase required to restore prices to their initial value, i.e., at point C'. Indeed, the new equilibrium would be at a point on the original GG curve G⁰G⁰ located to the southeast of E², with prices higher than at their initial value.

[28] Monetary and macroprudentai policies can also be complementary even if they are adjusted in opposite directions; see Agénor and Pereira da Silva (2021) for a formal example. This is because complementarity is fundamentally related to the need to match the number of instruments and the number of targets.

4.2. Quantitative models for integrated policy analysis

Simple analytical models of the type presented earlier are useful to provide intuition. However, to guide policy decisions in practice, quantitative models must be used. These models help to answer, on a case-by-case basis, several questions that simple models are simply not designed to address: does a more aggressive use of macroprudential policy obviate the need for policy interest rates to *lean against the wind*, i.e., to counter the build-up of financial imbalances? Should the macroprudential policy rule be limited only to financial stability considerations, or should it also account for output fluctuations? Should monetary policy and macroprudential regulation be supplemented by a systematic use of sterilised intervention, when central banks are also concerned with financial stability? Should temporary capital controls be viewed as a substitute to macroprudential regulation? These issues, as noted earlier, are critical in designing and operating an IIT regime.

The literature on open-economy DSGE models with financial frictions has gone a long way towards addressing these issues. Once again, this literature is too large to be reviewed here (see Agénor (2020)). One strand of this literature has built on the simple model presented earlier and has addressed a range of policy questions of relevance to implementing IIT in MICs.[29] A key aspect of these contributions — in addition to providing rigorous micro-foundations to behavioural functions, and being more explicit about the sources of financial frictions, the sources of price dynamics and asset accumulation, and so on — has been to systematically study the performance of monetary and macroprudential policy rules. Agénor *et al.* (2013), for instance, based on a calibrated DSGE model for MICs, support the view that a credit-augmented interest rate rule, combined with a countercyclical capital regulatory rule, is optimal for promoting macroeconomic and financial stability. They also provide insights on optimal monetary and macroprudential policies when there are strategic interactions between policy authorities.

---

[29] Issues that have been addressed in these studies include countercyclical capital requirements (Agénor *et al.*, 2013), dynamic provisions (Agénor and Pereira da Silva, 2017), reserve requirements (Agénor *et al.*, 2018), capital controls (Agénor and Jia, 2020) and foreign exchange interventional (Agénor *et al.*, 2020).

Because they are built to address well-specified policy issues, these models are often deliberately simplified in some dimensions. Moreover, to study the performance of alternative policy rules, they are often parameterised rather than estimated or rigorously calibrated. At the same time, they are designed in such a way as to replicate some stylised facts — regarding, for instance, the effects of a contractionary monetary policy on inflation, the impact of excessive credit growth on systemic financial risks or the macroeconomic effects of large capital inflows, as discussed earlier — in a benchmark scenario. Thus, while these models cannot be construed as applied policy models, in the sense that they are not aimed at fitting the reality of a particular country or providing country-specific policy advice, they are crucial in helping to move from simple analytical models to policy-oriented discussions.

Moreover, DSGE models with financial frictions, in discussing countercyclical regulation, often focus on a credit variable, an intermediate target for financial stability that is particularly important in the context of MICs. The empirical evidence suggests indeed that, even though episodes of rapid credit growth do not always lead to financial distress, episodes of financial distress are almost invariably preceded by periods of excessive credit growth. Thus, viewing the role of countercyclical macroprudential policy as being used to mitigate excessive credit expansion, viewed as the manifestation of an underlying distortion that can be addressed only by structural policies, is a sensible approach. This focus also provides a rationale for the use of simple macroprudential policy rules. At the same time, however, because credit fluctuations can be efficient, from a social welfare perspective, it is important to also examine how well narrowly-defined countercyclical rules (consistent with institutional mandates) perform relative to fully optimal policies.

5. Operational challenges to IIT implementation

Designing and implementing an IIT regime in MICs creates a number of operational challenges. These challenges include the extent to which central bank mandates must be altered, how enhanced transparency and communication should be addressed, how to implement integrated models in central banks and what role should international coordination play. We consider these issues in turn. The next section will consider

5.1. Redefining central bank mandates

In an IIT regime, as noted earlier, the central bank should have an explicit (albeit contingent) financial stability mandate. In countries considering altering the central bank's charter to officially reflect that mandate, whether hierarchical or concurrent with price and output stability, there is a risk of confusing markets and weakening credibility at first, given the lack of consensus around the very definition of "financial stability". This cost could be large in MICs where the central bank's perceived commitment to low inflation is not firmly established. However, it does not need to be permanent if sufficient effort is made to explain to the public: (1) the reason(s) for altering the central bank's mandate and the reasons why there should be a more prominent focus on credit growth as an intermediate target for financial stability; (2) the (state and time) contingent nature of the monetary policy response to perceived risks to financial stability and (3) why policy interest rates may need to be relied on to address financial stability concerns, either by themselves or in coordination with macroprudential instruments. Improving transparency and communication is thus essential, as emphasised previously, for the performance of an IIT regime. Naturally enough, the change in the official mandate of the central bank, should it be made, should occur in a stable economic and financial environment.

The empirical evidence suggests that narrow institutional mandates remain the norm for both central banks and macroprudential regulators. For the former, the mandate is generally formulated in terms of price stability and (less commonly) output stability, whereas for the latter, it is often in terms of an empirically-based (or operational) summary measure of financial stability, such as credit gaps, deviations in credit to GDP ratios, or broader measures of financial sector leverage. As documented by Archer (2017) and Calvo *et al.* (2018), there are five main arrangements currently being used in practice: (1) macroprudential policy is a shared responsibility of the central bank and the regulator, without an explicit coordination mechanism; (2) macroprudential policy is a shared responsibility, with an inter-agency coordinating body; (3) a separate, independent macroprudential agency, with decentralised implementation by existing regulators via structural interventions and variable regulatory add-ons to microprudential requirements; (4) macroprudential policy is the responsibility of the central bank, while at the same time there is a separate microprudential regulator; and (5) the central bank is responsible for both macro- and microprudential, with a regulator taking over responsibility for more specialised activities (such as financial product safety). The data suggest that in recent years the arrangement that has been the most popular is (2), in which the central bank is part of an inter-agency council (IAC). From the perspective of IIT, the key issue is whether the institutional mandate allows a close coordination between central banks and regulators in calibrating monetary and macroprudential policies; from that perspective, it is not obvious that IACs are the "best" arrangement, given the fact that by their very nature they do not embed clear mechanisms to resolve policy conflicts when they arise.

What remains clear is that if monetary and macroprudential policies must indeed be determined jointly, as should be the case under IIT, coordination between the central bank (or its Monetary Policy Committee, MPC) and the macroprudential authority (or its Financial Stability Committee, FSC) must be close and the ritual of their communication to markets carefully thought through.

5.2. *Addressing transparency and communication challenges*

As pointed out earlier, for a number of reasons, implementing and operating an IIT regime is more demanding in terms of communication and transparency than a standard IT regime. Explaining to the public the nature of the regime, the operational concept of "financial stability" and the hierarchy of objectives is an essential step to avoid confusing markets and destabilising expectations. In particular, the fact that final targets (inflation and output) are used to define macroeconomic stability, and that an intermediate target (most commonly a credit aggregate) is used to define financial stability, must be clearly explained to the public. The fact that policymakers may potentially need to adjust monetary and macroprudential policies in opposite directions (despite the fact that these policies are fundamentally complementary, as in the example discussed previously) creates added communication challenges.

A practical implication of these challenges is that, in an IIT regime, policymakers, rather than issuing independent reports on inflation and financial stability, as is the case in most IT countries at the present time, should instead focus on issuing a single, integrated report. This would help to provide a unified view of the challenges that the central bank faces with respect to all of its objectives. Indeed, an integrated IIT report is *not* a comprehensive financial stability report; responses, for instance, to the cross-section (structural) dimension of systemic risks to the financial system should be included only to the extent that they bear on the time dimension of these risks. Rather, the focus should be on countercyclical macroprudential policies, which need to be calibrated jointly with monetary policy. A case in point is Norway, which has switched since 2013 from producing a standard *Monetary Policy Report* to issuing a *Monetary Policy Report with Financial Stability Assessment*.[30] However, this report could still be improved upon in a number of dimensions, especially in terms of explaining the need for integrated policy decisions, the reasoning behind the joint calibration of monetary and macroprudential polices — should the case arise — and why policies may need to be operated in different directions.

To further promote transparency and communication with the public, the timing and design of meetings of the MPC and the FSC may also need to be revaluated. The regularity of these meetings, and transparency in their outcomes, would be important for markets to understand and foresee changes in the macroprudential regulatory regime, as well as their implications for macroeconomic and financial stability.

5.3. *Implementing integrated models in central banks*

As noted earlier, implementing integrated, quantitative models in the policy process is an essential step in adopting an IIT regime in which financial stability concerns play a significant role in macroeconomic policy decisions. These models allow policy analysts to study the

---

[30] See Monetary Policy Report with financial stability assessment (norges-bank.no).

performance of interest rate and macroprudential policy rules, and their ability to stabilise key macroeconomic and financial variables.

A common trigger variable in macroprudential policy rules — as well as in monetary policy rules, when the central bank engages in *leaning against the wind* — is the credit-to-GDP ratio. This is in line with the emphasis on credit as an intermediate target for financial stability. An important issue in that context is whether the credit variable should be measured in terms of deviations from a trend (in mechanical fashion) or from an equilibrium value (determined through econometric estimation). The reason is that rising credit-to-GDP ratios do not necessarily reflect a build-up of financial imbalances: they may also reflect financial inclusion — an important consideration for countries where the scope of the formal financial system, and access to credit and other financial services, remain limited to begin with. In fact, by reducing reliance on the unregulated financial system, and increasing opportunities for risk-sharing and consumption smoothing, financial inclusion may help to *promote* financial stability in the longer run.[31] Thus, using an equilibrium value, based on a country-specific econometric model that captures the determinants of credit demand (the urbanisation rate, the dependency ratio, access to banks and so on) is warranted. At the same time, as noted earlier, it is important to keep in mind that the credit-to-GDP ratio is a noisy indicator (Drehmann and Tsatsaronis, 2014); using it mechanically to guide monetary and macroprudential policies could produce unintended effects.[32]

The existing evidence suggests that central banks in IT-MICs have some way to go to upgrade their policy models to account for macroprudential regimes, and the broader set of instruments discussed earlier, namely, (sterilised) foreign exchange intervention and temporary capital controls. In a recent survey of the major IT countries in Asia, the

---

[31] A related issue is whether the central bank and the regulator should consider a broad measure of credit or only a component of aggregate credit. As noted earlier, working capital loans are related to the supply side, not the demand side, of the economy. See Agénor and Pereira da Silva (2019, Chapter 5) for a more detailed discussion.

[32] This potential difficulty in interpreting movements in the credit-to-GDP ratio represents an argument in favour of using credit growth as an intermediate target for financial stability.

Bank for International Settlements (2020) noted, in particular, that many of these models continue to use an uncovered interest parity condition and account only in part for macroprudential regulation. Thus, a stepped-up program of technical assistance to central banks in IT-MICs, is much needed to speed up the process.

5.4. What role for international coordination?

Most of the foregoing discussion has focused on decision-making at the individual country level. However, some of the issues that arise in an IIT regime relate to international policy interactions. Indeed, the GFC has also shown that differences in national regulatory regimes can trigger cross-border regulatory arbitrage, which in turn may lead to sharp swings in (bank-related) capital flows and magnify the international transmission of real and financial shocks. Such leakages may therefore create challenges to macroprudential policies, with possibly unwelcome spillover and spillback effects, which may in turn weaken their domestic policy impact (see Agénor et al., 2022).

To mitigate incentives for regulatory arbitrage requires some degree of coordination between macroprudential regulators across countries. Basel III's *Principle of Reciprocity* — a mechanism whereby the home country is required to maintain at least the same countercyclical capital requirement as the host country for lending to the host country from its banks in that jurisdiction — is a step in that direction. However, it is limited to countercyclical capital buffers only; broader efforts for international macroprudential policy coordination have so far proved elusive. Possible reasons for that include divergence in policymakers' views regarding how the world works, how policy spillovers and spillbacks operate and how large they are, the incentive to renege once cooperative agreements have been put in place, and so on (see Agénor and Pereira da Silva (2018)).

6. Towards an integrated macro-financial policy framework

In the foregoing discussion IIT was defined as a flexible IT regime in which (1) monetary and countercyclical macroprudential policies are calibrated jointly to achieve macroeconomic and financial stability, to ensure that interactions between these policies are accounted for, and the policy interest rate responds directly, but possibly in a state- and time-contingent fashion, to excessively rapid credit expansion; (2) the central bank is given an explicit (albeit contingent) financial stability mandate, which gives it scope — depending, in particular, on the nature and persistence of shocks, and on how quickly macroprudential tools can be deployed — for using the policy interest rate and other instruments of monetary policy to respond to financial imbalances, should such a course of action be deemed necessary; (3) the policy toolkit should involve foreign exchange intervention and temporary controls, to be deployed as needed, generally in conjunction with monetary and macroprudential policies; and (4) improved transparency and communication, in the form of the publication of an integrated policy report and closer coordination in running Monetary Policy Committee and Financial Stability Committee meetings. The foregoing analysis also discussed how an IIT regime should be implemented in MICs where banks dominate the financial system and bank credit plays a critical role on both the supply and demand sides of the economy.

To conclude, it is worth emphasising that, to achieve and maintain macroeconomic and financial stability, IIT should itself be part of a broader Integrated Macro-Financial Policy Framework (IMFPF).[33] In our view, such a framework should blend together IIT and a fiscal policy framework that involves the combination of fiscal rules, which help to enhance credibility, with a stabilisation fund — even in countries that are not highly exposed to commodity price shocks — in order to create fiscal space and allow fiscal policy to regain a countercyclical role.[34]

Indeed, in many countries, due to lack of flexibility in the budget (itself due to earmarking, the presence of fiscal rules, and so on), and the often

---

[33] The notion of an "integrated" macro-financial policy framework was discussed in the early mid-2000s; see, for instance, the references in Borio *et al.* (2022). However, in addition to the specific nature of our IIT proposal, our perspective on fiscal policy (as discussed next) differs substantially from existing approaches.

[34] For a discussion of the performance of fiscal rules in developing countries, see Ardanaz *et al.* (2020) and World Bank (2020). See also Agénor (2016) for a discussion of optimal allocation rules to stabilisation funds in response to commodity price shocks. A similar approach could be used for a broader analysis of the performance of these rules when combined with monetary and macroprudential policies.

highly politicised nature of spending and taxation decisions, this role has largely been lost.[35] Government spending does tend to increase during exceptional times, as vividly illustrated during the COVID-19 pandemic. However, the consequence is often a sharp increase in public debt, which can create subsequently a drag on the economy through higher interest rates. To increase the scope for countercyclical fiscal policy, countries — regardless of whether they are commodity exporters or not — should adopt a stabilisation fund. This would help them to create fiscal space (in terms of their ability to adjust and smooth expenditure) and allow them to step up in a timely fashion during booms and downswings, even when fiscal rules are in place. In so doing, fiscal policy may serve as an important complement to monetary and macroprudential policies in promoting macroeconomic and financial stability in an IMFPF. Of course, the issue of how to generate resources for the fund would need to be addressed; while for commodity exporters resource windfalls could be relied on, for the others, a low temporary tax on wealth initially, followed by a permanent tax on financial transactions, could be a viable option.

References

Adler, G and C Tovar (2014): "Foreign exchange interventions and their impact on exchange rate levels", CEMLA, mimeo.

Adler, G, K S Chang and Z Wang (2020): "Patterns of Foreign Exchange Intervention under Inflation Targeting", Working Paper No. 20/69, International Monetary Fund (Marc).

Adrian, T and N Liang (2018): "Monetary policy, financial conditions, and financial stability", *International Journal of Central Banking*, vol 14, no 1, January, pp 73–131.

Agénor, P-R (2002): "Monetary policy under flexible exchange rates: an introduction to inflation targeting", in N Loayza and R Soto (eds), *Inflation Targeting: Design, Performance, Challenges*, Central Bank of Chile, pp 79–169.

---

[35] In many countries, the lack of flexibility in budget outlays is related to the high share of wages and other non-discretionary spending. In addition, delays in approving and implementing fiscal policy changes tend to be unduly long, given their often politically contentious nature. In turn, a highly politicised appropriation process makes it difficult to go through regular budgetary channels to ensure a timely countercyclical response of fiscal policy.

_____ (2016): "Optimal fiscal management of commodity price shocks", *Journal of Development Economics*, vol 122, September, pp 183-196.

_____ (2020): *Monetary Policy and Macroprudential Regulation with Financial Frictions*, MIT Press (Cambridge, MA).

Agénor, P-R, K Alper and L Pereira da Silva (2013): "Capital Regulation, Monetary Policy and Financial Stability", *International Journal of Central Banking*, vol 9, September, pp 193-238.

_____ (2014): "Sudden floods, macroprudential regulation and stability in an open economy", *Journal of International Money and Finance*, vol 48, part A, November, pp 68-100.

_____ (2018): "External shocks, financial volatility and reserve requirements in an open economy", *Journal of International Money and Finance*, vol 83, May, pp 23-43.

Agénor, P-R and A Flamini (2022): "Institutional mandates for macroeconomic and financial stability", *Journal of Financial Stability*, vol 62, October, 101063.

Agénor, P-R, T Jackson and L Pereira da Silva (2020): "Foreign exchange intervention and financial stability", *BIS Working Papers*, no 889, September.

_____ (2022): "Cross-border regulatory spillovers and macroprudential policy coordination", *BIS Working Papers*, no 1007, March.

Agénor, P-R and P Jia (2020): "Capital controls and welfare with cross-border bank capital flows", *Journal of Macroeconomics*, vol 65, September.

Agénor, P-R and P Montiel (2015): *Development Macroeconomics*, 4th ed, Princeton University Press.

Agénor, P-R and L Pereira da Silva (2017): "Cyclically adjusted provisions and financial stability", *Journal of Financial Stability*, vol 28, February, pp 143-62.

_____ (2018): "Financial spillovers, spillbacks, and the scope for international macroprudential policy coordination", *BIS Working Papers*, no 97, April.

_____ (2019): *Integrated Inflation Targeting*, BIS Publications. https://www.bis.org/publ/othp30.htm.

_____ (2021): "Macroeconomic policy under a managed float: A simple integrated framework", *BIS Working Papers*, no 964, September.

Akinci, O and J Olmstead-Rumsey (2018): "How effective are macroprudential policies? An empirical investigation", *Journal of Financial Intermediation*, vol 33, January, pp 33-57.

Altunbas, Y, M Binici, and L Gambacorta (2018): "Macroprudential policy and bank risk", *Journal of International Money and Finance*, vol 81, March, pp 203-220.

Archer, D (2017): "Institutional Arrangements for Financial Stability", unpublished, Bank for International Settlements (November).

Ardanaz, M, E Cavallo, A Izquierdo and J Puig (2020): "Safeguarding public investment from budget custs through fiscal rule design", *Working Papers*, no IDB-WP-1083, February.

Bank for International Settlements (2018): *Annual Economic Report 2018*, June.

——— (2020). "Capital flows, exchange rates and policy frameworks in emerging Asia", Report of the Consultative Asian Council, November.

Basel Committee on Banking Supervision (2011): *Basel III: A global regulatory framework for more resilient banks and banking systems*, revised version, June.

——— (2017): *Basel III: Finalising post-crisis reforms*, December.

Behn, M, C Detken, T Peltonen and W Schudel (2013): "Setting countercyclical capital buffers based on early warning models: would it work?", *ECB Working Papers*, no 1604, November.

Borio, C, I Shim and H S Shim (2022): "Macro-financial stability frameworks: Experience and Challenges", see Chapter 1 of this publication.

Borio, C and H Zhu (2012): "Capital regulation, risk-taking and monetary policy: A missing link in the transmission mechanism?" *Journal of Financial Stability*, vol 8(4), pp 236–251.

Bruno, V, I Shim and H S Shin (2017): "Comparative assessment of macroprudential policies", *Journal of Financial Stability*, vol 28, February, pp 183–202.

Calvo, D, J C Crisanto, S Hohl and O Pascual Gutiérrez (2018): "Financial supervisory architecture: What has changed after the crisis?", *FSI Insights on Policy Implementation*, no 8, April.

Calvo, G and C Reinhart (2002): "Fear of floating", *Quarterly Journal of Economics*, vol 117, no 2, May, pp 379–408.

Cerutti, E, S Claessens and L Laeven (2017): "The use and effectiveness of macroprudential policies: New evidence", *Journal of Financial Stability*, vol 28, February, pp 203–24.

Cesa-Bianchi, A and A Rebucci (2015): "Does easing monetary policy increase financial instability?", *IMF Working Papers*, no 15/139, June.

Claessens, S, S R Ghosh, and R Mihet (2013): "Macro-prudential policies to mitigate financial system vulnerabilities", *Journal of International Money and Finance*, vol 39, December, pp 153–185.

Domanski, D, E Kohlscheen and R Moreno (2016): "Foreign exchange market intervention in EMEs: What has changed?", *BIS Quarterly Review*, September, pp 65–79.

Drehmann, M and K Tsatsaronis (2014): "The credit-to-GDP gap and countercyclical capital buffers: questions and answers", *BIS Quarterly Review*, March, pp 55–73.

Eichengreen, B and A Rose (2014): "Capital Controls in the 21st Century?", *Journal of International Money and Finance*, vol 48, November, pp 1–16.

Frankel, J A (2019): "Systematic managed floating", *Open Economies Review*, vol 30, April, pp 255–295.

Fratzscher, M, L Menkhoff, L Sarno and T Stöhr (2019): "When is foreign exchange intervention effective? Evidence from 33 countries", *American Economic Journal: Macroeconomics*, vol 11, January, pp 132–156.

Gadanecz, B, A Mehrotra and M Mohanty (2014): "Foreign exchange intervention and the banking system balance sheet in emerging market economies", *BIS Working Papers*, no 445, March.

Gambacorta, L and A Murcia (2017): "The impact of macroprudential policies and their interaction with monetary policy: An empirical analysis using credit registry data", *BIS Working Papers*, no 636, May.

Garcia, M (2011): "Can sterilized FX purchases under inflation targeting be expansionary?" PUC-Rio Department of Economics, *Texto para discussão*, no 589, October.

Garcia, M and T Volpon (2014): "DNDFs: A more efficient way to intervene in FX markets?", *SCID Working Papers*, no 501, May.

Gonzalez, R, D Khametshin, J-L Peydró and A Polo (2018): "Hedger of last resort: Evidence from Brazilian FX interventions, local credit and global financial cycles", Central Bank of Brazil, mimeo.

International Monetary Fund (2013): "Key aspects of macroprudential policy", *IMF Policy Papers*, June.

Kim, S and A Mehrotra (2018): "Effects of monetary and macroprudential policies — evidence from four inflation targeting economies", *Journal of Money, Credit and Banking*, vol 50(5), August, pp 967–992.

Patel, N and P Cavallino (2019): "FX Intervention: Goals, Strategies and Tactics", in Reserve Management and FX Intervention, BIS Paper No. 104, Bank for International Settlements (Basel).

World Bank (2020): *Fiscal Rules and Economic Size in Latin America and the Caribbean*, World Bank Publications (Washington DC).

Zhang, L and E Zoli (2016): "Leaning against the wind: macroprudential policy in Asia", *Journal of Asian Economics*, vol 42, February, pp 33–52.

© 2023 World Scientific Publishing Company
https://doi.org/10.1142/9789811259432_0031

Towards a New Monetary-Macroprudential Policy Framework: Perspectives on Integrated Inflation Targeting: A Discussion

Barry Eichengreen

University of California, Berkeley

Inflation targeting is in vogue in emerging markets. Why is clear to see. Inflation targeting as currently practised has its limitations, but it is the "least-worst alternative" for central banks requiring a monetary anchor. And every central bank requires a monetary anchor. Exchange rate pegs are fragile, especially in the presence of an open capital account, where emerging markets as a class are moving in the direction of greater capital-account openness. Monetary targets are unreliable, as historical experience has amply shown. However, having no anchor or well-articulated monetary policy strategy is not a viable option. So a growing number of central banks are led to some variant of inflation targeting by process of elimination.

In earlier work (Agénor and Pereira, 2019), the present authors showed that inflation targeting generally performed well compared to other monetary regimes. My own research is consistent with this conclusion. In a paper with Poonam Gupta (Eichengreen and Gupta, 2020), we studied the transition to inflation targeting in India. There we found that the transition was followed by declining inflation volatility, better anchored inflation expectations, declining inflation uncertainty and greater stability of ancillary variables such as the exchange rate and equity prices. Looking across countries, we also found that inflation-targeting central banks were able to implement significantly larger interest rate cuts in the early stages of the COVID-19 crisis, reflecting the policy credibility created by this nominal anchor.

However, whereas theorists tend to model inflation targeting in isolation, practitioners have to worry about integrating it with other policy instruments and targets. How to think about and implement this integration is the challenge that Agénor and Pereira set for themselves. Specifically, they ask how inflation targeting should be coordinated with macroprudential regulation, capital controls and fiscal policy. And they ask how the answers need to be tailored to the circumstances of middle-income emerging markets.

Consider first the coordination of macroprudential and monetary policies. The Tinbergen–Brainard Principle suggests assigning monetary policy to price stability and macroprudential regulation to financial stability, and leaving it at that. But what about Jeremy Stein's (2013) observation that only monetary policy can "get into all the cracks"? If valid, this observation creates an argument for monetary policymakers taking financial-stability considerations on board and leaning against credit booms. However, this is a second-best response; the first best is to improve the effectiveness of macroprudential policies. As a student of the 1920s, when the Federal Reserve leaned against a credit boom, with what were ultimately disastrous consequences, I am reluctant to endorse central banks orienting monetary policy towards financial stability targets. Safer — on all grounds — would be to instead invest heavily in strengthening macro- and microprudential tools.

Even then, there is the question of how macroprudential and monetary policies should be coordinated with one another. In the absence of formal coordination, it is possible to get unnecessarily large swings in both policies. Consider for example a positive supply shock that raises output and reduces inflation. The central bank presumably will cut interest rates in order to offset the decline in inflation. However, regulators will respond to the credit boom unleashed by the positive supply shock and easier monetary conditions by tightening macroprudential policies. This will lend more impetus to the incipient deflation that the central bank is concerned to offset, so it will cut rates by more. Regulators will then respond, however, by tightening more. This danger of destabilising policy spirals can be contained if the two policymakers coordinate (if, as it is put in the paper, they "solve jointly for the two policies"). In some countries, this need is addressed through a "twin peaks" structure, where there exist separate monetary policy and financial policy committees in the central bank, with the governor serving on both in order to facilitate coordination. Where macroprudential policy is made outside the central bank, such coordination is obviously harder.

In their chapter, the authors recommend giving inflation-targeting central banks an explicit financial-stability mandate. This is wise in cases where the central bank possesses its own macroprudential tools. However, in institutional set-ups where another agency of the government sets capital requirements, loan-to-value ratios and so forth, it would be better to give the central bank an explicit mandate to share information and coordinate with the macroprudential authorities, so as to avoid deflecting monetary policy from its inflation target.

The authors also advocate using temporary capital controls as a second-best form of macroprudential policy. I am also on board with this idea, having learned it at Michael Mussa's knee in my days at the IMF (see Eichengreen and Mussa, 1998). Implementation, however, is not straightforward. Policies initially conceived as temporary have a tendency to become permanent. Investors anticipating the application of temporary capital controls may have an incentive to scramble out in advance, bringing forward the very crisis that the policy is designed to avert. Then there is the uncomfortable fact that over time — meaning since 1970 — we have seen fewer countries, including fewer emerging markets, utilising capital controls (see Ito and Chinn, 2020). If the pursuit of sound macroprudential policy recommends the retention of capital controls, other mysterious forces seem to be pushing in the opposite direction.

Finally, there is the coordination of inflation targeting with fiscal policy. Post COVID-19, this is a problem with which every country, and not just middle-income emerging markets, is struggling. In this case, the traditional assignment is that monetary policy should again target inflation, while fiscal policy targets the output gap. For the same reasons described earlier, one can imagine that this assignment will work better when the two policies are set jointly. However, in practice, monetary and fiscal policies are adjusted at very different frequencies. There is also the danger of undermining central bank independence; there is the question of how central bankers can give fiscal policy advice without overstepping their mandates, in other words. And does not a commitment to coordinating monetary and fiscal policies open the door to fiscal dominance?

These reservations notwithstanding, I am broadly in agreement with the authors' conclusions. Central banks and governments need multiple instruments in order to hit multiple targets. Monetary policymakers need a clear mandate and operating strategy. Those responsible for macroprudential and monetary policies need to coordinate with one another. Setting policies jointly, or at least sharing information with other policymaking agencies, is likely to work better than setting them independently. This is good advice not just for bank-dependent, middle-income economies but for countries in general.

References

Agénor, Pierre-Richard and Luiz Awazu Pereira da Silva (2019), *Integrated Inflation Targeting: Another Perspective from the Developing World*, Basel: Bank for International Settlements.

Eichengreen, Barry and Poonam Gupta (2020), "Inflation Targeting in India: An Interim Assessment," World Bank Policy Research Working Paper no. 9422, Washington, D.C.: World Bank.

Eichengreen, Barry and Michael Mussa (1998), "Capital Account Liberalization: Theoretical and Practical Aspects," Occasional Paper 172, Washington, D.C.: International Monetary Fund.

Ito, Hiro and Menzie Chinn (2020), "Notes on the Chinn-Ito Financial Openness Index: 2018 Update," unpublished manuscript, Portland State University and University of Wisconsin, Madison.

Stein, Jeremy (2013), "Overheating in Credit Markets: Origins, Measurement and Policy Responses," Speech to the "Restoring Household Financial Stability after the Great Recession: Why Household Balance Sheets Matter" Research Symposium, St. Louis: Federal Reserve Bank of St. Louis.

Lightning Source UK Ltd.
Milton Keynes UK
UKHW021039120123
415162UK00002B/37